RIGOS PRIMER SERI

UNIFORM BAR EXAM (UBE) RE'

MULTISTATE BAR EXAM (MBE) *VOLUME 2*

2020 EDITION

Table of Contents

This 2020 MBE edition is updated for all NCBE content specification outline changes. We present the MBE seven subject coverage in two volumes. Volume 2 contains the below four subjects while MBE Volume 1 contains the other three subjects and a full MBE practice exam. Magic Memory Outlines, question maps, multiple-choice learning and practice questions and answer rationales are included. The MEE questions, answers, and related prior exam issue distribution charts covering all the seven MBE subjects are included. Consider purchasing the combined 2020 MBE and MEE three-volume set.

MBE Volume 1 contains the following three subjects with related questions and answers:

Volume 1

INTRODUCTION

Welcome to the 2020 Rigos UBE Review Series Uniform Multistate Bar Exam (MBE) Volume 2 which is updated for the new content specification outlines. Our comprehensive review course material and software are all you need to pass the United States MBE administered by the National Conference of Bar Examiners (NCBE) as a part of the Uniform Bar Exam (UBE). Carefully read the introductory portion of this text containing valuable information about the MBE exam and exam questions. The introduction information herein also serves as your planning session and roadmap for efficiently and successfully passing all parts of the bar exam. Begin your preparation by registering with us for free updates and helpful aids at http://www.rigos.net/BarReservation.asp.

EDITORIAL DIRECTION

James J. Rigos is an Attorney-CPA and a graduate of Boston University Law School. He is Editor-in-Chief of the creating team of this Bar Review Series. He has written and lectured for professional associations and bar and CPA exam review programs for almost 40 years. Over 100,000 students have used the Rigos courses to pass their professional entrance exams. Mr. Rigos is a national Director and past Officer of the American Academy of Attorney-CPAs and chairs the Academy's national ethics and dual practice committee.

ACKNOWLEDGEMENTS

This work product was substantially enriched because of the robust encouragement and editorial involvement of many thoughtful individuals. Laura Colberg, Matt Conrad, Tracy Duany, Drew Foerster, Lisa Goldoftas, Leah Golshani, Michelle Johnson, Steve Johnson, Gina Lowe, Carolyn Plant, Aaron Rocke, Joanna Roth, Tom Smith, Kevin Stemp, Jason Stonefeld, Sidney Tribe, and Tracy Wood made significant drafting contributions. Law school Professors Janet Ainsworth, Jim Bond, Mark Chinen, David DeWolf, Sam Donaldson, Christian Halliburton, Gregory Hicks, Jim Jurinski, Lisa Kelly, Rachel Levine, Tom Lininger, Peter Nicolas, John Parry, Elizabeth Porter, Chris Rigos, and Karl Tegland made helpful suggestions on substantive improvements and reviewed portions of the UBE textbooks. A special thanks to our past students for their many suggestions of substantive improvement and creative new learning aids. Their recommendations and successes are a part of every page of this Rigos UBE Review Series.

TRADEMARK PROTECTION

The Magic Memory Outlines® is a registered trademark owned by James J. Rigos and Rigos Professional Education Programs, Ltd.

COPYRIGHT PROTECTION

DESIRE TEXT OUTLINE AND PRACTICE SOFTWARE TO PERFECT YOUR MBE SKILLS?

UPGRADE TO OUR *FULL-SERVICE MBE CLASS*

Rigos *full service* MBE preparation program includes downloaded Magic Memory Outline (MMO) software template, complete MMO review by our graders, multiple-choice question drill software, and three full MBE practice exam sets. The MEE essay question grading improvement service covers the seven MBE subjects (as well as the other MEE subjects). This allows you to:

1. Create your own summary **Magic Memory Outlines**® using our Word software templates. Be concise: your self-created Outlines should be a summary that captures the essence of the applicable black letter law. We review, grade, and suggest improvements that can be incorporated into your Outlines. Well-crafted outlines, once memorized, will serve as your primary substantive knowledge base to be reviewed periodically.

2. Use the **Question Maps** as a guide to select questions that directly relate to the textual material you are then reviewing. This allows you to see how the examiners apply and test the subject and work on your weak topics. Use the class software to "drill down" through the outline to the question desired by clicking on the + sign for the section. The outline will expand when you "drill down" to show individual questions. You can select as many questions as you like from the question maps.

3. Use the **"Make Your Own Exam"** software feature to create your own mixed subject question drills randomly selected from all seven MBE chapters. The software program will automatically select your designated number of random questions (up to a maximum of 100). You can also print the questions for your drill exercises.

4. Our **MEE book** contains prior exam 30-minute multiple-part NCBE essay questions and answers which tests your knowledge in the seven MBE topics. Issue distribution charts indicate prior UBE testing frequency. Our full-service course includes grader essay feedback that complements and "fills-in" your MBE subject's application.

5. Work all **post-class quizzes** and four **practice exam sets** in 180-minute sets each. This will reinforce your knowledge and perfect your use of our proprietary **MBE Secret Weapon** technique. We will grade your multiple-choice, essays, and performance tasks. Our graders point out the MBE distractors and review the reasoning for any questions you missed.

Register at http://www.rigos.net/register_v2.asp.

PRACTICE MAKES PERFECT AND RIGOS MAKES PRACTICE EASY

OTHER RELATED BAR EXAM PREP BOOKS

If you **liked** this Rigos Uniform Multistate Bar Exam (MBE) course, you **will love** our other Multistate UBE 2020 Review Series publications. Included are:

1.   UNIFORM MEE SUBJECTIVE ESSAY EXAM

- **Succinct** explanation of the **most frequently tested NCBE essay** subject's rules. The Rigos text is very concise and focused, containing only the breadth and depth of the legal issues you need to answer the MEE essays.
- **Hundreds of acronyms-mnemonics and UBE tips** help you memorize frequently tested issues and perfect an essay checklist approach.
- **Five or more full essay questions per subject** with **summarized pointer sheet grading guides** and **full model answers** for all MEE subjects, the seven MBE subjects, and professional responsibility testing.
- Historical NCBE exam **distribution of issues tested** shows frequency of topic testing.
- Our MEE optional **essay grading and improvement** service complements and fills-in your understanding of the law tested on the two MBE sets.
- Our **Magic Memory Outline software**, **essay grading**, and **substance and presentation improvement guidance** are available in our full-service course.

2.   UNIFORM MPT PERFORMANCE TEST

- **Succinct** explanations of the most frequently NCBE tested MPT tasks contain **only the information you need to pass the MPT** portion of the exam.
- **"Tips and Traps" section** helps familiarize you with typical distracting characteristics that often confuse the Performance Test exam-takers.
- Advice on **the best approach, time scheduling, and format** for answering each of the four types of MPT questions helps strengthen your abilities to research and organize the library and file. This will focus your answers and increase efficiency.
- Text includes **professional responsibility** material covering a lawyer's or law firm's ethical rules application which has been recently tested on the performance tasks.
- Ten **simulated exam questions** categorized by topic **with full sample answers** help you gauge your progress and reinforce your MPT practice.
- Full course upgrade to **task grading and improvement suggestion** service available.

3.   UNIFORM MPRE ETHICS EXAM

- **Concise and focused** explanations of the most frequently tested MPRE subjects.
- **"Tips and Traps"** section helps familiarize you with typical distracters used to create question confusion for the MPRE exam-takers.
- **Question Maps** cross-reference the textual coverage to over **350 professional multiple-choice ethics questions** with **full answer rationales**.
- **Advice on the best approach, time scheduling, and format** for answering the MPRE questions helps increase your abilities to analyze answer choices.
- Full **simulated final exam with 60 MPRE questions with full answer rationales** help you to gauge your progress before you sit for the actual MPRE.

To order a specific book go to https://www.rigos.net/register_v2.asp.

OTHER QUESTIONS – Send us an email at bar@rigos.net

RIGOS UBE BAR REVIEW PRIMER SERIES

MULTISTATE BAR EXAM (MBE) REVIEW

2020 EDITION, VOLUME 2

INTRODUCTION AND SUCCESS ON THE MBE

Table of Contents

RIGOS UBE BAR REVIEW PRIMER SERIES

2020 MULTISTATE BAR EXAM (MBE) REVIEW VOLUME 2

INTRODUCTION AND SUCCESS ON THE MBE

I.   INTRODUCTION

A. Welcome

Congratulations on choosing the Rigos Primer Series for your Multistate Bar Exam (MBE) Review. This introduction covers our preparation framework to follow to be sure you score high on the MBE the first time you sit.

1. MBE Exam Overview: This introduction section describes the MBE process, including how exam questions are created and graded. It covers question characteristics and tips for approaching the MBE. Following our organized preparation program in this introduction section will ensure you score high the first time you sit. Study this information thoroughly before you start the review of the first substantive subject. Refer back periodically to review the question characteristics and make sure you are staying on track.

2. Essay Exam: Candidates in jurisdictions that administer the Multistate Essay Exam should also use the Rigos MEE in conjunction with this MBE program. The seven MBE subjects are now also tested using essay questions. Our MEE course contains NCBE style multi-part practice essay questions to supplement the text and multiple-choice questions contained in this MBE program.

3. Performance Exam: Candidates in jurisdictions that administer the Multistate Performance Test should also use our MPT book in conjunction with this MBE program. Our MPT course contains practice performance questions to supplement the task-focused analysis.

B. Focused, Positive Mental Attitude

What the mind can conceive, dedicated hard work can achieve. You must believe you can and will pass the bar exam and become a successful attorney.

1. Join the Winning Team: More than 100,000 professional alumni have used these structured Rigos Series programs to pass their professional entrance exams. Therefore, your objective of passing the MBE at the first sitting is very attainable.

2. Success-Focused Program: Exam confidence is the result of a well-organized and well-executed preparation program. Students following the complete Rigos Bar Review Series seamless program are trained for exam success.

C. MBE Exam in General

The MBE is a testing product of the National Conference of Bar Examiners (NCBE). The MBE takes one full day of testing and is scheduled for the last Wednesday in February and July. It is required in all but a handful of states. More than 60,000 students sit for the MBE annually.

The student must complete two sets of 100 multiple-choice questions in morning and afternoon sessions of three hours each. Both the actual MBE test booklets and this Rigos UBE Review Series text are printed in 12-point type.

II. QUESTION DETAILS

The MBE consists of 200 multiple-choice questions, each with four answer options. There are 100 questions in each morning and afternoon set, 10 of which are for pre-test evaluation purposes only. Contracts has 28 questions. Constitutional Law, Criminal Law and Procedure, Evidence, Federal Civil Procedure, Property, and Torts have 27 questions each. Both morning and afternoon exam sets have 13 to 15 questions for each subject, presented in random order that jump from subject to subject.

A. Question Source

1. Organization: The NCBE's MBE Drafting Committees create questions for the seven MBE subjects tested. There are five people per committee with broad representation from law school professors, professional bar examiners, and practicing attorneys.

2. New Questions: The NCBE creates and pre-tests new multiple-choice questions on an ongoing basis to refresh the test bank of potential questions and promote breadth of topic coverage. The objective is questions that discriminate between highly knowledgeable applicants and those less knowledgeable. Proposed new questions are subject to multiple reviews by content experts to ensure questions fairly test the subjects and are well-drafted, accurate, and unambiguous. State bar admissions authorities may submit comments about proposed new questions.

B. Grading System

1. Scoring: There is no penalty for a candidate's wrong answer choice selection on the MBE. Every correct answer is worth one point, regardless of the question's degree of difficulty or the time it takes to work.

 a. Scaled for Difficulty: The final number of right answers reported for a particular exam depends upon that particular exam's overall difficulty. Examiners test to meet the same pre-determined level of professional competence. The NCBE has a scaled ("equating" is the descriptive term) difficulty system, so the final score awarded to bar candidates is comparable from exam to exam. The additional scaling points typically run between 10 and 20 points. Thus, the final equated score averages around 135 to 140 nationally.

 b. Ensure Consistency: The examiners' analyses of answers and the scaling system are intended to correct the effect of any bad or especially difficult questions on a particular exam. This ensures grading consistency and comparisons from exam to exam.

2. State Passing Rate: Each jurisdiction decides how to combine the MBE scaled score with the essay and performance question testing. Nationally, about 60 to 70% of candidates receive a "passing" scaled score, although this percentage varies from state to state. Most UBE states require a minimum score of 135. For a year-by-year breakdown go to www.ncbex.org/ and click "Bar Examinations and Admission Statistics page." In states that permit students from non-ABA approved law schools to sit, the pass rate may be significantly lower.

 a. State Rules Vary: Non-UBE states combine the MBE and essay performance scores using various weights. Some allow a waiver on the essays if the candidate achieves a certain MBE score. While some states accept MBE scores from other jurisdictions, some do not.

 b. Particular State: For passing statistics and grading methods used in combining exam parts in your jurisdiction, check with your state bar association. Go to http://www.americanbar.org/groups/bar_services/resources/state_local_bar_associations.ht ml for an online listing of state-by-state bar information.

C. Question Approach

1. Focus: The MBE focuses on fundamental legal principles from the Restatements of Law, promulgated by the American Law Institutes (ALI). Statutes and local or minority case law positions and/or precedent are not usually tested. MBE objective questions concentrate on analysis and detailed black letter law rules, in contrast to broad concepts usually tested on bar exam essay questions.

2. Call of the Question: The facts of a question provide the situational foundation to test an application of the relevant controlling legal rule.

    a. Facts Lead to Requirements: The facts lead to a requirement sentence containing a "call of the question." The correct answer is one of the four following alternative legal theories presented. The best answer usually is most directly responsive to the call of the question as there may be two or more alternatives that are technically not inaccurate.

    b. Requirement Position: The student is usually required to take either the position of a judge (decide the court's likely decision outcome) or a client advocate (best/strongest or worst/weakest argument for P or D). A few questions ask the candidate to choose the most effective structuring of a transaction or legal problem. You may also be asked to give a client an opinion on the best course of action. The reasoning is more important than the likely outcome.

3. Develop Your Approach: Approximately one-fourth of the MBE questions are reasonably difficult. We recommend the following general approach:

    a. Active Reading Necessary: You may have time for only one read. Focus on the parties' relationships and interactions. Look for the facts the writer embedded in the fact pattern to raise legal issue arguments. Read for key words, which are often adjectives such as "oral" or "written," and adverbs such as "deliberate" or "intended." Think of the requirements of the applicable legal rule.

    b. Using a Systematic Approach: Your best strategy is a systematic approach to select the correct answer. An enlightened elimination-guessing system is also useful (see comprehensive suggestions *infra* on page 9). You need to make a detailed analysis of the legal theories in all four alternatives; instinctive answers are often wrong because fine-line distinctions are everywhere on the MBE.

    c. Tricks Abound: There is usually some merit in each of the four legal theories presented. Still, some small factual difference or nuance of the determinative legal rule makes one alternative the most compelling answer. The examiners work hard to make red herrings and distracting legal theory seem reasonable and occasionally quite attractive.

D. Subjects Tested

Seven substantive subjects are tested on the MBE. The NCBE does issue content specification outlines with rough percentage distributions but tends to confine testing to certain major areas of each subject. We have summarized the usual topic coverage as follows:

1. Torts: Expect up to half of the questions in this common law topic to cover various aspects of negligence and related defenses in some detail. Up to one-quarter of the questions may be on claims asserted under strict liability and product liability theories that do not require intent or carelessness. The remaining questions are spread fairly evenly over other torts topics. The MBE emphasizes the elements of the tort action P must prove to make a *prima facie* case and the various defenses that may be asserted by D.

2. Contracts and UCC Article 2: Expect broad testing with more than two-thirds of contracts questions on common law "SIR" topics (services, intangibles, and real estate). The MBE also covers various provisions of UCC Article 2 sale of goods, especially where there is a different or expanded treatment under the UCC as compared to the common law. Most of the questions focus on: (1) formation elements, especially offer and acceptance testing issues, defects in meeting of the minds, and statute of frauds compliance; (2) performance, especially reasons for non-performance; and (3) remedies. Contracts questions often are longer than the other five subjects and are tested both more broadly and more deeply.

3. Property and Future Interests: This text is updated for the 2017 NCBE changes. Property questions often feature a series of transactions. Future interests are usually in about 20% of the questions and may involve quite difficult issues. Transaction closing and acquisition of property by deed or adverse possession are heavily tested. Easements, conveyances, and recording are also frequent topics. Restrictive covenants have reasonable coverage and landlord-tenant issues receive some attention. Testamentary devises and rights in personal property are lightly tested.

4. Evidence: MBE evidence questions are relatively short but may involve several levels of analysis. Testing authority is the Federal Rules of Evidence (FRE). Questions usually ask you to analyze why a particular item of evidence is admissible or inadmissible under the facts presented in the question. The court's admission dilemma of barely relevant but highly prejudicial evidence and hearsay evidence (and exceptions) constitute at least half of the testing. Questions focus on the purpose for admission and rules that exclude or limit admissibility of evidence at issue.

5. Constitutional Law: The emphasis is on the U.S. Federal Constitution's effect on the actions and powers of the three branches of the federal government: the Executive, Legislative, and Judicial. The MBE also tests constitutional limits establishing what a state may or must do in regulating their laws. The commerce clause, due process, equal protection, and degree of judicial scrutiny are frequent topics. Approximately half the questions test individual rights and ask whether a statute is valid or invalid.

6. Criminal Law and Procedure: Criminal law questions focus on basic common law rules, although some questions focus on the modern majority rules of statutory modifications. The D's mental state relating to the intent requirements for different crimes comes up frequently. Criminal procedure comprises about one-third of the questions and emphasizes U.S. constitutional limitations on the states' abilities to introduce evidence to convict criminal defendants. Questions emphasize the controlling standards and appropriate procedural requirements states must meet in the prosecution process.

7. Federal Civil Procedure: The Federal Rules of Civil Procedure (FRCP) questions test current rules, although some origination matters involve state law issues. Local federal district court rules may supplement the nationwide procedural rules but must be consistent with them. The FRCP numbers are not necessary in your answers. Two-thirds of the questions are based on jurisdiction, venue, pretrial procedures, and various motions. The other one-third of testing comes from jury trials, verdicts and judgments, and appealability and review of decisions reached below.

MBE Tip: It may help to diagram the interaction between the parties in all subjects.

III. MBE QUESTION CHARACTERISTICS

A. <u>Comments and Pitfalls</u>

Developing your MBE skills and avoiding objective question pitfalls increases your correct choices on the exam multiple-choice questions. The MBE tests not only your knowledge of the legally significant black letter law rules, but also your MBE question analytical skills. These necessary skills can be developed only through practice. Thus, the following material is quite important and should be reviewed periodically during your preparation program.

1. Format: All MBE questions are multiple-choice with four alternatives. All levels of difficulty are represented, and there is no pattern to the MBE sequence.

2. Preferred Answer Objective: Look for the best legal conclusion and theory. Often two answers conclude that party A will prevail, while the other two conclude that party B will prevail. The legal rationale supporting the conclusion thus becomes the determining factor.

a. Objective: The key is to select the answer that is the most nearly correct or, conversely, the least incorrect. Each alternative usually has some merit; the best alternative will be the most completely correct, and it must relate to the facts. Look for detailed facts in the question that make one alternative more compelling than the others. Appreciate the difference between the command adverbs "may" (optional) and to "shall" or "must" (mandatory).

b. Problems: Typically, two of the four alternatives are the same or very close in outcome, and both may sound accurate. An alternative may reach the right conclusion for the wrong reason or for a reason less compelling than another alternative's rationale. Also, watch out for incomplete definitions of the determinative rules of law, particularly conclusions that have more than one requirement, but where only one requirement is given in the question.

3. Negatives: A few questions may have negatives in the facts, the call, or the alternatives. This means the correct choice becomes the worst, least helpful, least likely, or most false alternative. For example, "Which argument would be least helpful as a viable defense?" or "Which is the least sufficient basis for admitting this hearsay?" Reason very carefully through the alternatives and reverse the polarity of the normal frame of reference. The "true-false" approach discussed in item 4 directly below is often helpful in dealing with negatives.

4. Try a True-False Approach: It may help to use a true-false analysis for each of the four outcome alternatives. Evaluate each answer choice by asking "Is the statement asserted here true or false?" The true-false approach is especially useful for questions having a negative call. Ideally you will end up with a 3-1 split; the odd one out is usually the best answer.

5. Absolutes: Be on the alert for sweeping exclusionary words such as "all," "always," "none," "never," "under no circumstances," "solely," or "only." An answer containing such words is so broad or narrow it is unlikely to be correct. Ask yourself, "Is there any exception?" If the answer is yes, you can eliminate this answer option. A more narrowly stated and inclusive alternative is usually preferable. The word "reasonable" in an alternative often makes for an attractive answer outcome.

6. Unlikely Theory: Occasionally the MBE will include answer options containing an unlikely, even nonsensical principle, concept, or theory. Examples are the "doctrine of changed circumstances" or "*res ipsa loquitur*" in an evidence question. Such a rationale generally is wrong unless you have seen the theory similarly applied in our UBE Series texts.

7. **Be Selective:** The question often contains more facts or law than necessary.

   a. **Distracters:** Fact patterns may contain red herrings. The examiners may create attractive factual distracters supporting logic leading to wrong alternatives.

   b. **Detail May Be Coding:** Look for seemingly meaningless detail; it may be – and often is – a necessary fact for a controlling legal rule. For example, if a transaction is between a wholesaler and retailer, some UCC provisions may apply because both parties are considered to be "merchants" because they regularly deal in that good. In comparison, a neighbor selling a lawn mower does not qualify. If dates or dollar amounts are given in the facts, these usually are important factors necessary to reach the correct conclusion.

8. **Analyze Modifiers in the Alternatives:** Many answer alternatives begin with the conclusion – for instance, "P will prevail," "P will not prevail," or "D's defense will be effective." This is followed by a conditional or limiting modifying word ("because," "since," "if," "only if," or "unless") and a statement of a supporting legal reasoning or rationale. Picture the following three-element framework:

Conclusion │ Conditional or Limiting Modifier │ Supporting Reasoning or Rationale

   a. **"Because," "Since," or "As":** These conditional modifiers usually indicate the rationale that follows is legally necessary to satisfy the conclusion.

   (1) **Example:** "Alice prevails because she validly accepted thereby creating a contract that is binding on the offeror." "Alice prevails" is the conclusion, "because" is the conditional modifier, and "she validly . . . offeror" is the legal rationale.

   (2) **Reasoning Requirements:** The reasoning must be consistent with the facts given in the question. The reasoning also must resolve the central legal issue.

   b. **"If" and "Only If":** This limiting modifier indicates the rationale that follows need only be possible under the facts; it is not required to be totally consistent, as in "because" or "since" questions.

   (1) **Example:** "Baker prevails if" (or "only if") she reasonably relied on Smith's promise." "Baker prevails" is the conclusion; "if" (or "only if") is the conditional modifier; and "she reasonably relied . . ." is the legal rationale.

   (2) **Reasoning Requirement:** The "if" modifier can – and often does – go beyond the given question facts to create a more compelling factual argument to support the legal conclusion. "Only if" is similar, except it creates an exclusive condition that must be satisfied. An "if" or "only if" modifier also requires you to reason through the other three alternatives to be sure there is not a better "if" or "only if" argument.

   c. **"Unless":** This conditional modifier usually is followed by a rationale that addresses more required legal or factual elements than the other modifiers. Notice that "unless" usually is a mirror image of "if," and the usual modifier form of "no, unless. . . ." is the only way that alternative outcome could occur. Consider carefully any alternative with facts following "unless" or "if."

   (1) **Example:** "Carol prevails unless she had actual, constructive, or inquiry notice of the property encumbrance." "Carol prevails" is the conclusion; "unless" is the conditional modifier; and "she had actual, constructive, or inquiry notice of the property encumbrance" is the legal rationale.

(2) Reasoning Requirement: The "unless" reasoning can reverse the general rule outcome or provide a missing element. It must be necessary for controlling principles of law to apply. If there is any other way the result can occur, an "unless" alternative is incorrect. Reason through all other alternatives to make sure there is no better argument.

9. Remember Our Default Rules: Some MBE questions contain very challenging subjects. Examples are future interests in property and some convoluted constitutional rights question. It may not be efficient to spend the time necessary to totally analyze every detail. Every question is worth one point and you still may be uncertain after expending considerable time and effort. By eliminating wrong answers you can usually reduce the choice to two viable alternatives. Use the following default rules as a logical basis for an educated guess.

a. Longest Alternative: Everything else being equal, a longer narrative alternative is slightly more likely to be the correct answer than a shorter alternative.

(1) Rationale: A correct answer usually must contain all the required elements and reasoning of the governing black letter law necessary to be the best choice. This concept favors a more detailed and longer alternative over a shorter, fragmented choice.

(2) Exception: Still, there have been questions in which the right answer was only one word, such as "innocent" or "battery." The other alternatives in such a question typically involve incorrect or incomplete rationales.

b. Central Issue: Generally, the more precise the answer focus on the question's central issue, the better the choice; vagueness is not encouraged in black letter law questions application. The three incorrect alternatives in such a question may contain distracters to create confusion.

c. Easier to Prove: An answer choice that is easier to prove is preferable over one with more complicated legal requirements.

d. Opposite Answer: If two of the four alternatives are directly opposite (*e.g.*, "P wins because…" as contrasted with "P loses because…"), one of the two opposites is likely to be the best answer. This rule would also apply if a similar rationale supports opposite answer outcomes (*e.g.*, "P wins because…" as opposed to "D wins because …").

e. More Than One Legal Subject: An answer alternative that includes another legal subject is usually wrong. Questions infrequently have cross-overs between most subjects, so an answer covering two legal subject areas is unlikely to be the best answer.

f. Eliminating Wrong Answers: The NCBE examiners are very skillful at creating attractive wrong answer alternatives. Beyond learning the details of the law, it is helpful to know the three common general reasons why a MBE answer alternative is wrong:

(1) Legal Rule Misstatement: The statement of the rule is wrong or, more likely, incompletely states the legal principle at issue. For example, a key requirement of a rule is intentionally omitted, such as the D's *scienter* is required to prove fraud.

(2) Factual Omission or Misstatement: The facts required to support the choice are not stated in the question's fact pattern. A contract example is the "firm offer by a merchant" rule where the facts are silent as to whether there was a merchant involved. An alternative's facts may also go clearly beyond what is required by the question. Occasionally, the facts of the alternative directly contradict the facts in the question. The alert candidate will spot inconsistencies and synthesize the factual situation carefully.

(3) Legal or Factual Irrelevancy: The law or facts in an alternative answer are accurate, but do not focus on the central determinant issue of the question. For instance, the question involves an element of law that P must prove to establish a *prima facie* case, thus avoiding a summary judgment of dismissal or directed verdict, but the alternative answer focuses on less relevant facts that do not focus on the dispositive facts in the question.

B. Approach to MBE Questions

Parts of this section refer to practicing exam-type questions on paper. If you want to use the software feature for practice, also review the instructions on page 16 *infra*. You should still do many of your review questions on paper, since this is how you will take the test.

1. Stay Within Time Allocation:

a. Pace Yourself: Carefully manage your time as you proceed through the questions. The NCBE trend is toward longer fact patterns, rather than string questions. Answer every question, since there is no penalty for guessing. There are 100 questions in each of the two 180-minute (three-hour) sessions and you should begin by taking 10 minutes to categorize all the questions by subject. This leaves you an average of 1.7 minutes (100 seconds) per question. You will need to practice extensively to work up to this fast pace.

b. Build Time Performance: Start working questions with a 2 ½ minute maximum (150 seconds). One third of the way through your study period, drop to 125 seconds for each question. For the final third of your study period, reduce this to 100 seconds for each question. This intellectual strategy will get your pace up to the required exam timing.

c. Procedure: Start with quickly and carefully reading the call of the question for direction on the decision you have to make after full analysis. Then look over the four options for issues at play in the question. Analyze the fact pattern carefully because you usually only have time for one read. Underline and take marginal notes. If a particular question gives you difficulty, make your best educated guess and put a question mark notation in the margin so you can come back to it later if you have time.

2. Analyze Facts and Law:
Analyze both the relevant facts and the four legal choices presented below. Strive to understand the precise facts of the question separately from the four alternative answer choices presented. The facts in the question story develop chronologically. Read actively and circle all the parties' designated names or titles in the question book; every new person adds another potential legal relationship and set of claims. Candidates often select a wrong answer because they failed to appreciate the consequence of a significant fact. For more complicated questions, you might opt to quickly sketch a chronological diagram of the events in the margin.

3. Question Approaches:
Two sequencing methods are possible in working the 100 questions in the set. Under both methods, we recommend transposing all your 100 circled choices to the bubble answer sheet at one time just before the end of the exam set. Circle your answer choice – A, B, C, or D – on the question booklet itself as you work through the exam.

a. First Method – Do Questions in Order: This is the traditional method of doing every question in order regardless of subject. This requires that you shift your intellectual knowledge base up to 99 times, which loses time and dilutes subject concentration.

b. Second Method – "MBE Secret Weapon": This Rigos proprietary system focuses the mindset so that intellectually there are seven individual knowledge base subjects of about 25 minutes each. You contemplate the nuances of only one legal subject at a time, leading to greater mental concentration, accuracy, efficiency, and time control.

(i) Procedure: Go through the question booklet and marginally categorize each question subject. Use abbreviations of **K** for contracts, **T** for torts, **P** for property, **E** for evidence, **CN** for constitutional law, **CR** for criminal law and procedure, and **CP** for civil procedure. If the examiners allow it, use columns on a separate sheet of paper as below; if not, simply note the subject in the left margin of the test booklet alongside the question. Either way, our proprietary system allows you to work all the same subject questions at the same time.

(ii) Categorization: Only read enough of each question and the four answer choices to determine the subject category. Look for key words such as "offer" or "agreed" for contracts, "intent" or "injury" for torts, "land" or "lease" for property, "state law" or "challenge" for constitutional law, "admissible" or "hearsay" for evidence, "police" or "arrest" for criminal law and procedure, and "ruling" or "jurisdiction" for civil procedure.

(iii) Example: An example of the first 18 sorted questions by subject is:

T	K	P	E	CN	CR	CP
1	9	6	3	4	5	19
2	13	10	11	12	8	20
7	14	16	17	15	18	21

(iv) Do Each Subject Separately: Work all the questions at one time from a subject such as torts, **T** above (T number 1, 2, 7, etc.). The early questions will reinforce and increase your knowledge of the subject. This will help improve your time efficiency and choice effectiveness. Circle your answer choice in the booklet the first time through.

(a) Sure of Subject: Answer all of the subject's questions in order from your listing. This applies even if you are not 100% certain of the exact details of the critical issue being tested. If unsure, apply our default rules on page 9 and follow your gut instinct. Circle your alternative choice – A, B, C, or D – in the question booklet.

(b) If Unsure – Take Your Best Shot: If you are not sure which alternative is best, eliminate the wrong alternatives. Usually you will be down to two choices. If you have spent more than 20 to 30 seconds on the question, you must tentatively commit. There is just not enough time to waste second-guessing, so use our default rules. Circle the question number (such as 12) for possible review again later if you have time left.

(c) Review Circled Questions Last: After you have gone through all the questions from the subject once, look at the time left from the 26 minutes. Examine the circled questions to determine if you can identify anything new. Questions you have worked subsequently may jog your memory or give you a new perspective. If you still are uncertain, stick with your original instinctive choice; it is most likely your best shot at the correct answer.

4. Circle Answers in Question Book: Circle each of your answer choices in the question booklet before you go to the next question.

5. Answer Sheets Are Critical: Pay careful attention when transferring your choices from the exam booklet to the bubble answer sheet in the last ten minutes. A mistake here can be fatal. Candidates can avoid or reduce the chance of any of 100 mistakes by transposing their answers – A, B, C, or D – at one time in the last few minutes of the exam.

6. Mechanical Transfer: Transfer all of your choices at the end after you work the last question. Practice this process in advance so you know how long it will take.

Leave enough time to complete this critical function. Remember, don't leave a single question unanswered; always make your best educated guess – there is no penalty for wrong answers.

7. Practice the Techniques: If you pick our preferred answering method, you need to practice our subject sequencing system. Use it on the exam drills you create and on the practice exams so you become as efficient with our system as possible. Practice the ability to quickly put questions into the seven MBE categories. Also quite important is to practice your answer-transferring skills and time yourself when filling in the bubbles on the answer sheets. This is an important portion of our MBE practice exam exercises.

IV.   RECOMMENDED MBE PREPARATION PROGRAM

A. <u>Substantial Effort Necessary</u>

Make the commitment to put in sufficient time needed to pass the exam. It takes time to learn, absorb, and synthesize the legal rules into your Magic Memory Outlines®. You need to be able to channel your knowledge into the MBE multiple-choice method of testing.

1. Disassemble Book: Carefully take the books apart, a few pages at a time, punch three holes on the left margin, and place everything in three-ring binders. Tab the various subjects. This will help you study more efficiently, and you can spread out various parts of your book for easy cross-reference.

2. You Must Work Questions: You will become most familiar with the examiners' fine-line distinctions and various distractors by working hundreds of MBE-patterned questions. We have a compendium of more than 1,700 questions at varying degrees of difficulty (easy, average, and hard). Even if you miss some of the harder questions, you will benefit and learn by comparing and contrasting the alternatives explained in the answer rationales. Some of our questions are more factually complex than the MBE and contain more uncertainties. How you perform on the more difficult questions that most students get wrong is of special import in determining your position on the grading curve.

3. Time Commitment: Your total preparation time necessary depends on how long ago you studied the subjects and how efficient you are in the MBE learning process.

a. Time Variables: Our successful students report an average of 20 to 40 hours per chapter, or about 200 to 300 hours in total MBE study time. This does not include the time spent preparing for the other parts of the exam (essay and performance tasks), which many candidates often find also requires a comparable time commitment. Some people work relatively quickly; but for others, passing the bar exam requires greater effort.

b. Schedule: The traditional MBE review period followed by most commercial review courses is over the six or seven weeks beginning in early June or January. The problem is too long solid study periods (over 10 hours a day) reduce memory retention for most students. Many Rigos students therefore follow an early-bird philosophy. They start their MBE studying in April for the July exam or November for the February exam. These students complete the MBE subjects in early June or January and then turn to six weeks of essay and performance learning and practice. A "review of the review" period is also necessary.

c. Do It Right: It is a mistake to underestimate the necessary effort required to pass the MBE. This is a very challenging exam, and you never know when you cross the passing line. The prudent approach is to aim for a healthy margin of safety.

4. Schedule and Calendars: Your effort needs to be well-organized and cover all parts of the exam – MBE, MPT and MEE. Use our week-by-week calendars on pages 19 and 20 to schedule the time you need to devote to studying, both on a daily basis and subject-by-subject. The MBE subjects should be studied before the performance and essay exam subjects. Clear your schedule of all other commitments; you want to take the bar exam only once.

5. Three-Hour Time Blocks: Get used to studying in three-hour solid blocks of time without a break, which is the actual time for answering 100 MBE questions. Aim for three-hour learning blocks, six days a week, with a 60-minute break in between each block. You may have to work up to this. If you intend to use our recommended seven-part subject-by-subject MBE approach for the exam, try to work about 15 to 20 questions from each of the seven subjects in one sitting. This is a preview of how you will use our MBE Secret Weapon in the actual exam. Practice will improve your question subject classification skills.

B. Six Element Success Program

A multi-step approach works best because you are exposed to the substantive law and question nuances from many different viewpoints. The result is a complete preparation positive focused program and "seamless process" that leaves nothing to chance. Following it minimizes bar exam preparation natural fear. This total integrated preparation effort is more effective than the sum of the individual parts.

1. Preview Text Overview: Start by skimming through all the contents and text pages of this book to acquaint yourself with the MBE subjects covered on the exam. This will give you a sense of what is and what is not tested. Look for subject-by-subject breadth and depth coverage, as they may differ from what you experienced in related law school classes. Your Rigos Review course material covers only what is tested on the MBE, not the broader material found in some law school classes or other bar review courses.

2. Detailed Study of Each Chapter: Study every chapter slowly and carefully using pens and highlighters to mark up the text. You must know the black letter law thoroughly. Pay particular attention to the MBE Tips that point out areas of testing concentration or provide test-taking suggestions. Study the important facts or legal rules on which fine-line distinction answers frequently turn. Working the learning questions referenced in the text will reinforce your understanding of the applicable black letter law.

3. Prepare Your Own Magic Memory Outline® of Each Subject: Like law school success, it is essential that you prepare and memorize your own thorough outlines.

a. Summarize Your Knowledge: You need to prepare a summary of every chapter in your own words. This may be accomplished using the Magic Memory Outlines® that are printed both in the book and on optional downloadable software Word templates. These "keyword" outlines match the bold headings in this book's text.

b. Capture the Essence: Your job is to summarize the text following each bold heading. Capture the essence of the rules and enter your own streamlined wording into the outlines. Aim for concise, yet comprehensive, statements of the rule. Focus on the required technical elements of the legal principles. Integrate any helpful "learning question" information into your outline. An evidence example of a Magic Memory Outline can be found on page 4-71 *infra*. Doing your outlines well is the key to learning the law.

c. Memorize Your Outlines: After you complete your own Magic Memory Outline® for a chapter, carefully read it over once or twice. You need to commit your outline to memory. Read it over at least once each week during your review. Quick reads are good. Even as you progress into the review course's later stages, and are practicing the performance and essay subjects, it is helpful to keep the completed MBE subjects in your active memory.

4. Work Chapter Questions: Practice makes perfect. Once your outline is complete, work through the remaining chapter questions. Some of these questions are more complicated and dense than actual MBE questions. They are not necessarily in the same order as the topics in the chapter, but the Question Maps serve as a convenient cross-reference. The questions preceded by a bold F at the right refer to our optional final exam questions.

a. Procedure: If you took your book apart, lay the question sheets next to the answer sheets to save time flipping pages back and forth. Cover the answer sheet page and mask down to consider each alternative answer rationale only after you have actually worked the question. Test yourself by working every question before looking at the answer rationale. It is usually worthwhile to review rationales for all alternatives you missed. They reinforce relevant fine-line distinctions and distractors tested within that particular rule of law.

b. Do a Few at a Time: Start by working the book's practice questions in small bites of around 15 to 20 questions from one subject. Date and put an X through their number in your Rigos textbook margin as you work each question. An example is "5/25 7̶1̶" indicating that on May 25 you worked question 71. Stop and check the answer rationales right after you work each question. Review any question you missed or guessed on.

c. Software Option: The same book questions are also on the optional software so you can use this tool to work the questions in order. On Question Map software, a question pertaining to that topic will pop up if you click on the question.

d. Learn from Mistakes: Your preparation objective is to learn from your mistakes by reviewing the answer rationales while you still appreciate the details of the question. Expect to make mistakes; difficult questions will help you become familiar with the MBE nuances, distractors, and fine-line distinctions. Put a star in the margin of every question you missed. Rework your missed questions shortly before taking the actual exam.

e. Extra Questions: If you have worked most of our 1,500+ questions and want more we suggest the NCBE website as a source. They have numerous actual multiple-choice questions from prior exams that test at the current level of difficulty. We suggest the Value Pack at $150 at http://store.ncbex.org/the-ube-value-pack/.

5. Take the Practice Exam: MBE book 1 at page 573 contains a simulated MBE exam that is also on the software. There are 100 questions in random order. While some practice questions in your text are intentionally easier or more difficult and complex than the MBE, the Final Exam has approximately the same overall difficulty as the actual MBE.

a. Solid Blocks of Time: It is most beneficial to create actual exam conditions. The best schedule is 9:00 a.m. to 12:00 p.m., or from 1:00 to 4:00 p.m. Time yourself and work as quickly as you can without sacrificing accuracy. This gives you a three-hour time block in which to answer 100 multiple-choice questions.

b. Correct and Analyze Your Answers: Correct and review all your answers only after you complete the full practice exam. Review the answer rationales for all four alternatives in each missed question. This reinforces the details of the relevant issue.

(1) Learn from Your Mistakes: When you refer to the answer rationales for missed questions be sure to understand why you picked the wrong choice. Fine-line distinctions are critical. More than one answer rationale may be identical or substantially similar to others if the alternatives are incorrect for the same reason. Determine whether you misread or failed to recognize the importance of a key fact or omission.

(2) Mark Mistakes: Again, put a star in the margin next to every question you missed and work them again the day right before sitting for the actual MBE.

(3) Assess Your Skill Level: Based on your scores on all the questions, award yourself a competency grade of 1 to 6 for every area. Spend more time reviewing your lower score subjects.

6. Revise and Memorize Magic Memory Outlines®: After you work the end of the chapter and the practice exam questions, you may want to update your Magic Memory Outlines®. Key determinative fact patterns have a tendency to repeat themselves on the MBE, even though the scene of the questions may be superficially different. Consider adding a short favorite fact statement following the legal rule summary. Commit your Magic Memory Outlines® to memory by reading them over at least once a week until the exam.

C. Other Study Tips

1. Keep Working Questions: Continue to work practice MBE questions by mixing topics from different chapters. You can make your own exam drills with our optional Rigos software. You may work 5, 10, 20, or 100 random questions at a time. When you have a few spare minutes, do a number of short exams.

2. Learn from Your Mistakes: Shortly before sitting for the actual exam, review every practice question you missed in the review. Each of these questions should have a star next to it. This attention will help you avoid making the same mistakes on the exam.

3. Study Time Blocks: Concentration during your study time is critical. We recommend you increase your studying time to full three-hour blocks without breaks. This will not be easy at first, but you can work up to it. Build up your stamina and concentration intensity so you maintain focus and work quickly during the actual exam. Turn off your cell phone and e-mails during the three-hour study block.

4. Improve Morning Performance: If you are usually a late riser, the week before the exam you should begin to get up early every morning. At exactly 9:00 a.m. during the week before the MBE, do one or two dozen questions from varied subjects. This will get your test-taking mental routine strong as you start the day. Perhaps use the "Make Your Own Exam™" feature on the downloaded software to pick the morning "get going" questions.

D. Additional Rigos Bar Review Series Products

If you like these MBE volumes, consider using other Rigos UBE Review Series publications covering your Uniform Multistate Essay Exam (MEE), Multistate Performance Test (MPT), and Multistate Professional Responsibility (MPRE) examinations. The MEE covers essay testing from the seven-subject MBE text coverage. It contains prior exam distributions and listings of "primary rules" of the most frequently tested issues.

V. DOWNLOADING AND USING THE SOFTWARE

Register at www.rigos.net to download the optional software template for the Magic Memory Outlines, Question Maps and "Make Your Own Exam" question drills. There are numerous ways to work the questions contained on the software and you can mix and match the techniques below. With more than 1,600 questions, you won't soon run out of new challenges.

A. Straight Through Chapter Questions

You can answer practice questions from one subject at a time, usually in order.

1. How It Works: The chapter questions will appear on your screen one at a time beginning with Learning Question Number 1. Work the questions in order.

2. How to Use It: Go to the main page and choose a chapter – for example, click on Chapter 1, Torts. The questions will appear in the same sequence as in the text, and you can work them from beginning to end. If you are reading the text material you can use this software feature to work through the Learning Questions in order. Read the fact pattern and call of the question thoroughly, and then click on selection, "A," "B," "C," or "D." When you make your answer selection, a window will open and indicate whether your choice was correct or incorrect, and present the answer rationale.

B. Final Assessment

1. How It Works: The optional add-on Final Exam is a mock MBE test with approximately the same number of questions, difficulty range, and time constraints as the actual MBE. The software version is timed at 180 minutes per 100-question set. It is designed to be an electronic practice run for the MBE. It should give you confidence when you go in for the real MBE.

2. How to Use It: You may purchase a Final MBE exam which is available from the Rigos website. If you use the software, go to the main page and click "Chapter 7, Final Exam." The MBE exam has 200 questions: 100 for the morning set and 100 for the afternoon. It is timed at 180 minutes for each set. Work the a.m. exam straight through without stopping. Take a one-hour break, then work the p.m. set. The correct answers will show up after you complete the entire exam.

C. Make Your Own Exam™

This optional feature allows you to use the software to create practice sessions in sets of 5, 10, or 20. You can select any specified number of questions of your own choosing.

1. How It Works: Questions appear in random order from all seven MBE subjects. You can use this feature as often as you wish, and you will constantly get new combinations of questions. Work up to answering many questions in a row, which builds your stamina.

2. How to Use It: Click the "Make Your Own Exam" button on the main page. Choose the number of questions that you want to work and click "5," "10," "20," or type any whole number into the white box and click "X." The questions will come on the screen one at a time. Read the fact pattern and call of the question thoroughly, then click on your selection of A, B, C, or D. When you make your answer selection, a window will show whether your choice was correct and why (or why not). You may find it helpful to read all four answer rationales to gain a more thorough understanding of the subject.

3. Do Some from the Book: Even if you favor the software drill, work some questions printed in the books so you gain experience with the format of the actual exam. With the Make Your Own Exam feature, there is no attempt to cover the exam with a subject-by-subject approach. Instead, you practice answering questions in random subject order.

VI. EXAM-TAKING TIPS

A. Be Punctual

1. Consider a Convenient Hotel: Unless you live close to the exam site, consider booking a hotel room nearby. Many authorities advise getting your own room so you have no commuting distractions. It is best to walk from your hotel room to the exam site if possible to avoid all the uncertainties and stresses of travel.

2. Arrive Early: The morning of the actual MBE, an early fully engaged start is especially important. Know where you are going, and do not rush on the morning of the exam. Arrive well before the scheduled starting time and expect to wait in line. Avoid hurrying or arriving late because that will likely adversely affect your performance. Check in at the registrar's desk. Look over the facilities and restroom locations.

B. What to Bring

1. Admission Card and ID: Bring to the exam site your written instructions and admission card provided by your state bar testing authority. Also bring backup identification bearing your signature and picture, preferably a driver's license or passport. Take an accurate watch to both the morning and afternoon exam sessions.

2. Comfort and Practicality: Dress comfortably in clothes that make you feel the best. Layered clothing is recommended as it allows you to compensate for a too warm or cold testing room. Hats and headphones (including earbud headphones) are not allowed. Some states allow candidates to use earplugs, but some do not – check with your local bar association. If allowed, use them while working questions during the preparation period.

3. Snacks: Do not consume a large meal or too much liquid before the exam. Although restroom breaks are possible in most states, they cost you valuable time and break your concentration intensity. Time is very precious in this exercise. Your study practices should have expanded your ability to sit and concentrate for full three-hour blocks. Eat foods that provide energy and are easy to digest (raisins, peanuts, apples, oranges, bananas, energy bars), but do not give you a letdown or make you feel tired.

4. Pre-exam Warm-up: Some candidates use our Make Your Own Exam™ drills first thing in the morning to get into the mental intensity routine beginning at 9:00 a.m. Do this same warm-up the morning of the actual MBE.

C. Focus Only on the MBE

1. Preserve Your Mental Energy: Get a full night's sleep before you take the exam. Some advocate at least one short stretch break per exam set. Fight to keep mentally sharp and intense for both of the MBE three-hour testing sessions. If you find your focus weakening towards the end of the exam, pause, close your eyes, and take four deep breaths.

2. Concentrate on the Task: Do not check your smart phone or e-mails in the morning or at lunch as the outside world may detract from your exam concentration. Imagine you and the exam booklet are in a glass box. During the 180 minutes in each MBE session, the only thing that matters is that you make your best effort on this exam. Leave personal problems outside the exam room. Use the time management techniques you have learned and practiced.

D. Be Confident

1. Relax: Consciously attempt to relax; deep, slow breathing will facilitate this mental state. Don't listen to the pre-exam chatter of nervous candidates; you do not want their test anxiety to affect you. It is too late to add anything to your knowledge base and this distraction may confuse and drain you. It is better not to talk to anyone. If other candidates are bothering you, take a little walk by yourself if that is allowed at your test site.

2. Confidence and Poise: Get psyched to make the MBE (and the rest of the bar exam) your finest intellectual effort. Approach the exam with mental confidence and poise. Think of the MBE as a game that you are going to win. Don't get discouraged by any difficult early questions; some MBE questions are intentionally created to be very rigorous. Think of such questions as opportunities to use your keenly developed analytical

MBE skills. Many of your competitors have not followed a "seamless process" review program and are there essentially "for practice." Rigos Bar Review Series candidates are there to pass.

3. Contemplate the Moment: Just before the examination proctor says, "Start your exam," contemplate the moment. Close your eyes and picture the bar admission ceremony in which you will be sworn in. Every lawyer has been there. This is our professional rite of passage and you will only do it once. Prepare yourself mentally to go for every point and make a commitment not to leave any exam session early. Come off the blocks strong, focused, and determined. The most important race of your professional life has just begun.

E. Exam Performance

1. MBE Secret Weapon: Use our confidential proprietary trade secret patent applied for system to increase time efficiency and answer accuracy. The actual exam will likely seem easier than the Rigos questions you have mastered. See *supra* at 10 for details.

2. Go the Distance: Work to the end of both MBE exam sessions and leave ample time at the end to transfer all your choices to the bubble answer sheet. Keep working until the examiner calls time. The difference between a passing and failing score can get down to one or two extra correct questions and you never know for sure when you cross the line.

3. Use All of the Time: To leave any exam session early implies all your choices are correct. Perfection is not possible on the MBE. Use all of the time to reconsider close answers. Also, leave no question unanswered; it is better to guess than leave answers blank.

VII. CONCLUSION

The 2020 MBE portion of the UBE is passable the first time. Our "seamless process" preparation program works well for candidates committed to success. You can upgrade to our full-service course at www.rigos.net. Included is our software, practice drills, grading service, and four full practice final exam sets. There is simply no shortcut to planning and following a thorough preparation program. Spend the time necessary and distribute all seven subjects over at least seven weeks. You must also master the essay and performance testing.

Use the planning and daily schedules on pages 19 and 20 and incorporate the planning dates into your electronic calendar. The recommended schedule allows you to break your effort into manageable modules to create your own paced review program. Review your completed Magic Memory Outlines® at least weekly while you master the essay and performance exam subjects. Mark your mistakes as you go along for revisiting during the final "review of the review." Plan for success and stay on schedule!

After you get your results, please take the time to fill out the evaluation at the end of this book. It will help us improve our course for the students who will follow you, and we may publish your thoughts and ideas. Good luck on the MBE and in your legal career.

James J. Rigos,
Editor-in-Chief
Rigos UBE Review Series
January 1, 2020

RIGOS PRIMER SERIES UNIFORM BAR EXAM (UBE) REVIEW

15 and 7 WEEK UBE ALL-PART 2020 PREPARATION PLANNING SCHEDULE

For Bar Exam dates of _____

15 WEEK LEARNING SCHEDULE

Weeks To Go	Date Completed	Exam Part
15	_____	Orientation Sessions and Performance Task study and work question
14	_____	Torts, Volume 1
13	_____	Contracts, Vol. 1
12	_____	Property, Vol. 1
11	_____	Evidence, Vol. 2
10	_____	Constitutional Law, Volume 2
9	_____	Criminal Law, Volume 2
8	_____	Civil Procedure, Volume 2
7	_____	Practice Exam 1 Business Entities
6	_____	Conflicts of Law and Family Law
5	_____	Trusts, Wills, and Estates
4	_____	UCC Article 9 and Performance Exam Review
3	_____	Professional Responsibility and Practice Exam 2
2	_____	Double Practice Set 3 and 4
1	_____	Review all essay and missed MBE questions

Get books and do what you can on your own before your formal start date focusing on the seven MBE subjects

7 WEEK LEARNING SCHEDULE

Weeks To Go	Date Completed	Exam Part
7	_____	Orientation Sessions, Tort, and Performance Task study and question
6	_____	Contract Law and Property
5	_____	Constitutional Law and Evidence
4	_____	Civil Procedure and Criminal Law
3	_____	Practice Exam 1, Business Entities, Conflicts of Law, Family Law
2	_____	UCC, Trusts and Wills, Practice Exam 2
1	_____	Professional Responsibility, MPT Review, Double Practice Set 3 and 4

The UBE students should use our Weekly Planning Sheets and daily schedules on the next page to study text and prepare MMOs. Work all built-in learning and essay testing questions.

EXAM WEEK "REVIEW OF THE REVIEW"

Saturday – Score both MBE practice exams and review the rationales to the questions you missed.

Sunday – Read over all your MMOs, review acronyms-mnemonics, write a few essays and tasks.

Monday – Review all essay and performance questions not previously worked in the program. Focus on the law and fact clusters used to raise issues, especially those subjects in which your graded scores were low. Go over and commit to memory our recommended boilerplate wording and acronyms one last time.

Tuesday evening – Review all MBE questions you missed during the MBE review program.

RIGOS UBE REVIEW SERIES

MULTISTATE BAR EXAM (MBE) REVIEW

WEEKLY AND DAILY PLANNING SHEET

WEEK: From Monday _____ **to Sunday** _____ .

THE BAR EXAM IS _____ **WEEKS AWAY**

WEEKLY OBJECTIVES:

	Subject Studied	Do Learning Questions	Prepare MMO	Do Chapter Questions	Memorize MMO and Acronyms
Mon					
Tues					
Wed					
Thurs					
Friday					
Sat/* Sun					

*We recommend students schedule one day a week without substantial bar exam study.

DAILY SCHEDULE BY HOUR

Time	Monday	Tuesday	Wednesday	Thursday	Friday	Saturday	Sunday
8-9:00							
9-10:00							
10-11:00							
11-12:00							
12-1:00pm							
1-2:00							
2-3:00							
3-4:00							
4-5:00							
5-6:00							
6-7:00							
7-8:00							
8-9:00							
9-10:00							
10-11:00							

CHAPTER 4

EVIDENCE

RIGOS UBE REVIEW SERIES

UNIFORM MULTISTATE BAR EXAM (MBE) REVIEW

CHAPTER 4 – EVIDENCE

Table of Contents

RIGOS UBE REVIEW SERIES

UNIFORM MULTISTATE BAR EXAM (MBE) REVIEW

CHAPTER 4

FEDERAL RULES OF EVIDENCE

I.   INTRODUCTION

A. Preliminary Matters

1. MBE Evidence Focus: 27 of the 200 MBE multiple-choice questions test evidence. Up to half of the questions test the two main topics of the hearsay rule (and exceptions) and relevance (and the reasons for excluding relevant evidence). The remainder of the questions are evenly spread over this chapter's contents. Study them closely and carefully review the answer rationales for any questions you missed. See MEE at 10-445 for 14 prior NCBE exam question issues tested distribution.

2. Workbook Format: This chapter on Evidence has four sections: (1) a substantive outline, (2) Magic Memory Outlines®, (3) question maps, (4) practice questions, and (5) answer rationales at the end of the chapter. Within the Substantive Outline, you will find references to Learning Questions (1-71) that directly relate to each of the topics you have just studied. When prompted in the text, go and work the referenced Learning Questions. This will reinforce your learning and build your confidence!

3. Learning Questions: When answering the evidence multiple-choice Learning Questions, the analysis is more important for your learning of the concepts than arriving at a correct answer. Analyze not only why a certain answer is correct, but also why the other answers are incorrect or less correct than the preferred answer.

4. Practice Questions: Once you have completed the entire chapter on Evidence, answer the remaining practice questions in the chapter to assess your strengths and weaknesses in the subject. NCBE has additional sample MBE exams that can be purchased from their website if you feel you need more. Most students find what we have here is sufficient.

5. Crossover Testing: Evidence questions often crossover to civil procedure and criminal law and procedure, particularly *Miranda* warnings and related.

6. Federal Rules of Evidence: The MBE tests the Federal Rules of Evidence (FRE) exclusively – not the common law or state variation thereof. A fertile area for testing is where there is a different treatment between the FRE and common law. Know these rules particularly well. It is not necessary to memorize rule numbers for the MBE or MEE.

B. Answer Strategies – 4 Ws

The thrust of most of the MBE evidence questions is the basis or reasoning upon which a person's testimony or an item of evidence will be determined to be admissible or inadmissible. Also tested is the best reason for determining the evidence admissibility or non-admissibility conclusion. Ask yourself "why is this testimonial evidence being introduced," "whom is trying to offer it," "when in the proceeding," and whether it is a civil or criminal case? – 4 Ws.

1. Admissibility for Other Purposes:

a. Objective: First, determine just what the proponent of the evidence is trying to accomplish. It may seem the proponent is trying to introduce character evidence when in actuality the evidence is being offered to impeach a witness. An item of evidence inadmissible for one purpose may be admissible for some other purpose.

b. Impeachment Purpose: Evidence of an accused's prior conviction for perjury may be admitted at a present trial to impeach him if he takes the stand as a witness. This evidence may have been excluded in the case-in-chief under the "evidence of other crimes or acts" rule, FRE 404(b). However, even though the evidence may also tend to show action in conformity with those past acts, this does not prohibit its admission during impeachment.

2. Process of Elimination:
The correct answer may often be arrived at by eliminating two or three of the answers. Try a true-false approach for every alternative.

3. Nonsensical Answers:
If an answer states a doctrine you do not recognize, chances are it is not correct. After studying the following Rigos UBE Review Series text, you should feel confident in recognizing all the important rules that the MBE tests.

4. Old Common Law Rules:
An answer may seem correct under the Common Law or state Rules of Evidence you learned in law school. The MBE tests only the U.S. Federal Rules of Evidence (FRE). Although the MBE does not specifically test on differences between the two, mastery of the Federal Rules is important to prevent picking a wrong answer.

5. Overruled or Sustained:
When you see this type of answer option, remember that overruled means the objection fails and the evidence may be admitted and considered by the trier of fact. If sustained, the objection is successful and the evidence is excluded.

C. Common Answers

The following evidence answer rationales are found on the MBE with some regularity. Some are illusive, but others require closer scrutiny as they are possibly correct.

1. Inadmissible Because of Witness Incompetency:
This answer is very often incorrect because the threshold of required competency is normally very low.

2. Inadmissible Unless Offered in Rebuttal:
Evidence that may not be admitted in the case in-chief may be introduced in rebuttal to the other party's testimony.

3. Inadmissible Because Prejudice Outweighs Probative Value:
Be sure that the prejudice substantially outweighs the probative value. Generally, only the evidence that would cause the jury to decide on emotion rather than on the facts will reach this threshold.

> **MBE Tip:** A common argument is to assess very damaging evidence as "unduly prejudicial." Remember that all evidence is prejudicial to some extent; that is why attorneys try to get it admitted at trial. Only if the evidence is unhelpful to the case and is introduced primarily to make the jury like or dislike the defendant will it be inadmissible.

4. Inadmissible Because Declarant is Available to Testify:
This only applies to the hearsay **DAAL** exceptions in Rule 804 and Rule 807 on page 4-60 *infra*.

5. Best Evidence Rule: This is a frequent MBE distracter. The best evidence rule applies only to proving the contents of writings and documents. It does not, as many seem to infer from the name of the rule, operate to exclude inconclusive, poor, or "weak" evidence.

II. GENERAL PROVISIONS UNDER THE FRE

A. Sources and Applicability of Law

1. Federal Rules Orientation: The MBE questions are based only on the Federal Rules of Evidence (FRE).

2. Application – FRE 1101: The Federal Rules of Evidence apply to all Federal Courts, except in the following situations listed in Rule 1101(d) & (e) where the rules do not apply:

a. Preliminary Questions of Fact: Preliminary questions of fact necessary to determine admissibility are to be evaluated by the Court under FRE 104.

b. Grand Jury Proceedings: The FREs do not apply to Grand Jury Proceedings.

c. Miscellaneous Proceedings: FREs do not apply to extradition, issuing warrants, criminal summonses, sentencing phases in criminal proceedings, immigration matters, and bail releases.

3. Preliminary Questions – FRE 104: The rules do not apply to preliminary court determinations necessary to decide the admissibility of evidence except the rules concerning privileges. For example, whether a privilege exists or the qualifications of an expert witness can be established by evidence that would otherwise be inadmissible (*e.g.*, hearsay). Such evidence admissibility hearings shall usually be conducted outside the jury's presence.

B. Court Discretion

There are few absolutes in the world of Evidence. Nearly all of the rules give the court discretion to do what seems reasonably fair based on the facts and circumstances presented in the particular case. Always keep your mind flexible and imagine what a court would do to avoid a manifest injustice if the facts seem extreme. Rule 102 states: "These rules shall be construed to secure fairness in administration, eliminate unjustifiable expense and delay, and promote the development of evidence law to the conclusion of ascertaining the truth and securing a just determination."

> **MBE Tip:** The Federal Rules of Evidence reflect reasonable guidelines with the overall objective of fairness. Thus, if you spot an issue but forget the particular details of the rule, employ a common-sense approach to the issue promoting fairness in the pursuit of the truth.

C. Judicial Notice – FRE 201

1. Basic Rule: In a civil case, judicial notice of a fact conclusively establishes that particular fact for the jury. In a criminal case, the prosecution's burden of production on that issue is satisfied, but the court should instruct the jury that it is not necessary they accept it as conclusive. A court may take judicial notice of an adjudicated fact or one not subject to reasonable dispute and so instruct the jury. This will arise in one of two circumstances:

a. Generally Known: If the fact is generally known by the public at large and not reasonably disputable, it is subject to judicial notice. "The sun sets in the west" is an example of this kind of fact.

b. Capable of Accurate and Ready Determination: If consultation of "sources whose accuracy cannot be reasonably questioned" (like a dictionary, atlas, or a calendar) will reveal the fact, it is appropriately subject to judicial notice.

2. Examples: Examples of such unquestionable facts would be that Los Angeles is in California, or that July 17, 2014 was a Monday. Taking notice of lesser known facts may be error. For example, it would be error to take judicial notice of the fact that headrests in automobiles are standard safety equipment; evidence of this fact would be necessary. While most people know that headrests come standard in modern automobiles, the fact that they are safety equipment (as opposed to comfort or some other use) is lesser known.

3. Discretionary Notice: The court has discretion to take judicial notice of certain kinds of facts. The court may take such notice *sua sponte* (on their own initiative) or upon the request of one of the parties. The kinds of facts subject to discretionary notice are:

    a. Laws of Foreign Countries;

    b. Regulations of Private Agencies;

    c. Municipal Ordinances; and

    d. Matters of Local Geography.

4. Mandatory Notice: If a party so requests, a court must take judicial notice of the following kinds of facts:

    a. Federal and State Law; and

    b. Indisputable Facts and Scientific Propositions.

5. Any Time: Judicial notice may be requested and/or taken at any time during the proceeding. Parties have the right to be heard regarding the propriety of taking judicial notice.

> **MBE Tip:** Any time a court accepts a fact without testimony, look for an answer discussing judicial notice.

D. Evidentiary Rulings – FRE 103

Although rulings on evidence are usually final at the trial level, erroneous rulings (either to admit or to exclude) can be the basis for an appeal. A substantial right of a party must be affected and a timely objection and/or motion to strike stating specific grounds must be made. An offer of proof is also usually required to preserve the issue for post-trial motions and appeal. The court is under no obligation to enforce the rules of evidence on its own initiative.

1. Objection: If the ruling is to admit evidence, opposing counsel seeking to exclude must make a timely and specific objection in order to preserve the right to appeal the admission decision. An offer of proof may be required. The objection must be made before the evidence is admitted, or as soon thereafter as possible by a motion to strike.

2. Specific Grounds: The basis and specific grounds for the evidentiary objection must be stated. There are two exceptions, but in practice they are not frequent.

a. Obvious: If the grounds for the objection are obvious from the context, a general objection will suffice. For example, if a witness is recounting a telephone conversation and counsel has already stated "Objection, hearsay" nine times in a row, and the tenth time counsel says simply, "Again, objection," this will likely suffice.

b. Plain Error: If the admission or exclusion of the evidence in question constitutes "plain error," it may constitute denial of a fair trial, and thus grounds for appeal, even in the absence of an objection.

3. Offer of Proof: If the court ruling is to exclude evidence, counsel must make an affirmative offer of proof detailing the substance of the evidence at issue. The only exception is if the substance of the evidence is apparent from the context of the questions asked.

4. Harmless Error: Reversal on appeal of an evidence ruling below is rare and usually only possible if it would have made a difference in outcome or involved a significant constitutional right violation and counsel entered detailed objections below.

E. Preliminary Questions and Conditional Relevance – FRE 104

In a pre-trial meeting, a court may determine preliminary facts such as to whether a witness is qualified, a privilege exists, or evidence is admissible.

1. Burden of Proof: In establishing preliminary facts, the burden of submitting evidence of proof is on the party seeking to establish the facts (the proponent). The proponent must establish the preliminary facts by a preponderance of the evidence.

2. Ruling Not Conclusive: Although the court may rule that preliminary facts are admissible, it is still up to the jury to determine the weight and credibility of those facts.

3. Conditional Relevance: When the relevancy of evidence is dependent upon a condition precedent, the Court will admit the evidence subject to fulfillment of the condition.

4. No Fifth Amendment Waiver: A criminal defendant does not waive his Fifth Amendment privilege against self-incrimination by testifying on a preliminary matter.

5. Privileges Apply: Although the evidentiary standards are relaxed at this preliminary stage (for example, hearsay may be used) the rules regarding privilege still apply.

6. No Cross-examination: By testifying upon a preliminary matter, a defendant in a criminal case does not become subject to cross-examination on other matters.

F. Limited Admissibility – FRE 105

1. Permissible Purpose: Under Rule 105, evidence may be inadmissible for one purpose but admissible for another. For example, a prior conviction may be barred by Rule 404(b) to prove the D is a criminal type, but admissible under Rule 609 to impeach the D if he or she testifies as a witness. In this situation, the court gives a limiting instruction, instructing the jury to consider the evidence only for the permissible purpose and not others.

2. Analysis: Any question regarding admissibility will involve more than one analysis. For example, an out of court statement must be analyzed on relevancy and hearsay. Character evidence, if admissible, may also be subject to an FRE 403 prejudice analysis. A jury limiting instruction is possible. In short, keep your mind open. On the exam, there are often several valid objections to the admissibility of a given piece of evidence.

> **MBE Tip:** On the MBE, the admissibility of evidence may turn on the purpose for which it is being offered. Be sure you understand the purpose before answering the question.

G. Remainder of Related Writings or Recorded Statements – FRE 106

This rule is also called the rule of "completeness." If one party introduces part of a recorded statement or document, that party has waived the right to object to another part of that same statement or document being admitted. The court may require other related submissions be produced that in fairness should be considered at the same time.

H. Presumptions and Burden of Proof – FRE 301

1. Burden of Production: If P has the original burden of production on issue X, P must produce evidence that X exists. If P does not satisfy this burden, the court will decide the issue as a matter of law and will not permit the jury to consider it.

2. Burden of Persuasion: If P has the burden of persuasion on an issue, that means if the jury is not convinced to the level of the required standard of proof, P loses on that issue.

a. Standard of Proof: For criminal cases, the standard is always "beyond a reasonable doubt." For most civil cases, the standard is a "preponderance of the evidence" or "more likely than not." For civil cases involving fraud, attorney disbarment, and the validity of a deed or will, the standard is "clear and convincing evidence."

b. Example: On a claim of negligence, plaintiff will always have the initial burden of persuasion to prove all four required A, B, C, and D elements. Defendant will then have the burden of persuasion on any affirmative defenses.

> **MBE Tip:** The examiners like to know that a candidate can distinguish between the burden of production and the burden of persuasion.

3. Effect of Presumptions: In a civil case, a presumption satisfies one party's burden of production. This "shifts" the burden to the other party to come forth and produce sufficient credible and convincing evidence to rebut the presumption. If so, the "bubble bursts" and the issue goes to the jury. In a criminal case, presumptions are not allowed against the D on an essential element of the crime charged because the burden of persuasion always remains with the prosecution.

I. Federal Law in Civil Actions and Proceedings – FRE 302

In federal district court civil cases, the effect of a presumption regarding a claim or defense raised pursuant to that state law is governed in accordance with the rules of that state.

> **STOP!** Go to page 91 and work Learning Questions 1 to 6.

III. RELEVANCE

A. Definition of Relevant Evidence – FRE 401 and 402

Relevant evidence is that which (1) has some probative value and (2) is material to the case. Although the evidence must be reliable, it does not have to be conclusive to be admissible.

1. Probative Value: The rule requires only that there be any significant tendency to make the existence of any consequential fact more or less probable than it would be without the evidence. Do not confuse this requirement with degree of sufficiency, which is for the jury to decide. The evidence offered need not be enough by itself to sustain a verdict, so long as it is relevant and has probative value. Circumstantial evidence is acceptable.

2. Materiality: The evidence must be of some consequence in determining the action. Therefore, it must bear directly on a fact in issue: look for a link between the evidence offered and the applicable controlling substantive law (*i.e.*, elements of a tort, defense, or crime).

3. Both Elements: Evidence must meet both **PM** elements – **P**robative and **M**aterial – to be relevant. However, relevant evidence is not automatically admissible. Relevant evidence is still subject to constitutional requirements, federal statutes, or other Federal Rules of Evidence. Evidence that is not relevant and material is not admissible.

4. Collateral Matter Evidence Excluded: Facts unconnected to an issue or matter in dispute are inadmissible. At best they are irrelevant and may be mischievous if they significantly distract and mislead the jury. When a witness is cross-examined concerning a collateral issue, the cross-examining party is bound by the answer and the lawyer cannot usually call another witness to contradict the first.

B. Examples

1. Undisputed Evidence: Evidence that is not in dispute may be probative, but not necessarily material because it is already established.

2. Rebuttal: Evidence that is irrelevant during the P's case in chief may become relevant during the D's case in chief. For example, evidence rebutting an affirmative defense.

3. Conduct Suggesting Guilt: Evidence of such behavior is nearly always relevant and admissible. Examples are fleeing from the scene of a crime, hiding from police, changing appearance, using an alias, or refusing to take a field breath or sobriety test in a DUI case.

4. Inadmissible Relevant Evidence:

a. Similar Accidents or Injuries: Unless substantially similar circumstances exists, past occurrences are inadmissible to show a negligence pattern. Such evidence may be admissible on a narrower issue or for a limited purpose (*i.e.*, to show notice or knowledge of a dangerous condition). If admissible, such evidence is usually accompanied by a limiting instruction to the jury. For example, in a products liability case, reports to the manufacturer about similar previous injuries are admissible to show danger awareness.

   b. Similar Contracts: These are inadmissible to show terms of the contract in question, but may come in for the limited purpose of showing definitions, industry or trade usages, past course of dealings, etc.

   5. Violation of Law or Industry Standard: In a civil case, D's violation of an applicable statute or administrative regulation may be admissible to demonstrate negligence or unsafe product. D's violation of an industry standard or similar standard not having the force of law may likewise be admissible relevance. The proponent must demonstrate that:

   a. Applies: The law or standard at issue applies to D's conduct and to the situation presented, and

   b. Probative and Material: The violation of statute or regulation must be both probative (a tendency to prove a fact at issue) and material (of significant consequence) on the issue of negligence or unsafe product. The question of whether the violation constitutes negligence *per se* is governed by tort law, not evidence law.

   6. D's Financial Condition: In a criminal case in which D is charged with theft or a similar crime, D's poverty, alone, is inadmissible to show a motive for the crime. However, it becomes admissible when coupled with additional evidence, such as a sudden improvement in D's financial condition after the alleged crime.

   7. Demonstrative Evidence: Photos, video, diagrams, etc., are generally favored by the court, as long as it is a reasonable representation of the facts depicted.

> **MBE Tip:** Keep clear the difference between demonstrative and admissible evidence. While demonstrative evidence may be used, it cannot be taken back to the jury room during deliberations unless it is properly admitted.

   a. Admissibility: The test is whether the demonstrative evidence is a reasonable representation of the facts depicted. Usually this is satisfied by testimony from an authenticating witness, who says the photo, the model, or the like, is an accurate depiction. However, if the demonstrative evidence is for illustrative purposes only, the evidence is not admitted as an exhibit and is only viewed by the jury during the proceedings.

   b. Photos: Photos must be recent and clear enough to be relevant.

   c. Models: A model must be accurate enough to be useful to the jury.

   8. "Real" Evidence: Something that actually played a part in the case (weapon used in a robbery) requires a showing of the chain of custody (where item has been and who has handled it) to rule out tampering. This is especially important for fungible substances.

   9. Witness Bias: Bias is nearly always relevant to their testimony credibility.

C. Balancing Against Prejudice – FRE 403 - MUUC

Relevant evidence may be excluded if its probative value and need for the evidence is substantially outweighed by any of the four **MUUC** factors:

1. Marginally Relevant: This applies when the mere fact of a prior conviction is an element of the crime presently charged (*e.g.*, the crime of owning a firearm with a prior felony conviction). The prosecution may be required to accept D's offer to stipulate to the prior conviction, thus keeping the details of the prior conviction from the jury. The reason for this is usually that the nature of the prior crime is marginally relevant yet could be highly prejudicial.

> **MBE Tip:** The court's decision of prejudice and resulting exclusion usually applies unless it is clear on the facts that the probative value of the evidence substantially trumps the prejudice.

2. Unfair Prejudice Danger: Some prejudice is allowable; only "unfair" prejudice is excluded. The danger is that unfairly prejudicial evidence may inflame the jury into making a decision on the basis of emotion rather than relevant fact. Evidence may be excluded that is barely relevant but highly prejudicial, such as the murder defendant is a gang member.

a. "Too Good" Not Enough: Evidence that is simply "too good" or "too powerful" cannot be excluded on that basis alone. All negative evidence is prejudicial to a party. The probative value must be substantially outweighed by prejudice.

b. Examples: Possibly unfairly prejudicial evidence would include a prosecutor's introduction of gruesome autopsy photographs and related high-impact evidence. One example is the trial of the D.C. snipers: the court excluded the testimony of grief-stricken relatives of people who were allegedly murdered by the defendant in the same "killing spree." That evidence was not the subject of the prosecution before the court.

> **MBE Tip:** Look for the words "substantially outweighed," not merely "outweighed."

3. Unproductive / Cumulative: Introduction should not waste court time, such as needless presentation of cumulative repetitious evidence. "Asked and answered" is the usual objection. The rule could also be used to exclude a photograph that is too fuzzy to be helpful. There are no hard and fast rules here though, and the trial court has wide discretion.

4. Confusion: The evidence should not create confusion of the issues or mislead the jury. This does not mean that confusing evidence is by definition irrelevant. Rather, irrelevant evidence is confusing because the jury does not know what purpose it serves.

> **MBE Tip:** Marginally relevant evidence may be excluded if **MUUC** applies. Rule 403 does not authorize a judge to exclude evidence on the ground that it lacks credibility. Credibility and weight are for the jury alone to decide, after hearing all of the evidence.

STOP! Go to page 92 and work Learning Questions 7 to 11.

IV. CHARACTER EVIDENCE – FRE 404 and 405

A. Character Evidence Generally – FRE 404(a)

Evidence of a person's character or trait concerns a person's natural tendencies and general reputation showing what kind of person he or she is. Examples would be evidence of honesty, peacefulness, sobriety, etc. By definition, this evidence is partly judgmental and is generally not admissible for the purpose of proving action in accordance with that character or trait on a particular occasion. There are different exceptions for civil and criminal cases:

> **MBE Tip:** The issue of introduction of character evidence as opposed to specific conduct is frequently tested. Pay attention to the type of case (civil or criminal), the person against whom the evidence is offered (plaintiff/victim/defendant/witness), and the purpose of the evidence.

1. Civil Proceeding:

a. Character at Issue: If character traits, credibility, or truthfulness is actually directly at issue, evidence is admissible (*i.e.*, truth of a defamatory libel/slander accusation, employing a person of questionable character, parental character fitness in a custody dispute).

b. Character Not at Issue: Where character is not at issue (the typical civil case), such extrinsic evidence is not admissible to prove negligence or other liability. Character evidence may only be admissible for impeachment under FRE 608. See *infra* at 4-45.

2. Criminal Proceeding:
Evidence of criminal character or a trait thereof is not usually admissible to prove that D's present action was in conformity therewith, except:

a. Character of Accused – FRE 404(a)(1):

(1) Offered by Accused: A criminal D is entitled to introduce pertinent evidence of historical tendency towards good character relevant to the criminal act with which he is charged. The character or trait evidence must be relevant to the act which created the criminal charge at issue. This is usually peacefulness and/or truthfulness. Unrelated specific prior acts to prove innocence are still excluded.

(2) Offered by Prosecution: The prosecution may not introduce evidence to impugn the D's character except under two circumstances:

(a) Rebuttal: To rebut the accused's character evidence when the D "opens the door," with their own related character evidence or

(b) Victim: If the accused offers a victim's character trait under 404(a)(2), the prosecution may introduce the same character trait of the accused.

b. Character of Victim – FRE 404(a)(2): A pertinent trait of the victim's character may be offered:

(1) Accused in Criminal Proceeding: If offered by the accused, it is limited to circumstances where the victim's character is pertinent, which is rare. If evidence of the victim's character is allowed, the prosecution may offer victim character evidence in rebuttal such as the peacefulness of the victim.

(2) Victim's Peacefulness in Homicide Where Self-Defense is Raised: As in the case of homicide, the prosecutor may introduce character evidence of the peacefulness of the victim to rebut a D's claim of self-defense in that the victim was the first aggressor.

(3) Sexual Assault: A victim's character is only rarely admitted because the law tries to protect victims. See FRE 412 *infra* at 4-37 for more detail on introducing evidence of the victim's alleged character.

c. Character of Witness – FRE 404(a)(3): See Rules 607, 608, and 609 *infra* for evidence regarding the character of a witness.

B. Prior Crimes, Wrongs, or Other Related Acts – FRE 404(b)

This rule applies to both civil and criminal cases. It essentially prohibits the use of evidence of past misdeeds or good behavior in an attempt to prove action in conformity therewith in the current matter. Evidence of D's prior conduct, both misconduct to demonstrate a propensity for bad behavior, such as gang membership, or to suggest a propensity for subsequent good behavior, such as community service, is inadmissible. The rule has exceptions.

1. Inadmissible as to Character or General Propensities: A person's prior misconduct is not admissible to show that the person is a certain "type" or has a certain trait that makes it more likely that the person committed the crime charged or was negligent. The law shuns the notion that "once a criminal, always a criminal" or "once negligent, always negligent." In other words, a person's prior misconduct is inadmissible to demonstrate the person's general propensities. For an exception in cases of sexual assault, see Rule 413 *et seq.*

2. Admissible for Other Purposes: Character evidence may be admissible for other purposes, so long as the prosecution gives reasonable notice of intent to do so. The Rule lists some non-exclusive other purposes such as *modus operandi*, motive, opportunity, intent, preparation, plan, knowledge, identity, absence of mistake or accident. Examples include:

a. Rebutting Claim of Accident: D is accused of assaulting V, but claims it was an accident. Evidence that D assaulted V last week is inadmissible to show D as violent, but may come in to rebut Ds defense that the assault was merely an "inadvertent accident."

b. Common Scheme or Plan: D is charged with only one of multiple crimes. The other crimes are inadmissible to show D has a criminal tendency, but may be allowed to show that this crime was part of a larger criminal scheme (D's "*modus operandi*").

c. Intent: The prosecution charges that on May 15, D possessed an ounce of methamphetamine with intent to distribute. D admits that he possessed the drugs on May 15, but insists in his direct examination that he possessed the drugs solely for his personal use and not for sale to others. The prosecution may now introduce evidence that D sold methamphetamine on April 1, April 15, and May 1. The evidence of these prior acts helps to show D's intent to distribute the drugs he possessed on May 15.

> **MBE Tip:** The key to admissibility of character evidence is to be able to articulate how in some way the evidence is relevant other than to demonstrate a person's subsequent action in conformity with the previous character trait. The court may create a limited jury instruction.

C. FRE 404 Character Evidence Chart

Type of Case	Type of Character Evidence	Party Offering	Purpose of Introduction of Evidence	Admissible?
Civil	General	Either	Prove conformity therewith	NO
Civil	General	Either	Character is at issue	YES
Civil	General	Either	Impeach witness	YES
Civil	Other Crimes, Wrongs, or Acts	Either	Prove conformity therewith	NO
Civil	Other Crimes, Wrongs, or Acts including Misdemeanors	Either	Proof of motive, opportunity, intent, preparation, plan, knowledge, identity, absence of mistake	YES

Type of Case	Type of Character Evidence	Party Offering	Purpose of Introduction of Evidence	Admissible?
Criminal	General	P	Prove conformity therewith	NO
Criminal	General	D	Prove innocence; impeach witness; challenge witness' character	YES
Criminal	General	P	Rebut; impeach witness (if D "opens the door")	YES
Criminal	Other Crimes, Wrongs, or Acts	P	Prove conformity therewith	NO
Criminal	Other Crimes, Wrongs, or Acts	P	Proof of motive, opportunity, intent, preparation, plan, knowledge, identity, absence of mistake	YES
Criminal	Other Crimes, Wrongs, or Acts	D	Prove innocence; impeach witness; challenge witness' character	YES

Type of Case	Type of Character Evidence	Party Offering	Purpose of Introduction of Evidence	Admissible?
Criminal – Rape	General	P/D	Character of Victim	NO
Criminal – Rape	Other Crimes, Wrongs, or Acts	P/D	Character of Victim	NO
Criminal – Rape	Other Crimes, Wrongs, or Acts	P/D	Prove D was not source of semen; prove consent via past sexual acts	YES

> **MBE Tip:** Remember that all evidence is still subject to a balancing test for prejudicial harm under Rule 403. Keep this in mind in any Rule 404(b) analysis on the exam.

D. Methods of Proving Character – FRE 405

If it is admissible for one of the permitted purposes under 404(b), past incidents of character or trait evidence may be introduced in one of two ways. The choice depends on whether the character trait in question is essential to the charge, claim, defense, or proof:

1. Reputation or Opinion: If the character trait is not essential, then evidence of the trait may be introduced by reputation or opinion.

a. Reputation: Reputation evidence must relate to a party's reputation in a neutral and generalized community, such as the party's neighbors or co-workers. A party's reputation in a smaller or non-neutral community (*e.g.*, among law enforcement officers or within the party's family) will usually be inadmissible.

b. Opinion: Opinion evidence is the testimony of one person as to his or her own generalized opinion regarding the D's character. Examples of specific instances of conduct leading to a reputation/opinion may be inquired about on cross examination if the other party "opens the door," but may not usually be introduced on direct.

2. Specific Conduct: Evidence of specific instances of conduct may be admitted if the character or trait is an essential element of a charge, claim or defense.

MBE Tip: FRE 404 and 405 must be read together to make sense. FRE 404 describes those circumstances in which evidence of a character trait is admissible. If the evidence passes the 404 test, then proceed to a 405 analysis to determine which kind of evidence is permissible. The answer will depend on whether the character trait at issue is an essential element of the charge or claim. This concept is tested reasonably frequently on both the MBE and MEE.

E. Victim's Sexual History – FRE 412

1. General Rule of Inadmissibility: In any civil or criminal proceeding, a victim's other sexual behavior or sexual predisposition is generally not admissible.

MBE Tip: For the purposes of the MBE, it is not too likely that the examiners would write a question where the correct response is the admission of a victim's past sexual behavior. If in doubt, choose the response that excludes the evidence under FRE 412.

---

2. Exceptions: Instances of admissible sexual behavior include:

a. Criminal Proceedings:

(1) Proof of Physical Evidence: Evidence of a victim's specific sexual acts with others offered to prove that the accused was not the source of the semen, injury, or other physical evidence;

(2) Proof of Victim Consent: Evidence of past sexual behavior between the victim and person accused of sexual misconduct to prove consent in the present case;

(3) Protection of Constitutional Rights: Other evidence for which exclusion would violate the constitutional rights of the accused.

b. Civil Proceedings:

(1) Probative Value High: Evidence of a victim's sexual behavior or sexual predisposition if otherwise admissible by these rules and the probative value substantially outweighs the danger of harm to any victim or potential prejudicial value;

(2) Reputation Placed at Issue: Evidence of a victim's reputation is only admissible if the victim places their reputation in controversy.

3. Procedure: A party intending to present such victim criminal evidence must file a motion to be heard by the court *in camera* at least 14 days before trial. All parties including the alleged victim must receive notice specifically describing the evidence at issue in the hearing. Unless the court orders otherwise, the record and all related papers must be sealed.

**F. Evidence of Similar Crimes in Sexual Assault and Child Molestation Cases –
FRE 413, 414, and 415**

This regularly tested rule is an exception to the Rule 404(b) prohibition on propensity evidence. In both civil and criminal proceedings involving sexual assault or child molestation, evidence of past conduct in sexual assault or child molestation is admissible for "its bearing on any matter to which it is relevant." The D must receive at least 15 days prior notice.

| STOP! | Go to page 93 and work Learning Questions 12 to 19. |

V. HABIT AND ROUTINE PRACTICE – FRE 406

A. Establishing Habit or Routine Practice

1. Conformity: Evidence of a person's habit or of the routine practice of an organization is generally admissible to show conformity with a particular set of circumstances, whether corroborated or not and regardless of the presence of eyewitnesses.

2. Habit: "Habit," however, is narrowly defined. It means regular automatic behavior without significant premeditation or advance thought. Examples include always turning right coming out of the driveway or always blowing a whistle at a railroad crossing.

3. Routine Practices: "Routine practices" of an organization are usually admissible to show conformity therewith on the occasion in question (*i.e.*, mailroom procedures or a standard chain of review of common forms). This is usually very effective evidence.

4. Method of Proof: Evidence of habit may be introduced either by general opinion testimony or by specific instances of conduct. If specific instances are offered, they must be sufficient in number and frequency to constitute a finding that the behavior is a habit or routine practice.

MBE Tip: A habit is a semi-automatic regular response. The test is whether you would have acted the same way if the stimulus were removed; if you would have had to think about it (the act), then it is not a habit. If the response is characterized in the MBE fact pattern as "often," "frequently," or "sometimes" occurring, the odds are that the behavior will fall short of the definition of a "habit" according to the rule. If the response is characterized as "always" or "regularly" occurring, then it is probably a habit and admissible.

B. Habit Distinguished from Character

Habit is distinguishable from reputation character evidence. Character is a general pattern of behavior or a personality trait; habit is more automatic when a party always performs a specific act or set of reactions when a particular set of circumstances occurs.

VI. SUBSEQUENT REMEDIAL MEASURES – FRE 407

A. Generally Inadmissible

The law encourages parties to take remedial or corrective measures after an accident to avoid or reduce the chances of similar future injury or harm. When such measures are taken, evidence of subsequent remedial measures is not admissible to prove negligence or culpable conduct in connection with the product or event in question. This arises in product liability cases if a product was redesigned after an injury even if it would prove feasibility of design.

B. Examples of Inadmissible Remedial Measures

Examples of such subsequent remedial measures which would have made the injury or harm less likely to occur include posting warning signs, systemic product improvements, safety measures, retraining, redesign of a product, etc. Although some states admit evidence of subsequent changes in design to prove prior defects, the Federal Rules do not allow this.

C. Exception Purposes

Evidence of subsequent remedial measures may be offered for more narrowly defined purposes such as (1) proving disputed ownership or control of an asset, (2) proving feasibility of precautionary measures if the potential success of such measures is in controversy and the introduction does not have a strong tendency to prove negligence, or (3) impeachment. For these purposes, an exception is made and the subsequent remedial evidence is admissible.

> **MBE Tip:** Questions that demonstrate the above exception are common. For example, look for cases where P seeks to admit a subsequent remedial measure to establish D's disputed ownership or control of the property involved in a negligence action. The remedial measure is admissible for this purpose.

VII. OFFERS OF COMPROMISE – FRE 408, 410

Settlement negotiations in both the civil and criminal contexts are usually inadmissible. The law intends to encourage compromise and settlement of disputes prior to trial.

A. Civil Proceeding – FRE 408

1. Generally Inadmissible: Offering, negotiating, or agreeing to an offer of compromise in a pending contested claim is not admissible to prove validity of the claim or liability.

> **MBE Tip:** The rationale for this no-severance rule is to remove what would otherwise be a disincentive toward settlement negotiations. Therefore, the statement does not have to be particularly damaging or compromising to be excluded.

2. Compromise Exception: An exception may be made to allow evidence of a settlement to show bias or prejudice of a witness, or to negate or rebut an accusation of undue delay. However, such may still be excluded as too prejudicial under Rule 403, *supra* at 32.

3. "No Severance" Rule: A party may not circumvent the rule against introducing offers of compromise by severing statements of culpability from the actual offer of settlement.

a. Example: For example, just following an automobile collision, the D approaches the P and says, "I'm so sorry this happened, it's all my fault. Please let me pay for your damages." The P cannot introduce the first sentence by omitting the second – both are considered statements made as an offer of compromise and are excluded.

b. Exception: When the offer is specifically an offer to pay medical expenses, statements of same may be severed from other settlement particulars. See Rule 409, *infra* at 40.

B. **Criminal Proceeding – FRE 410**

1. Generally Inadmissible: The fact that a party entered into discussions and/or negotiation in a criminal case regarding the entering or withdrawal of a settlement or *nolo contendere* plea is inadmissible. Statements made to the prosecutor during plea discussions are also inadmissible. But admissions made during police questioning are usually admissible.

2. Borderline Situations: In borderline criminal cases, the test is to ask: (1) did D subjectively believe he/she was then engaged in plea negotiations, and (2) if so, was the belief reasonable from an objective point of view, based on the circumstances?

3. Exception: Such pleas, offers, or statements are admissible in a criminal proceeding to evidence perjury or false statement if the statement was made by the D under oath, on the record, and in the presence of counsel. Also, another contemporaneous statement already admitted may in fairness allow for admission of the first statement.

VIII. PAYMENT OF MEDICAL EXPENSES – FRE 409

Evidence of furnishing, offering to pay, or paying someone's medical, hospital, or similar expenses is generally made from desirable human impulses are therefore inadmissible against the defendant for public policy reasons to encourage such activities. If made as a settlement offer, it is inadmissible to prove liability for the underlying injury. This is a narrower exclusion than in rules 408 and 410. Statements regarding offers to pay medical expenses as settlement are not subject to the "no severance" principle under FRE 408. This means that statements of general culpability made in connection with D's offer to pay P's medical expenses may be introduced, as long as the actual liability admission itself is omitted.

IX. LIABILITY INSURANCE – FRE 411

A. Generally Inadmissible

Evidence that a person was or was not insured against liability is not admissible to prove liability for negligence, contributory negligence, or wrongful conduct.

B. Exception

When offered for another permissible purpose, such as proof of agency, ownership, control, or bias or prejudice of a witness, insurance evidence may come in. The exceptions are narrowly construed and must still pass the Rule 403 danger of unfair prejudice analysis.

> **STOP!** Go to page 94 and work Learning Questions 20 to 24.

X. PRIVILEGES – FRE 501 and 502

Privileges are exclusionary rules designed to serve the higher purpose of fostering confidentiality where client disclosure to a professional are essential. Privileges apply to all stages of legal proceedings, including discovery as well as the Constitutional right to refuse to be an incriminating witness against oneself.

> **MBE Tip:** The source of privileges in Federal Courts is the common law, rather than statute or formal rule of evidence as in many state courts. This area is not heavily tested.

A. General Approach to Privileges

1. Legitimate Relationship Required: There must be a professional relationship or legitimate marriage in fact on the date of the communication at issue.

2. Confidentiality Intended: Any protected communication offered within the privileged relationship must have been made under an intention of confidentially. A third party cannot have overheard the protected communication unless the third party's presence was necessary to promote the relationship (*e.g.*, nurse, legal secretary, guardian).

3. "Holder" May Choose to Assert or Waive Privilege: Each privilege belongs to a natural person "holder" who is then entitled to assert or waive the privilege. Only a criminal D can use the privilege to avoid taking the witness stand.

a. Assertion: The "holder" is usually the non-professional in the relationship (*i.e.*, doctor's patient, lawyer's client, etc.). The professional may also assert the privilege on behalf of the holder (*i.e.*, attorney may assert privilege concerning confidential communications with one of his clients), but cannot waive the protection on behalf of the holder.

b. Knowledgeable Waiver: Waiver is often an affirmative act (disclosing privileged information to a third party, or filing suit against the hearer of the communication). Waiver can also follow a failure to assert the privilege while under oath. The general rule is that once privilege is waived, it is forever waived as to the information disclosed.

c. Inadvertent Waiver: If the protected communication was disclosed by mistake and the holder took prompt reasonable steps to rectify the mistake the court may hold that such communication does not constitute waiver if overall a waiver would be unfair.

4. More Than Just Verbal Communications: Much like the rules about freedom of expression, privilege rules have been expanded to include not just written and spoken verbal conveyances, but also assertive conduct (like a "thumbs-up" gesture or nodding head).

B. Attorney-Client and Work-Product Privilege

The client is the holder of this privilege and can assert it to prevent his or her own testimony or to prevent the testimony of their attorney. An attorney can also assert this privilege on behalf of the client. Attorney work-product prepared in anticipation of litigation is also protected, but planning a future crime or fraud in the presence of a lawyer has no privilege.

1. Necessary Element – Relationship Must Exist: The privilege does not arise until an attorney-client relationship exists. In general, the test is whether the communications were made when the client believed he or she was consulting a lawyer and manifested an intention to seek professional legal advice. A private lawyer's office is not necessary.

2. Necessary Element – Confidentiality Expectation: The privilege applies only to communications intended as confidential. The presence of third persons may destroy the privilege. Examples are conversations made in a public place like an elevator, a courthouse hallway, or in the presence of an unprivileged third party.

3. Exceptions:

a. Crime or Fraud: If the communication was made in furtherance of a future crime or fraud, then communication is not protected.

b. Attorney-Client Dispute: The privilege is not applicable if the communication is relevant to an attorney/client dispute such as a client lawsuit for malpractice or collection of fees.

c. Attesting Witness: If the communication concerns a document to which the lawyer was an attesting witness, an exception applies. For example, if a client tells the lawyer that he believes the opposing party lied, and that statement is then made part of the lawyer's sworn affidavit, communications relevant to that statement in that affidavit are not privileged.

d. Joint Clients: If former joint clients are currently involved in their own dispute, communications to the lawyer relevant to a matter of common interest, made during the time when joint representation was still in effect, are not privileged as to both joint clients. But as to the rest of the world, the privilege remains.

MBE Tip: Look for the presence of a third person at the communication. If the person's presence is necessary for the communication to occur, privilege is not destroyed. For example, a nurse who keeps the client awake or an interpreter who facilitates communication with a lawyer will not destroy a privilege.

C. Marital Communication Privilege and Spousal Incompetency

There are two types of spousal privileges to be distinguished: (1) spousal privilege for communications made during marriage then intended to be confidential and (2) spousal incompetency. Each operates independently of the other.

1. Traditional Privilege for Confidential Communications: This is available in both civil and criminal cases. This privilege protects the (confidential) communication made or exchanged between spouses during the marriage – even if the spouses are later divorced. The holder is the non-testifying spouse; thus one spouse can prevent the testimony of the other.

2. Exceptions: The marital Communication Privilege is not applicable to the following four situations:

a. Lawsuit: In a lawsuit between the spouses where they are directly adverse;

b. Competency: In a competency proceeding against one of the spouses by the other spouse or by a third party;

c. Prosecution of Crime against the Other Spouse: When one spouse is prosecuting the other spouse for a crime against them or the family children; or

d. Planning Crime or Fraud: The communication at issue was made to aid the planning or commission of a crime or fraud.

MBE Tip: The Marital Communication Privilege applies to statements made between spouses only. This would not prevent a spouse from testifying as to the other spouse's actions. Spousal incompetence may prevent a spouse from testifying about the other spouse's action.

---

3. Adverse Spousal Testimony Privilege: The principle of spousal privilege prevents a spouse from testifying against the other spouse about confidential communications that were made between the spouses during marriage. The privilege may be waived and expires upon divorce. An exception applies to testimony in a criminal action against any child of whom the testifier is the spouse or parent of the child.

MBE Tip: Marital and Adverse Spousal Privilege may overlap, such as when the spouses are still married and the testimony sought is regarding a confidential marital communication.

TIME OF COMMUNICATION	SPOUSAL INCAPACITY "PRIVILEGE" (WITNESS INCOMPETENCY) Available?	MARITAL COMMUNICATION PRIVILEGE Available?
Before Marriage	Yes, spouse is incompetent to testify as to any and all communications made before or during marriage	No, confidential communications prior to the marriage date are not protected
During Marriage	Yes, unless waived	Yes, unless waived
After Marriage Termination	No, spouse may now testify as to any communications made at any time (except those during marriage)	Yes, but only as to confidential communications that occurred during the marriage

D. Physician-Patient Privilege

Communication or disclosures made for the purpose of medical diagnosis or treatment are privileged. There is a waiver if the patient places her medical condition "at issue."

The Supreme Court in *Jaffee* recognized a general psychotherapist privilege intended to encourage mental patients to seek professional psychiatrist assistance requiring full disclosure for treatment. The doctor or psychotherapist may assert the privilege on behalf of the patient. Note that this privilege does not apply to personal injury suits or to malpractice claims that the patient may bring against the psychotherapist.

> **STOP!**   Go to page 95 and work Learning Questions 25 to 29.

XI. WITNESS COMPETENCY

A. General Rule of Competency – FRE 601

Every person is deemed competent to be a witness except very young children, or as provided by statute or by court rule. The state law of witness competency governs. Therefore, state Dead Man's Statutes control questions of disallowing testimony of the decedent's statements because of age, mental capacity, or financial interest.

B. Disqualification of a Witness – LULU

1. **Lack of Observation:** Witness lacks observation/perception. See Rule 602.

2. **Untruthfulness:** Witness has a lack of appreciation for truthful testimony.

3. **Lack of Memory:** Witness lacks recollection of the events in question.

4. **Uncommunicative:** Witness lacks ability to communicate.

MBE Tip: Do not assume that a particular witness class (*e.g.*, insane, infant) automatically meets the above criteria. Look for facts referring to an applicable state law on point.

C. Personal Knowledge – FRE 602 and 603

A lay witness must testify under oath on the basis of personal knowledge of the matter. For example, if the witness did not see the stoplight, she cannot testify as to what color it was.

1. Own Testimony: Evidence of personal firsthand knowledge may consist of the witness's own testimony such as "I saw the light and it was green." However, simply stating "The light was green" requires a factual foundation that the witness saw the light itself.

2. Equivocating Witness: This rule does not prevent a witness from qualifying her knowledge with words like "I think," "As I recall," or "Probably . . .," etc. Equivocation goes to the weight, not admissibility of the testimony. Weight is for the jury to consider.

> **MBE Tip:** This rule seldom results in the exclusion of testimony. Objections are often mistakenly made regarding weight, not admissibility.

D. Judge as a Witness – FRE 605

The judge presiding at the trial may not testify in that trial as a witness. No objection needs to be made to prevent this basic role conflict.

E. Juror as Witness – FRE 606

A member of the jury may not testify as a witness in the trial of the case in which the juror is sitting. Objections to calling such a witness must be made out of the presence of the jury. After a verdict has been published, a juror may testify about extraneous prejudicial information considered, outside influence imposed upon jurors, or verdict form mistake.

XII. WITNESS CREDIBILITY / IMPEACHMENT

A. Generally – FRE 607

1. Impeachment Defined: Impeachment is introducing evidence not on the merits of the case itself, but to cast doubt upon the credibility or reliability of a witness. The prosecutor must disclose such in a criminal case. To exclude such evidence, the probative value of their testimony must be substantially outweighed by the danger of unfair prejudice. Impeachment evidence is usually offered to demonstrate the following:

a. Bias: Witness personal bias, either actual (witness states a bias in favor of a particular outcome) or implied (witness has a personal relationship with a party or attorney) is a strong ground for impeachment.

b. Mental or Sensory Perception Problems: If an impairment would interfere with the witness' proper recitation of an event, this may be a ground for impeachment. For example, bad eyesight (without glasses) or hearing loss (without hearing aid), or a poor memory.

c. Contradiction of a Witness' Testimony: Usually a material direct contradiction is grounds for impeachment. A witness' mere different recollection about an unimportant detail will not usually suffice.

d. Character or Prior Conduct of a Witness: In some circumstances, the character or prior conduct of a witness is admissible to impeach if it is relevant. See FRE 608.

e. Prior Convictions of Witness: Criminal convictions for crimes involving untruthfulness.

f. Inconsistent Statements of a Witness: Prior statements made to police or in preliminary proceedings can be used to impeach.

2. Contradiction with Extrinsic Collateral Evidence Prohibited (Collateral Facts Rule): When not otherwise prohibited, extrinsic evidence used to impeach a witness by contradiction must be relevant to a substantive issue in the case.

a. Example: Witness 1 states "I saw D run the red light. I was wearing a blue jacket at the time." Witness 2 could testify "D did not run the red light," because it directly contradicts a substantive factual issue stated by Witness 1. Witness 2 cannot state, "Witness 1 was wearing a red jacket at the time, not blue." Though this casts doubt upon Witness 1's memory by contradicting his testimonial statement, this contradictory evidence is not material to the issues at trial and its only purpose is to cast doubt upon Witness 1's memory. The color of Witness 1's jacket is collateral to the issues at trial.

b. Exception: If there were a videotape of the collision, and the tape showed Witness 1 wearing a red jacket, the tape would not be collateral because it is relevant to a substantive issue. Witness 1 can be cross-examined on the color of the jacket because such questioning is not extrinsic evidence.

> **MBE Tip:** The credibility for recollection of a witness may not be attacked with introduction of extrinsic evidence if the facts in the evidence have no other purpose than to cast doubt on the credibility of the testimony. This is known is the "Collateral Facts Rule."

3. Use of Impeachment Evidence as Substantive Evidence: Evidence that impeaches a witness may be used as substantive evidence as well, so long as the evidence is not excluded under any other rule such as hearsay.

a. Admission with Limiting Instruction: If the impeachment evidence is not admissible substantively, then the Court gives a limiting instruction to the jury that the evidence may be considered only for witness impeachment purposes.

b. Example: Extrinsic evidence of a prior inconsistent statement by a witness (not a party) would be admissible as impeachment evidence under FRE 613 (see *infra* at page 47). This evidence may be inadmissible as substantive evidence under hearsay rules.

> **MBE Tip:** Once a criminal accused testifies, under FRE 404(a)(3), he or she becomes a witness subject to impeachment rules 607, 608, & 609, which includes impeachment by prior conviction.

B. Character or Conduct of the Witness – FRE 608

1. Opinion or Reputation Evidence of Witness's Veracity – FRE 608(a): The veracity and credibility of a witness may be attacked or supported by evidence in the form of opinion or reputation for truthfulness, untruthfulness, or credibility.

a. Reputation in Neutral Community: Reputation evidence must relate to the witness's reputation in a neutral and generalized community, such as the witness's neighbors or co-workers. A witness's reputation in a smaller or non-neutral community (*e.g.*, a witness's reputation among local law enforcement officers) is inadmissible.

b. Truthfulness: Evidence of the witness's truthful character may be introduced only in rebuttal to evidence of untruthfulness.

2. Specific Instances of Conduct – FRE 608(b): Evidence showing specific instances of conduct, other than conviction of a crime, which concerns a witness's character for truthfulness or untruthfulness may be introduced only by cross-examination of that individual witness. Conduct may not be proven by extrinsic evidence such as calling witness 2 to testify about an unrelated collateral issue involving witness 1's truthfulness or untruthfulness.

a. Witness' Own Acts: A witness may be asked upon cross-examination about his or her own prior acts that reflect upon their untruthfulness.

b. Other Witness' Acts: This is where witness 2 is called by witness 1's lawyer and testifies to the character of witness 1. The general rule is that witness 2 may testify about witness 1's prior acts only upon cross-examination, not upon direct.

C. Impeachment by Evidence of Conviction of Crime – FRE 609

> **MBE Tip:** Rules 608 & 609 allow for the introduction of character evidence of an accused on cross examination if he chooses to testify. For example, if a criminal D on trial for perjury takes the stand, his prior perjury conviction may be introduced for the purpose of attacking his credibility at the same time collaterally implying that the D has a propensity for perjury.

1. General Rule: For the purpose of attacking the credibility or truthfulness of a party or witness, evidence of the following types of crimes may be admitted:

a. Felonies: For any witness other than the accused, all crimes punishable by death or more than one year in prison (typically felonies) are admissible. When the witness is the accused, evidence of a prior felony conviction may be admitted if the court determines that the probative value substantially outweighs the prejudicial effect.

b. Dishonesty: Any prior crime that involves dishonesty (fraud, theft, etc.) or false statement as an element of the offense – *i.e.*, that which the prosecution must necessarily prove to win the case – regardless of the punishment prescribed by the statute is admissible.

c. Other Crimes: Crimes not falling into the above two categories are not admissible to attack the credibility of the witness under this rule. Typically, misdemeanors will not be admissible.

2. Time Limit – 10 Years: Conviction of a felony or a crime involving dishonesty is not admissible in a civil action if the conviction (or prison release) was more than ten years ago.

3. Exception: However, if the court determines that the probative value of the prior conviction supported by those specific facts and circumstances substantially outweighs its prejudicial effects, the court may admit evidence of a conviction that occurred earlier than the ten-year limit. This is allowed in the interest of justice, so long as the offering party gives advance, written notice of such intent.

4. Effect of Pardon, Annulment, or Certificate of Rehabilitation: Evidence of a conviction is not admissible under this rule if the conviction was the subject of a pardon, annulment, or equivalent procedure where one of the following applies:

a. No Subsequent Felony: The person has not been convicted of any subsequent felony, or

b. Innocent of Charge: The pardon, etc., was based on a finding of innocence.

5. Juvenile Adjudications: Evidence of juvenile adjudications is not admissible against the D in a criminal case. Such evidence may be admissible against another witness in a criminal or civil case, so long as the juvenile adjudication meets all the above-listed requirements for adult convictions, and the admission of the juvenile conviction is necessary for a fair determination of the issue of guilt or innocence.

MBE Tip: The restrictions on impeachment evidence in Rules 608 & 609 do not apply to evidence showing bias. Bias may always be shown by prior acts that might otherwise be inadmissible character or credibility evidence. Example: Witness's membership in the same violent gang as the D is sometimes admitted to show bias in favor of the D.

D. Religious Beliefs – FRE 610

Religious beliefs or related opinions thereupon (or the absence thereof) are not admissible for the purpose of enhancing or impairing the credibility of a witness. However, religious beliefs may be admissible for another purpose such as personal interest or to show bias such as an affiliation with a church that is a party in the lawsuit.

E. Witness Prior Statements – FRE 613

1. Inconsistent: A prior witness statement or identification that is inconsistent with or casts doubt upon her present trial testimony may be admitted into evidence for impeachment.

2. Example: Witness A states that D ran a red light. That testimony is material to P's case. If witness B heard A previously state that the light was green, B may testify to such. However, witness A must be given an opportunity to explain or deny their prior statement and opposing counsel must have an opportunity to interrogate the witness about the statement. This provision does not apply to an admission by party opponent under Rule 801(d)(2).

3. Purpose of Evidence: A statement offered only for impeachment is not admitted substantively so not subject to the hearsay rule. This is because the statement is not offered to prove the truth of the matter asserted, rather the fact that the statement was made.

4. Collateral Facts Rule Applies: As explained above, if a prior inconsistent statement is revealed with extrinsic evidence (FRE 613(b)), that evidence must be highly relevant to a substantive issue at trial.

MBE Tip: Extrinsic evidence may be used to introduce a witness's prior inconsistent statement. Don't confuse the prior statement with specific instances of conduct that may not be introduced with extrinsic evidence. Compare FRE 608(b) and FRE 613(b). Prior witness statements are still subject to the prohibition on impeachment evidence of collateral matters.

| STOP! | Go to page 95 and work Learning Questions 30 to 38. |

XIII. WITNESS PRESENTATION AND INTERROGATION

A. Mode and Order of Interrogation and Presentation – FRE 611

The court has discretion to control the mode and order of interrogation to avoid needless waste of time and to protect witnesses.

1. Scope of Cross-Examination: Cross-examination is normally limited to the subject matter of the direct examination and matters affecting the credibility of the witness. Still, the trial court has discretion to permit inquiry into additional relevant related matters.

2. Leading Questions: Leading questions – suggesting a "yes" answer to the witness - are permitted on hostile witness cross-examination. Leading questions should not be used on direct examination except as may be necessary to develop the witness's testimony.

3. Exception: When a party calls a hostile witness, an adverse party, or a witness identified with an adverse party, leading questions may be used on direct examination. A hostile adverse witness will not usually want to be "led" so leading questions are harmless.

4. Compound Question: Only one question at a time is allowed.

B. Writing Used to Refresh Memory – FRE 612

Rule 612 relates to helping a friendly witness recall factual details. If a witness is forgetful, a writing or anything else (*i.e.*, song, scent, photograph) may be used to help jog the witness's memory. This applies to refreshing memory while or before testifying.

1. Oral Testimony: The witness may testify orally after refreshing his memory. He/she may not read from the document used to refresh, but must testify from memory.

2. Need Not Be Admitted: Note that the writing or other item need not be introduced as evidence but must be available to the opposing party.

3. Opposing Counsel May Review Writing: Opposing counsel has the right to inspect anything used to refresh the witness's memory and may cross-examine thereon. Such a writing may be introduced into evidence if it meets other requirements of admissibility.

4. Privileges Are Waived: If the material was previously protected from disclosure by a privilege, counsel using the material to refresh the witness's memory is deemed to waive the protection.

> **MBE Tip:** If the writing itself is introduced as evidence, it must meet the other requirements of admissibility such as authenticity and hearsay.

C. Witness Prior Statements – FRE 613

1. Examining Witnesses Concerning Prior Statement: The attorney who seeks to use a prior inconsistent statement need not show the statement to the witness, but must show the statement to opposing counsel upon request.

2. Extrinsic Evidence of Prior Inconsistent Statement: Sometimes the attorney examining a witness will want to bring in extrinsic evidence of prior inconsistent statements, such as a transcript or other record of inconsistent statements in the past. Such evidence will not be admissible unless the witness has an opportunity to explain or deny the allegedly inconsistent statements and the opposing party has a chance to interrogate the witness about these statements. This rule does not apply to admissions by the party opponent.

D. Calling and Interrogation of Witness by Court – FRE 614

The Court may call or interrogate any witness *sua sponte* (on their own motion) or the request of a party. Objections may be made when the jury is not present. During such questioning, the Court must refrain from demonstrating or suggesting any bias or partiality to any witness or argument.

E. Exclusion of Witness – FRE 615

At the request of a party, the Court shall order a future witness excluded or sequestered from the courtroom proceeding, so that he/she cannot hear the testimony of other witnesses prior to giving their own. This eliminates the possibility of the excluded witness framing their testimony based upon something besides their own recollection or opinion. A party to the action may not usually be excluded from the full trial.

XIV. OPINION AND EXPERT TESTIMONY

A. Opinion Testimony by Lay Witnesses – FRE 701

Opinion testimony by a lay witness is not automatically excluded by the FREs, including an arresting police officer. (Such opinions are usually excluded under the common law rules of evidence). Therefore, it is the judge's discretion whether to admit opinion testimony, so long as any opinion testimony meets the following criteria:

1. Rationally based on the Witness' Perception: This witness focus is consistent with the Rule 602 requirement of prior personal knowledge for any witness testimony. A lay fact witness may also qualify as an expert based upon their separate non-technical skill or specialized knowledge that may be helpful to the judge or jury.

2. Helpful to Understand:

a. Factual Testimony: The trial judge has discretion to admit evidence that is helpful to the jury. Lay opinions may be used to help determine a fact in issue. For example, a witness would be allowed to draw a conclusion that a certain liquid she observed at a fire scene was gasoline. This reflects most people's familiarity with gasoline although the witness could be wrong. The alternative would be limiting testimony to only the witness's observation that the liquid was amber in color, gave off strong fumes, and ignited when a match was set to it.

b. Fact in Issue: Since the jury may not otherwise reach the conclusion that a liquid described in technical terms was gasoline, the witness's conclusion is helpful to a clear understanding. Of course, opposing counsel would be allowed to cross-examine the witness on the witness's experience with gasoline that could cast doubt on the witness's testimony.

3. Not Based on Knowledge within Scope of FRE 702: A lay witness may not give an opinion based on scientific, technical, or other specialized knowledge governed by FRE 702. If the witness can qualify as an expert, then an opinion may be given, but it must avoid personal opinions on creditability of D or other witness and the expression of legal conclusions.

4. Lay Witness Examples:

a. Opinion: "Jim was happy." "My house is worth $200,000." "This is Sandra's handwriting."

b. Perception: "Jim was smiling." "She was driving very fast." "Houses just like mine sell for $200,000." "This handwriting has these distinct characteristics, which I have also seen in Sandra's other handwriting."

c. Observation: The above opinions are based on firsthand factual observation, which is still a strict requirement of admissibility. Therefore, counsel will need to lay the foundation of firsthand knowledge before eliciting such opinions from the witness.

d. Legal Conclusion: Words having legal significance, such as "promised" or "agreed," may be objectionable unless the witness is relating a conversation in which said words were actually spoken.

> **MBE Tip:** Because the allowance of lay opinion is within the court's discretion, it is unlikely that a correct answer on the exam will be exclusion of the testimony because it is an opinion. Because Rule 701 favors inclusion to help the jury, look for other reasons to exclude such as lack of personal knowledge (see Rule 602).

B. Testimony by Experts – FRE 702

If scientific, technical, or other specialized knowledge is relevant and it will be helpful to assist the trier of fact to understand the evidence or to determine a technical fact in issue, a qualifying expert witness may testify in the form of an opinion. The trial judge serves as a "gatekeeper" for admitting scientific expert testimony. Typically, the party objecting to the expert files a motion *in limine* to exclude their testimony prior to trial.

1. Requirements: Most questions concerning expert witness testimony requirements are usually left to the sound discretion of the trial judge.

2. Qualification of Experts - SKEET: The expert witness must be qualified by s̲kill, k̲nowledge, e̲xperience, e̲ducation, and/or t̲raining in the technical field. An expert does not necessarily have to be currently licensed in the discipline.

> **MBE Tip:** Any essay discussion of experts should include the five qualification variables. The relative weight the individual **SKEET** characteristic should take in deciding to admit depends in part of the subject complexity and are to be decided by the trial court.

3. Helpfulness: The expert opinion must be helpful to the jurors in understanding the relevant "scientific or technical knowledge" at issue in the dispute. This means that the subject matter is usually beyond the common understanding and normal knowledge of lay jurors. Expert opinion is not admissible if the jury does not need help understanding a matter of common experience such as intoxication or identifying gasoline.

> **MBE Tip:** Note that formal education is not required; for example, a lifelong hobby can qualify a witness as an expert in that particular hobby. If **SKEET** qualification as an expert is raised on the MBE, don't forget informal experience.

4. _Daubert_ Reliable Methods – SRA: Rule 702 charges trial judges with the enhanced responsibility of "gate keepers" to exclude questionable expert testimony that may overcome the jury's even and fair consideration. Three **SRA** _Daubert_ reliability conditions are required for an expert's methods and opinions to be deemed reliable and helpful enough to survive an expert witness admissibility challenge:

    a. <u>Sufficient Authority</u>: The facts and authorized data upon which the opinion testimony is based must be sufficient to qualify as "scientific knowledge." A factual foundation must be presented or the expert opinion is objectionable as speculation.

    b. <u>Reliable Principles and Techniques</u>: The expert's opinion testimony must be based on reliable principles and sound scientific methodology which is well established and generally accepted in that particular scientific professional community. "Generally accepted" must be more than an "educated guess" but does not have to rise to the level of the majority view. Peer reviews help establish credibility. Can the theory be tested or is it just a "naked opinion?" "Junk science" theory may violate this requirement.

    c. <u>Applied Reliably</u>: Has the expert applied the principles and methods reliably to the facts? This may put the reasonableness of the factual assumptions at issue.

5. Example: The expert is an astrologer who will testify that it was physically impossible for D to have committed the crime because Aries was ascending into Capricorn that day thereby precluding D's ability to get out of bed. Before _Daubert_, the judge had discretion to admit this testimony if astrology could be proved a reliable principle or method and it is reliably applied to the facts of the case. Acceptance of the principles in the scientific or specialized community in question is a factor for the judge's consideration prior to qualification.

6. Some State Rules Differ: Some states follow the strict exclusion rule that the scientific basis of expert testimony must be well accepted in that particular scientific or professional community. Other states allow the court to let the jury hear and weigh the merits of questionable ("junk science") expert testimony proffered by both sides.

C. <u>Basis for Expert Opinion</u> – FRE 703

Expert opinion testimony must be based on more than mere conjecture or speculation; there must be some reasonable basis for an opinion.

1. Facts Known to Expert: The facts or data upon which an expert bases an opinion may be those perceived by or made known to the expert at or before the hearing. This includes hypothetical facts upon which the expert is asked to offer an opinion or conclusion.

2. Need Not Be Admissible Facts: The facts or data need not be admissible into evidence (may be hearsay) if they are of a type reasonably relied upon by experts in the particular field in forming opinions or inferences upon the subject. Hypothetical situations are possible. As a practical result, assuming the expert's reliance is reasonable, counsel cannot object that the expert is basing an opinion on "facts not in evidence."

3. Proponent May Not Disclose Inadmissible Facts: If the opinion is based on inadmissible facts, those facts may not be disclosed by the proponent to the jury. There is no prohibition on opposing counsel conducting a cross-examination of the witness on the inadmissible facts.

> **MBE Tip:** Courts may exclude expert opinion because it was based upon nothing but assumptions and speculation without a reliable foundation. More often, however, such objections go to the methodology and weight of the facts upon which the expert is relying, not admissibility. The court has discretion to make this determination.

D. Opinion on the Ultimate Issue of Fact – FRE 704

1. Not Objectionable: Testimony by either experts or lay witnesses in the form of an opinion that would otherwise be admissible is not objectionable simply because it embraces an ultimate issue to be decided by the trier of fact. Examples: "D was driving too fast for the conditions."; "D was intoxicated."; or "The substance found in D's car was cocaine."

2. Legal Conclusion Prohibited: The witness cannot, in a criminal case, give an opinion on the ultimate legal issue conclusion to be made by the jury. An example is whether D did or did not have a mental state or condition constituting an element of the crime charged or a defense. The test for determining admissibility is usually whether the words chosen are ordinarily understood by the jury as lay persons or are legal terms of art with meanings of which the jury might be unaware.

3. Examples of Legal Conclusions: "D is guilty as charged."; "D had no reason to defend himself."; and "D was not negligent." A witness can say there was a "murder," or say that the guardrail was "inherently dangerous." However, an expert witness cannot testify "D committed second degree assault;" these ultimate elements of the crime are for the jury. Similarly, an expert can testify "D had a serious mental disorder," but not "D was legally insane."

> **MBE Tip:** A witness cannot expressly tell the jury what result to reach or verdict to render.

E. Disclosure of Facts or Data Underlying Expert Opinion – FRE 705

1. Foundation Unnecessary: The expert testifies in terms of opinion and thus may give reasons for their opinion without prior disclosure of the facts or data underlying the opinion, unless the court requires disclosure. There is no need to "lay a foundation" by bringing out the factual basis first. However, the expert may be required to disclose the underlying facts or data on cross-examination.

2. Hearsay: If there is a serious question the court may require the expert to disclose the basis or underlying data relied upon if that information would otherwise be inadmissible as hearsay. The answer is that the expert may reveal the basis, but the court will give a limiting instruction, directing the jury not to consider it as substantive evidence. The court also has discretion to exclude such evidence altogether under Rule 403's prejudicial balancing test.

F. Court Appointed Experts – FRE 706

The court may *sua sponte* or on the motion of any party enter an order to show cause why a compensated expert witness should not be appointed. The court may appoint the expert of its own selection and/or ask the parties to submit nominations. Experts are entitled to receive reasonable compensation.

> **STOP!** Go to page 97 and work Learning Questions 39 to 46.

XV. HEARSAY

> **MBE Tip:** The hearsay rule and the numerous exceptions are up to one-third of the testing. Again, focus on the **4 Ws** admissibility variables - "**w**hy is this evidence being introduced," "**w**hom is trying to offer it," "**w**hen in the proceeding is the evidence offered," and **w**hether the proceeding is a civil or criminal case? See MEE 10-445 for prior exam issue tested distribution.

A. Rule of Exclusion – FRE 802

Hearsay is excluded from evidence unless specifically allowed by rule. The evidence offered must first meet the definition of hearsay. Even if the statement is not hearsay it may still be subject to other rules of exclusion (relevance, character, prejudicial).

B. Definitions – FRE 801

1. Hearsay: Hearsay is an assertive statement, made by the declarant outside of the particular trial or hearing proceeding and the statement is offered to prove the truth of matter asserted in the statement. A statement must meet this definition to be excluded as hearsay. Notice the witness must recount the declarant's words verbatim to be considered hearsay.

> **MBE Tip:** A statement that does not fit the definition of hearsay is non-hearsay, while a statement that fits the definition is, but may be subject to an exception. This is an important distinction, since the MBE may test knowledge of non-hearsay as well as the exceptions. Multiple valid exceptions may be presented in the same question, so be selective.

a. Statement: A "statement" is a person's (1) oral or written assertion or (2) nonverbal conduct intended as an assertion of fact, such as pointing or nodding. Computer-generated "statements" like credit card receipts or GPS device "statements" are admissible.

b. Declarant: A "declarant" is the person who makes the statement in question.

c. Truth of the Matter Asserted: Logically, to be excluded under Rule 802, a statement must meet the definition of hearsay. A statement offered for a purpose other than to prove the truth of the matter asserted is not hearsay. If the jury's belief in the truth of the statement is necessary to the proponent's case, then the statement is usually hearsay.

d. Examples of Non-Hearsay: The following are typical examples of statements not offered to prove the truth of the matter asserted therein:

(1) Statements of Independent Legal Effect: These statements have legal effect regardless of the truth or falsity of the statement. "I give you my WorldCom stock" conveys a property interest by the mere utterance; whether the statement is true or not.

(2) Statements Offered to Prove the Statement Was Made: Typically, this is to prove notice or a reason for duress or other injury.

(a) Example: A witness at the scene stating "these floorboards are loose," can demonstrate notice to an owner in a premises liability case when knowledge of condition is an element; "Sign this contract or I'll break your knees," can show duress; "Professor Smith is a communist," can establish defamation.

(b) Statement Sufficient: The truth of the statement need not be believed to support a party's case, rather just the fact it was said. Note that the jury may infer the truth, but that is not the purpose for which the statement is offered.

(3) Statements Offered to Show Declarant's Perception: When the mental perception of a person based upon a statement is relevant to the case, then the truth or falsity of a statement is not at issue.

(a) Example: To assert a claim of self-defense, D could testify, "Bob told me Victim wanted to kill me." This establishes the D's fear of imminent harm. Whether or not it is true that Victim did want to kill D does not matter; only the fact that D heard the statement. The declarant's description of an item or event may be offered not to prove that the perception was accurate, but rather to prove that the declarant perceived the item or event.

(b) Example: Declarant's statement "Old Main at the University of Arizona is painted white on the inside," may be offered to support a contention that declarant has been inside of Old Main. This does not support a contention that the walls are indeed white, only the inference the declarant learned the color by personal observation at the site.

e. Conduct as an Assertion: This is testimony about what the declarant did that was intended by the declarant to be an assertion at the time.

(1) Inference: A verbal or written statement is usually intended as an assertion. However, certain types of conduct may lead a witness to infer a critical fact. Only if the conduct was intended to assert a fact, will the conduct be hearsay.

(2) Example: To prove it was raining during an automobile accident, an investigator asks the declarant "were people walking by using their umbrellas?" In response the declarant says yes, implicitly asserting that he had knowledge it was indeed raining on the street of the accident. This testimony about this out-of-court conduct - that it was raining – is not treated as hearsay since the testimony is deemed an implied assertion.

> **MBE Tip:** Be careful when assessing conduct as an assertion. It will almost always be in response to a request for information. If the fact pattern describes the conduct as an unsolicited assertion, it is probably not assertive conduct.

f. Silence as an Assertion: See adoptive admission in 2(b)(2) below. Obviously, an adoptive admission is also an assertion.

2. Statements that are Non-Hearsay Despite Meeting Definition – FRE 801(d): A statement may meet the above hearsay definition, but still be non-hearsay under rule if it meets the criteria of either **a** or **b** below:

a. Prior Statement by Witness – FRE 801(d)(1): The declarant testifies at the trial or hearing and is subject to cross-examination concerning the statement then made, and the statement is:

(1) Inconsistent: Prior testimony is inconsistent with the declarant's current testimony and the prior testimony was given under oath at a prior formal legal proceeding such as a trial, hearing, deposition, or grand jury session; or

(2) Consistent: Prior testimony is consistent with the declarant's testimony and is offered to rebut an express or implied charge of recent fabrication or improper influence or motive, provided that the statement predates the inception of the motive to lie; or

(3) Identification: A prior identification of a person made after perceiving the person (*i.e.*, identification in a lineup or shortly after a crime) is not hearsay.

> **MBE Tip:** A good rule of thumb is that a statement is non-hearsay under 801(d)(1) only when the declarant is also a witness.

b. Opposing Party Statement – FRE 801(d)(2): The statement is offered against a party and is:

(1) Own Statement: That party's own admission, or assertive conduct, in either an individual or a representative capacity such as a corporate officer.

(2) Adoptive Statement: A statement that the party has adopted as his own or has manifested a belief in its truth (also known as an "adoptive admission"). An adoptive statement must meet all of the below three **HEN** criteria to be admissible:

(a) <u>H</u>eard: The party heard and understood the import of the statement.

(b) <u>E</u>xpected Denial: The statement was of such a nature and significance that a reasonable person would feel compelled to deny it if it were not true. An example is a co-D states "we robbed the bank."

(c) <u>N</u>o Response: The party was able to respond to the statement, but did not. Therefore, silence in response to a police statement at the scene may usually be introduced.

(d) Silence and Fifth Amendment: There must be no reasonable basis inferring the silence was based on the Fifth Amendment criminal privilege of silence. And if a suspect chooses to remain silent after receiving *Miranda* warnings, evidence of that silence is not admissible. See page 6-345 for related constitutional law restraints.

> **MBE Tip:** The admissions exception is very broad and opens the door to virtually anything the opposing party has said, written, or agreed to expressly or implicitly. It does not have to be a statement "against interest." Typical MBE examples are letters or diaries written by the opposing party, opposing party's deposition, or answers to interrogatories.

(3) Authorized: A statement by a person authorized by the party to make a statement concerning the subject; or

(4) Agent: A statement by the party's agent or employee who:

(a) Scope of Agency: Acts within the scope of the agency or employment, and

(b) During Agency: Made the statement during such agency or employment (under the Federal Rules, the agent or employee need not have authority to make the admission).

(5) Co-Conspirator: A statement by a co-conspirator of a party during the course and in furtherance of the conspiracy. An example is A and B conspire to import illegal drugs and A tells C that he (A) and his partner B will transact with C concerning drugs. A's testimony could be introduced against B.

STOP! Go to page 98 and work Learning Questions 47 to 51.

C. Hearsay Exceptions; Availability of Declarant Immaterial – FRE 803

Admissible hearsay must meet a specific exception. The following statements are **PETSRR** exceptions to the exclusion general conclusion under the rule because they are likely accurate. They apply in all cases, civil and criminal, whether the declarant is available to testify or not. The presence or absence of the declarant makes no difference.

> **MBE Tip:** Again, a good analytical approach for hearsay exceptions is to start by asking yourself "<u>w</u>hat is the reason that this evidence is being offered, by <u>w</u>hom, <u>w</u>hen in the proceeding, and <u>w</u>hether it is a civil or criminal action?" – **4 Ws**

1. Present Sense Impression – FRE 803(1): This is a spontaneous statement describing or explaining an event or condition made to police while the declarant was observing the event or condition, or immediately thereafter. Usually the statement is made to assist the police in resolving an ongoing emergency at the criminal event site itself. An emergency 911 oral crime report usually qualifies. Another emergency declaration example is a statement about a phone call, immediately after hanging up: "That was Herman on the phone and he told me he was coming over here."

> **MBE Tip:** The present sense impression exception requires that the witnesses' statement was contemporaneous with the event. The passage of significant time eliminates this exception. Distinguish from a situation where the declarant described the event some time period after its occurrence so the primary purpose was to create an out-of-court substitute for trial testimony.

2. Excited Utterance – FRE 803(2): A statement relating to (but not necessarily describing) a startling event or condition made while the declarant was then under the stress of excitement caused by the event. The event causing the emotional excitation usually has occurred immediately prior to the utterance. Examples are a hysterical statement made to police describing a horrific automobile accident; or a victim's sobbing declaration at the crime scene. The Supreme Court has held the admission of some 911 calls does not violate a D's Sixth Amendment right to confront the witness who is not available for trial.

> **MBE Tip:** The above two exceptions are heavily tested. To distinguish from present sense impression, an excited utterance can occur with less immediacy than what is required by present sense impression. The time between the event and the statement can be somewhat longer. The key here is the declarant's emotional stress or excitement existing at the time of the statement. Watch for exclamation points or verbs suggesting significant excitement.

3. Then-Existing Mental, Emotional, or Physical Condition – FRE 803(3): A statement concerning the declarant's then-existing state of mind, emotion, sensation, or physical condition. An example is a physician's statement made for purposes of diagnosis.

    a. Includes: This includes intent, plan, motive, design, mental feeling, pain, and bodily health as currently being experienced by the declarant. Watch for phrases like "I do," "I intend," "I will," "I am," as they all indicate a then-existing state of mind or intention.

    b. Excludes: However, statements regarding a declarant's state of mind, emotion, or beliefs are not admissible to prove causation such as intent or motive. Thus, "I believe my current leg pain was caused by yesterday's car collision," is inadmissible as part of the statement relates to a past event. A statement describing a past mental, emotional, or physical condition is not admissible unless the statement relates to the validity or terms of the declarant's will.

4. Statements Made for Medical Treatment – FRE 803(4):

a. Relevant to Treatment: This is a statement made to a medical clinician or doctor to help the clinician diagnose or treat the declarant's medical illness or injury, even if the clinician is retained only for expert testimony. However, the facts in the hearsay statement must be relevant to the medical diagnosis or treatment.

b. Fault Excluded: Statements attributing fault are technically excluded. "I was beaten" would be admissible as the cause of injury because it might assist the clinician in her treatment or diagnosis. "I was beaten by my husband," is not because who caused the injury does not assist the clinician in her diagnosis or treatment. However, many courts will admit these statements on the theory that they are necessary to prevent future injury to the patient (*i.e.*, potentially recurrent spousal or child abuse).

5. Recorded Recollection – FRE 803(5):

This applies when a knowledgeable witness presently has insufficient recollection to testify fully and accurately about a historical matter or event. If an accurate or factually correct record concerning the matter was made or adopted by the witness when the matter was fresh in the witness's memory, the record may be reconsidered to refresh memory. The record may be inspected by the opposing side, but not itself be entered as an exhibit unless offered by an adverse party.

a. Examples: Some examples of past recorded recollection refreshed are police reports and notes taken at the scene of the incident, court reporter's notes, journalist's notes, and entries in business records (note that some of these may also be records of regularly conducted activity).

b. Foundation – PIFA: To lay a proper record foundation for introduction, the following facts must be shown. Failure to meet any of these four "**PIFA**" elements will render the recollection inadmissible.

(1) Pertinent: The record pertains to a matter about which the witness once had personal knowledge;

(2) Insufficient Present Recollection: The witness now has insufficient recollection to testify fully and accurately (thus partial recollection or insufficient recollection of details would not negate this element, but a total lack of recall would);

(3) Fresh When Adopted: The record was made or adopted (witness agreed to accuracy at the time of preparation) by the witness when the matter was fresh in the witness's memory; and

(4) Accurate: The record reflects the witness's prior knowledge accurately.

6. Records of Regularly Conducted Activity (Business Records Exception) – FRE 803(6): Records made and kept in the regular course of business are admissible. The rationale is that the business has an incentive to keep accurate records for the purposes of taxation, accounting, etc. To qualify as a business record, the document must meet the following requirements through the testimony or certification of a witness with knowledge that:

a. Regularly Conducted: The record entry, memo, and/or report is of regularly conducted business activity.

b. Near in Time: The record was created in the regular course of business at or near in time to the activity, condition, or event at issue in the case.

c. Personal Knowledge: A custodian, supervisor or witness has personal knowledge of or is the person in the business who made the business record at issue.

d. Regular Practice: The record involved must have originated in a regular routine practice of the business. Special purpose documents made in anticipation of litigation or created on a one-time basis do not qualify under this business record exception.

e. Reliable: The record is reliable for truthfulness (no apparent motive to fabricate) – again, records prepared in anticipation of litigation fail this element.

> **MBE Tip:** Remember **PETSRR** and watch for hearsay within hearsay, *infra* at 62. If a business record entry is based on a statement obtained by a declarant not in the business, then it will not be admissible unless the statement qualifies under another hearsay exception.

> **STOP!** Go to page 99 and work Learning Questions 52 to 54.

D. Other Hearsay Exceptions; Availability of Declarant Immaterial

> **MBE Tip:** The following exceptions are not heavily tested, but are presented here for completeness of your hearsay study.

1. Absence of Entry in Records – FRE 803(7): Lack of an entry of an activity that would normally be recorded and admissible as a Record of Regularly Conducted Activity is admissible as a hearsay exception to show lack of an occurrence or nonexistence of a matter.

2. Public Records – FRE 803(8):

a. Rule: Copies of all records and documents on record or on file in the offices of the various departments of the United States and of any State or Territory within the United States, when duly certified (under seal where appropriate) by custodial officers of such documents, shall be admitted into evidence. The record must be government generated and simply state facts. Public records prepared by police may not usually be admitted.

> **MBE Tip:** A record that expresses an opinion or discretionary finding (such as an administrative determination) does not fall within this exception. Note that these records are also self-authenticating under FRE 902.

b. Examples: Driving records, official weather reports, official records of births and deaths, or a sheriff's written proof of service (often called a "return of service").

3. Public Records of Vital Statistics – FRE 803(9): Records or data compilations, in any form, of births, fetal deaths, deaths, or marriages are admissible, if the report was made to a public office pursuant to requirements of law.

4. Absence of a Public Record – FRE 803(10): The absence of such a record where one should or is alleged to exist may also be introduced and is not hearsay. For example, if a D claims to be 28 years old and after a diligent search there is no entry of her birth record 28 years prior, that absence of record may be introduced.

5. Records of Religious Organizations – FRE 803(11): Births, deaths, marriages, ancestry, or other personal or family history contained in regularly kept religion records.

6. Marriage, Baptismal, and Similar Certificates – FRE 803(12): Statements of fact contained within the certificate that the maker performed the marriage or other sacrament.

7. Family Records – FRE 803(13): Statements by family members concerning family history contained in bibles, genealogies, charts, engravings, or inscriptions.

8. Records of Documents Affecting an Interest in Property – FRE 803(14): Deeds and mortgages recorded in a public office and a statute authorizes recording.

9. Statements in Documents Affecting an Interest in Property – FRE 803(15): A statement within a document purporting to establish or affect an interest in property if the statement is relevant to the purpose of the document.

10. Statements in Ancient Documents – FRE 803(16): Statements in a document in existence 20 years or more whose authenticity is established are admissible. See Rule 901 for authenticity requirements. Examples are old newspapers, reference books, and deeds.

11. Market Reports and Commercial Publications – FRE 803(17): Reliable market quotations, tabulations, lists, directories, or other published compilations generally used and relied upon by the public or persons in a particular occupation are admissible.

12. Learned Treatises – FRE 803(18): Portions of a learned written treatise or periodical may be read into evidence if there is an expert to establish credibility of the treatise. It is used to supplement the testimony of an expert on either direct or cross-examination.

a. Foundation: As a matter of foundation, counsel must establish that the expert relied upon the publication and that it is authoritative. The expert may only read relevant portions to the jury. The publication itself is not admitted as documentary evidence.

b. Cross-Examination: A learned treatise or periodical may also be used on cross-examination of an expert for purposes of impeachment. On cross-examination, counsel must establish that the publication is authoritative, but not that the expert actually relied upon it. The contents of the treatise may be substantive as well as impeachment evidence.

> **MBE Tip:** Questions frequently suggest the jury wants to examine the expert's learned treatise themselves in their deliberations. This is not usually permitted.

13. Reputation Concerning Personal or Family History – FRE 803(19): Reputation among family members concerning a person's birth, adoption, marriage, divorce, death, ancestry, or other personal or family history.

14. Reputation Concerning Boundaries or General History – FRE 803(20): Reputation in a community, arising prior to the controversy, as to boundaries of or customs affecting lands in the community, or general historical events of significance to the relevant community, state, or nation.

15. Reputation as to Character – FRE 803(21): Reputation of a person's character among associates or in the community.

16. Judgment of Previous Conviction – FRE 803(22): A final judgment after trial or guilty plea (but not *nolo contendere* plea) adjudging guilt of a crime punishable by death or imprisonment of more than one year is admissible, but only to support a fact essential to sustain the judgment against the defendant.

17. Judgment as to Personal, Family, or General History, or Boundaries – FRE 803(23): Judgments as proof of matters of personal, family, or general history, or boundaries of land that was essential to the judgment, if the same would be provable by evidence of reputation.

> **MBE Tip:** The list of 803 exceptions is long and daunting. Use common sense to evaluate whether an 803 exception applies: is it the kind of information generally relied upon in society?

E. Hearsay Exceptions; Declarant Unavailable – FRE 804

Unlike Rule 803 exceptions, the following FRE 804 testimony exceptions require that the declarant be unavailable as a witness.

1. Definition of Unavailability – DAAL: "Unavailability as a witness" includes situations in which:

a. Death or Infirmity: The declarant is unable to be present or to testify at the hearing because of their death or then-existing physical or mental illness or infirmity; or

b. Asserted Privilege: The declarant is exempted from testifying on the ground of privilege (such as spousal marriage); or refuses to testify concerning the subject matter of the declarant's statement despite a court order; or

c. Absence: The declarant is absent from the hearing and the proponent has been unable to procure the declarant's attendance by subpoena or other reasonable means. If the proponent is trying to use the hearsay exceptions in FRE 804(b)(2), (3), or (4), the proponent will need to show that the declarant could not be summoned to trial or to a pretrial deposition.

d. Lack of Memory: The declarant testifies to a lack of memory of the subject matter of the declarant's statement; or

e. **Wrongdoing by Proponent:** A declarant does not meet the definition of unavailable if the exemption, refusal, claim of lack of memory, inability, or absence is due to the procurement or wrongdoing of the proponent of a statement for the purpose of preventing the witness from attending or testifying at trial. Examples are counsel flew the declarant to another country or affirmatively instructed the declarant not to say anything.

2. Hearsay Exceptions – FRE 804(b): The following **FAB** exceptions are not excluded by the hearsay rule if the declarant is unavailable as a witness, such as dead, ill, protected by privilege, or otherwise not amenable to subpoena service.

> **MBE Tip:** Remember **FAB** for the major hearsay statement exceptions of **F**ormer testimony, **A**gainst the declarant's interest, and **B**elief of impending death.

a. **Former Testimony – FRE 804(b)(1):** Testimony given by a witness at a prior trial hearing or deposition (but not grand jury), if the current opponent of this evidence (or, in a civil case, a predecessor in interest of the current opponent) had an opportunity and similar motive to develop the testimony on that prior occasion by direct, cross or redirect examination. For example, W testifies in D's criminal trial. A mistrial is declared, but before the second trial, W dies. W's testimony from the first trial is admissible under this exception.

> **MBE Tip:** Do not confuse the Rule 804(b)(1) Former Testimony exception with a Rule 801(d)(1) Prior Statement by Witness. Prior Statement by Witness refers to situations where the witness is available, but there is a potential inconsistency.

b. **Against Interest – FRE 804(b)(3):** A statement that is significantly contrary to the declarant's pecuniary or proprietary interest, such as subjecting the declarant to criminal or civil liability, or rendering invalid a claim by the declarant against another, is admissible. A reasonable person in the declarant's position would not have made the statement unless the declarant then believed it to be true. This demonstrates the inherent trustworthiness.

(1) Not Merely Embarrassing: Statements that simply expose the declarant to ridicule or disgrace do not qualify. Personal knowledge by the declarant is required.

(2) Criminal Case: An exception is in a criminal case, a statement tending to expose the declarant to criminal liability and exculpating the accused or self-inculpating the witness is not admissible unless corroborating circumstances clearly indicate the trustworthiness of the statement.

> **MBE Tip:** Do not confuse a statement against interest with an admission by party opponent. A party opponent is available, so Rule 804 exclusions do not apply. Conversely, in order to be excepted under Rule 804 the declarant cannot be a party; the declarant must be unavailable. Also, a Rule 801 admission may be self-serving, a statement against interest cannot be.

c. **Belief of Impending Death – FRE 804(b)(2):** A dying declaration made by a declarant (1) while believing that his or her death was imminent, and (2) concerning the cause or circumstances of his or her imminent death is admissible. This rule applies in all civil cases, but in criminal prosecutions only for the homicide of the declarant. The declarant need not be dead, but only unavailable. Other non-death related declarations remain non-admissible.

> **MBE Tip:** Exam questions often include facts that specify the declarant expressed a belief of impending death, though the declarant need not subsequently die. Conversely, the fact that the declarant did die does not necessarily establish the required pre-death belief in imminent death.

d. Statement of Personal or Family History – FRE 804(b)(4): This is either:

(1) Own Statements: A statement concerning the declarant's own birth, adoption, marriage, divorce legitimacy, relationship by blood, adoption, ancestry, or other fact of family history even despite the declarant's lack of personal knowledge, or

(2) Other Statements: A statement concerning the birth, adoption, marriage, divorce legitimacy, relationship by blood, adoption, ancestry, or death of another person, if the declarant was related to the other by blood, adoption, or marriage or was so intimately associated with the other's family as to be likely to have trustworthy information concerning the matter declared.

e. Forfeiture by Wrongdoing – FRE 804(b)(6): A statement may be offered against a party who procured the unavailability of the declarant as a witness.

> **MBE Tip:** Frequently the previous declarant of the statement identifying the criminal D is dead. This by itself does not meet any of the FRE 804 exceptions and thus such evidence is to be properly excluded, unless it is former sworn testimony.

F. Hearsay Within Hearsay – FRE 805

Hearsay included within hearsay is not excluded if each part or level of the combined out-of-court statements conform to an exception or exceptions to the hearsay rule. For example, at trial a written police accident or hospital admission report is offered into evidence which states "An occurrence witness at the accident scene talked to V who identified D as his slayer before he died." The report and V's statement are hearsay but may be introduced under the Dying Declaration and Business or Public Record exceptions.

> **MBE Tip:** Think of "levels" or "layers" of out-of-court hearsay statements. For each layer, does the statement meet the definition of hearsay? If so, does a separate exception apply? If any layer of hearsay does not meet an established exception, then the statement is inadmissible.

G. Credibility of Declarant – FRE 806

1. Impeachment: When hearsay, or a statement defined under Rule 801(d)(2)(C-E), is admitted pursuant to a hearsay exception, the out-of-court declarant's credibility may be attacked by their inconsistent statements just as if he were present in the courtroom and testifying live as a witness. The opportunity for the declarant to deny or explain is not required.

2. Cross-Examination: A party against whom a hearsay statement was admitted may call the declarant as a witness and interrogate him or her for credibility or otherwise as to substance of the testimony as if on cross-examination.

H. Residual Exception – FRE 807

Hearsay not excepted from exclusion under Rules 803 & 804 may still be admitted if it appears to be trustworthy and the following three criteria are met:

1. Material Fact: The statement is offered as evidence of a material fact,

2. Probative: The statement is more probative on the point for which it is offered than any other evidence that the proponent can procure through reasonable efforts, and

3. Interest of Justice: The general purposes of these rules and the interests of justice will best be served by admission of the hearsay statement into evidence.

> **MBE Tip:** This exception is rarely directly tested, but it might apply if the hearsay in question is the most probative of any other available evidence.

I. Confrontation Clause

Hearsay testimony statements might conflict with the right of the criminal accused to confront witnesses against him as guaranteed by the Confrontation Clause of the Sixth Amendment. In *Crawford* the Supreme Court held in a criminal case that testimonial hearsay is not admissible even if it falls within an exception to a hearsay rule. A trial witness cannot be an effective conduit for out-of-court witness statements. Here are the main points you need to know.

1. In What Settings Does the Confrontation Clause Apply? The confrontation right only arises in criminal trials, not in pretrial or post-trial sentencing hearings, and not in any civil proceedings. The Confrontation Clause applies to evidence offered by the government against the accused, not vice versa.

2. Clause is Limited to "Testimonial" Evidence: The term "testimonial" means that the offered out-of-court statement is akin to trial testimony. A statement could be testimonial if the declarant could reasonably foresee the later prosecutorial use of the statement. A statement could also be testimonial if the police elicited the statement while investigating a past crime, even where the police duped the declarant into believing that she was not speaking to a police officer. Statements made in certain settings are almost always deemed testimonial: trials, hearings, grand jury sessions, affidavits, and formal police interrogations.

3. "Emergency" Exception: The Supreme Court has held that if police take a statement from a declarant while responding to an ongoing emergency, that statement will not be testimonial. For example, if police come to the scene of apparent domestic violence, and if police ask a few brief questions while securing the scene, the responses to those questions will be deemed non-testimonial. Once the scene is secure and the police begin to investigate a past crime, the answers to their questions will be deemed testimonial.

4. Forfeiture of Confrontation Rights: If the accused caused the absence of the declarant with the specific intent of making the declarant unavailable at trial, the accused cannot complain that the government's use of the declarant's hearsay violates the Confrontation Clause. Mere causation of unavailability is not enough to effect a forfeiture. Even if the evidence shows that the accused killed the declarant, the prosecution cannot prove forfeiture unless the prosecution shows that the accused likely killed the declarant for the specific purpose of thwarting trial testimony.

5. What Constitutes Sufficient Confrontation? The Confrontation Clause requires that the accused must have the right to cross-examine declarants of testimonial hearsay. The prosecution can introduce hearsay statements, and even play videotapes of out-of-court statements by the declarants, so long as the prosecution makes the declarants available for cross-examination at trial. Transcripts or pretrial hearings or depositions could be admitted at trial without further cross-examination, so long as the accused had an opportunity to conduct cross-examination in the pretrial setting.

J. Hearsay Summary

1. Definition: It must be a "statement offered for the truth of the matter asserted." Not meeting the definition are statements of independent legal effect, statements indicating the state of mind, prior inconsistent statements offered to impeach, or an admission by a party's opponent.

2. Rule 803 Exceptions: The most important "declarant not available" exceptions include present sense impression, excited utterances, then existing state of mind or physical conditions, regular business and government records, and learned treatises.

3. Rule 804 Exceptions: If the declarant is not available, include statements in former testimony, impending death, against interest, or personal and family interest.

> **MBE Tip:** Hearsay is the most heavily tested topic in the evidence section of the MBE and is frequently tested in essay questions. 911 emergency calls are one of the examiner's favorite.

> **STOP!**   Go to page 100 and work Learning Questions 55 to 60.

XVI. DOCUMENT AUTHENTICATION AND IDENTIFICATION

A party may give pretrial notice of intent to introduce a document and unless an opponent makes a timely objection to the document it is usually automatically admissible at trial. Documentary evidence cannot stand on its own if admissibility is questioned. It must be proved to be what the proponent claims it to be. The document can be self-authenticating or authenticated by other means.

A. Authentication and Identification Required – FRE 901(a)

Document authentication and identification, as a condition precedent to admissibility, is satisfied by evidence sufficient to support a finding that the matter in question is what its proponent claims. In practice, the requirement is easily satisfied in most cases but the opposing party remains free to challenge the reliability. This rule pertains mainly to documents and other tangible evidence such as photographs, and the identification of voices.

B. Acceptable Methods – FRE 901(b)

The following is a list of acceptable methods of authentication and identification.

1. Testimony of Witness with Knowledge: This is testimony by one who would have reason to know that the document is what it purports to be, and not a fake or forgery. The maker of, or a witness to, the creation of the document may testify to authenticity.

a. Special Knowledge: The authenticating witness may have knowledge that facts in the writing were known only to herself and the writer. For example, A told the witness, "I wrote to Madame Versant that I was admitting liability due to my bad horoscope." The witness could relate this special knowledge to establish that the memo was written by A.

b. Maker's Admission: The maker may testify that she did indeed make the writing.

c. Witness to the Creation: A witness can testify that she saw the writer create the writing.

d. Out-of-Court Admission: An out-of-court statement regarding the authenticity of the document is subject to hearsay rules.

e. Expert Opinion on Handwriting: An expert can compare the signature on a document with an authentic signature.

2. Photograph or Drawing: Testimony by a witness who saw the scene in question and testifies the photograph or drawing is a fair and accurate representation. If the witness took the picture, then she is a witness with knowledge.

3. Non-Expert Opinion on Handwriting: Non-expert opinion as to the genuineness of handwriting is based upon familiarity acquired prior to litigation. Examples include a sister testifying as to her sibling's writing in a journal, correspondence, or on a deed.

4. Distinctive Characteristics: Appearance, contents, substance, internal patterns, or other distinctive characteristics are usually sufficient, taken in conjunction with circumstances. For example, the authenticity of page three of a five page letter is in dispute. Assuming the other pages are authentic, if page three "fits" within the letter, it will be authentic.

MBE Tip: The bar frequently tests the admissibility requirements of authentication. An expert is not usually required; only someone with personal familiarity.

---

5. Voice Identification: Identification of a voice, whether heard firsthand or through mechanical or electronic transmission or recording, by opinion based upon hearing the voice at any time under circumstances connecting it with the alleged speaker. Of course, the witness must have prior knowledge of the maker's voice.

6. Telephone Conversations: Telephone conversations, by evidence that a call was made to the number assigned at the time by the telephone company to a particular person or business, if

a. Identification: In the case of a person, circumstances, including self-identification, show the person answering to be the one called, or

b. Reasonable Content: In the case of a business, the call was made to a place of business and the conversation related to business reasonably transacted over the telephone.

c. Return Call: If caller calls Bob at his place of business, leaves a message, and someone returns the call identifying himself as Bob returning the prior call, there is a *prima facie* showing so the voice of Bob is authenticated.

7. Electronic Mail (email) and Text Messages: Testimony by a person with knowledge of the author and particular email address, date, and time sent or received.

8. Ancient Documents or Data Compilation: Evidence that a document or data compilation, in any form:

a. Not Suspicious: Is in such condition as to create no authenticity suspicion;

b. Likely Place: Is in a place where it, if authentic, would likely be found, and;

c. 20 Years Old: Has been in existence 20 years or more at the time it is offered.

C. Self-Authentication – FRE 902

Due to the typical accuracy of the following documents, additional evidence of authenticity is not usually required as a condition to admissibility:

> **MBE Tip:** Self-authentication only refers to official documents. If self-authentication is an option, be wary unless it is an official publication or under some kind of seal or oath.

1. Domestic Public Documents Under Seal: Public documents bearing a proper seal and an attesting or executing notarized signature.

2. Domestic Public Documents Not Under Seal: Authenticity of non-sealed public documents is established if 1) the signing officer had no seal to use when the document was signed, and 2) a current public officer who works for the same public entity certifies under seal that the signature is genuine.

3. Foreign Public Documents: A foreign public document is authenticated by the fact it is signed by a public official authorized to do so under the laws of a foreign country, and has a final certification by a U.S. Consular agent.

4. Certified Copies of Public Records: Copy of an official record certified by the custodian as authentic.

5. Official Publications: Books, pamphlets, or other publications purporting to be issued by public authority.

6. Newspapers and Periodicals: Newspapers, magazines, and other periodicals.

7. Trade Inscriptions: Signs, tags or labels purporting to have been affixed in the course of business and indicating ownership, control, or origin.

8. Acknowledged Documents: Documents accompanied by a certificate of acknowledgement by a notary public of the identity of the person acknowledging.

9. Commercial Paper and Related Documents: Commercial paper, signatures thereon, and documents relating thereto.

10. Act of Congress: Any signature, document, or other matter declared by Act of Congress is presumed to be authentic.

11. Certified Domestic Record of Regularly Conducted Activity: A record accompanied by a declaration of its custodian or other qualified person certifying that the record was kept properly. The proponent must give reasonable notice to adverse parties and make the declaration available for inspection. For a record to be kept "properly" means that:

a. Near in Time: The record as made at or near in time to the occurrence by or through information transmitted by a person with knowledge,

b. Regular Course: The record was kept in the course of regularly conducted activity, and

c. Regularly Conducted Activity: The record was made as part of a regularly conducted activity, as opposed to a unique record made in response to an extraordinary event.

12. Certified Foreign Record of Regularly Conducted Activity: This falls under the same requirements as 11 above, but is applicable in civil cases only. Also, the declaration must be made under the penalty of the criminal laws of perjury of the country of origin.

XVII. BEST EVIDENCE RULE

The best evidence rule simply states that to prove the contents of a writing, the original writing should preferably be produced. The best evidence rule applies only when attempting to prove the actual content of a writing, recording, or photograph. It does not apply when attempting to prove underlying or related events. For example, a business keeps written records of certain transactions. If the business wishes to use the records themselves as evidence, it must comply with the best evidence rule. But employees may give oral testimony about the underlying transactions from memory without satisfying the best evidence writing rule.

A. Definitions – FRE 1001

1. Writings and Recordings: "Writings" and "recordings" consist of letters, words, sounds, numbers, or their equivalent, set down by handwriting, typewriting, printing, photographing, magnetic impulse, mechanical or electronic recording, or other forms of data compilation.

2. Photographs: "Photographs" include still photographs, x-ray films, sound recordings, video tapes, and motion pictures.

3. Originals: An "original" of a writing or recording is the writing or recording itself or any counterpart intending to have the same effect by a person executing or issuing it. An "original" of a photograph includes the negative or any print from the negative. If data is in a computer, any printout or other readable output shown to reflect the data accurately is an "original."

4. Duplicate: A "duplicate" is a counterpart produced (1) by the same impression as the original, (2) from the same matrix, (3) by means of photography, including enlargements and miniatures, (4) by mechanical or electronic recording, (5) by chemical reproduction, or (6) by other equivalent techniques that accurately reproduce the original.

B. Requirement of Original – FRE 1002

To prove the content of a writing, recording, or photograph, the original is required, except where the FREs or law provide otherwise. FRE 1003 below is the biggest exception.

> **MBE Tip:** An answer purporting to exclude the evidence as failing the best evidence rule is a common MBE trap. The best evidence rule applies only when content at issue is a material term of a writing or the witness is testifying relying on the writing. If the witness is testifying to a collateral matter, the best evidence rule does not apply.

C. Admissibility of Duplicates – FRE 1003

A duplicate, such as a photocopy, is admissible to the same extent as an original unless (1) a genuine question is raised as to the authenticity of the original or (2) in the circumstances it would be unfair to admit the duplicate in lieu of the original.

> **MBE Tip:** Look for a credible allegation that the duplicate has been tampered with. In this instance the original document is required.

D. Other Evidence of Contents – FRE 1004

To prove the content of a writing, recording, or photograph, the original (or a duplicate) is required, unless:

1. Original Lost or Destroyed: All originals are lost or have been destroyed, unless the proponent lost or destroyed them in bad faith; or

2. Original Not Obtainable: No original document can be obtained by any available judicial process or procedure and there is a credible reason for the absence; or

3. Original in Possession of Opponent: At a time when an original was under the control of the party against whom offered, that party was put on notice, by the pleadings or otherwise, that the contents would be a subject of proof at the trial or hearing, and that party does not produce the original at the trial or hearing; or

4. Collateral Matters: The writing, recording, or photograph is not closely related to a controlling issue in the case. The terms in question must be material.

E. Public Records – FRE 1005

Contents of official public records or documents properly recorded or filed may be authenticated in accordance with Rule 902 or by testimony of a witness who has compared the copy to the original. If a certified correct copy cannot be obtained with reasonable diligence, other evidence of the contents may be given.

F. Summaries – FRE 1006

Where the contents of voluminous writings, recordings, or photographs cannot conveniently be examined in court, they may be presented in the form of a chart, summary, or calculation. The summary must be sponsored by the preparer who testifies the summary accurately reflects the cumulative details of the underlying documents. To qualify the summary, the originals, or duplicates shall be made available for examination or copying, or both, by other parties in the matter at a reasonable time and place. The court may also order that the underlying documents in question be produced in court.

G. Content Admission – FRE 1007

Authenticity of the writing, recording, or photograph may be proved by testimony, deposition, or written admission by a party against whom the document is offered. The proponent need not account for the original.

H. Function of Court and Jury – FRE 1008

When admissibility is conditioned on the truth of another fact, the fulfillment of that fact is to be determined by the Court. But if a jury trial, the jury determines issues as to the existence of the writing, the originality of the writing, and/or whether other evidence accurately reflects the contents.

STOP!   Go to page 101 and work Learning Questions 61 to 71.

XVIII. FINAL CHAPTER REVIEW INSTRUCTIONS

1. Completing the Chapter: Now that you have completed your study of the chapter's substantive text and the related Learning Questions, you need to button up Evidence. This includes preparing your Magic Memory Outlines® and working all of the subject's practice MBE questions.

2. Preparing Your Own Magic Memory Outline®: This is helpful to your MBE success. The book paper outline works but consider purchasing our software template for your creation process. Do not underestimate the learning and memory effectiveness derived from condensing the text chapter into succinct summaries using your own words. This important exercise is covered in much more detail in the introduction and on the downloaded software.

    a. Summarize Knowledge: You need to prepare a summary of the chapter in your own words. An example is at page 4-71. The words in the outline correspond to the bold headings in the text.

    b. Capture the Essence: Your job is to summarize the substance of the text by capturing the essence of the rule and entering summarized wording into your own outlines. Use the text coverage to craft your own tight, concise, but comprehensive statements of the law.

    c. Boilerplate Rule Statements: Our related MEE volume at 10-447 contains primary issue statements that are helpful in both outline creation and MEE answer boilerplate language rule statements. Take pride in your skills as an author; your Magic Memory Outlines should be the finest written document you have ever created.

    d. Focus: Focus your attention and wording on the required technical elements necessary to prove the relevant legal principles. Look for fine-line distinctions. Integrate any helpful "learning question" information into your outline.

3. Memorize Outline: After you have completed your own Magic Memory Outline® for the whole chapter, read it over carefully once or twice. Refer back to your outlines frequently in quick reads during your preparation period.

4. Work Questions: The next step is to work all the regular questions in this chapter beginning on page 4-102. Questions vary in degree of difficulty, but the ones toward the end tend to concentrate on the most difficult fact patterns and issues. Date and put an X through their numbers as you work each question. Use the Question Map for cross-reference to the textual coverage so you can work on your weak topics. If you use the software, you can click on the questions under the subject and topic you have just studied.

    a. Question Details: It is usually worthwhile to review the explanatory answer rationales, as they reinforce the relevant principles of law. If you are still unsure of the controlling rule, refer back to the related portion of the text using the Question Map for cross-reference. This will help you to appreciate the fine-line distinctions on which the MBE evidence questions turn.

b. Do a Few Questions at a Time: Work the final chapter practice questions in sequence. Make sure you stop after no more than a few to check the answer rationales. Do this frequently so that the facts of the individual question are still in active memory.

c. Mask Down: Lay a mask over the answer rationales. Mask the answers for the questions to be worked. Pull the mask down to expose that question's answer rationale. Do not look down at future answers until after you work the relevant question. Test yourself.

d. Best to Work Them All: We have tried to pick questions with an average or higher probability of reappearing on the MBE. Work as many as you can, but at least read all of the questions in our book and ponder their answer rationales. Every question and answer has some marginal learning and/or reinforcement value. Many of the actual MBE questions are very similar to the ones in your Rigos UBE Review Series review books.

e. Learn from Mistakes: The objective is to learn from your mistakes by reviewing the explanatory rationales while you still remember the factual and legal details of the question. It is good to miss a few; this will help you become familiar with the MBE fine-line distinctions. The bar examiners' use of distracters, tricks, and red herrings is repetitive.

f. Flag Errors: Put a red star in the margin of the book alongside every question you missed. Missed questions should be worked again the day right before the MBE so that you do not make the same mistakes on the exam.

5. Take the Practice Exams: You can order our two optional simulated MBE exam sets that provide a helpful assessment. It contains 200 questions in random order broken down into two three-hour groups of 100 each. The bold question numbers listed on the right side of the Question Map refer to these final exam questions. While some practice exam questions in your text are intentionally easier or more difficult and complex than the MBE, both parts of the Final Exam have approximately the same overall difficulty as the actual MBE questions.

6. Make Your Own Exam: The optional UBE Review Series software allows you to pick 5, 10, 20, or 100 questions at random from all seven MBE subjects. This is an important feature because you must become intellectually comfortable with all the different subjects. If you are not an early riser and/or get going slowly when you first get up, try working 10 or 20 questions using the "Make Your Own Exam" software the first thing every morning.

7. Update Your Magic Memory Outline®: The fine-line distinctions in the question and answer rationales will improve your understanding of how the MBE tests the law. Consider updating your Magic Memory Outline® while the question testing environment is still fresh in your mind.

8. Essays: Candidates in jurisdictions that administer the Multistate Essay Exam *(MEE)* should refer to the *Rigos UBE Review Series Multistate Essay Exam Review* for the listing of primary issue statements. That volume contains sample MEE evidence essay questions and answers that relate to this chapter.

9. Performance Questions: Candidates in jurisdictions that administer the Multistate Performance Exam should refer to the *Rigos UBE Review Series Multistate Performance Test (MPT) Review* for practice task performance questions.

10. Next Chapter: It is now time to go to the beginning of the next subject in your review. Begin by previewing the chapter. Scan the topical coverage and major issues.

> **MBE Tip:** This Magic Memory Outline® is intended to be the platform upon which you create your own outline. Capture the essence and concentrate on using streamlined wording.

I. INTRODUCTION

A. Preliminary Matters – *27 evidence questions over both MBE sets* ....
1. MBE Evidence Focus – *half of questions cover relevance and hearsay rule with all the exceptions* ....
2. Workbook Format ....
3. Learning Questions – *Specified as student goes along in book. They reinforce and apply the text coverage. Stop and work them* ....
4. Practice Questions, Essays, and Sample Exam – *work all other questions after the learning questions at end of chapter* ....
5. Crossover Testing – *Frequent to issues of criminal law, especially Miranda* ......
6. Federal Rules of Evidence – *exclusive testing source* ....

B. Answer Approach Strategies – 4 **W**s – *<u>w</u>hy introduced, by <u>w</u>hom, <u>w</u>hen in proceeding, and <u>w</u>hether it is a civil or criminal case* ....
1. Admissibility Issues ....
   a. Objective – *introduce character v. impeach a witness* ....
   b. Impeachment Purpose – *prior conviction for perjury* ....
2. Process of Elimination – *and/or try a true-false approach* ....
3. Nonsensical Answers – *doctrines you do not recognize are likely distractors and thus wrong* ....
4. Old Common Law Rules – *only FRE tested on MBE* ....
5. Overruled or Sustained – *overruled means objection to admission failed so offered evidence comes in* ....

C. Common Answers ....
1. Inadmissible Because of Witness Incompetence – *usually wrong* ....
2. Inadmissible Unless Offered in Rebuttal – *frequently tested and often the best choice* ....
3. Inadmissible Because Prejudice Outweighs Probative Value – *must be substantial prejudice* ....
4. Admissible if Declarant is not Available to Testify – *Former testimony, against interest, and belief of impending death all qualify for this exception* ......
5. Best Evidence Rule – *only applicable to writing and documents* ....

II. GENERAL PROVISIONS UNDER THE FRE

A. Sources and Applicability of Law ....
1. Federal Rules Orientation – *all MBE questions* ....
2. Application – FRE 1101 – *applies to all federal courts* ....
   a. Preliminary Questions of Fact – *court determines admissibility* ....
   b. Grand Jury Proceedings – *FRE non-applicable* ....

RIGOS UBE REVIEW SERIES

UNIFORM MULTISTATE BAR EXAM (MBE) REVIEW

CHAPTER 4

EVIDENCE

Text to Question Distribution Map

> **MBE Tip:** Numbers immediately following the topic are the chapter question numbers. The **boldface** numbers preceded by "F" are the final exam question numbers. For example, for the topic "IIC. Judicial Notice" below, questions 1, 2, 3, and 103 are in the chapter question section on pages 4-91, 4-91, 4-91, and 4-108, respectively. Questions in bold at the right margin are in the final exam.

> **MEE Candidates:** Please refer to the *Rigos UBE Review Series Multistate Essay Exam (MEE) Review* for practice essay questions and sample answers covering evidence.

LEARNING QUESTIONS

Assume all jurisdictions use the Federal Rules of Evidence.

1. In a civil case, when the Court takes judicial notice of a fact, that fact is
    (A) Conclusively established.
    (B) Still must be proved with other evidence.
    (C) The moving party's burden of production is satisfied.
    (D) Established but the other party may rebut with other evidence.

2. In a criminal case, when the Court takes judicial notice of a fact
    (A) That fact is conclusively established.
    (B) That fact must still be proved with other evidence.
    (C) The prosecution's burden of production is satisfied.
    (D) A text or other reference source must be consulted.

3. For which of the following facts, would it be error to take judicial notice in a civil case?
    (A) The fact that the sky is blue.
    (B) The fact that New York City is in New York State.
    (C) The fact that the Columbia River empties into the Pacific Ocean.
    (D) The fact that air bags are standard safety equipment on automobiles.

4. D is on trial for embezzlement. During the prosecution's case in chief, evidence of D's prior conviction for embezzlement is offered into evidence. The Court sustains the objection, ruling that prior convictions may not be admitted to demonstrate that D is a criminal type or committed this particular embezzlement. During D's case in chief, D testifies that he is honest and would never do such a thing. In rebuttal, the prosecution again offers the evidence of conviction to impeach D's testimony. What must happen for the evidence to be admitted?
    (A) The Court must tell the jury that they may consider the evidence only to determine the D's credibility and reliability.
    (B) The Court must tell the jury that they may consider the evidence not only as impeachment evidence, but also for its substantive value.
    (C) The Court may tell the jury that evidence of a prior conviction is determinative of a witness's credibility and reliability.
    (D) The Court must not comment on the evidence in any way.

5. A controlling statute provides that it is negligence *per se* to allow your dog to run loose without a collar and leash. D's dog, while running loose, bites P. P sues in a civil action and during his case in chief, produces evidence that D's dog was running loose at the time he was bitten. This evidence has what effect?
    (A) The D's negligence is presumed.
    (B) The D's negligence is presumed unless and until he offers substantial evidence in rebuttal.
    (C) The jury may consider whether the dog running loose and biting P was negligent.
    (D) P has not proved anything.

6. A statute provides that it is negligence *per se* to allow your dog to run loose. D's dog, while running loose, bites and seriously injures a passerby. D is charged with criminal negligence based on the same facts. What effect does the prosecution's introduction of the fact that D's dog was running loose at the time of the bite have?

(A) The D's negligence is presumed.

(B) The D's negligence is presumed until he offers evidence in rebuttal.

(C) The jury may consider whether the dog running loose and biting P was criminally negligent.

(D) The prosecution has not proved anything.

7. P is suing D for negligence (failure to exercise due care) resulting from a rear-end automobile collision. Which of the following facts is relevant to P's case?

(A) The fact that D was not carrying a license to drive.

(B) The fact that D was driving too fast for the weather conditions.

(C) The fact that the license plate on D's car was expired.

(D) The fact that D was driving a Gremlin.

8. P is suing D for negligence for failure to exercise due care resulting from a rear-end automobile collision. P is able to establish D's negligence on summary judgment. P then moves to admit evidence that D was not carrying a license to drive at the time of the accident and that he was driving too fast for the rainy weather conditions. How should the court rule?

(A) Irrelevant, not probative of negligence.

(B) Irrelevant, not material to establishing P's case at trial.

(C) Relevant, material to establishing D's negligence.

(D) Relevant, probative of D's negligence.

9. D is on trial for embezzlement. The prosecution wishes to introduce evidence that D makes only $15,000.00 per year and has a net worth of $5.00 to establish a motive for the embezzlement which occurred in the D's department. What else, if anything, must the prosecution offer to establish the relevance of this evidence?

(A) None, poverty alone is sufficiently relevant to show motive for embezzlement.

(B) The fact that after the money disappeared, D bought a very expensive sports car.

(C) The fact that D is a compulsive gambler.

(D) The fact that D inherited two million dollars.

10. Doctor Witness testifies on behalf of P in P's suit for personal injuries. Which of the following questions will be permitted on cross-examination of the witness?

(A) "Isn't it true that the only way your bill will be paid is if P recovers?"

(B) "Isn't it true that you were once cited for sleeping in a park?"

(C) "Isn't it true that your wife is a communist?"

(D) "Isn't it true that your Doctoral Degree is in Post-Modern Feminist Thought?"

11. P is suing D for breach of contract. P needs to prove that D failed to personally deliver 20 widgets at 2:00 p.m. on Friday as required by the contract. D denies he failed to do this claiming he delivered the widgets at the specified time. Which item of evidence will not be admitted?

- **(A)** The fact that D was seen at Safeco Field at 2:00 p.m. on Friday.
- **(B)** Testimony by a witness who states "I read a letter that said D stated he failed to deliver the widgets as required by the contract."
- **(C)** Testimony by a witness who states "D told me that he couldn't perform on the contract because he wanted to attend a pro-Taliban rally in downtown New York at 2:00 p.m. on Friday where he had been invited to speak against the U.S. and in favor of Osama bin Laden."
- **(D)** The fact that D was at a bar drinking beer at 2:00 p.m. on Friday.

12. D is on trial for assault. Prosecutor (P) offers evidence of D's prior conviction of assault. Which of the following must occur first to admit this evidence?

- **(A)** Expert testimony establishing that once a person has assaulted, they are more likely to commit a subsequent assault.
- **(B)** Testimony that D has always been a peaceful person who would never harm a fly, much less assault anyone.
- **(C)** Testimony that the victim was a peaceful person.
- **(D)** None – the evidence comes in on its own.

13. D is on trial for a robbery that occurred in Los Angeles on January 1. P offers evidence that D was charged with assault in an unrelated incident on the same day in Los Angeles. Which of the following is a condition precedent to the admission of the assault evidence?

- **(A)** The assault victim was first aggressor.
- **(B)** The robbery involved an assault as well.
- **(C)** The robbery victim was first aggressor.
- **(D)** D claims that he was in Las Vegas on January 1.

14. Heather is a radical leftist who is charged with giving the middle finger to a police officer. The Prosecution offers Heather's previous five convictions for giving the finger to police officers. Which of the following is a condition precedent to admission of the previous convictions?

- **(A)** Heather claims she was giving the finger to a rich capitalist who was walking behind the police officer.
- **(B)** Heather must testify.
- **(C)** Testimony that Heather has a reputation for such acts.
- **(D)** There is no condition precedent, the evidence comes in on its own.

15. In a divorce proceeding, the court orders a parental fitness hearing. The wife offers evidence that the husband is a violent drunk. Characterize this evidence.

- **(A)** Inadmissible character evidence.
- **(B)** Inadmissible to prove that the husband will be a drunk in the future.
- **(C)** Admissible because character is at issue.
- **(D)** Admissible provided the evidence is offered for a purpose other than to prove action in conformity therewith.

16. Professor McGaff sues Garrett for defamation because Garrett stated "Professor McGaff is a communist, a liar, and stupid." Which of the following is not admissible?

- **(A)** Professor's membership card in the Communist Party.
- **(B)** Professor's five previous perjury convictions.
- **(C)** Professor's law school transcript.
- **(D)** Professor's previous Driving While Intoxicated conviction.

17. D is charged with a daring nighttime burglary during which the Crown Jewels were stolen from the Tower of London (ignore international jurisdictional issues). The burglar left a single red rose as a calling card in the empty jewel case. The prosecution offers the testimony of five burglary victims, for which burglaries D was convicted, who testify that a single red rose was left at the scene of each of their burglaries. For which purpose may this evidence be admitted?

    (A) To show that D is the likely crown jewel burglar.

    (B) To show that D is the criminal type.

    (C) To rebut D's denial that he is not the criminal type.

    (D) To bolster the credibility of the five witnesses.

18. D is on trial for perjury. D claims to be an honest person while on the stand. Which of the following is not a permissible method of proving character?

    (A) On direct examination: "In my opinion, D is a dishonest person."

    (B) On direct examination: "In the general community, D has a reputation as a dishonest person."

    (C) On direct examination: "On January 1, I heard D lie to his wife."

    (D) On cross-examination: "My poor opinion of D as a liar is due to my witnessing him lie to his family numerous times."

19. D is on trial for molesting Child V. Which of the following may be admitted into evidence?

    (A) D's previous conviction of molesting children.

    (B) D's previous conviction for perjury.

    (C) D's previous conviction for assault.

    (D) D's previous conviction for burglary.

20. Which of the following qualifies as routine practice, as opposed to a habit?

    (A) A train engineer who has blown the train whistle at every crossing for the past 20 years.

    (B) Washing one's hands before every meal one's entire life.

    (C) A factory that fills out an incident report every time a worker is injured.

    (D) A factory worker who runs a machine, resetting the safety lever 30 times per day.

21. In regards to evidence of a subsequent remedial measure, which of the following is not correct?

    (A) Admissible to prove negligence.

    (B) Admissible to prove notice.

    (C) Admissible to prove feasibility of safety measures.

    (D) Admissible to prove ownership or control.

22. In which situation will the statement by D, "I am so sorry that I was negligent and you were hurt as a result" be admissible at trial?

    (A) If the statement was made right after D offered to settle P's claims.

    (B) If the statement was made during a meeting with the prosecutor regarding a plea agreement for criminal negligence.

    (C) If the statement was made right after D offered to pay P's medical expenses.

    (D) If the statement was made in a settlement letter sent to P in which the D discusses P's medical expenses.

23. With respect to evidence that the D did or did not possess liability insurance, which of the following is not correct?

    (A) Admissible to prove ownership or control over an automobile.

    (B) Admissible to prove the existence of an agency relationship.

    (C) Admissible to prove witness bias.

    (D) Admissible to prove negligence.

24. P is suing D for injuries sustained when P slipped on an icy sidewalk allegedly owned by D. D denies owning the portion of the sidewalk upon which P slipped. Which of the following is not admissible at trial?

    (A) The fact that D subsequently contracted with Bob to keep the sidewalk clear of ice.

    (B) The fact that D sent a letter to P offering to pay P a large amount of money because as D stated in the letter "I may be subject to liability."

    (C) The fact that D added a "slip and fall" endorsement to his premises liability insurance policy.

    (D) The fact that upon offering to pay P's medical bills, D admitted to owning the sidewalk.

25. In which of the following situations does a privileged communication exist?

    (A) Doctor Bob asks Lawyer a legal question at a cocktail party with others adding to the conversation.

    (B) A married couple loudly arguing in public.

    (C) Larry consults with his Lawyer in a private office in order to plan an insurance fraud scheme.

    (D) A surgeon husband tells his wife privately "I think I was negligent in that operation today."

26. In which of the following situations could a spouse be compelled to testify regarding a communication between the two?

    (A) A communication made before marriage between a couple now divorced.

    (B) A communication made between a currently married couple during their marriage.

    (C) A communication made between a currently married couple before their marriage.

    (D) A communication made during marriage between a couple now divorced.

27. In which situation will the client be able to invoke attorney-client privilege?

    (A) When the client refuses to pay the attorney's fees.

    (B) When the client consults with the attorney as to the best way to avoid detection of a continuing fraud.

    (C) When the client asks the attorney to represent him in defending against a charge of fraud.

    (D) When the client discusses a legal matter in the presence of a "man on the street."

28. In which of the following situations is marital privilege present?

    (A) In a divorce proceeding.

    (B) In a mental competency proceeding.

    (C) In the planning or commission of a crime.

    (D) In a lawsuit by a third party against one of the spouses.

29. In which of the following may a physician assert a patient privilege?

    (A) Psychotherapist-patient privilege.

    (B) Medical treatment of a patient with cancer.

    (C) Non-diversity of citizenship case.

    (D) A malpractice action that the patient brings against a psychotherapist.

30. In which of the following situations will a witness be competent to testify?

    (A) The witness refuses to take the oath to testify truthfully.

    (B) The witness is completely deaf and just had her larynx removed and has not yet learned sign language.

    (C) The witness has been stricken with complete amnesia.

    (D) The witness is insane.

31. Which of the following witness statements is not admissible in and of itself?

(A) "The traffic light was green."

(B) "I was watching the traffic light at the time of the collision and it was green."

(C) "If I remember correctly, I saw that the traffic light was green."

(D) "I'm not exactly sure, but I'm fairly certain that when I saw the traffic light it was green."

32. P is suing D for damages resulting from D's throwing a brick through the P's window. D states that it was not him who threw the brick. Witness testifies "I saw D throw the brick and he was drinking a Daff Beer at the time." Which of the following evidence is inadmissible as impeachment evidence?

(A) A videotape showing someone other than D throwing a brick through the window drinking Daff Beer.

(B) Testimony of D stating that he could not have been drinking Daff Beer because he is allergic to alcohol.

(C) Testimony of D that he did not throw the brick through the window, rather it was his twin brother E.

(D) The fact Witness is a convicted perjurer.

33. D is accused of car theft. D calls Homer to testify that at the time of the theft, Homer and D were together at a pool hall. What question may be asked on cross-examination?

(A) "Isn't it true that D was once arrested for shoplifting a pen?"

(B) "Isn't it true that D has a reputation for theft?"

(C) "Isn't it true that D threatened you to get you to testify in his favor?"

(D) "Isn't it true that at the time of the crime, you were not playing pool, but air hockey?"

34. W1 testifies on behalf of P. P would like to ask W2 to confirm and reinforce W1's good reputation for truthfulness. What if anything must happen before W2 can testify about that?

(A) The accused must put his character in issue.

(B) The credibility of W1 must be attacked.

(C) Nothing, a witness can be impeached by any party including the party calling the witness.

(D) Nothing, specific instances of conduct cannot be proved with extrinsic evidence.

35. P calls Witness to testify on his behalf. Witness testifies very favorably for P. D knows about an incident where Witness lied to his landlord about his ability to pay rent. How can D get this into evidence?

(A) Call the landlord to testify about the incident.

(B) Introduce Witness's bank statement that shows Witness had enough money to pay the rent.

(C) Question Witness about the incident on cross-examination.

(D) He can't. P must first bolster the credibility of Witness before D can attack it.

36. D is on trial for assault. D takes the stand in his own defense and denies being the assailant. If the prosecutor wishes to attack D's credibility, which of the following is permissible?

(A) Introduce D's five-year-old conviction for embezzlement.

(B) Introduce D's misdemeanor conviction for reckless driving.

(C) Introduce D's 7-year-old juvenile conviction for perjury.

(D) Call a witness who will testify that D kicked her dog on one occasion.

37. In which situation will a witness's religious beliefs be admissible?

(A) To show that the witness is less likely to lie.

(B) To show that the witness takes the oath seriously.

(C) To show that the witness is more likely to lie.

(D) If religious belief is an essential element of a claim or defense.

38. Witness testifies on P's behalf. Witness states "I saw D's car run the red light." D knows that Witness stated to a police officer that the light was green when D entered the intersection. Which of the following is not a permissible way to impeach the witness?

(A) Question the Witness about the statement on cross-examination.

(B) Call the police officer to testify as to what Witness told him.

(C) Call another witness who will state that Witness told him "I did not see the color of the light."

(D) Call another witness who will state that Witness also said that the incident happened on a Tuesday when it actually happened on a Wednesday.

39. On direct examination Witness CPA is questioned as an expert by P regarding her knowledge of accounting professional standards. On cross-examination, D asks Witness "Isn't it true that an attorney must also adhere to professional standards?" Upon objection what result?

(A) Sustained, outside the scope of direct.

(B) Sustained, leading question.

(C) Overruled, within the scope of direct.

(D) Overruled, leading questions allowed to develop witness's testimony.

40. Witness is being questioned by P. P asks, "Please describe in detail the events of last Tuesday." Witness answers, "I don't recall in detail those events, but I took down some notes that I have with me. I'll look at them to help me remember." What must happen in order for the witness to use the notes?

(A) The notes must be offered and admitted into evidence.

(B) Opposing counsel must be allowed to inspect the notes.

(C) The notes must be read into the record, but the notes themselves not admitted into evidence.

(D) Nothing; the witness may use the notes.

41. Which of the following is not permissible lay witness trial opinion testimony?

(A) "D was obviously intoxicated when I saw him on the roof."

(B) "The substance upon which I saw P slip looked like grease."

(C) "I observed them both sign the legal agreement."

(D) "The roof on my house was not designed or built to industry standards."

42. Which of the following opinions is admissible?

(A) "The D is guilty."

(B) "The P's injuries were proximately caused by the automobile collision."

(C) "The D was negligent."

(D) "I examined the D, and in my opinion, he is not mentally capable of having the *mens rea* for the crime."

43. Which of the following will not qualify a witness as an expert?

(A) In an admiralty case, the witness spent 20 years as master of a commercial vessel and will testify as to standards of care in commanding a vessel at sea.

(B) In a case for negligent design, the witness holds a Master's Degree in Engineering and will testify as to the proper design required.

(C) In a case of legal malpractice, the witness is a law school professor who has studied the legal subject area and will testify as to the proper application of the law.

(D) In a medical malpractice case, the witness is a truck driver who has had an injury similar to the one claimed by P and will testify as to the causation of such an injury.

44. Upon which of the following facts may an expert opine?

(A) Those facts personally perceived by the expert witness.

(B) Those facts made known to the expert witness.

(C) Both A & B.

(D) Neither A nor B.

45. The facts upon which an expert bases her opinion must be

(A) Known to or perceived by the expert.

(B) Accepted within the scientific community.

(C) Admissible in and of themselves (may not rely on hearsay for example).

(D) Of a type reasonably relied upon by experts in the field.

46. If an expert gives an opinion based on certain underlying facts, those facts must be testified to by the expert

(A) Prior to giving the opinion.

(B) If elicited upon cross-examination.

(C) During the expert's qualification hearing.

(D) Only if the expert is court appointed.

47. Which of the following statements is made by a witness to prove the truth of the matter asserted therein?

(A) In a defamation case: "D was accused of stating that P has a sexually transmitted disease."

(B) In a murder prosecution: "Sally said she saw D kill victim."

(C) In a premises liability case: "Mr. Shopkeeper, did you know there is ice on the sidewalk in front of your store?"

(D) In a prosecution for kidnapping: "Victim told me that the inside of D's apartment was painted with pink and green stripes."

48. Which of the following is non-assertive conduct as to whether it is/was raining outside?

(A) Bob's secretary sees Bob glance out a window on his way out of the office, turn around, and take an umbrella off the coat rack.

(B) Upon Bob's return, the Secretary asks, "Is it raining outside?" Bob takes off one of his shoes and pours water out of it onto her desk.

(C) Upon Bob's return, the Secretary says, "It's raining." Bob looks at her and furiously shakes out his umbrella.

(D) Upon Bob's return, the Secretary asks, "Is it raining outside?" Bob shakes his head.

49. Determine which of the following out-of-court statements by a witness is hearsay.

(A) A statement given to an insurance adjuster in their claims office that is inconsistent with the witness's current trial testimony.

(B) A statement made at a previous trial inconsistent with the witness's current trial testimony.

(C) A statement made at a deposition inconsistent with the witness's current trial testimony.

(D) A statement made to a police officer identifying D as the perpetrator of a robbery.

50. The President personally and his corporation are being sued for an intentional tort. Determine which of the following out-of-court statements offered against the D is hearsay?

(A) D's wife said, "Of course my husband's company is liable."

(B) D states to an investigating officer, "I did it on purpose."

(C) D states to a friend, "I don't remember what happened."

(D) D Corporation's Public Relations Spokesperson states, "The President of Mega Co. has asked me to say we are very sorry that our toxic chemicals spilled into the public aquifer."

51. Which of the following is an adoptive admission?

(A) In the presence of a witness, P accuses D of negligent driving. D says nothing.

(B) Same as A, except D is deaf.

(C) Same as A above except after hearing the accusation, D faints from his injuries.

(D) Same as A above except D responds, "You are a filthy liar."

52. Which of the following statements will most likely not be admitted into evidence?

(A) Declarant is standing on a street corner with her friend witness. Declarant then says, "Hey, that car [driven by D] just ran a red light."

(B) Declarant is crossing the street when her ex-husband clips her in his car sending her onto the ground. She shouts, "John, you jerk! Watch where in the hell you are going!"

(C) Declarant returns home from work. Her husband asks how her day went. "Well, this morning on my way in to work, I saw [D] run a red light, and strike a poor innocent woman."

(D) Declarant returns home from work and tells her husband, "Don't ask me about my day. I'm so upset."

53. In order to admit a past recorded recollection as an exception to hearsay, which of the following are not required?

(A) The witness once had personal knowledge of the events or facts recorded.

(B) The witness has a total but inaccurate recollection of the events.

(C) The events or facts were fresh in the witness's knowledge when recorded.

(D) The record is an accurate reflection of the witness's knowledge at the time of the recording.

54. P is an employee in the factory owned by D Corp. P is injured on the job. P's supervisor immediately calls the risk management department who tells him, "Have all the witnesses make a written statement as per our established procedure. We want to be prepared for any potential lawsuit by the government." Would the statements qualify as Records of a Regularly Conducted Activity?

(A) Yes, because D Corp. took the statements pursuant to established procedure near in time to the incident.

(B) Yes, because the statements were made by persons with personal knowledge of the incident.

(C) No, because the statements were made in anticipation of litigation.

(D) No, because taking witness statements was not a regular practice of D Corp.

55. P Patient is suing D Doctor for medical malpractice. P alleges that D used an improper surgical technique when removing P's appendix. P calls Expert Witness who on direct examination states "According to the book 'Appendectomy Illustrated' upon which I relied in forming my opinion and which is authoritative within the surgical community, an appendix should be removed using a number four scalpel." On-cross examination, D's attorney would like to bring to the jury's attention a passage in "Appendectomy Illustrated" that states that a number five scalpel is also acceptable. What is the permissible way to get that passage to the jury?

(A) Offer the relevant passage into evidence.

(B) Have the expert read the relevant passage into the record.

(C) Admit the entire treatise into evidence with a limiting instruction that the evidence therein is for impeachment purposes only.

(D) Admit the entire treatise into evidence for impeachment or substantive evidence.

56. In which of the following situations, is the declarant unavailable for the purposes of a hearsay exception?

(A) The declarant is on the witness stand yet refuses to answer questions even though ordered to do so by the Court.

(B) The declarant is on vacation when service of process was attempted for the first time a week prior to trial.

(C) The declarant was murdered by the proponent of the statement.

(D) The declarant has suffered partial amnesia, but can remember most of the subject matter of the statement.

57. Which of the following does not qualify as admissible under a hearsay exception?

(A) "Bob shot me and I'm going to die." Declarant lives.

(B) "Bob shot me, but he missed anything vital, so I think I'll pull through." Declarant then dies.

(C) Declarant testifies in a trial involving two parties. A mistrial is declared. Before the second trial, declarant dies. The proponent offers the transcript of declarant's testimony from the first trial.

(D) Declarant states, "I do not have title to Blackacre even though everyone thinks I do."

58. P's medical records contain the following written statement by P's doctor, "Patient complains of arm pain secondary to motor vehicle accident." P offers the records into evidence. Which of the following hearsay exceptions will get this record into evidence?

(A) Then existing mental, emotional, or physical condition.

(B) Record of a regularly conducted activity, and Statements for purpose of medical diagnosis.

(C) Recorded recollection, and Statements for purpose of medical diagnosis.

(D) Present sense impression, and then existing mental, emotional, or physical condition.

59. P successfully introduced into evidence an out-of-court statement made by Henry, a witness not available for trial. D now wants to attack Henry's credibility with a contradictory statement also made by Henry. What is P's best argument against allowing such impeachment?

(A) Henry made the contradictory statement 15 years ago.

(B) The contradiction is not relevant to substantive issue in the case.

(C) Henry has no opportunity to explain or deny the contradiction.

(D) The contradictory statement offered is inadmissible hearsay.

60. Which of the following is not an element of the residual hearsay exception?
- (A) The statement is evidence of a material fact.
- (B) The statement is the most probative piece of evidence.
- (C) The admission of the evidence will best serve the purposes of the Rules and the interest of justice.
- (D) The statement can be corroborated for reliability.

61. What is the burden of proof a proponent must satisfy in order to authenticate the evidence?
- (A) Evidence sufficient to support a finding of plausible authenticity.
- (B) Evidence sufficient for the trier of fact to find authenticity by a preponderance of the evidence.
- (C) Clear and convincing evidence, which supports a finding of authenticity.
- (D) Proof beyond a reasonable doubt, which supports a finding of authenticity.

62. Which of the following is not an acceptable method of authenticating a document?
- (A) A lay witness compares the signature on the document with an authentic signature.
- (B) An expert witness testifies that she created the document.
- (C) A witness testifies that she witnessed the creation of the document.
- (D) A witness testifies that she heard the D admit to creating the document.

63. Which is a correct statement as to authenticating a photograph?
- (A) The photographer must testify as to taking the photograph.
- (B) Testimony by a witness who has been at the scene that the photograph is a fair and accurate representation thereof.
- (C) The photograph must have distinctive characteristics.
- (D) The opposing party must admit that the photograph is authentic.

64. In which situation is a voice over the telephone not authenticated?
- (A) X calls Y's place of business and leaves a message for Y. X gets a telephone call five minutes later and the caller states, "Hello, this is Y returning your telephone call."
- (B) X receives a telephone call where the caller identifies himself as Y.
- (C) X looks up Y's telephone number in the directory, dials the number, and the call is answered by "Hello, Y speaking."
- (D) X calls Y's place of business and speaks to a person identifying himself as Y and the two discuss business.

65. Which is not an acceptable way to authenticate a page in a letter?
- (A) Have a witness familiar with the maker's handwriting testify that the handwriting belongs to the maker.
- (B) Bring to the Court's attention that the page in question states in the margin "Maker's letter page 3 of 5." Authentication of the other pages is already established.
- (C) Have the maker's sister testify that the handwriting is the maker's.
- (D) The letter is proved to be fifteen years old.

66. Which of the following is most likely to negate authenticity of an "ancient document"?
- (A) The document is proved to be 225 years old.
- (B) The document was found in the County Recorder's Office where such documents are located.
- (C) Neither party disputes authenticity.
- (D) The document is printed in Times New Roman font on a sheet of clean white paper. All other documents of the same age are handwritten on yellowing, crumbling paper.

67. Which of the following is not a self-authenticating document?

    (A) Market reports or commercial publications.

    (B) A certified copy of a deed.

    (C) A book published by the Federal Government.

    (D) The New York Times.

68. Which of the following is considered "Best Evidence" under the Federal Rules?

    (A) Live testimony regarding the contents of a document.

    (B) Testimony of a witness with firsthand knowledge instead of hearsay.

    (C) An original document in order to prove the contents thereof.

    (D) An original document that records a witness's observations of an event.

69. In which of the following scenarios would it be impermissible to prove the contents of a document with evidence other than the document itself?

    (A) The document does not regard an issue central to the case.

    (B) The document was lost through no fault of either party.

    (C) The original is located in another country with no functioning courts.

    (D) Only a duplicate is available.

70. What effect does an opposing party's admission to the contents of a document have?

    (A) None, the document must still be produced.

    (B) The proponent need not produce the original.

    (C) None, provided that the original is not obtainable.

    (D) A presumption of the contents of the document arises.

71. In order to admit a summary of voluminous documentation, what must the proponent do?

    (A) The underlying documents must be admitted into evidence.

    (B) The underlying documents must be produced in court.

    (C) The party against whom the summary is offered must not object to the summary.

    (D) The underlying documents must be made available to opposing parties.

REGULAR QUESTIONS

72. Jones is on trial for vandalism in Seattle during the World Trade Organization riots. The State introduces a videotape of Jones throwing a garbage can through the window of a coffee shop in the Skinner Building. In his defense, Jones calls his chapter president of Rich College Kids United who testifies that Jones has a reputation for honesty within the college activist community. The prosecution timely objects. What result?

    (A) Admissible, relevant to show Jones' character for truth.

    (B) Admissible, relevant to dispute the charges.

    (C) Not admissible, character evidence cannot be introduced by the accused unless first attacked by the other party.

    (D) Not admissible, not a relevant character trait.

73. James is charged with assaulting a police officer. The primary evidence is the testimony of the officer who states that a black clad and masked person with a red "A" on his shirt spit in his face. The prosecution then introduces a certified copy of a State Court judgment finding James guilty 14 years ago for spitting in a police officer's face while wearing black clothing with a red "A" and a mask. Upon a timely objection, what result?

    (A) Admissible, probative value outweighs prejudicial effect.

    (B) Admissible, but not to prove that James has a propensity for spitting in police officer faces.

    (C) Not admissible, conviction is more than ten years prior.

    (D) Not admissible, specific acts cannot be proved with extrinsic evidence.

74. Henry is charged with lewd conduct after allegedly "mooning" the World Trade Organization delegate from Uruguay in a Chicago street demonstration. The prosecution wishes to introduce documents charging Henry with previous "hate speech" after he referred to another delegate in a racially derogatory way. In that offense Henry was charged but not convicted. If Henry timely objects, what result?

(A) Inadmissible, Henry was never convicted.

(B) Inadmissible, prejudice outweighs probative value.

(C) Admissible, probative nature of the evidence outweighs prejudice.

(D) Admissible, shows common scheme or plan.

75. Jerry was able to secure a new high paying job and buys a speed boat. His friend Heather scoffs, "That is an obscene monument to capitalism, and I'd like to use it to run down the President of Floor Mart because he deserves it. He has gotten rich off the backs of his employees and exploited his customers. Jerry hands the keys to Heather and says "Have fun." Heather takes the boat and sees the President of Floor Mart swimming. She runs him down, killing him. His estate sues Heather (wrongful death) and Jerry (negligent entrustment).

The estate wishes to call Peter who will testify that Jerry was aware that Heather had a propensity to run down prominent businessmen using various vehicles. Upon Heather's objection, what ruling?

(A) Not admissible, evidence of Heather's character is not relevant.

(B) Not admissible, specific instances of conduct cannot be introduced by extrinsic evidence.

(C) Admissible because the evidence goes to Jerry's knowledge of Heather's dangerous propensities.

(D) Admissible, but cannot be used for any purpose against Heather, only Jerry.

76. Gunther is charged with animal cruelty involving Lumbo the elephant. The prosecution wishes to introduce testimony that Lumbo exhibits fright whenever Gunther approaches, but not when anyone else approaches. If Gunther objects, what result?

(A) Not admissible, the prosecution must produce the best evidence.

(B) Not admissible, prejudice outweighs probative value.

(C) Admissible, evidence of guilt.

(D) Not admissible, evidence is immaterial and insufficient to sustain prosecution's burden.

77. Anthony sues Bob for battery. Anthony offers the testimony of Charlie who will state that he saw Bob drinking one beer two hours before the alleged battery. Bob timely objects to the testimony as irrelevant. The judge should rule

(A) For Anthony because it will help establish Bob's intoxication.

(B) For Anthony because intoxication may be a defense to the tort of battery.

(C) For Bob because intoxication is not a defense to an intentional tort.

(D) For Bob because drinking a beer does not help establish any of the elements of battery.

78. Dave is on trial for the murder of Erin. The prosecution offers the testimony of Frank who heard Erin accuse Dave of embezzling from their partnership. Dave timely objects to Frank's testimony as irrelevant. The judge should rule

(A) For the prosecution because Erin's accusation may have motivated Dave to murder her.

(B) For the prosecution because Erin's accusation demonstrates that Dave was dishonest.

(C) For Dave because Frank's testimony is insufficient to sustain a guilty verdict.

(D) For Dave because Frank's testimony is circumstantial evidence.

79. Dave is on trial for the murder of Erin. Frank testifies that he saw Dave dispose of bloody clothing after returning home from his work as a butcher. Dave timely objects. What ruling and why?

(A) For the prosecution because disposing of bloody clothes demonstrates that Dave was trying to hide something.

(B) For the prosecution because the testimony is relevant.

(C) For Dave because the testimony is prejudicial.

(D) For Dave because the testimony is irrelevant.

80. Dave is on trial for the murder of Erin and the defense asks Dave whether he was reprimanded by his law school for claiming to be on the Law Review when he was not. Dave states on the stand that his law school never reprimanded him. The prosecution offers into evidence a letter from the dean of the law school to Dave reprimanding Dave for going overtime on an exam. If Dave objects, what result?

(A) Sustained, because the letter is extrinsic evidence.

(B) Sustained, because Dave has not had an opportunity to explain or deny the statement in the letter.

(C) Overruled, because the letter is a prior inconsistent statement.

(D) Overruled, because the letter is offered to refresh the witness's memory.

81. Dave is on trial for the murder of Erin and calls his best friend Goler to the stand to testify as a character witness. Goler testifies "It has always been my opinion that Dave is honest and peaceful." The prosecution on cross-examination asks "Is it not true that you once sent a letter stating 'Dave is a violent liar.'" What ruling on Dave's timely objection?

(A) Sustained, the statement is extrinsic evidence.

(B) Overruled, prior inconsistent statement by witness.

(C) Sustained, the letter was not disclosed to Goler before questioning about it.

(D) Overruled, unless the letter is merely used to refresh Goler's memory.

82. Dave is on trial for the murder of Erin and his best friend Goler is on the stand testifying as a character witness. The prosecutor cross-examines Goler and raises doubt about his credibility as a witness. Upon further cross-examination, the prosecutor asks "Is it not true that Dave saved your life during the Gulf War?" Dave timely objects, what result?

(A) Sustained, irrelevant to Goler's credibility.

(B) Sustained, prejudicial.

(C) Overruled, shows possible witness bias.

(D) Overruled, shows Goler's propensity for truth.

83. P is suing D for breach of contract. P then telephones D and says "I'll settle for twenty dollars because it is questionable whether the terms of the contract were clear." D rejects the offer. At trial, D tries to testify about P's statement. On P's timely objection, what result?

(A) Not admissible, hearsay.

(B) Not admissible, but only the offer itself, not the fact P admitted the weakness of his case.

(C) Admissible, hearsay, but subject to an exception.

(D) Not admissible, both offer and admission are inadmissible.

84. Delores was furiously chatting on her cell phone while driving down the expressway when she ran down Penelope. Delores was quite concerned and the next day visited Penelope in the hospital. Delores said, "I will pay for all your medical expenses." As she left, Delores said, "I am very sorry I was negligent." At trial, Penelope wishes to testify about the statement. Upon Delores' objection, what result?

    (A) Delores' entire statements are admissible.
    (B) Only Delores' offer to pay is admissible.
    (C) Only Delores' admission of negligence is admissible.
    (D) Delores' entire statement is not admissible.

85. In which of the following situations is the evidence most likely to be admitted?

    (A) P's attorney examines Witness about their relationship with D. Upon cross-examination, D's attorney questions P further about the relationship.
    (B) P is suing D for damages arising from negligence. In his answer, D admits to negligence, but denies the damages. P calls Witness to testify as an expert that D's conduct was negligent.
    (C) In a murder trial of D, P offers into evidence autopsy photos in order to prove that the victim was killed.
    (D) P calls Witness as the tenth witness to testify that D has a reputation for dishonesty.

86. Doris is walking by Henry's store when she trips over a dislodged piece of sidewalk. She sues Henry alleging that he knew or should have known of the dangerous condition. Henry takes the stand and testifies that since he had the sidewalk installed no one has tripped over it, so Doris was also responsible for her injury. Doris objects to this testimony. What result?

    (A) Overruled, relevant to an issue in the case.
    (B) Overruled, but subject to a limiting instruction.
    (C) Sustained, negative evidence is inadmissible.
    (D) Sustained, not relevant to an issue in the case.

87. Dr. Witness testifies as a witness for P on the causation of P's injuries. On cross-examination D's attorney reads from a textbook "Astrological causation of injury" a passage that disagrees with the doctor's testimony. The doctor scoffs at the passage and declares that the text is both mere fiction and non-authoritative. Upon P's objection what ruling on the admissibility of the passage?

    (A) Not admissible, not authenticated.
    (B) Not admissible, not determined as authoritative.
    (C) Admissible, but only to impeach the doctor's testimony.
    (D) Admissible, to impeach and as substantive evidence.

88. Polly is suing Domingo for injuries resulting from an automobile collision. She alleges that he ran a stop sign. Domingo states that there were no stop signs, and as the car on the right he had the right-of-way. The collision happened at night. Polly introduces a photograph taken the next day in daylight. The photograph clearly shows a stop sign on the street upon which Domingo was traveling. Polly testifies that the photo is an accurate depiction of the placement of the stop signs at the time of the collision. Domingo objects, what result?

    (A) Sustained, the photo does not depict the intersection at the time of the collision.
    (B) Sustained, unless the photographer testifies to authenticity.
    (C) Overruled, the photo is authenticated.
    (D) Overruled, photographs do not need authentication.

89. Captain Ron contracts with Meteorologist Mary to notify him in the event of rapidly dropping barometric pressure, which is a good sign of an approaching storm. Before his last departure, Mary tells Ron that the pressure is holding steady. Twelve hours later a Nor'Easter strikes, sinking Ron's ship. Ron sues Mary alleging that she broke her contract to warn of dropping pressure. In her defense, Mary offers into evidence a certified copy of a National Weather Service report for the day the storm struck that recorded the barometric pressure, which states that the pressure never fell. She then calls a famous meteorologist as an expert witness. Mary's attorney's first question to the witness is "What was the barometric pressure on the day of the storm?" Ron objects. What result?

(A) Overruled, experts may testify based on hypothetical information.

(B) Overruled, the witness's fame establishes his expertise.

(C) Sustained, expert witnesses must base their opinions on admissible evidence.

(D) Sustained, foundation for the opinion must first be established.

90. Sally is called as a witness in Paul's suit against Deidre. Sally testifies "I did not see the collision, but Deidre must have been going at least seventy miles-per-hour." Upon Deidre's objection what result?

(A) Excluded, not based on personal knowledge.

(B) Excluded, Sally is not an expert.

(C) Admitted, expert opinion is not required because it does not take specialized knowledge or training to testify as to a car's speed.

(D) Admitted, best evidence available.

91. Bob is prosecuted for possession of cocaine. The prosecution's chief witness is a ten-year crime-lab technician who will testify that he tested a sample of a substance taken from Bob by police. The test came up positive as cocaine under a standard test used by most crime labs across the country. The testimony is

(A) Admissible, expert opinion.

(B) Not admissible, whether or not the substance is cocaine is an ultimate issue for the trier of fact.

(C) Not admissible, the opinion is not based on items in evidence.

(D) Not admissible, the expert does not have personal knowledge of the arrest facts.

92. Billy-Joe and Bobbie-Sue are a married couple with nothing better to do. While dining together in a crowded restaurant one night, Billy-Joe confesses "Before we were married, I shot a man while robbing his castle." Billy-Jack, a detective was eating dinner in the next booth, overhears the conversation and arrests Billy-Joe. At Billy-Joe's murder trial, Bobbie-Sue is called by the prosecution and asked about Billy-Joe's statement. Which objection will the judge sustain?

(A) Hearsay.

(B) Marital Communication Privilege.

(C) Specific instances of conduct cannot be proved by extrinsic evidence.

(D) None, the statement is admissible.

93. Jerry goes to an attorney's office where in the presence of attorney and a court reporter working for the attorney, he gives a sworn statement confessing to the conspiracy of the murder of JFK and implicating several others in the plot. Jerry meets a mysterious death some days later. JFK's estate sues Jerry's estate for the murder and calls the court reporter to testify to the contents of Jerry's statement. What result?

(A) Admissible, privilege ends on the death of the client.

(B) Admissible, the presence of the court reporter destroyed any privilege.

(C) Not admissible, the privilege is not destroyed.

(D) Not admissible, hearsay.

94. Gary is a bartender at the Unicorn Tavern. He is serving Bob and Cheryl when he hears Cheryl say "Bob, if you leave me, I will kill you." Bob then says "Let's talk about this disagreement at home." Bob's body is then found at his and Cheryl's house. Cheryl is placed on trial for Bob's murder. Gary is called to the stand to testify to Bob and Cheryl's statements made in the Unicorn Tavern. Which of the statements are admissible?

(A) Bob's statement only because he is not available at trial.
(B) Cheryl's statement only because it is not hearsay.
(C) Both statements are excepted from the hearsay exclusion rule.
(D) Neither, both statements are hearsay subject to no exception.

95. Gary testifies for the prosecution at Cheryl's murder trial that he heard Cheryl threaten to kill Bob. The first trial ends in a hung jury. Gary's National Guard unit is activated and he is serving in Kerblekistan during the time of the second trial. The prosecution would like to offer the transcript of Gary's testimony from the first trial in lieu of his live testimony. What additional facts are needed to admit the transcript?

(A) That the prosecutor contrived Gary's assignment because he is not credible on the stand.
(B) That the testimony regards the state of mind of the declarant.
(C) That Gary reiterates his testimony to his company chaplain after being wounded on the battlefield.
(D) That Gary is beyond service.

96. Richard was inspecting a roof when he stepped on a portion of the roof that he did not know was weak, fell through, and landed three stories below. A witness who comes to his aid hears Richard whisper, "The roof was rotted." Witness looks up and clearly sees rotted wood in the spot Richard fell through. Richard dies and his estate brings a wrongful death action against the owner of the building. The owner approaches Witness and says, "I will give you $50,000.00 to testify that the wood was not rotted." If the Witness testifies to the owner's statement, what result?

(A) Admissible, hearsay subject to an exception.
(B) Admissible, not hearsay.
(C) Not admissible, hearsay not subject to an exception.
(D) Not admissible, no indication Richard thought he was dying.

97. Ronald is sued civilly by Betty for damages caused by the tort of assault and battery. Ronald calls Warren to testify that Ronald has a reputation for peacefulness in the general community. If Betty objects what result?

(A) Admissible, character evidence may be offered by the accused.
(B) Admissible, for other purposes.
(C) Not admissible, character evidence may not be offered to show action in conformity therewith.
(D) Not admissible, Betty must first attack Ronald's character.

98. Percy is involved in an automobile collision that leaves several dead. One of the estates sues the bar at which Percy had been drinking just prior to causing the automobile collision. The estate calls Dave a bar patron who will testify that he saw and heard Doris tell the bartender, "Look at Percy, he's stumbling around drunk and vomiting." Percy objects, what result?

(A) Admissible, hearsay subject to the medical treatment statement exception.
(B) Admissible, not hearsay.
(C) Not admissible, Doris is not an expert on intoxication.
(D) Not admissible, hearsay not subject to any exception.

99. Hamlet brings a wrongful death action against his uncle for his father's death. Hamlet wishes to enter into evidence the records of the church showing that his father died on January 2, a day the uncle was present. The uncle testifies that he was in Norway negotiating with Fortinbras on the day of the death. He offers into evidence the guest logbook of Fortinbras' castle filled out by the gate guard showing January 2 as the entry date. What is the admissibility of each of these documentary exhibits?

(A) The church records are not admissible, hearsay.
(B) The logbook is not admissible, hearsay.
(C) Neither are admissible, hearsay.
(D) Both are admissible.

100. Hadley is suing Baxendale for defective design of a driveshaft. His allegation is that the diameter of the driveshaft when made was too big. Hadley wishes to introduce blueprints showing the specifications of the shaft. The blueprints, unfortunately, are thirty (30) years old. Assuming the parties have stipulated the blueprints are authentic, what ruling on their admissibility?

(A) Not admissible, hearsay.
(B) Not admissible, age makes the blueprints unreliable.
(C) Admissible, hearsay but subject to an exception.
(D) Admissible, not hearsay.

101. Stone and Hauser are well known to be enemies. Hauser's wife returns home to find him lying in a pool of his own blood. With his last breath, Hauser says, "That Stone tried to stab me to death. Call 911 and I will live." Hauser's wife, who also hates him, does nothing. He dies. The prosecution calls the wife to testify about Hauser's last words in Stone's murder trial. What is the best objection to this testimony?

(A) Hearsay.
(B) Irrelevant.
(C) Prejudicial.
(D) Dead Man's Statute.

102. Patricia is called to the stand to testify regarding events from ten years ago. Her memory of the detailed events is not clear; however, she did take notes at the time. How can the notes be used?

(A) The witness may not look at the notes.
(B) The witness may look at the notes, so long as they are then entered into evidence as a documentary exhibit.
(C) The witness may look at the notes, so long as the notes are available at the hearing for opposing counsel to examine.
(D) The witness may only read the notes into the record, but then counsel must enter the notes into evidence as documentary evidence.

103. Hoffman is on trial for criminal assault. The prosecution must establish that the assault occurred in King County, the venue of the trial. The victim testified that the assault occurred in Seattle, Washington. The judge takes judicial notice of the fact that Seattle is located in King County, in the State of Washington. What effect does judicial notice have?

(A) The prosecution's burden of production is satisfied.
(B) The fact is conclusively established.
(C) The burden of production is shifted to the D.
(D) The fact is conclusively established unless the D objects.

104. Percy is suing Anarchist for damage to Percy's store window. Clancy Cleancut testifies that Anarchist threw a brick through Percy's window. Anarchist cross-examines Clancy and asks, "Isn't it true that you were wearing a blue coat that day?" Clancy replies, "No, my coat was red." Anarchist then seeks to introduce videotape showing Clancy next to the smashed window in a blue jacket. How should the judge rule on the admissibility of the tape?

(A) Not admissible, because specific instances of conduct cannot be proved by extrinsic evidence.

(B) Admissible, because it casts doubt on Clancy's recollection.

(C) Not admissible, because the color of Clancy's jacket is collateral to the issues at the trial.

(D) Admissible, because it is impeachment evidence.

105. Able brings an action against Betty for breach of contract for the lease of commercial property to be used by Betty for her retail business. A material term of the lease contract required Betty to procure liability insurance, which Able alleges she has not done. At trial, Able's attorney seeks to introduce the testimony of Betty's employee Carol who will state "Betty told me she does not have liability insurance on her leased property." Betty objects based on both hearsay and evidence of insurance coverage. How should the judge rule on Betty's timely objection, specifically on the evidence of insurance coverage?

(A) For Betty because evidence of insurance coverage, or lack thereof, is not admissible upon the issue of whether she acted negligently or otherwise wrongfully.

(B) For Betty because Carol's testimony is in regards to an out-of-court statement offered for the truth of the matter asserted.

(C) For Able because the testimonial evidence is offered for a purpose other than negligent or wrongful conduct.

(D) For Able because all relevant evidence is admissible.

106. Able brings an action against Betty for breach of contract for the lease of commercial property to be used by Betty for her retail business. A material term of the contract required Betty to procure liability insurance, which Able alleges she has not done. At trial, Able's attorney seeks to introduce the testimony of Betty's employee Carol who will state "Betty told me she does not have liability insurance on her leased property." How should the judge rule on Betty's timely objection of hearsay to Carol's testimony?

(A) For Betty because Carol's testimony is in regards to an out-of-court statement offered for the truth of the matter asserted.

(B) For Able because Carol's testimony is being offered against Betty and is Betty's own statement.

(C) For Betty because Carol's testimony is in regards to insurance coverage.

(D) For Able because Carol's testimony is being offered against Betty and is a statement by her agent or servant.

107. Jeff, who was convicted 12 years ago of sexual assault for which he served one year and a day in prison, is called to testify on behalf of Larry in Larry's personal injury suit. Jeff testifies as to his observations of how Larry's injuries have affected his daily life. On cross-examination, defense counsel asks "Is it true that you were convicted of sexual assault?" Larry's attorney timely objects. What ruling and why?

    (A) For D because past sexual assaults are admissible for its bearing on any matter to which it is relevant.

    (B) For D because past crimes punishable by death or imprisonment greater than one year are admissible to impeach a witness.

    (C) For Larry because Jeff's conviction was not for a crime involving dishonesty and false statement.

    (D) For Larry because more than ten years has elapsed since Jeff's release from prison.

108. Sal is on trial for the murder of Tom, his business partner. Tom was killed by a single gunshot fired from a rifle of the same caliber as one owned by Sal. In fact, there are millions of rifles that use the same caliber bullet as the one that killed Tom. This is the only evidence that could possibly link Sal to the murder. The prosecution seeks to introduce Sal's rifle into evidence. The rifle is a Remington "Widowmaker" sniper rifle, the same model used by SWAT teams and military Special Operations forces. Sal timely objects. The judge should

    (A) Exclude the rifle from evidence because the possible prejudice of the model name "Widowmaker" outweighs the probative value.

    (B) Exclude the rifle from evidence because as the only prosecution evidence it is insufficient to sustain a guilty verdict.

    (C) Admit the rifle into evidence because it is relevant.

    (D) Admit the rifle into evidence, and take judicial notice that the "Widowmaker" model rifle is commonly used by the military and law enforcement.

109. Sal is on trial for the murder of Tom, his business partner. Tom was killed by a single gunshot fired from a rifle of the same caliber as one owned by Sal. Sal calls Vernon as a witness to testify that Sal has a high reputation in the community for peacefulness. Sal then wishes to call Wendy who will testify to Vernon's reputation for truthfulness. The prosecution objects to Wendy's testimony. The judge should

    (A) Allow Wendy's testimony as a character witness for another witness.

    (B) Allow Wendy's testimony because it supports another witness's credibility.

    (C) Bar Wendy's testimony because Sal has opened the door to prosecution attack of his character.

    (D) Bar Wendy's testimony because Vernon's character has not been attacked by the prosecution.

110. Sal is on trial for the murder of Tom, his business partner. Tom was killed by a single gunshot fired from a rifle of the same caliber as one owned by Sal. Tom was killed at 6:30 p.m. on a Saturday night. Sal wishes to offer the testimony of his friend Bruce who will state that he has seen Sal with his rifle at the gun club on every Saturday from 5:00 p.m. until 6:00 p.m. for the last ten years. Bruce will then testify that every time Sal finished shooting, he always disassembled and cleaned his rifle, which always takes until 7:00 p.m. On the evening in question, Bruce went with Sal to the gun club, but had to leave early for a church function. The prosecutor objects to Bruce's testimony. The judge should rule to

(A) Exclude the testimony because it is not based on firsthand knowledge.
(B) Exclude the testimony because it attempts to use religious beliefs to enhance Bruce's credibility.
(C) Allow the testimony because it is relevant to demonstrate that Sal had probably disassembled his rifle at the time Tom was killed.
(D) Allow the testimony because it may be admissible for another purpose such as intent, plan, preparation, or knowledge.

111. Sal is on trial for the murder of Tom, his business partner and Tom's estate files a wrongful death suit against Sal. The attorneys for each party enter into lengthy and extensive settlement negotiations, but do not conduct any discovery or other pre-trial pleadings. After one year, with settlement negotiations continuing Sal brings a motion to dismiss the suit alleging the estate has taken no action on the suit. The estate's attorney prepares an affidavit detailing the numerous settlement offers given by each party. Sal moves to strike the affidavit. What result?

(A) Strike the affidavit because evidence of settlement offers is not admissible.
(B) Strike the affidavit because an attorney cannot be a necessary witness in a case he is involved in as counsel.
(C) Allow the affidavit because it is not evidence of plea discussions.
(D) Allow the affidavit because it rebuts Sal's contention that the estate has taken no action in the case.

112. Sal is on trial for the murder of Tom, his business partner. Tom was killed by a single gunshot fired from a rifle of the same caliber as one owned by Sal. Tom did not die until several days after he was shot, though he was never conscious. Tom's wife saw Sal in public and loudly accused him of shooting Tom. Sal replied "I will pay for Tom's medical bills." Tom's estate wishes to offer the testimony of the wife repeating Sal's statement. Which is the best answer to the question of admissibility of the Wife's testimony?

(A) Admissible as an admission by party opponent.
(B) Inadmissible because it regards an offer to compromise.
(C) Inadmissible for the purpose of proving liability for Tom's death.
(D) Inadmissible because the prejudice outweighs the probative value.

113. Tenant falls down stairs lacking a handrail at his apartment building, injuring himself. He sues Landlord, Inc., a large property management company he believes owns the building, alleging that the lack of a handrail is negligence. Landlord, Inc. answers by denying ownership of the building. To rebut this denial, Tenant offers into evidence the testimony of Contractor who will state that he was hired by Landlord, Inc., to install a handrail after the injury. Landlord, Inc., objects. What result?

(A) Admissible to show Landlord, Inc.'s ownership of the apartments.

(B) Admissible because Contractor can authenticate any written work orders.

(C) Inadmissible because actions taken after an injury that could have prevented the injury cannot be used to prove negligence.

(D) Inadmissible because Contractor's testimony is hearsay.

114. Cathy sues Arnold Attorney for legal malpractice resulting from Arnold's failure to file Cathy's personal injury suit within the applicable statute of limitations. Arnold intends to testify on his own behalf. Cathy brings a motion to bar Arnold from discussing the fact that Cathy ordered him not to file the suit. What result?

(A) Arnold's testimony is barred because Cathy has not waived the Attorney-Client privilege.

(B) Arnold's testimony is barred because he is offering an out of court statement for the truth of the matter asserted.

(C) Arnold will be allowed to testify because Cathy cannot assert Attorney-Client privilege because the privilege is inapplicable.

(D) Arnold will be allowed to testify because an inequitable result would otherwise occur.

115. Donald is called as a witness by P to testify regarding a collision he witnessed. Defense counsel objects as to Donald's competency. The judge holds a competency hearing in which Donald confirms that he is under psychiatric care for schizophrenia. The court then hears testimony by Donald's brother who states, "In my opinion, and according to his reputation in the community, Donald is a liar." What should the judge decide?

(A) Donald is competent to testify notwithstanding his mental illness and reputation as a liar.

(B) Donald is competent to testify because his credibility may be attacked by any party.

(C) Donald is incompetent to testify due to his mental illness.

(D) Donald is incompetent to testify because he is a known liar.

116. Alan is on trial for armed robbery. Alan calls Bob to testify regarding Alan's reputation for peacefulness and honesty. Upon cross-examination, the prosecution asks "Isn't it true that you and Alan were members of a prison gang that requires absolute loyalty to each other?" Alan objects. How should the judge rule?

(A) Sustain the objection because the prosecutor seeks to establish Alan's propensity to commit crime.

(B) Overrule the objection because it attacks Bob's credibility as a witness.

(C) Sustain the objection because Alan has not placed his character in issue.

(D) Overrule the objection because this is a specific instance of conduct concerning Bob's character for untruthfulness elicited under cross-examination.

117. Alan is on trial for armed robbery and calls Bob to testify regarding Alan's reputation for peacefulness and honesty. Upon cross-examination, the prosecution asks "Isn't it true that you and Alan were members of a prison gang that requires absolute loyalty to each other?" Alan calls Charlie who testifies that Bob has a high reputation for truthfulness due to his devout religious beliefs. On cross-examination the prosecutor asks "Isn't it true that Bob has lied to his priest?" Alan objects. How should the judge rule?

(A) Sustain the objection because references to a witness's religion are inadmissible.

(B) Sustain the objection because this statement can only be elicited by cross-examination of Bob.

(C) Overrule the objection because conduct probative of untruthfulness may be inquired into by cross-examination.

(D) Overrule the objection because the prosecutor failed to timely object to Charlie's testimony.

118. Alan is on trial for armed robbery and takes the stand in his own defense. After his testimony, the prosecution offers into evidence a certified copy of a guilty judgment on the verdict entered against Alan five years ago for "Spitting on a sidewalk," a crime punishable by three months in jail. If Alan objects, which of the following is the best argument in support of exclusion of the evidence?

(A) The judgment is extrinsic evidence of a specific instance of conduct.

(B) The crime involved dishonesty or false statement.

(C) The prosecution failed to give the defense adequate notice (pursuant to 404(c)(1)) of its intent to introduce the past crime.

(D) The crime was not punishable by death or imprisonment greater than one year.

119. Alan is on trial for armed robbery. At Alan's trial, the prosecution calls the store clerk who was robbed at gunpoint. The clerk testifies that the robber wore a Halloween mask of Bill Clinton and said "I did not have sexual relations with that woman." The prosecutor then offers into evidence Alan's 20-year-old conviction for numerous armed robberies during which he wore Halloween masks of various presidents and uttered a famous phrase of each president. Alan objects. The judge should rule as follows:

(A) Overrule the objection because the evidence is offered for a purpose other than to prove action in conformity therewith.

(B) Sustain the objection because it has been more than 10 years since his conviction.

(C) Overrule the objection because the evidence is that of a habit.

(D) Sustain the objection because this evidence may lead the jury to believe that Alan has a propensity to commit robbery.

120. Alan is on trial for armed robbery and calls David as an alibi witness. David states "I was with Alan at the Spar Tavern shooting pool at the time of the robbery." On cross-examination the prosecutor asks David if he told Mary that he was home alone at the time of the robbery. Alan objects. How should the judge rule?

(A) Sustain the objection because of hearsay.

(B) Overrule the objection because prior inconsistent statements are always admissible.

(C) Sustain the objection because David was not afforded an opportunity to explain or deny the statement.

(D) Overrule the objection because a witness may be examined regarding his or her own prior statement.

121. Alan is on trial for armed robbery and calls David as an alibi witness. David states "I was with Alan at the Spar Tavern shooting pool at the time of the robbery." The prosecutor asks David, "Do you remember the statement you gave to the detective who was investigating the robbery?" David says "no I don't," but acknowledges giving the statement. After showing the detective's notes regarding the statement to Alan's attorney, the prosecutor asks David to read the detective's notes and then asks "What did you tell the detective?" Alan objects. How should the judge rule?

(A) Overrule the objection because the notes are a recorded recollection.
(B) Overrule the objection because the notes are writings used to refresh witness memory.
(C) Sustain the objection because the prosecution has not demonstrated that the notes were made or adopted by David when the matter was fresh in his memory.
(D) Sustain the objection because the prosecution has not demonstrated that the notes accurately reflect David's knowledge correctly.

122. P is suing D for breach of contract. Counsel for defense calls P as a witness. The first question is "Sir, when did you stop beating your wife?" Counsel for P objects. What is the best objection to make?

(A) Leading.
(B) Prejudicial.
(C) Outside the scope of direct examination.
(D) Defamatory.

123. Witness is called to testify regarding a motor vehicle collision that occurred at a four-way stop intersection. Witness confirms she did not witness the actual collision, but came upon the scene shortly afterwards. She saw two cars with obvious damage, but not touching each other. One of the cars had a smashed front-end with steam escaping from the radiator. The other had a dented door. If asked what she saw, what response is least likely to arouse an objection.

(A) "Two cars that had collided with each other."
(B) "Two cars that had collided, one of which obviously ran the stop sign."
(C) "The car with the front-end damage ran the stop sign."
(D) "The car with the door damage entered the intersection first."

124. Cancer patient P calls a medical Professor to testify regarding his condition. Professor states, "Based on my ten years of research into possible cancer-causing effects of cell phones, my examination of P, and statements by my faculty colleagues conducting similar research, it is my opinion on a more probable than not basis that P's brain cancer was proximately caused by using the cell phone he purchased from D." Which of the following is the most likely?

(A) The judge must exclude the testimony because the mainstream scientific community has not yet accepted that cell phones cause cancer.
(B) The judge must exclude the testimony because it contains hearsay.
(C) The judge must admit the testimony because Professor has substantial expertise regarding the possible link between cell phones and cancer.
(D) The judge must admit the testimony because Professor stated that there was a causal link between cell phones and cancer.

125. Doug sees Paul run a red light. Later, Doug tells Wendy "Paul ran a red light." At Paul's trial, the prosecutor calls Wendy who states, "Doug told me Paul ran the red light." What objection?

(A) Hearsay.
(B) Lack of personal knowledge.
(C) Prejudicial.
(D) Irrelevant.

126. Albert is being sued for premises liability. A necessary element of liability is that the landowner had notice of the condition. P alleges she slipped on ice in front of Albert's business. Prior to P's slipping, Bob told Albert in the presence of David, "There is ice in front of your business and you are under a legal duty to remove it." David is called to testify about what Bob said to Albert. After timely objection, what ruling?

(A) Exclude as hearsay.

(B) Admit because it is not hearsay.

(C) Admit because it is an admission by party opponent.

(D) Admit as a prior statement by witness.

127. In a capital murder case, possible exculpatory evidence is that it was raining on the day of the murder. Unbelievably, the only person who has knowledge of that fact is Cindy. Cindy will testify that on the day after the murder she asked her now deceased husband if it had rained the previous day. He responded by holding up his $200.00 Italian loafers that were obviously ruined by water. Cindy knows he had worn those shoes outside on the day of the murder. What is the best way to characterize Cindy's testimony?

(A) Not hearsay, admissible.

(B) Hearsay, but admissible.

(C) Hearsay, not admissible.

(D) Not hearsay, inadmissible.

128. P calls Whitney who testifies that D ran the red light. P then calls Xavier who testifies that Whitney told him the same thing shortly after the incident. Which of the following is correct regarding Xavier's testimony of Whitney's statement?

(A) Admissible because Xavier is subject to cross-examination regarding the statement.

(B) Admissible because Xavier's testimony is one of identification.

(C) Not admissible because the defense has not attributed an improper motive to Whitney.

(D) Not admissible because Xavier's testimony is extrinsic evidence of Whitney's truthfulness.

129. Paul sues Dan for breach of contract for the sale of Paul's property to Dan. Paul testifies that he verbally offered $100 for the property and Dan said "I accept your offer." Dan objects to Paul testifying to Dan's statement. Which ruling is the judge most likely to make?

(A) Admissible, exception to hearsay exclusion.

(B) Admissible, not hearsay.

(C) Not admissible, hearsay not subject to any exception.

(D) Not admissible, subject to exclusion by another rule of evidence.

130. In a contract dispute, Drake asserts an affirmative defense of duress. He takes the stand and testifies "Piper told me 'Agree to my offer or I will kill your cats.'" Piper objects to Drake testifying regarding the statement. What ruling and why?

(A) Not admissible, hearsay.

(B) Not admissible, self-serving.

(C) Admissible, hearsay but excepted as statement against interest.

(D) Admissible, not hearsay.

131. Peter is called to testify in Paul's robbery trial. Peter testifies, "Paul robbed me at gunpoint." Paul then calls David who testifies, "Peter told me 'Oh my God! I was just robbed by Sal.'" How should the judge rule?

(A) Admissible, non-hearsay.

(B) Admissible, hearsay, but subject to an exception.

(C) Not admissible, hearsay not subject to any exception.

(D) Not admissible, extrinsic evidence.

132. Jack and Jill are on trial for murder. The prosecutor calls Bob who testifies, "Jack and I were sitting around drinking beer and he told me 'I killed him myself, but Jill will take the blame.'" What is the best way to characterize Jack's statement to Bob?

    (A) Admissible, admission by party opponent.

    (B) Admissible, impeachment of Jack.

    (C) Admissible, statement by coconspirator.

    (D) Not admissible, hearsay not subject to an exception.

133. Pure-hearted P is suing Mega, Inc., a large, evil corporation accused of polluting the habitat of baby ducks. At issue is whether Mega, Inc.'s Chief Engineer altered a diversion valve to spew pollution onto the baby ducks. The case is made possible by Whistleblower Wally, the human resources manager who told Sierra Club Sue, "Even though I have nothing to do with the Engineering Department, I know for a fact that this company did alter the valve." Sue now wants to testify as to Wally's statement. What ruling?

    (A) Admissible, hearsay, residual exception because stopping a polluter is in the interest of justice.

    (B) Admissible, not hearsay, admission by party opponent.

    (C) Admissible, hearsay subject to an exception.

    (D) Not admissible, hearsay subject to no exception.

134. Pure-hearted P is suing Mega, Inc., a large, evil corporation accused of polluting the habitat of baby ducks. At issue, is whether Mega, Inc.'s Chief Engineer altered a diversion valve to spew pollution onto the baby ducks. Sue wishes to testify that she was speaking with Whistleblower Wally, Mega's human resources manager, over the phone when he said, "Sue, you won't believe this, but I'm looking out my window watching those goofballs from Engineering alter a diversion valve." What ruling?

    (A) Admissible, hearsay, residual exception because stopping a polluter is in the interest of justice.

    (B) Admissible, not hearsay, admission by party opponent.

    (C) Admissible, hearsay subject to an exception.

    (D) Not admissible, hearsay subject to no exception.

135. Pure-hearted P is suing Mega, Inc., a large corporation accused of polluting the habitat of baby ducks. At issue, is whether Mega, Inc.'s Chief Engineer altered a diversion valve to spew pollution onto the baby ducks. Wally Whistleblower is now suing Mega, Inc., for emotional distress. Mega, Inc., has alleged that Wally made up his symptoms well after the spill. Sue will testify that before the spill, but after the alteration of the valve Wally told her "Sue, I am so sad and disillusioned with this company; I am sick to my stomach and am losing sleep." What ruling?

    (A) Not admissible, hearsay not subject to any exception.

    (B) Admissible, hearsay subject to an exception.

    (C) Admissible, not hearsay.

    (D) Not admissible, excluded under admission by party opponent exception.

136. Bob is an employee of Mega, Inc., the same evil corporation that polluted the habitat of baby ducks. Bob sees his physician Dr. Julius Hibbert and tells him "My hair and teeth are falling out, I am suffering from abdominal cramps, and I am convinced it is due to Mega Inc.'s use of Dihydrogen Monoxide to which I have been exposed." Which is the best reason to admit Dr. Hibbert's testimony regarding what Bob told him?

    (A) None.

    (B) Present sense impression.

    (C) Then-existing mental, physical, or emotional condition.

    (D) Statements for purposes of medical diagnosis or treatment.

137. Joe, a Mega, Inc. employee, is suffering physical ailments and believes they are caused by exposure to Dihydrogen Monoxide, which Mega, Inc. uses. In his suit against Mega, Inc. Joe calls Wally as a witness to testify regarding an injury that occurred on the job. Wally witnessed the injury, and filled out a company injury report on the spot. In the report he states, "I saw Joe, an independent contractor, get injured. Joe told me that he was in pain." On the stand, Wally admits that he fills out at least three injury reports each day and states that even if he reviewed the report he would not remember the events. You are Joe's Attorney. What should you do?

(A) Offer the report into evidence as a self-authenticating document.

(B) Have Wally read the entire report into evidence.

(C) Have Wally read the report except for Joe's statement to him because it is hearsay.

(D) Offer the report into evidence, but strike Joe's statement because it is hearsay.

138. Joe is suing Mega, Inc. for damages resulting from injuries sustained when the diversion valve failed. Mega, Inc. denies that valve failure caused the injuries. No report was created at the time of the injury. After Joe files suit, the V.P. of Legal Affairs directs Wally to investigate and take statements from other witnesses to the injury to help prepare Mega, Inc.'s defense. Several witnesses state "Joe was 100% at fault for his own injury, he failed to relieve the pressure on the valve before opening it," which Wally dutifully records in a report to the V.P. Unfortunately, all of the witnesses meet mysterious and untimely deaths. Counsel for Mega, Inc. offers the report into evidence. What result?

(A) Not admissible, hearsay not subject to any exception.

(B) Admissible, hearsay subject to an exception.

(C) Admissible, not hearsay.

(D) Not admissible, not hearsay, but excluded under another rule of evidence.

139. Sara is suffering from a broken arm sustained in a motor vehicle collision. She brings suit, but needs an expert to testify as to causation. She goes to Dr. Flibble and tells him, "My arm is in tremendous pain, it broke due to striking it on my car door in a motor vehicle collision, when the D ran a stop sign." How much of Sara's statement may Dr. Flibble relate via testimony?

(A) None, Dr. Flibble was retained exclusively for expert testimony, not treatment.

(B) "My arm is in tremendous pain."

(C) "My arm is in tremendous pain, it broke due to striking it on my car door in a motor vehicle collision."

(D) "My arm is in tremendous pain, it broke due to striking it on my car door in a motor vehicle collision, when the D ran a stop sign."

140. Arnie is on trial for the murder of Bret. The prosecution calls Mr. Tallman who found a dying Bret and heard him exclaim with his last breath, "That jerk Arnie stabbed me! But I think he missed anything vital." What ruling and why?

(A) Not admissible, hearsay not subject to any exception.

(B) Admissible, hearsay but subject to the dying declaration exception.

(C) Admissible, hearsay but subject to the excited utterance exception.

(D) Admissible, not hearsay.

141. Earl's will is offered for probate. Dan contests the will by testifying as to Earl's deathbed statement, "I am about to die. I now know that at the time I executed the will, I was suffering from a delusion." Is Earl's statement admissible and why or why not?

(A) Admissible, statement under belief of impending death.

(B) Admissible, then existing emotional, mental, or physical condition.

(C) Admissible, not hearsay.

(D) Not admissible, not hearsay, but excluded under another rule of evidence.

142. Percy P is suing Donald for the tort of battery. Percy calls Wendy to testify that she saw Donald strike Percy. However, Wendy testifies that it was not Donald who struck Percy. This answer was a surprise to the examiner. Percy then calls Xavier to testify that he saw Donald strike Percy. How should the judge rule on Xavier's testimony?

(A) Admissible because Percy was caught off-guard by Wendy's testimony.

(B) Admissible because Xavier's testimony is relevant to issues at trial.

(C) Not admissible because one may not impeach their own witness.

(D) Not admissible because it is unfair to Donald.

143. Percy P is suing Donald for the tort of battery. Percy calls Xavier to testify that, while Xavier was standing 15 feet away, he saw Donald strike Percy. On cross-examination, Donald's attorney asks Xavier if he was wearing eyeglasses at the time of the battery. Xavier replies, "No, I do not wear eyeglasses or need them to see." Donald then calls Dr. Smith, Xavier's optometrist to testify that Xavier wears reading glasses, despite excellent distance vision. What ruling as to Dr. Smith's testimony and why?

(A) Admissible to impeach Xavier's credibility.

(B) Admissible to impeach Xavier's memory.

(C) Not admissible because a witness's prior acts cannot be proved through extrinsic evidence.

(D) Not admissible because whether or not Xavier wears reading glasses is collateral to the issues at trial.

144. Percy P is suing Donald for the tort of battery. Percy calls Wendy to testify that she saw Donald strike Percy. However, Wendy testifies that it was not Donald who struck Percy. Percy calls Xavier to testify that he saw Donald strike Percy. Donald calls Ray to testify regarding Xavier's reputation for truth in the community. Ray admits he has never met Xavier. What ruling as to Ray's testimony?

(A) Not admissible because Ray does not know Xavier.

(B) Not admissible because it is character evidence.

(C) Admissible because it will impeach Xavier's testimony.

(D) Admissible because Ray does not know Xavier and is thus more credible.

145. Paul was a passenger in Dan's car when he was injured. Paul sues Dan for negligence. Dan denies any negligence or that Paul was injured. Paul's attorney seeks the introduction of a transcript from Dr. Jones' deposition. In the deposition, Dr. Jones stated that he examined Paul one week after the injury occurred and found a recently incurred broken arm. Dr. Jones dies one week before trial. What ruling on the admissibility of the Doctor's testimony?

(A) Admissible, present physical, mental, or emotional condition.

(B) Admissible, former testimony.

(C) Not admissible, irrelevant.

(D) Not admissible, hearsay not subject to any exception.

146. P sues D Corporation for injuries. D's attorney requests the risk manager memorialize the incident in a letter to the attorney. P demands that the letter be produced at trial. What result?

(A) Produce the letter because it is a record of a regularly conducted activity.

(B) Produce the letter because it is not privileged.

(C) Withhold the letter because it is attorney-client communication.

(D) Withhold the letter because it is hearsay not subject to an exception.

147. D Dirk is on trial for armed robbery. At trial, the prosecution offers evidence of Dirk's past armed robberies and his reputation in the community as a thief and robber. What ruling on this evidence?

(A) Admissible to prove that it is more likely than not that Dirk is the robber.

(B) Admissible to impeach the credibility of Dirk's testimony.

(C) Not admissible to prove Dirk committed the robbery in question.

(D) Not admissible because the prosecution failed to provide reasonable notice of its intention to use the evidence.

148. A blue car skids through an intersection into a red car. The red car's driver does not know which of two people were driving the blue car. Dave and Tom were in the blue car and approach the red car. Dave states in the presence of the red car driver, "Tom, you idiot. Didn't you see that stop sign?" Tom says nothing. The red car driver sues Tom and wishes to testify at trial as to the exchange between Dave and Tom. What ruling and why?

(A) Admissible, statement of a co-conspirator.

(B) Admissible, adoption of opposing party's statement.

(C) Not admissible, silence is never an adoptive admission.

(D) Not admissible, unless Dave is also a party.

149. James is attacking the validity of his father's will executed ten years ago. James offers a contemporaneous affidavit by the father's doctor opining that the father was mentally incompetent at the time of the execution. What ruling on the admissibility of the affidavit?

(A) Not admissible, dead man's statute.

(B) Not admissible, hearsay without exception.

(C) Admissible, ancient document.

(D) Admissible, statement for the purpose of medical diagnosis.

150. Jane is being sued for breach of contract. The P's evidence consists of a letter purporting to bear Jane's signature. Jane denies the signature is hers. P calls a former co-worker to identify the signature on the letter. The former co-worker states that she is familiar with Jane's signature and the letter does indeed bear Jane's signature. Will the letter be admitted into evidence?

(A) No, the co-worker has not been qualified as an expert witness.

(B) No, unless the co-worker can testify that she saw Jane sign the letter.

(C) Yes, a lay witness may testify regarding a signature with which he or she is familiar.

(D) Yes, the co-worker's familiarity with Jane's signature makes her an expert.

151. Clumsy Clancy slips and falls on some ice on a sidewalk in front of a video store and dry cleaner, which are located side by side. It is unclear which of the two businesses had control over the sidewalk. The elements of premises liability are notice and control over an unsafe condition. Clancy sues both. Both allege contributory negligence as an affirmative defense. The video store offers evidence that to the best of its knowledge no patrons have ever slipped and injured themselves when the sidewalk has been icy. Is this evidence admissible?

(A) Yes, because it is relevant to the Video Store's notice of a dangerous condition.

(B) Yes, because it is relevant to show that Clancy did not exercise the same care as have other patrons.

(C) No, because it is irrelevant to the Video Store's exercise of due care.

(D) No, because it is prejudicial to Clancy.

152. Clumsy Clancy slips and falls on some ice on a sidewalk in front of a video store and dry cleaner, which are located side by side. It is unclear which of the two businesses had control over the sidewalk. The elements of premises liability are notice and control over an unsafe condition. Clancy sues both. Both allege contributory negligence as an affirmative defense. Clancy wishes to introduce evidence that after his fall the video store received a letter from the landlord acknowledging that the video store shoveled the ice off of the sidewalk as required by the lease. Is this letter admissible?

(A) Yes, because it shows that the video store had knowledge of the unsafe condition.

(B) No, subsequent remedial measures are not admissible.

(C) No, unless Clancy can prove that the ice was more dangerous than a bare sidewalk.

(D) Yes, because it goes to control over the sidewalk.

153. Lynx sues Golden Eagle after he is hit by a golf ball. Lynx alleges that Golden Eagle failed to yell "Fore" after swinging at the ball. On cross-examination Lynx testifies that he was wearing a maroon shirt that day. Golden Eagle proposes to call Steve to testify that Lynx's shirt was orange. Upon objection, Steve's testimony is

(A) Admissible, relevant.

(B) Admissible, impeaches Lynx's memory.

(C) Not admissible, irrelevant to Lynx's memory.

(D) Not admissible, extrinsic evidence of a collateral matter.

154. P sues D Railroad Company for injuries after P drove his car across tracks and was struck by a train. P alleges that the crossing signals were not operating nor did the train blow its warning whistle. The Railroad Company calls Witness 1, a passenger in P's car, to testify that "We should not have tried playing chicken with the approaching train." What ruling on the admissibility of this testimony?

(A) Admissible, admission by party opponent.

(B) Admissible, not hearsay.

(C) Not admissible, hearsay with no exception.

(D) Not admissible, lack of personal knowledge.

155. P sues D Railroad Company for injuries after P drove his car across tracks and was struck by a train. P alleges that the crossing signals were not operating nor did the train blow its warning whistle. The Railroad Company calls Witness 1, a passenger in P's car, to testify that "We should not have tried playing chicken with the approaching train." The Railroad Company calls Witness 2 to corroborate Witness 1's testimony by confirming that right after the collision, Witness 1 told him the same thing. Witness 2 is called to testify that he was standing with Witness 3 right before the collision when Witness 3 exclaimed, "Oh my! That car is trying to play chicken with the train! They are going to be killed!" Witness 3 then died from fright. What ruling?

- (A) Admissible, dying declaration.
- (B) Admissible, present sense impression.
- (C) Admissible, declarant unavailable.
- (D) Not admissible, hearsay with no exception.

156. Mega Co. and its vendor, Vend Co., consult with the senior partner of Dewey, Cheatum, & Howe about a product liability case initiated by P for injuries caused by a Mega Co. product of which a part was made by Vend. Co. Both parties discussed their potential liability. In its answer, Mega. Co. cross-claims against Vend Co. P calls Vend Co. and asks Vend Co. to repeat statements made by Mega Co. at a joint conference. What ruling on the admissibility of the statements?

- (A) Not admissible, privileged conversation.
- (B) Admissible, no privilege.
- (C) Admissible, admission by party opponent.
- (D) Not admissible, hearsay with no exception.

157. Mega Co. and its vendor, Vend Co., consult with the senior partner of Dewey, Cheatum, & Howe about a product liability case. The matter was initiated by P for injuries caused by a Mega Co. product in which a significant part was made by Vend. Co. Both parties discussed their potential liability. In its answer, Mega. Co. cross-claims against Vend Co. P calls Vend Co. and asks Vend Co. to repeat statements made by Mega Co. at a joint conference. Vend Co. calls a coffee server who was present at the conference to testify as to Mega Co.'s statements. What ruling?

- (A) Admissible, relevant to rebut Mega Co.'s cross-claim.
- (B) Admissible, no privilege.
- (C) Not admissible, hearsay without an exception.
- (D) Not admissible, still a privileged conversation.

158. A Seccna 172 (a light single propeller airplane) stalls short of the runway, killing all aboard. After the crash, Seccna begins installing a stall warning indicator on all of its production aircraft. The estate of a passenger sues for defective design in not installing a stall warning indicator. Is the evidence of the subsequent installation admissible?

- (A) Yes, relevant to prove Seccna manufactured the airplane that crashed.
- (B) Yes, relevant to prove Seccna's negligence.
- (C) No, subsequent remedial measures are not admissible.
- (D) No, installation of the warning indicator insufficient to prove that lack of a warning indicator proximately caused the crash.

159. A Seccna 172 (a light single propeller airplane) stalls short of the runway, killing all aboard. After the crash, Seccna begins installing a stall warning indicator on all of its production aircraft. The estate of a passenger sues for defective design in not installing a stall warning indicator. Seccna alleges that it was not feasible to install the indicator in the 172. Seccna introduces evidence that the pilot had failed to take his heart medication. The evidence is a statement in the pilot's wife's diary that the pilot refused to take his medication. What ruling on this writing?

    (A) Admissible, the wife is unavailable due to marital privilege.
    (B) Admissible, best evidence.
    (C) Not admissible, hearsay.
    (D) Not admissible, best evidence.

160. A Seccna 172 (a light single propeller airplane) stalls short of the runway, killing all aboard. After the crash, Seccna begins installing a stall warning indicator on all of its production aircraft. The estate of a passenger sues for defective design in not installing a stall warning indicator. Seccna alleges that it was not feasible to install the indicator in the 172. Seccna introduces evidence that the pilot had failed to take his heart medication. The evidence is a statement in the pilot's wife's diary that the pilot refused to take his medication. The pilot's wife is called to testify that her husband stopped taking his medication. What result?

    (A) Admissible, subject to an offer of proof on relevance.
    (B) Admissible, provided that the diary is made available to opposing counsel.
    (C) Not admissible, the contents of a writing must be proved with the writing admitted into evidence.
    (D) Not admissible, hearsay.

161. A Seccna 172 (a light single propeller airplane) stalls short of the runway, killing all aboard. After the crash, Seccna begins installing a stall warning indicator on all of its production aircraft. The estate of a passenger sues for defective design in not installing a

stall warning indicator. Seccna alleges that it was not feasible to install the indicator in the 172. Seccna calls an air traffic controller who was talking to the pilot and will testify that the pilot stated, "I forgot to put fuel in the airplane." Is this statement admissible?

    (A) Yes, admission by party opponent.
    (B) Yes, exculpates Seccna.
    (C) No, hearsay with no exception.
    (D) No, irrelevant to negligence claim.

162. Bubo brings an action to eject some squatters from his home after returning from Lovely Mountain. The squatters allege an affirmative defense of adverse possession. Central to the case is the date upon which Bubo left for his adventure. Bubo testifies that it was on a Thursday and he remembers the fact because the day before he hosted Elf for tea and wrote on his engagement tablet "Elf Tea Wednesday." Is the testimony regarding the engagement tablet admissible?

    (A) Yes, provided the underlying document is made available to opposing counsel.
    (B) Yes, because the engagement tablet is collateral to the issues at trial.
    (C) No, best evidence: The engagement tablet itself must be offered into evidence.
    (D) No, hearsay not subject to any exception.

163. Witness finds victim lying in a pool of blood. Victim states, "Peter stabbed me. Since I am dying, I must clear my conscience. I shot T.R." Victim survives and is prosecuted for the shooting of T.R. Can witness testify as to Victim's statement?

    (A) No, hearsay.
    (B) Yes, dying declaration.
    (C) Yes, opposing party's statement.
    (D) No, declarant is available.

164. Polly comes home to find her apartment trashed and graffiti scrawled on the wall. Knowing her ex-boyfriend, Justin, probably did it, she telephones his home. A voice picks up and says, "Hello, Justin speaking." Polly says, "You SOB. How could you trash my apartment like this?" The voice starts laughing and hangs up. If Polly brings suit against Justin, what is the best way to characterize this conversation?

(A) Hearsay subject to an exception, and authenticated telephone voice.
(B) Hearsay with no exception, and unauthenticated telephone voice.
(C) Hearsay subject to an exception, but unauthenticated telephone voice.
(D) Hearsay with no exception, but authenticated telephone voice.

165. Polly comes home to find her apartment trashed and graffiti scrawled on the wall. Polly offers a photograph of her apartment to prove the extent of the damages. What else is needed to admit the photograph?

(A) The testimony of the photographer.
(B) Testimony that the photograph was taken within a reasonable time of Polly's arrival home.
(C) Testimony that the photograph accurately depicts the damage to the apartment.
(D) Testimony that the photograph is actually of her apartment.

166. Polly comes home to find her apartment trashed and graffiti scrawled on the wall. She is fairly certain that her ex-boyfriend, Justin, is the culprit. Polly calls Handyman to testify that he, erroneously thinking Justin still lived in the apartment, let Justin in to Polly's apartment. Polly then offers a copy of a log supposedly filled out by Handyman every time he lets a tenant into an apartment. Justin objects to the log. What result?

(A) Admitted, the log is an admission that Justin was in the apartment.
(B) Admitted, hearsay subject to an exception.
(C) Not admitted, hearsay not subject to an exception.
(D) Not admitted, no authentication.

167. Polly comes home to find her apartment trashed and graffiti scrawled on the wall. She is fairly certain that her ex-boyfriend, Justin, is the culprit. Justin was subsequently charged with breaking and entering. Justin calls his employee George to testify that Justin is very religious and is not the type of person who would do such a thing. Is George's testimony admissible?

(A) Yes, this kind of character evidence is admissible.
(B) No, character evidence is not admissible to prove or disprove action in conformity therewith.
(C) No, religious beliefs are not admissible.
(D) Yes, hearsay subject to an exception.

168. Polly comes home to find her apartment trashed and graffiti scrawled on the wall. She is fairly certain that her ex-boyfriend, Justin, is the culprit. Justin has been charged with breaking and entering. Justin calls his employee George to testify that Justin is very religious and is not the type of person who would do such a thing. On cross-examination, George is asked, "Are you aware that Justin has trashed the apartments of his last three girlfriends?" George answers, "Yes." Upon a timely motion to strike, what ruling?

(A) Admissible to impeach George's testimony.
(B) Admissible as substantive evidence of Justin's propensity to trash apartments of ex-girlfriends.
(C) Not admissible, prior bad acts cannot be proved with extrinsic evidence.
(D) Not admissible, collateral matter.

169. The police are called to Polly's apartment. They find Justin shot to death and recover Polly's handgun which has been fired. Polly is charged with murder. Her defense is that Justin came to her apartment to kill her and she shot him in self-defense. Polly calls three of Justin's friends who testify that Justin had a reputation for being aggressive and intimidating. Is this testimony admissible?

    (A) Yes, not hearsay.

    (B) No, character evidence of one not accused is not admissible.

    (C) No, the victim is not available to rebut the character evidence.

    (D) Yes, character evidence of the victim is generally admissible.

170. The police are called to Polly's apartment. They find Justin shot to death and recover Polly's handgun which has been fired. Polly is charged with murder. Her defense is that Justin came to her apartment to kill her and she shot him in self-defense. The prosecution calls Officer Friendly who will testify that Justin was not dead when he arrived at the apartment and that Justin told him, "Polly just shot me and now I'm going to die." What ruling on the admissibility of this statement?

    (A) Admissible, dying declaration.

    (B) Admissible, declarant unavailable.

    (C) Not admissible, irrelevant.

    (D) Not admissible, prejudicial.

171. The police are called to Polly's apartment. They find Justin shot to death and recover Polly's handgun which has been fired. Polly is charged with murder. Her defense is that Justin came to her apartment to kill her and she shot him in self-defense. Polly wishes to call three of Justin's ex-girlfriends who testify that Justin had a propensity to come to their apartments, assault them, and threaten them with a deadly weapon. Assume that the judge excluded the testimony of the three ex-girlfriends. Polly takes the stand and testifies that Justin was the first aggressor. The prosecution now wishes to call George to testify that Justin had a peaceful nature. Is George's testimony now admissible?

    (A) Yes, a victim's character is admissible to rebut self-defense.

    (B) No, a victim's character is admissible only when the D brings it up first.

    (C) Yes, the victim is not the accused.

    (D) No, Justin is not a witness, therefore he cannot be impeached.

172. The police are called to Polly's apartment. They find Justin shot to death and recover Polly's handgun which has been fired. Polly is charged with murder. Her defense is that Justin came to her apartment to kill her and she shot him in self-defense. Justin's estate sues Polly for wrongful death. The estate calls Officer Friendly who will testify that Polly said, "Oops, I was cleaning my pistol and it went off striking Justin. I sure was negligent." Is this testimony admissible?

    (A) Yes, statement against interest.

    (B) No, hearsay without an exception.

    (C) Yes, statement of an opposing party.

    (D) No, opinion on an ultimate issue that must be left for the jury.

173. The police are called to Polly's apartment. They find Justin shot to death and recover Polly's handgun which has been fired. Polly is charged with murder. Her defense is that Justin came to her apartment to kill her and she shot him in self-defense. Justin's estate sues Polly for wrongful death. The estate calls the Personal Representative who will testify that Polly said, "Hey, can we try to work this out between the two of us? I am so sorry that I was partially at fault; here's ten thousand dollars to settle your claim against me." Is this statement admissible?

    (A) No, offer of compromise or settlement.

    (B) Yes, the statement embraces issues in addition to an offer of compromise.

    (C) No, embraces an ultimate issue to be decided by the jury.

    (D) Yes, but only the part of the statement admitting negligence.

174. The police are called to Polly's apartment. They find Justin shot to death and recover Polly's handgun which has been fired. Polly is charged with murder. Her defense is that Justin came to her apartment to kill her and she shot him in self-defense. Justin's estate sues Polly for wrongful death. The estate calls Surprise Witness Wendy who will testify that she heard Dana say, "Polly said, 'I confess. I called Justin over telling him I wanted to get back together. Then I shot him. I would have gotten away with it too if it weren't for you meddling kids.'" What result?

- (A) Inadmissible, embraces ultimate issue.
- (B) Inadmissible, hearsay without exception.
- (C) Admissible, admission by party.
- (D) Admissible, statement against interest.

175. Wally Witness saw a complex series of events resulting in an injury. He wrote a detailed account of what he saw. At trial, he testifies to the events he saw. He can't remember one detail, so Wally pulls the writing from his pocket to consult it. What must happen next?

- (A) The writing must be entered into evidence.
- (B) Opposing counsel must be allowed to inspect the writing and to cross-examine Wally about it.
- (C) Wally must read the writing into evidence.
- (D) Wally must state that he regularly records such events.

176. Doctor Doomuch is called as a P's witness in a wrongful dog death case. The Doctor testifies that he performed an autopsy on "Muffin," the P's 250-pound Bull Mastiff. The Doctor states that he followed the procedures established by the Board of Certified Dog Pathologists in performing the autopsy and found a surgical instrument inside Muffin, which the Doctor opines was the cause of death. The instrument has not been entered into evidence. Is the Doctor's testimony admissible?

- (A) No, dog autopsies are not recognized in the veterinary community.
- (B) No, an expert cannot base testimony on items not in evidence.
- (C) Yes, provided that the instrument is merely admissible, but not necessarily in evidence.
- (D) Yes, an expert may base testimony upon items not in evidence.

177. Bob is on trial for burglary, a crime punishable by two years in prison. The prosecution wishes to enter a certified copy of a prior burglary conviction in which Bob spent two days in prison. What is the best way to characterize the prosecutor's offer to admit this evidence?

- (A) Admissible to prove Bob's character and propensity to commit burglary.
- (B) Admissible to impeach Bob's trial testimony.
- (C) Not admissible because Bob's jail time was less than 30 days.
- (D) Not admissible, character evidence.

178. Clumsy Clancy trips on uneven pavement in front of Carl's house. Carl denies that the sidewalk belongs to him and asserts that it is county property. Clancy sues Carl for injuries and seeks to admit the testimony of Nosy Neighbor who saw Carl repairing the sidewalk a week after Clancy tripped. Is Nosy's testimony admissible?

- (A) Inadmissible, repairing a dangerous condition would be discouraged otherwise.
- (B) Inadmissible, too much time has passed since the injury.
- (C) Admissible, it is evidence of Carl's ownership of the sidewalk.
- (D) Admissible, it proves the sidewalk was in a dangerous condition.

179. Clumsy Clancy trips on uneven pavement in front of Carl's house. Carl denies that the sidewalk belongs to him and asserts that it is county property. Clancy sues Carl for injuries and seeks to admit the testimony of Nosy Neighbor who saw Carl repairing the sidewalk a week after Clancy tripped. Nosy is called to the stand by Clancy and refuses to testify even after being thrown in jail for contempt. Clancy offers Nosy's deposition transcript in lieu of Nosy's testimony. Carl objects. What result?

(A) Admissible, former testimony.

(B) Admissible, prior statement by witness.

(C) Inadmissible, declarant is available.

(D) Inadmissible, hearsay not subject to an exception.

180. Captain Ahab runs his ship aground. The owners of the ship then sue Ahab alleging he negligently failed to order the ship to turn away from the shore. Ahab testifies that he gave the order to turn away from the shore, but the helmsman failed to respond in time. All orders given on the ship are recorded in the ship's log. The owners object to Ahab's testimony. What result?

(A) Inadmissible, when the contents of a writing are sought to be proved, the writing itself must be produced.

(B) Inadmissible, hearsay not subject to an exception.

(C) Admissible, Ahab's firsthand knowledge.

(D) Admissible, hearsay subject to an exception.

181. Jones is arrested for driving under the influence of a controlled substance, marijuana. The prosecution wishes to introduce a videotape from a pot party showing Jones sucking on a four-foot bong and saying "That's great weed, man." Assuming the prosecutor can establish the proper foundation, is this videotape admissible?

(A) Yes, hearsay, admission by party.

(B) Yes, not hearsay.

(C) No, hearsay not subject to any exception.

(D) No, this evidence must be elicited upon cross-examination.

182. Jones is arrested for driving under the influence of a controlled substance, marijuana. The prosecution wishes to introduce a videotape from a pot party showing Jones sucking on a four-foot bong and saying "That's great weed, man." At a pre-trial hearing, Jones' attorney alleges that the police did not have probable cause to pull Jones over. At the hearing, the police officer testifies that he was following Jones and saw Jones driving erratically. Jones' attorney then wishes to introduce an affidavit of the officer stating that he pulled Jones over because he "looked like a dirty hippie freak." What result?

(A) Admissible, but only to impeach the testimony of the officer.

(B) Admissible, as substantive evidence of why the officer pulled Jones over.

(C) Inadmissible, hearsay not subject to any exception.

(D) Admissible, unlimited purpose.

183. Jones is arrested for driving under the influence of a controlled substance, marijuana. The prosecution wishes to introduce a videotape from a pot party showing Jones sucking on a four-foot bong and saying "That's great weed, man." At a pre-trial hearing, Jones' attorney alleges that the police did not have probable cause to pull Jones over. At the hearing, the police officer testifies that he was following Jones and saw Jones driving erratically. Jones testifies on his own behalf and states, "I am an honest person. I absolutely did not drive erratically. On cross-examination, the prosecutor asks, "Isn't it true you lied in your divorce trial last year?" Upon objection, what result?

    (A) Admissible, goes to Jones' credibility as a witness.
    (B) Admissible, so long as the prosecutor produces a certified copy of the conviction.
    (C) Not admissible, specific instances of conduct cannot be proved with extrinsic evidence.
    (D) Not admissible, irrelevant.

184. Frank is on trial for burglary. Frank was caught after Wally Witness told a Police Officer, "I saw Frank enter that building twenty minutes ago and come out with an armload of stuff." The Officer then went to Frank's house and arrested him. Prior to trial, Wally meets a mysterious and untimely death. The prosecutor wishes to have the Officer testify as to Wally's statement. Is the Officer's testimony admissible?

    (A) Yes, present sense impression.
    (B) Yes, declarant unavailable.
    (C) No, hearsay with no exception.
    (D) No, all testimony must be subject to cross-examination.

185. Bob is on trial for the strangulation of a security guard. The County Coroner testifies that the Guard had petechiae in the eyelids, which she claims is conclusive for death by asphyxiation. Bob's expert testifies that petechiae can be caused by many conditions. The expert then justifies her opinion by citing *Pathology of Asphyxiation*, a treatise recognized as authoritative in this subject area. The expert then reads the relevant passage to the jury. If the prosecution objects, what result?

    (A) The passage will be read to the jury.
    (B) The treatise must be entered into evidence as an exhibit.
    (C) The judge will prohibit the expert from reading the passage.
    (D) The judge will prohibit the expert from referring to the treatise.

186. Frank is on trial for burglary. Frank was caught when Wally Witness told a Police Officer, "I saw Frank enter that building twenty minutes ago and come out with an armload of stuff." The Officer then went to Frank's house and arrested him. Prior to the trial, Wally met a mysterious and untimely death. The prosecutor wishes to introduce a letter signed by Frank addressed to the Prosecutor during a plea-bargaining session. The letter stated, "Yes, I am guilty of the burglary. However, because your best witness is now dead, I will only plead guilty to littering." Is this letter admissible?

    (A) Yes, admission by party.
    (B) Yes, statement against interest.
    (C) No, plea discussions are inadmissible.
    (D) No, hearsay subject to no exception.

187. Caesar is on trial for treason. He takes the stand in his own defense. On cross-examination the prosecutor asks, "Isn't it true that you were convicted of rape three years ago?" Upon objection, what must the prosecutor argue to get his question answered?

(A) That rape has a logical nexus to treason.
(B) Nothing, the Prosecutor may always ask such questions on cross-examination.
(C) That rape somehow involves dishonesty or false statement.
(D) That the prosecutor will offer into evidence a certified copy of the conviction, authority that rape is punishable by one year or more in prison, and that the probative value outweighs its prejudicial effect.

188. Ethel Expert is called to testify and give her opinion in regard to causation of a certain mechanical failure. Which of the following is not correct in regards to the type of facts an expert may rely upon?

(A) Facts known personally to the expert.
(B) Facts made known to the expert at trial.
(C) Facts of the type reasonably relied upon by experts in the field in forming an opinion.
(D) The facts upon which the expert bases her opinion must be admissible, but not necessarily admitted into evidence.

189. Ethel Engineer is an expert who was called to testify and give her opinion in regards to causation of a certain equipment's mechanical failure. Wally Weasel is called to testify as to Ethel's reputation for truth and veracity. Wally says, "Ethel does not have a good reputation for truthfulness. In fact, she falsified test data for her Doctoral Dissertation." Which of the following parts of Wally's statement is admissible?

(A) The first sentence only.
(B) The second sentence only.
(C) Both sentences.
(D) Neither sentence.

190. Ethel Expert is called to testify and give her opinion in regards to causation of a certain mechanical failure. Wally Weasel is called to testify as to Ethel's reputation for truth and veracity. Wally's wife is called to testify about a statement Wally made to Ethel prior to the Wife's marriage to Wally. Can the Wife be compelled to testify?

(A) Yes, the communication occurred before marriage.
(B) Yes, opposing counsel failed to make a hearsay objection.
(C) No, a spouse cannot be compelled to testify against her spouse.
(D) No, despite the lack of objection, the Court may not allow inadmissible hearsay evidence.

191. Dudley is an engineer called by P to testify in a trial concerning the application of automotive engineering standards. Dudley testifies that he has a degree in Mechanical Engineering and has studied automotive engineering standards in his spare time. On cross-examination, opposing counsel asks, "Isn't it true that you have never worked as an automotive engineer?" If Dudley answers "Correct" what result?

(A) He is disqualified as an expert because he has not worked in the field.
(B) His authority as an expert may be undermined in the eyes of the jury.
(C) No adverse results because specific instances of conduct must be proved with extrinsic evidence.
(D) Strike the question because it does not go to truth or veracity.

192. What is the best way to authenticate a disputed signature on a document for a jury's consideration?

- (A) Right before trial, have a lay witness compare the signature with an already authenticated signature.
- (B) Have the jury make a finding of fact that the signature is indeed authentic.
- (C) Have an expert compare the disputed signature with an already authenticated signature.
- (D) When the alleged signatory answers "No" when asked if the signature is his, follow up with the question, "Are you sure?"

193. P is suing D for fraud. P takes the stand and says, "I was one of D's investment clients for ten years. D defrauded me and several other investors out of our life savings." In rebuttal, D testifies that P was a client for only two years, and ceased to be a client one year prior to the alleged fraud. Is D's rebuttal testimony admissible?

- (A) Inadmissible, evidence on a collateral matter is not admissible for impeachment only.
- (B) Inadmissible, irrelevant.
- (C) Admissible, testimony that is substantive evidence of whether D could have been defrauded.
- (D) Admissible, because it impeaches P's credibility.

194. P sues D Accountant for negligent calculation of the amounts due on P's tax returns. P calls Price Airhouse, an accountant, to present a summary of the taxes reported in the years in which D was P's accountant. If the summaries are to be admitted into evidence, what must occur?

- (A) The underlying tax returns must be admitted into evidence.
- (B) The witness must testify that the summaries are accurate and based upon the relevant tax returns.
- (C) Nothing, the summaries are admissible in and of themselves.
- (D) The underlying tax returns may not be produced in Court.

195. Carl Criminal is on trial for "Disturbing the Social Order" by criticizing an elected official. The main witness against Carl is Sally Socialist, the elected official Carl allegedly criticized. Carl does not take the stand in his own defense. He does call Percy who will testify that Carl volunteers at the local orphanage to read bedtime stories to the poor urchins. Is the testimony admissible?

- (A) Not admissible, not here a pertinent character trait.
- (B) Admissible, goes to witness bias.
- (C) Admissible, an accused may always put on favorable character evidence.
- (D) Not admissible, character evidence may not be admitted to prove action in conformity therewith.

196. Case law holds that evidence of a violation of a statute creates a rebuttable presumption of negligence. P offers evidence that D ran a stop sign thus raising the presumption. D offers evidence that there was not a stop sign. What instruction should the Court give to the jury?

- (A) Negligence is presumed, thus a verdict for P must be returned.
- (B) D has the burden of persuasion in rebutting the presumption.
- (C) P has not met his burden, so a verdict in favor of D must be returned.
- (D) P has the burden of persuasion to establish negligence.

197. P sues D for injuries suffered in an automobile collision. P calls Doctor to testify that during an exam to determine injuries from a collision, P stated, "I had no pain in my back prior to the collision even though I had a prior back injury." Is Dr. Evil's testimony admissible?

- (A) No, hearsay not subject to any exception.
- (B) No, physician-patient privilege.
- (C) Yes, then existing physical condition.
- (D) Yes, statement for the purpose of medical diagnosis.

198. D and Cool Mo are hanging out on the street corner. They are joined by Mr. Big, who is actually an undercover police officer. Mo says to D, "That is some expensive jewelry you are wearing. You must have been one of the folks who knocked over that jewelry store last week." D looked down and said nothing. D is later arrested for the heist and Mr. Big testifies that upon the accusation by Mo, D was silent. Upon objection to entering Mo's statement and D's lack of response at the robbery scene, which result?

(A) Admitted, statement of defendant.

(B) Admitted, witness' personal knowledge.

(C) Excluded, hearsay with no exception.

(D) Excluded, only spoken utterances can be hearsay.

199. A court was hearing a complicated lawsuit involving liability and interpretation of coverage language in a fire insurance contract. Both sides had multiple parties and expert witnesses testifying on different aspects of the controversy. Which of the below rulings would be in error by the court?

(A) The plaintiff requests the court to exclude the defendant's witness from hearing the testimony of the plaintiff's witness and the court denies the motion.

(B) The court calls a witness based upon the suggestion of a party and the other party objects.

(C) The plaintiff calls a hostile witness and begins to cross examine him. The defendant objects and the court denies the objection.

(D) A lay witness testified that he thought the substance he observed at the fire scene was gasoline, opposing counsel objected as expert testimony, and the court denied the objection.

200. Robert Raper had dated Victoria Victim for a month when they went out for a Saturday night of drinking and dancing. When the nightclub closed, Robert drove Victoria home and Victoria suggested he come up to her flat for a nightcap. Robert agreed. They had a cup of coffee and Victoria passed out. In the morning, Victoria allegedly discovered semen and bruises so she filed criminal and civil charges against Robert alleging rape. Robert's attorney offered evidence of Victoria's intercourse with another man on Friday evening to show Robert was not the source of the semen. In addition, he offered evidence that on the previous Saturday, Robert had intercourse with Victoria to which Victoria consented. If Victoria's attorney objects, the court should admit

(A) Neither the proof that the semen was from another nor testimony about Victoria's prior consent.

(B) The proof that the semen was from another, but not the testimony concerning Victoria's prior consent.

(C) The testimony about Victoria's prior consent, but not the proof that the semen was from another.

(D) Both the proof that the semen was from another and testimony about Victoria's prior consent.

> **MBE Tip:** Put a piece of paper over the answers and "mask down" while working through the questions so you don't accidentally peek at the next answer.

1. **/A/** The fact is conclusively established when the court takes judicial notice of a fact in a civil case. **(B)** is incorrect because the fact is conclusively established. **(C)** is not the best answer because it describes the effect of judicial notice in a criminal case. **(D)** is incorrect because if the fact is conclusively established, rebuttal is not allowed.

2. **/C/** Unlike a civil case, judicial notice of a fact in a criminal case merely satisfies the prosecution's burden of production on the fact. **(A)** is incorrect because in a criminal case, the defense may still rebut. **(B)** is not the best answer because the prosecution's burden of production has been satisfied, although the defense may still rebut. **(D)** misstates the law: a court may take judicial notice of a universally accepted fact without reference to outside sources.

3. **/D/** This is a factual question that must be proved with evidence. The basic rationale of judicial notice is to save time. This is different from the court ruling as a matter of law that the fact is established, which it can do upon proper motion. However, that is a civil procedure issue, not an evidentiary one, so summary judgment will not be granted. **(A)** would not be error. This fact is known to everybody who does not live in a cave. **(B)** would not be error. The fact that New York is in New York is not subject to reasonable dispute. **(C)** is not error. This can be readily verified in an atlas or other generally accepted text, making it capable of accurate and ready determination.

4. **/A/** This is a necessary limiting instruction under FRE 105. The evidence is not admissible to prove that D has a history of embezzlement, but it is admissible to show that his testimony ("would never do such a thing") is unreliable. **(B)** misstates the rule: the conviction may only be admitted for impeachment purposes. **(C)** is incorrect because a prior conviction's effect on a witness' credibility is for the jury to weigh and decide. **(D)** is incorrect because FRE 105 requires a limiting instruction in this circumstance.

5. **/B/** In a civil case, a presumption can be raised by the evidence and will exist until the other party offers evidence rebutting the presumption. At that point, the presumption disappears and the question becomes simply an issue of fact for the jury to decide. If D did not offer any evidence in rebuttal, then the presumption becomes conclusive and is established as a matter of law. **(A)** is not the best answer because D's negligence is presumed only until he offers significant rebuttal evidence. **(C)** is incorrect because P has proved negligence *per se* according to the statute, and the jury must find D negligent unless he adequately rebuts the presumption. **(D)** is incorrect because here P has established negligence *per se* according to state law.

6. **/C/** In a criminal case, a presumption merely satisfies the prosecution's burden of production. The jury must still determine whether the D has violated all the statutory requirements of the crime. **(A)** is incorrect because the jury may merely consider the evidence in its ultimate determination of criminal negligence. **(B)** is incorrect because the jury may merely consider the evidence in its ultimate determination of criminal negligence. **(D)** is incorrect because the prosecution has proved a fact for the jury's consideration in its determination of whether criminal negligence applies.

7. **/B/** This evidence goes to lack of due care which makes it relevant. **(A)** is incorrect because it has no tendency to make the existence of D's negligence more or less likely and is thus irrelevant. **(C)** is incorrect because it has no tendency to make the existence of D's negligence more or less likely and is thus irrelevant. **(D)** is incorrect because it has no tendency to make the existence of D's negligence more or less likely and is thus irrelevant.

8. **/B/** Though probative of negligence, it is immaterial to any issue at trial here because negligence has already been conclusively established. **(A)** is not the best answer because the evidence is probative, it is just not material because negligence has already been established. **(C)** is incorrect because the evidence is not material if negligence has already been established. **(D)** is not the best answer because the evidence is probative but not material because negligence has already been established.

9. **/B/** This fact may show not that D was a pauper, rather it creates a suggestion that a pauper would not normally be able to buy an expensive sports car. Thus, the jury could then infer that D got the money for the sports car from the embezzlement. **(A)** is incorrect because poverty alone is not relevant to show motive of embezzlement. **(C)** is not relevant unless it could be established that D had large gambling debts. **(D)** is relevant to the defense's case and does not help the prosecution.

10. **/A/** This question shows a motivation for bias, which is nearly always relevant. A corollary to this is that witness impeachment evidence will never be excluded for irrelevancy, but it must conform to Rules 608-609. **(B)** is irrelevant absent further proof that such a "crime" is probative of a material issue at trial. Also, this type of crime does not meet the Rule 609 criteria for impeachment evidence. **(C)** involves a question that is irrelevant to any issue at trial. **(D)** is also irrelevant absent proof that Witness is testifying as a medical expert. Witness could be a friend testifying upon personal knowledge of the effect of injuries upon P. Don't assume "Doctor" always means a medical doctor or some type of expert.

11. **/C/** Though probative of D's possible breach, the prejudicial effect of the evidence seems to substantially outweigh the probative value. The witness could testify that D said he had another engagement at that time without creating such potential prejudice. The other three answers are prejudicial (as is all evidence) but the prejudice does not substantially outweigh the probative value to the point where the jury would make a decision based on emotion rather than reason. FRE 403. **(A)** is incorrect because it is relevant and not unfairly prejudicial. **(B)** is not the best answer even though it might be admissible as a report containing an opposing party's statement. **(D)** would likely be admitted because it is relevant and although prejudicial, not unfairly so.

12. **/B/** Under FRE 404(a) character evidence may be introduced to rebut character evidence offered by the accused. **(A)** is incorrect because character evidence cannot be used to show a propensity to commit the crime. **(C)** is incorrect because character evidence of the victim's peacefulness can be introduced only to rebut an accused's character evidence of the victim or to rebut a charge that the victim was first aggressor when the accused claims self-defense. **(D)** is incorrect because character evidence cannot be used to show a propensity to commit the crime.

13. **/D/** Under FRE 404(b) other crimes, wrongs, or acts may be admissible for other purposes such as to establish the identity of the robber. In this case, since D placed his whereabouts in issue, the fact that he was charged with a crime becomes admissible to rebut his claim that the robber was not him. **(A)** is incorrect since this trial is for robbery not assault. **(B)** may be correct if there is other evidence to establish a common scheme or plan between the two assaults. **(C)** is incorrect unless D is charged with murder.

14. **/A/** This would allow the prosecution to introduce the evidence to rebut Heather's claim of mistake if she defended herself based upon the fact she intended her gesture towards another. FRE 404(b). Otherwise, the evidence is inadmissible as propensity evidence. **(B)** is incorrect unless the previous crimes conformed to the definition in FRE 609, which the facts do not address. **(C)** is incorrect because reputation for such acts is another form of character evidence. **(D)** is obviously incorrect because without Heather's claim of mistake, the evidence is inadmissible because it is propensity evidence.

15. **/C/** Character is at issue in this case as it relates directly to fitness as a parent. **(A)** is incorrect because character is at issue in this case as it relates directly to fitness as a parent. **(B)** is incorrect because the evidence may be used to show a propensity for conduct that would render one an unfit parent. **(D)** is incorrect because the evidence may be used as propensity evidence in this case.

16. **/D/** This alternative is simply not relevant to any issue at trial. In a defamation case, the truth is a defense. **(A)** would establish the truth of Garrett's statement and thus is admissible to establish a defense to defamation. **(B)** would establish the truth of Garrett's statement and thus is admissible to establish a defense to defamation. **(C)** would establish the truth of Garrett's statement and thus is admissible to establish a defense to defamation.

17. **/A/** This is *modus operandi* evidence that may be used to link D from the previous burglaries to the current one by demonstrating a repetitive method of operation. **(B)** is incorrect because it may not be used to show that D is a criminal type as that would be general propensity evidence. **(C)** is incorrect because propensity character evidence may not be used to rebut a mere denial, otherwise every defendant who denies the crime would be subject to this, effectively eliminating the prohibition on propensity character evidence. **(D)** is not the best answer because evidence is not usually relevant solely for the purpose of showing that various witnesses agree with each other. For example, if all five witnesses were introduced just to prove that the crime happened at night, this would likely be cumulative and irrelevant. Some other reason (like propensity) must be offered.

18. /C/ Specific instances of conduct may be elicited upon cross-examination only, unless the character trait is an essential element of a charge or claim. In this instance, it is not necessary to use character evidence to convict for perjury. **(A)** is a permissible way to prove character once character evidence is deemed admissible. **(B)** is a permissible way to prove character once character evidence is deemed admissible. **(D)** is a permissible way to prove character once character evidence is deemed admissible.

19. /A/ FRE 413 allows propensity character evidence in cases of sexual assault. **(B)** is incorrect because although FRE 413 does allow propensity character evidence in sexual assault cases, the evidence must be related to propensity for a sexual crime. **(C)** is incorrect because although FRE 413 does allow propensity character evidence in sexual assault cases, the evidence must be related to propensity for a sexual crime. **(D)** is incorrect because although FRE 413 does allow propensity character evidence in sexual assault cases, the evidence must be related to propensity for a sexual crime.

20. /C/ This is a routine practice performed in certain circumstances, but not an automatic response as found in a habit. The action of filling out the report is premeditated. **(A)** is habit: an automatic response conditioned by the amount of time elapsed. **(B)** is habit: the length of time establishes this automatic response to sitting down to eat. **(D)** is habit: an automatic response not involving premeditation.

21. /A/ Evidence of a subsequent remedial measure is inadmissible to prove negligence. **(B)** is incorrect because evidence of a subsequent remedial measure is admissible for any "other purpose" besides as proof of negligence (notice). **(C)** is incorrect because evidence of a subsequent remedial measure is admissible for any "other purpose" besides as proof of negligence (feasibility of safety measures). **(D)** is incorrect because evidence of a subsequent remedial measure is admissible for any "other purpose" besides as proof of negligence (ownership or control).

22. /C/ Under FRE 409 an offer to pay a person's medical expenses is inadmissible to prove negligence, but other statements made during the course of such an offer are admissible. This is a narrower restriction on admissibility than is contained in rules 408 and 410. Whether the offer of settlement was verbal or written makes no difference. **(A)** is incorrect because settlement negotiations are inadmissible under FRE 408. **(B)** is incorrect because details of plea negotiations are inadmissible under FRE 410. **(D)** is incorrect because the letter is a settlement offer. The fact that medical expenses are "discussed" does not make the rest of the settlement letter admissible.

23. /D/ Evidence of liability insurance is not admissible to prove negligence. **(A)** is incorrect because evidence of insurance may be admissible to prove ownership or control of an automobile. **(B)** is incorrect because evidence of insurance may be admissible to prove existence of an agency relationship. **(C)** is incorrect because evidence of insurance may be admissible to prove witness bias.

24. /B/ This is a statement contained in an offer of compromise and therefore inadmissible. **(A)** is admissible to show ownership and control over the sidewalk since D placed control in issue by denying ownership. **(C)** is admissible to show control over the sidewalk since D placed control in issue by denying ownership of the property. **(D)** is admissible because such statements which are other than an offer to pay medical bills may be admissible.

25. **/D/** This is a confidential communication that was made during marriage. Privacy is one of the necessary elements of a privileged communication. **(A)** is missing the element of privacy, one of the necessary elements of a privileged communication. **(B)** is missing the element of privacy, one of the necessary elements of a privileged communication. **(C)** is a communication about a future crime, which is not privileged.

26. **/A/** A spouse need not testify against the other either during their marriage or regarding a communication made during marriage. However, in **(A)** neither is present. The other options have at least one of these two criteria present so a spouse there will not be compelled to testify. Marital privilege is applicable to communications made during marriage. Spousal incompetence applies during marriage. These two can overlap. **(B)** is incorrect because one spouse cannot be compelled to testify against the other during their marriage. **(C)** is incorrect because one spouse cannot be compelled to testify against the other during their marriage. **(D)** is incorrect because one spouse cannot be compelled to testify against the other regarding communications made during their marriage period, even if the marriage is now over.

27. **/C/** This is a confidential communication where the client is seeking representation for a past crime. **(A)** is incorrect because when an attorney is engaged in a fee dispute or the client sues for malpractice, the privilege disappears. **(B)** is incorrect because here the client is consulting in the furtherance of a continuing crime. **(D)** is incorrect because the "man on the street" is a third party and not necessary to the communication as opposed to an interpreter or attorney support staff.

28. **/D/** This is the best answer because it does not constitute an exception to the marital privilege. **(A)** is incorrect because divorce proceedings are an exception to the marital privilege. **(B)** is incorrect because a mental competency proceeding against a spouse is an exception to a marital privilege. **(C)** is incorrect because statements regarding the planning or furtherance of a crime are excepted from marital privilege.

29. **/A/** In *Jaffee*, the Supreme Court recognized a general psychotherapist-patient privilege to encourage candid and full disclosure by mentally-impaired patients. **(B)** is incorrect because the federal rules do not have a general physician-patient privilege. **(C)** is incorrect because only if the case is a diversity case in which one of the states recognizes the physician-patient privilege would this be recognized. **(D)** is incorrect because the psychotherapist may not assert a privilege if sued for malpractice by their client.

30. **/D/** Insanity of a witness alone will not necessarily disqualify a witness from testifying. An insane person may be able to recall some events and communicate about them with an appreciation of truthfulness. **(A)** is incorrect because witnesses are not competent unless they take the oath to testify truthfully. **(B)** is incorrect because witnesses are not competent if they cannot communicate to the trier of fact. **(C)** is incorrect because witnesses are not competent if they cannot recall events at issue in the lawsuit.

31. **/A/** There is no foundation as to the witness' personal knowledge of the green light. **(B)** is incorrect because it establishes that witness saw the light and thus has personal knowledge. The fact that witness may use equivocal language goes to weight and not admissibility. **(C)** is incorrect because it establishes that witness saw the light and thus has personal knowledge. The fact that witness may use equivocal language goes to the evidence's weight and not admissibility. **(D)** is incorrect because it establishes that witness saw the light and thus has personal knowledge. The fact that witness may use equivocal language goes to weight and not admissibility.

32. **/B/** This is a collateral matter that goes only to casting doubt on the witness' memory. Impeachment evidence must be material to the case. The other options is evidence that is material to the case while casting doubt upon the veracity of the witness' testimony. **(A)** shows that someone other than D threw the brick, so it is substantive evidence that also impeaches witness. **(C)** is admissible because material to the case. **(D)** A fact witness' prior crimes are admissible under FRE 609.

33. **/C/** This question shows potential testimony bias, which is nearly always admissible. **(A)** is inadmissible propensity character evidence. **(B)** is inadmissible propensity character evidence. **(D)** is incorrect because it is not material (what game the two were playing at the time) and would only cast doubt on the witness, not contradict the fact that Homer and D were together.

34. **/B/** Before bolstering the credibility of a witness with reputation evidence, the credibility must first be attacked. **(A)** would apply to a situation where the prosecution offers character evidence under FRE 404. **(C)** is a correct statement of FRE 607, but is still subject to FRE 608. **(D)** is not applicable because the party is not offering extrinsic evidence but rather character evidence.

35. **/C/** This is the only way to question the witness about specific instances of conduct. FRE 608(b). **(A)** is incorrect because extrinsic evidence of a collateral matter may not be used to attack a witness' credibility. **(B)** is incorrect because extrinsic document evidence may not be used to attack a witness' credibility. **(D)** is incorrect because there is no condition precedent to a party attacking another party's witness.

36. **/A/** Under FRE 609(a)(2), conviction for a crime of dishonesty may be used to impeach any witness. Embezzlement is a crime of dishonesty. **(B)** is incorrect because under FRE 609(a)(1) a misdemeanor conviction (other than for dishonesty or false statement) cannot be offered against the accused. **(C)** is incorrect because a juvenile adjudication is not admissible against the accused. **(D)** is not evidence of a crime or dishonest behavior. It is irrelevant and likely inadmissible.

37. **/D/** For instance, a defeasible fee simple estate may require that the grantee remain Catholic. Thus, if the grantee becomes Lutheran, evidence of religious belief becomes an issue in a quiet title action. **(A)** is incorrect because evidence of religious belief is inadmissible to bolster or attack a witness' credibility. **(B)** is incorrect because evidence of religious belief is inadmissible to bolster or attack a witness' credibility or truthfulness. **(C)** is incorrect because evidence of religious belief is inadmissible to bolster or attack a witness' credibility or tendency to be truthful.

38. **/D/** This is a collateral matter, so it could be held not admissible. If the day the incident happened were in issue then it would not be collateral, but there is not enough information given here to infer that. **(A)** is a permissible way to impeach a witness with a prior statement under FRE 613 (just hope that the witness doesn't lie). **(B)** is permissible extrinsic evidence of a prior inconsistent statement under FRE 613(b). **(C)** is also permissible even though the statement is not directly contradictory of W's testimony. The prior statement need only cast significant doubt upon W's testimony. Note that the prior statement may be elicited for impeachment evidence only. If offered as substantive evidence, then it is hearsay that must come in under an exception.

39. **/A/** The witness scope of direct testimony here is focused on accounting professional standards. Thus any other professional standards seem here to be irrelevant and outside the scope. **(B)** is incorrect because leading questions may usually be asked on cross-examination. **(C)** is incorrect for the same reason (A) is correct. **(D)** is a trick answer. Leading questions may certainly be asked to develop testimony, but as an exception to the prohibition on leading questions on direct. This exception is not required on cross-examination, where leading questions are allowed.

40. **/B/** When a writing is used to refresh the witness' memory, the opposing counsel must be allowed to inspect the writing. FRE 612. **(A)** is incorrect because the writing may be offered into evidence, but admission is not required merely to refresh the witness' memory. **(C)** is incorrect and is the rule for admitting a Recorded Recollection under FRE 803(5). **(D)** is incorrect because opposing counsel must be allowed to inspect the writing.

41. **/D/** This type of opinion requires an expert in roofing because the opinion requires the specialized knowledge of best practices in roof design and build procedures. Also, it is not clear from the statement that the witness perceived the event. **(A)** is based upon the witness' perception, pertains to subjects not requiring specialized knowledge and will help the jury when stated as a conclusion. **(B)** is based upon the witness' perception, pertains to subjects not requiring specialized knowledge and will help the jury when stated as a conclusion. **(C)** is based upon the witness' personal perception of the parties' actions, pertains to subjects not requiring specialized knowledge, and will help the jury when stated as a conclusion.

42. **/B/** An opinion on an ultimate issue of fact on causation and damages is admissible. **(A)** is a legal conclusion, which in a criminal case is not admissible. **(C)** is a legal conclusion, which in a criminal case is not admissible. **(D)** is incorrect because such an opinion is specifically inadmissible in a criminal case under FRE 704(b).

43. **/D/** An expert may be qualified by experience, but a case involving medical malpractice usually requires an actual medical practitioner expert. A lay person with experience with a particular injury is not qualified to testify as to medical issues. **(A)** is incorrect because the witness here qualifies as an expert based on experience. **(B)** is incorrect because the witness here qualifies as an expert based on education. **(C)** is not the best answer because the witness may qualify as an expert based on knowledge, even if the professor cannot demonstrate actual experience in the area.

44. **/C/** An expert may draw an opinion from facts either perceived by or made known to the witness. **(A)** is incorrect because an expert may draw an opinion from facts either perceived by or made known to the witness. **(B)** is incorrect because an expert may draw an opinion from facts either perceived by or made known to the witness. **(D)** is incorrect because an expert may draw an opinion from facts either perceived by or made known to the witness.

45. **/A/** The facts themselves need only be known to or perceived by the expert. It is the methods and principles that the expert uses to arrive at an opinion that may be accepted within the scientific community, so **(B)** is incorrect. The facts upon which an expert relies need not be admissible, so **(C)** is incorrect. The facts must be the type relied upon by experts in the field only when the opinion is based on facts not in evidence, so **(D)** is incorrect.

46. **/B/** An expert need not testify to facts underlying the opinion unless specifically asked to on cross-examination. FRE 705. An expert need not testify to facts underlying the opinion unless asked about such details on cross-examination, so **(A)** is incorrect. An expert need not testify to facts underlying the opinion unless asked to on cross-examination, so **(C)** is incorrect. An expert need not testify to facts underlying the opinion unless asked to on cross-examination, so **(D)** is incorrect.

47. **/B/** This is a hearsay statement that is offered to prove the guilt of defendant, so it is asserting the truth therein. **(A)** is incorrect because in a defamation case, the fact that a defamatory statement was uttered is an element of the claim. Thus, the statement is offered to prove that it was uttered, not for the truth of the statement. **(C)** is incorrect because a statement offered to show notice to a person does not turn on the truth of the statement. Whether or not the statement is true, it would put the shopkeeper on notice to inspect and remedy a hazardous condition. **(D)** is incorrect because this statement shows that the victim perceived the location of his captivity, not that the perception was accurate.

48. **/A/** This is the best answer because Bob's actions were not meant as an assertive communication to anyone that it was raining outside, so such actions are not hearsay. Assertive conduct is usually in response to an inquiry. **(B)** is incorrect because the conduct is in response to an inquiry, and therefore it is assertive. **(C)** is incorrect because although the secretary was not making a direct inquiry, Bob's conduct of shaking the umbrella was meant to communicate to her the truth of her assertion. **(D)** is incorrect because the conduct is in response to an inquiry, and therefore it is assertive.

49. **/A/** Under FRE 801(d)(1) a witness's prior inconsistent statement must have been given while under penalty of perjury so an oral statement to an insurance adjuster is hearsay. **(B)** is not hearsay because the prior inconsistent statement was made under penalty of perjury. **(C)** is not hearsay because the prior inconsistent statement was made under penalty of perjury. **(D)** is not hearsay because statements regarding identification of a person are generally admissible.

50. **/A/** This is hearsay. In the case of intentional torts, the spouse is not a party unless he/she specifically participated in the tort. Therefore, the admission is not by a party. FRE 801(d)(2). **(B)** is not hearsay, but rather a statement of an opposing party. FRE 801(d)(2). **(C)** is a statement of an opposing party even though the defendant is not necessarily "admitting" liability. A statement of an opposing party includes almost any statement by a party-opponent. FRE 801(d)(2). **(D)** is not hearsay because a statement by a person authorized by the party to make the statement is a statement of an opposing party. FRE 801(d)(2).

51. **/A/** An adoptive admission requires that the party heard the statement, the statement was not denied, and the party was able to respond. All three are present, so D's silence is an adoptive admission of the statement. **(B)** is incorrect because D could not hear the statement, so it is not an adoptive admission. **(C)** is incorrect because D fainted before he could answer, he was unable to respond to the statement, so there is not an adoptive admission. **(D)** is incorrect because D denies the statement, so it is not an adoptive admission.

52. /C/ This alternative likely does not fit under any of the hearsay exceptions and it is too attenuated in time to be a Present Sense Impression. **(A)** is a Present Sense Impression, a statement made during or immediately after perceiving the event. **(B)** is an Excited Utterance, a statement made about a startling event while under the stress of the event. **(D)** is a statement of a Then Existing Emotional, Mental, or Physical Condition. The statement must describe the declarant's condition at the time the statement is made. Here the declarant is describing her then-current condition of being upset.

53. /B/ To qualify for the FRE 803(5) past recorded recollection hearsay exception, the witness must have an insufficient present recollection of the record to testify fully as well as accurately. Thus, total recall, as here, negates this exception. **(A)** is not the best answer because it correctly states an element of the Recorded Recollection hearsay exception. **(C)** is not the best answer because it correctly states an element of the Recorded Recollection hearsay exception. **(D)** is not the best answer because it correctly states an element of the Recorded Recollection hearsay exception.

54. /C/ Due to the risk manager's statement, these statements were made in anticipation of litigation even if the litigation was not yet underway. This gives the D Corp. a motive to at least slant the statements, if not outright fabricate them. **(A)** is incorrect because failure of any of the requirements negates this exception even though this particular requirement was met. **(B)** is incorrect because failure of any of the requirements negates this exception even though this particular requirement was met. **(D)** is incorrect because the facts state that the procedure is established, which makes the taking of statements a regular practice.

55. /B/ The expert may only read the relevant passage of a learned treatise into the record. The treatise itself cannot be admitted into evidence. **(A)** is incorrect because the treatise itself cannot be admitted into evidence. **(C)** is incorrect because the treatise itself cannot be admitted as documented evidence. **(D)** is incorrect because the treatise itself cannot be admitted into evidence.

56. /A/ A witness who refuses to testify despite a court order to do so is treated as an unavailable witness under FRE 804(a). **(B)** is incorrect because absence requires that the proponent was unable to procure the declarant's attendance or testimony by reasonable means. The proponent had plenty of time to subpoena the witness prior to trial, so the proponent's failure to do so does not render the declarant unavailable. **(C)** is incorrect because a declarant is not unavailable if the inability to testify is due to the proponent's wrongdoing. FRE 804(a). **(D)** is incorrect because under FRE 804(a)(3), the declarant must testify to a lack of memory of the subject matter of the statement. Since the declarant remembers most of the subject matter, she is available.

57. **/B/** The best answer because the fact that the declarant did not then believe his death was impending even though he subsequently died, does not allow introduction of the statement under the exception. Even so, some of Bob's comments might come in under a Then-Existing Mental, Emotional, or Physical Condition exception. **(A)** is incorrect because it is a statement made under belief of impending death regarding the cause of the impending death. Since the declarant is making a statement concerning the cause of his (believed) impending death, the exception applies. **(C)** is incorrect because the exception applies in this case because the party against whom the statement is offered had the opportunity to cross-examine the declarant at the first trial. **(D)** is incorrect because it is a statement against interest. This statement was contrary to the declarant's proprietary interest, so the hearsay exception applies.

58. **/B/** This is hearsay within hearsay. The record of the doctor and the plaintiff's statement the doctor recorded are their own statements each of which must have its own exception. The medical records are Records of a Regularly Conducted Activity and the statement of plaintiff was a Statement for the purpose of Medical Diagnosis. **(A)** is not the best answer because only one of the hearsay statements is addressed. The motor vehicle accident statement is not covered by this exception. **(C)** is incorrect because the recorded recollection exception requires the declarant's insufficient recollection which is not indicated in the facts. **(D)** is incorrect as neither exception applies to the doctor's medical records, though they may apply to plaintiff's statement.

59. **/B/** When hearsay is admitted, FRE 806 generally allows a non-available declarant to be impeached just as if he were present and testifying at trial. However, a witness cannot be impeached with collateral facts that are irrelevant to any substantive issue in the case at bar. **(A)** is incorrect because FRE 806 places no express time limitation on inconsistent statements introduced under this rule. **(C)** is incorrect because FRE 806 does not necessarily require an opportunity for the declarant to explain or deny the inconsistent statement. **(D)** is incorrect because D is not trying to prove the truth of the matter asserted, and therefore, the inconsistent statement is not hearsay.

60. **/D/** FRE 807 residual exception to hearsay exclusion applies and reliability corroboration of the hearsay statement is not required. **(A)** is incorrect because it is a requirement of the residual hearsay exception. **(B)** is incorrect because it is a requirement of the residual hearsay exception. **(C)** is incorrect because it is a requirement of the residual hearsay exception.

61. **/B/** There must be sufficient evidence for the trier of fact to conclude the evidence is more likely than not authentic. **(A)** is incorrect because it understates the required burden of proof. **(C)** is incorrect because the proponent need only satisfy a preponderance of the evidence standard, thus answer **(C)** overstates the required burden of proof. **(D)** is incorrect because the proponent need only satisfy a preponderance of the evidence standard, thus this alternative overstates the required burden of proof.

62. **/A/** This type of comparison requires an expert. FRE 901(b)(3). A lay witness who is familiar with the signature may authenticate based on familiarity, but not based on a comparison. FRE 901(b)(2). **(B)** is incorrect because this is an acceptable method of authentication. **(C)** is incorrect because this is an acceptable method of authentication. **(D)** is incorrect because this is an acceptable method of authentication (Note: the statement is not excludable as hearsay because it is an admission by a party opponent and thus falls under that exception).

63. **/B/** Testimony of a witness who has been at the scene is an acceptable method under FRE 901 (b)(1). **(A)** is not the best answer because the word "must" renders it incorrect even though it may be an acceptable method of authentication. It is not required to authenticate a photograph, but may be used to authenticate a photograph. The word "must" in option **(C)** renders it incorrect even though it is an acceptable method of authentication. It is not required to authenticate a photograph, but may be used to authenticate a photograph. The word "must" in option **(D)** renders it incorrect even though it is an acceptable method of authentication. It is not required to authenticate a photograph, but may be used to authenticate a photograph.

64. **/B/** This is not sufficient to identify the caller's voice as someone could be posing as Y. **(A)** is not the best answer because it has a higher degree of reliability as a person identifying himself as "Y" was called at a phone number assigned by the phone company to Y. The difference between (A) and (B) is the fact that in (A) 'Y' stated he was returning the previous call. Otherwise, the situation would be the same as (B). **(C)** is incorrect because it has a higher degree of reliability as a person identifying himself as "Y" was called at a phone number assigned by the phone company to Y. **(D)** is incorrect because it has a higher degree of reliability, as a person identifying himself as "Y" was called at a phone number assigned by the phone company to Y.

65. **/D/** An incorrect answer because an ancient document must be in existence for at least 20 years to qualify for authentication under FRE 901(b)(8). **(A)** is usually an acceptable method of authentication under FRE 901(b)(2). **(B)** is usually acceptable as a distinctive characteristic under FRE 901(b)(4). **(C)** is usually acceptable under the lay witness opinion on handwriting.

66. **/D/** An ancient document under FRE 901(b)(8) must be in such a condition so as to not raise suspicions concerning its authenticity. Given that the document does not match the other similarly aged documents, there are serious questions regarding the reliability of the document's authenticity. **(A)** is incorrect because it satisfies the requirement for an ancient document. **(B)** is incorrect because it satisfies the requirement for an ancient document. **(C)** is incorrect because it would render the need for authentication moot.

67. **/A/** This is an exception to hearsay, not a self-authenticating document. **(B)** is usually self-authenticating under FRE 902(4). **(C)** is usually self-authenticating under FRE 902(5). **(D)** is usually self-authenticating under FRE 902(6).

68. **/C/** The "Best Evidence" rule simply states that an original document must be produced to prove the contents thereof. FRE 1002. **(A)** is incorrect because it is contrary to the Best Evidence rule and describes exactly what the rule forbids. **(B)** is incorrect because it goes to credibility and weight rather than admissibility of the document, which is the focus of the Best Evidence Rule. **(D)** is incorrect because if the witness can testify from first hand regarding the events, it makes the Best Evidence Rule irrelevant.

69. **/D/** Under the "Best Evidence" rule, duplicates are generally admissible in lieu of the original unless a genuine question is raised about the original's authenticity. [FRE 1003] **(A)** is incorrect because neither an original nor a duplicate is required to prove a collateral matter. [FRE 1004(d)] **(B)** is incorrect because other evidence is admissible if the original has been lost, and the proponent did not act in bad faith. [FRE 1004(a)] **(C)** is incorrect because other evidence is admissible if the original is unobtainable through any judicial process or procedure. [FRE 1004(b)]

70. **/B/** B is the best answer because an admission to the document's contents eliminates the need to produce the original under FRE 1007. **(A)** is incorrect because opposing party's admission to the document's contents eliminates the need to produce the original under FRE 1007. **(C)** is incorrect because obtainability is not part of the Rule 1007 analysis. **(D)** is incorrect because the arising of a presumption is a matter of substantive law. FRE 301 merely governs the treatment of a presumption once arisen.

71. **/D/** FRE 1006 applies and the only requirement to admit a summary of the four alternatives presented is that originals or duplicates of the underlying documents be made available to opposing parties for examination and copying. **(A)** is incorrect because the underlying documents need not be admitted, though they must be admissible. **(B)** is incorrect because a requirement to produce the underlying document in court is at the judge's discretion. **(C)** is incorrect because opposing parties need not stipulate to the admission of the summary.

72. **/D/** Here it helps to eliminate the incorrect alternatives. This is the best answer because prior honesty is not relevant to vandalism and seems to be highly prejudicial. Watch for the accused trying to introduce his own positive character evidence, which is admissible, so long as it is also relevant to the criminal charge. **(A)** is incorrect because Jones here is the D, not a witness. **(B)** is incorrect because honesty is not relevant to the issue of a character trait, or lack thereof, to commit property damage. If Jones were on trial for perjury, evidence of his honesty would be relevant. **(C)** is incorrect because character evidence may be introduced by the accused; however, he opens the door to rebuttal questioning by the prosecution and thus this alternative states the opposite of the rule.

73. **/A/** This evidence is admissible for other purposes to show identity (Rule 404(b)). Again, eliminate the alternatives. **(B)** is not the best answer because the evidence may imply action in conformity therewith, so long as the evidence is admissible for another purpose. **(C)** is incorrect because Rule 609 applies to crimes committed by witnesses only; James is not on the stand. **(D)** is incorrect because this answer applies to impeaching witnesses under Rule 608. Watch for answers that seem to impeach the accused when he does not take the stand; such an answer will always be wrong.

74. **/B/** By eliminating the incorrect alternatives one arrives at (B). This evidence will prejudice Henry because its shock value outweighs the very slight probative value. **(A)** is attempting to distract you from the main issue by referring to the requirements of impeaching a witness with a prior crime. **(C)** is incorrect because this evidence will prejudice Henry (its shock value outweighs the very slight probative value). **(D)** is incorrect because the two incidents are not similar enough to show a scheme or plan.

75. **/C/** This evidence is admissible as establishing Jerry's negligence by entrusting Heather with the boat when he knew or should have known she would make good on her threat. **(A)** is incorrect because evidence of Heather's character is admissible, not to prove action in conformity therewith, rather to establish Jerry's knowledge, thus it is permissible for the jury to infer Heather's liability therefrom. **(B)** seeks to confuse you with the general rule for impeaching witnesses. **(D)** is incorrect because the evidence can be used against Heather, so long as it is admissible for another purpose other than to prove action in conformity therewith.

76. **/C/** Though this evidence in and of itself is not sufficient to sustain the prosecutor's burden, it does have some probative value in suggesting Gunther's guilt. **(A)** is incorrect; the best evidence rule applies to documentary evidence. **(B)** is incorrect because prejudice must substantially outweigh probative value to justify exclusion of the evidence. This situation is the opposite. Remember that all evidence is prejudicial to some extent. **(D)** is incorrect because evidence need not be sufficient, merely relevant.

77. **/D/** This is the correct answer because drinking a beer does not make the occurrence of the battery any more or less probable. **(A)** is incorrect because Bob's intoxication does not make the fact of the battery any more or less probable. **(B)** is incorrect even if intoxication is a defense to battery because the existence of an affirmative defense does not make the battery any more or less probable. **(C)** is incorrect because the question of relevancy is again the establishment of battery, not an affirmative defense.

78. **/A/** This is the correct answer because even though it is not direct evidence (such as a witness to the murder) it is circumstantial in that it establishes a motive for the murder. **(B)** is incorrect because the fact Dave is dishonest does not make it more or less likely that he murdered Erin. **(C)** is incorrect because a piece of evidence need not in and of itself sustain a guilty verdict. As stated by McCormick it need only be "one brick in the wall of evidence" that the prosecutor must build to sustain a verdict. **(D)** is incorrect because circumstantial evidence can be very relevant.

79. **/B/** This is the best answer because the disposal of the bloody clothing is consistent with both innocent and guilt. The fact that Dave is a butcher goes to the weight of this evidence, rather than its admissibility. **(A)** is not the best answer because Dave's work as a butcher makes this less likely. **(C)** is incorrect because all negative evidence is prejudicial to some extent. To be inadmissible, the prejudice must substantially outweigh the probative value. **(D)** is not the best answer the testimony could be relevant because it may imply he was disposing of the clothes he wore during the murder.

80. **/A/** This is correct because the letter is extrinsic evidence of a specific instance of conduct under Rule 608(b), which here is very collateral to a murder charge and thus is not admissible. **(B)** is meant to confuse you with Rule 613, prior statement by witness. However, the letter was not a statement made by Dave. **(C)** is meant to confuse you with Rule 613, prior statement by witness. However, the letter was not a statement made by Dave. **(D)** is incorrect because the prosecutor is offering the letter itself into evidence, not giving it to Dave to refresh his memory.

81. **/B/** This is correct because a prior written or verbal statement by the witness may be the subject of questioning for impeachment. Rule 613. **(A)** is incorrect because extrinsic evidence may be used to prove a prior inconsistent statement. **(C)** is incorrect because under Rule 613 the statement need not be shown to the witness prior to questioning. **(D)** is nonsensical because the prosecutor is not producing the letter, merely asking Goler about it.

82. /**C**/ This is correct because it shows possible witness bias, which is generally admissible. **(A)** is incorrect because the question is relevant to Goler's possible bias. **(B)** is incorrect because any prejudice does not substantially outweigh the probative value of Goler's bias. **(D)** is not the best answer. Although bias does go to truthfulness, (C) is a better way of stating it. The Prosecutor has no desire to show G's propensity for truth on cross; she would be trying to show the opposite.

83. /**D**/ This is the best answer because statements made during settlement negotiations are not usually admissible. **(A)** is incorrect because a statement by an opposing party is non-hearsay under FRE 801(d)(2), but subject to an exception (admission by party opponent). **(B)** is incorrect because the entire statement is inadmissible under Rule 408: the settlement offer itself and statements made during negotiations stay out. **(C)** is incorrect because though the statement is subject to a hearsay exception, it is still inadmissible under Rule 408.

84. /**C**/ Unlike Rule 408, Rule 409 excludes only the evidence of offering to pay medical bills; it does not exclude an independent admission made during the offer. Note that if Penelope had said "I'm sorry I was negligent; I'll pay your medical bills if you agree not to sue me" it would be a settlement offer. **(A)** is incorrect because Rule 409 excludes only the offer to pay; it does not exclude an independent admission made during the offer. **(B)** is incorrect because Rule 409 excludes only the offer to pay; it does not exclude an independent admission made during the offer. **(D)** is incorrect because Rule 409 excludes only the offer to pay; it does not exclude an independent admission made during the offer.

85. /**A**/ The cross-examination concerns a matter within the scope of direct examination, so the court would normally allow further exploration on the same concern. You can also arrive at this answer through elimination of the other alternatives. **(B)** is incorrect because the offered evidence of negligence is irrelevant; Defendant has stipulated to negligence, thus any evidence of such is not needed. **(C)** is incorrect because here the prejudicial effect likely outweighs the probative value and there are other ways to prove that the victim is dead. **(D)** is incorrect because the cumulative nature of the testimony makes it prejudicial and wastes court time.

86. /**A**/ This evidence could rebut Doris' allegation that Henry knew or should have known of the dangerous condition and support his contention she had comparable fault therefore his testimony on point is admissible. **(B)** is incorrect because it is relevant to an issue in the case; therefore, no limiting instruction is necessary. **(C)** is incorrect because negative evidence is admissible if it is relevant. **(D)** is incorrect because evidence could rebut Doris' allegation that Henry knew or should have known of the dangerous condition.

87. /**B**/ The text must be established as authoritative to fall under the Learned Treatise exception to hearsay evidence being excluded. **(A)** is incorrect because the evidence is a reading of the passage, not the document itself. **(C)** is incorrect because the text must be established as authoritative to fall under the Learned Treatise exception to hearsay. **(D)** is incorrect because the text must be established as authoritative to fall under the Learned Treatise exception to hearsay. Note that if the treatise were determined as authoritative then (D) would be correct as a treatise passage can impeach and be substantive evidence.

88. **/C/** The issue to be proved is the placement of the stop sign. So long as Polly can testify that the photo is an accurate depiction of the placement of the sign at the time of the collision, the photo is authenticated. **(A)** is incorrect because so long as Polly can testify that the photo is an accurate depiction of the placement of the sign at the time of the collision, the photo is authenticated. **(B)** is incorrect because the creator of the photo need not testify, rather a witness with personal knowledge that it is an accurate depiction of the item to be proved may testify. **(D)** is incorrect because a photo needs to be authenticated.

89. **/D/** An expert's opinion must be based on facts known to her and her status as an expert beyond a layperson must be established to the court's satisfaction. **(A)** is incorrect because, though it is true, it is not applicable to the facts. No hypothetical information has been introduced. **(B)** is incorrect because an expert's credentials must be established in court, not in public. **(C)** is incorrect because an expert need not base her opinion on admissible evidence but must base it on facts relied upon by the scientific community in reaching such an opinion.

90. **/A/** The best answer because Sally did not see the collision, so she has no personal knowledge of the car's speed. **(B)** is incorrect because it does not take an expert to establish something as ordinary as the approximate speed of a car. **(C)** is true, but not applicable to these facts because Sally has no personal knowledge. **(D)** is incorrect because this goes to weight not admissibility.

91. **/A/** The technician is an expert based on experience in this scientific knowledge, and his opinion is based on his perception of the facts. **(B)** is incorrect because an expert may opine on an ultimate issue. **(C)** is incorrect because opinions need not be based on facts in evidence, only upon the perception of the expert using methods accepted by the scientific community. **(D)** is incorrect because he does have personal knowledge of the test results which is the matter upon which the technician is offering an opinion.

92. **/D/** Communications between spouses are privileged while they are married. However, no privilege exists where there was no expectation of confidentiality, such as in a crowded restaurant. **(A)** is incorrect because the statement is non-hearsay under FRE 801(d)(2). as an admission by party-opponent. **(B)** is incorrect because there was no expectation of privacy. Marital Communication Privilege should not be confused with spousal incompetence, which is not a choice in this question. **(C)** is meant to confuse you with impeaching of a witness.

93. **/C/** The presence of the court reporter in this case does not destroy the privilege because her presence was necessary to the attorney-client communication. **(A)** is incorrect because privilege survives the death of the client. **(B)** is incorrect because the presence of the court reporter in this case does not destroy the privilege because her presence was necessary to the attorney-client communication. **(D)** is incorrect because it is an admission by party opponent, thus not hearsay.

94. **/C/** Both statements are then existing state of mind excepted from the hearsay exclusion under Rule 803(3). *"Let's talk about this disagreement at home,"* is a "statement of the declarant's then-existing state of mind. **(A)** is incorrect because it does not matter if Bob is available for trial or not. **(B)** is incorrect because her statement is hearsay; it is not an admission. **(D)** is incorrect because the statements are subject to hearsay exceptions.

95. /D/ Former testimony may be admitted when the declarant is unavailable. One of the factors making a declarant unavailable is that he is beyond process. Rule 804(a)(5). Overseas military assignment would most likely qualify. **(A)** would operate to bar Gary's former testimony because procuring a declarant's unavailability negates this hearsay exception. Note that in the first trial, Gary was not the declarant; he was a witness repeating a declaration. His former testimony makes him the declarant at the second trial – the substance of his testimony is hearsay within hearsay. **(B)** is trying to confuse you with Rule 803(3) in which availability is immaterial. **(C)** is incorrect because a Rule 804(b)(2) dying declaration is admissible only for the declarant's perception of the cause of death.

96. /B/ Admission by party opponent applies so the statement is admissible. The statement is an admission of owner's knowledge of his culpability, and a statement by a co-conspirator of a party during the course and in furtherance of the conspiracy. **(A)** is incorrect because the statement is not hearsay (note the difference from a hearsay statement subject to an exception). **(C)** is incorrect because the statement is not hearsay (note the difference from a hearsay statement subject to an exception). **(D)** is a distracter. The statement being offered is owner's not Richard's.

97. /C/ By elimination C is the best answer because such testimony does not go to the battery, as such, and thus is not admissible. **(A)** may seem correct if this were a criminal case, but it is civil. **(B)** is incorrect because reputation does not show motive, opportunity, intent, or the others listed in Rule 404(b). **(D)** is incorrect because again this is a civil case. If it were a criminal case, Betty could only rebut Ronald's character evidence, not the other way around.

98. /B/ The statement was not being offered for its truth, but rather to show the bartender was on notice of Percy's intoxication. **(A)** is incorrect because the statement was made to a bartender, not a medical clinician. **(C)** is incorrect because the statement need only be based on the personal observation of the witness. **(D)** is incorrect because the statement was describing an event as it was happening and falls under the present sense impression exception to the hearsay rule.

99. /D/ The logbook is a record of a regularly conducted routine activity; the church records are records of a religious organization. Both are exceptions to hearsay under Rule 803. **(A)** is incorrect because the logbook is a record of a regularly conducted activity. **(B)** is incorrect because the church records are records of a religious organization. **(C)** is incorrect because the logbook is a record of a regularly conducted activity and the church records are records of a religious organization.

100./C/ Under Rule 803(16) the blueprints are ancient documents and excepted from the hearsay rule. **(A)** is incorrect because the blueprints are ancient documents and excepted from the hearsay rule. **(B)** is a nonsensical answer. Evidence is either (1) hearsay and is inadmissible, or (2) not hearsay/subject to an exception and is admissible. It is never both. **(D)** is incorrect as the blueprints do meet the definition of hearsay.

101. /A/ This is hearsay and the belief of impending death exception does not apply because Hauser was confident he would live, so there was no belief of impending death. **(B)** is incorrect because the statement is certainly relevant. **(C)** is incorrect because the statement is not prejudicial (just because it's bad for someone's case doesn't make it prejudicial!). **(D)** is a red herring and incorrect. The examiners will occasionally throw this in to confuse you. The Dead Man's Statute makes a decedent's statements inadmissible when the statement is offered to prove a contractual or other claim against the estate. It would not apply to a statement under belief of impending death.

102. /C/ Rule 612 writing used to refresh memory. **(A)** is incorrect because a witness may refer to notes to refresh her recollection. **(B)** is incorrect. It is possible to have the witness read the notes into evidence under Rule 803(5), but the notes themselves may not be entered as exhibits. **(D)** is incorrect. It is possible to have the witness read the notes into evidence under Rule 803(5), but the notes themselves may not be entered as exhibits. Note that under Rule 803(5) the notes must have been made while the matter was fresh in the witness's memory.

103. /A/ In a criminal case, the prosecution's burden of production is satisfied when judicial notice is taken, but the court should instruct the jury that it is not necessary that they accept it as conclusive. **(B)** is incorrect because the facts specify that this is a criminal case, not civil. **(C)** is incorrect because the defendant in a criminal case does not need to produce any evidence to the contrary; the prosecutor always has the burden of persuasion. **(D)** is incorrect even in a civil case; the fact would be conclusive.

104. /C/ This is the best answer because though the color of the jacket may cast doubt on Clancy's memory, the color of the jacket is not central to the plaintiff's claim. The memory of a witness can only be attacked with contradictory facts central to the case such as a videotape showing the policeman throwing an object through the window. **(A)** is incorrect because specific acts are not involved. **(B)** is incorrect because evidence that casts doubt on witness testimony is not automatically admissible. **(D)** is incorrect because evidence that casts doubt on witness testimony is not automatically admissible.

105. /C/ Able is offering the testimony for purposes other than proving a likelihood of negligent or wrongful conduct. He is offering it to prove an essential element of breach of contract. **(A)** is incorrect because Able is offering the testimony for purposes other than proving a likelihood of negligent or wrongful conduct. He is offering it to prove an essential element of breach of contract. **(B)** is a hearsay objection, but this is non-hearsay as an admission by party opponent. **(D)** is correct, but not the best answer because all relevant evidence is admissible unless otherwise excluded by rule. Though relevant, the fact that the offered evidence regards insurance coverage brings Rule 411 into play requiring an analysis beyond Rules 401 and 402.

106. /B/ Rule 801(d)(2)(A) allows for the admission of a party's own statement against him or her. Betty made the statement herself and it is offered against her to prove breach of contract. **(A)** is incorrect for the reason **(B)** is correct. Though the statement was not made by the declarant (Carol) and is offered to prove the truth of the matter asserted (lack of coverage), it is not hearsay. **(C)** is not the best answer because the subject of insurance is not offered to prove negligence. It would be admissible. **(D)** is incorrect because even though the testimony is made by Betty's employee, the statement was made by Betty herself.

107. /D/ Rule 609(b) prohibits admission of a witness' past crime for impeachment purposes if the witness was convicted or released (whichever is later) more than ten years ago. If the court determines that the probative value of the conviction supported by specific facts and circumstances substantially outweighs its prejudicial effects, the court may admit evidence of a conviction that is outside the ten year limit if in the interest of justice; that seems unlikely here since this conviction is not for a crime that is highly probative of truthfulness. **(A)** is incorrect because evidence of past sexual assaults is admissible only against an accused not a witness. See Rule 413 *et seq.* **(B)** would be correct if Jeff's conviction or release was less than ten years ago. **(C)** is not the best answer, though technically correct, because evidence of past crimes other than for dishonesty or false statement can be admissible to impeach a witness (though not in this case because of the ten year lapse). See Rule 609(a).

108. /C/ Sal's ownership of the rifle is relevant to establish that he possessed the means to kill Tom. **(A)** is not the best answer because it is unlikely that the name and use of the rifle creates prejudice greater than the probative value. Further, the judge could instruct the jury not to be prejudiced by the "Widowmaker" name. **(B)** is incorrect because the insufficiency of the evidence does not make it inadmissible. Don't confuse the standards for a directed verdict with the standards for admissibility. **(D)** is not the best answer because the military and law enforcement use of this particular rifle model is neither generally known nor "capable of accurate and ready determination" without evidence. It would therefore be improper for the judge to take judicial notice. See Rule 201.

109. /D/ Evidence of a witness' truthful character is not admissible unless the witness' character has been attacked by the other party. Rule 608(a)(2). **(A)** is incorrect because evidence of a witness' truthful character is not admissible unless the witness' character has been attacked by the other party. **(B)** is incorrect because evidence of a witness' truthful character is not admissible unless the witness' character has been attacked by the other party. **(C)** is incorrect because Sal calling a character witness does not bar Wendy from testifying.

110. /C/ This is evidence of a habit. Rule 406. The key is the similarity of circumstances between the night in question and every Saturday for the past ten years. If any circumstances had changed, such as Sal not going to the club that night, Bruce's testimony would be barred. **(A)** is incorrect because Bruce's testimony is based on firsthand knowledge, though it implies circumstances beyond his firsthand knowledge. **(B)** is incorrect because the fact Bruce left for church is a collateral matter not used for the purpose of enhancing his credibility. **(D)** is incorrect because Rule 404(b) is not applicable in these circumstances.

111. /D/ Evidence of compromise or offers thereof is admissible to rebut a contention of delay. Rule 408. **(A)** is incorrect because evidence of compromise or offers thereof is admissible to rebut a contention of delay. **(B)** is incorrect because it is an ethics question not an evidentiary question. **(C)** is technically correct, but not the best answer because any evidence other than plea discussions is not barred by Rule 410.

112. /C/ Evidence of offering to pay for Tom's bills is inadmissible to prove liability. Rule 409. **(A)** may be correct, but even if the statement clears the hearsay hurdle it cannot get past Rule 409, so it is not the best answer. **(B)** is incorrect because the statement is not an offer of compromise. **(D)** could be correct, but (C) is the better answer because of the bright line prohibition on payment of medical expense evidence.

113./A/ Subsequent remedial measures are not admissible to prove negligence, but may be admitted for other purposes such as to prove ownership. Since Landlord, Inc. has denied ownership Tenant may introduce the installation of the handrail to prove such. **(B)** is incorrect because Tenant has not offered any documentary evidence, only testimonial. **(C)** is incorrect because a subsequent remedial measure is not admissible to prove negligence, but may be admitted for another purpose such as to prove ownership. **(D)** is incorrect because Contractor is merely identifying who hired him; he is not relating an out of court statement.

114./C/ The Attorney-Client privilege is not applicable when the client sues the attorney for malpractice. **(A)** is incorrect because the Attorney-Client privilege is not applicable when the client sues the attorney for malpractice. **(B)** is not the best answer because Cathy's statement is most likely an admission by party opponent; hearsay would not bar her statement. **(D)** is not the best answer because there is a concrete rule available: the exception to Attorney-Client privilege when a client sues for malpractice. Therefore, (D) is not the best way to articulate the rule.

115./A/ Rule 601 assumes every witness is competent unless otherwise provided by the Rules. Though he is mentally ill, defense counsel has not proved that Donald does not appreciate truthfulness or cannot recall the events he witnessed. **(B)** is not the best answer because the fact his credibility may be attacked does not support his competency. **(C)** is incorrect because Rule 601 makes every witness competent unless otherwise provided by the Rules. Though he is mentally ill, defense counsel has not proved that Donald does not appreciate truthfulness or cannot recall the events he witnessed. **(D)** is incorrect because the brother's testimony goes to Donald's credibility, not competence. Credibility is a question for the jury alone. The brother may testify against Donald's character under Rule 608.

116./B/ Do not be distracted by the subject matter of Bob's testimony. The prosecutor is trying to establish Bob's bias as a witness. **(A)** is incorrect because evidence inadmissible for one purpose may be admissible for another. In this instance, Bob and Alan's prison time is elicited to show Bob's bias even though it collaterally demonstrates a propensity to commit crime. **(C)** is incorrect because by eliciting character testimony from Bob, Alan has opened the door to prosecution attack of his character. **(D)** is incorrect because being in a gang is not a specific instance of conduct concerning truthfulness. If the facts showed that Bob had lied for Alan in the past, then (D) would be the correct alternative.

117./C/ This is a classic Rule 608(b) situation: Specific instances of conduct, other than conviction of a crime, concerning a witness's character for truthfulness or untruthfulness may be introduced only by cross-examination of a witness. **(A)** is incorrect because the fact that a priest is referenced does not invoke the Rule 610 prohibition of religious beliefs. The prosecutor is trying to attack Bob's credibility by virtue of his lying, not by virtue of his religious affiliation. However, the prosecutor missed a good Rule 610 objection when Charlie testified to Bob's reputation for truthfulness due to his religious beliefs. **(B)** is meant to confuse you by making you think Charlie's answering of the question is extrinsic evidence of Bob's character, but a witness may be impeached by the cross-examination of a second witness when the second witness has testified on direct to the first witness' character. Note that it is arguable whether Alan could solicit Charlie's testimony of Bob's truthfulness because Bob's character has not been attacked (though his bias has been exposed). **(D)** is incorrect and is meant to confuse you with the fact the prosecutor did not object to Charlie's testimony establishing Bob's truthfulness due to his religious beliefs.

118./D/ Under FRE 609 an accused who takes the stand cannot be impeached by a crime not punishable by death or imprisonment greater than one year, unless it only involved dishonesty or false statement. Impeachment by crimes punishable by more than one year in prison applies only to witnesses. **(A)** is not a good answer because it is a Rule 608(b) argument, which applies to conduct other than conviction of a crime. Since this involves a crime Rule 609 is applicable. **(B)** is incorrect because spitting on the sidewalk does not involve dishonesty or false statement. **(C)** is not the best answer because **(B)** is a much stronger argument (the crime must involve dishonesty or false statement to be admitted) than this weaker procedural argument.

119./A/ The prosecutor is offering the evidence for a purpose other than propensity evidence. This is evidence of identity due to the unique *modus operandi* of the robbers in both cases. See Rule 404(b). **(B)** would be correct if the prosecutor were offering the evidence of the past conviction to impeach Alan's own testimony. Rule 609(b). **(C)** is incorrect because a habit is an automatic response to identical stimuli, which these facts are not. **(D)** is incorrect despite the fact that the jury could draw a conclusion that the evidence shows a propensity. The test for admissibility under Rule 404 is not based on what conclusion the jury may reach but rather the reason for which the proponent offers the evidence.

120./D/ Rule 613(a) permits examination of a witness regarding his or her own prior statement. Note that David's prior statement does not meet the definition of hearsay because a hearsay statement is one made by a person other than the witness. See Rule 803(c). **(A)** is incorrect because rule 613(a) permits examination of a witness regarding his or her own prior statement. **(B)** is incorrect (watch out for universal statements with the words "never" or "always") because under Rule 801(d)(1)(A) a prior inconsistent statement that meets the definition of hearsay must have been made under oath subject to the laws of perjury to be admissible. **(C)** is incorrect because this opportunity to explain or deny must be afforded when a prior inconsistent statement is offered using extrinsic evidence. Here, the evidence is elicited under cross-examination. Compare Rule 608(b) with 613(b).

121./B/ This question is meant to mislead you into a hearsay analysis. However, so long as the prosecutor allows Alan or his attorney to inspect the notes, it is permissible under Rule 612 for David to review the detective's notes to refresh his memory regarding the statement he gave to the detective. **(A)** is not applicable because the prosecution has not offered the notes into evidence, so a hearsay analysis does not arise. **(C)** is not applicable because the prosecution has not offered the notes into evidence, so a hearsay analysis does not arise. **(D)** is not applicable because the prosecution has not offered the notes into evidence, so a hearsay analysis does not arise.

122./B/ This is the best answer because the question posed by defense counsel is very prejudicial and appears to offer little probative value. **(A)** is incorrect because leading questions may be asked of an adverse party on direct examination. **(C)** is incorrect because P is apparently testifying after being called by the opposing party so it is not clear that there was a direct examination to produce potential scope restrictions. **(D)** is incorrect because it is a nonsensical objection since there is a judicial immunity from defamation.

123. /A/ Even though this is an opinion, the opinion is admissible because it is based only on her own perception and thus is more helpful to the trier of fact than a mere recitation of exactly what she saw. Though (A) is also somewhat based on an inference, it is the most likely inference. **(B)** is incorrect because the witness makes a conclusion not based on her perception, but upon an inference from what she saw. **(C)** is incorrect because the witness makes a conclusion not based on her perception, but upon an inference from what she saw. **(D)** is incorrect because the witness makes a conclusion not based on her perception, but upon an inference from what she saw.

124./C/ This is the best answer under the *Daubert* standard. Professor is undoubtedly an expert in this area, even if other experts disagree with his research. **(A)** is not the best alternative because acceptance of the scientific community is merely one factor for the judge to consider in her discretion, rather than a strict rule of exclusion of such expert opinion. **(B)** is not the best alternative because an expert may testify that he or she relied upon statements of others to arrive at the opinion. See Rule 703. **(D)** is not the best alternative because it goes to the weight of the testimony, not the admissibility.

125./A/ Wendy is not testifying to a fact she witnessed, but rather to what Doug told her which makes it hearsay. **(B)** is incorrect because she has personal knowledge of Doug's statement. **(C)** is incorrect because the statement's probative value outweighs its prejudice. **(D)** is incorrect because the evidence of Paul running the light is central to the prosecution's case.

126./B/ The statement is not offered for the truth of the matter asserted (the presence of ice), rather to prove notice to Albert (the fact the statement was made). This does not meet the core definition of hearsay. **(A)** is incorrect because the statement is not offered for the truth of the matter asserted (the presence of ice). **(C)** is incorrect because the declarant, Bob, is not a party-opponent. **(D)** is incorrect because it is not a prior statement by the witness, David.

127. /C/ The husband's holding up of the shoes was intended as a non-verbal assertion that it had rained the previous day, and the testimony is offered to prove the fact that it was raining the day before. No hearsay exception applies, making it inadmissible hearsay. **(A)** is incorrect because the statement is hearsay and no hearsay exception applies. **(B)** is incorrect because the holding up of the shoes was not a present sense impression admissible under Rule 803(1) (the assertion was not made contemporaneously with the event). **(D)** is incorrect because the statement is hearsay.

128. /C/ Xavier's testimony does not fall under the Rule 801(c) definition of non-hearsay because a consistent prior statement may not be admitted unless the witness' credibility is attacked. **(A)** is incorrect because a consistent prior statement may not be admitted unless the witness' credibility is attacked. **(B)** is incorrect because Whitney's statement is not one identifying a person. **(D)** is incorrect because there is no prohibition in the hearsay rules against using extrinsic evidence of a witness' prior inconsistent or prior consistent statement. Compare with the Rule 608(b) prohibition on extrinsic evidence used to prove a witness' prior acts.

129. /B/ Dan's statement has independent legal effect regardless of the truth or falsity of his statement. It is not being offered for the truth of the matter asserted. It is also arguable that the statement is an admission by party opponent. Thus the statement is not hearsay. **(A)** is incorrect because the statement is not hearsay thus an analysis under Rule 803 is moot and the fact Dan is a party makes him available under Rule 804. **(C)** is incorrect because the statement does not meet the definition of hearsay. **(D)** is incorrect because there is no other rule of exclusion applicable to the testimony.

130. /D/ Drake is not offering the statement to prove Piper actually intended to kill his cats, rather he is trying to prove that the statement was made as evidence of the duress. **(A)** is incorrect because it is not offered for the truth of the matter asserted. **(B)** is incorrect because testimony can be self-serving (watch for answers that seem out of left field like this one). **(C)** is incorrect because the declarant must be unavailable to take advantage of this exclusion and because the statement is not hearsay.

131. /B/ Peter's statement to David is hearsay, but is excepted from exclusion as an excited utterance. Rule 803(2). **(A)** is incorrect because Peter's prior statement, though inconsistent, was not given under oath thus Rule 801(d)(1)(A) is not applicable. **(C)** is incorrect because the statement is an excited utterance. **(D)** is incorrect because extrinsic evidence may be used to prove prior inconsistent statements, Rule 613(b), but not specific instances of conduct. Rule 608(b).

132. /A/ This is an opposing party's statement under Rule 801(d)(2)(A) Party's Own Statement. **(B)** is incorrect because impeachment is attacking the credibility of a witness even though Jack's statement is arguably against his interest. Here, the facts give no indication that Jack has testified, and he has a Fifth Amendment right not to take the stand. **(C)** is incorrect because the statement is not a Rule 801(d)(2)(E) statement by a co-conspirator because no other evidence of a conspiracy is present. **(D)** is incorrect because this is an admission by a party opponent, under Rule 801(d)(2)(A).

133./D/ This statement is hearsay with no exception and not within the scope of the human resource topical duties. **(A)** is incorrect because there is no evidence that the statement is more probative than any other available evidence. **(B)** is incorrect. A statement by a party-opponent's employee must concern a matter within the scope of the employment to be an admission, or the declarant must be authorized to make the statement. An engineering issue is not within the course and scope of a human resource manager's employment. If this were an employment discrimination case, the result would be different. **(C)** is incorrect because there are no facts supporting a hearsay exception.

134./C/ The statement is a present sense impression. Rule 803(1). Wally is describing an event as it is happening. If he were more excited, the statement would also be an excited utterance. **(A)** is not the best answer because the present sense impression exception applies. **(B)** is incorrect because a statement by a party-opponent's employee must concern a matter within the scope of the employment to be an admission, or the declarant must be authorized to make the statement. **(D)** is incorrect because the statement is a present sense impression and excepted from the hearsay rule.

135./B/ The statement to Sue is excepted from hearsay as either a Present Sense Impression or Then Existing Mental, Emotional, or Physical Condition, because Wally's emotional, mental, and physical condition is at issue to the case. Thus **(A)** is incorrect because Wally's statement is admissible. **(C)** is incorrect because the statement falls under the Present Sense Impression or Then-Existing Emotional or Physical Condition Exceptions. **(D)** is incorrect because Wally himself is offering the statement; it is not being offered by his opponent.

136./D/ With this hearsay exception – statement made for medical treatment – the entire statement would be admitted because it is all significant to treatment. **(A)** is simply incorrect, as at least part of Bob's statement would be admissible under the three exceptions given in the question. **(B)** would allow only complaints of his symptoms, not the statement regarding how he acquired the symptoms. **(C)** would allow only complaints of his symptoms, not the statement regarding how he acquired the symptoms.

137./B/ This is hearsay within hearsay. The company injury report is hearsay but is excepted either as a Recorded Recollection or a Record of a Regularly Conducted Activity; and Joe's statement is hearsay but is excepted as a then existing physical condition. Because Wally has insufficient recollection the report would be read into evidence. **(A)** is incorrect because the report does not qualify as self-authenticating under Rule 902. **(C)** is not the best answer because although Joe's statement is hearsay within hearsay, it is excepted as a then existing physical condition, so it can be admitted. **(D)** is not the best answer because Joe's statement is admissible, so there is no need to strike it.

138. **/A/** This is not a record of a regularly conducted activity because this report was prepared in anticipation of litigation. Neither is it a present sense impression of the witnesses because of the passage of time. **(B)** is incorrect because the report is not a record of a regularly conducted activity (the report was prepared in anticipation of litigation). Nor is it a present sense impression of the witnesses because of the passage of time. **(C)** is incorrect because the statements are offered for the truth of the matter asserted: Joe's own fault. **(D)** is incorrect because the statement is hearsay and inadmissible unless the court determines that (1) the statement is offered as evidence of a material fact; (2) the statement is more probative on the point for which it is offered than any other evidence which the proponent can procure through reasonable efforts; and (3) the general purposes of these rules and the interests of justice will best be served by admission of the statement into evidence.

139. **/C/** Statements for purposes of medical diagnosis or treatment are admissible including statements regarding causation. How the injury occurred is important to the treatment or diagnosis. [FRE 803(4)] **(A)** is incorrect, the fact that the statement was made to a physician retained exclusively for expert testimony does not make the entire statement inadmissible. A medical expert still needs to diagnose the problem as any treating physician would. **(B)** is not the best answer because the statement of causation is important to the treatment and diagnosis. **(D)** is incorrect because the statement of defendant's actions is not for the purpose of diagnosis and treatment and would most likely be excluded.

140. **/C/** The best answer because this hearsay would come in as an excited utterance under 803(2) or a then existing mental, emotional, or physical condition under 803(3). **(A)** is not the best answer because at least two hearsay exceptions apply. **(B)** is incorrect because the statement was not made under belief of impending death, as Bret thought his injuries were not life-threatening. **(D)** is incorrect because the statement is hearsay, as it was made out of court, and the prosecution is offering it for the truth of the matter asserted.

141. **/B/** Typically, a then-existing mental condition cannot be admitted into evidence to prove a prior existing condition. However, it may be admitted when, as here, it relates to the execution of a will. **(A)** is incorrect because the statement does not concern the cause or circumstances of an impending death. **(C)** is incorrect because the statement is used to prove the truth of the matter asserted: the fact that Earl was delusional when he executed the will. **(D)** is incorrect because the statement is hearsay since the declarant is now dead.

142. **/B/** Whether Donald struck Percy is the central issue at trial. **(A)** is incorrect because "being caught off guard" is not a legitimate basis on which to admit or deny evidence. **(C)** is incorrect because a party may certainly impeach its own witness (FRE 607). The fact that Wendy's testimony was detrimental to Percy's case does not prohibit Xavier from testifying. **(D)** is incorrect because "fairness" is a broad policy abstraction, but is very subjective when applied to individual cases.

143. /D/ Even though it would cast doubt on Xavier's testimony, Xavier's credibility may not be impeached with this evidence because the fact that he wears reading glasses is collateral to the issues at trial. **(A)** is incorrect because Xavier's credibility may not be impeached with this evidence because the fact that he wears reading glasses is collateral to the issues at trial. **(B)** is incorrect because Xavier's credibility may not be impeached with this evidence because the fact that he wears reading glasses is collateral to the issues at trial. **(C)** is incorrect because there is no prior act being elicited. Xavier should be impeached with evidence that Donald did not strike Percy or that Donald was not present.

144. /C/ Ray merely needs personal knowledge of the reputation. FRE 602. He need not know Xavier personally. **(A)** is incorrect because Ray merely needs personal knowledge of the reputation. FRE 602. He need not know Xavier personally. **(B)** is incorrect because character evidence is admissible pursuant to FRE 404(a)(3). **(D)** is incorrect because credibility is not a basis for admitting or excluding evidence.

145. /B/ Under FRE 804(b)(1) former testimony is admissible if the declarant is unavailable. Death certainly meets this requirement. The party against whom the testimony is now offered must have had an opportunity or motive to develop the testimony by direct, cross or redirect examination. **(A)** is incorrect because a then existing physical condition must be the declarant's condition. Here the declarant is talking about someone else's condition. Note that if the Doctor said, "Paul told me that his arm was broken," it would then fit within this exception. **(C)** is incorrect because an injury is relevant to plaintiff's damages. **(D)** is incorrect because there is a valid exception. Note that the Doctor's statement is hearsay, but it is subject to an exception.

146. /C/ Because the risk manager wrote the memo to the attorney, it is attorney-client communication. **(A)** is incorrect because the memo was not created as a routine matter following the injury and is not a business record exception to the hearsay rule. **(B)** is incorrect because the risk manager wrote the memo to the attorney so it is attorney-client communication. **(D)** is not the best answer because hearsay would exclude the memo from evidence, but would not prevent its production in discovery.

147. /C/ This is classic propensity evidence; the prosecution is trying to show that Dirk is the kind of person more likely than not to have committed the armed robbery. **(A)** is incorrect because this is classic propensity evidence; the prosecution is trying to show that Dirk is the kind of person more likely than not to have committed the armed robbery. **(B)** is incorrect because Dirk has not taken the stand. Even if he did, only character evidence of truth or veracity may be introduced for the limited purpose of impeaching his testimony. **(D)** is incorrect because the prosecution need not notify the defendant of its intent to impeach Dirk. (D) attempts to confuse with the requirement of FRE 807 to disclose the intent for this type of hearsay evidence.

148. /B/ A party may make an admission by failing to contradict such a statement when a reasonable person would be expected to contradict such a statement. **(A)** is incorrect because there is no evidence of a criminal conspiracy. **(C)** is incorrect because silence can be an adoptive admission. **(D)** is incorrect because there is no indication Dave should be party to the suit. Note that Tom is the declarant, even though he is silent.

149./B/ This is the best answer out of the options presented. No valid exception to hearsay is presented. **(A)** is incorrect because the Dead Man's Statute bars claims against a decedent's estate. **(C)** is incorrect because a document must be twenty years old to be ancient. **(D)** is incorrect because it is unknown if the diagnosis is based upon a statement by decedent.

150./C/ FRE 901(b)(2) allows a non-expert familiar with the signature to authenticate it. **(A)** is incorrect because an expert is not required to authenticate a signature. **(B)** is incorrect because the witness need not have seen Jane sign the letter, though if she had, that also would be authentication evidence. **(D)** is incorrect because an expert is not required to authenticate a signature.

151./A/ While past behavior is not usually admitted, here it goes directly to notice of a dangerous condition. **(B)** is incorrect because lack of prior injuries does not prove Clancy was contributorily negligent and is thus irrelevant. **(C)** is incorrect because the evidence is offered for control not due care. **(D)** is incorrect because prejudice must substantially outweigh the probative value.

152./D/ This evidence goes directly to the issue of control over the area where Clancy fell. **(A)** is incorrect because it would then be characterized as a subsequent remedial measure if offered for proof of negligence. **(B)** is incorrect because the evidence is not offered to prove negligence. FRE 407. **(C)** is incorrect because it is not relevant to negligence.

153./D/ The color of Lynx's shirt is collateral to the issues at trial and when a witness is cross-examined as to collateral facts, the party cross-examining will be bound by the answers, and cannot contradict him by another witness. **(A)** is incorrect because even if the color of the shirt is relevant, relevancy is the threshold inquiry still subject to other rules of admissibility. **(B)** is incorrect because relevancy is the threshold inquiry still subject to other rules of admissibility, even though it is good evidence of Lynx's memory. **(C)** is incorrect because the question may be marginally relevant to Lynx's memory, but is still excluded under the collateral matters rule.

154./B/ This is direct testimony by a witness based on first-hand knowledge. There is no out of court statement. **(A)** is incorrect because this is direct testimony by a witness based on first-hand knowledge. There is no out of court statement. **(C)** is incorrect because this is direct testimony by a witness based on first-hand knowledge. There is no out of court statement. **(D)** is incorrect because the witness was a passenger in the car.

155./B/ Excited utterance would also be correct, but (B) is correct because Witness 3 was describing the event as it occurred. **(A)** is incorrect because the statement did not encompass the cause of the declarant's death. **(C)** is incorrect because mere unavailability does not constitute an exception in and of itself. Unavailability is a condition precedent to the exceptions under FRE 804, which do not apply to this question. **(D)** is incorrect because Witness 3 was describing the event as it occurred.

156./A/ Despite the presence of both parties, in relation to third parties this conversation was privileged because both parties are required for the communication to occur. **(B)** is incorrect because there is attorney-client privilege. **(C)** is incorrect because of the privilege. Just because a statement may be admissible under a hearsay exclusion, it may still be inadmissible under another rule of evidence. **(D)** is incorrect because it is arguably an admission by party opponent.

157. /B/ This is permissible because there is no privilege between the two parties present, unless employee's presence was reasonably required in the product liability case meeting and a mere coffee server would not seem to qualify. **(A)** is not the best answer because even if relevant, it may still be subject to a privilege. **(C)** is incorrect because it is arguably an admission by a party. **(D)** is incorrect because there is no privilege.

158. /C/ Subsequent remedial measures are not ordinarily admissible to prove negligence. **(A)** is incorrect because the facts do not suggest a dispute over who manufactured the airplane. **(B)** is incorrect because a subsequent remedial measure is inadmissible to prove negligence. **(D)** is incorrect because it argues to the sufficiency of the evidence, not the admissibility. The analysis turns on the purpose for which the remedial measure is offered.

159. /C/ The diary is an out-of-court statement offered for the truth of the matter asserted. The wife could testify, but admission of her diary alone is not an option. **(A)** is incorrect because unavailability is not an exception in and of itself. Also, the marital privilege is inapplicable because the diary was not a marital communication, thus she is available as a witness. **(B)** is incorrect because the best evidence rule applies to proving the contents of writings. The wife could testify that the husband stopped taking medication, but not that she wrote that in her diary. **(D)** is incorrect because the best evidence rule applies to proving the contents of writings. The wife could testify that the husband stopped taking medication, but not that she wrote that in her diary.

160. /A/ This is the best answer, subject to relevancy to the cause of the crash. **(B)** is incorrect because the witness is not testifying to the contents of a writing. **(C)** is incorrect because the witness is not testifying to the contents of a writing. **(D)** is incorrect because the wife is testifying from personal knowledge of facts not out of court statements.

161. /C/ This is an out of court statement offered by Seccna to prove the truth of the matter asserted: the pilot's own negligence and not admissible unless allowed under the residual exception of FRE 807. **(A)** is incorrect because the pilot is not a party. **(B)** is incorrect because the fact that Seccna is exculpated does not make the statement admissible, though the statement would certainly withstand a relevancy challenge. **(D)** is incorrect because the statement is relevant to a negligence claim.

162. /B/ The best evidence rule does not extend to writings collateral to the issues at trial. The issue is what date Bubo left, which he testifies to out of personal knowledge. The fact that he remembers the date because he wrote it down is collateral to the issue of when he left. **(A)** is incorrect because the engagement tablet need not be admitted to prove a collateral matter. If the contents of the engagement tablet were in issue, then the tablet would have to be offered into evidence. **(C)** is incorrect because the engagement tablet need not be admitted to prove a collateral matter. **(D)** is not the best answer because the evidence is testimony regarding the engagement tablet, not the tablet itself.

163. /C/ Victim is now a party and the confession is an admission. **(A)** is incorrect because there is an exception. **(B)** is incorrect because the Victim's confession did not address the manner of his impending death. **(D)** is not the best answer, though the availability of victim would preclude the admission of a dying declaration, witness can testify based on another exception.

164. /A/ Admission by party opponent as to the laughing (note the adoptive admission) and the fact the voice identified itself as Justin at his telephone number of record authenticates the voice as his. FRE 901(b)(6). **(B)** is incorrect because there is an admission by a party opponent as to the laughing (note the adoptive admission) and the fact the voice identified itself as Justin at his telephone number of record authenticates the voice as his. FRE 901(b)(6). **(C)** is incorrect because the voice was authenticated. **(D)** is incorrect because the statement is an admission by party opponent.

165. /C/ So long as Polly states that the photograph accurately depicts the damage to the apartment, the photo is authentic under FRE 901(a); the matter in question is what it is claimed to be. **(A)** is not the best answer as the photographer would also have to testify that the photo accurately depicts the damage, thus the photographer's testimony alone is superfluous. **(B)** is not the best answer as it does not prove that the photograph depicts what it claims to depict. **(D)** is not the best answer as it is not as detailed as (C), which is the best rationale for authentication.

166. /D/ There needs to be evidence of the log's authenticity, such as Handyman testifying that he filled out the log. **(A)** is incorrect because the log is not an admission by Justin. **(B)** is not the best answer, though the log is a record of a regularly conducted activity, the authentication hurdle to admissibility is not surmounted. **(C)** is incorrect because the log is a record of regularly conducted activity.

167. /A/ The accused may offer character evidence that shows he is not the type of person that would commit the crime. **(B)** is incorrect because the accused may offer character evidence to show he is not the type of person that would commit the crime. **(C)** is incorrect because religious beliefs are inadmissible to establish credibility of a witness; Justin is not a witness. **(D)** is incorrect because here there is no out of court statement.

168. /A/ When a witness offers character evidence of another, that witness may be cross-examined on specific instances of that person's prior conduct under FRE 405(a). **(B)** is incorrect because this evidence cannot have substantive value to show Justin's character for trashing apartments; it may be offered to rebut Justin's character evidence under FRE 404(a)(1). **(C)** is incorrect because FRE 405 does allow the evidence to be offered to rebut Justin's character evidence under FRE 404(a)(1). **(D)** is incorrect because the testimony bears directly on the statement made by George that Justin would not "do that sort of thing," so it is not collateral.

169. /D/ FRE 404(a)(2) allows a pertinent character trait of the victim to be admitted and the word "generally" makes this choice compelling. But see FRE 412 *et seq.* (Sex assault victims). **(A)** is not the best answer because though the evidence is admissible it is not because of a hearsay exception. **(B)** is incorrect because FRE 404(a)(2) allows a pertinent character trait of the victim to be admitted. **(C)** is incorrect because there is no requirement that the victim must have the opportunity to rebut the evidence.

170. /A/ The best answer. A dying declaration must be made by a declarant while believing his or her death is imminent, and must concern the cause or circumstances of his or her imminent death. Justin's statement to the police officer seems to satisfy both of these requirements. **(B)** is incorrect because unavailability is not in and of itself a hearsay exception allowing introduction. **(C)** is not the best answer because the relevancy standard is a low bar and this evidence seems somewhat relevant here. **(D)** is incorrect because to deny admissibility the prejudice must substantially outweigh the probative value.

171. /A/ In a homicide case, the prosecution may offer a victim's character as evidence once the accused alleges the victim was the first aggressor. FRE 404(a)(2)(C). **(B)** is incorrect because the defendant need not make the victim's character an issue, but rather allege that the victim was the first aggressor. **(C)** is incorrect because the character of the victim is analyzed differently from the character of the accused under FRE 404. **(D)** is incorrect because the character evidence under FRE 404 has nothing to do with FRE 608 witness character evidence.

172. /C/ Polly is a party and the statement is an admission of negligence. **(A)** is incorrect because the statement is an admission by party opponent, making it non-hearsay. In addition, Polly is available, thus this exception would not apply. **(B)** is incorrect because the statement is non-hearsay. **(D)** is incorrect because FRE 704 allows opinions embracing an ultimate issue.

173. /A/ All statements made in the course of settlement negotiations in a contested claim are inadmissible. Here, the partial fault statement by Polly seems sufficient to meet the contested claim requirement. **(B)** is incorrect because all statements made in settlement negotiations are not admissible. **(C)** is incorrect because FRE 704 allows opinions on ultimate issues. **(D)** is incorrect because all statements contemporaneous with settlement negotiations are inadmissible if the claim is contested.

174. /B/ There are two levels of out-of-court hearsay in this statement – Polly's statement to Dana and Dana's statement to Wendy. Polly's statement is non-hearsay as an admission by opposing party. However, Dana's statement to Wendy is hearsay without an exception and thus is inadmissible. **(A)** is incorrect because FRE 704 allows opinion on an ultimate issue. **(C)** is incorrect because Dana is not a party. **(D)** is incorrect because both declarants are available.

175. /B/ The writing is used to refresh the witness' memory under FRE 612 and is not required to be entered into evidence though it may be offered into evidence by opposing counsel. **(A)** is incorrect because it is not required to be entered into evidence. **(C)** is incorrect because it is not an FRE 803(5) recorded recollection because the witness must have insufficient recollection of the events recorded. **(D)** is incorrect because the writing need not be a record of a regularly conducted activity to be used to refresh a witness' recollection.

176. /D/ An expert may opine on facts not in evidence, so long as the facts are those relied upon by other experts in the field. **(A)** is incorrect because the Doctor testified that the procedures are recognized. **(B)** is incorrect because an expert may base an opinion on facts not in evidence. **(C)** is incorrect because the facts need not be admissible.

177. /B/ Impeachment of the defendant is the only way this evidence could be admitted. **(A)** is incorrect because character evidence is not normally admissible to prove subsequent action in conformity therewith. **(C)** is incorrect because a conviction is a matter of public record excepted from hearsay under FRE 803(8) and the rule has no *de minimus* exception. **(D)** is not the best answer because while it may be character evidence, it is admissible to impeach Bob.

178. /C/ FRE 407 allows subsequent remedial measures to be admitted to prove, *inter alia*, ownership. **(A)** is incorrect, though it is a correct statement of the policy rationale, because the repairs are not offered to prove negligence, thus the policy rationale for excluding such evidence is not present. **(B)** is incorrect since the passage of time does not enter an FRE 407 analysis. **(D)** is incorrect because it is directly contrary to the purpose of FRE 407.

179. /A/ Nosy's refusal to testify renders her unavailable under FRE 804, thus former testimony is excepted from hearsay under FRE 804(b)(1). **(B)** is incorrect because a prior statement by witness under FRE 801(d)(1) must be inconsistent with present courtroom testimony to rebut a claim to the contrary. **(C)** is incorrect because under FRE 804(a)(2) Nosy is not available. **(D)** is incorrect because an exception does exist.

180. /C/ Ahab is testifying to his firsthand knowledge of events, not to out of court statements or the log record. **(A)** is not correct; Ahab is not testifying as to the contents of the log but the events as he perceived them first hand; the log would certainly corroborate his testimony. **(B)** is incorrect because he is testifying to events, not to an out-of-court statement. **(D)** is incorrect because Ahab is testifying to events, not to an out-of-court statement, but would be correct if the log itself were being offered since it is a record of a regularly conducted activity.

181. /B/ So far as Jones' action is an admission, it is not hearsay under FRE 801(d). **(A)** tries to trick you by defining the action as an admission and calling it hearsay at the same time, so B is a better answer. **(C)** is incorrect because Jones' action is an admission and is not hearsay under FRE 801(d). **(D)** is incorrect unless the prosecution is trying to impeach Jones under FRE 608(b), but he has yet to be a witness and the actions do not go to his character for truthfulness.

182. /A/ Impeachment evidence need not comply with hearsay rules because it is not offered to prove the truth of the matter asserted, rather to impeach the witness. This is not a prior statement by witness inconsistent with the declarant's testimony under FRE 801(d)(1)(A) because the affidavit was not a statement made at trial, hearing, or deposition. **(B)** is incorrect because impeachment evidence is not offered to prove the truth of the matter asserted but to impeach the witness. **(C)** is incorrect because impeachment evidence is not offered to prove the truth of the matter asserted but to impeach the witness. **(D)** is incorrect because admissibility is limited.

183. /A/ This is a specific instance of conduct that is admissible to prove the character of the witness under FRE 608(b). Although the illegal conduct did not result in a conviction, it is still admissible, but only upon cross-examination. Note that Jones could lie, and the prosecutor could do nothing about it. **(B)** would be correct if Jones had been convicted of perjury. **(C)** would be correct had the prosecutor called another witness to testify or introduced some document regarding the lie. **(D)** would be correct if Jones were asked about a prior act not concerning the witness' character for truthfulness.

184./C/ Wally is not a party, and though unavailable, his statement does not fall under any hearsay exception unless the court determines the circumstances guarantee trustworthiness and it goes to a material fact. **(A)** is incorrect because he did not make the statement while observing the event. **(B)** is incorrect because mere unavailability of the declarant is not an exception. **(D)** is incorrect because hearsay exceptions allow for introduction of statements without the opportunity for cross-examination. Note that this statement would be admissible as a prior statement by a witness of identification of a person. FRE 801(d)(1). However, that option was not available for this question.

185./A/ FRE 803(18) allows for a relevant passage of a learned treatise to be read into evidence once the authority of the treatise is established. **(B)** is incorrect because the treatise itself may not be admitted into evidence. **(C)** is incorrect because the passage may be read into evidence. **(D)** is incorrect because an expert may refer to a treatise.

186./C/ FRE 410(4) makes any statement made in the course of plea discussions inadmissible. **(A)** would be correct if the statement were not made in the course of a plea discussion. **(B)** is incorrect because under this exception (FRE 804(b)(3)) the declarant must be unavailable. **(D)** is incorrect because but for the plea discussion, the statement is an admission.

187./D/ FRE 609(a)(1) allows evidence of a conviction punishable by one year or more in prison to be introduced provided the probative value of the evidence outweighs the prejudicial effect. **(A)** is incorrect because a nexus between the current crime and a past crime does not determine admissibility. **(B)** is incorrect because there are limits on what the prosecution may ask regarding conviction of a crime. **(C)** is incorrect because the conviction need not be for dishonesty or false statement.

188./D/ Under FRE 703 facts upon which the expert bases her opinion need not necessarily be admissible into evidence. **(A)** is a proper basis for an expert opinion and therefore an incorrect response. **(B)** is a proper basis for an expert opinion and therefore an incorrect response. **(C)** is a proper basis for an expert opinion and therefore an incorrect response.

189./A/ The first sentence is reputation testimony admissible under FRE 608(a). The second sentence is extrinsic evidence of a specific instance of conduct inadmissible under FRE 608(b). **(B)** is incorrect because the second sentence is extrinsic evidence of a specific instance of conduct inadmissible under FRE 608(b). **(C)** is incorrect because the second sentence is extrinsic evidence of a specific instance of conduct inadmissible under FRE 608(b). **(D)** is not the best answer because the first sentence is reputation testimony admissible under FRE 608(a).

190. /C/ A spouse may not be compelled to testify against the other regarding any matter. This is marital incompetence and is distinguished from marital privilege which only covers communications during marriage. **(A)** is incorrect because marital incompetence still prohibits the testimony. If Wife had divorced Wally prior to trial, she could be compelled to testify. **(B)** would be correct but for marital incompetence, in which a spouse may not be compelled to testify against the other regarding any matter. **(D)** is incorrect because an objection not timely made is waived. FRE 103.

191. /B/ The best answer because this impeachment evidence can reduce the expert witness' credibility in the eyes of the jury. **(A)** is incorrect because a witness can be an expert based on knowledge even if they do not have related experience. FRE 702. **(C)** is incorrect because it misstates the rule prohibiting extrinsic evidence, and even if correctly stated, prior acts – or the lack of same – may be elicited upon cross-examination. **(D)** is incorrect because the cross-examination question goes to credibility as an expert, not credibility for truth.

192. /C/ The best answer to a confusing question because under FRE 901(b)(3) an expert in handwriting may authenticate a signature with an already authenticated specimen. **(A)** is incorrect because a lay witness must be familiar with the signature for reasons other than purposes of trial. **(B)** is incorrect because the jury must have an authenticated specimen with which to compare the contested signature and this alternative does not so indicate. **(D)** is incorrect because it will prove nothing.

193. /C/ This testimony goes directly to rebut plaintiff's claim of fraud by proving that plaintiff was not a client at the time of the alleged fraud. Thus, the testimony is not regarding a collateral matter, but goes directly to the issues at trial, though it will have the effect of also impeaching plaintiff by casting doubt upon her memory. **(A)** is incorrect because the testimony is not regarding a collateral matter, but goes directly to the issues at trial, though it will have the effect of also impeaching plaintiff by casting doubt upon her memory. **(B)** is incorrect because the testimony is very relevant. **(D)** is not the best answer because if this were the only reason to admit the testimony it might be viewed as collateral. The fact that the testimony impeaches the witness does not in and of itself make it admissible.

194. /B/ This is the best answer: the witness must lay the foundation for the accuracy of the summary of the tax returns. **(A)** is incorrect because FRE 1006 does not require that the underlying documents be admitted, though there is no prohibition on admission either. **(C)** is incorrect because a witness must at least identify the exhibit as a summary. **(D)** is incorrect because the court may order the production of the underlying tax returns.

195. /A/ The character of the accused is admissible if offered by the accused and pertinent to the charge. In this case, Carl's compassion for children is not pertinent to the charges against him. **(B)** is incorrect because the facts state that Carl never took the stand. **(C)** is incorrect because the favorable character evidence must be pertinent. **(D)** is incorrect because an accused may offer evidence of a pertinent character trait that may tend to prove he did not commit the crime.

196./D/ Plaintiff always has the burden of proof in establishing the presumption, so this is the best answer. **(A)** is incorrect because the presumption is rebuttable and defendant offered some rebuttal evidence. **(B)** is incorrect because the establishment of the presumption does not shift the burden of proof to defendant; plaintiff still has the burden of proof and persuasion. **(C)** is incorrect because plaintiff has offered evidence in favor of the presumption.

197./D/ Statements for the purpose of medical diagnosis are admissible. Note that FRE 803(4) allows the description of past symptoms, which would not be admissible under an FRE 803(3) then existing physical condition. **(A)** is incorrect because there is an applicable exception. **(B)** is incorrect because plaintiff waives this privilege by bringing suit where his physical condition is at issue. **(C)** is incorrect because the symptoms must be contemporaneous with the statement.

198./A/ Here, D's silence is being offered as an effective out-of-court assertion that he is guilty of the robbery crime. A reasonable person in this situation would likely have denied the accusation that they "knocked over a jewelry store last week." By failing to respond, D has effectively adopted Mo's statement, making it an admissible opposing party's statement at trial. Note that there is no facts here suggesting the D's silence was in assertion of Fifth Amendment silence rights. **(B)** is incorrect because personal knowledge is not an exception to the hearsay rule. **(C)** is incorrect because D's silence amounted to an effective admission that he did, in fact, rob the jewelry store. As such, it is an opposing party's statement. **(D)** is incorrect because assertive conduct can be an admission.

199./A/ This alternative would be error for the court because FRE 615 requires the court to order witnesses excluded at the request of a party so they cannot hear the testimony of other witnesses. **(B)** is incorrect because FRE 614 allows a court to call a witness at the request of a party. **(C)** is incorrect because FRE 611(c) authorizes interrogation (examination) by leading questions when a party calls a hostile witness as an exception to the general rule that leading questions are not allowed on direct. **(D)** is incorrect because, while lay witnesses may not usually give expert opinion testimony, here it is a matter of personal perception which is allowed under FRE 701.

200./D/ The best answer because both the evidence that the semen could have been from another person and proof of victim's prior consent is likely to be admitted under FRE 412. While the general rule of the "rape victim shield rule" is that a victim's other sexual behavior or predispositions are to be excluded, the exceptions to the rule include the two categories present in this fact pattern. **(A)** is incorrect because the testimony about Victoria's prior consent is admissible as an exception to FRE 412. **(B)** is incorrect because the evidence concerning Victoria's prior consent is admissible as an exception to FRE 412. **(C)** is incorrect because the proof that the semen could have been from another is admissible as an exception to FRE 412.

CHAPTER 5

CONSTITUTIONAL LAW

RIGOS UBE REVIEW SERIES

UNIFORM MULTISTATE BAR EXAM (MBE) REVIEW

CHAPTER 5 – CONSTITUTIONAL LAW

Table of Contents

The most frequent constitutional amendment subjects tested on the MBE and MEE are:

Amendment	Rights and Interests Covered
1	Religion, speech, press, assemble, and petition
2	Right to bear arms
4	Prohibition on searches and seizures
5	Self-incrimination privilege, double jeopardy and property takings
6	Right of criminal D to assistance of counsel and confront witnesses
7	Right to a jury trial of at least six members
8	Excess bail or fine prohibited, cruel or unusual punishment outlawed
10	Rights not addressed and general "police power" reserved to states and
11	Bars private citizen's suits for damages against a state in federal court
13	Enabling Clause – slavery and racial discrimination prohibited
14	Equal protection, due process, suspect class, right to abortion
15	Voting rights for all citizens, poll taxes, and literacy tests outlawed

RIGOS UBE REVIEW SERIES

UNIFORM MULTISTATE BAR EXAM (MBE) REVIEW

CHAPTER 5

CONSTITUTIONAL LAW

I.   INTRODUCTION

A. Bar Exam Focus Generally

1. Constitutional Law Testing: 27 of the 200 multiple-choice MBE and one out of three MEE exams historically test topics from the subject of Constitutional Law. They are segregated into five areas: Federal Courts' Authority (approximately 4 questions); Separation of Powers (6 questions); Federalism (5 questions); First Amendment (6 questions); and other Individual Rights (6 questions). Constitutional law issues covering criminal procedure are covered in the next chapter. Constitutional law issues tested in civil procedure are covered in Chapter 7. See MEE at 11-465 for prior NCBE exam question issues tested distribution.

> **MBE Tip:** Over half the constitutional questions deal with individual liberties and rights.

2. Source of Questions: Questions mainly cover controlling Supreme Court case decisions and the text of the Constitution that distributes power among the branches. Memorize the powers of Congress and the Executive branch. Knowing the locations (which Article or Amendment) of certain powers and protections is helpful in remembering who is restricted (federal or state government) and who is protected (*e.g.*, states, people, residents).

3. Ambiguity: There are some constitutional issues that are unresolved and many doctrines turning on criteria that leaves a great deal of room for judgment and debate. As a general matter, the more uncertain the test or doctrine, the less likely it is that the MBE will test the issue in a detailed way. You may be asked to identify the proper approach to resolve such an issue, but it is unlikely for the examiners to ask you what specific result is correct. But, where applicable doctrine or criteria is clear, the MBE may ask for more specific answers.

B. Checklist Approach

In order to spot and answer the constitutional issues present in most MBE questions, mentally walk through the following checklist:

1. Who is Acting: If individual liberties and rights are at stake, is there state action or an individual acting on the state's behalf? If validity of a statute is in question, ask first "who – Congress or a state legislature – is enacting the legislation?"

2. Identify Individual Rights or Subject Matter Involved: If legislative power is questioned, what category is the regulation (*e.g.*, economic regulation, safety)? If Congress has enacted the legislation, what enumerated power allows it to do so? If individual rights are threatened, are the rights "fundamental" (*e.g.*, freedom of speech, religion, liberty), or not? If an agency is acting, are there any crossover issues?

3. Test Applicable: If legislative power has been exercised, then determine the appropriate power. If rights are infringed, then determine which test to apply: strict scrutiny for fundamental rights and suspect classes; intermediate or rational basis scrutiny for other classes. MBE Tips throughout the text help identify the facts supporting the best answer.

4. Eliminate Wrong Legal Standards: If legislative power is challenged, does the government have power over the issue; or may the means (power) used justify the ends achieved? If individual rights are challenged, does the government (strict scrutiny) or the challenger (rational basis scrutiny) have the burden of proof?

5. Be Aware of Subtle Differences: Part of the reason Constitutional Law on the MBE is challenging is because the tests and levels of scrutiny often contain slight variations. Both of these variables depend on which Constitutional provision is being challenged. A solid mastery of these variations will prevent confusion.

MBE Tip: The MBE requires specific and detailed knowledge not only of the Constitution, but also of the constructs that courts use to evaluate it (levels of scrutiny, fundamental v. non-fundamental rights, etc.). Make sure you understand these intricacies.

II. FEDERAL COURTS' AUTHORITY – ORGANIZATION

A. Article III Courts

Article III of the Federal Constitution vests judicial power over all federal cases and controversies in one Supreme Court. Lower courts (*e.g.*, federal district and appellate courts) may be established by Congress. Federal Courts may hear cases involving diversity of citizenship (*e.g.*, parties from different states) involving a federal question (arising under the Constitution or federal law), admiralty, and/or those in which a state is a party.

1. Supreme Court: Article III provides for only one Supreme Court but Congress may establish or eliminate lower federal courts. The Supreme Court has original jurisdiction over cases in which a state is a party between individual states, or a private party seeking damages from a state. Most normal federal cases begin in federal district court and proceed to the federal courts of appeal.

MBE Tip: It is a frequently held misconception that all levels of the federal judicial branch are immune from elimination by an act of Congress. There is little case law on this issue. But, remember, only the Supreme Court is established and protected by the Constitution.

---

2. Article III Judges: These judges are nominated by the President, with the advice and consent of the Senate majority. They have life tenure (dismissal only for cause by act of Congress) and salary protection (Congress may not lower salary). Non-Article III judges do not have this protection and may usually be terminated at will.

B. Article I Courts

Congress creates other courts (*e.g.*, Tax Courts, District of Columbia Courts, military courts), which may be vested with administrative as well as judicial functions. Judges on such courts are not necessarily tenured or salary protected. The Supreme Court has said, however, that the "essential attributes of judicial power" must remain with Article III courts. Consequently, in certain circumstances, such as when life, liberty, or property is at stake, an Article I court's decision is reviewable by an Article III court. As a result, the Constitution places some limits on Congress's ability to shift cases from Article III courts to Article I courts. If Article III courts have the ability to hear appeals from the decisions of Article I courts, then the Supreme Court is likely to find that such an arrangement is constitutional.

III. FEDERAL COURTS' AUTHORITY – FEDERAL JUDICIAL REVIEW

A. Original Jurisdiction – Supreme Court

The Supreme Court sits as a trial court in cases involving **PACS** – **P**ublic ministers, **A**mbassadors, **C**onsuls, or a **S**tate is a party. Congress may neither enlarge nor restrict the Supreme Court's jurisdiction but may grant concurrent jurisdiction to lower courts. Cases between two or more states must be heard in the Supreme Court; lower federal courts have concurrent jurisdiction to hear other cases where a state is a party.

> **MBE Tip:** There may be a case "between states" where one state is a party via *parens patriae* (which allows a state to sue on behalf of its citizens if there is a separate sovereign injury or interest). This derivative standing does not confer original jurisdiction on the Supreme Court.

B. Appellate Jurisdiction – Supreme Court

Congress may broadly regulate which cases may be appealed to the Supreme Court. The extent of this power is unsettled because, although there have been many proposals in Congress to limit Supreme Court jurisdiction over certain kinds of cases, such as abortion or school prayer, few have been enacted into law. Many commentators believe that Congress has plenary power over the Supreme Court's appellate jurisdiction, but others disagree. Even if Congress can prevent Supreme Court appellate jurisdiction over particular classes of cases, it cannot violate other constitutional principles, such as equal protection or the suspension clause.

> **MBE Tip:** Compare "Congress passes a law preventing the Supreme Court from exercising jurisdiction over decisions that upheld temporary injunctions under the Clean Air Act," which is constitutional; with "Congress passes a law that only Republicans may seek Supreme Court review of redistricting decisions," which is probably unconstitutional under the First Amendment.

Appeals can be made via two different procedures:

1. *Writ of Certiorari*–Discretionary: The U.S. Supreme Court may hear all cases from Federal courts of appeal as well as from a state high court decision when the constitutionality of a treaty or any statute is questioned, and all cases from federal courts of appeal. This review is usually discretionary with the Supreme Court.

2. Appeal–Mandatory: Since the late nineteenth century, Congress has repeatedly narrowed the Supreme Court's mandatory appellate jurisdiction. Today, mandatory appeals to the Supreme Court can be taken only from final judgments of three-judge federal district courts.

C. Federal Court Jurisdiction – District Courts

1. Federal Question: Federal District Courts may hear any case arising under a federal statute, treaty, or the Constitution. However, the mere existence of an affirmative defense under Federal Law is not usually sufficient to create federal question jurisdiction.

2. Diversity Jurisdiction: District courts may hear cases between citizens of different states, provided that the amount in controversy is greater than $75,000. Diversity must be "complete;" e.g., no plaintiff may be a citizen of the same state as any of the defendants.

3. Supplemental Jurisdiction: A Federal Court usually has supplemental subject matter jurisdiction over claims related to the "same case or controversy" where Federal Subject Matter Jurisdiction exists. Supplemental jurisdiction may include claims that involve the joinder or intervention of additional parties.

> **MBE Tip:** Be sure to check out our chapter 7 coverage on Civil Procedure for more details on jurisdiction. The subtle differences between "jurisdiction" and "venue" are important.

D. Judicial Restraint – Justiciability

The Constitution confined federal courts to adjudicating only "cases or controversies." A number of discrete doctrines have evolved from this restriction.

1. Advisory Opinions: Federal courts may neither offer advisory opinions nor settle abstract or hypothetical questions or disputes. They can only hear actual cases and controversies involving real and substantial disputes that are not hypothetical.

2. Political Questions: Courts cannot hear and decide political questions. The Supreme Court has said that several factors control whether an issue falls under the political question doctrine. The two most important factors are:

a. Constitutional Commitment of the Decision to Another Branch: Does the Constitution textually commit final decision of the matter at issue to another branch of government (*e.g.*, time to ratify a pending constitutional amendment)?

b. Lack of Standards: Is there a lack of clear judicially manageable standards by which to decide the case (*e.g.*, organizing, disciplining, and arming the military)?

> **MBE Tip:** Perhaps the best way to summarize these factors is to ask whether there is a need for a unified pronouncement on the issue by the federal government, and perhaps especially by the political branches (*e.g.*, foreign policy matters, respect for states).

c. Examples of Political Questions: Political questions include most congressional membership issues (*e.g.*, age, residency, and citizenship), Presidential pardons, or Senate impeachment hearings. Whether the "guarantee clause" (also referred to as "republican form of government") allows a particular structure of government is a political question. Cases that raise foreign affairs issues are not necessarily political questions, but decisions about such things as military action or diplomatic relations probably qualify as political questions.

d. Examples of Non-Political Questions: Often tested are non-political questions such as state legislative election voting apportionment lines known as "gerrymandering" cases, or whether a tax is for the purpose of raising revenue. These cases sound like political questions because they involve political elections, but they do not fall within the political question doctrine, which is why the examiners like to use such fact patterns.

> **MBE Tip:** Just because an issue involves politics doesn't necessarily make it a "political question." Government employees and agencies are bound by laws, and courts adjudicate legal disputes. Remember, political questions are those which the Constitution would prohibit a court from deciding.

3. Ripeness:

a. Balancing Test: A case is ripe if there is a genuine, immediate threat of harm. The Court must balance whether future developments in the case may more narrowly clarify the dispute versus the hardship on the P of denying review now.

> **MBE Tip:** To analyze a ripeness question, ask: Has this case been brought too early? Will there be additional harm if the case is brought later?

b. Examples: Individuals have standing to invalidate a statute suppressing free speech even if it has not yet been enforced against them, because the harm prevented by free speech laws is unlawful prior restraint. However, a state law prohibiting purchase of the game of Scrabble that has not been enforced in 70 years does not threaten imminent harm.

> **MBE Tip:** A threat of future harm can create ripeness, but the harm must be actual, not speculative. For example, if a zoning law directly harms the value of A's property, A has standing. But if the law applies to another neighborhood, and A only suspects that it may be applied to her neighborhood in the future, her suit is probably premature.

c. Finality: To be ripe for review on appeal, a case must be "final" below. This means that a final order, judgment, dismissal, etc. must have been entered that ended the case at the previous level. The only exception is when a particular issue of law must be settled for the case to proceed, in which case an interlocutory appeal can be filed.

4. Mootness:

a. Test: Is the case being brought too late or after the controversy has been resolved? An actual controversy must exist at all stages of the litigation, including appeal. A case is moot if it is settled, or if the activity that produced the controversy has ended. But do not be misled by a defendant's "voluntary cessation" of the challenged activity. If the defendant could resume the activity, then the controversy is not technically moot.

b. Exceptions:

(1) Capable of Repetition, But Evading Review: If the duration of the actual harm is shorter than the typical court cycle, this exception may come into play. It also applies if the D voluntarily stops injuring P, but could resume injuring P at any time.

(2) Class Actions: Even if the class representative's particular case is moot by the time of the court action, the representative may proceed as long as remaining class members' claims are still ripe.

c. Examples:

(1) Mootness: A farmer sues a manufacturer because his cows were poisoned by the manufacturer's illegal distribution of cow feed containing toxic chemicals and it will require expensive veterinarian's fees to restore their health. However, halfway through the treatment his cows are all killed by a tornado. The farmer's case is moot.

(2) Capable of Repetition: The classic case of "capable of repetition yet evading review" is the constitutionality of a state abortion law. Inevitably, the party bringing the challenge is no longer pregnant by the time the case goes to trial or appeal, but the party or another party could become pregnant again and face the same issue.

5. Standing: Is the proper party bringing the suit? P must establish a "personal stake" in the outcome of a "case or controversy" by having suffered harm or is threatened with impending harm. To meet the constitutional requirements of standing, P must establish:

a. Injury: A personal and direct injury in fact, which usually requires a present economic harm or violation of a personal right;

b. Causation: Injury must be fairly traceable to or connected with the D's government unit conduct; and

c. Redressability: The relief sought from the court must be able to eliminate the harm alleged. Threat of imminent harm is required for injunctive relief.

d. Prudential Factors: The Supreme Court sometimes also employs non-constitutional "prudential factors" that further restrict standing for review. These include avoiding decisions on "generalized grievance" issues and requiring that the case fall within the "zone of interests" protected by the law at issue.

> **MBE Tip:** Frequently tested standing issues include government statutes – if the case involves a federal statute and the P is in the "zone of interests" that the statute was enacted to address, then a P suffering damages will have standing. Third party rights are usually inadequate.

e. Organization Standing: If there is an injury in fact to members for which those members could sue, and the injury has some connection to the organization, the organization will normally have standing to sue on behalf of its members.

> **MBE Tip:** Generally, there is no "citizen standing" for an abstract or generalized grievance (*i.e.*, no right to sue merely as a citizen claiming the government is functioning improperly).

6. Third Party Standing: Generally, third-party standing is not sufficient. The P must assert his own rights, not the rights of other parties. The major exceptions to this rule are:

a. Close Relationship: P and the actual injured party must have a close relationship. Examples are doctor/patient; school/student, labor union/member, and association/member. This ensures adequate representation of the real party's interests. An association has standing to assert the rights of its members if the right is related to the association's purpose.

b. Special Need to Adjudicate: Injury suffered by P adversely affects his relationship with third parties (*e.g.*, doctor cannot perform abortion if patients' right to abortion is hindered).

c. Limited Taxpayer Standing: A federal taxpayer usually lacks standing to constitutionally challenge federal taxes or related expenditures because the impact on them is too remote. One narrow exception is that one may make an Establishment Clause challenge to an expenditure enacted under the congressional tax/spending power. A state taxpayer may have standing to challenge measurable state expenditures.

> **MBE Tip:** A person may seek judicial review if **SERF** – she has **s**tanding to contest, has **e**xhausted all administrative remedies, the issue is **r**ipe, and the administrative decision is **f**inal.

7. State Sovereign Immunity – Eleventh Amendment:

a. Rule: A state cannot be sued in federal court by its own citizens, citizens of another state, or citizens of a foreign country, unless the state expressly waives immunity. This rule applies regardless of whether the case involves federal question or diversity jurisdiction.

b. Exceptions: There are numerous exceptions to the rule barring suits against states in federal courts:

(1) Local Governments: Immunity does not bar suits against state's political subdivisions and local agencies (*e.g.*, counties, cities, municipalities, school boards).

(2) Limited Actions Against State Officers (Instead of Against States):

(a) Injunctions Against Future Constitutional Violations: A person can sue a state itself or a state officer in a federal court to enjoin a future violation of the Federal Constitution, so long as that person has standing to bring the suit.

(b) Personal Actions: A party can sue a state officer in his personal capacity in a federal court for damages and/or injunctive relief if the officer acted "under color of law" purporting to perform official duties even if the actions were outside the scope of his state authority. Note that this exception applies even if the state will indemnify the official.

(3) Express Consent: If a state gives express consent to be sued in federal court on a particular issue or pursuant to a particular area of law, it is permissible. The Court has held that "consent" covers the situation in which a state was sued in state court, removed the case to federal court, and then sought dismissal on Eleventh Amendment grounds.

(4) Federal Taxation: Similarly, states are immune from federal taxation unless the state activity at issue is a proprietary business. See *infra*.

(5) Congress Abrogates: Congress can remove a state's immunity from suit in federal court pursuant to Section 5 of the Fourteenth Amendment, which empowers Congress to enforce its provisions. The Court has explicitly held, however, that Congress cannot abrogate state sovereign immunity when legislating under the Commerce Clause. Any abrogation must be clear and explicit.

> **MBE Tip:** State immunity is frequently tested. There are so many exceptions to absolute state immunity from suit that "Eleventh Amendment immunity of the state precludes a lawsuit" is usually a wrong answer.

8. Abstention Doctrine:

a. State Law: The general rule is that federal courts abstain from hearing cases involving underlying questions of state law that are presently unsettled. This policy encourages state courts to interpret state statutes without federal court involvement.

b. Pending Claims: Additionally, federal courts will only hear cases where relief below has been exhausted and is final – pending claims will not be reviewed unless some sort of showing of extreme bad faith on the part of the D governmental unit is made.

9. Adequate and Independent State Grounds:
When the decision coming to the Supreme Court is based on "adequate and independent state grounds" (*i.e.*, issues of state law), the Court will refrain from hearing the case because the federal question (which

is required by the jurisdiction-granting statute) is not necessary to decide the case. Failure of criminal defendants to comply with state procedural rules is an adequate state ground so long as the rule is applied consistently.

> **MBE Tip:** Look for a state statute that violates the state and federal constitutions. A court will not review the case if state decisional grounds are (1) clearly independent from the federal grounds and (2) adequate to decide the case, even if the state court erroneously decided a federal constitutional issue.

STOP! Go to page 227 and work Learning Questions 1 to 9.

IV. SEPARATION OF POWERS – FEDERAL CONGRESSIONAL POWER

Congress makes the laws, which are executed by the CEO President and interpreted by the judiciary branch. All congressional legislation must find a basis in one of Congress's enumerated powers.

A. General "Police Power" of the State

There is no federal police power. Under the 10th Amendment, the states have a general "police power" to legislate for health, safety, and welfare of their citizens. Such legislation is subject to rational basis scrutiny if challenged, for example, under the equal protection clause.

B. Congressional Enumerated Powers

The enumerated federal powers include commerce, admiralty/maritime, military/war, foreign affairs, tax and spend, citizenship/immigration/naturalization, postal, trademark, bankruptcy, and laws for the District of Columbia. These powers are magnified by the necessary and proper clause, which allows Congress to use reasonable means to carry into execution any power granted to another federal branch. There is a general immunity for speeches and debate in legislative matters.

> **MBE Tip:** If the necessary and proper clause is offered independently as an alternative, it is likely to be wrong answer.

1. Commerce Clause: Congressional power in this area is broad. As there is no national police power, most legislation is enacted via the interstate commerce clause power. Under the Commerce Clause, Congress has plenary authority to regulate:

a. The Channels of Interstate Commerce: Examples are waterways and interstate highways.

b. Instrumentalities: This is persons or things in interstate commerce. Examples are trucks and drivers transporting goods between states.

c. Substantial Relationship: Economic activities having a substantial relation to and effect upon interstate commerce are covered.

d. Determination: In order to determine whether an activity has a "substantial effect" on interstate commerce, the Court will consider aggregate or cumulative instances of the activity. In addition, the activity in question must be economic in some sense (including production, distribution, and consumption of goods).

e. Non-Economic Purposes: Congress may achieve purely non-economic purposes by regulating commerce. For example, the Civil Rights Act of 1964 sought to advance civil rights by outlawing discrimination in employment and public housing rentals and accommodations. Laws with non-economic regulatory purposes are likely to receive greater scrutiny into whether they at least take the form of regulating commercial activity, particularly in areas of criminal and tort law. Compare the Civil Rights Act to *U.S. v. Lopez* (federal crime to possess a firearm in school zone had no substantial relation to interstate commerce, unless gun traveled across state lines); *U.S. v. Morrison* (federal tort for victims of gender-based violence was not proper use of commerce clause).

f. 10th Amendment Limits: All rights not granted to the U.S. are reserved to the states. Congress may not regulate states directly, but may dictate applicable laws (*e.g.*, federal government may require all employers, including states, to comply with minimum wage and overtime provisions). Congress may not commandeer the legislative processes of the states by directing the state to enact a state regulatory program or compel the state to enforce a federal program. Federal funding for the general welfare is constitutional. Congress can force state courts to hear federal causes of action.

> **MBE Tip:** The "10th Amendment controls" is usually a wrong answer if asked about the constitutionality of a federal statute restricting or directing a state action. Do not choose an answer that strikes a federal funding merely because it regulates "an integral state function."

2. Tax and Spend Power:

a. Taxing: Congress has broad powers to lay and collect taxes from even a state government unless it interferes with a state's basic functions. Courts will defer to Congress's taxation decisions if the dominant intent is fiscal, meaning the tax produces revenue. The U.S. Supreme Court in *National Federation* 2012 construed the Affordable Care Act's requirement to purchase insurance as imposing a constitutionally valid mandatory tax.

b. Spending: Under the general Welfare Clause, Congress may spend for any public purpose. Also known as "Federal Appropriations," Congress may attach conditions to its spending. For example, Congress can withhold federal money from states unless the state raises the alcohol drinking age, lowers the speed limit, or restricts illegal activity. There must be some reasonable relationship between the condition imposed and the money appropriated (*i.e.*, requiring states that receive highway funds to set a certain maximum speed limit). Also, the federal conditions cannot be too coercive in terms of what states must do to receive the money, and in terms of how much funding is at stake.

> **MBE Tip:** Congress cannot regulate merely for the general welfare like states can – "general welfare" is not an independent power but a limitation on Congress's power to tax and spend.

3. Postal Power: Federal mail can be restricted, regulated, priced, and classified, but no individual or group may be excluded from the national postal system.

4. Immigration and Citizenship: Congress may establish rules of immigration and naturalization. Although the Supreme Court has sometimes suggested that Congress (and the President) has plenary authority over immigration – which would mean that it may admit or deport aliens as it sees fit – there are still due process limits, especially once an alien is lawfully inside the United States. On June 24, 2012 the U.S. Supreme Court refused to strike an Arizona Law requiring police to demand proof of citizenship if they suspect illegal alienship.

5. Bankruptcy: Congress may regulate bankruptcies, but its power is not exclusive like the postal power. States may legislate in the field of bankruptcy as long as the laws do not conflict with federal laws.

6. Property: Congress controls the disposition of all federal property and lands.

7. Takings / Eminent Domain: The Government can appropriate private property for the public good, provided that the private owner is justly compensated for the taking (Fifth Amendment). The takings power may also be exercised pursuant to some other enumerated constitutional power such as property required by the government for a military base or emergency. Actual appropriation or physical invasion is a taking. See *infra* at 195.

a. Public Use: Any public use rationally related to a legitimate government purpose will usually suffice to justify a taking. Thus, the federal and state governments may take private residential property and give that property to commercial developers or businesses with the goal of revitalizing a neighborhood.

b. Regulations: If the reduction in property value is due to a regulation to protect the public health, safety, or welfare for a compelling reason rather than a taking, no compensation is due. An example is the U.S. Forest Service destroying a cabin in the path of a forest fire. However, in rare cases, there is a category of regulation, a "regulatory taking," that requires compensation. A permanent reduction of value will qualify.

(1) Complete Devaluation: If the law or regulation deprives the owner of all economic value in the land, this will be a taking unless the restraint existed at the time the property owner acquired the property.

(2) Rough Proportionality: If the property owner retains some value in the land, there is a benefit-detriment balancing test:

(a) Benefit Increase: Weigh the social value increase of the regulation against the detriment to the property owner.

(b) Value Decrease: The reduction in value and the property owner's reasonable expectations *vis a vis* the property.

c. Personal Property: While personal property is afforded less protection than real property, the Supreme Court held in 2015 that a federal agency does not have the right to take a farmer's raisin crop without compensation under a federal price support program.

8. Investigation: Congress has an implied right to investigate. There must be express or implied authorization by the congressional house conducting the investigation. Witnesses are afforded the protection of the Fifth Amendment (unless they have immunity) and are only required to answer relevant questions.

C. Delegation of Legislative Power

Congress may vest in an agency, committee, the executive, or the judiciary with the authority to write rules and regulations that have the force of law. Sometimes this is described as the delegation of legislative power, but some judges and commentators maintain that it is only a grant of discretion to the executive branch (or judiciary). To be valid, the delegation must include comprehensive and clear "intelligible principles" to guide the entity that is receiving the delegated authority.

1. No Veto: If Congress disagrees with the action of an agency that is exercising its delegated authority, then Congress must pass a law to override that action, not simply overturn the agency decision. Such a law would itself be subject to Presidential veto. The legislation that sets up the delegation authority may not reserve to Congress the power to veto by legislative action alone (*i.e.*, without presentment to the President). The presentment clause requires a bill passed by Congress to be presented to the President for signature or veto within 10 days. 2/3 House vote may override a Presidential veto.

2. Powers Unique to Congress: The powers to appropriate funds, impeach, and declare war are not delegable.

D. Fourteenth Amendment

1. Implementing Procedures: Congress may create appropriate enforcement legislation to implement due process, equal protection, the privileges or immunities of citizens of the United States, or any right incorporated through the Fourteenth Amendment.

2. Limitation Interpretations: This is the main source of any limited "police power" that the federal government may have. It is also the primary way in which Congress can abrogate state sovereign immunity. However, the Supreme Court has made clear that "appropriate legislation" means laws that enforce the Fourteenth Amendment as the Court has interpreted it. Congress has no power to advance interpretations that depart from what the Court has held. Instead, all statutes passed under Section Five must be "congruent and proportional" to the Court's interpretations of the Fourteenth Amendment.

3. Commerce Clause Alternatives: Remember that Section 5 addresses only the federal government's power to regulate states. A statute that cannot regulate state action because of Section 5 may still be valid as against private action under the Commerce Clause.

V. SEPARATION OF POWERS – FEDERAL EXECUTIVE POWERS

A. Execution of the Laws

The President must faithfully execute the laws but may affirmatively veto a legislative bill passed by the House and Senate. The President's line item veto has been declared unconstitutional but they have significant discretion to execute the laws, which in practice means the President's power to favor certain laws and not to enforce others. The Justice Department personnel choose which laws to prosecute. The constitutional anti-bribery Emolument Clause prohibits the President from accepting payment from foreign governments or their agents because it may compromise the President's loyalty to the U.S. Governmental administrative agencies that engage in rulemaking and internal adjudicative proceedings of their own are also ultimately under the control of the Executive Branch.

B. Appointment Clause and Judicial Nominations

The President, with "advice and consent of the Senate," appoints all "Officers of the United States," including ambassadors, federal judges, and cabinet members. Congress vests the power to appoint "Inferior Officers" in the President, the heads of departments, and the federal courts. Congress cannot appoint anyone to a position in which that person would qualify as an officer or inferior officer. This remains the exclusive Presidential authority. Presidential nominations for open judicial positions are reviewed by the Senate Judiciary Committee and confirmation must be approved by a simple majority of the Senate.

C. Removal of Appointed Officials

The Constitution does not address the power to remove executive officials. As a result, the doctrine in this area is not always clear. The general outline of the doctrine is as follows:

1. At Will Status: Any officer of the United States who exercises "purely executive power" is an "at will" employee and therefore cabinet members are subject to Presidential termination.

2. Independent Agencies: Congress can create positions, usually in "independent agencies" such as the Federal Trade Commission and the Federal Communications Commission, in which an officer exercises "quasi-legislative and quasi-judicial" power. When it creates these positions, Congress can provide that the officer will hold the position for a fixed term of office, subject only to good cause removal.

3. Impedes Duties: The Supreme Court has suggested that the test for the constitutionality of any restrictions on Presidential removal power is whether the restriction impedes the President's ability to perform his constitutional duty.

4. For-Cause Removal: Although for-cause limits on the removal power are valid with respect to both officers and inferior officers, the Court has indicated that the President must either be able to make the for-cause termination decision or have unfettered removal power over the officer who makes that decision (*Free Enterprise Fund v. Public Company Accounting Board*, 2010).

D. Pardons

Art. II, Sec. 1 specifies that the President may pardon individuals for federal crimes but not state crimes. This Presidential power cannot be limited by Congress.

MBE Tip: Watch for this issue – a fact pattern where a case involving a state crime goes to the Supreme Court on a constitutional question and then a presidential pardon occurs. Even though the case ends up in federal court on appeal, it is the sovereign that is prosecuting the crime that dictates whether a pardon is appropriate. The federal pardon in this case would be invalid, because it is a state crime. Only the state governor, not the President, can issue a pardon here.

E. Commander-in-Chief

The president may commit and deploy troops during the outbreak of hostilities (even though only Congress – not the President – may formally declare war). The president may activate state militias into federal service and is given broad discretion in emergencies. The President also has the broad power to conduct day-to-day business with foreign countries.

F. Foreign Affairs and Policy

The president has three power sources for conducting the business administration of foreign affairs and policy: his power as Commander-in-Chief, treaty power, and congressional authorization (which is a delegation of the commerce power).

1. Treaty Power: A treaty with a foreign government must receive at least two-thirds consent of the Senate. If there is a conflict between a treaty and a federal law, the most recent in time controls. In some instances, a treaty will vest power directly in the President.

2. Executive Agreements: These are agreements made by the President and the head of a foreign country. They are less formal than a treaty because they are never submitted to the Senate for its advice and consent. Executive agreements are to be distinguished from executive orders, which deal with domestic policy.

3. Congressional – Executive Agreements: These are similar to executive agreements and distinct from treaties, because they are not subject to the two-thirds senatorial advice and consent rule. Instead, both houses of Congress vote on the agreement and if a majority is achieved, the agreement is enacted into law. The North American Free Trade Agreement is an example of a congressional-executive agreement.

G. Executive Privilege / Immunity

Executive privilege provides grounds to refuse disclosure of sensitive information. This right is absolute for military or diplomatic secrets and is qualified (*i.e.*, limited) for other information. The President and executive branch personnel have immunity against civil suits for money damages resulting from actions taken while in office. They are not immune from suit for acts that occurred before they took office. Executive officials also are not immune.

MBE Tip: Although Presidential immunity is broad, watch for limiting facts. Criminal actions and actions taken prior to inauguration will not be subject to immunity.

H. Impeachment and Removal of Elected Executives

The president, vice president, and all other civil officers are subject to the impeachment clause. This applies where a majority of the House determines grounds for impeachment exist ("Treason, Bribery, or other high Crimes and Misdemeanors"), and the Senate convicts by a two - thirds vote. Exactly what conduct qualifies as "high Crimes and Misdemeanors" is probably a political question to be answered, first, by the House (which impeaches) and, second, by the Senate (which tries the impeachment). If the president or other official is convicted, he must then leave office and remains subject to potential criminal liability.

VI. FEDERALISM – INTERGOVERNMENTAL IMMUNITIES AND TAXATION

A. Taxation and Power

The federal government and its agencies are generally immune from state taxation and other regulations interfering with their authorized function (subject to (2) below).

1. State Commerce Taxation: A state may tax commerce in their borders if:

a. Non-Discriminatory: The tax must be non-discriminatory between states and between residents of different states. The result may not be protectionist.

b. Nexus: There must be a substantial nexus between an articulated state interest and the activity taxed. Residency creates the right of a state to tax income.

c. Fairly Apportioned: The tax must also be reasonably fairly apportioned, so the tax is not disproportionate to the business conducted in the state.

d. Not in Stream of Commerce: States may tax goods at the beginning, end, and any break in transit, but not in the stream of commerce between states.

2. State Tax on Federal Government: States may levy non-discriminatory state (1) property tax on federal government buildings, (2) state income tax on resident federal employees, (3) sales tax on items sold from estates, and (4) tax on private contractors. The legal incidence of the tax may not fall directly on the federal government.

3. Federal Property Clause: Article IV, Section III of the Federal Constitution limits State power – Congress has the power to purchase and dispose of and make all needful rules and regulations regarding the territory of and the real and personal property of the U.S.

> **MBE Tip:** To spot a Federal Property clause issue, look for state law or action intruding on federal land, federal buildings or enclaves (group of buildings), military ships and airplanes, wild animals on federal land, or Indian reservations.

4. Federal Taxation of States: The States are partially immune from federal taxation. The federal government may only tax an activity of a state if:

a. Uniform Tax: The tax is uniform (applied equally to all the states); and

b. On a Proprietary Activity: The activity taxed is "proprietary," meaning one that could also be operated by the private sector. For example, property taxes levied on the state capitol building are not allowed, but they would be on a government-operated parking lot.

B. Article IV – Interstate Privileges and Immunities Clause

This clause prohibits discrimination by a state against citizens or residents of another state regarding important state rights. There is no protection for aliens and corporations.

1. Fundamental Rights: Only fundamental state rights or essential activities are protected by the Privileges and Immunities Clause. This includes rights involving commercial activities to pursue a livelihood and civil liberties protections. Private sector hiring preference to state residents, commuter taxes, and charging higher license fees to nonresident commercial fishermen are examples of violations. Note that these rights are different from "fundamental rights" such marriage, voting, or free speech.

2. Exception: If there is a substantial justification for the different treatment because the nonresidents are a particular cause or part of the harm sought to be prevented, the state regulation may be upheld. Examples are limited state issued sport fishing licenses to promote species increases or restricting the use of a natural resource such as conserving scarce water. The regulation must use the least restrictive means available.

3. Full Faith and Credit: This requires each state to respect the judicial proceedings and judgments entered in other states.

> **MBE Tip:** Don't confuse Article IV Privileges and Immunities with two other clauses: the Dormant Commerce Clause and Fourteenth Amendment Privileges or Immunities. Keep them straight this way: (1) if the discrimination is against a citizen or resident of another state based on a state preference right, then use Article IV – Interstate Privileges and Immunities; (2) if the discrimination is against an entire business or industry, then use the Dormant Commerce Clause; (3) if the discrimination is based on a federal national citizenship right, then look to the 14th Amendment Privileges or Immunities.

C. Supremacy Clause

Article VI of the Constitution makes federal law "the supreme law of the land," preempting state laws when they conflict.

1. Federal Law Controls: The Supremacy Clause provides that the Constitution, federal statutes, and treaties are the supreme law of the land. This means that any federal law, regulation, or order controls trumps and/or pre-empts any inconsistent state law or state constitutional provision. Note, however, that a treaty will trump state law only if (1) it is self-executing, meaning that it applies of its own force without the need for implementing legislation, or (2) if Congress has passed legislation to implement it.

2. Preemption: The doctrine of preemption addresses the extent to which state law is displaced by federal law. There are three kinds of preemption: (1) express preemption, when a federal statute contains a provision that refers to preemption and declares what kinds of state laws are preempted; (2) field preemption, when the federal regulatory scheme is so powerful, dominant, and pervasive that courts conclude there is no room left for state regulation; and (3) conflict preemption, when it is impossible to comply with both federal and state law, or state law creates an obstacle to the full implementation of federal law.

STOP! Go to page 228 and work Learning Questions 10 to 18.

VII. FEDERALISM – DORMANT COMMERCE CLAUSE

This doctrine is also known as the negative Commerce Power Clause. Congress regulates interstate commerce, and the Supremacy Clause is used to strike down inconsistent state laws, such as a state environmental regulation. States are free to regulate areas where there is no uniform regulation required by the federal government, unless Congress preempts by occupying the field. But the negative or dormant impact of the Commerce Clause is that state regulations must be both non-discriminatory against out-of-state interests and not unduly burden interstate commerce.

MBE Tip: Close cases involving the Dormant Commerce Clause are usually resolved against the state. When in doubt, choose the option in which the state law is struck down.

A. State Commerce Taxation

The state may tax commerce if it is non-discriminatory (not protectionist) and there is a substantial nexus between state interest and the activity taxed (due process). The tax must be fairly apportioned between in-state and out-of-state actors. States may tax goods at the beginning, end, and any break in transit, but not in the stream of interstate commerce.

B. Non-Discrimination

State discrimination against commerce originating from external states is "facially *per se* invalid." A state may not favor or protect local interests over foreign interests unless:

1. No Other Means to Advance a Legitimate State Interest: To survive a dormant commerce clause review, a discriminatory law or tax must be narrowly tailored to (1) further a legitimate non-protectionist state purpose and (2) be the only means to advance that state interest. The Court has described this as "rigorous scrutiny." Generally, the only state laws that have survived such scrutiny are legitimate quarantine laws. But state laws somewhat similar to quarantine laws, such as bans on importation of out-of-state trash, have been struck down.

2. Market Participant: If the state is a "market participant" (*i.e.*, a buyer and seller of goods in the market) the Dormant Commerce Clause does not apply. Contrast state market participation with their own funds to becoming a market regulator solely for the purpose of favoring local vendors. A state, acting as a "market participant," may favor in-state vendors over out-of-state vendors when using taxpayer funds to purchase goods and services.

MBE Tip: Be careful of the "market participant" concept. If the state actor is trying to control the market only through preferential rules and regulations, then the state is not a market participant and favoritism of local interests is improper discrimination. However, if the state is actually participating in commerce by buying and selling goods it is a "market participant."

C. Undue Burden on Interstate Commerce

If there is no overt "facial" discrimination against out-of-state commerce (*i.e.*, the statute is facially neutral), a state law may still be vulnerable under the Dormant Commerce Clause because of the undue burden it places on interstate commerce.

1. Legitimate Interest: To determine whether the state regulation imposes an undue commerce burden, courts first consider whether the state is pursuing a legitimate interest (*e.g.*, furthering health, safety or employment of its citizens).

2. Balancing Test: If the answer is yes, balance the extent to which the regulation advances the benefit to the putative in-state interest against the negative impact of the regulation on interstate commerce. If the negative impact on interstate commerce outweighs the extent to which the regulation advances legitimate state interests, the regulation is invalid.

D. Congressional Consent

Congress may enact legislation approving state discrimination against out-of-state residents. Such a congressional act will usually reverse negative court rulings.

E. Taxation

There are a number of different kinds of state and local taxes that may not discriminate against interstate commerce or unfairly burden interstate commerce participants.

1. Use Taxes: These are taxes imposed on the transaction price of goods purchased outside the state but used by the buyer within the state.

2. Sales Tax (Seller's State): If the sale takes place physically within the state, a state sales tax (price x tax rate) is valid even if the buyer removes the item from the state. If the sale takes place outside the state, the state sales tax on the item is usually invalid.

3. Sales Tax (Buyer's State): A sales tax is valid if the seller has substantial marketing contacts with the state, even if the goods are delivered from outside the state.

4. *Ad Valorem* Property Tax: This is a tax based on the value of the property asset. Commodities in interstate transit are exempt. Instrumentalities of transport (trucks, planes, boats, etc.) may only be taxed if they have sufficient connections (receive benefits or protection of the state). The tax must also be apportioned fairly.

5. Net Income, License, Franchise, & Occupational Taxes: These are taxes on doing business and must be apportioned to the business activity conducted in that state.

6. Stream of Commerce Taxation: States are prohibited from taxing goods in the stream of commerce through the state under the "internal consistency" test. This includes tax credits only available to state-based businesses.

> **MBE Tip:** State taxation should be evaluated first on whether it is contrary to any federal legislation, and if not, then whether it unduly burdens interstate commerce.

VIII. INDIVIDUAL RIGHTS – STATE ACTION

The Constitution prohibits discrimination or deprivation of rights only by state actors, not private individuals, businesses, or a private school or university. State action depriving a person of a right granted by the federal government is actionable. (The only exception is the 13th Amendment prohibition of slavery, which does not require state action.) There must be significant state involvement in a private actor to meet the requirement of a "state action." Nevertheless, the actions of private persons may be state actions in the following circumstances:

A. Public Function Doctrine

Public schools are included and it also applies where a private party carries on an activity that is traditionally a state function. A company town providing the organization and necessities of life (security system, utilities, schools, etc.) for all the town's inhabitants is the functional equivalent of a state actor. In comparison, privately-owned shopping malls are not.

B. Mutual Contacts or Symbiotic Relationship

Significant state business involvement, pervasive regulation, a "sweetheart" low rent lease, or a state subsidy may justify finding a "state action." *Moose Lodge 107.* For example, a private company working under government contract would be a state actor for the purposes of that contract. However, there is no state action by operating independently under a liquor license despite a high amount of state regulatory involvement in the process.

> **MBE Tip:** The exam often tests the concept of significant state involvement with a private actor. For example, a state-owned building with a business tenant with racially discriminatory policies or a private school with a racist policy that uses state-supplied textbooks or operates rent-free. Such arrangements are potentially subject to constitutional challenge.

C. State Command or Encouragement

If the private actor is working at the behest, encouragement, or order of the state, then a private actor becomes a public one for the purpose of constitutional limitation. An example would be the police suggesting to a private actor that the private actor conduct a search.

D. State Courts: Racially Restrictive Covenants and Defamation

In at least some circumstances, a state court's adjudication of private rights constitutes state action, such that the state court cannot enforce a private right that is in tension with constitutional principles. For example, when a property deed or lease negotiated between private parties contains a covenant excluding a particular race, state action is present if the contract is enforced by a court (this is a narrow rule that was established in *Shelley v. Kramer*). Also, a state court cannot enforce common law defamation rules in actions brought by public figures without also taking account of First Amendment doctrine (*New York Times v. Sullivan*).

IX. INDIVIDUAL RIGHTS – EQUAL PROTECTION

A. Equal Protection Clause

Fourteenth Amendment Equal Protection analysis is used when similarly situated persons or groups are treated differently by a state action or statutory classification. The Supreme Court has held that the Due Process Clause of the 5th Amendment similarly restricts the federal government from engaging in different treatment.

1. Facially Discriminatory: The first step in your analysis is to determine if the law is discriminatory on its face. If the law in question is facially discriminatory, go immediately to the next two steps: (1) identify the class being discriminated against and (2) subject the law to the appropriate level of judicial scrutiny.

2. Facially Neutral: A law that is facially neutral but has a disparate impact on a protected group does not violate equal protection unless the P can prove a discriminatory intent.

JUDICIAL REVIEW CATEGORIES

Class Affected	"Suspect"	"Quasi-Suspect"	"Non-Suspect"
Includes Discrimination Concerning	Race, Alienage, National Origin	Sex/Gender and Illegitimacy	All Other
Standard Applied	Strict Scrutiny	Intermediate Scrutiny	Rational Basis
Governmental Interest	"Compelling"	"Important"	"Legitimate"
Burden of Proof	Government	Probably Government	Complainant P

B. Classifications

If the fact pattern includes facial discrimination, or disproportionate impact and discriminatory intent against members of one class, identify the class as either "suspect," "quasi-suspect," or "non-suspect." Your final step is to identify and apply the appropriate test and allocate the burden of proof to the government or complainant.

1. Suspect Class: Memorize the following **RAN** classifications for the suspect classes.

a. Race: Ethnic ancestry or national background. See *infra* for details.

b. Alienage (or citizenship): State discrimination is subject to strict scrutiny so state actions denying aliens employment or welfare or medical benefits will usually be struck. Aliens may be excluded from being teachers, police, or important government employees but children of illegal aliens are entitled to free public education. The Federal government may legislate over illegal alienage under a rational basis standard. Illegal aliens are not a suspect class.

   c. <u>National Origin</u>: This is the nation where the individual was born.

   2. Quasi-Suspect Class: Specific sex/gender and "illegitimacy" laws which benefit children born to married parents and prejudice children not born to married parents are unconstitutional. The court would focus on the purpose of the statute or regulation, not merely the sex/gender effect. An example is hiring the most appropriate applicants for women's locker room attendants. This class is subject to intermediate scrutiny.

   3. Non-Suspect Class: All other classifications, including a person's poverty, wealth, age, education, and mental retardation, or social and economic regulatory measures are not suspect classes. As such they are only subject to rational basis scrutiny.

C. <u>Level of Scrutiny – SIR</u>

   The applicable level of judicial scrutiny and burden of proof will depend on which of the above three classifications applies. Memorize the following three **SIR** categories or levels of scrutiny. Distinguish between "compelling," "important," and "legitimate" necessary governmental interests.

   1. <u>S</u>trict Scrutiny: If the class is a suspect class (**RAN** – <u>r</u>ace, <u>a</u>lienage, <u>n</u>ational origin), then the governmental unit (or equivalent) has the burden to show that the law is necessary and "narrowly tailored to promote a compelling governmental interest." A law is narrowly tailored if it is not overly broad and no less restrictive means are available to achieve the compelling government interest (such as national security). The government unit advocating the law has the burden of proof in this highest category of judicial scrutiny.

   2. <u>I</u>ntermediate Scrutiny: If the law affects an expressive liberty activity (such as speech) or a "quasi-suspect" class (gender or illegitimacy), it must be "substantially related to a legitimate and important governmental interest" (such as taxation, gender, and labor laws). The state probably has the burden of proof on this mid-level intermediate standard of review.

   3. <u>R</u>ational Basis Test: This default category applies if the class of people affected is one of age, education, handicap, voting, jury service, or economic regulation (such as forced age retirement, zoning restrictions, public housing, welfare, taxation, or requiring a license or permit, etc.). If so, the law at issue must merely be "rationally related to a legitimate governmental interest." P has the burden of proof to show that the challenged measure lacks a legitimate rational basis government interest when weighted against the burden it would impose.

D. Racial Classifications

Race-based governmental plans (also called benign discrimination or affirmative action) involve a suspect class and thus are subject to strict scrutiny. A state action is present if a state court enforces a contract containing racially restrictive covenants.

1. Invidious Discrimination: Under the 14th Amendment, a government scheme or attempt to treat a particular racial group less or more favorably will be struck down. Unequal administration may qualify. Examples are intentional separation by race such as "separate but equal" facilities or a redistricting plan using race as a predominate factor.

2. Education Affirmative Action: If prior discrimination related to the problem area can clearly be shown, an action by government to remedy the problem may overcome strict scrutiny. Resulting affirmative actions to create diversity in a school's student body by considering race as one plus factor is acceptable (*Gratz*) unless tied to quotas or fixed percentages (*Grutter*). Pupil assignment to a particular school through bussing to create racial percentage does not meet the required strict scrutiny standard of review.

3. Employment Preferences: While a racial hiring preference would likely be struck down, employer promotion under a race-based remedial effort to cure past discrimination would likely meet the strict scrutiny standard of review.

4. Sex Discrimination and Affirmative Action: Note that gender-based affirmative action plans involve a quasi-suspect class and thus are subject to intermediate review level scrutiny. Distinguish this from a new law that merely has a disparate impact on women.

> **MBE Tip:** Because of the recent Supreme Court decision in *Gratz* approving affirmative action to promote school student body diversity, this issue seems likely to appear on the MBE. Remember that using race as one factor among others in university admissions is acceptable, but using it as the exclusive factor or imposing racial quotas is unconstitutional.

E. Peremptory Challenges

Peremptory challenge of a potential juror by any party made solely on the basis of race or sex is unconstitutional in both civil and criminal cases. *Batson*.

F. Interstate Travel

Discrimination or denial of the right to domestic U.S. travel (*e.g.*, durational residency requirements) on a limited class of persons is subject to strict scrutiny under Equal Protection. International travel is subject to a lower intermediate scrutiny review level.

> **STOP!** Go to page 229 and work Learning Questions 19 to 27.

X. INDIVIDUAL RIGHTS – DUE PROCESS

Fundamental individual rights generally arise from those protections guaranteed in the Bill of Rights. Most of the Bill of Rights (the first ten amendments to the United States Constitution) apply directly to limit the federal government and have been selectively incorporated into the Fourteenth Amendment to apply to the states. The rights that do not apply to the states include the right to a grand jury in criminal cases, right to a jury trial in civil cases, and a right against excessive bail. The Supreme Court has held that the Second Amendment right to bear arms is incorporated in due process. There are two categories.

A. Procedural Due Process

Procedural due process asks "what process is due?" Notice and the opportunity to be heard are required whenever a state deprives a person of a life, liberty, or property interest which is broadly defined. The Fifth Amendment restricts the federal government the same way the Fourteenth Amendment restricts the states. *Mathews v. Eldridge* established a balancing test for determining whether state pre-deprivation due process is warranted.

> **MBE Tip:** Procedural Due Process does not distinguish between "a right or a privilege." Both are protected.

1. Liberty Interests: A liberty interest involves both physical and non-physical liberties. These include: right to contract, right to engage in gainful employment, natural parents' care and custody of children, right to refuse unwanted medical procedures, and freedom of movement to travel.

2. Property Interests: A property interest can be tangible or intangible, but usually involves some kind of economic stake. These include: welfare and disability benefits, public education, continued public employment absent good cause for termination (*e.g.*, tenured teachers and civil service employees who are not "at will" employees), and a license required to do business or practice a profession such as public accounting.

3. Minimum Due Process: Minimum due process requires both adequate notice and a meaningful opportunity to be heard in a judicial review hearing by an unbiased tribunal.

a. Notice: Notice must be "reasonably calculated under the circumstances" to reach the affected person(s). Service of process or some kind of official delivery letter or contact must occur to inform the person threatened with deprivation by the action.

b. Opportunity to be Heard: The party must have a meaningful right to give input into the hearing process leading to the tribunal's decision in a matter revoking a person's liberty and/or property interest.

4. Timing of Due Process: All persons' lives and some liberty and property rights are deemed too important to be taken away without a pre-deprivation due process proceeding. Apply the following test to determine when the hearing should occur, *i.e.*, pre or post deprivation of the property interest.

a. *Mathews v. Eldridge* Pre-Deprivation Balancing Test: Balance the importance of the interest and the risk that the person affected will be deprived erroneously against the cost and administrative burden on the government to provide additional procedure.

Importance of individual interest involved + Risk of erroneous deprivation	VS	Cost to government of pre-deprivation procedure + Administrative burden and Availability of additional safeguards

b. Post-Deprivation Due Process: When the cost to the government and the administrative burden of additional safeguards outweighs the importance of the deprived interest and low risk of erroneous deprivation, the person adversely affected retains the opportunity to be heard after the deprivation.

> **MBE Tip:** MBE examiners do not usually use the terms "procedural" or "substantive" in due process questions. "Procedural" tells us what and when process is due. "Substantive" due process isn't really "process" at all. It refers to the category of rights and privileges that may not be infringed upon without proper procedural due process.

B. Substantive Due Process

Substantive Due Process asks "may the government infringe on this individual right?" For the purposes of the MBE, ask yourself two questions:

1. Category of Right: Is the right one of life, liberty, or property?

2. Fundamental Right: Is the right fundamental? (See list below.) If so, then apply strict scrutiny to determine whether the challenged law or action is valid. If the right is not fundamental, then the right is viewed as only a liberty or property interest, and the challenged law or action is subject only to rational basis scrutiny.

> **MBE Tip:** Substantive Due Process protects fundamental rights from laws which affect all persons, compared to Equal Protection, which protects against two persons similarly situated from being treated differently.

3. Liberty Interests: This refers to basic personal freedom to move about such as driving a car or changing residence, raising a family, or practicing a profession. Look for governmental action affecting someone's freedom (such as jail or civil commitment). Restrictions on non-fundamental liberty interests are subject only to rational basis scrutiny.

4. Property Interests: A property interest is a legitimate claim to something of value. The property may be tangible or intangible. Examples on the exam include the right to a public education and to own real and personal property. There is also a right to keep a government job if tenured. The organization's rule book often specifies some cause procedure is necessary for dismissal.

> **MBE Tip:** Punitive damages may violate substantive due process if they are "grossly excessive" of actual compensatory damages.

5. Non-Fundamental Right Test: If the right being infringed upon is not fundamental, then the action is presumed valid and must merely be "rationally related to a legitimate governmental interest." The burden is on the challenger to prove the action invalid.

6. Fundamental Right Test: If the right deprived of is fundamental, then strict judicial scrutiny will be applied. The state government has the burden of persuasion to show:

a. Compelling Interest: The state restriction must be necessary to advance a compelling (beyond "legitimate") governmental interest, and

b. No Less Intrusive Means: There also must be no less reasonable intrusive means available to mitigate the right deprivation. As with equal protection, courts sometimes ask whether the restriction is "narrowly tailored."

> **MBE Tip:** Under the "rational relation" test the affected individual has the burden of persuasion, but if a fundamental right the government bears the justification burden.

7. Particular Fundamental Rights: The following liberty rights are fundamental and subject to frequent UBE testing:

a. First Amendment Rights: This heavily tested subject includes the freedoms of religion, speech, press, assembly, and to petition the government for redress of grievances.   Speech is covered in detail *infra* at page 199 and citizens have the right to assemble and associate freely for those ends not prohibited by criminal law.

b. Voting: State reasonable non-discriminatory voter qualifications, such as residence requirements, and legislative boundary apportionment (population equivalency rules) are permissible.   Gerrymandering schemes that deliberately distort voting districts for political party purposes are unconstitutional.

(1) Apportionment: Geographical boundaries of voting districts may not be defined so as to prevent numerical equality among voting groups (one person, one vote).   An exception is a special limited purpose district (*e.g.*, water storage district) which can be limited to landowners and apportioned based on the percentage of land owned.

(2) Ballot Access: States may make reasonable restrictions (*e.g.*, pay a reasonable filing fee or gather a small percentage of voter signatures).   The state may require minimum age and residency requirements for candidate eligibility.

c. Interstate Travel: There is a fundamental right to travel domestically freely from state to state in the U.S.   This pertains to the right to travel itself, not to the right to engage in certain activities once the traveler has arrived.   For example, if a state prohibits someone from doing business in that state, the right to travel is not implicated, although there might be Commerce Clause or Article IV Privileges and Immunities concerns.   If a state requires duration-based residency as a condition of benefits, the right to travel may be violated.

(1) Residency Requirement: While the state may require residency for some government paid benefits, durational residency requirements are unconstitutional prerequisites for medical aid, welfare benefits, and library services.   They are allowed in determining reduced tuition for state universities, marital dissolutions, or voter registration.

(2) Foreign Travel Restraints: Unlike domestic travel foreign travel restrictions are reviewed under a rational basis scrutiny for national internal security reasons.   A law regulating the right to change residency should be evaluated for Due Process considerations if it is a general limitation on all persons' ability to travel.   See Equal Protection section *supra*.

MBE Tip: If the question deals with the basic right to vote, apply the Fifteenth Amendment.   If there is discrimination in voting (*e.g.*, race or sex), apply the Fourteenth Amendment Equal Protection Clause.   Duration-based residency requirements are a right to travel issue (Substantive Due Process), not a right to vote issue.

---

d. Refuse Medical Treatment: A mentally competent adult has the right to refuse life prolonging medical treatment and necessary nutrition.   In comparison, affirmative suicide may be criminalized by a state, including assistance from a medical professional.   A person probably has the right to medication that will relieve severe and unrelenting pain, even if that medication will lead to that person's death.   Requiring a patient to accept a blood transfusion usually violates the right to privacy.

e. Privacy Rights – "CAMPER": The privacy rights listed below are fundamental and subject to strict scrutiny review standards of review:

(1) Contraception: Strict scrutiny applies to this privacy right and states cannot prohibit the sale of contraceptive devices to adults. *Griswold v. Connecticut.*

(2) Abortion: *Roe v. Wade* held states may regulate but not prohibit or unduly burden a woman's fundamental personal right to obtain an abortion. Prior to the end of the first trimester of pregnancy (pre-viability period), a state may not interfere with or regulate a patient's and physician's decision to terminate a pregnancy. A state may require parental consent for an abortion for a minor, but it must make judicial review available. States cannot require spousal consent. Patients have no right to state funding for abortion.

(3) Marriage: Absent a compelling interest, states may not unduly restrict the fundamental right to marry but may set a minimum age without requiring parental consent. For example, a state cannot prohibit an ex-spouse from remarrying in order to force him to make past due child support payments, even if there is a compelling state interest in doing so. Requiring a marriage license is not a restriction on the right to marry *per se* but is a condition of receiving certain benefits of the legal status of marriage. In 2015, the Supreme Court held in *Obergefell v. Hodges* prohibitions on same sex marriages to be unconstitutional.

(4) Procreation: States may not interfere excessively with individual's procreative activities. This is closely related to contraception and abortion rights protections.

(5) Education: Parents have a right to privately educate their own children (*i.e.*, home-school). Although there is no absolute right to free public education, a complete deprivation of education is probably unconstitutional.

(6) Relations in Families: Related people (nuclear family) have the right to live together and natural parents have the right to have custody of their children.

MBE Tip: Privacy now protects homosexuals from prosecution under state sodomy statutes. While the Supreme Court has *not* held that there is a fundamental right to engage in such activity, it nonetheless concluded that there is "no legitimate state interest" in criminalizing same-sex sodomy. *Lawrence v. Texas.* This landmark ruling may be tested.

STOP! Go to page 230 and work Learning Questions 28 to 37.

XI. OTHER INDIVIDUAL RIGHTS

A. Privileges or Immunities Clause

This is also known as the rights of national citizenship. This clause protects rights fundamental to national unity from intrusion by the federal government or by a state against its own citizens. The Supreme Court has interpreted this clause very narrowly, and the rights restricted must be quite important such as denying a person the right to work or vote. The right to travel from state to state (also protected by Equal Protection Clause) or treat new state residents less favorably than existing residents are commonly tested topics on the MBE.

B. Contracts Clause

Article I, Section 10 prohibits states government (not the federal government or state courts) from retroactively impairing public or private contracts unless a significant public need applies. The state's police power (power to regulate for the health, safety, and morals of the state) generally satisfies the public need and the court applies the intermediary scrutiny test.

> **MBE Tip:** Because of the broad police power, "impairment of contracts" is often a wrong answer. Focus on whether the new law retroactively impairs past contracts.

C. "Taking" of Property

States, like the federal government, may not take private property for public use without just compensation. Allowable public uses have traditionally included utilities, railroads, and road expansions, but recently local governments requiring businesses to install floodlights and cameras to deter criminal activity have been upheld.

1. Methods of Taking: Property appropriation is government "taking" by eminent domain, inverse condemnation (reduction in value by restricting the owner's future use), or a regulatory statute which permanently deprives the owner of all viable economic use of land.

2. Restrictions: States may usually restrict use of property without paying compensation unless such renders the property useless (*e.g.*, land use, zoning). *Penn Central* held a court must balance (1) the negative economic impact of the regulation, (2) the extent of the interference with investment expectations, and (3) the character of the government action.

> **MBE Tip:** Traditionally the taking must be for a "public use." The Supreme Court held that a private developer's building project for condemned property intended to stimulate the local economy qualified as a public use. *Kelo v. City of New London.* A question alternative stating "The government taking is invalid because it is not for a public use" may be a wrong answer.

D. Right to Bear Arms

The Second Amendment protects the right of the people to own and carry guns and related weapons. States and local government prohibitions are so limited but private property owners can prohibit side arms on their premises and property. Similarly, local governments may require gun owner applications, licensing and deny gun permits to felons. Concealed weapons may be banned in public places like libraries, court rooms, and sporting events. It is also usually permissible to ban assault and automatic firing weapons, and require trigger locks.

E. *Ex Post Facto* Law

After an act has occurred, the government may not then retroactively (1) make that conduct criminal, (2) increase the punishment level for the act, or (3) decrease the burden necessary to convict the D. This prohibition does not apply to mere procedural changes or to civil actions such as changes in standards of civil liability if a final judgment has been rendered.

> **MBE Tip:** Striking a law on *ex post facto* grounds is usually a wrong answer on the MBE.

F. Bills of Attainder

A legislative act cannot punish a named or ascertainable group or individual members for past conduct without a proper judicial trial (criminal or civil punishment). For example, the state cannot pass a law punishing a person for prior political beliefs or activities.

> **MBE Tip:** An alternative that the action "is an inappropriate bill of attainder" is usually a wrong answer. Remember, for a bill of attainder to exist, the law must single out a named person or group of persons without a trial. If the law happens to affect only a small group, but does not name that group, it is not a bill of attainder. The equal protection clause would apply instead, and the level of scrutiny would be rational basis unless the group is a protected class.

XII. FIRST AMENDMENT RIGHTS – RELIGION CLAUSES

Freedom of religion is a fundamental right and the government must be religion neutral. The statute may not help or hinder religion. Any law must be religion-neutral. If the law interferes, distinguish between the "religious belief" itself and the "conduct" stemming from the belief. If the law endorses or supports religion, look at the purpose of the law, the effect of the law, and whether there is excessive government entanglement between church and state.

A. Free Exercise Clause

When the issue is one of free exercise of religion, identify whether the law pertains to a religious belief or the conduct or practice stemming from that religious belief. For example, if there is a religion that believes that clothing is evil, distinguish between the belief that clothing is evil and walking around naked in public.

1. Beliefs: Religious beliefs are absolutely protected, no matter how far outside the norm they are. A law that outlaws a particular religious belief is *per se* unconstitutional. Also, clerics may not be excluded from holding public office, and requiring religious oaths for government jobs is prohibited. In comparison, an oath to uphold the Constitution is usually permissible.

2. Conduct: Conduct stemming from a particular religious belief may be regulated if there is a secular reason for doing so. For example, the government may not enact a law making it illegal to believe that clothes are evil, but it may make it against the law to walk around naked in public. Similarly, the army may not generally prohibit Muslims from wearing head coverings, but a ban on all non-army headgear while on duty would likely be upheld.

3. Scrutiny: The degree of scrutiny for some free exercise claims is uncertain.

a. Lower Scrutiny: The Supreme Court has said that neutral laws of general applicability do not violate the Free Exercise Clause. Thus, if the law is generally applicable and not intentionally discriminatory, then favor the answer that upholds the law, especially criminal laws.

b. Strict Scrutiny: If the law expressly targets religious practices it is subject to strict judicial review scrutiny. There must be no less restrictive means available to achieve a compelling secular objective. For strict scrutiny to apply, one of the following must be proven:

(1) Governmental Intent to Interfere: This applies where there is some evidence or indication that the state was deliberately trying to create, interfere, prohibit, restrict, or regulate religious conduct.

> **MBE Tip:** The Supreme Court is slow to find government intention to interfere, but if it is very clear or given in the facts, then apply strict scrutiny. Look for facts that suggest an obviously devious or improper purpose.

(2) Support by Another Fundamental Right: If the regulation also interferes with another fundamental right then apply strict scrutiny. Compare these examples:

(a) Religion – Control of Child's Education: Amish parents' right to educate their children at home combines religious conduct with the free exercise right to educate one's children in a manner the parent chooses. Strict scrutiny will apply because this prefers one religion.

(b) Religion – Property Right: If a "for cause" state employee quits her job for religious reasons (*e.g.*, a new work rule requiring her to work on her Sabbath day), unemployment benefits cannot be withheld. This is true despite the fact that the loss of work is a "voluntary quit" not normally covered by unemployment compensation laws. Strict scrutiny will apply because a property right (state employment) is combined with freedom of religion.

> **MBE Tip:** Many candidates assume that strict scrutiny will apply whenever any freedom of religion issue is in play. Study the above distinctions and remember that strict scrutiny only applies in limited circumstances.

4. Examples: Examples of permissible regulations that affect religious conduct are:

a. Use of Controlled Substances: Laws prohibiting the use of hallucinogenic peyote in religious ceremonies have been upheld.

b. Polygamy: State laws prohibiting the practice of polygamy encouraged by the person's religion have been upheld.

c. Public Safety and Health: *Bona Fide* individual religious freedom usually controls (*e.g.* Jehovah Witnesses can't be forced to take a blood transfusion) unless the religious belief creates a public danger (such as a local health authority requiring all residents to be vaccinated to prevent spreading a serious flu epidemic).

d. Graduation on Sabbath: A school holding graduation ceremonies on a Saturday, which is the Sabbath for some students, has been tested. The Saturday graduation policy is designed to promote the secular end of administrative and family convenience. This interest must be balanced against the degree of indirect infringement on religious belief. An acceptable alternative used by many institutions is to hold a second event on a Sunday.

> **MBE Tip:** First Amendment religion in a school context is an examiner's favorite fact pattern.

B. Establishment Clause

Government may not sponsor religious observances, prefer or advance one religion over another religion, or over non-religion. Statutes and regulations must be enacted for a secular purpose and must not cause the government to become too involved in religion. Remember, however, that the government may "accommodate" religious practices, so long as the accommodation does not create or amount to a preference.

1. The *Lemon* Test: There is a three-part **SEEE** test for determining whether an Establishment Clause violation has occurred. The law may not have a **s**ecular purpose, **e**ffect to benefit/diminish religion, or result in **e**xcessive government **e**ntanglement in religion.

a. Secular Primary Purpose: The legislative purpose of the law must not be religious. It must be for the benefit of the public at large without religious considerations. However, if there is a mixed secular and religious purpose, this requirement is probably satisfied. Sunday business closure laws are permitted as a secular day of rest but requiring students to observe two minutes of silence for prayer and meditation is an Establishment Clause violation if primarily motivated to aid religion.

b. Effect Neutral: The law at issue must neither advance nor inhibit religion. While it may have incidental effects, the primary effect must be neutral and neither force nor encourage people to worship or refrain from worshipping.

> **MBE Tip:** Look for a government action advancing a general important public interest that has an incidental effect on a particular religion. As long as the effect on religion is only incidental, the action passes this prong of the *Lemon* test.

c. Excessive Government Entanglement: The law must not foster excessive government entanglement or require close government monitoring of lesson plans. Allowing a church to veto a liquor license application unconstitutionally entangles churches in government activities because the church is delegated government decision-making.

d. Endorsement: Separate from the *Lemon* test, the Court sometimes asks whether a reasonable person would interpret the government action or entanglement as an endorsement of religion (as opposed to a mere accommodation). Bargain sale of government assets to a religion may constitute an effective religious endorsement.

2. Examples:

a. Religious Activity: Government-sponsored religious activity or teaching religion in public schools are generally unconstitutional. This likely includes requiring a moment of prayer, forbidding the teaching of evolution, or demanding the teaching of creationism.

b. Financial Aid: Government aid directed solely to private religious schools is unconstitutional in the K-12 grades, but probably not at the university level. University athletic program funding is usually approved. Tuition vouchers, free textbooks, or funded teachers provided to all schools on the same terms, including religious schools, is constitutional.

> **MBE Tip:** If a government action benefits all students it likely is constitutional even though religious students may benefit more than non-religious students.

3. Conflict: Distinguish between the Free Exercise Clause (government non-interference with religious belief) and the Establishment Clause (intermingling of government and religion). Government may hire chaplains to work in the military, prisons, or hospitals but not at a public school. Religious displays taken as a whole, which celebrate the secular holiday season, are constitutional. A display in a government building consisting of two reindeer, Santa, a Jewish menorah symbol, an 18' Menorah and 45' Christmas tree was upheld. In comparison, allowing the Catholic Church to put a nativity scene alone in a city building was held unconstitutional.

4. *Van Orden* Test: In 2005, the Supreme Court decided two cases concerning the public religious symbol display of the Ten Commandments and the Establishment Clause. They did not overrule *Lemon*, but in *Van Orden v. Perry*, the Supreme Court noted that it does not always consistently use the *Lemon* test and held that a 40+-year-old "passive monument" inscribed with the Ten Commandments and set among over 35 other monuments on the Texas State Capitol grounds did not violate the Establishment Clause.

5. *McCreary* Test: On the other hand, in *McCreary County v. ACLU of Kentucky*, the Supreme Court applied *Lemon* in invalidating the stand alone posting of the Ten Commandments display in courthouses.

6. Suggested Approach: In cases matching these fact patterns determine the context in which the religious symbol is displayed and the history of the display. In all other Establishment Clause cases, apply the *Lemon* **SEEE** test but also use the "endorsement" test to help you apply your common sense.

> **MBE Tip:** Religious issues connected with some government-approved event, religious display, or free/bargain purchase of government assets appear on almost every exam.

> **STOP!** Go to page 231 and work Learning Questions 38 to 43.

XIII. FIRST AMENDMENT RIGHTS – FREEDOM OF EXPRESSION

A. Overall Approach

1. Identify the Law: If the law (regulation, edict, etc.) affects speech or expressive conduct, it may raise a First Amendment Freedom of Expression issue.

> **MBE Tip:** Even if the law is not aimed at speech or intended to affect speech, there are freedom of expression implications if speech is only indirectly affected. Justice Kennedy wrote the First Amendment "protects the speech we detest as well as the speech we embrace."

2. Content Question: Second, determine whether the idea expression restricting law is content-neutral or content-specific. This usually is fairly obvious from the facts: if a particular type of speech is identified as prohibited, then the law is content-specific.

a. Content Neutral – Public or Private Forum: If the restricting law is content neutral (does not specify a type of speech or idea expression that is prohibited), intermediate scrutiny applies. Next, identify the forum as public, limited public or private.

b. Content Specific Protected or Unprotected: If the law is content specific, identify the idea expression as either protected (political usually) or unprotected speech (defamation, fighting words). If the speech is unprotected such as those urging sedition, the government may ban it outright. If the idea expression is banned, the law must be necessary to promote an important and specifically articulated compelling governmental interest.

> **MBE Tip:** Freedom of speech analysis is intricate and a very heavily MBE and MEE tested subject. Watch your facts carefully for clues about the forum and the type of speech affected.

B. Facial Attacks

A law restricting speech or association may be attacked as unconstitutional on its face or as applied by the government. A facial attack alleges the law as written is *per se* unconstitutional, regardless of the context in which it is enforced. An example is *Citizen United*, which held that political speech and related contributions do not lose First Amendment protection simply because its source is a corporation. Facial attacks of the statute are usually made on the basis of vagueness, overbreadth, and allowed unfettered discretion.

1. Vague: A law must give fair and reasonable notice of what speech is prohibited. A vague law is so unclear that persons of ordinary intelligence must guess as to its meaning in application. A law which states that one needs a permit to speak about "morally repugnant issues" is unconstitutionally vague, because the concept of moral repugnance is vastly malleable. What is morally repugnant to one person may be morally uplifting to someone else.

2. Overbroad: Overbroad laws are written in such sweeping language that they punish both protected and unprotected speech. The test is whether the regulation restricts substantially more speech than is necessary. A law restricting all speech on government land or in a city park would likely be struck because it is overbroad and lacks specificity.

3. Unfettered Discretion: Officials may not have arbitrary discretion to or not to grant licenses to appear or speak (*e.g.*, parade license issued only if police chief says so).

MBE Tip: "Unfettered discretion" applies to the topic of Administrative Law. Any administrative agency or employee must have some kind of minimal legislative non-vague guidance in decision-making regarding issues of fundamental rights. Otherwise, constitutional violations are likely.

C. Content Neutral Regulations of Speech

Content neutral regulations of speech are limited to restrictions on the time, place, and manner of its expression. Prior restraints prevent idea expression from taking place and are therefore subject to a heavy presumption against constitutional validity. Public and private forums have different analysis.

1. Public Forum: A traditional public forum is that in which the public assembles and engages in expressive conduct. Traditional public forums include streets, sidewalks, parks, and town squares where speeches, debates, leafleting, and broadcasting take place. Spaces that are not traditional public forums may still qualify as "designated" public forums. To pass constitutional muster, content neutral place, time, and manner restrictions on speech in a public forum must be facially valid and must conform to the following:

a. Narrowly Tailored to Advance a Significant Interest: The idea repression law must be narrowly tailored (least apparent restrictive means available) to achieve a significant or substantial governmental interest, and

b. Reasonable Time, Place, and Manner Restrictions: The law must leave open alternative channels of speech communication that are somewhat comparable to the channels restricted. For example, restricting all public speeches in a park is not acceptable simply because the speaker could call people on the phone to deliver the same message.

MBE Tip: Note that the interest furthered by the government need only be "significant" rather than "compelling." This is different from the strict scrutiny standard applied in equal protection and due process cases. If the fact pattern indicates any reasonable policy reason for the expressive activity law, it will probably survive this intermediate level of scrutiny.

---

c. Examples of Allowable Activities: Nazi parades on public streets, virtually all peaceful demonstrations, protests near military events and funerals, literature distribution, and charitable solicitations must be allowed in traditional public forums open to the public.

d. Restrictions Allowed: Loudspeaker use may be limited as to time of the day and volume. A restriction on picketing normally tailored to protect a homeowner's privacy may be upheld if similar demonstrations at some other close forum is allowed. Similarly, an eight-foot space separation restriction on abortion clinic picketing which prohibited pamphlets and argument with customers was held constitutional as it was content neutral, narrowly tailored, and alternative time, place, and manner of expression were available.

2. Nonpublic Forum: Basically, this is any land or space that is not a public forum, including private residences, shopping malls, airports, newspapers, jails, military bases, and courtrooms. Reasonable regulation is allowed as long as the time, place, and manner restrictions on speech in a private forum are not facially invalid and conforms to the following:

a. Viewpoint Neutral: The legal regulation must be viewpoint and subject matter neutral. Both sides must be able to present their opposing opinions and views.

b. Rationality Test: The legal regulation must bear a rational relationship to a legitimate articulated governmental interest. Essentially, it is almost impossible to fail this test unless the law at issue is utterly absurd and meaningless.

MBE Tip: Notice that the scrutiny tests are similar to those described previously, but slightly different. For example, "strict scrutiny" as described in section XII in the context of free exercise of religion analysis is "narrowly tailored to achieve a compelling government interest," but in the context of free speech analysis, the level is closer to "intermediate" scrutiny," which is "narrowly tailored to achieve a significant government interest."

---

c. Door-to-door Solicitation: A total prohibition is not allowed, but requiring registration of canvassers and sales persons for personal home solicitation may be upheld if registration could promote crime prevention. In comparison, attempted religious conversion by Jehovah's Witnesses and distributing handbills to homes may not be restricted.

3. Licensing and Registration: A licensing statute, such as requiring a parade or demonstration permit, must be content neutral and cannot give the licensing official unrestricted discretion to issue or deny. To meet constitutional requirements there must be a narrowly defined criteria such as place, time, and duration if the organizer is required to obtain a permit. If the application is denied, an appeal must be taken if the organizer wishes to go forward; one cannot just disregard the official decision.

4. Limited Public Forum: This is a government-owned forum open only to certain subjects or speakers. Possible examples include libraries, schools, and fairgrounds. This forum may be regulated in the same manner as private forums.

D. Content Specific Speech

Content specific speech may be categorized as protected or unprotected. Unprotected speech is afforded no legal protection whatsoever. For constitutional law analysis purposes, unprotected speech is non-speech. If you have identified the speech prohibitive law as content specific, determine whether it is protected or unprotected speech.

1. Unprotected Speech: The following categories of speech are not protected including obscenity, child pornography, and false statements of fact. The Supreme Court has made clear that it probably will not expand this category (for example, it rejected the argument that depictions of animal cruelty are unprotected speech).

a. Defamation: The definition of defamation is a "false statement, of or concerning the P, intentionally communicated to third persons, which results in injury to P's reputation." Oral defamation is "slander" and special damages must be proven. Written defamation is "libel" and general damages are presumed. The requisite proof for defamation will differ depending upon the jurisdiction's defamation rules, whether the subject of the defamatory statement is a public official or figure, and whether the factual matter published is of public or private concern.

(1) Public Official, Candidate, or Figure – Matter of Public Concern: This category includes anyone whose job, position, or reputation has a connection to public life or the public welfare. The burden of proof, which is on the P, is a preponderance of the evidence. The P must show falsity of the statement and actual malice. "Actual malice" is defined as "knowledge of falsity, or reckless disregard for the truth or falsity of the statement."

> **MBE Tip:** As discussed in the Criminal Law chapter, "malice" is a pre-Model Penal Code term that is somewhat misleading as applied to defamation. There does not need to be any evil or ill will involved for "malice" to occur, only wrongful intention or recklessness.

(2) Public Official – Matter of Private Concern: Damages are presumed if the defamation involves one of the four **LUNI** subject matters. This includes **L**oathsome disease, **U**nchastity or other serious sexual misconduct, **N**otorious criminal allegation, and **I**njury in trade, business, or profession. (These are discussed in detail in MBE Volume 1 at page 1-67 in our tort chapter.) The burden is on the D to show the truth of the statement.

> **MBE Tip:** Keep in mind that what is considered a matter of "private concern" when a public figure is involved may be restricted compared to those matters considered private to a private figure. For example, the sexual conduct of a public figure might be considered a matter of public concern if such conduct is considered to compromise that figure's character or suitability for public office.

(3) Private Figure – Matter of Public Concern: The burden is on the P, who must show falsity of the statement and negligence by the D.

(4) Private Figure – Not Matter of Public Concern: Only falsity and ordinary negligence must be shown. Damages are presumed, and burden is on the D to show the truth of the statement. Some jurisdictions shift the burden and require the P to show falsity.

b. Fighting Words: These are specific threats that would naturally incite immediate physical violence in the person to whom they are directed. Contrast racist opinions to displaying a noose to a black person. A statute that bans "all fighting words" is unconstitutionally overbroad and vague. Merely annoying or nuisance speech does not rise to the level of fighting words, as the speech must incite violence.

> **MBE Tip:** The Supreme Court has rejected prohibition of "fighting words" that are based on a particular category of speech, for example, a restriction only on racially provocative speech or speech that inflames based on religion. This is too close to political speech, which is guarded by the First Amendment.

c. Commercial Speech: Commercial advertising is generally protected as long as it is truthful and not proposing illegal activity or promoting the sale of illegal products.

(1) Commercially Illegal Speech: Advertisements for illegal products or services may be outlawed.

(2) Commercially Misleading Speech: False or deceptive advertising may be prohibited if it has a clear tendency to significantly mislead the public.

(3) Unique Level of Scrutiny: Censorship of commercial speech that is not about an illegal activity and is not misleading is subjected to a slightly different standard of scrutiny than any described thus far.

(a) **Substantial Government Interest**: The law must involve and serve a substantial government interest;

(b) **Directly Advance:** The law must directly advance that government interest;

(c) **Narrowly Tailored**: The law must be narrowly tailored to protect that interest.

(4) **Examples:** States may prohibit advertising for any illegal activity, such as prostitution. Untruthful, misleading, or deceptive commercial speech may usually also be prohibited. Similarly, billboards may be limited in size or lighting or outright prohibited if they create traffic risks. Regulation, but not a total ban, is allowed for tobacco, gambling, and liquor advertising. Professional licensing rules, such as bar-imposed minimum fee schedules and a ban on lawyer advertising, or locating newsstands in a public area, are unconstitutional.

> **MBE Tip:** Commercial speech is essentially all forms of advertising. It is potentially subject to more government – imposed restrictions than political speech.

d. **Obscenity:** Obscene material may be banned outright. The test consists of:

(1) **Prurient Interest:** The material taken as a whole must appeal to the prurient interest in sex, using a community standard, and;

(2) **Patently Offensive:** The material must depict sexual conduct in a patently offensive way and be an affront to current community standards; and

(3) **Lacks Value:** The material may be banned if, taken as a whole, it lacks serious objective literary, artistic, political, or scientific value and/or merit.

(4) **Standards Used:** Elements 1 and 2 apply the contemporary community (local) standards, and element 3 is subject to an objective reasonableness standard. Radio and television broadcasting do not have all of the same constitutional protections as other forums (such as video sales), so the government may regulate obscene material in public broadcasting.

> **MBE Tip:** Private possession of obscene material – beyond mere pornography – in the home is protected, but not in theaters or other modes of distribution. The location of obscenity is more likely to be tested than the general question of whether something is deemed to be obscene.

(5) **Zoning and Liquor Regulations:** States may use zoning ordinances to limit the location and number of adult theaters or bookstores. States may use the 21st Amendment to regulate live sexual entertainment locations that the state licenses to serve liquor. Seizure of allegedly obscene books to block their distribution must be preceded by a full adversarial hearing and a judicial determination of obscenity (see prior restraint).

e. **Child Pornography:** Viewing obscene material in one's home is not usually punishable. However, states can criminalize possession of child pornography anywhere, even in one's home. The standard for child pornography is easier for the government to satisfy than other "obscenity." It is the visual depiction of any sexual context involving a child, even if the lewd depiction would not be obscene if adults were the actors and actresses.

f. **Incite Unlawfulness:** This type of speech may be prohibited if it is (1) intended to produce and (2) is likely to incite (3) imminent unlawful conduct.

g. Audience Veto: The government must take reasonable steps to allow even unpopular speakers to speak. Even a threat of violence does not justify prior police suppression.

h. Speech Integral to Criminal Conduct: A person who solicits a crime, verbally agrees to be part of a conspiracy, or tries to commit fraud by oral or written means cannot raise the First Amendment as a defense against prosecution.

2. Protected Speech: A strict scrutiny standard applies to protected speech which is the highest form of speech recognized under the Constitution. Any restraint must be minimized and serve an important government interest. Examples of protected speech include:

a. Political Speech and Speech on Matters of Public Concern: This includes all speech on matters of public interest which is not intended to incite imminent lawless behavior and is not likely to produce such action.

b. Commercial Speech: This includes commercial speech such as advertising that is not commercially illegal, false, or misleading.

c. Non-Obscene, Sexually Explicit Speech: Sexually explicit speech that is not "obscene" is protected.

d. False Statements Lists: The U.S. Supreme Court recently struck down the Stolen Valor Act, which made it a crime to misstate military awards and decorations. The opinion focused on the theory that the government may not compile a list of subjects about which false statements are deemed to be criminal.

E. Freedom of the Press

The press and media generally stand on the same constitutional footing as individuals. The media can report information that is in the public domain. This includes an unconditional privilege to report what occurs in open court or republish documents in the court file.

1. Some Restrictions: The press right is not totally unfettered. For example:

a. Judicial Closure Order: A judge may find that a narrow closure (gag) order is necessary to promote a substantial interest. This is rare; an example of when such an order may be appropriate is when it protects the identities of children who are victims of sex crimes. More common are judicial orders to parties and their representatives not to speak to the press; this limited type of "gag order" is allowable if there is a "substantial likelihood" of material prejudice in a court proceeding that could result from such extra-judicial statements.

b. Equal Time: Broadcast media may be required to give equal air-time to ideas (not candidates).

c. Government Privilege: Some records may be redacted (portions blocked out) or classified and hence made unavailable to the press for national security reasons.

d. Grand Jury Testimony: Reporters and other members of the press may be required to testify in grand jury proceedings unless there is a state shield law.

2. Regulations of Broadcast Media: Television and radio broadcast media can be more regulated than print or internet media. The key interest protected is the interest of viewers and listeners to receive information that is of public interest or concern. However, patently offensive broadcasts may be prohibited to protect the privacy interest of children.

> **MBE Tip:** Contrary to popular belief, the press has no greater First Amendment protection than any other citizen. If an MBE question involves freedom of the press, remember to analyze the question from a freedom of speech standpoint as well.

> **STOP!** Go to page 232 and work Learning Questions 44 to 50.

F. Prior Restraints on Speech

A prior restraint is a law that prohibits future speech, rather than punishing inappropriate speech after the fact. Common examples of prior restraints on speech are the necessity to get a permit before speaking and movie censorship before a film release. Prior restraints are presumptively unconstitutional; the preference is to allow the speech and then punish it if necessary. This presumption may be overcome if the following elements are present:

1. Unprotected Speech: If the speech that is being restrained is clearly dangerous or unprotected, such as child pornography, prior restraint is usually allowed.

2. Important Governmental Interest: If the prior restraint serves an important governmental interest, it will usually be held enforceable. Examples of justified prior restraint include classified military information the disclosure of which raises significant safety or security concerns, or prohibiting speech expression urging sedition or terrorist activities.

3. Not Vague or Overbroad: As elsewhere, the language of a valid prior restraint law must be narrowly drawn and definite. Statutes generally prohibiting vagrants, "agitating speech," "annoying unwelcome speech," or "loitering" especially where police officers have absolute discretion in determining if there was a violation are examples of overbreadth.

> **MBE Tip:** "Vagueness or overbreadth" is a common MBE answer. Restricting a large category of speech does not make a restraint necessarily overbroad, nor does restricting a general type of speech make it vague. Generally, vagueness and overbreadth arguments fail.

4. Reasonable Notice: Reasonable notice of the prior restraint must be given.

5. Uniformly Applied: The prior restraint must be uniformly applied.

6. Prompt Judicial Review / Burden on Censor: Upon denial of a permit to speak, prompt judicial review is allowed. The burden of proof is on the government censor to show either an important governmental interest, or that the speech is unprotected.

G. Nonverbal or Symbolic Conduct as Speech

Speech is not always mere words or writings. Non-verbal expressions may qualify. Other means of idea expression, such as display conduct, may qualify.

1. Political Conduct as Speech: Burning an American flag, defacing an effigy, and tearing up a draft card are examples of political conduct treated as protected speech. In general, political conduct is afforded the same degree of protection as political speech, but the test is more complex.

2. Test: A regulation of symbolic speech must be (1) otherwise within the constitutional power of the government (*i.e.*, the government has the power to create and regulate a draft), (2) in furtherance of an important or substantial government interest, (3) furthering a government interest unrelated to the suppression of free expression, and (4) creating incidental restriction on First Amendment freedoms no greater than is essential to the suppression of free expression. *U.S. v. O'Brien* (1968). Thus, the government must show any prohibition is "necessary to promote a compelling governmental interest."

3. Commercial Conduct as Speech: Wearing a sandwich board or dressing up as a giant stuffed animal and parading around a street corner to lure customers into a used car lot are examples of commercial conduct as speech. Any law prohibiting such commercial conduct must promote a "substantial governmental interest" and the regulation must "directly advance" such interest.

H. Loyalty Oaths

Loyalty oaths as a precondition to public employment, such as "I swear under penalty of perjury that I am not a communist," or mandatory public school flag salutes by students, are invalid. Exceptions include an oath to support and uphold the Constitution and oppose the violent or unconstitutional overthrow of the government. The key is that the loyalty oath may not be vague or overbroad and may only consist of promises to refrain from actions.

MBE Tip: Loyalty oaths are an example of where the government may not compel a particular kind of speech. While rare, look for this type of issue in a free speech context.

I. Freedom of Association

Freedom of association is different from the right to assemble. It is not explicitly protected by the words of the Constitution but is an unquestionable right that is implied by other language and supported by Supreme Court case law.

1. Group Membership: Membership in a group cannot be punished (such as denial of public employment), unless the group advocates unlawfulness (such as the violent overthrow of the government), the member is a knowing and active member, and the member has specific intent to further unlawful behavior and activities. An example is communist party membership. Organizations may be compelled to disclose their membership lists only if the government can show clear illegal activities.

2. Not Absolute: Like any constitutionally protected freedom, the freedom of association is subject to some restrictions, however those restrictions are subject to the strict scrutiny standard of review. Any restrictions will be upheld only if they **CUL**:

    a. **C**ompelling State Interest justification;

    b. **U**nrelated to the Suppression of Ideas; and are the

    c. **L**east Restrictive Means of protecting the intellectual interest involved.

J. Bar Admission Constitutional Related Issues

State bar associations can set reasonable admission character and fitness requirements. Past membership in the Communist Party does not necessarily indicate a lack of character and fitness sufficient to disqualify a bar applicant but must be disclosed. Still, a state has the right to inquire into membership in subversive organizations. Requiring in-state residency by a state bar is a violation of the Privileges and Immunities Clause. However, prior felonies or unpaid child support may be constitutionally permissible grounds for denial of admission.

STOP! Go to page 233 and work Learning Questions 51 to 54.

XIV. FINAL CHAPTER REVIEW INSTRUCTIONS

1. Completing the Chapter: Now that you have completed your study of the chapter's substantive text and the related Learning Questions, you need to button up constitutional law. This includes working all of the subject's practice questions.

2. Preparing Your Own Magic Memory Outline®: This is helpful to your MBE success. The book paper outline works but consider purchasing our software template for your creation process. Do not underestimate the learning and memory effectiveness derived from condensing the text chapter into succinct summaries using your own words. This important exercise is covered in much more detail in the introduction and on the downloaded software.

a. Summarize Knowledge: You need to prepare an outline of the chapter in your own words. An example is at page 5-209. The words in the outline correspond to the bold headings in the text.

b. Capture the Essence: Your job is to summarize the substance of the text by capturing the essence of the rule. Enter summarized wording to prepare your own outlines. Use the text coverage to craft your own tight, concise, but comprehensive statements of the law.

c. Boilerplate Rule Statements: Our related MEE volume at 11-467 contains primary issue statements that are helpful in both outline creation and MEE answer boilerplate language rule statements. Take pride in your skills as an author; your Magic Memory Outlines should be the finest written document you have ever created.

d. Focus: Focus your attention and wording on the required technical elements necessary to prove the relevant legal principles. Look for fine-line distinctions. Integrate any helpful "learning question" information into your outline.

3. Memorize Outline: After you have completed your own Magic Memory Outline® for the whole chapter, read it over carefully once or twice. Refer back to your outlines in quick reads during your preparation period.

4. Work Old Questions: The next step is to work all the regular questions in this chapter beginning at page 5-234. These vary in degree of difficulty, but the ones toward the end tend to concentrate on the more difficult fact patterns and issues. Date and put an X through their numbers as you work each question. Use the Question Map for cross-reference to the textual coverage so you can work on your weak topics. If you use the software, you can click on the questions under the subject and topic you have just studied.

a. Question Details: It is usually worthwhile to review the explanatory answer rationales, as they reinforce the relevant principles of law. If you are still unsure of the controlling rule, refer back to the related portion of the text. This will help you to appreciate the fine-line distinctions on which the MBE constitutional law questions frequently turn.

b. Do a Few Questions at a Time: Work the final chapter practice questions in sequence. Make sure you stop after no more than a few to check the answer rationales. Do this frequently so that the facts of the individual question are still in active memory.

c. Mask Down: Lay a mask over the answer rationales. Mask the answers for the questions to be worked. Pull the mask screen down to expose that question's answer rationale. Do not look down at future answers until after you work the relevant question. Test yourself.

d. Work Them All: We have tried to pick questions from subjects and issues with an average or higher probability of reappearing on the MBE. Work as may as you can, but at least read all of the questions in our book and ponder their answer rationales. Every question and answer has some marginal learning and/or reinforcement value. Many of the actual MBE questions are very similar to the ones in your Rigos UBE Review Series review books.

e. Learn from Mistakes: The objective is to learn from your mistakes by reviewing the explanatory rationales while you still remember the factual and legal details of the question. It is good to miss a few; this will help you become familiar with the MBE fine-line distinctions. The bar examiners' use of distracters, tricks, and red herrings frequently reoccurs.

f. Flag Errors: Put a red star in the margin of the book alongside every question you missed. Missed questions should be worked again the day right before the MBE so that you do not make the same mistakes on the exam.

5. Take the Practice Exam: You can order two optional full simulated MBE exam sets that provide a helpful assessment. It contains 200 questions in random order broken down into two three-hour groups of 100 each. While some practice exam questions in your text are intentionally easier or more difficult and complex than the MBE, both parts of the Final Exam have approximately the same overall difficulty as the actual MBE questions.

6. Make Your Own Exam: The optional UBE Review Series software allows you to pick 5, 10, 20, or 100 questions at random from all seven MBE subjects. This is an important feature because you must become intellectually comfortable with all the different subjects. If you are not an early riser and/or get going slowly when you first get up, try working 10 or 20 questions using the "Make Your Own Exam" software the first thing every morning.

7. Update Your Magic Memory Outline®: The fine-line distinctions in the question and answer rationales will improve your understanding of how the MBE tests the law. Consider updating your Magic Memory Outline® while the question testing environment is still fresh in your mind.

8. Essays: Candidates in jurisdictions that administer the Multistate Essay Exam should refer to the *Rigos UBE Review Series Multistate Essay Exam Review (MEE)* for further depth and practice essay questions. That volume contains sample MEE constitutional law essay questions and answers in the three NCBE styles that relate to this chapter coverage.

9. Performance Questions: Candidates in jurisdictions that administer the Multistate Performance Exam should refer to the *Rigos UBE Review Series Multistate Performance Test (MPT) Review* for practice performance task questions.

10. Next Chapter: It is now time to go to the beginning of the next subject in your review. Begin by previewing the chapter. Scan the topical coverage and major issues.

Magic Memory Outlines®

> **MBE Tip:** This Magic Memory Outline® is intended to be the platform upon which you create your own outline. Capture the essence and concentrate on using streamlined wording.

I. INTRODUCTION

A. Bar Exam Focus Generally – *Federal Courts authority and requirements*................

1. Constitutional Law Testing – *Federal Courts Authority (4 questions), Separation of Powers (6 questions), Federalism (5 questions), First Amendment (6 questions), Individual Rights (6 questions)*................

2. Source of Questions – *State Court., Constitution, Congress, Executive branch* ..

3. Ambiguity – *uncertain constitutional tests or doctrine unlikely to be tested* ....

B. Checklist Approach – *Best sequence of approach is usually*................

1. Who is Acting – *Congress, State, or individual acting*................

2. Identify Individual Rights or Subject Matter Involved – *category of regulation*................

3. Test Applicable – *Strict, intermediate, or rational basis scrutiny*................

4. Eliminate Wrong Legal Standards – *Legislative power or individual rights*........

5. Be Aware of Subtle Differences – *Tests, level of scrutiny, constitution provision*

II. FEDERAL COURTS' AUTHORITY – ORGANIZATION

A. Article III Courts – *Federal cases and controversies, diversity, admiralty*................

1. Supreme Court – *Protected by Constitution, other courts by Congress*................

2. Article III Judges – *Appointed by President, life tenure, salary protection* ....

B. Article I Courts – *Congress may create other courts (tax, military, etc.)*................

III. FEDERAL COURTS' AUTHORITY – FEDERAL JUDICIAL REVIEW

A. Supreme Court Original Jurisdiction – ***PACS*** – *Public, Ambassador, Consuls, or State*

B. Appellate Jurisdiction – Supreme Court – *Constitutional equal protection*................

1. *Writ of Certiorari* – Discretionary – *Fed. Cts. of Appeal or constitution question* ....

2. Appeal – Mandatory – *Final judgment of federal district court*................

C. Federal Court Jurisdiction – District Court ....

1. Federal Question – *Arising under federal statute, treaty, or constitution* ....

2. Diversity Jurisdiction – At least *$75,000 and complete citizen diversity* ....

3. Supplemental Jurisdiction – *part of same case or controversy*................

D. Judicial Restraint – Justiciability – *actual "cases and controversies" required*........

XIII. FIRST AMENDMENT RIGHTS – FREEDOM OF EXPRESSION

RIGOS UBE REVIEW SERIES

UNIFORM MULTISTATE BAR EXAM (MBE) REVIEW

CHAPTER 5

CONSTITUTIONAL LAW

Question Distribution Map

> **MBE Tip:** Numbers immediately following the topic are the related chapter question numbers. The **boldface** numbers preceded by "F" are the final exam question numbers. For example, for the topic "II. A. Article III Courts" below, questions 1, 82, and 97 are in the chapter questions on pages 5-227, 5-240, and 5-243, respectively. Question **F129** is from one of our final exams.

IX. INDIVIDUAL RIGHTS – EQUAL PROTECTION

X. INDIVIDUAL RIGHTS – DUE PROCESS – 64, 75, 77, 85, 87, 154, 158, 184

MEE Candidates: Please refer to the *Rigos UBE Review Series Multistate Essay Exam (MEE) Review* for practice essay questions and sample answers covering constitutional law.

Learning Questions

1. Which of the following is not within the jurisdiction of the Federal Courts?
   (A) Suits between two states.
   (B) Admiralty suits.
   (C) Suits between one state and the citizen of another state.
   (D) Suits against the United States.

2. Which of the following will not be reviewed by the U.S. Supreme Court?
   (A) A California Supreme Court decision in a Quiet Title action.
   (B) A Michigan Supreme Court decision interpreting the federal Clean Air Act.
   (C) A decision of the Ninth Circuit interpreting Texas State Law.
   (D) A decision of the Ninth Circuit interpreting state minimum wage regulations.

3. A P's prayer for injunctive relief to stop oil drilling on a federal wildlife reserve is heard in federal court by a three-judge panel. Relief is denied. What will be the result of an appeal to the Supreme Court?
   (A) Certiorari will be granted because environmental protection of federal lands is a federal issue.
   (B) Certiorari will be denied because the docket is overloaded with more pressing issues.
   (C) Appeal will be granted because it is mandatory.
   (D) Appeal will be denied because the Supreme Court does not have jurisdiction.

4. A labor union learns that one of its members, a law professor, was wrongfully discharged by the law school. Does the union have standing to file suit?
   (A) Yes, because the close relationship between union and member creates third-party standing.
   (B) Yes, because when injury occurs to a member of an organization, direct injury to the organization is imputed.
   (C) No, because there is no concurrent injury to the union.
   (D) No, because third-party standing is not generally allowed.

5. If a citizen files a suit in federal court claiming that his state's governor has not balanced the state budget, what result?
   (A) The case will be removed to state court.
   (B) The case will be dismissed because there is no "citizen standing" for generalized grievances.
   (C) The case will be heard only if the citizen can demonstrate that he has suffered some loss as a result of the governor's malfeasance.
   (D) The case will be dismissed because the governor has immunity.

6. The U.S. Forestry Department approves the sale of federally owned forest lands to a logging company. A taxpayer files suit in federal court to stop the sale. What is the likely outcome?
   (A) The case will be dismissed because the injury is not redressable.
   (B) The case will be dismissed because the P has no standing.
   (C) The case will be heard because a challenge to an expenditure enacted under the tax/spend power is an exception to the general preclusion of taxpayer standing.
   (D) The case will be dismissed unless the P can prove damages.

7. A state enacts a law prohibiting all abortions, except to save the life of the mother. A pregnant woman files suit to invalidate the law. By the time the case reaches the Supreme Court, she has

traveled to another state to have the abortion. The respondent argues that the case is moot. Will the case be allowed to continue?

(A) Yes, because there may still monetary damages at issue.
(B) No, because the respondent is correct, the case is moot.
(C) No, because the Supreme Court does not engage in a mootness inquiry.
(D) Yes, because the injury in question was one capable of repetition, yet presently evading review.

8. Which of the following is not an example of a political question?
(A) Whether the U.S. Army should be restructured to eliminate racial disparities.
(B) Whether the President should be impeached.
(C) Whether a legislative district is properly apportioned.
(D) Whether the Guarantee Clause prohibits the use of the electoral college system.

9. "Abstention" refers to
(A) When federal courts delay hearing a case in which an unsettled issue of state law exists.
(B) When federal courts refrain from hearing a case which is not ripe.
(C) When state courts refrain from hearing an issue of federal law.
(D) When federal courts refrain from deciding an issue upon motion for summary judgment.

10. If Congress were to outlaw the growing of wheat over a certain quantity by individual farmers even if the wheat is for the farmer's personal use or consumption only, what is the likely source for that power?
(A) Commerce Clause.
(B) Necessary and Proper Clause.
(C) Exclusive Legislation Clause.
(D) General Welfare Clause.

11. Which of the following is a proper exercise of Congress' power to regulate interstate commerce?

(A) Providing a Federal civil cause of action for victims of gender-based violence.
(B) Criminalizing the possession of firearms on state public school property.
(C) Outlawing racial discrimination rental by hotels not located near any interstate highway.
(D) Prohibiting a person from driving over 55 miles per hour.

12. Which is a proper delegation of Congress' legislative authority?
(A) Granting authority to the Department of Transportation to promulgate regulations, but reserving a legislative "veto" on the regulations.
(B) Granting authority to the president to designate certain acts as criminal and to promulgate an appropriate penalty.
(C) Granting authority to the Supreme Court to promulgate rules of evidence for use by the Federal Judiciary.
(D) Granting authority to the president to reject only certain portions of a bill.

13. Which of the following is not a proper exercise of state taxing authority?
(A) State property tax on federal property.
(B) State income tax on federal employees.
(C) State tax on goods manufactured in a neighboring state.
(D) State tax on all goods warehoused in the state.

14. Congress passes a law establishing that arsenic in water must be less than 50 parts per billion. Which of the following subsequent state laws would not be effective?
(A) A law establishing maximum arsenic in water at 100 parts per billion.
(B) A law establishing maximum arsenic in water at 10 parts per billion.
(C) Any law regulating arsenic in the water.
(D) A law establishing maximum lead in water at 100 parts per billion.

15. Congress does not have the power to do which one of the following?
- (A) Require employers to limit the workweek to 40 hours.
- (B) Prohibit gender discrimination in places of public accommodation.
- (C) Change the command structure of the Coast Guard.
- (D) Compel the executive branch of a state to enforce a federal jobs program.

16. Which of the following categories is not an enumerated power of Congress subject to rational basis scrutiny?
- (A) Admiralty and Maritime.
- (B) Trademarks.
- (C) Laws of the District if Columbia.
- (D) Energy production.

17. Congress appropriates $4 billion for domestic abuse prevention programs, to be distributed only to states that enact tougher penalties for perpetrators of domestic violence. Is Congress' action valid?
- (A) Yes, because it is an appropriate exercise of its power under the Commerce Clause.
- (B) Yes, because Congress may attach conditions to its spending.
- (C) No, if such action was rejected and invalidated by the President.
- (D) No, the 10th Amendment prohibits Congress from compelling states to enforce a federal program.

18. For the president to enter into a treaty with a foreign country, he must obtain:
- (A) The advice and consent of Congress.
- (B) 2/3rds consent of the Senate.
- (C) 3/4ths consent of the Senate.
- (D) An executive agreement.

19. A state enacts a law allowing the licensed hunting of sporting game in the federal Greenboughs National Park, which is entirely within its state borders. Is the law valid?
- (A) No, because the law infringes on Congress' power under the Property Clause.
- (B) No, because the law exceeds state power under the Dormant Commerce Clause.
- (C) Yes, because minor state intrusion on federal land is permissible if its boundaries are entirely within that state.
- (D) Yes, because wildlife is not a fixture and therefore the law does not affect the land directly.

20. Congress has occupied the field of nuclear safety. It passes a law setting the maximum permissible radiation output of a nuclear generator as 100 millirads per day. The State of Syracuse enacts a law establishing a maximum output of 50 millirads per day. What result?
- (A) The state law is valid because it exceeds the federal standard.
- (B) The state law is valid because states have general police powers.
- (C) The state law is invalid.
- (D) The state law is valid because of the vital state interests involved.

21. Which of the following is not a "state action" for the purpose of a constitutional violation?
- (A) A court ruling upholding a privately negotiated restrictive covenant in a deed that prohibits selling the property to certain racial groups.
- (B) A private tenant of a state-owned office building that refuses to hire members of a certain racial group.
- (C) A private citizen conducts a search of a tenant's room at the behest of police.
- (D) A state licensed liquor store that refuses to hire members of a certain racial group.

22. The State of Hamilton bans the slaughter of beef within its borders. As a result, the price of kosher beef increases by a factor of two, but the price of non-kosher beef stays the same. Which argument is most likely to prevail within the context of an equal protection violation claim?
- (A) The law is facially discriminatory.

(B) The law was intended to discriminate against the Jewish community.

(C) The law will be subject to rational basis scrutiny.

(D) The State has a compelling governmental interest in preventing the consumption of beef.

23. Which of the following is a "non-suspect" class requiring only a rational basis level of scrutiny?

(A) Race.

(B) Citizenship.

(C) Disability.

(D) National Origin.

24. Which of the following is a permissible state action?

(A) A law that gives illegitimate children the same inheritance rights as legitimate children.

(B) A law that excludes a foreign national from attendance at state universities.

(C) A law that limits the rights of Pakistanis to own real property.

(D) A law that limits the voting rights of members of a certain racial group.

25. The State of Columbus passes a law giving government job preference to members of a certain racial group. If the state is sued for racial discrimination, what must the state prove?

(A) The law is a quota to bring employment levels of the racial group to reflect their proportion within the population.

(B) The law is narrowly tailored to remedy past discrimination.

(C) The group continues to experience daily discrimination.

(D) The group is a racial minority recognized by the EEOC.

26. Anystate, USA passes a law requiring that anyone who moves into the state be financially self-sufficient. What is the proper analysis that will be used by the court?

(A) Any restrictions on travel are unconstitutional.

(B) The law must be rationally related to a legitimate governmental interest.

(C) The law must be narrowly tailored to achieve a compelling governmental interest.

(D) The law must be substantially related to an important governmental purpose.

27. A peremptory challenge of a potential juror on the basis of gender in a criminal case

(A) Is unconstitutional and prohibited.

(B) Must be proven by the party making the challenge to have a rational basis.

(C) Must be proven by the party making the challenge to serve a compelling interest.

(D) May be made only by the D.

28. In which of the following situations is a fundamental right violated?

(A) The State of Washington prohibits entering the state by swimming across the Columbia River.

(B) A state legislature redraws a Congressional District boundary to reflect the growth in population.

(C) A state legislature requires a certain amount of time residing in the state before a student may get reduced state university tuition.

(D) A state legislature passes a law that states a person may not have a child without attending a state approved child-care class.

29. Which of the following does not involve a fundamental right?

(A) The purchase of contraceptives by minors.

(B) Educating one's child at home or at a private school.

(C) Getting married without a license.

(D) A father's right to live with his child.

30. If a right is not fundamental, a law infringing upon it is

(A) Presumed invalid and must be rationally related to a legitimate governmental interest.

(B) Presumed valid and must forward a compelling governmental interest.

(C) Presumed valid and must be rationally related to a legitimate governmental interest.

(D) Presumed valid but there must be no less intrusive means available to achieve the state's goal.

31. Procedural due process is not required when the state deprives a person of

(A) Welfare benefits.

(B) Public education.

(C) Employment.

(D) The right to engage in gainful employment.

32. Which of these is not a factor in the *Mathews v. Eldridge* balancing test?

(A) Risk of erroneous deprivation.

(B) Cost to government.

(C) Timing of due process.

(D) Administrative burden.

33. A municipal ordinance provides that no one may vote without showing proof of age. A voter challenges the ordinance. The ordinance will likely be

(A) Subjected to strict scrutiny and upheld.

(B) Subjected to rational basis scrutiny and upheld.

(C) Subjected to strict scrutiny and overturned.

(D) Subjected to rational basis scrutiny and overturned.

34. Harbor State may not prohibit newly-hired college professors from leaving the state for 180 days because

(A) It is an unconstitutional restriction on the right to education.

(B) It is an unconstitutional restriction on the right to interstate travel.

(C) Such a rule has no rational relationship to a legitimate government interest.

(D) It is an equal protection violation.

35. Which of the following describes a fundamental right?

(A) The right of a terminally ill person to receive a painless lethal dose of morphine.

(B) The right of the wife of a man in an unrecoverable coma to order the withdrawal of artificial life support.

(C) The right of a mentally competent adult to refuse intravenous nutrition and breathing assistance, when such methods may save his life.

(D) The right of parents of a mentally competent adult to terminate intravenous nutrition and breathing assistance, when such methods may save his life.

36. All but which of the following are acceptable restrictions on the fundamental right to marry?

(A) Requiring proof of marriage before allowing a spouse to be covered by the medical plan of a state employee.

(B) Requiring parties who are divorced to wait 6 months before remarrying.

(C) Requiring issue of a license if parties intend the marriage to be legally recognized.

(D) Requiring parental consent below a certain age.

37. A state agency is accused of racial discrimination regarding the right to vote. A challenge to the action would properly be brought under the

(A) 14th Amendment.

(B) 15th Amendment.

(C) 10th Amendment.

(D) 16th Amendment.

38. Which of the following is most likely the basis for a successful 14th Amendment Privileges or Immunities Clause challenge?

(A) A citizen of State A moves to State B but is refused employment at the office of the Secretary of State because of a past felony conviction for fraud.

(B) A business entity incorporated in State A is refused a license to operate in State B because State B wants an in-state corporation to retain its monopoly.

(C) A citizen of State A is refused entry to the federal courthouse.

(D) A citizen of Country Y is refused employment in State A because he is not an in-state resident.

39. "Inverse condemnation" is a principle related to the law of

(A) Takings.

(B) Bills of attainder.

(C) Free exercise.

(D) 14th Amendment privileges or immunities.

40. The first step in analyzing a freedom of religion issue is identifying

(A) Whether there is excessive government entanglement.

(B) Whether the law pertains to a religious belief or conduct stemming from the belief.

(C) Whether the law pertains to "free exercise" or "establishment."

(D) The level of scrutiny to be applied.

41. State Q enacts a law restricting the use of 27 kinds of food additives considered dangerous. One such additive is used in preserving kosher meats. Citizen R challenges the law as a burden on his free religious exercise. The law will likely be upheld if

(A) There are no less restrictive means available to achieve the desired end.

(B) It is generally applicable and not intentional discrimination.

(C) It is selectively enforced.

(D) There is no evidence that one religion is preferred over another.

42. Which of the following is not an example of excessive government entanglement in religion?

(A) Allowing a church to veto the issuance of a liquor license.

(B) Allowing a church to install a nativity scene in a city building.

(C) Government aid given solely to religious private elementary schools.

(D) A law requiring businesses to be closed on Sundays.

43. Pursuant to its Commerce Clause power, Congress passes a law requiring that all federal public contracts be verified by a separate oversight agency. As a result, certain executory public contracts are suspended. The law is likely

(A) Valid, because only private, not public, contracts are subject to the Contracts Clause.

(B) Valid, because the federal government contracts are not subject to the Contracts Clause.

(C) Invalid, because there is substantial interference with public contracts without a significant public need.

(D) Invalid, because the federal government has no broad police power.

44. A law in State M prohibits "speaking about lewd topics within 100 feet of a schoolyard." If challenged, this law will likely be

(A) Upheld, because it leaves open alternative channels of communication.

(B) Upheld, because it is narrowly tailored to achieve a significant government interest.

(C) Invalidated, because the law is unconstitutionally vague.

(D) Invalidated, because the law is unconstitutionally overbroad.

45. The Chaplin County Council established a local authority to organize, oversee, and approve plans for public assemblies and holiday parades. The enabling act authorized a county overseer to "issue appropriate permits to acceptable public and private groups who wish to march and speak." A local group advocating the legalization of marijuana use applies for a permit to march and speak in an upcoming Veteran's Day parade. The permit is denied. Upon challenge, what result?

(A) The decision will be affirmed, because the group's position is inappropriate and therefore the commissioner acted within his discretion.

(B) The decision will be affirmed, because the group advocates unlawful behavior.

(C) The decision will be reversed, because the enabling act is overbroad.

(D) The decision will be reversed and the statute invalidated, because it allows the commissioner unfettered discretion.

46. Content neutral restrictions on speech in a public forum must not be facially invalid and must

(A) Be narrowly tailored to achieve a significant government interest.

(B) Bear a rational relationship to a legitimate government interest.

(C) Be viewpoint and subject matter neutral.

(D) Be narrowly tailored to achieve a significant government interest and leave open alternative channels of communication.

47. Defamatory speech is not protected by the First Amendment. What must a public official show to prevail in a defamation case?

(A) Falsity of the statement and negligence by the D.

(B) Falsity of the statement and knowledge of falsity or reckless disregard for the truth by the D.

(C) Damages are presumed and the burden is on the D to show the truth of the statement.

(D) Reckless disregard of the truth by the D.

48. Which of the following is an example of unprotected speech?

(A) A lecture advocating the legalization of prostitution.

(B) A commercial advertisement for a car that suggests its owner will be considered more sexually attractive.

(C) A man shouting "The government wants to jail you, riot, riot!" into a megaphone at a public rally about racial discrimination.

(D) A magazine depicting graphic sexual acts, found in the owner's home.

49. State police set up and execute a successful "sting" operation. Their objective was to seize shipments of allegedly obscene material to block their public distribution. Before the material was destroyed, the distributors challenged the police action and demand the return of the material. Was the police seizure action proper?

(A) No, because the seizure was not preceded by a full adversary hearing.

(B) Yes, because obscene material is unprotected speech.

(C) Yes, because police are capable of ascertaining the community standards to judge obscenity.

(D) No, because non-broadcast printed material is protected speech, even if it is considered obscene.

50. A law requiring newspapers to give equal time to all political candidates is likely

(A) Valid, if the information is not in the public domain.

(B) Valid, because "equal time" requirements do not infringe on the freedom of the press to report the news.

(C) Invalid, because only broadcast entities may be subject to equal time requirements.

(D) Invalid, because political speech is protected.

51. A prior restraint on speech is

(A) Presumed unconstitutional, but the presumption can be overcome.

(B) Presumed constitutional unless demonstrated to burden protected speech.

(C) *Per se* unconstitutional.

(D) *Per se* constitutional.

52. Under the 1st Amendment, burning a voter registration card is likely

(A) Unprotected, because it is not speech.

(B) Protected.

(C) Unprotected, because it is intentional destruction of an important government document.

(D) Unprotected, if the government can demonstrate a rational basis for prohibiting their destruction.

53. A loyalty oath as a precondition to public employment is

(A) Always unconstitutional.

(B) Constitutional if it is an oath to oppose the violent overthrow of the government.

(C) Constitutional only if it does not involve religious language.

(D) Always constitutional.

54. Membership in a group can be punished if:

(A) The group advocates unlawfulness.

(B) The member is a knowing and active member.

(C) The group advocates unlawfulness, the member is a knowing and active member, and the member has specific intent to further unlawful behavior.

(D) The member has specific intent to disseminate knowledge of the group's activities to others.

REGULAR QUESTIONS

55. HardTime Inc., a private corporation, owns and operates a proprietary prison in the State of South Carobama. The State Prison System needed to outsource some of the overflow of the prison population, due to the increase in jail penalties for drug crimes. HardTime gets $85 per inmate, per day. Terry McNichols is being kept in solitary confinement costing HardTime $175 per day because the warden is afraid that Terry will be confused with another criminal, and the other inmates will harm Terry. Terry wants to sue to make HardTime move him back into the general population of the prison. The HardTime rules allow the warden complete discretion, but Terry wants to claim that his liberty is infringed. In a suit against South Carobama and HardTime, will HardTime be considered a State Actor?

(A) No, because it is private corporation.

(B) No, because South Carobama does not excessively regulate HardTime.

(C) Yes, because running prisons is deemed to be a public function.

(D) Yes, because the contract encourages cost cutting.

56. The Evergreen State University charges resident students $1,200 per year, and nonresident students $4,800 per year in tuition. The University considers a student a nonresident if the student's primary residence was outside the state at any time during the previous school year.

Imma Grant transferred from Sunshine State University to Evergreen as a junior. She paid nonresident tuition that year. She filed a declaratory judgment action against the Evergreen Registrar to have her considered a resident and asked for no money damages. Fourteen groups filed amicus briefs in support of changing Evergreen's protectionist regulation. Now that she is a senior, and spent all of her last year within Evergreen, she is considered a resident student. The federal court should

(A) Dismiss the suit as moot.

(B) Dismiss the suit, because she lacked standing to sue initially.

(C) Hear the case if it appears that Ms. Grant is diligently prosecuting.

(D) Hear the case due to the amicus interests.

57. T.J. Simpson, an African American man, was a defendant in a civil suit represented by Johnny Tortrun, an African American attorney. Johnny used three peremptory challenges to strike individuals from the jury pool. Johnny struck Barney, an African American man, because of his race. Barney was the only African American on the panel. Johnny struck Albert because he was Catholic. The third strike was against Mark, because Mark was a white racist. Which of these is/are likely unconstitutional peremptory strike(s)?

(A) None, because a defense attorney is not a state actor.

(B) Barney

(C) Albert.

(D) Mark.

58. Evergreen State requires all persons between the ages of 6 and 16 who reside in the state to attend a state accredited elementary or secondary school. The state school system is funded by local property taxes. The accreditation committee is funded by the state's education allotment of the general fund. St. Pious is a private school run by the Catholic Church and fully accredited by the State. Catherine, a 15-year-old, was suspended from St. Pious for refusing to say the Lord's Prayer during the morning announcements and prayer time. Catherine's parents sue St. Pious on her behalf, claiming her First Amendment

rights were violated. In the suit, St. Pious will

(A) Win, because the parents have no standing.
(B) Lose, because Catherine may not be forced to speak.
(C) Win, because there is no state action.
(D) Win, because the school has a compelling interest in her praying.

59. State has had a criminal statute making it illegal to knowingly interfere with the operation of government with malicious intent. Criminal is a computer hacker, who shut down the government's website by infecting it with a virus. The virus entered the electronic mail of users and mailed itself to every e-mail address listed in each user's address book every two hours. The website was crippled for the last week of January. The state passed a law in February clarifying that knowingly infecting the state's internet server with a computer virus met the definition of interference in the statute. During the criminal trial against Criminal, the state asked for a jury instruction based on the statutory computer virus clarification. The defense objects to the requested instruction. How should the state court judge rule?

(A) Reject the instruction, based on *ex post facto.*
(B) Reject the instruction as a violation of due process.
(C) Admit the instruction, because the law was passed before the prosecution was initiated.
(D) Admit the instruction, as a bill of attainder.

60. The National Collegiate Athletic Association (NCAA) is a voluntary association of public and private universities. The NCAA adopted rules governing member institutions' recruiting, admissions, academic eligibility, and financial aid standards for student athletes. Member schools agree contractually to the discipline of NCAA, but may withdraw from the association at will. The NCAA Policing Committee imposed sanctions on Coach N. Tice, the head football coach for Farm State

University. The NCAA scheduled a backroom hearing for Farm State, at which it would impose further sanctions if the university did not fire Coach Tice. Farm State fired Coach Tice. Tice sued the NCAA claiming that the backroom committee violated his rights. Which constitutional right will a court analyze?

(A) None, because NCAA is not a state actor.
(B) Due Process, because Tice had no notice.
(C) Due Process, because Tice had no opportunity to be heard.
(D) None, because Tice contracted away his constitutional rights.

61. Congress passed the Davis Energy Act, which requires commercial energy users to reduce their consumption by a specified percentage, and authorizes the president to set that percentage by executive order. The Act delineates standards for determining the percentage. The provision that allows the president to set the exact amount is probably

(A) Constitutional, because it creates a limited administrative power to implement the statute.
(B) Unconstitutional, because it delegates legislative power.
(C) Constitutional, because the president has inherent power to execute laws.
(D) Unconstitutional, because it violates Due Process.

62. Bob, a Pakistani American, was fired from New Yorsey State University the day after unknown terrorists ran a hotdog cart into the campus Starcups Coffee Shop. Bob claimed the University fired him only because of his heritage. He filed a suit in federal court against his supervisor, Dean Neechurk, pleading for reinstatement and back pay. Bob used a federal statute that created a private civil action for the violation of civil rights if the D acted "under color of state law" to deny him "equal protection under the law." Dean Neechurk filed for summary judgment claiming the statute was invalid. The court will take what action on the motion?

(A) Grant it, because the 11th Amendment bars the suit.

(B) Grant it, because there is no substantial effect on commerce.

(C) Deny it, if due process was denied.

(D) Deny it, because Congress validly passed the statute.

63. North Wisconsin State legislature banned the importation of milk from other states to avoid harm to its citizens by adulterated milk. The U.S. Supreme Court struck down the North Wisconsin law as unconstitutional. The president, however, is a connoisseur of cheese and especially likes North Wisconsin's domestic sharp cheddar. While speaking to the North Wisconsin governor about the problem, he learns that milk is the major ingredient in cheese. The president twists arms on the hill and gets Congress to pass a new law forbidding the importation of milk into North Wisconsin. Which of the following best describes the constitutionality of this federal statute?

(A) Constitutional, because federal government may legislate for the general welfare.

(B) Unconstitutional, because the Dormant Commerce Clause forbids it.

(C) Constitutional under the Commerce Clause.

(D) Unconstitutional, because the Supreme Court is the final authority for interpreting the Constitution.

64. Nebraskahoma passed a statute providing for the incarceration of any person with AIDS in a special state facility, regardless of whether that person has engaged in criminal activity. The incarceration occurs after a full, adversarial trial results in a judicial determination that the person suffers from AIDS. The statute also provides for an attorney for indigent persons, and an appeal as a matter of right. The statute is

(A) Unconstitutional, denial of due process.

(B) Unconstitutional, denial of right to a trial by jury.

(C) Constitutional, as a health and safety measure.

(D) Unconstitutional, denial of equal protection.

65. Stan is a certified public accountant in the State of Kansitaw. Stan specialized in debt adjusting until the state passed a law restricting the business to attorneys. Stan sues the Kansitaw Attorney General in state court to enjoin him from enforcing the new law claiming it violates his federal constitutional rights of due process and equal protection. Which answer best describes the burden in the case?

(A) Stan must show that the law serves no important government interest.

(B) Kansitaw must show that the law serves an important government interest.

(C) Kansitaw must show a rational relationship to the interest served by the law.

(D) Stan must show that the law serves no legitimate state interest.

66. Alablaintiff State Court entered a judgment for P, Mr. Gan, and against D, McDan's, for not disclosing to its customers that its french fries contained "animal flavoring." The jury awarded Mr. Gan $4,000 in damages (he ate a lot of french fries), and $4 million in punitive damages. Assuming no remitittur is granted, what is McDan's recourse?

(A) Pay $4,004,000, because the judgment is rational economic regulation.

(B) Appeal claiming punitive damages are so grossly excessive as to violate due process.

(C) No recourse. Jury awards are not reviewed under due process.

(D) Appeal, claiming a taking in violation of the constitution.

67. The State of Tropicana is composed of dozens of islands. State law criminalizes participating in an abortion procedure performed by anyone other than a licensed physician, but the New East Coast Journal of Medicine and the Association of American Medical People agree that a physician's assistant is qualified to perform the operation. Three fourths of the Tropicana population live on the main island. Candice is four weeks pregnant and wants an abortion. She is on state assistance. She lives on an island where there are no licensed physicians, only physician's assistants and midwives. It would cost a minimum of $125 to take a boat or plane round trip to the main island where there are many licensed physicians. She and her physician's assistant attack the constitutionality of the criminal statute, and in the alternative, they seek state assistance in getting Candice to the main island. The most likely outcome is that

- (A) The criminal statute is a facially unconstitutional violation of due process rights.
- (B) The statute violates the contracts clause with respect to the physician's assistant.
- (C) Not getting Candice to the main island violates due process and equal protection.
- (D) The criminal statute is a facially constitutional exercise of police power.

68. Trail State passes a law requiring state civil service employees to retire no later than their 65th birthdays. Congress passes a law in reaction forbidding employers from requiring anyone to retire prior to age 70, unless there is a compelling interest in a younger person performing the job. Cletus has worked for Trail for the past 50 years as a janitor in the state capital building. He is in great shape, and the staff likes his quick wit. Because of the state mandatory step raises, he earns almost as much as the Beaver University Football Coach. Trail will save $40,000 per year by hiring a new employee. Cletus, on his 65th birthday, files a complaint in federal court using the federal statute as protection from mandatory retirement. The Court will likely rule that

- (A) Cletus may continue working, because the Trail law violates equal protection.
- (B) Cletus must retire, because the state has a legitimate interest in saving money.
- (C) Cletus may continue working, because the federal law relates to the integral governmental function of operating a public building.

- (D) Cletus may continue working, because the federal law voids the inconsistent state law.

69. The Jellystone National Park is an exclusively federal jurisdiction. Federal law prohibits hunting wild animals in the park. Wherehouser hires Rutger and pays for his state-issued hunting license to shoot any spotted owls who try to leave Jellystone and inhabit Wherehouser's adjacent wooded property. Rutger is prosecuted for violating the federal law. What is the strongest argument for upholding the statute?

- (A) The law is necessary and proper for protecting federal property.
- (B) Hunting is a privilege, not a right, so due process is not affected.
- (C) Federal police power supersedes inconsistent state laws.
- (D) Animals crossing boundaries are in interstate commerce.

70. The State of Wazacomy passed a law requiring employers to hire only state "residents" to work on the State's new oil pipeline project. A "resident" under this statute is a person who has lived in the state for 20 of the last 24 months. Wazacomy will impose civil penalties against general contractors who hire nonresidents. Cal, who is a nonresident, challenges the statute's constitutionality. Cal's strongest argument is that the statute violates the

- (A) Privileges and Immunities Clause of Article IV.
- (B) Dormant Commerce Clause.
- (C) Equal protection clause.
- (D) *Ex post facto* clause.

71. Charles Dahmer is on trial in Gallows State Court for murder in the first degree. During jury selection, the prosecuting attorney uses peremptory challenges to eliminate three Catholics from the jury pool. The defense objects, but the judge grants the challenges. Dahmer's lawyer appeals claiming the peremptory challenges violate a Gallows State Court Rule and the Federal Constitution. The Gallows Supreme Court overturns the conviction. In the opinion, the State Court says that peremptory challenges violate the court rule and the Federal Constitution. The State appeals to the U.S. Supreme Court claiming State Court error. The U.S. Supreme Court will likely

(A) Accept review, because the Gallows Court misinterpreted the Constitution.

(B) Accept review to clarify that the U.S. Constitution does not protect religion in this manner.

(C) Deny review for lack of standing.

(D) Deny review, because the Gallows Court Rule itself is an adequate state ground.

72. An earthquake devastated northern Mexico and disrupted water, power, and civil services, including medical and police functions. The President of Mexico pleaded for U.S. involvement and because Congress was not in session over a holiday break, the President acted on his own. The President sent the 82nd Airborne from North Carolina and other units from Texas to assist in a humanitarian capacity. The Army Corps of Engineers dedicated 1,000 soldiers and $1 million in equipment to clear rubble and debris. Which alternative is true of the President's use of soldiers in Mexico?

(A) Unconstitutional, because the President cannot act without Congress delegating authority.

(B) Valid exercise of the President's power as Commander-in-Chief.

(C) Valid under the plenary powers of the President to use the Army for humanitarian purposes.

(D) Unconstitutional aid to foreign nation, because Congress was not involved.

73. Senator Watt, distinguished gentleman from New Dakota, determined that there should be a uniform law for fluorescent lights used in commercial buildings, and sponsored the Federal Lit Building Act, which was referred to in debate as the Dim Watt Act. Which constitutional provision could most easily be considered as the basis of the Act?

(A) Commerce Clause.

(B) Necessary and Proper Clause.

(C) 3rd Amendment.

(D) Federal Police Power.

74. The Republic of Lone Star, in the United States, passed a law authorizing the use of force and trespass to apprehend terrorists, and posted a $1,000 reward for each terrorist captured. John Ruger, a private citizen, breaks into Lin Bowden's house. John finds evidence of bomb manufacturing, and captures Lin in the home. Lone Star gave John a $1,000 check. Will John's actions be considered state action?

(A) No, because John is a private citizen.

(B) Yes, because there is state endorsement.

(C) No, because the 11th Amendment bars the suit.

(D) Yes, if John cashes the check.

75. Young was convicted of his third rape offense in 1989 and sentenced to 20 years in prison by Kansington State Court. The Kansington Legislature passed the Sexual Predator Act of 1990, which allowed for the "civil commitment" of persons found to be sexually violent predators. When he was being released early in 1995 for good behavior, Young was put on trial for being a sexually violent predator. He was given assigned counsel, and after a trial, the jury found him to be a sexually violent predator. He was civilly committed to the Kansington Rehabilitation Center. He is confined to his cell or cell unit most of the time. He participates in mandatory group counseling and individual counseling. In 2001, he filed a *habeas corpus* suit in federal court after being told that he was not close to being released. Many experts agree that sexually violent predators have no hope of recovery by the time they reach this level. The federal court will likely have him

(A) Remain, because the state has a compelling interest in treating him and protecting the community.

(B) Released, because it violates the due process clause.

(C) Released, because it violates the *ex post facto* clause.

(D) Released, because it violates double jeopardy.

76. Kennedy Middle School, a public school, allows groups to rent the gym and cafeteria after school hours and on weekends. Fearing a lawsuit, the school restricts the use of the school to groups with a non-religious purpose. The Great News Club applied for and was denied use of the cafeteria on Sundays. They offered to pay the usual fee, require parental consent from minors who attended, and clean up any juice and cookie spills. The school denied the request, because the Great News Club wanted to conduct religious activity on school grounds. Great News filed suit in federal court. The likely outcome based on federal constitutional issues would be that Great News

(A) Prevails, if the school is deemed a limited public forum.
(B) Prevails, because the school violated equal protection.
(C) Loses, because the school has a legitimate fear of lawsuits.
(D) Loses, because the school cannot get entangled with the club.

77. City of Brotherly Love passed a tough gun ordinance. The ordinance prohibits the private ownership of a long list of guns and related weapons that are "unreasonably dangerous." Under the ordinance, the owner may reside in the city and store the guns outside the city limits. The ordinance becomes effective in 90 days. Fourteen of the seventeen guns owned by Harry Dirt were made illegal under this ordinance. What is the best characterization of the city ordinance?

(A) Unconstitutional, as a violation of the Second Amendment.
(B) Unconstitutional, as a violation of Privileges of National Citizenship.
(C) Constitutional, as an exercise of the police power.
(D) Constitutional, as a proper exercise under Section 5 of the Fourteenth Amendment.

78. In response to growing concern about the use of airplanes in terrorist attacks on the government facilities, the President issued an executive order banning the exportation of flight training or flight simulation materials to a list of 50 countries. Congress had previously passed a law granting the Executive wide authority to restrict foreign trade, and gave standards for selecting methods of new restrictions. Big Fox, a Redmond State corporation, sells software games nationally and internationally. Big Fox had contracts to sell Plane Simulator software to retailers in 30 of the listed countries. All of these contracts are now expressly prohibited by the executive order. Which of the following statements best describes the order?

(A) The executive order is constitutional, because the President has inherent power to conduct foreign affairs.
(B) The executive order is constitutional, because Congress has plenary power to regulate commerce with foreign nations and authorized the President to issue such orders.
(C) The executive order is an unconstitutional violation of the Contracts clause.
(D) The executive order is unconstitutional because Big Fox has a property interest in the existing contracts.

79. The Dry State legislature is convinced that women mature at an earlier age than men and fight less frequently than men. Dry State passes a law lowering the drinking age for women to 18, but keeping the drinking age for men at 21. What best describes the constitutionality of the statute?

(A) Unconstitutional, unless the State shows a compelling state interest.
(B) Unconstitutional, unless the State shows the age minimum is rationally related to a legitimate state interest.
(C) Unconstitutional if the law is not substantially related to an important government interest.
(D) Unconstitutional if the law is not narrowly tailored.

80. The State of East Tennessee wanted to protect its citizens from lending institutions by passing an anti-usury statute. The law made 12% the highest interest rate legally permissible for in-state banks to lend at, with a small exception for credit cards. The interest rate jumped suddenly after the stock markets improved. The Federal Reserve raised rates, and banks followed suit. Soon, inflation began to occur. A Wall Avenue Journal article reported that no bank could make a mortgage loan for less than 15%. It came to the point in East Tennessee that only wealthy people could afford to buy real estate. Is the East Tennessee anti-usury statute constitutional?

(A) Yes, because the state acted properly to protect its citizens.
(B) Yes, because the law is not in an area specifically reserved to the federal government.
(C) No, because the law denies equal protection to less wealthy people.
(D) No, because it violates the negative implications doctrine.

81. Congress adopted a statute years ago, which provided for student aid at colleges and universities. A recent change requires colleges and universities that receive federal money to offer aid to students solely on the basis of need. Which is the best source of federal power authorizing the statute?

(A) Police power.
(B) Power to enforce Equal Protection.
(C) Power to tax and spend for the general welfare.
(D) Power to enforce Privileges and Immunities.

82. After conservatives gained eight seats in the Senate, Congress decided to take action against judges on the west coast. Citing the high percentage of cases from one circuit that have been overturned by the Supreme Court, Congress passes a law making changes to the Supreme Court and the Ninth Circuit. The U.S. Supreme Court will now sit six Justices in Washington, D.C., and three Justices in California to hear Ninth Circuit appeals. This provision will bypass the liberal judges in the Ninth Circuit. What is the likely result based on the Constitution?

(A) Unconstitutional, because the Supreme Court must have nine members.
(B) Unconstitutional, because there is only one Supreme Court.
(C) Unconstitutional, because Congress has no power to eliminate a circuit court.
(D) Unconstitutional as a denial of equal protection.

83. Which of the following cases is least likely to be heard under the Supreme Court's original jurisdiction?

(A) *Washington v. Oregon*, over which state breached its duty to prevent a forest fire.
(B) *New York v. New Jersey*, over which state owns part of an island.
(C) *Texas v. U.S.*, regarding a state challenge to an executive order reducing federal funding to a highway.
(D) *California v. U.S.*, regarding state citizens' interest in continued diplomatic ties with Japan.

84. Congress held hearings regarding the shrinking middle class in America. Economists testified that the wealth gap between rich and poor has not been this big since Louis XIV reigned in France. The wealthiest five percent own 85% of the property when government property is excluded. Reacting to "hate the rich" sentiment in the population, Congress passes a statute substantially raising the estate tax. The law eliminates loopholes. The government will get $1 billion from the tax. After the cost of auditing and accounting is accounted for, the net revenue generated will be about $10 million. What is the likely result if the Court reviews the constitutionality of the statute?

(A) Constitutional, if the dominant intent of the tax was fiscal.
(B) Constitutional, because Congress has the power to tax the estates of persons.
(C) Unconstitutional, because the revenue does not substantially outweigh the burden on the estate.
(D) Unconstitutional, because the Court will conclude that it is a penalty, not a tax.

85. Brook stored his personal handguns at Flagg's Mini-Storage. Brook became delinquent in payment for his storage space. Flagg's informed him that his property would be sold pursuant to state law that permitted the private sale of stored goods under such circumstances. Brook filed an injunction against Flagg's in federal court, claiming the sale violated his rights. What constitutional rights are at issue?

(A) 14th Amendment Due Process.
(B) 2nd Amendment Right to Bear Arms.
(C) Dormant Commerce Clause.
(D) None, because no state action.

86. Congress passed an amendment to the federal tax code. The amendment creates a one-time deduction for a very narrow class of taxpayers. The deduction allows twin brothers who simultaneously inherit a corporation, which owns land that produces farm crops during the taxable year, from the estate of a common paternal parent, if the taxpayer receives one-half share of the corporation and the taxpayer has natural hair color of brown and is thirty-eight years old during the fiscal year. Earnest and Julio Gallon met all of the requirements and fortunately inherit their father's wine company during the one year that the deduction is effective. John Crest, a competitor of the Gallons, files a declaratory judgment in federal court to have the tax law declared unconstitutional. What is the likely outcome?

(A) The court will declare the deduction is an unconstitutional bill of attainder.
(B) The court will declare the deduction is unconstitutional as not rationally related to a legitimate government interest.
(C) The court will declare the deduction is a constitutional exercise of the tax power.
(D) The court will not hear John's case on the merits.

87. Attorneys and accountants are bitterly fighting in Evergreen State regarding the ability of attorneys to form partnerships with non-attorneys. Accountants want to be able to hire attorneys to give legal advice to clients of the accounting firm. Accountants accuse the legal profession of economic protectionism. Some attorneys view the proposal as a danger to the independent professional judgment of attorneys to work for non-attorney management. The Evergreen Legislature was holding hearings to hear public comment on the issue. Tom Iman called the legislators, who were primarily lawyers, "Cowards for not allowing the accounting firms to practice law." The Legislature passed a statute declaring that Mr. Iman would never be able to obtain a license to practice law in Evergreen State. What is the best characterization of the statute?

(A) An unconstitutional *ex post facto* law.
(B) An unconstitutional bill of attainder.
(C) Unconstitutional, because it violates due process.
(D) Unconstitutional, because it violates his rights of state citizenship.

88. The City of West Angeles needs to protect its beaches from excessive development. Significant public outrage against the overabundance of large new beachfront condominiums convinced city planners to increase the environmental protections of the City's waterfront. A commission redrew the local zoning plans. Pursuant to state law, the City stopped issuing new permits for all new building within 200 feet of the high-water mark of the ocean. Buildings completed previously must be taken down within 180 days. Fran Kavalon owns an acre of property on the beach. The acre is a long stretch of beach, and only extends 215 feet from the high-water mark. She had just signed a contract with a general contractor to build 45 condominiums overlooking the water. The contractor sent her notice of intent to terminate performance under the contract due to the recent law changes. The property still has a wonderful view of the ocean. What is Fran's best argument?

(A) The City owes her money under the inverse condemnation doctrine.
(B) The City violated due process by taking her land.
(C) The City violated the Contracts Clause.
(D) Both B and C .

89. Syscom, a Dover State corporation, had a contract with the federal government to install direct server lines to bring the Internet to "all American Embassies." The president then issued an executive order cutting off foreign relations with Jamaica, because the country lowered trade barriers with Cuba. Marines were scheduled to close the American Embassy in Jamaica the following day. If Syscom filed suit in federal court to enjoin the closing of the embassy, what would be the most likely outcome?

(A) Dismissed, because the Court would not consider the action on motion for injunction as it is an issue committed to another branch of government.

(B) Dismissed, because the Constitution's Takings Clause applies.

(C) Dismissed, because Constitution's Contracts Clause applies.

(D) Dismissed, because Syscom lacks an injury in fact.

90. During the World Commerce Organization's convention in Emerald City, several members of the Resist One-World Government (ROWG) protested. Some of the protesters caused damage to the convention center and local businesses. ROWG has many members, some of whom overlap with the ACLU. Members rely on the loose-knit leadership to keep their names secret. Some of the members who work for corporations and local governments fear retaliation for being members. ROWG does not endorse violence or property damage, but many of the members actively profess it. The Emerald City Attorney subpoenaed the organization for the membership list. Emerald asserts that ROWG should have known that some of its members would resort to lawbreaking. ROWG files a motion to resist the subpoena. What is the most likely outcome?

(A) ROWG's motion denied, because ROWG lacks standing to protect individual member rights.

(B) ROWG's motion granted, because the members had the right to peaceably assemble.

(C) ROWG's motion granted, because membership is lawful.

(D) ROWG's motion denied if the state can show a compelling state interest.

91. Alabarkansa Legislature passed a law stating that if state elementary schools teach children about George Washington, then they must also teach children about Moses, a person described in the Bible.

What is the likely result if the constitutionality of the statute was tested?

(A) Unconstitutional, because it violates free exercise clause.

(B) Constitutional, unless there is no secular purpose.

(C) Unconstitutional, because the teachers cannot be forced to teach an idea.

(D) Constitutional if applied generally to public and private schools.

92. The City of Rhode, in the State of Pawtucket Island, erects an annual Christmas display during the Christmas season. In the display are Santa Claus and other related characters, colored lights, and a nativity scene with Mary, Joseph, and the infant Jesus. Does the display survive constitutional scrutiny?

(A) No, because it depicts a religious scene.

(B) No, if government employees erected it and taxpayers paid for it.

(C) Yes, if the inclusion of Jesus was to celebrate the season and depict the origins of the holiday.

(D) Yes, if the scene is in a limited public forum.

93. Congress passed a law authorizing and directing the Food and Drug Administration (FDA) to regulate genetically modified crops. Congress was reacting to the fervor of activists and a "20 Minutes" television news report suggesting the dangers of genetically altered foods. The law has standards for determining congressional intent and boundaries for the regulation. If the law is interpreted broadly, the FDA will have the authority to pass a regulation allowing it to seize crops and finished products anywhere in the stream of commerce or in the home. Under the law, the FDA will not take action on the crops and produce, until it passes a rule about how the seizure will proceed. Fearing government storm troopers in the homes of its members, the Americans for Liberal Civilities Union files suit in federal court to enjoin the FDA from conducting seizures. What is the court most likely to do?

(A) Dismiss, because the FDA has not passed a rule.

(B) Abstain from ruling, but retain jurisdiction over the case.

(C) Enjoin the FDA from making an unconstitutional rule.

(D) Dismiss, because of the 11th Amendment Immunity.

94. Cornhusk City denied the Crew Cut Clan's permit application for the city's Autumn Parade on November 11th in favor of a Veteran's Day parade. What is the constitutionality of this denial?

(A) Unconstitutional, because it is prior restraint on free speech.

(B) Unconstitutional if the Clan can show that their speech is protected.

(C) Constitutional if a prompt judicial review finds an important governmental interest for having a Veteran's parade that day instead of the Clan's parade.

(D) Constitutional if the state articulates a viewpoint neutral reason that shifts the burden to the Clan.

95. Congress has passed a statute which provides that no federal court, including the United States Supreme Court, shall have jurisdiction to decide any case involving the validity under the Constitution of any law limiting the rights of children under age 15 to obtain an abortion without parental consent. If properly challenged, the statute would be held

(A) Constitutional because of the plenary power of Congress to determine jurisdiction of the federal courts.

(B) Constitutional because a series of Supreme Court decisions have upheld the constitutionality of similar statutes.

(C) Unconstitutional because Congress cannot regulate the jurisdiction of the United States Supreme Court.

(D) Unconstitutional because Congress may not preclude an entire class of cases from judicial review.

96. Jones, a 21-year-old white male, applied to law school at Missibama State University, a prominent southern university which had been found ten years before to have unlawfully refused applicants based upon their race. His index score, which combines law school aptitude test score and grade point average, was below the lowest score of white applicants admitted. Jones' score, however, was substantially above 15 of the 20 black students admitted. The university agreed to grant bonus points to black students' index score and had a numerical goal of 20 black students, pursuant to a consent decree entered in 1980. If Jones brings suit to require that he be admitted because the university has unlawfully discriminated against him because of his race, the Court would

(A) Grant relief because a classification solely based on race, even to achieve a worthy purpose, is not necessary to achieve a compelling state need, and therefore violates the Equal Protection Clause.

(B) Grant relief because a state may not use race as a criterion in making admissions decisions.

(C) Deny relief because a state may consider race as a factor in admissions when it is attempting to aid disadvantaged minorities and penalizes no particular group.

(D) Deny relief because the racial classification is designed to remedy past unlawful discrimination.

97. The State of Mountain is operating a large nuclear power plant on the Green River. The plant uses river water for cooling and discharges water back into the river ten degrees warmer than it was at the point of entry. While this temperature differential quickly dissipates, it has adversely affected the business of North Pole, a downstream ice-cutting operator, located in the State of Valley. Primarily as a result of North Pole's urging, Valley has sued Mountain in the U.S. Supreme Court, alleging damage to its environment and seeking an injunction against thermal discharge. The U.S. Supreme Court should

(A) Dismiss the suit because the suit it is barred by the Eleventh Amendment.

(B) Hear the matter on the merits because Valley is suing in its own right and jurisdiction is proper.

(C) Dismiss the action because it does not have original jurisdiction.

(D) Hear the matter on the merits because Valley is suing *parens patriae*.

98. The school-age population in Metro City is 15% black and 85% white. Metro City has fifteen schools within its district. Seventy percent of the pupils in five intercity schools in the city are black. Other schools have no black pupils. Which of the following statements concerning these facts is most accurate?

(A) The facts establish a violation of the Equal Protection Clause of the Fourteenth Amendment.

(B) The facts set forth are not sufficient to establish an Equal Protection violation unless it could be shown that the predominantly black schools were the five oldest schools in the system.

(C) The facts are insufficient to establish a violation of the Equal Protection Clause of the Fourteenth Amendment, but a violation would be established if it could be shown that there was a higher percentage of tenured teachers in the predominantly white schools.

(D) The facts are insufficient to establish a violation of the Equal Protection Clause of the Fourteenth Amendment even if the facts shown in Choices (B) and (C) are established.

99. The town of Arlex has enacted a zoning ordinance that restricts all land in the town to single-family residences that can only be constructed (except for a small business zone in the center) on lots with a frontage of 200 feet and an area of 60,000 square feet. An out-of-state developer who plans to build townhouses in Arlex has brought suit in the federal court to enjoin the operation of the statute. Which is the weakest argument for the city if it tries to obtain a dismissal of the suit before a trial on the merits?

(A) The case is moot.

(B) There is no case or controversy.

(C) The P lacks standing.

(D) The issues are not ripe.

100. Pursuant to a state enabling statute, the city of Easton enacted a rent control ordinance affecting all residential buildings containing ten or more dwelling units. As of the effective date of the ordinance, the maximum rent allowed was the rent charged on that dwelling unit one year prior to the effective date. Landlord had entered into a two-year lease with Tenant six months prior to the effective date of the ordinance at a rental higher than was charged one year prior to the effective date. If Landlord challenges the constitutionality of the city ordinance, his most effective argument will be that it

(A) Impairs the obligation of contract.

(B) Violates the Due Process Clause because it operates retroactively.

(C) Violates the Equal Protection Clause because it classifies large landlords differently from small landlords.

(D) Violates the Due Process Clause because the rent charged was controlled without giving him a hearing.

101. Roman is the leader of a religious cult in Thogam City. He holds a weekly "service" in the public park and during his sermon, uses insulting expletives directed at persons in his audience who are not members of the cult. The audience has become boisterous and several times fights have almost broken out between members of the audience and members of the cult. After a particularly boisterous rally, the attorney for the city of Thogam obtained an *ex parte* injunction prohibiting Roman from conducting any further rallies "which tend to disturb or annoy the average member of the community." If challenged on appeal, a judge would find the injunction

(A) Valid because the threats of imminent violence justify the injunction.

(B) Invalid because the injunction is overly broad and vague.

(C) Invalid because the injunction was obtained in a manner that violates procedural due process.

(D) Invalid for the reasons set forth in choices (B) and (C).

102. Dolly Belle was a guest on a television talk show called "Fernwood Today," which is on the air between 4 p.m. and 6 p.m. The host of the show spent five minutes asking Dolly specific questions about the size and shape of her breasts. Dolly answered all the questions in a full, frank, and candid manner. The Federal Communications Commission issued a letter of reprimand to the station because of the program's content, and the station has appealed on the ground that the Commission does not have the constitutional power to issue the reprimand. Which of the following is the strongest argument to uphold the validity of the Commission's action?

(A) Because the airwaves are public property and limited in number, the government may regulate broadcasts under the police power.

(B) The pervasive nature of television makes it likely that a show scheduled in the late afternoon will reach an immature audience whom the government has a right to protect.

(C) The material present on the show was obscene and not entitled to First Amendment protection.

(D) The show was staged for the purpose of raising advertising revenue, and is therefore commercial speech that is subject to reasonable regulation.

103. William Pierce was addressing an audience in a park in New City on the subject of salvation. He uttered words highly offensive to the religious crowd that gathered to hear him speak. After a while, about three men indicated that if the police officer did not "get that S.O.B. off the stand," that they would do it themselves. At this point, a police officer stepped in to stop a fight from breaking out and demanded that Pierce cease speaking. When he refused, the police officer arrested Pierce and he was convicted of disorderly conduct. Upon appeal

(A) The conviction will be reversed by the Supreme Court of the United States because Pierce's arrest constituted an interference with his First Amendment right to freedom of speech.

(B) The conviction will be reversed by the Supreme Court of the United States because Pierce's arrest constituted undue interference with his audience's right to assemble peaceably under the First Amendment.

(C) The conviction will be sustained by the Supreme Court of the United States because Pierce had a duty to obey a police officer where there were other times and places to convey his message.

(D) The conviction will be sustained by the Supreme Court of the United States because his speech caused an immediate and substantial threat to public order.

104. State Q enacts a statute that is narrowly drawn and defines obscenity in accordance with the latest decision of the U.S. Supreme Court. When the police searched D incident to a motor vehicle arrest, they found a DVD in his coat pocket. D is arrested for the illegal transportation of obscene material. Assuming that the material found on his person is an indecent pornographic film, what is his best defense?

(A) Others have carried similar material with the knowledge of the police and have not been prosecuted.

(B) He received the DVD as a gift.

(C) He only had the DVD because he just bought it and was taking it home.

(D) Parts of the DVD have literary merit.

105. Dandruff is the owner of a beauty shop, which employs only male hairdressers and caters only to female customers. An ordinance of the City of Tinsel makes it unlawful for any person to operate a hairdressing salon catering to female customers if the hairdressers are male. Dandruff brings an action in federal court challenging the constitutionality of the ordinance. If the D city moves to dismiss the lawsuit on the grounds that Dandruff lacks standing, the city would

(A) Prevail because the ordinance does not prohibit the operation of beauty salons *per se*, but only the right of the male employees to service female customers.

(B) Prevail because only the employees can raise their rights of association.

(C) Not prevail because the employees and the beauty shop operators have rights that are harmed by the ordinance.

(D) Not prevail because the ordinance prevents the employees from exercising their First Amendment rights.

106. Smith, a citizen of England, operates an adult theater that shows films that are obscene in the constitutional sense. Pursuant to a narrowly drawn statute, Smith is prosecuted in state court for the exhibition of an obscene motion picture, and he asserts as a defense the right of privacy. Which of the following best explains the effectiveness of his defense?

(A) An alien may not assert an invasion of privacy defense.

(B) The right to possess obscene material does not extend beyond the home.

(C) The right of privacy allows the possession of obscene motion pictures in one's home.

(D) Theaters may show obscene films to adults.

107. When he was interviewed on a radio show, an assistant district attorney made three statements:

A. His boss, the district attorney, was on a witch-hunt, trying to convict prominent citizens so that he could further his political career.

B. Many times he did not produce all of the evidence that the police had gathered if he felt that the D should not be convicted.

C. He was going to ask the legislature to appropriate more funds for the public defender's office because he felt that the quality of their representation of criminals was not as good as the state representation by the district attorney's office.

The district attorney could dismiss him for making:

(A) Statement A.
(B) Statement B.
(C) Statement C.
(D) None of the statements.

108. A zoning ordinance of Carmel prevents the keeping of any animals, except dogs and cats, within city limits. Chusetts is a member of a religious cult that believes in ancestor worship and uses monkeys as part of their daily religious worship. Consequently, he keeps a monkey in a separate bedroom in his home. If the town should sue to require Chusetts to remove the animal from the premises because its presence violates the zoning ordinance, and Chusetts challenged the constitutionality of the statute on First Amendment grounds,

(A) Chusetts will prevail if he proves that the City passed the law with religious motivation, and if Carmel fails to prove that the zoning ordinance is not narrowly tailored to a compelling government interest.

(B) Chusetts will prevail only if he proves that the application of the statute to him is not rational.

(C) The city will prevail only if it can show that the statute is necessary to satisfy a compelling state need.

(D) The city will prevail if it can show a rational basis for the statute.

109. Chinook, a resident of State A, was a commercial salmon fisherman who fished for two months per year in the Red River in State B. Effective this year, State B's legislature provided that the fee for a salmon fishing license was $5 per year for a resident and $500 per year for a non-resident. If Chinook challenged the constitutionality of the law under the Privileges and Immunities Clause of Article IV, the Court would find that

(A) It was constitutional because the state has a proprietary interest in the fish within its borders, and therefore may discriminate against nonresidents.

(B) It was constitutional because no fundamental interest was infringed.

(C) It is unconstitutional discrimination against nonresidents because it does not bear a substantial relationship to the fact that there is a limited number of salmon.

(D) It is unconstitutional because a state may not deny an alien a livelihood unless that action is necessary to satisfy a compelling state need.

110. A new statute in the State of Regina requires all residents to submit a certificate of fetal health during the fourth month of each pregnancy. The certificate must be signed by a doctor, which declares that the baby is healthy and free of AIDS and genetic defects. The certificate must still be submitted if the prospective mother has an abortion prior to the fourth month. Mary files suit in state court to enjoin the statute. She alleges the law impinges on her federally guaranteed constitutional right to privacy. The state court upholds the statute. The state supreme court upholds the statute on emergency appeal. Mary appeals to the U.S. Supreme Court. In her distress, Mary has a miscarriage prior to oral arguments. Which answer best describes whether the Supreme Court should dismiss the suit?

(A) Yes, the Court lacks jurisdiction to hear the case because it is moot.

(B) Yes, the Court lacks jurisdiction to hear the case because it originated in state court.

(C) No, the Supreme Court has jurisdiction because a constitutional issue is raised.

(D) No, the Court has jurisdiction because she may become pregnant again and be subject to the law, yet not reach the high court in time.

111. The city of Madison, in Willis state, enacts an ordinance that requires a city inspection of all milk products coming into the city from outside the state of Willis. A Willis state law requires an identical inspection of all milk, both intra- and interstate, for health purposes. The Good Milk Company sues, alleging that requiring the city inspection is a Commerce Clause violation. What is the most likely result in the case?

(A) Madison will prevail because the statute is designed to protect the health and welfare of Madison citizens.

(B) Madison will prevail because it has been given implicit authority

by the Willis statute to conduct the inspection.

(C) The Good Milk Company will prevail because the city inspection, which is identical to the state inspection, is an undue burden on interstate commerce.

(D) The Good Milk Company will prevail because the statute is discriminatory on its face.

112. The President of the United States has entered into an executive agreement with the President of Mexico. The agreement provides that all Mexicans in prison in the U.S. will be repatriated to serve the remainder of their sentences in Mexican prison, and all Americans in Mexican prison will be repatriated to serve the remainder of their sentences in American prison. Pursuant to this agreement, federal marshals arrived at a local prison in Texanis to take Lopez, a convicted murderer of Mexican citizenship, and deliver him to Mexican authorities. A state statute requires that murderers convicted in Texanis must be incarcerated in Texanis prisons. The local sheriff therefore brings an action in federal court to enjoin the marshal on the ground that he is acting pursuant to an unconstitutional order. The court should:

(A) Grant the injunction because the agreement violates the sovereign powers reserved to the states under the Tenth Amendment.

(B) Grant the injunction because executive agreements cannot supercede state law.

(C) Deny the injunction because of the Supremacy Clause.

(D) Deny the injunction because a sensitive area of foreign policy is nonjusticiable.

113. Furman has been convicted of a federal offense carrying the death penalty, and has been sentenced to death by a federal court during a time when the death penalty was constitutional. The Supreme Court rejected all appeals, including an appeal claiming ineffective assistance of counsel by Furman's trial attorney. The President of the United States decided that there may have been valid arguments tending to show ineffective assistance of counsel. The President proceeded to commute the sentence from the death penalty to life in prison subject to the condition that Furman would never be eligible for parole. At a later date, the death penalty is declared unconstitutional and Furman seeks parole. The federal district court will decide that

(A) This is a valid exercise of the President's pardoning power under Article II.

(B) The commutation must be set aside because it is not authorized by legislation.

(C) The commutation must be set aside because the President may not decide constitutional issues.

(D) The commutation must be set aside because the national death penalty was subsequently declared unconstitutional.

114. The United States House of Representatives asks the judiciary committee to recommend a law regulating the conditions for marriages and divorces. The committee would like to respond with a law that would most likely withstand constitutional analysis. That law would

(A) Only apply to marriages and divorces by members of the armed services.

(B) Only apply to marriages performed by federal judges and divorces in federal courts.

(C) Only apply to marriages implemented by an executive agreement seeking to define basic human rights.

(D) Apply only to marriages and divorces in the District of Columbia.

115. Jersey State sues York State over which state owns Sille Island, which is located in the navigable water between the two states. Jersey files its complaint in the U.S. Supreme Court initially. York brings a motion to dismiss. What is the most likely outcome on the motion?

(A) Dismiss as a political question.

(B) Remand the case to federal district court.

(C) Overrule the motion and hear the case on the merits.

(D) Dismiss the case as a violation of the 11th Amendment.

116. Pat sues Don in state court for trespass and battery. Pat prevails in a bench trial on the merits, but Don continues to object to evidence admitted regarding a deed. Don claims the deed was erroneously admitted, and violated the rules of evidence. Don appeals his evidence issue to the state supreme court, but the court upholds the trial court in a published opinion. Don files in the U.S. Supreme Court. The Court should:

(A) Refuse to hear the case, unless there is a final judgment on the merits from highest state court.

(B) Deny the *writ of certiorari*, because the court has no jurisdiction.

(C) Decline to hear oral arguments, if the case can be easily decided.

(D) Decline the appeal, because it is not an interesting issue.

117. The city of Big Apple passed a municipal ordinance making spray painting on public buildings a misdemeanor, if it is done with the intent to criticize a public officer. Spary is arrested and charged for "tagging" the County Jail, which sits inside city limits. Spary painted "Juliani sucks." Spary is assigned a public defender. The public defender believes the ordinance violates both the State and Federal Constitutions. If the public defender files a declaratory action in federal district court on Spary's behalf to have the ordinance declared unconstitutional, the district court would most likely do what to the federal action?

(A) Dismiss, because Big Apple has not consented to suit in federal court.

(B) Abstain, if the prosecution has initiated.

(C) Hear the case, because one party is a city not a state.

(D) Hear the case, because it is a flagrant violation of the Constitution.

118. The city of Big Apple passed a municipal ordinance making spray painting on public buildings a misdemeanor, if it is done with the intent to criticize a public officer. Spary is arrested and charged for "tagging" the County Jail, which sits inside city limits. Spary painted "Juliani sucks." Spary is

assigned a public defender. The public defender believes the ordinance violates both the State and Federal Constitutions.

The Big Apple continues the prosecution within the state system and the court convicts Spary after a bench trial. Spary's attorney appeals claiming the conviction violates both state and federal constitutional protections of free speech. The highest court in the state concludes that the statute does violate the state constitution, but does not reach the federal issue. The state's constitution has a free speech provision, but the language and case history are distinct from the Federal Constitution. For that reason, the Americans for Liberal Civilities Union (ALCU) convinces Spary to appeal the decision to the U.S. Supreme Court. What is the weakest argument for declining review by the Supreme Court?

    (A) The ALCU has no standing.
    (B) Spary's conviction is already overturned.
    (C) The decision would be merely advisory.
    (D) The case is non-justiciable.

119. Manning received unemployment benefits from Great Lake State for one year more than the state statute allowed. When the federal government sent a memorandum to the Great Lake Attorney General resulting from an audit, the state sought to recover the funds from Manning. Kennedy was an assistant attorney general for Great Lake who filed an action in federal court against Manning to recover the payments, relying on an obscure regulation that allows a jurisdiction to recover government money accepted under misleading circumstances. Manning files a motion to dismiss in federal district court. What is the most likely outcome?

    (A) The court will dismiss based on the State's Sovereign Immunity in federal court.
    (B) The court will dismiss based on lack of standing.
    (C) The court will hear the case.
    (D) The court will find for Manning based on the *ex post facto* clause.

120. Congress enacted a statute prohibiting states from intentionally discriminating in hiring based on the applicant's race. The statute further provided individuals may file a suit for money damages in federal court based on the violation. What is the best characterization of the statute?

    (A) Constitutional exercise of the Fourteenth Amendment.
    (B) Unconstitutional as an abridgment of the 11th Amendment.
    (C) Unconstitutional as a regulation of an integral state function.
    (D) Constitutional exercise of the Commerce Clause power.

121. Congress enacted a law limiting the number of passengers allowed in each train car. The bill was drafted the day after a terrorist attack on a passenger train. It also criminalized all of the common law crimes if committed while on a train scheduled for interstate travel. During debate, it became clear that the law would be solely for the purpose of deterring terrorists. What is the constitutionality of the statute?

    (A) Constitutional exercise of the commerce clause.
    (B) Constitutional exercise of the federal police power.
    (C) Unconstitutional regulation in a traditional state area.
    (D) Unconstitutional as enacted for a non-economic purpose.

122. The State of Tennesville enacted a law criminalizing certain speech. The legislature intended to punish the use of "fighting words." A recent law review article by a third-year law student argued that the law is a fairly well-worded, good faith attempt at the constitutional requirements. The student argued that a reasonable person could decide what conduct or speech was prohibited, but that the law is borderline constitutional. The law student decided to write the article because there were no state cases interpreting the statute, and the new governor had talked about enforcing it. Americans for Free Speech (AFS) initiate a declaratory judgment action in federal district court. The Governor of Tennesville claims that the law prohibits another, yet unrecognized category of unprotected free speech. The district court will most likely

(A) Not hear the case because the state court has not interpreted the law.
(B) Not hear the case, because the state is immune from suit in federal court.
(C) Hear the case, if the AFS has membership in the state.
(D) Hear the case, because of the law's effects on interstate commerce

123. South Georgia has had a statute on the books prohibiting the use of contraceptives by any person since the year condoms were invented. The state has not prosecuted anyone under the statute in 80 years, and sales have been brisk. Bill and Sally Process are married and living in South Georgia. Bill Process wanted to join a gang of liberals. As an initiation, Bill was ordered to file a lawsuit against the State. Bill sued the state in federal court alleging the old contraceptive law in place was unconstitutional. What is the court's most likely course of action?

(A) Dismiss the case, as the outcome would have no practical legal effect.
(B) Dismiss the case, because Bill does not have standing.
(C) Dismiss the case as a violation of the 11ᵗʰ Amendment.
(D) Hear the case on its merits and find the law unconstitutional.

124. More than ten years ago, Congress created the United States Sentencing Commission and delegated to it the power to promulgate sentencing guidelines that would bind the federal courts to impose sentences within prescribed ranges. Last year, Congress authorized the Commission to update sentence recommendations in light of prison overcrowding. The Commission adopted new guidelines effective May of this year, but only for drug crimes. The law creating the Commission set general policies and principles to guide the creation of the Guidelines.

In April of this year, Kris Rock was arrested for assault and battery of a postal worker and tried in federal court. He was convicted in June. At the sentencing hearing, the judge imposed a sentence at the high end of the standard range. Had the Commission lowered the sentence range for assault and battery in proportion with how much lower the new drug crime range is, Kris's sentence would be outside the range. Kris's attorney is arguing on appeal that the sentence is improper. What is the likely outcome on appeal?

(A) The sentence violates the *Ex Post Facto* clause.
(B) The sentence was valid.
(C) The sentence violates the Equal Protection clause.
(D) Congress improperly delegated to the Sentencing Commission.

125. Last year, the Key Lime Supreme Court struck down the statute that sets the procedure for implementing the death penalty for capital crimes in the state. This year, Key Lime State prosecuted Birddog for murder. On the next New Year's Day, Birddog shot and killed two nuns and a firefighter in a crosswalk while he was on parole for armed robbery. Key Lime had a statute since 1901 stating that this crime was a capital offense. Key Lime legislature passed a statute that would survive current constitutional standards for the death penalty procedures. In June, Birddog was convicted and sentenced to death in accordance with the new law. What is the likely outcome on appeal of the case?

(A) Because the sentence was unconstitutional, Birddog will be released.
(B) The sentence will be upheld, because it comports with the Constitution.
(C) The conviction violates the *Ex Post Facto* clause if the new statute was not in effect when the crime was committed.
(D) The conviction will be upheld, but the sentence violates the Constitution.

126. The Richmond State Constitution has always had a provision prohibiting aliens from inheriting certain property. The United States signed a treaty over a century ago with Great Britain providing that no restrictions shall be placed on the rights of the citizens of either country to inherit property in the country of the other. Arthur, a citizen and resident of Great Britain, stands to inherit 34 acres of land in Richmond. This type of conveyance falls within the prohibition in the State Constitution. What is the likely outcome?

(A) Arthur inherits the land if he can show no compelling state interest for the prohibition.
(B) Arthur inherits the land, because the treaty overrides the prohibition.
(C) Arthur does not inherit the land, because the Richmond State constitution prohibits it.
(D) Arthur inherits the land, because the prohibition violates Equal Protection.

127. The State of Ilwa requires a license for those "who engage in the trade of barbering." Ilwa grants licenses to people who meet three conditions: graduate from an Ilwa licensed barber college, reside in the state for at least two years, and are United States citizens. The requirement that a license applicant have graduated from an Ilwa barber school is likely

(A) Constitutional, because barbering is a privilege not a right.
(B) Constitutional, because the state does not know the quality of barber schools outside of Ilwa.
(C) Unconstitutional because it is a violation of the 14th Amendment Privileges or Immunities clause.
(D) Unconstitutional as an undue burden on interstate commerce.

128. The State of Ilwa requires a license for those "who engage in the trade of barbering." Ilwa grants licenses to people who meet three conditions: graduate from an Ilwa barber school, reside in the state for two years, and are United States citizens. The requirement that a license applicant must be a United States citizen is

(A) Constitutional as an exercise of the state's police power.
(B) Constitutional as an effort to ensure that barbers speak English adequately.
(C) Unconstitutional as a denial of equal protection.

(D) Unconstitutional as a bill of attainder.

129. The State of Ilwa requires a license for those "who engage in the trade of barbering." Ilwa grants licenses to people who meet three conditions: graduate from an Ilwa barber school, reside in the state for two years, and are United States citizens. Which of the following is (are) good argument(s) to challenge the two-year residency requirement?

(A) Art. IV Privileges and Immunities.
(B) 14th Amendment Privileges or Immunities.
(C) 14th Amendment Equal Protection.
(D) Both A and C.

130. The State of Ilwa requires a license for those "who engage in the trade of barbering." Ilwa grants licenses to people who meet three conditions: graduate from an Ilwa barber school, reside in the state for two years, and are United States citizens. Jake Elwood, a resident of the State of Eastern, was not allowed to sit for the hairdresser's licensing exam in Ilwa because he graduated from an Eastern barber school. If Jake files a suit in federal court to contest the denial of the license, what is the likely outcome for Jake?

(A) Dismissed, because of the abstention doctrine.
(B) Prevail, because Ilwa violated due process.
(C) Prevail, because the law violates the Art. IV Privileges and Immunities Clause.
(D) Decided on the merits, because federal jurisdiction extends to controversies between two states.

131. Ronald McDowell is convicted for speaking out about the oppression of clowns by the state government. Ronald is convicted under a statute prohibiting the "disturbance of the peace by shouting political nonsense." While Ronald was known for his outbursts when he forgot to take his medication, some of his statements on this occasion could be defensible if interpreted favorably.

On appeal to the state's highest court claiming a violation of his right to free speech, the court refused to hear the case. In a single page decision, the court invoked a widely ignored rule of appellate procedure requiring litigants to attach a copy of the statute in the appendix of the brief. As a result, Ronald's conviction stands. In an appeal to the U.S. Supreme Court, what is the most likely result?

(A) The Court will hear the case if Ronald claims the state violated due process by applying the appellate rule.

(B) The Court will hear the case, because the state may not preclude high court review by applying the appellate rule inconsistently.

(C) The Court will hear the case, because it is a facially invalid statute.

(D) The Court will not hear the case, because the appellate rule issue is not a federal constitutional matter.

132. Congress passed a statute requiring each state to arrange for the disposal of toxic waste generated within its borders. If the toxic waste is not disposed of or contained pursuant to federal guidelines within five years, the state will be deemed to "take title" to the waste and thereby become liable for tort damages stemming from it. The federal statute contemplates that every state with toxic waste within its boundaries will pass legislation funding containment. It will take New Power State five years to build containment facilities to handle all of the nuclear waste it currently has to meet the new federal standards. New Power files an action in federal court to have the law declared invalid. What is the likely outcome of the case?

(A) The court will invalidate the law, which improperly requires the state to pass laws to implement a federal program.

(B) The court will dismiss the case, because it violates 11th Amendment sovereign immunity.

(C) The court will dismiss the case, because New Power will not suffer any injury for five years, so the case is not yet ripe.

(D) The court will find for the United States, because the federal law is constitutionally valid.

133. The State of North Island entered into a contract with Roads, Inc., for the construction of a four-lane turnpike. Prior to commencement of construction, the legislature, in order to provide funds for parks, repealed the statute authorizing the turnpike and canceled the agreement with Roads. Roads sued North Island to enforce its original agreement. In ruling on this case, a court will likely hold that the state statute canceling the agreement is

(A) Valid, because constitutionally the sovereign is not liable except with its own consent.

(B) Valid, because the legislature is vested with constitutional authority to repeal laws it has enacted.

(C) Invalid, because a state is equitably estopped to disclaim a valid bid once accepted by it.

(D) Invalid, because of the constitutional prohibition against impairment of contracts.

134. Green is cited for contempt by the House of Representatives after she refused to answer certain questions posed by a House Committee concerning compensation received from a foreign government while serving as a United States Ambassador. A federal statute authorizes the Attorney General to prosecute contempt of Congress charges. Pursuant to this law, the House directs the Attorney General to begin criminal proceedings against Green. A federal grand jury indicts Green, but the Attorney General refuses to sign the indictment. Which of the following best describes the constitutionality of the Attorney General's action?

(A) Illegal, because the Attorney General must prosecute if the House of Representatives directs.

(B) Illegal, because the Attorney General must prosecute those who violate the federal law.

(C) Legal, because ambassadors are immune from prosecution for acts committed in the course of their official duties.

(D) Legal, because the decision to prosecute is an exclusively executive act.

135. Green is cited for contempt by the House of Representatives after she refused to answer certain questions posed by a House Committee concerning her acts while serving as a United States Ambassador. A federal statute authorizes the Attorney General to prosecute contempt of Congress. Pursuant to this law, the House directs the Attorney General to begin criminal proceedings against Green. A federal grand jury indicts Green, but the Attorney General refuses to sign the indictment. If the Attorney General signs the indictment, the strongest defense Green could offer is that

(A) Green may refuse to answer the questions if she can demonstrate that they are unrelated to matters upon which Congress may legislate.

(B) The House may question Green only on matters pertaining to the expenditure of funds appropriated by Congress.

(C) Only the Senate may question Green on matters that relate to the performance of her duties.

(D) Congress may not ask questions relating to the performance of duties executed by an officer of the executive branch.

136. Congress decided that the application of the Uniform Consumer Credit Code (UCCC) should be the same throughout the United States. To that end, it enacted the UCCC as a federal law directly applicable to all consumer credit, small loans, and retail installment sales. The law is intended to establish uniform national standards to protect borrowers and buyers against unfair practices by suppliers of consumer credit. Which of the following constitutional provisions may most easily be used to justify federal enactment of this statute?

(A) The obligation of Contracts Clause.

(B) The Privileges or Immunities Clause of the 14th Amendment.

(C) The Commerce Clause.

(D) Section 5 of the Fourteenth Amendment.

137. Congress decided that the application of the Uniform Consumer Credit Code should be the same throughout the United States. To that end, it enacted the UCCC as a federal law directly applicable to all consumer credit, small loans, and retail installment sales. The law is intended to protect borrowers and buyers against unfair practices by suppliers of consumer credit. A national religious organization makes loans throughout the country for the construction and furnishing of churches. The federal UCCC would substantially interfere with the successful accomplishment of that organization's religious objectives. The organization seeks to obtain a declaratory judgment that the federal law may not be applied to its lending activities. As a matter of constitutional law, which of the following best describes the burden that must be sustained?

(A) The federal government must demonstrate that the application of this statute to the lending activities of this organization is necessary to vindicate a compelling governmental interest.

(B) The federal government must demonstrate that the religious conduct affects commerce.

(C) The organization must prove that the activity is central to their religion and substantially interfered with.

(D) The organization will prevail by showing intentional discrimination by the federal government only if it also shows the law is not narrowly tailored to a compelling government interest.

138. The Federal Endangered Species Act imposes criminal penalties for killing certain specified animals, among which is the rare Plaid Squirrel. Trail State classifies all species of squirrels as varmints, which may be destroyed by anyone with a Trail State hunting license. Rambo, who possesses a Trail State hunting license, regularly shoots Plaid Squirrels that trespass on his land. If Rambo is prosecuted under the federal statute, and challenges the constitutionality of the law, which of the following is the strongest constitutional argument in support of the statute?

(A) The Commerce Power.
(B) The Necessary and Proper Clause.
(C) The Police Power.
(D) The power to regulate federal lands.

139. The Macrosoft Corporation is headquartered in Evergreen State. To keep the corporation within the state, Evergreen passes a massive funding bill, which includes direct subsidies to Macrosoft. Several state attorneys general and private software competitor companies file an injunction against Evergreen subsidizing Macrosoft claiming a violation of the Dormant Commerce Clause. The most likely disposition of this suit will be that the injunction will be:

(A) Granted, because the subsidies violate the Dormant Commerce Clause by unduly burdening out-of-state companies that must compete with Macrosoft.
(B) Granted, because the subsidies violate the Dormant Commerce Clause by effectively insulating the in-state corporation from out-of-state competition.
(C) Granted, because the Ps have standing to challenge such state subsidies as measurable expenditures.
(D) Denied, because the states are not prohibited from using state tax dollars to subsidize local industry.

140. The State of Northwest requires imported apples to be inspected for parasites and diseases to reduce the risk of infecting local apple crops. The inspections are relatively low in cost and do not delay shipments more than a few hours. Unfortunately, a new breed of apple maggot found only in the State of Oleon south of Northwest cannot be identified with any existing test due to its small size. The Oleon Apple Maggot devastates any crop it comes in contact with. Northwest apple growers successfully lobbied their state legislature into passing a law banning the importation of apples from Oleon. Those in Oleon who challenge the statute as unconstitutional will

(A) Prevail, because the law discriminates against interstate commerce.
(B) Prevail, because the law violates the Article IV Privileges and Immunities of those in Oleon.
(C) Lose, because the law only burdens one state not several states.
(D) Lose, if there is no less restrictive way to prevent the Oleon Apple Maggot infestation from reaching the State of Northwest.

141. The U.S. Department of Agriculture distributes surplus farm products acquired in exchange for farm subsidies. To reduce fraudulent claims, the agency implemented a test program in its distribution of government cheese. Each household is allowed up to one pound of cheese per month. Any household in which unrelated persons were living together would be ineligible for the cheese. Bill and Hillary, two unmarried people, each applied for surplus cheese and were both denied because they lived together. What is the most appropriate provision for challenging the agency's withholding of the cheese?

(A) First Amendment.
(B) The equal protection implications of the Fifth Amendment.
(C) The Due Process Clause of the Fourteenth Amendment.
(D) The Privileges and Immunities Clause of the Fourteenth Amendment.

142. After two-thirds majorities of the House and Senate passed the Campaign Finance Amendment to the U.S. Constitution, it was submitted to the states for ratification. Several years passed while states were considering the amendment. The State of Mountain's legislature subsequently took up the issue. While the matter was pending before the Mountain legislature, an action was filed in federal district court seeking to enjoin the legislature from voting on the ratification issue. The grounds cited were that the Campaign Finance Amendment was no longer viable because fewer than three-fourths of the states necessary for ratification had ratified it, and no other states were currently considering whether to ratify it. How should the district court rule on this issue?

(A) Dismiss the matter as untimely, since the Mountain legislature has not yet voted on the issue of ratification.

(B) Dismiss the action as a nonjusticiable political question.

(C) Abstain so that the state's highest court may authoritatively interpret state law on the subject.

(D) Decide the matter on its merits.

---

143. The local chapter of the Libertarians wants to secede from Snow County and form Freedom County. In an effort to raise awareness of the oppressive nature of the government, Jeb contacted the advertising department of the local AM talk radio station. Jeb wants to run a campaign of political ads on the radio, and he thinks this station is the best way to reach his target audience. The advertising department manager refuses to run the ads. Jeb files an action seeking a federal court order to force the radio station to air the advertisements. What is the trial court's strongest justification in denying Jeb relief?

(A) The radio station's commercial time is not a public forum.

(B) Jeb has a reasonable alternative to get his message out to his target audience.

(C) The Fourteenth Amendment provides no basis upon which to compel the radio station to air Jeb's ads.

(D) The radio station's decision is based on a content neutral reason.

---

144. University of Michel conducted a test, using state tax subsidies, to determine the cause of the recent increase in fatalities from car accidents. Professor Thunderbird concluded that Yokobishi Manufacturing had produced a defective electronic speedometer. Neither Congress nor any other state took any action on the issue. Rather than naming the particular manufacturer Yokobishi, the Michel State Legislature banned the use of all electronic speedometers within the state effective 60 days from the passage of the law. What is the best argument to defeat the law?

(A) It is a violation of the Equal Protection Clause because it treats electronic speedometers differently from conventional speedometers.

(B) It is a violation of the Commerce Clause, because it unduly burdens interstate commerce.

(C) It is a violation of the Due Process Clause because it is a taking without just compensation.

(D) It is a violation of the Constitution as a Bill of Attainder.

---

145. Congress enacted the Health Information Act, which disbursed funds from the federal treasury to the public educational systems of each state ($500 per pupil enrolled in the state college system). It also provided that the school system includes in its curriculum accurate information about the human reproductive system and sexual behavior, including the manner of transmission of the AIDS virus. If these provisions of the federal act are challenged as unconstitutional, they should be held

(A) Invalid, because education about human sexuality is not a proper subject of federal regulation.

(B) Invalid, because Congress may not achieve through conditional grant of funds an object that would be unconstitutional if it were the subject of direct regulation.

(C) Valid, as a proper exercise of congressional power to spend to promote the general welfare.

(D) Valid, but only if the health education has a significant impact upon interstate commerce.

---

146. Responding to the economic downturn, New Gingrich State passed a law terminating all welfare programs effective in 90 days. Ninety days later, the State cuts off Sally's benefits. Sally, a mother of two who is currently on welfare, files suit. The court will most likely

(A) Find that the hardship on Sally outweighs the administrative convenience of terminating the benefits.

(B) Deny Sally's claim.

(C) Find the action invalid as the State did not provide Sally an opportunity to be heard.

(D) Find that the State must give Sally a post-deprivation hearing to determine her benefits.

147. Soon after a small private plane crashed near the White House, Congress enacted a law prohibiting private planes from flying over Washington, D.C. An organization representing private plane pilots brought suit in the federal court seeking to invalidate this law. The federal statute could best be supported by

(A) The Supremacy Clause.

(B) The General Welfare Clause.

(C) Congress's plenary power to make regulations protecting government property.

(D) Congress's police power over the District of Columbia.

148. Marymore State purchases old junk cars, or "hulks" and disposes of them. The state purchases these hulks from in-state owners for $200, and from out-of-state owners for $10. Were an out-of-state owner to challenge the program, the court would find that it was

(A) Constitutional, because the state created the financial market in question using its own funds.

(B) Unconstitutional, because it substantially interferes with interstate commerce.

(C) Unconstitutional, because it violates the negative implications of the commerce clause.

(D) Unconstitutional, because it is in-state economic protectionism.

149. Congress enacted a $100 tax on the sale of any handgun to a private individual not for use in law enforcement or military duties. Will this tax survive a constitutional challenge?

(A) Yes, but only if Congress could have banned possession of handguns outright.

(B) Yes, if the dominant intent of Congress was that the tax would produce revenue.

(C) No, if the tax does not result in any significant collection of revenue.

(D) No, because the tax is clearly intended as a penalty on handgun ownership.

150. Dixie State requires a competency test granting people a license to teach elementary or secondary school within the state. The test covers skills and knowledge taught in high school, as well as other skills. Caucasian test-takers pass the test twice as often as African-American test-takers. Regina, a black woman who failed the test, sues Dixie State. An expert testifying on behalf of the P opines that Caucasians score 35% higher than minority groups on multiple-choice question format tests, but that other formats reduce the margin substantially. The expert further opines that the choice of the multiple-choice format in the face of such evidence is clearly intentional discrimination. The court will most likely find that the competency test is

(A) Constitutional, as rationally related to a legitimate government interest.

(B) Unconstitutional, as a violation of equal protection due to its discriminatory impact.

(C) Unconstitutional, as a violation of equal protection due to its discriminatory intent.

(D) Constitutional, because teachers constitute participation in government.

151. Belt State Legislature sent Belt University, a private religious school, a $1 million cash grant for the school to acquire a new kitchen facility in the student union building. The grant was a part of a larger series of state awards of higher education grants to schools. If the grant is challenged by a P who has proper standing, the court will likely find it

(A) Valid, as an incidental benefit to a private school in higher education.

(B) Valid, as a property clause disbursement.

(C) Invalid, as an excessive entanglement.

(D) Invalid, as an improper religious benefit

152. Sam Blocky was married to Eve. Eve won custody of their two children and support payments from Sam in the divorce decree. Readjustment was hard on Sam. Sam got behind in his support payments. Then Sam met Rebecca and asked her to marry him. The state refused to issue a marriage license unless he could make a showing that his two children from Eve would never have to go on welfare. This denial of the marriage license was pursuant to a state statute. What is the probable outcome if the statute were properly challenged as to its constitutionality?

- (A) Valid, as rationally related to the legitimate end of protecting children of a prior marriage.
- (B) Valid, as the state has general power to enact legislation.
- (C) Invalid, as the statute is not narrowly tailored to promote a compelling government interest.
- (D) Invalid, as the statute does not treat applicants with children the same as similarly situated applicants without children.

153. A state law banning the sale of which substance would be least likely to be subject to strict scrutiny?

- (A) Milk.
- (B) Condoms.
- (C) Rubber tires.
- (D) Both B and C.

154. Mr. Dole is a welfare recipient. The state passed a law ending welfare in the state. The department ceases paying benefits to Mr. Dole in reaction to the law. What best describes the constitutionality of this?

- (A) Constitutional, as rationally related to legitimate ends.
- (B) Unconstitutional, because the state ended his benefits prior to a hearing.
- (C) Unconstitutional, because the state has assumed the duty of his care.
- (D) Constitutional, if the state grants him a hearing as soon as practicable after the benefits are ceased.

155. In Farstate, USA the examinations for driver's licensing are contracted out to a private company. The contractor refuses to hire anyone but white males. Assume that there are no state or federal civil rights statutes that would prevent such hiring practices. Which of the following is the correct analysis and conclusion?

- (A) Race is a suspect class, so the policy most likely violates strict scrutiny because there is no compelling governmental interest being advanced.
- (B) The private company is not a state actor, so unless there are statutes preventing race discrimination, the action is not prohibited by the equal protection clause.
- (C) Because race and gender are both at issue, the proper level of scrutiny is intermediate because the lesser of two classes is evaluated in a "double classification" case. The decision will be for the contractor because driver licensing is an important governmental purpose.
- (D) Because there is no constitutional right to drive, the proper level of scrutiny is rational basis.

156. Farstate grants funding to a private nursing home to care for indigent patients. The nursing home has a practice of hiring only women who are members of a minority racial group. Assume that there are no state or federal civil rights statutes to prevent such a hiring practice. Which of the following is the correct analysis and conclusion?

- (A) Race is a suspect class, so the hiring practice most likely violates strict scrutiny because there is no compelling governmental interest being advanced.
- (B) The nursing home is not a state actor, so unless there are statutes preventing race discrimination the action is not prohibited by the equal protection clause.
- (C) Race is a suspect class, but since the hiring practice is remedying past discrimination the practice will satisfy strict scrutiny.
- (D) Because government funding is involved, the proper level of scrutiny is rational basis.

157. The Farstate Department of Wealth Equality is an agency dedicated to taking from the rich to give to the poor in the finest Marxist tradition. The head of the department has promulgated the following hiring rule: "Because the rich are the source of all problems of society and cannot understand the plight of the poor, anyone who has a net worth over $100,000.00 is ineligible for employment with this department." Immediately, 25 department employees are fired due to their net worth. They sue the state. Which of the following is the most correct analysis and conclusion?

(A) The action is arbitrary and capricious, so it is unconstitutional under strict scrutiny.

(B) The action is not by a state actor because wealth redistribution is not an essential government function.

(C) The right to public employment is a protected property interest and the employees would likely prevail because of lack of procedural due process.

(D) Wealth is a quasi-suspect class, so the rule must promulgate an important governmental purpose. Because eliminating poverty is so important, the rule meets this level of scrutiny.

158. The State of Oppression passes a law that authorizes the Department of Environmental Quality to seize "any motor vehicle that pollutes an unconscionable amount." The law then states that the seizure becomes permanent after a "reasonable time." The department decides to be generous in that no seizure will become permanent until after a hearing. The department then posts the hearing dates on its website. At the hearing, the owner is allowed a fair opportunity to present his or her case. Under this scheme, which option is the correct result?

(A) The owners have been granted sufficient notice and an opportunity to be heard.

(B) The owners do not have sufficient notice.

(C) Notice may be constructive when the regulated subject matter is an important governmental function like pollution.

(D) The owners have sufficient notice, but the hearing itself does not meet due process because the burden of proof beyond a reasonable doubt is not upon the state.

159. The State of Coast has a law that all state employees are "at-will" employees, which means the employees may be fired without cause. Professor Leftofski is a university associate professor who attends public rallies critical of U.S. foreign policy. He often cancels his classes and has been late on several deadlines because of his activities. The university president tells the professor "Get your lazy rear end off my campus. You're fired." Which of the following is the correct analysis and conclusion?

(A) Employment is a fundamental right requiring due process. Due process was denied, so the professor's termination was illegal.

(B) A job with the government is a property right requiring due process. Due process was denied, so the professor's termination was illegal.

(C) The professor had no property interest in the job, so his termination did not violate due process.

(D) The professor was exercising his protected free speech rights, and so his at-will termination was unconstitutional.

160. The State of Coast has a law that all state employees are "at-will" employees, which means the employees may be fired without cause. Professor Leftofski is an associate professor who attends public rallies critical of U.S. foreign policy. He often cancels his classes and has been late on several deadlines because of these activities. The university president tells the professor, "Get your lazy rear end off my campus. You're fired." The former Professor is now a private citizen. He gets on a soapbox in downtown and begins a diatribe against the U.S., capitalism, and democracy. The busy capitalists walking by pay no attention to him. In frustration, he throws an American flag to the ground and shoots it with his .357 Magnum to get people's attention. Which is the proper analysis and conclusion?

(A) Freedom of speech is a fundamental right, which includes the right to be heard. Therefore, getting people's attention with the pistol was a protected exercise of expression.

(B) He may be prosecuted for discharging a firearm, but not desecrating the flag. This is because desecrating a flag is protected political speech, but discharging a firearm is not, due to a rational basis in protecting public safety.

(C) He may not be prosecuted for discharging a firearm because the second amendment prohibits such, but may be prosecuted for desecrating a flag if prohibited by state law.

(D) He may be prosecuted for both discharging a firearm and desecrating a flag because there was no prior restraint on his speech.

161. The North American Association to Promote Strictly Traditional Religions (NAAPSTR) has successfully lobbied the State of Texarkana for a statute named "Equal Rights for All Religions." The law requires broadcasters that air segments discussing Christianity to allow equal time for segments on Judaism, Hinduism, and Buddhism.

The American Atheism Association (AAA) is devoted to the study and promotion of the belief that there is no supreme power or creator. AAA has put together a segment about atheism for broadcast on five major television stations in Texarkana. However, four of the five stations have declined to air the segment because they believe it would violate the statute. AAA has sued the four stations and has filed suit against the state challenging the constitutionality of the statute.

What is the strongest argument AAA can make in support of striking down the Equal Rights for the All Religions statute?

(A) The First Amendment prohibits government interference with freedom of the press.

(B) The fact that the statute involves only broadcast media and not print media is an Equal Protection violation.

(C) The First Amendment prohibits government interference with the free exercise of religion.

(D) The statute is not narrowly tailored to promote a compelling secular governmental interest.

162. The North American Association to Promote Strictly Traditional Religions (NAAPSTR) has successfully lobbied the State of Texarkana for a statute named "Equal Rights for All Religions." The law requires broadcasters that air segments discussing Christianity to allow equal time for segments on Judaism, Hinduism, Islam, and Buddhism.

The American Atheism Association (AAA) is devoted to the study and promotion of the belief that there is no supreme power or creator. AAA has put together a segment about atheism for broadcast on five major television stations in Texarkana. However, four of the five stations have declined to air the segment because they state it would violate the statute. AAA has sued the four stations and has filed suit against the state challenging the constitutionality of the statute.

The state files a motion to dismiss, claiming that AAA lacks standing. What result?

(A) Motion granted, because the stations were under no obligation to air the segment and therefore no injury has occurred.

(B) Motion granted, because only individual members of AAA (and not the organization itself) have standing.

(C) Motion denied, because the stations refused to air the broadcast segment based on the statute.

(D) Motion granted, because the statute does not actually prohibit the stations from broadcasting the segment.

163. The North American Association to Promote Strictly Traditional Religions (NAAPSTR) has successfully lobbied the State of Texarkana for a statute named "Equal Rights for All Religions." The law requires broadcasters that air segments discussing Christianity to allow equal time for segments on Judaism, Hinduism, and Buddhism.

The American Atheism Association (AAA) is devoted to the study and promotion of the belief that there is no supreme power or creator. AAA has put together a segment about atheism for broadcast on five major television stations in Texarkana. However, four of the five stations have declined to air the segment because they believe it would violate the statute. AAA has sued the four stations and has filed suit against the state challenging the constitutionality of the statute.

NAAPSTR files suit against the station that agreed to air the AAA segment, claiming that the station violated the statute. What is the likely result?

(A) The suit will be dismissed because NAAPSTR lacks standing.

(B) The suit will be dismissed because only the state has the power to enforce the statute.

(C) NAAPSTR will prevail because the station violated the statute.

(D) The station will prevail because atheism is not a religious belief and therefore the broadcast did not violate the statute.

164. The states of Allen and Burns share a border straddled by a beautiful mountain range. Atop the range are two state parks, one run by the state of Allen and one run by the state of Burns. Visitors may take gondolas to the top of the mountains and take state-guided tours that overlap both parks. According to the federal Parks & Recreation Employment Act, employees of any park or recreational facility that engages in interstate activities must be paid a minimum wage of $15.00. Tour guides are employed by both states. Tour guides from Allen are paid $10.00 per hour, which is the minimum wage of that state. Guides from Burns are paid $12.50 per hour, although that state's minimum wage is only $6.00.

Employees from the State of Burns sue the state in federal court for back pay, claiming they are entitled to the difference between their wages and the $15.00 per hour wages mandated by the Parks & Recreation Employment Act. What is the likely result?

(A) The employees will prevail, because of the Supremacy Clause.

(B) The case will be dismissed or remanded pursuant to the Eleventh Amendment.

(C) The state will prevail, because Congress has no authority to regulate the wages of state employees not engaged in interstate commerce.

(D) The state will prevail, because the management of state parks is a traditional state function.

165. The states of Allen and Burns share a border straddled by a beautiful mountain range. Atop the range are two state parks, one run by the state of Allen and one run by the state of Burns. Visitors may take gondolas to the top of the mountains and take state-guided tours that overlap both parks. According to the federal Parks & Recreation Employment Act, employees of any park or recreational facility that engages in interstate activities must be paid a minimum wage of $8.00. Tour guides are employed by both states. Tour guides from Allen are paid $6.75 per hour, which is the minimum wage of that state. Guides from Burns are paid $7.50 per hour, although that state's minimum wage is only $6.00.

State of Allen park employees sue the State of Allen in state court for back pay, claiming they are entitled to the difference between their wages and the $7.50 per hour paid to State of Burns park employees. What is the likely result?

(A) The state will prevail, because it is not required to pay its employees the same wage as similarly situated employees in Burns.

(B) The employees will prevail, because of the Article IV Privileges and Immunities Clause.

(C) The employees will prevail, because of the Equal Protection Clause.

(D) The case will be dismissed, because it is barred by the Eleventh Amendment.

166. Rebecca is a married woman living in the State of Serendipity. She has three children and is a homemaker. In which of the following situations is she most likely to successfully challenge the constitutionality of a state statute?

(A) A statute is passed that prohibits unmarried persons from engaging in "unnatural" sexual acts. Rebecca wants to challenge the statute as a violation of the right to privacy and for vagueness.

(B) A statute is passed that gives a state income tax credit to married persons with children. Rebecca wants to challenge the statute under the Equal Protection Clause.

(C) A statute is passed that deprives citizens of the State of Serendipity from receiving unemployment benefits if they were dismissed for refusing to work on their Sabbath day. Rebecca wants to challenge the statute under the Establishment Clause.

(D) A statute is passed that prohibits speeches in Serendipity public squares that "incite strong negative emotions" about the state government. Rebecca has no plans to make any public speeches, but wants to challenge the statute for overbreadth and as a violation of the right to free speech.

167. Due to decades of overfishing by commercial and game fisherman, the South Pacific Red Tuna has become an endangered species. Congress has passed a law that prohibits the importation of all rare tuna into the United States. However, the President, with the consent of two-thirds of the Senate, has a long-standing treaty with the country of Ivaronia that includes trade agreements approving the importation of South Pacific Red Tuna.

The President has vetoed the law, but both houses of Congress have overridden the veto by a three-fourths majority. What is the best argument for why the importation of tuna from Ivaronia should cease?

(A) Only a two-thirds majority of Congress is required to override a Presidential veto.

(B) When a treaty and a federal law are in conflict, the one that is last in time prevails.

(C) When a treaty and a federal law are in conflict, the federal law prevails whenever the law relates to commerce.

(D) The Executive Branch has ultimate authority regarding foreign affairs.

168. Congress has passed the Career Horizons Act which provides educational grants to U.S. citizens who meet specific qualifications. Hans Kleimer is a German citizen who has been studying in the United States under a valid visa. Hans applies for a grant under the Career Horizons Act. Despite meeting all of the other specified qualifications, Hans is turned down because he is not a U.S. citizen. If Hans challenges the constitutionality of his denial, what is the most likely decision that a court would reach?

(A) Hans will not prevail, because Congress has the right to attach limiting conditions to its spending.

(B) Hans will prevail, because he is in the country legally and is entitled to constitutional protections.

(C) Hans will not prevail, because Congress has broad powers to restrict the entitlements of aliens.

(D) The case will be dismissed, because aliens have no right to bring suit in courts of the United States.

169. Cheminol is a corporation operating in the State of Nebar. The company produces and ships flammable chemicals for use in the manufacture of certain types of hard plastics. For years, Cheminol has been burying bithium, a toxic waste product, in metal drums in a storage trench on Cheminol property. Some of the drums have suffered metal fatigue and begun to leak, but the company has not instituted clean up procedures.

Kasan, a city in Nebar located near the Cheminol plant, has recently been detecting rising levels of bithium in its groundwater, attributable to the Cheminol dumpsite. One test completed on April 3 revealed that the bithium level had reached 100 parts per billion. The federal government regulations regarding bithium set the maximum permissible level in groundwater at 250 parts per billion. Neither the State of Nebar nor the city of Kasan has any law regarding bithium on the books.

The Kasan City Council is concerned about a new study indicating that even lower levels of bithium – 75 parts per billion – could be dangerous to humans. On July 17, the council passed a municipal ordinance limiting the permissible amount of bithium in groundwater to 50 parts per billion and cites Cheminol for violation. After a full and fair hearing, the city fined Cheminol $100,000 and ordered the immediate cleanup of the dumpsite within 60 days.

Cheminol brings suit to challenge the fine. What is the likely result?
- (A) The city council will prevail, because it has the right to regulate for the health and safety of its citizens.
- (B) The city council will prevail, because Cheminol had notice and an opportunity to be heard.
- (C) Cheminol will prevail, because the city ordinance amounts to a bill of attainder.
- (D) Cheminol will prevail, because the city ordinance was an *ex post facto* law.

170. Cheminol is a corporation operating in the State of Nebar. The company produces and ships flammable chemicals for use in the manufacture of certain types of hard plastics. For years, Cheminol has been burying bithium, a toxic waste product, in metal drums in a storage trench on Cheminol property. Some of the drums have suffered metal fatigue and begun to leak, but the company has not instituted clean up procedures.

Kasan, a city in Nebar located near the Cheminol plant, has recently been detecting rising levels of bithium in its

groundwater, attributable to the Cheminol dumpsite. One test completed on April 3 revealed that the bithium level had reached 100 parts per billion. The federal government regulations regarding bithium set the maximum permissible level in groundwater at 250 parts per billion. Neither the State of Nebar nor the city of Kasan has any law regarding bithium on the books.

The Kasan City Council is concerned about a new study indicating that even lower levels of bithium – 75 parts per billion – could be dangerous to humans. On July 17, the council passed a municipal ordinance limiting the permissible amount of bithium in groundwater to 50 parts per billion and cites Cheminol for violation. After a full and fair hearing, the city fined Cheminol $100,000 and ordered the immediate cleanup of the dumpsite within 60 days.

Cheminol brings suit to challenge the constitutionality of the city ordinance. What is the LEAST effective argument Cheminol could make?
- (A) Congress has occupied the field of regulation of toxic waste contaminant levels.
- (B) The city ordinance is in conflict with the federal law and is therefore invalid.
- (C) The city ordinance was enacted as a result of improper procedural methods.
- (D) The city ordinance amounted to a taking of Cheminol's property because there is no way to operate its plant without a minimum contamination rate of 60 parts per billion.

171. Cheminol is a corporation operating in the State of Nebar. The company produces and ships flammable chemicals for use in the manufacture of certain types of hard plastics. For years, Cheminol has been burying bithium, a toxic waste product, in metal drums in a storage trench on Cheminol property. Some of the drums have suffered metal fatigue and begun to leak, but the company has not instituted clean up procedures.

Kasan, a city in Nebar located near the Cheminol plant, has recently been detecting rising levels of bithium in its groundwater, attributable to the Cheminol dumpsite. One test completed on April 3 revealed that the bithium level had reached 100 parts per billion. The federal government regulations regarding bithium set the maximum permissible level in groundwater at 250 parts per billion. Neither the State of Nebar nor the city of Kasan has any law regarding bithium on the books.

The Kasan City Council is concerned about a new study indicating that even lower levels of bithium – 75 parts per billion – could be dangerous to humans. On July 17, the council passed a municipal ordinance limiting the permissible amount of bithium in groundwater to 50 parts per billion and cites Cheminol for violation. After a full and fair hearing, the city fined Cheminol $100,000 and ordered the immediate cleanup of the dumpsite within 60 days.

Cheminol refuses to obey the order to clean up its site, and after 90 days an additional non-compliance fine of $200,000 is assessed. If the ordinance is valid, can the new fine be enforced?

- (A) Yes, because Cheminol had a full and fair hearing and refused to obey the order.
- (B) Yes, because Cheminol had no liberty or property interest at stake in performing the cleanup.
- (C) No, because the order was an *ex post facto* law.
- (D) No, because the order was in conflict with federal law.

172. In an effort to smooth relations between two troubled countries, the President of the United States signs an executive agreement with the Premier of the Sovereign Nation of Zimtar. The stated purpose of the agreement is for the president to "create the best possible public image" for Zimtar in the U.S. media. The Editor-in-Chief of the New York Times files suit on behalf of the paper, claiming that the agreement violates the First Amendment guarantee of a free press. The president's best argument for the constitutional validity of the executive agreement is

- (A) Executive agreements have no actual force of authority or law.
- (B) Congress can override an executive agreement if it so chooses.
- (C) The executive agreement does not place any restrictions whatsoever on the press.
- (D) The president has broad discretion when entering into executive agreements.

173. A state law requires state employees over the age of 60 who drive 3 or more hours a day as part of their job to take a periodic eyesight and reflex test. Males must take the test annually, and females must take it every two years. Which of the following, if true, would most likely make this law constitutionally valid?

- (A) Studies have shown that males are more likely than females to be involved in automobile collisions.
- (B) Studies have shown that males over the age of 60 lose their vision and reflexes twice as fast as females over the age of 60.
- (C) Congress has passed a law declaring gender discrimination in state employment to be legal.
- (D) In the past, female employees have been subjected to discrimination in hiring for state jobs that require three or more hours of driving per day.

174. After two disasters involving chemical explosions, Palray City enacted an ordinance banning the transportation of flammable chemicals within three miles of the city center. Chemlab, a manufacturer of volatile chemicals, is located in the heart of the industrial sector of Palray, one mile from the downtown area.

Employees of Chemlab protested the city's action, carrying signs and banners down to Palray City Hall. Many of them blocked traffic, and a number of city workers inside the building came to the windows when they heard the people below. Six Chemlab employees were arrested pursuant to Palray City Ordinance 35.598, which makes it a misdemeanor to "engage in protests, marches, gatherings, or demonstrations that create a disturbance or hinder the work of city employees."

Chemlab filed suit in state court, alleging that it was entitled to just compensation pursuant to the Fifth Amendment to the United States Constitution. What is the likely outcome?

(A) Palray will prevail, because the Fifth Amendment does not apply to cities or other non-federal governmental entities.

(B) Palray will prevail, because the regulation does not amount to a taking.

(C) Chemlab will prevail, unless Palray City can demonstrate that the ordinance serves a compelling interest and is the least restrictive means available.

(D) Chemlab will prevail, because it has been deprived of economic use of its property.

175. After two disasters involving chemical explosions, Palray City enacted an ordinance banning the transportation of flammable chemicals within three miles of the city center. Chemlab, a manufacturer of volatile chemicals, is located in the heart of the industrial sector of Palray, one mile from the downtown area.

Employees of Chemlab protested the city's action, carrying signs and banners down to Palray City Hall. Many of them blocked traffic, and a number of city workers inside the building came to the windows when they heard the people below. Six Chemlab employees were arrested pursuant to Palray City Ordinance 35.598, which makes it a misdemeanor to "engage in protests, marches, gatherings, or demonstrations that create a disturbance or hinder the work of city employees."

The six employees arrested at the protest filed suit against the city, claiming that Ordinance 35.598 is in violation of the United States Constitution. What is the strongest argument the employees can make in support of their claim?

(A) The ordinance violates the Equal Protection Clause.

(B) The ordinance prohibits exercise of the right to freedom of association.

(C) The ordinance prohibits the exercise of the First Amendment right to free speech.

(D) The ordinance is vague and overbroad.

176. After two disasters involving chemical explosions, Palray City enacted an ordinance banning the transportation of flammable chemicals within three miles of the city center. Chemlab, a manufacturer of volatile chemicals, is located in the heart of the industrial sector of Palray, one mile from the downtown area.

Employees of Chemlab protested the city's action, carrying signs and banners down to Palray City Hall. Many of them blocked traffic, and a number of city workers inside the building came to the windows when they heard the people below. Six Chemlab employees were arrested pursuant to Palray City Ordinance 35.598, which makes it a misdemeanor to "engage in protests, marches, gatherings, or demonstrations that create a disturbance or hinder the work of city employees."

The six employees arrested at the protest filed suit against the city, claiming that Ordinance 35.598 is in violation of the United States Constitution. In response to the employees' claim, Palray City argues that the statute is constitutional under Article X Section 5 of the Palray State Constitution, which gives cities greater discretion to regulate for public safety than federal law. This argument will likely

(A) Fail, because of the Supremacy Clause.

(B) Fail, because the federal government has ultimate police power.

(C) Succeed, because the federal government cannot interfere with a state's interpretation of its own constitution.

(D) Fail, because of the 14th Amendment Privileges or Immunities Clause.

177. The State of Waldorf and the State of Statler share a border at their eastern and western edges, respectively. Because

Waldorf has a lower sales tax than Statler does, many residents of Statler go to Waldorf to make major purchases, such as automobiles, expensive jewelry, etc. As a result, the otherwise quiet stretch of interstate highway connecting Eastern Waldorf and Western Statler is plagued with constant traffic jams and accidents.

Due to these problems and lost in-state revenues caused by interstate purchasers from Statler, Representative Moneypenny from the State of Waldorf lobbies the state to pass the Waldorf Business Defense Act. This bill would allow Waldorf to tax residents of Statler at a higher rate than residents of Waldorf for single consumer purchases over the cost of $1,000. The bill passes by a narrow majority.

Maggie Mardelene lives in the State of Statler. She takes a vacation to the nearby State of Waldorf to see her sister's new baby. While in Waldorf, Maggie drives her rental car past Sid's Sizzling Streetlegals, a used car lot incorporated and licensed in Waldorf. Sid's is selling a beautiful 1999 Lexus for $9,000. Maggie can't resist the great deal and goes to Sid's to purchase the car. However, when the salesman asks for her identification and discovers she is a resident of Statler, Maggie is charged sales tax amounting to $2,400. A resident of Waldorf would have paid only $900 in sales tax.

Maggie's best chance for challenging the constitutionality of the sales tax would be to bring a claim pursuant to the
- (A) Congressional Tax and Spend Power.
- (B) Commerce Clause.
- (C) Article IV Privileges and Immunities Clause.
- (D) Fourteenth Amendment Privileges or Immunities Clause.

178. The State of Waldorf and the State of Statler share a border at their eastern and western edges, respectively. Because Waldorf has a lower sales tax than Statler does, many residents of Statler go to Waldorf to make major purchases, such as automobiles, expensive jewelry, etc. As a result, the otherwise quiet stretch of interstate highway connecting Eastern

Waldorf and Western Statler is plagued with constant traffic jams and accidents.

Due to these problems and lost in-state revenues caused by interstate purchasers from Statler, Representative Moneypenny from the State of Waldorf lobbies the state to pass the Waldorf Business Defense Act. This bill would allow Waldorf to tax residents of Statler at a higher rate than residents of Waldorf for single consumer purchases over the cost of $1,000. The bill passes by a narrow majority.

Maggie Mardelene lives in the State of Statler. She takes a vacation to the nearby State of Waldorf to see her sister's new baby. While in Waldorf, Maggie drives her rental car past Sid's Sizzling Streetlegals, a used car lot incorporated and licensed in Waldorf. Sid's is selling a beautiful 2015 Lexus for $9,000. Maggie can't resist the great deal and goes to Sid's to purchase the car. However, when the salesman asks for her identification and discovers she is a resident of Statler, Maggie is charged sales tax amounting to $2,400. A resident of Waldorf would have paid only $900 in sales tax.

Which of the following taxes would be constitutionally permissible?
- (A) A sales tax by Statler levied against Maggie and a use tax by Statler levied against Maggie.
- (B) A sales tax by Waldorf levied against Sid's.
- (C) A sales tax by Statler levied against Maggie.
- (D) A use tax by Statler levied against Maggie and a net income tax by Waldorf levied against Sid's.

179. The State of Waldorf and the State of Statler share a border at their eastern and western edges, respectively. Because Waldorf has a lower sales tax than Statler does, many residents of Statler go to Waldorf to make major purchases, such as automobiles, expensive jewelry, etc. As a result, the otherwise quiet stretch of interstate highway connecting Eastern Waldorf and Western Statler is plagued with constant traffic jams and accidents.

Due to these problems and lost in-state revenues caused by interstate purchasers from Statler, Representative Moneypenny from the State of Waldorf lobbies the state to pass the Waldorf Business Defense Act. This bill would allow Waldorf to tax residents of Statler at a higher rate than residents of Waldorf for single consumer purchases over the cost of $1,000. The bill passes by a narrow majority.

Maggie Mardelene lives in the State of Statler. She takes a vacation to the nearby State of Waldorf to see her sister's new baby. While in Waldorf, Maggie drives her rental car past Sid's Sizzling Streetlegals, a used car lot incorporated and licensed in Waldorf. Sid's is selling a beautiful 2015 Lexus for $9,000. Maggie can't resist the great deal and goes to Sid's to purchase the car. However, when the salesman asks for her identification and discovers she is a resident of Statler, Maggie is charged sales tax amounting to $2,400. A resident of Waldorf would have paid only $900 in sales tax.

Sid's experiences a sharp drop in business because of the new tax against residents of Statler. The company files suit challenging the constitutionality of the state tax law. What is the least effective argument that the state can make in defense to Sid's claim?

(A) Sid's claim does not involve a fundamental right.

(B) There is statistical evidence that the problems on Waldorf's eastern highway are caused by residents of Statler.

(C) The Waldorf Business Defense Act is constitutional.

(D) Any other measure would not solve the problem.

180. In a stunning front-page article in the New York Times, it is revealed that the President of the United States, Geoff Brush, has participated in insider trading. On November 7, 2000, Brush was elected to his first term of office. On November 27, he resigned as CEO of his father's tobacco company, Fillup Maurice. On January 16, 2001, Brush was golfing with the CFO of Fillup Maurice. The CFO said that the company was about to

fold. Apparently, there had been some shady bookkeeping going on (of which Brush had no knowledge when he was CEO). On January 18, 2001, Brush dumped his stock. The dump greatly exacerbated the stock's plummet and caused a number of other stockholders to be financially ruined. On January 20, 2001, Brush was inaugurated.

On December 10, 2001, Brush is indicted under the Federal Insider Trading Act and is sued by the aggrieved stockholders. He argues that he has Executive Immunity as to the civil suit. Will his argument succeed?

(A) Yes, because the President is immune from suits for money damages while he is in office.

(B) No, because the act that is the basis for the suit took place two days prior to the President's inauguration.

(C) Yes, because only Congress can initiate civil litigation against a sitting President.

(D) No, because the President has also been indicted for a crime, and therefore his immunity to a related civil suit is waived.

181. In a stunning front-page article in the New York Times, it is revealed that the President of the United States, Geoff Brush, has participated in insider trading. On November 7, 2000, Brush was elected to his first term of office. On November 27, he resigned as CEO of his father's tobacco company, Fillup Maurice.

On January 16, 2001, Brush was golfing with the CFO of Fillup Maurice. The CFO said that the company was about to fold. Apparently, there had been some shady bookkeeping going on (of which Brush had no knowledge when he was CEO). On January 18, 2001, Brush dumped his stock. The dump greatly exacerbated the stock's plummet and caused a number of other stockholders to be financially ruined. On January 20, 2001, Brush was inaugurated.

Brush is tried and convicted of violating the Insider Trading Act. As a result, the House determines that grounds for impeachment exist. The vote is a majority of 223 to 212. The Senate convicts by a majority vote of 56 to 44. What are the consequences for President Brush?

(A) He is impeached.
(B) He is removed from office.
(C) He is impeached and removed from office.
(D) He is neither impeached nor removed from office.

182. In a stunning front-page article in the New York Times, it is revealed that the President of the United States, Geoff Brush, has participated in insider trading. On November 7, 2000, Brush was elected to his first term of office. On November 27, he resigned as CEO of his father's tobacco company, Fillup Maurice.

On January 16, 2001, Brush was golfing with the CFO of Fillup Maurice. The CFO said that the company was about to fold. Apparently, there had been some shady bookkeeping going on (of which Brush had no knowledge when he was CEO). On January 18, 2001, Brush dumped his stock. The dump greatly exacerbated the stock's plummet and caused a number of other stockholders to be financially ruined. On January 20, 2001, Brush was inaugurated.

Following a similar scandal in 1986, Congress enacted legislation to limit the Executive pardon power so that the vice president who was the direct successor to an impeached president could not pardon that same president. Brush's successor, Vice President Greely, is now president and wants to pardon Brush. He files suit in federal court challenging the legislation as unconstitutional. What should the federal court do?

(A) Dismiss the case as a non-justiciable political question.
(B) Strike down the law as involving a political question.
(C) Dismiss the case as moot, because the Presidential pardon power extends only to state crimes, not federal crimes.
(D) Uphold the law, because it is permissible under Article IV, Section III.

183. Kelly is a property developer who owns 110 acres in a suburb of Baysurf. She has subdivided the property into 1-acre plots and wants to sell them to private parties to build single-family dwellings. She receives all of the necessary licensing and zoning approval, and registers her business with the Secretary of State and other appropriate state agencies. Concerned about property values and safety, she wants to include in each deed a covenant stating that the purchaser will not resell the property to anyone of Arabic descent.

The O'Neills buy a piece of property and build a house. Three years later, they wish to sell, and get an outstanding offer from a man whose parents are both responsible Syrian nationals. They sell the property and move. However, Kelly files a breach of contract suit in state court for violation of the covenant. Kelly prevails, and the O'Neills appeal, claiming that enforcing the covenant amounted to unconstitutional racial discrimination. Kelly argues that there was no state action. What is the best argument that the O'Neills can make in support of their claim?

(A) The housing development is a place of public accommodation.
(B) There are mutual contacts between Kelly and the state.
(C) Housing citizens is a traditional public function.
(D) The lower court enforced the contract.

184. Congress recently passed a new comprehensive Labor and Employment Act, which greatly expanded the rights of American employees. In anticipation of an overwhelming amount of litigation, Congress created the federal Labor and Employment Court. The court's jurisdiction is to hear cases brought pursuant to the Labor and Employment Act. Since litigation will settle much of the controversy surrounding the Act, Congress has provided that the court will be eliminated after 10 years. Since the Labor and Employment Court will have expertise in adjudicating disputes about the act, no appeals will be allowed, and the U.S. Supreme Court will not have the power of judicial review.

The Minimum Wage Act provides that the federal minimum wage will increase by a certain percentage every two years. The next increase will occur in eleven months and will bring the federal minimum wage up to $9.15 per hour. The State of Dakola's minimum wage is currently $9.00 per hour.

What is the strongest ground for challenging the constitutionality of the Labor and Employment Act?

(A) It limits the jurisdiction of the federal Labor and Employment Court.

(B) It eliminates judicial review of an inferior federal court by the U.S. Supreme Court.

(C) It eliminates all possibility of appeal.

(D) It violates the constitutional provision that all federal court judges serve for a life term as long as they do not act improperly.

185. Congress recently passed a new comprehensive Labor and Employment Act, which greatly expanded the rights of American employees. In anticipation of an overwhelming amount of litigation, Congress created the federal Labor and Employment Court. The new court's jurisdiction is to hear cases brought pursuant to the Labor and Employment Act. Since litigation will settle much of the controversy surrounding the Act, Congress has provided that the court will be eliminated after 10 years. Because the Labor and Employment Court will have expertise in adjudicating disputes about the act, no appeals will be allowed, and the U.S. Supreme Court will not have the power of judicial review.

The Minimum Wage Act provides that the federal minimum wage will increase by a certain percentage every two years. The next increase will occur in eleven months and will bring the federal minimum wage up to $9.15 per hour. The State of Dakola's minimum wage is currently $9.00 per hour.

An employer in Dakola challenges the constitutionality of the Minimum Wage

Act in the Labor and Employment Court. The employer argues that when the new increases take effect, Dakola's minimum wage will increase and he will not be able to afford to stay in business. The State of Dakola moves to dismiss. What result?

(A) Dismissed because the case is not ripe because the employer has not been injured.

(B) Dismissed because the court does not have jurisdiction.

(C) Motion to dismiss denied because the employer will be injured by the law when it takes effect and the case should be heard by the Labor and Employment Court.

(D) Dismissed because the case is moot because the federal law will have no effect on Dakola's minimum wage.

186. The State of North Caretarna has a law that allows public funds to be used in financial assistance programs to schools. In North Caretarna, a few schools at each academic level are run by religious organizations. In which of the following situations is the law most likely to be constitutionally valid?

(A) The law allows payment to all elementary schools, provided the school can demonstrate that the funds are not used in furtherance of religion.

(B) The law allows payment to all high schools, provided the funds are used only for athletic programs.

(C) The law allows payment to all high schools, provided the school can demonstrate that students of all religions are admitted without discrimination.

(D) The law allows payment to all colleges, provided the funds are used for athletic programs.

187. An outbreak of waterborne illness has ravaged the State of Pensacola. The illness has been traced to seepage from slaughterhouses engaged in unsafe disposal of animal byproducts. A recently enacted state law requires the "sanitary disposal of all animal carcasses, including organs, at a designated state disposal site." Jerry is a devoutly religious man whose faith requires him to bury a whole goat carcass in his backyard each month as an offering. Two weeks after the law is enacted, he is arrested while performing the act of burial.

If Jerry is prosecuted for violating the state law, what is his best defense on constitutional grounds?

(A) Enforcement of the law in Jerry's case is a violation of his freedom of religion.
(B) The act of burying the goat is expressive conduct and is therefore protected speech under the First Amendment.
(C) His belief that his religion requires him to bury a goat is sincere and therefore the prosecution is a Free Exercise Clause violation.
(D) The statute excessively entangles the government with religion, and is an Establishment Clause violation.

188. An outbreak of waterborne illness has ravaged the State of Pensacola. The illness has been traced to seepage from slaughterhouses engaged in unsafe disposal of animal byproducts. A recently enacted state law requires the "sanitary disposal of all animal carcasses, including organs, at a designated state disposal site." Jerry is a devoutly religious man whose faith requires him to bury a whole goat carcass in his backyard each month as an offering. Two weeks after the law is enacted, he is arrested while performing the act of burial.

Which of the following is the court prohibited from considering in its evaluation of Jerry's constitutional challenge to the statute?

(A) Whether Jerry is the owner of a slaughterhouse.
(B) Whether Jerry's belief in the sanctity of goat-burying is sincere.
(C) Whether the ritual that Jerry performs is mandated by his faith.
(D) Whether a reasonable person would agree that belief in the sanctity of burying a goat is a "religious" belief.

189. The State of Illiho is located on the West Coast of the United States. To get from Illiho to almost any other U.S. state requires travelling through Tassen, a neighboring state that shares an eastern border. To the North of Illiho is the State of Starket, the only state accessible to Illiho without going through Tassen.

Ace Trucking Company has its national headquarters in the State of Illiho but ships goods throughout the United States. Due to the heavy use of its roads by trucks from Illiho, Tassen has imposed a privilege tax on trucks from Illiho of $10 for every shipment across Tassen. Trucks from other states are taxed 50 cents per shipment, regardless of the amount of use. Tassen trucks are exempted from the tax, regardless of how much they use Tassen roads. Tassen also imposes a tax of 4% of the value of the goods in each truck that travels through Tassen, regardless of where the truck originated and whether the truck stops in the State of Tassen or not.

Ace Trucking files suit challenging the constitutionality of the Tassen privilege tax. Which of the following is the strongest argument in support of Ace's claim?

(A) Tassen is taxing goods in the stream of commerce.
(B) There is no substantial nexus between the state interest and the activity taxed.
(C) The tax is protectionist.
(D) No legitimate state interest is furthered by the tax.

190. The State of Illiho is located on the West Coast of the United States. To get from Illiho to almost any other U.S. state requires travelling through Tassen, a neighboring state that shares an eastern border. To the North of Illiho is the State of Starket, the only state accessible to Illiho without going through Tassen.

Ace Trucking Company has its national headquarters in the State of Illiho but ships goods throughout the United States. Due to the heavy use of its roads by trucks from Illiho, Tassen has imposed a privilege tax on trucks from Illiho of $10 for every shipment across Tassen. Trucks from other states are taxed 50 cents per shipment, regardless of the amount of use. Tassen trucks are exempted from the tax, regardless of how much they use Tassen roads. Tassen also imposes a tax of 4% of the value of the goods in each truck that travels through Tassen, regardless of where the truck originated and whether the truck stops in the State of Tassen or not.

In a summary judgment hearing on the privilege tax case, the court determines that the imposition of a privilege tax by Tassen is constitutional, but that Tassen must change its tax code to include a tax on Tassen trucks. Tassen then moves to dismiss. What is the likely result?

(A) Motion denied, there is another issue of apportionment.
(B) Motion denied, there is another issue of preemption.
(C) Motion granted, because there are no other constitutional issues raised.
(D) Motion denied, any privilege tax is an undue burden on interstate commerce.

191. The State of Illiho is located on the West Coast of the United States. To get from Illiho to almost any other U.S. state requires travelling through Tassen, a neighboring state that shares an eastern border. To the North of Illiho is the State of Starket, the only state accessible to Illiho without going through Tassen.

Ace Trucking Company has its national headquarters in the State of Illiho but ships goods throughout the United States. Due to the heavy use of its roads by trucks from Illiho, Tassen has imposed a privilege tax on trucks from Illiho of $10 for every shipment across Tassen. Trucks from other states are taxed 50 cents per shipment, regardless of the amount of use. Tassen trucks are exempted from the tax, regardless of how much they use Tassen roads. Tassen also imposes a tax of 4% of the value of the goods in each truck that travels through Tassen, regardless of where the truck originated and whether the truck stops in the State of Tassen or not.

In a separate action, a trucking company from Illiho that ships goods through Tassen challenges the Tassen goods tax under the dormant commerce clause. Is the trucking company's claim valid?

(A) No. The dormant commerce clause only prohibits states from enacting protectionist legislation that burdens interstate commerce.
(B) Yes. The dormant commerce clause prohibits the taxing of goods in the stream of commerce.
(C) No. States are permitted to tax out-of-state interests at the same rate as in-state interests.
(D) Yes. The dormant commerce clause prohibits states from taxing goods unless a legitimate state interest is served.

192. The House of Representatives conducts a two-year study investigating the negative effects of domestic violence on the larger economic and social fabric of society. It is determined that a decrease in domestic violence would result in an increase in economic productivity nationwide. As a result of the study, Congress enacts a law prohibiting violence against women within the District of Columbia. What is the best argument in favor of the constitutionality of the law?

(A) The law does not violate the Necessary and Proper Clause.
(B) Congress has expansive powers to research and explore issues affecting society.
(C) The law is a proper exercise of Congressional authority pursuant to the Commerce Clause.
(D) Congress has police power over the District of Columbia.

193. In response to a rising problem with homelessness and panhandling, the State of Wollstone enacts legislation that requires those earning less than $20,000 per year to register with the state Department of Health and Human Services. The registration list is intended to track those who may eventually become homeless, and also to register eligibility for certain state services. Earl, a food service worker earning $18,000 per year, challenges the law on Equal Protection grounds. Under what test will Wollstone's law be evaluated?

(A) Earl must demonstrate that the law is not rationally related to an important governmental purpose.

(B) The state must demonstrate that the law is rationally related to a compelling governmental interest.

(C) Earl must demonstrate that the law is not rationally related to a legitimate governmental interest.

(D) The state must demonstrate that the law is substantially related to an important governmental purpose.

194. The State of Calibama enacts a new statute that requires drivers who are stopped and cited for traffic violations which have fines of less than $50 to pay the amount of the fine directly to the officer. The driver may then challenge the citation at a hearing. If the driver wins his or her case, the amount of the fine is returned along with reasonable court costs. If constitutional challenges to Calibama's statute are raised, it will most likely be because the statute threatens rights to

(A) Procedural due process.

(B) Substantive due process.

(C) Equal protection.

(D) Liberty interests.

195. The State of Calibama enacts a new statute that requires drivers who are stopped and cited for traffic violations which have fines of less than $50 to pay the amount of the fine directly to the officer. The driver may then challenge the citation at a hearing. If the driver wins his or her case, the amount of the fine is returned along with reasonable court costs. Joe challenges the validity of the Calibama statute under *Mathews v. Eldridge*. What fact, if true, most strongly supports the state's defense of its procedure?

(A) The statute is rationally related to a legitimate governmental interest.

(B) More than 70% of the citations issued under the old law were dismissed at hearing.

(C) To most people, $50 is a *de minimis* amount of money that is not important.

(D) Under the old law, citizens rarely paid their tickets and the state incurred substantial costs in pursuing those who evaded the fines.

196. Ty is the owner of a disreputable, run-down theater in the heart of the City of Statley's central business district. He specializes in screening films that "push the envelope of society" and advertises to that end. A number of local residents are upset by the graphic nature of some of his films and make complaints to the local police. Ty's theater is shut down pursuant to Statley's municipal code prohibiting the public screening of obscene films. Which of the following arguments would assist Ty in his suit to reopen his theater?

(A) The films his theater screens have artistic value.

(B) The films he screens have artistic value and a reasonable person would agree that the films he screens do not depict any deviant sexual activity.

(C) The films he screens have artistic value, a reasonable person would agree that the films he screens do not depict any deviant sexual activity, and the films he screens have been shown in theaters all across the United States.

(D) Most of the citizens of Statley agree that the films he screens have serious political value and a reasonable person would agree that the films he screens do not depict any deviant sexual activity.

197. Ty is the owner of a disreputable, run-down theater in the heart of the City of Statley's central business district. He specializes in screening films that "push the envelope of society decency" and advertises to that end. A number of local residents are upset by the graphic nature of some of his films and make complaints to the local police. Ty's theater is shut down pursuant to Statley's municipal code prohibiting the public screening of obscene films. Ty wins a lawsuit to reopen his theater. Before he can say "constitution," he is slapped with another lawsuit regarding his advertisements. Apparently, Statley also has an ordinance prohibiting the publication of advertisements promoting obscene material. For Statley's law to pass constitutional muster, a court must find that

(A) Statley's definition of "obscene" comports with the federal standard.
(B) The law serves a compelling governmental interest.
(C) The law is narrowly tailored to achieve a substantial government interest.
(D) The law is rationally related to the Statley's interest.

198. Virgenessee and Alabraska are neighboring states that share the Blue Ridge River as a border. For three years, Virgenesee has been relaxing its environmental laws, including water pollution controls, in the hope of enticing more manufacturing businesses to move to the state. It worked, and mercury levels in the Blue Ridge River have tripled. Citizens of Alabraska are no longer able to use the river for recreation and fishing. The State of Alabraska files suit in the Federal District Court of Virgenessee, requesting that Virgenessee compensate Alabraska citizens for the harm resulting from the increased mercury levels.

Virgenessee files a 12(b)(6) motion for dismissal of the case, arguing that the court has no jurisdiction to hear the matter. The motion will likely be

(A) Denied, because lower courts have concurrent jurisdiction to hear cases between two or more states.
(B) Denied, because of Alabraska's *parens patriae* status.
(C) Granted, because the Supreme Court has mandatory original jurisdiction.
(D) Granted, because in cases between states, the Supreme Court must first deny *certiorari* before a suit in a lower court can be filed.

199. Virgenessee and Alabraska are neighboring states that share the Blue Ridge River as a border. For three years, Virgenesee has been relaxing its environmental laws, including water pollution controls, in the hope of enticing more manufacturing businesses to the state. It worked, and mercury levels in the Blue Ridge River have tripled.

Citzens of Alabraska are no longer able to use the river for recreation and fishing. The State of Alabraska files suit in the Federal District Court of Virgenessee, requesting that Virgenessee compensate Alabraska citizens for the harm resulting from the increased mercury levels.

Alabraska is also suing to have Virgenesee's environmental laws declared invalid. Alabraska will most likely prevail in its suit if which of the following is true?

(A) Virgenessee's water pollution regulations are less stringent than Alabraska's regulations.
(B) The Virgenesee legislature lowered water pollution regulations without conducting a study of the possible impact on Alabraska citizens.
(C) Virgenessee's water pollution regulations do not comport with regulations promulgated by the Federal Water Board.
(D) Virgenessee's water pollution regulations are less stringent than those required under the Federal Clean Water Act.

200. With the approval of the majority of Congress, United States President John Taylor appoints Simon LeBon as head of the Environment Protection Aency for a term of 3 years. After a bitter political disagreement, Taylor revokes the appointment on the grounds that LeBon serves "at the pleasure of the President." LeBon protests and files suit. What is the likely result?

(A) LeBon will prevail, because he was appointed for a term.
(B) LeBon will prevail, because Taylor may not remove him without Congress' consent.
(C) Taylor will prevail, because the Executive Branch may dismiss administrative appointees at will.
(D) Taylor will prevail, because the Executive does not need Congressional approval to remove administrative appointees.

Answers

Question Answer Rationales

> **MBE Tip:** Put a piece of paper over the answers and "mask down" while working through the questions so you don't accidentally peek at the next answer.

1. /C/ Originally a lawsuit between a state and a citizen of another state was within the jurisdiction of the Federal Courts under Article III, but this principle was abrogated by the 11th Amendment. **(A)** is incorrect because suits between states are within the jurisdiction of the Federal Courts. **(B)** is incorrect because admiralty suits are within the jurisdiction of the Federal Courts. **(D)** is incorrect because suits against the United States are within the jurisdiction of the Federal Courts.

2. /A/ A State Supreme Court has the final word on state law issues that rest upon an adequate and independent state law grounds; here, a quiet title action regards property and is a state law matter. **(B)** is incorrect because it contains a Federal issue, so the Supreme Court will review the State Court decision. **(C)** is incorrect because the Supreme Court, absent limitation by Congress, may review Circuit Court decisions. The subject matter of the Circuit Court decision is not dispositive to the analysis. **(D)** is incorrect because the Supreme Court, absent limitation by Congress, may review Circuit Court decisions. The subject matter of the Circuit Court decision is not dispositive in the analysis.

3. /C/ When a case seeks injunctive relief involving federal land and is heard by a three-judge panel in federal court, acceptance of the appeal to the Supreme Court is mandatory. **(A)** is not the best answer because *certiorari* involves discretion; the Supreme Court does not have discretion to deny in these circumstances. **(B)** is incorrect because when a case involves injunctive relief and is heard by a three-judge panel in federal court, appeal to the Supreme Court is mandatory. **(D)** is incorrect because when a case involves injunctive relief and is heard by a three-judge panel in federal court, appeal to the Supreme Court is mandatory.

4. /A/ Although third-party standing is not generally allowed, an exception exists for certain close relationships, such as that between a union member and the union. **(B)** is not the best answer because a direct injury is not imputed, the third party is simply allowed to take the place of the injured party. **(C)** is incorrect because although third-party standing is not generally allowed, an exception exists for certain close relationships, such as that between union member and union. **(D)** is incorrect because although third-party standing is not generally allowed, an exception exists for certain close relationships, such as that between union member and union.

5. /B/ There is no citizen standing for generalized grievances. **(A)** is incorrect because there is no citizen standing for generalized grievances. **(C)** is incorrect because there is no citizen standing for generalized grievances. **(D)** is not the best answer because standing is a preliminary threshold analysis. An immunity analysis would only be reached after the court was satisfied that the P had standing.

6. **/B/** There is no general "taxpayer standing" and the possible injury here is too remote to the P. **(A)** is not the best answer because theoretically, the injury could be redressed by stopping the sale. **(C)** correctly states the law but is incorrect because property disposal under the property clause is not included in the exception. **(D)** is incorrect because there is no general "taxpayer standing."

7. **/D/** Because any pregnancy will always be significantly shorter than the appeals process, this falls under the mootness exception, so the case may be considered. **(A)** is not the best answer because regardless of monetary damages, the mootness exception applies. **(B)** is incorrect because a legal issue surrounding a pregnancy falls under the exception for injuries "capable of repetition yet evading review." **(C)** is incorrect because a legal issue surrounding a pregnancy falls under the exception for injuries "capable of repetition yet evading review."

8. **/C/** Voting apportionment (*a.k.a.* "gerrymandering") cases are frequently heard by the courts and are not considered as falling under the political questions doctrine. **(A)** represents a political question not addressable by the judicial branch. **(B)** represents a political question not addressable by the judicial branch. **(D)** represents a political question not addressable by the judicial branch.

9. **/A/** Federal courts will abstain from hearing, but keep jurisdiction over, cases in which a significant unsettled issue of state law exists. **(B)** is not the best answer because it describes a legal scenario other than abstention. **(C)** is not the best answer because it describes a legal scenario other than abstention. **(D)** is not the best answer because it describes a legal scenario other than abstention.

10. **/A/** This is the best answer because Congress may use the Commerce Clause to achieve enumerated ends, particularly since here it involves personal use. **(B)** is not the best answer because the Necessary and Proper Clause usually requires a nexus to or affect upon interstate commerce. Since here the farmers are not engaged in interstate commerce, but rather growing for his own use, that clause is not likely to be the source of this Congressional power. **(C)** is incorrect because Congress exercising exclusive legislation takes place in Washington, D.C., or other property purchased from the states with the consent of the legislature. **(D)** is incorrect because the General Welfare clause refers to taxing and spending.

11. **/C/** This option actually relates to commerce, so it is a subject falling within Congress' power. **(A)** is an actual case and does not have a sufficient nexus to commerce to be regulated. **(B)** is an actual case and does not have a sufficient nexus to commerce to be regulated. **(D)** is incorrect unless some nexus to interstate commerce is demonstrated. States enacted the 55-mile-per-hour law as a condition of receiving federal funding.

12. **/C/** Congress may delegate rule-making ability to other branches of government. **(A)** is incorrect because Congress may not reserve a "veto" on agency rules. **(B)** is incorrect because Congress cannot give the President a "blank check" and here the delegation is too broad. **(D)** is incorrect because a line-item veto is unconstitutional.

13. **/C/** A state may not burden interstate commerce with its tax policy or favor local interests over out-of-state interests generally. **(A)** is incorrect because a state may usually levy property tax on federal property as part of its general property tax scheme. **(B)** is incorrect because a state may also tax the income of federal employees. **(D)** is incorrect because a state may tax all goods within their state that encounter a break in transit.

14. **/A/** A state may set higher health and safety standards than the federal government, but not lower. **(A)** is ineffective because it sets a lower standard. **(B)** is incorrect because it sets a higher standard. **(C)** is incorrect because the state may generally regulate as long as their regulation does not fall below the federal standard (unless the federal government has totally preempted the field, which is not indicated in these facts). **(D)** is effective because it pertains to lead, not arsenic.

15. **/D/** The 10th Amendment prohibits Congress from commandeering the legislative or executive processes of the state to enforce a federal program. **(A)** is not the best answer because as long as the law at issue is generally applicable, it is a legitimate exercise of the Commerce Clause. **(B)** is incorrect because non-economic ends may be achieved by regulating public accomodation. **(C)** is incorrect because the structure of the military is an enumerated federal power.

16. **/D/** This is the only choice that is not an enumerated power. **(A)** is incorrect because Admiralty and Maritime law is an enumerated power of Congress. **(B)** is incorrect because Trademark law is an enumerated power of Congress. **(C)** is incorrect because laws of the District of Columbia are an enumerated power of Congress.

17. **/B/** Congress may attach conditions or "strings" to its spending appropriations that states may accept or reject. **(A)** is not the best answer because in this fact pattern Congress is exercising its Tax and Spend power, not its Commerce Clause power. **(C)** is incorrect because Article II obligates the President to execute the laws. **(D)** is incorrect because the 10th Amendment only limits Congress' power to directly control state legislative and executive functions.

18. **/B/** Consent of two-thirds of the Senate is required to enter into a treaty. **(A)** is not the best answer because it refers to "Congress" and does not indicate the level of consent required. **(C)** is incorrect because two-thirds Senate consent is required to enter into a treaty. **(D)** is incorrect because an executive agreement is separate from a treaty. It is merely an informal agreement regarding everyday business with foreign countries.

19. **/A/** The Federal Property Clause allows Congress to dispose of and make reasonable rules regarding federal land, and limits states' power in that regard. **(B)** is not the best answer because states have general police powers and may enact laws outside the realm of commerce. **(C)** seems reasonable, but it misstates the law; no such "minor intrusion" is permissible. **(D)** is incorrect because wildlife is property for the purposes of the Property Clause.

20. **/C/** When Congress occupies a field involving national concerns, preemption applies and states may not usually regulate in that same direct area. **(A)** is incorrect because when Congress occupies a field, states may not regulate in that area. **(B)** is incorrect because when Congress occupies a field, states may not regulate in that area. **(D)** is incorrect because when Congress occupies a field, states may not regulate in that area.

21. **/D/** Mere state licensing of an individual business, without more, is usually insufficient to constitute significant state involvement or direction. **(A)** is incorrect because it precisely describes the factual situation in *Shelly v. Kramer*, in which the Supreme Court held that state action existed. **(B)** is incorrect because a private lessee of state-owned property is considered to have "significant state involvement" such that state action is inferred. **(C)** is incorrect because a private citizen performing an act at the request or urging of police becomes a state actor for constitutional purposes.

22. /C/ Because the law is facially neutral and religion is not usually a suspect class for equal protection purposes, the law will be subject to the default rational basis level of judicial scrutiny. **(A)** is incorrect because the law here is facially neutral, and the facts do not reveal any discriminatory intent though the impact here is disproportionate. **(B)** is incorrect because religion is not a suspect class for equal protection analysis (Note: The call of the question involves an equal protection claim, not a free exercise challenge. First Amendment protections are still available). **(D)** is not the best answer because it is unlikely a court would find a compelling interest, but may find a rational purpose (politics is a strange animal, pun intended).

23. /C/ Disability is not a suspect class. There is no intuitive way to classify group membership. The level of scrutiny for each class must simply be memorized. It is easier to memorize the suspect classes (race, national origin, citizenship) and assume the rest to be non-suspect. **(A)** is incorrect because race is a suspect class. **(B)** is incorrect because citizenship is a suspect class. **(D)** is incorrect because national origin is a suspect class.

24. /A/ Legitimacy is subject to intermediate scrutiny and a law violates equal protection if it prejudices illegitimate children. Here the law seems to benefit that class, so the state action is permissible. **(B)** is incorrect because citizenship may only be a criterion for participation in government or government jobs. **(C)** is incorrect because national origin is subject to strict scrutiny and the purpose of the law probably does not meet a compelling governmental need. **(D)** is incorrect because race is a suspect class.

25. /B/ This is the scrutiny level required of affirmative action programs. **(A)** is incorrect because racial quotas are not constitutional. **(C)** is incorrect because continuing racial discrimination need not necessarily be proved, only past discrimination prompting corrective action. **(D)** is incorrect because the racial group need not be "recognized" by a government agency.

26. /B/ Because economic status is not a suspect or quasi-suspect class, the level of scrutiny is the default rational basis. **(A)** is incorrect because not every restriction on travel is *per se* unconstitutional. **(C)** is incorrect because the level of scrutiny stated here is incorrect. **(D)** is incorrect because the level of scrutiny stated here is incorrect.

27. /A/ According to *Batson* a peremptory challenge of a juror on the basis of race or gender in either a civil or criminal case is *per se* unconstitutional. **(B)** is incorrect because according to *Batson* a peremptory challenge of a juror on the basis of race or gender in either a civil or criminal case is *per se* unconstitutional. **(C)** is incorrect because according to *Batson* a peremptory challenge of a juror on the basis of race or gender in either a civil or criminal case is *per se* unconstitutional. **(D)** is incorrect because according to *Batson* a peremptory challenge of a juror on the basis of race or gender in either a civil or criminal case is *per se* unconstitutional.

28. /D/ Procreation is a fundamental right that may not be interfered with absent a compelling governmental interest. Since most people are able to raise children without formal education in how to do so (like we have since the dawn of time), there is no compelling state interest. **(A)** is incorrect because the legislature is not prohibiting entry into the state, rather only one very dangerous method of doing so. **(B)** is incorrect because apportionment in accordance with population growth is permissible. **(C)** is incorrect because in-state tuition may be subject to residency requirements.

29. **/A/** Prohibiting the sale of contraceptive devices to adults violates a fundamental constitutional right, but not to minors. **(B)** is incorrect because self-educating children is in the "CAMPER" list of fundamental rights. **(C)** is incorrect because getting married is in the "CAMPER" list of fundamental rights. **(D)** is incorrect because a parent's custodian rights are in the "CAMPER" list of fundamental rights.

30. **/C/** This is the proper statement of the non-fundamental right test. **(A)** is incorrect because the law is not presumed invalid. **(B)** is incorrect because it states an element of the strict scrutiny analysis. **(D)** is incorrect because it states an element of the strict scrutiny analysis.

31. **/C/** Although "for cause" employment termination is a protected property interest, due process is not required when the employee is "at will." Therefore, a blanket statement that employment is protected is inaccurate. **(A)** is incorrect because welfare benefits are a protected property interest. **(B)** is incorrect because public education is a protected property interest. **(D)** is incorrect because the right to engage in gainful employment is a protected liberty interest.

32. **/C/** The goal of the *Mathews* test is to determine the appropriate timing of due process, it is not a factor of the test. The test balances the importance of the individual interest + the risk of erroneous deprivation against the cost to the government + the administrative burden and availability of additional safeguards. **(A)** is an element of the *Mathews* test and thus an incorrect answer. **(B)** is an element of the *Mathews* test and thus an incorrect answer. **(D)** is an element of the *Mathews* test and thus an incorrect answer.

33. **/A/** Voting is a fundamental constitutional right, and thus infringement is evaluated under strict scrutiny. However, a reasonable non-discriminatory voting rule such as minimum age will likely be upheld because it advances a compelling government interest (ascertaining that all those voting are of the proper age) and there is no less intrusive means available ("proof of age" requirement is narrowly tailored to accomplish the interest). **(B)** is not the best answer because it states the incorrect level of scrutiny. Voting is a fundamental right and therefore subjected to strict scrutiny. **(C)** is not the best answer because the law is non-discriminatory, advances a compelling government interest, and is narrowly tailored; therefore, it will likely be upheld. **(D)** is not the best answer because it states the incorrect level of scrutiny. Voting is a fundamental right and therefore subjected to strict scrutiny.

34. **/B/** Restrictions on the right to enter or leave the state aimed at a specific group may be an unconstitutional restriction on the right to interstate travel. **(A)** is not the best answer because the fundamental right to "education" refers to school attendance. **(C)** is incorrect because the right to interstate travel is fundamental and therefore subject to strict scrutiny. **(D)** is not the best answer because an equal protection claim would be harder to prove than the clear restriction on the right to travel implicated by the facts.

35. **/C/** The right to refuse medical treatment is the fundamental constitutional right of all mentally competent adults. **(A)** is incorrect because the right to refuse medical treatment does not extend to assisted suicide. **(B)** is incorrect because the right to refuse medical treatment is only available to the person requiring the treatment, not a relative. **(D)** is incorrect because the right to refuse medical treatment is only available to the person requiring the treatment, not a relative.

36. /B/ A flat restriction on the right to marry when the parties would otherwise be free to marry (*i.e.*, they are not already married and are adults) is unconstitutional. **(A)** is incorrect because requiring proof of legal marriage for the purpose of distributing state benefits is acceptable. **(C)** is incorrect because requiring proof of legal marriage for the purpose of distributing state benefits is acceptable. **(D)** is incorrect because states may generally establish a minimal age to marry without parental permission.

37. /A/ A challenge of racial discrimination would be a 14th Amendment equal protection challenge. **(B)** is incorrect because the 15th Amendment is applicable when the law deals with restricting a person's right to vote based upon race or color. **(C)** is incorrect because the 10th Amendment reserves all power to the states unless delegated to the federal government by the Constitution. **(D)** is incorrect because the 16th Amendment allows the Congress to levy a national income tax.

38. /C/ The right to enter federal lands is a right of national citizenship that is protected by the 14th Amendment. **(A)** is not the best answer because there is just cause for not hiring – he is not refused employment on the basis of his state citizenship. **(B)** is incorrect because 14th Amendment Privileges and Immunities applies to people, not corporations. **(D)** is incorrect because only citizens of the United States are protected by the clause.

39. /A/ Inverse condemnation refers to a government regulation that restricts the use of property, thereby reducing its value and giving rise to a monetary takings inquiry of just compensation to the owner. **(B)** is incorrect because inverse condemnation is a principle related to the law of government takings. **(C)** is incorrect because inverse condemnation is a principle related to the law of government takings. **(D)** is incorrect because inverse condemnation is a principle related to the law of government takings.

40. /C/ The two possible issues in any religious freedom issue are whether the law in question advances or inhibits an individual's right to free exercise of his or her religious beliefs, or whether the law creates excessive government entanglement or endorsement of an establishment of religion. **(A)** is incorrect because the threshold question of whether the law pertains to "free exercise" or "establishment" must be answered before any other analyses can occur. **(B)** is incorrect because the threshold question of whether the law pertains to "free exercise" or "establishment" must be answered before any other analyses can occur. **(D)** is incorrect because the threshold question of whether the law pertains to "free exercise" or "establishment" must be answered before any other analyses can occur.

41. /B/ Unless there is evidence of intentional discrimination or the regulation interferes with another fundamental right, a generally applicable law is subject to lower scrutiny. **(A)** is not the best answer because it defines the strict scrutiny standard. **(C)** is incorrect because selective enforcement suggests an invalid law, not a valid one. **(D)** is not the best answer because preference of religion involves an establishment clause analysis.

42. /D/ Look for the alternative that least advances or inhibits religion. Sunday business closure laws have been permitted, even though their purpose is partially religious in nature. **(A)** is an example of government unconstitutional entanglement in religion. **(B)** is an example of government unconstitutional entanglement in religion. **(C)** is an example of government unconstitutional entanglement in religion.

43. **/B/** The retroactive Contracts Clause of the 14th Amendment applies only to the states, not the federal government. **(C)** is incorrect because the Contracts Clause applies only to the states, not the federal government. **(D)** is incorrect because the Contracts Clause applies only to the states, not the federal government. **(A)** is not the best answer because the Contracts Clause does include public contracts.

44. **/C/** The law does not sufficiently define what "lewd" speech is, making it constitutionally vague. **(A)** is incorrect because a law must first survive a facial attack before further analysis becomes necessary. **(B)** is incorrect because a law must first survive a facial attack before further analysis becomes necessary. **(D)** is not the best answer because "lewd" speech, similar to obscene speech, is probably not protected speech, and because free speech rights are more limited in the proximity of a school.

45. **/D/** The term "appropriate" places no restrictions on the county overseer. Unfettered discretion in a licensing official makes a law restricting speech facially unconstitutional. **(A)** is incorrect because it assumes the commissioner has appropriate authority to deny the permit. **(B)** is incorrect because it assumes the commissioner has appropriate authority to deny the permit. **(C)** is not the best answer because the enabling act does not punish any particular kind of speech, so it cannot punish protected speech.

46. **/D/** The best and broadest answer because the test of a content neutral restriction on speech in public forums is that it must be narrowly tailored to achieve a significant government interest and also leave open alternative channels of communication. **(A)** is incorrect because it is an insufficient reason as compared to D. **(B)** is incorrect because it comprises the test for content neutral speech in private forums. **(C)** is incorrect because it comprises the test for content neutral speech in private forums.

47. **/B/** This is the appropriate standard of proof in a defamation case involving a public official. **(A)** is incorrect because it describes the standard of proof when the suit involves a private figure regarding a matter of public concern. **(C)** is incorrect because it describes the standard of proof when the suit involves a private figure regarding a matter of private concern. **(D)** is not the best answer because it does not mention the requirement that the statement be proven false.

48. **/C/** Speech that is intended and likely to produce imminent serious unlawful conduct is unprotected speech; promoting a riot would seem to qualify. **(A)** is incorrect because it is political speech which is protected. **(B)** is not the best answer because only significantly misleading commercial speech is unprotected. **(D)** is not the best answer because obscene material in the home is ordinarily protected speech.

49. **/A/** Seizure of printed materials to block their distribution must be preceded by a full judicial adversary hearing. **(B)** is incorrect because seizure of printed materials to block distribution must be preceded by a full adversary hearing and a judicial determination of obscenity. **(C)** is incorrect because seizure of printed materials to block distribution must be preceded by a full adversary hearing and a judicial determination of obscenity. **(D)** is not the best answer because only printed obscene material in private homes is protected, not when it is in the public forum.

50. /C/ Although radio and television media may be subject to equal time restrictions, the print media outlets are not. **(A)** is incorrect because print media outlets are not subject to "equal time" restrictions. **(B)** is incorrect because print media outlets are not subject to "equal time" restrictions. **(D)** is not the best answer because a freedom of speech analysis does not completely answer the question without examining freedom of the press issues.

51. /A/ Prior restraints on speech are presumed unconstitutional, but the presumption can be overcome if a number of elements are shown, including that the speech is unprotected, the prior restraint serves an important governmental interest, it is not vague or overbroad, etc. **(B)** is incorrect prior restraints on speech are presumed unconstitutional. **(C)** is incorrect because the restriction must be shown "necessary to promote a compelling governmental interest" to pass constitutional muster. **(D)** is incorrect because the restriction must be shown "necessary to promote a compelling government interest" to pass constitutional muster.

52. /B/ Burning a voter registration card is likely conduct qualifying as protected political speech. **(A)** is incorrect, because political conduct is afforded the same protection as political speech. **(C)** is incorrect because burning a voter registration card is conduct qualifying as protected political speech. Unless the prohibition is necessary to promote a compelling governmental interest, the conduct may not be prohibited. **(D)** is wrong because it misstates the test: unless the prohibition is necessary to promote a compelling governmental interest, the conduct may not be prohibited.

53. /B/ A loyalty oath that only requires the employee to uphold the constitution and/or oppose the violent overthrow of the government is acceptable, but all others are not. **(A)** is incorrect because it contains the absolute word "always" and a loyalty oath that only requires the employee to uphold the constitution and/or oppose the violent overthrow of the government is acceptable, but all others are not. **(C)** is incorrect because a loyalty oath that only requires the employee to uphold the constitution and/or oppose the violent overthrow of the government is acceptable, but all others are not. **(D)** is incorrect because it contains the absolute word "always" and a loyalty oath that only requires the employee to uphold the constitution and/or oppose the violent overthrow of the government is acceptable, but all others are not.

54. /C/ The First Amendment freedom of association protection only allows punishment for membership in a particular group if all three of these elements are shown. **(A)** is incorrect because First Amendment freedom of association protection only allows punishment for membership in a particular group if all three elements are shown. **(B)** is incorrect because First Amendment freedom of association protection only allows punishment for membership in a particular group if all three elements are shown. **(D)** is incorrect because First Amendment freedom of association protection only allows punishment for membership in a particular group if all three elements of C are shown.

55. /C/ This is the best answer because HardTime is performing a public function, as punishment for crimes is traditionally and exclusively performed by the state. Similar public functions are running a primary election, or a company town. **(A)** is incorrect because although private actors are generally not state actors, this situation squarely fits the public function exception. **(B)** is incorrect because although private actors are generally not state actors, this situation squarely fits the public function exception. **(D)** is incorrect because although state encouragement can be an exception, the fixed contract price actually encourages not using expensive solitary confinement.

56. **/A/** This is the best answer because she is now a resident and did not ask for money damages. **(B)** is incorrect because she was the right P to bring the suit when she was considered a nonresident. **(C)** is incorrect because it ignores mootness. This does not meet the capable of repetition exception, because as a senior she will never again be a nonresident at Evergreen – unlike *Roe*, who could get pregnant again. **(D)** is incorrect because *amici* are not parties to the lawsuit, so their interests do not sustain the case.

57. **/B/** Strikes based solely on race or gender are improper under *Batson*. **(A)** is incorrect because a defense attorney is subject to peremptory challenges rules. **(C)** is incorrect because Albert can probably be struck for his religious beliefs. **(D)** is incorrect because racists can be struck, but the facts do not state whether the race of the juror was the sole reason for striking him.

58. **/C/** This is the best answer because mere accrediting by a state agency does not usually make a private actor a state actor. This is a close call and the closest case holding to the contrary was a racially discriminatory private school using state-supplied textbooks. **(A)** is incorrect because there is no standing problem with parents suing on behalf of their minor children. **(B)** is incorrect because the First Amendment does not apply to private actors such as St. Pious. **(D)** is incorrect because even if the First Amendment did apply, it must be a governmental interest, not the school's interest.

59. **/A/** This is the best answer because the *ex post facto* clause prohibits the government from making something criminal after it has occurred. The prosecution could argue that it is an interpretation of the old law, but such a choice is not given. **(B)** is not the best answer because the *ex post facto* principle is more clearly on point. **(C)** is incorrect because the law must be effective before the criminal act. **(D)** is incorrect because it is nonsensical in that Bills of Attainder are also prohibited, and this isn't one of them.

60. **/A/** This is correct because there was no state action. Although it is a close call to a "symbiotic relationship," a majority held otherwise in *NCAA v. Tarkanian*. The university made the decision to fire him rather than suffer sanctions, but they could have withdrawn from the Association. **(B)** is incorrect because there is no state action. **(C)** is incorrect because there is no state action. **(D)** is incorrect because he is not under contract with the NCAA and couldn't have contracted any rights away under these facts.

61. **/A/** This is a garden-variety delegation of legislative power. Just because it gives limited administrative power to the Executive, that doesn't invalidate the provision. **(B)** is incorrect because giving limited administrative power does not invalidate a delegation. **(C)** is not the best answer because although executing the law requires fixing a percentage, the focus of the question is on the provision of the law, not the presidential power. **(D)** is incorrect because the facts do not suggest loss of property without due process of law.

62. **/D/** This is the best answer because a statute created by Congress has the power to enforce the equal protection clause in section V of the 14th Amendment. The provision "under color of state law" will be interpreted as nearly equivalent to state action, which is met by a state employee, Dean Neechurk, acting in his official capacity. **(A)** is incorrect because the statute is a valid exercise under the 14th Amendment, which will trump the 11th Amendment, and the state is not named. **(B)** is incorrect because Congress is not using the commerce clause, but the 14th Amendment. **(C)** is not the best answer, because the statute says "equal protection" in the language.

63. /C/ The Court properly struck the initial state law as a violation of the dormant commerce clause (also known as the negative implications doctrine). This is the best answer because Congress can effectively consent to state discrimination in commerce and actively legislate it. **(A)** is incorrect because there is no federal general welfare clause (only spending for the general welfare). **(B)** is incorrect because this clause is a limit on the states – not the federal government. **(D)** is incorrect because here the state law was only unconstitutional because Congress had not yet authorized it.

64. /A/ This is correct because a liberty interest is at stake and this is not the least restrictive means to serve the state's interest. **(B)** is incorrect because the right to a jury trial in civil cases has not been selectively incorporated against the states. **(C)** is incorrect because the state's police power may not be used in violation of due process. **(D)** is incorrect because similarly situated persons are treated the same under the law.

65. /D/ To overturn an economic regulation pursuant to the Equal Protection Clause, the challenger (Stan) has the burden of proving that the law is not rationally related to a legitimate government interest. The applicable equal protection analysis would be the same for the class of CPAs under these facts. Stan would prevail if no legitimate state interest is served. **(A)** is incorrect because it states too high an interest and is therefore not the best answer. **(B)** is incorrect because the burden is on the challenger under rational basis scrutiny. **(C)** is incorrect because the burden is on the challenger under rational basis scrutiny.

66. /B/ The court can strike "grossly excessive" punitive damages as a violation of substantive due process. **(A)** is incorrect because the court can strike "grossly excessive" punitive damages as a violation of substantive due process. **(C)** is incorrect because the court can strike "grossly excessive" punitive damages as a violation of substantive due process. **(D)** is incorrect because the takings clause justifies reasonable compensation for the state taking private property for public use, and judgments have never been seen as takings.

67. /D/ This is the best answer of those presented in the question because states can regulate for health and safety purposes (police power), unless it unduly burdens a person's right to an abortion; here that burden seems *de minimus*. The state may rationally authorize only physicians to perform abortions, despite credible evidence that it is not necessary. **(A)** is incorrect because while there is a strong argument for the law being unconstitutional as applied, it is facially valid. Facial attacks prevail if the law cannot be enforced against anyone. This law is valid against the women on the main island who are not unduly burdened by this requirement. **(B)** is incorrect because police power ordinarily trumps private contracts. **(C)** is incorrect because there is no due process right to assistance in getting an abortion, and poverty is not a suspect class under equal protection (rational basis scrutiny).

68. /D/ The employee may continue working, because the supremacy clause usually voids and preempts inconsistent state laws, even against the state as employer. **(A)** is incorrect, because age is not a suspect class. The State could use age 65 as rationally related to the legitimate end of health, safety, or welfare. **(B)** is incorrect because the employee may continue working. **(C)** is not the best answer because the federal law voids the inconsistent state law.

69. **/A/** This is the best answer because Congress has the power to regulate and dispose of federal property. **(B)** is incorrect (and is a common incorrect answer) because the Necessary and Proper Clause does not itself confer any power, it is simply a means by which Congress can carry out its other enumerated powers. **(C)** is incorrect because there is no federal police power. **(D)** is not the best answer because there are no facts presented providing a jurisdictional argument to a substantial effect on interstate commerce.

70. **/A/** This is the best answer because this situation is exactly what the clause prohibits and there is no market participant exception to this clause. **(B)** is not the best answer, because the discrimination is against residents, not an entire industry, profession, or product. Also at issue is the market participant exception for states. **(C)** is not the best answer, because residency is not a suspect class. **(D)** is incorrect because the *ex post facto* clause restricts criminal punishment.

71. **/D/** This is the best answer because there are adequate state grounds clearly independent from the Constitution that resolve the issue. **(A)** is incorrect because the Supreme Court will not hear the case, even though the state court got the constitutional issue incorrect. **(B)** is incorrect because the Supreme Court will not hear the case, even though the state court got the constitutional issue incorrect. **(C)** is a good answer, but not the best because there are strong arguments that Gallows has no injury in fact, or that the case is moot, but adequate state grounds is on all fours.

72. **/B/** This is the best answer because the Constitution enumerates specific powers of the President, including Commander-in-Chief of the armed forces. **(A)** is incorrect because it assumes the President has no inherent independent authority. **(C)** is incorrect because it assumes inherent plenary power, which is too broad a description of the President's enumerated powers. **(D)** is incorrect because it assumes the President has no inherent independent authority.

73. **/A/** The Commerce Clause is the workhorse for the federal government regulation of economic activity. **(B)** is incorrect because the Necessary and Proper Clause only enhances other enumerated powers and has no reach of its own. **(C)** is incorrect unless there are quartered soldiers involved. **(D)** is incorrect because there is no federal police power.

74. **/B/** This is the best answer because Lone Star encouraged and endorsed John's conduct. **(A)** is incorrect because John's actions are attributed to Lone Star due to their active encouragement. **(C)** is incorrect because the question does not ask whether Lin may sue Lone Star in federal court for money damages. **(D)** is not the best answer because the state action probably occurred when John entered the property, not when he cashed the check.

75. **/A/** This is the correct answer by process of elimination. The facts say that the commitment is civil, not criminal, and due process has been satisfied. **(B)** is incorrect because he was given procedural due process at trial and the statute satisfies substantive due process by attempting to treat him. **(C)** is incorrect because the commitment is civil treatment, not criminal punishment so *ex post facto* does not apply. **(D)** is incorrect because the commitment is civil treatment, not criminal punishment so double jeopardy does not apply.

76. /A/ This is correct because the Club's free speech rights were infringed upon by viewpoint discrimination when the school would not allow religious activity. Public schools are state actors, not private property, and the restriction was content specific – it did not allow religious activity. **(B)** is incorrect because religion is not a suspect class. **(C)** is incorrect because content specific restrictions must be a compelling interest. **(D)** is incorrect because there was no excessive entanglement (establishment clause) due to it being after-school hours and asked for parental consent.

77. /C/ This is the best answer because the law is a constitutional exercise of police power. Cities and states may usually regulate guns in a reasonable way to protect the public. **(A)** is incorrect because the Second Amendment restricts all units of government of the right to prohibit citizens owning guns. **(B)** is incorrect because gun ownership is probably not a national citizenship right. **(D)** is incorrect because it authorizes the federal not the state government to enforce the 14th Amendment.

78. /B/ This is the best answer because Congress does have plenary power to regulate foreign commerce, which can be done by delegating authority to the Executive. **(A)** is incorrect because the President's foreign affairs power is largely delegated by Congress – not inherent. **(C)** is incorrect because the Contracts clause restricts states actions – not the federal government or courts. **(D)** is incorrect because the executive order is valid. The contract expectancy is probably a valid property interest, but it can be limited by a compelling federal interest.

79. /C/ On double classification problems, the law must pass both the (age, gender) tests. **(C)** most properly articulates the mid-tier scrutiny for gender under the equal protection doctrine. The law would likely allow the age designation under the rational basis standard, if that was the only problem. **(A)** is incorrect because the compelling standard is more difficult to prove than rational basis and is only half the test. **(B)** is incorrect because the challenger has the burden under the rational basis standard, and the law is not saved by satisfying the age problem alone. **(D)** is incorrect because narrowly tailored is too strict a standard for mid-tier scrutiny.

80. /A/ This is correct as an indirect way of testing the police power of the state to protect their citizens. **(B)** is not the best answer because the state may indeed be prohibited from passing laws that are not reserved to the federal government. **(C)** is incorrect because poverty is not a suspect class. **(D)** is not the best answer, because there are no given conflicting federal laws and the law burdens in-state banks – not out-of-state banks.

81. /C/ This is correct because Congress can always attach strings to the receipt of federal funds and can reach areas outside the commerce clause with spending. **(A)** is incorrect because there is no federal police power. **(B)** is incorrect because equal protection issues are not raised by these facts. **(D)** is incorrect because privileges and immunities issues are not raised by these facts.

82. /B/ This is the best answer because judicial power is vested in one Supreme Court. **(A)** is incorrect because nowhere in the Constitution is the number nine specified. **(C)** is not true, Congress can eliminate any lower court. **(D)** is interesting, but no case law suggests a violation based on it.

83. **/D/** This is the least likely to be heard because it is a state asserting the rights of its citizens – rather than a right of its own – and probably a political question. The Supreme Court *may* hear any case where a state is a party. **(A)** is incorrect because it is a suit between two states. **(B)** is incorrect because it is a suit between two states. **(C)** is incorrect because it could be heard by concurrent jurisdiction in either Supreme or District Court as a case with a state as party.

84. **/A/** This is correct because the Courts defer to Congress if the intent of the tax – as here – is to produce revenue. **(B)** is not the best answer because the tax could be invalid for more than that one reason. **(C)** is incorrect because it incorrectly states the test. **(D)** is incorrect because the Courts defer to Congress if the intent of the tax is to produce revenue.

85. **/D/** This is correct because Flagg's exercise of its statutory right to sell Brook's property does not make Flagg a state actor. **(A)** is incorrect because there is no state action. **(B)** is incorrect because the Second Amendment right to bear arms restricts the federal government, not private actors. **(C)** is incorrect because nothing suggests that the state law conflicts with a federal scheme.

86. **/D/** John Crest, a third party, has no standing here because he has no personal injury. Federal taxpayers generally have no standing. **(A)** is incorrect because this is not a bill of attainder that is punishing anyone. **(B)** is not the best answer because while it might be true, nobody has standing to challenge the amendment. **(C)** is incorrect because the court will not hear the case.

87. **/B/** This is the best answer because this is legislative punishment of a named person. **(A)** is incorrect because the new statute is not necessarily criminal and does not make any act a retroactive crime. **(C)** is not the best answer because the law is clearly an unconstitutional bill of attainder and no due process analysis is required. **(D)** is not the best answer because the new law is clearly an unconstitutional bill of attainder (although a license to practice law is a privilege that can be restricted in some cases).

88. **/A/** This is the best argument here because the state may take private property for public use but must pay the owner reasonable compensation. Inverse condemnation is the remedy when the government restricts the use of the land to such an extent that it eliminates all reasonable viable economic use of the land. **(B)** is incorrect because the state may restrict use of the land under its police power to preserve the environment. **(C)** is incorrect because police power generally trumps contracts clause claims. **(D)** is incorrect because the state may restrict use of the land under its police power to preserve the environment.

89. **/A/** This is correct because the court will not prevent the executive from closing down a foreign embassy. The political question doctrine applies to issues textually committed to another branch of government. **(B)** is incorrect because the Takings Clause refers to private property being taken for public use, not loss of business opportunities. **(C)** is incorrect because the Contracts Clause does not apply to the federal government, only to states. **(D)** is not the best answer, because (depending on the interpretation of the contract) Syscom only has to allege that it suffered, or is threatened imminent economic loss or that the U.S. breached the contract to satisfy the "injury in fact" requirement of standing.

90. /C/ This is the most likely outcome because the government cannot compel disclosure of membership – unless it could make a showing that membership is illegal. ROWG is a lawful group. **(A)** is incorrect because ROWG can assert association standing on behalf of its members – because its members could assert this privilege. **(B)** is incorrect because the right to be present does not mean they had the right to assert a privilege to resist membership disclosure. **(D)** is incorrect because it misstates the test—the government can only compel disclosure of the membership list if it could make membership illegal due to the illegal nature of the organization.

91. /B/ This is the best answer because the state is trying to prefer one religion over others by teaching a character from the Bible (analogous to requiring the teaching of creation with evolution). The court will likely find either no secular purpose and strike the law or find both a secular and religious purpose and uphold the law. **(A)** is incorrect because this presents an establishment clause problem – not a free exercise problem. **(C)** is incorrect because this presents an establishment clause problem – not a free speech problem. **(D)** incorrectly states a part of free exercise analysis to an establishment problem.

92. /C/ This is the best answer because the display must have a secular purpose (prong 1), and may have an incidental, but not the primary effect of advancing religion (prong 2). **(A)** is too broad of a rule, because the government may depict religious scenes if they pass the *Lemon* test. **(B)** is not the best answer because it states two factors that may influence the decisions, but the test is the three prongs of *Lemon*. **(D)** is incorrect because the limited public forum is a category of free speech – not establishment analysis.

93. /A/ This is the best answer because the case is not ripe yet. There is no imminent injury, because the FDA could choose to pass a constitutional regulation. **(B)** is incorrect because abstention restricts federal courts from interfering with state court prosecutions. **(C)** is incorrect because the FDA could choose to pass a constitutional regulation. **(D)** is incorrect, because the 11th Amendment is state sovereign immunity – not federal agency immunity.

94. /C/ The government may use prior restraints on protected free speech if a prompt judicial review finds a very important governmental interest is advanced. **(A)** is incorrect because the government may use prior restraints on protected free speech if a prompt judicial review finds an important governmental interest. **(B)** is incorrect because the government may use prior restraints on protected free speech if a prompt judicial review finds an important governmental interest. **(D)** misstates the rule for analyzing prior restraints.

95. /D/ This is the best choice because the Supreme Court is the final interpreter of the Constitution and Congress may not exclude an entire class of cases from all judicial review. **(A)** is incorrect because although Congress has substantial power to regulate the appellate jurisdiction of the federal courts, this power may not be used to effectively overrule a Supreme Court prior decision. **(B)** is incorrect because although Congress has substantial power to regulate the appellate jurisdiction of the federal courts, this power may not be used to effectively overrule a Supreme Court decision. **(C)** is incorrect because Congress can regulate the appellate jurisdiction of the Supreme Court.

96. **/D/** This is the best answer because the Court will probably analyze the case using strict scrutiny; here, the program will likely survive scrutiny because it is narrowly tailored to achieve a compelling interest – this particular school intentionally discriminated in the past in this particular area of admissions. **(A)** is incorrect because the Court has ruled that the use of racial classifications by school authorities to implement the desegregation of an intentionally segregated school system is not only constitutionally permissible, but mandated by the 14th Amendment. **(B)** is incorrect because the Court has ruled that the use of racial classifications by school authorities to implement the desegregation of an intentionally segregated school system is not only constitutionally permissible, but mandated by the 14th Amendment. **(C)** is not the best answer because of the "penalizes no particular group" language and also because it does not categorize this case as a remedy for past intentional discrimination.

97. **/A/** This is the best choice because the suit is really between North Pole and the state of Mountain, and North Pole is barred by the sovereign immunity principle of the 11th Amendment from suing Mountain in federal court. Valley has no separate sovereign interest and has not alleged an injury in fact. **(B)** is incorrect because Valley does not have a sovereign interest. Valley could sue if the warm water was injuring the state's resources, but that was not given. **(C)** is incorrect because the Supreme Court has original jurisdiction to hear cases where a state is a party. That jurisdiction is exclusive if between two states, and concurrent if not. **(D)** is incorrect because Valley does not have a sovereign interest. Valley could sue if the warm water was injuring the state's resources, but that necessary fact was not given in the question.

98. **/D/** This is correct because this question tests whether the candidate can select the correct facts, rather than recall the words used in equal protection analysis. The facts are given, so the question does not test burdens of proof and the facts fail to establish the existence of an intention to discriminate. **(A)** is incorrect because the existence of segregation due to residential patterns or other neutral classification does not, by itself, establish a violation of the Equal Protection Clause. Some intentional act by the state that created the segregation must be proven before a violation of the Equal Protection Clause will be found. **(B)** is incorrect because the change in the racial composition of a school does not prove intentional discrimination by the government. **(C)** is incorrect because the fact that there are more tenured teachers in the white schools can be attributed to the individual choices of the teachers and does not by itself show an intention to discriminate by the school board or the city.

99. **/A/** Mootness applies to the case brought too late. All three of the other answers are similar in that they address the case brought too early, which is ripeness. **(B)** is incorrect because this is a strong argument since the city may argue that since the developer is merely planning the project and has not yet begun to implement his plans, there is not yet a case or controversy. **(C)** is incorrect because while the developer may meet the constitutional requirement for standing, he may not meet the prudential rules of standing since he has not yet shown how, when, or where he plans to build. **(D)** is incorrect because the case will be better decided when the developer provides the specifics of his development, the town may argue that the issues are not ripe.

100./A/ This is the best answer offered because the ordinance retroactively impairs the obligation of Tenant to Landlord on a contract legally in existence on its effective date even though the State would merely need to show that this is reasonable action furthering a legitimate interest. A Contracts Clause argument is a slightly better argument than Equal Protection. **(B)** is incorrect because the statute does not operate retroactively; it sets a future maximum rent limited to a past benchmark. **(C)** is not the best answer because here there is a rational basis for treating them differently. **(D)** is incorrect because the legislature passed the generally applicable law and no hearing right was specified.

101./B/ This is the best answer because the injunction fails to sufficiently define what acts are prohibited. **(A)** is incorrect because there is no threat of imminent violence. **(C)** is not the best answer because there does not appear to be a due process deficiency. **(D)** is not the best answer because there does not appear to be a due process deficiency.

102./B/ This is correct because the federal government has broader discretion to regulate broadcast media and can regulate the use of airwaves because there is a substantial interest in protecting children who would likely view the broadcast during that time scheduled. **(A)** is incorrect because there is no federal police power. **(C)** is incorrect because it is not bad enough to be obscene if there is some literary merit. **(D)** is incorrect because the speech was not "commercial speech" and this alternative states the incorrect rule.

103./D/ This is the best answer because the "audience veto" of unpopular speech can only be stopped when there is imminent danger of uncontrollable violence, and the police must use reasonable means to protect the speaker's rights. The officer waited and allowed the speaker to continue until the situation was getting out of hand. **(A)** is incorrect because the police officer gave the speaker an opportunity to be heard and only intervened when the situation was getting out of control. **(B)** is incorrect because the audience's right to assemble does not grant him his right to speak. **(C)** is incorrect because the police may not require obedience to an unconstitutional law.

104./D/ This is correct because the film may be protected if it has literary, artistic, political, or scientific merit. **(A)** is incorrect because selective prosecution is not a defense. **(B)** is incorrect because possession outside the home can be made illegal (criminal procedure may have a defense for unwitting possession). **(C)** is incorrect because possession outside the home can be made illegal (criminal procedure may have a defense for unwitting possession).

105./C/ This is the best answer because Dandruff and his employees are harmed by the statute and they have standing to contest the ordinance. **(A)** is incorrect because Dandruff alleges a sufficient injury for standing. **(B)** is not the best answer because association is neither the only right, nor the strongest right asserted. **(D)** is incorrect because it presents an issue on the merits – not for standing.

106./B/ This is the correct alternative because the line is drawn at the home for personal use, not the theater. One may possess obscenity in the home. Remember, there is a distinction between "obscenity" and mere pornography. **(A)** is incorrect because the Constitution does protect aliens as persons. **(C)** is incorrect because a person is constitutionally protected to possess (not buy or sell) obscenity in their home. **(D)** is incorrect because the State may prohibit obscenity, even for adults.

107./B/ This is obviously a free speech question. **(B)** is the best answer because it is an admission of his failure to discharge his duty as an attorney. **(A)** is a weak answer because the district attorney is a public figure and the comment is a public concern. **(C)** is incorrect because political activity is protected. **(D)** is incorrect because Statement B is an admission by the assistant district attorney that he had failed to discharge his duty, which is grounds for dismissal.

108./A/ This is the best answer because the law here is subject to strict scrutiny if there is intentional discrimination. **(B)** is incorrect because "irrational as applied" is probably not a defense if the statute is rational as generally applied. **(C)** is incorrect because strict scrutiny would apply only to a generally applicable law if the state is found to be intentionally discriminating, like answer **(A)**. **(D)** is not the best answer because it is not as clear that rational basis applies if the law places a direct burden on a person's religious practices and does not allow him to practice his religion at all.

109./C/ This is correct because the state must show a substantial direct relationship. **(A)** is incorrect because a state may not discriminate against a non-resident merely because it has a proprietary interest in the resource. **(B)** is incorrect because earning a living is a fundamental interest. These facts are distinct from recreational fishing. **(D)** is incorrect because the standard applied is not strict scrutiny.

110./D/ This is the best answer because an exception to the mootness doctrine is when an injury is repeatable yet may evade review. **(A)** is not the best answer because mootness is the issue, but this case probably meets an exception. **(B)** is incorrect because the Supreme Court has appellate jurisdiction over constitutional issues. **(C)** is not the best answer because it does not acknowledge the mootness concern.

111./C/ This is the best answer because the application of the inspection rule creates an unnecessary burden on interstate commerce by requiring double inspection and, therefore, the rule is not the least restrictive means of protecting its citizens. **(A)** is incorrect because the state must use the least burdensome means to protect its citizens. **(B)** is incorrect because the federal government must approve restrictions on interstate commerce so state authority is insufficient. **(D)** is incorrect because it is the application of the rule that is unconstitutional, not that it is discriminatory on its face.

112./C/ This is correct because executive orders (domestic policy) and executive agreements (foreign policy) preempt and invalidate inconsistent state law under the Supremacy Clause. **(A)** is incorrect because it does not pervasively interfere with state sovereignty and does serve an important national·interest. **(B)** is incorrect because executive orders (domestic policy) and executive agreements (foreign policy) invalidate inconsistent state law under the Supremacy Clause. **(D)** is not the best answer because this is not a political question. A standard exists by which the court can decide the issue, and that standard is the Supremacy Clause.

113./A/ This is correct because the President has plenary power to pardon offenses against the U.S. (federal law) and set conditions of pardon, including conditions Congress did not establish by statute. **(B)** is incorrect because the President has plenary power to pardon offenses against the U.S. **(C)** is incorrect because the President can pardon for nearly any reason, whether or not based in fact or law. His pardon does not alter the Court's interpretation of the Constitution. **(D)** is probably incorrect because the death penalty was constitutional when the pardon was made so the conditions are enforceable after it was declared unconstitutional.

114./D/ All the answers are arguably plausible, but **(D)** is the clearest example that could likely be upheld. The House of Representatives is the body with authority to regulate marriages (traditionally a state function) in the District of Columbia (D.C.). **(A)** is not the best answer because while it might be sustained under the War Powers Act, it could be an Equal Protection violation. **(B)** is not the best answer because it could be an Equal Protection violation. **(C)** is not the best answer because it involves a complex use of executive branch power to establish foreign policy, which is not the most likely of these four options to be upheld.

115./C/ This is the best answer because the U.S. Supreme Court actually did hear this case since the high court has original and exclusive jurisdiction over cases between two states. **(A)** is incorrect because ownership of property within the U.S. is not a political question. **(B)** is incorrect because the high court has original and exclusive jurisdiction over cases between two states. **(D)** is incorrect because the 11th Amendment bars suit by a person against a state in federal court.

116./B/ This is the best answer because the U.S. Supreme Court may only hear cases that have a federal question (constitutional or other federal law). While interesting issues may be more likely to be heard, the court must have jurisdiction to hear them. One way to the Supreme Court is after a final judgment from the state's highest court, but there must be some type of federal question at play. **(A)** is incorrect because the U.S. Supreme Court may only hear cases that have some type of federal question. **(C)** is incorrect because the U.S. Supreme Court may only hear cases that have some type of federal question. **(D)** is incorrect because the U.S. Supreme Court may usually only hear cases that have some type of federal question.

117./B/ This is correct because the Abstention doctrine restricts federal court review of pending state court criminal prosecutions. **(A)** is incorrect because it hints at 11th Amendment sovereign immunity, and sovereign immunity neither applies to declaratory judgments nor protects municipalities. **(C)** is incorrect because it hints at 11th Amendment sovereign immunity, and sovereign immunity neither applies to declaratory judgments nor protects municipalities. **(D)** is incorrect, because the civil suit was filed after the criminal action began.

118./A/ This is the best answer because the ALCU does not need standing if it convinces Spary to appeal. The other three answers are merely different ways to say the same thing. **(B)** is incorrect because the case is an advisory opinion if Spary's conviction is already vacated or overturned. **(C)** is incorrect because federal courts may not usually issue advisory opinions. **(D)** is incorrect because non-justiciable is another way of describing certain reasons, including advisory opinions and mootness, why the Court will not hear a case.

119./C/ This is the best answer assuming there is a federal question to provide the tribunal with jurisdiction. **(A)** is incorrect because sovereign immunity was waived when the state filed as P. **(B)** is incorrect because the state has standing if it alleges that their money was taken fraudulently. **(D)** is not the best answer because the court hearing the case is more certain statement than how the case is decided.

120./A/ This is the correct answer because Congress can overcome the state's immunity under the 14th Amendment if clearly expressed. **(B)** is incorrect because Congress may waive 11th Amendment immunity pursuant to the 14th Amendment provided that it does so explicitly. **(C)** is a common incorrect nonsense answer on the constitutional law questions. **(D)** is not the best answer because it is incomplete since Congress can lift states' immunity under the 11th Amendment pursuant to the Commerce Clause only if it does so explicitly. Also, the statute described in the facts appears to be enacted pursuant to the Fourteenth Amendment, not the Commerce Clause.

121./A/ This is the best answer because Congress may make criminal statutes and regulate instrumentalities of interstate commerce for non-economic ends. **(B)** is incorrect because there is no federal police power. **(C)** is a common incorrect answer on the MBE because traditional state area is not a winning argument. **(D)** is incorrect because Congress may make criminal statutes and regulate instrumentalities of interstate commerce for non-economic ends.

122./A/ This is the best answer because the Abstention Doctrine restrains federal courts from addressing federal constitutional law concerns until any unsettled issues of state law have been resolved. If the state court interprets the law to prohibit fighting words only, then there is no reason to interpret the Constitution further. **(B)** is incorrect because the 11th Amendment does not apply to most declaratory judgments. **(C)** is the not the best answer because although the P needs associational standing to sue in federal court, the court will likely abstain in this case. **(D)** is incorrect because if the law affects speech, then the Constitution is implicated. Adding the Commerce Clause to that does nothing to the justiciability of the case.

123./A/ This is the best answer because the rationale describes the mootness doctrine, which results in dismissal. **(B)** is not the best answer because it is arguable that Bill has an injury in fact if the law could be enforced, but it is a clear case under mootness. **(C)** is incorrect because the 11th Amendment does not bar declaratory judgments generally where the declaratory P is not seeking money damages. **(D)** is not the best answer because although the statute is unconstitutional (*Griswold*) Bill's motivation for the suit and the total lack of prosecution of the statute would likely lead a judge to decide the case is moot in the interests of judicial economy.

124./B/ This is the best answer because there seem to be no strong challenges to the sentence. **(A)** is incorrect because this act was criminal long before Kris committed it and the punishment has not changed. **(C)** is incorrect because the class of violent crime convicts is not a suspect class. Rational basis scrutiny will be applied, and there will be a rational basis for distinguishing drug crimes from violent crimes. **(D)** is incorrect. The delegation was proper because it contained guidelines, and it did not violate separation of functions by restricting judges.

125./B/ This is correct because the *ex post facto* clause prohibits punishing an act that was legal when it was committed and subsequently made illegal afterwards or increases the punishment. **(A)** is incorrect because after overturning criminal sentences, appeal courts typically remand cases back to the trial court for resentencing and here the sentence was not unconstitutional. **(C)** is incorrect because aggravated murder was a death penalty crime before the act was committed. So, both the conviction and sentence are constitutional under the *Ex Post Facto* challenge. **(D)** is incorrect because this is an appeal of the entire constitutional challenge. If it doesn't violate *ex post facto* rule, it is valid.

126./B/ This is the best answer because the Supremacy Clause preempts and strikes state laws, including constitutions, that conflict with federal laws, including treaties. **(A)** is not the best answer because the restraint is invalid, whether or not it survives Equal Protection analysis. **(C)** is incorrect because the Richmond State Constitution is preempted by the treaty under the Supremacy Clause. **(D)** is not the best answer because the restraint is invalid, whether or not it survives Equal Protection analysis.

127./D/ This is the best answer because the state is preferring in-state colleges over out-of-state colleges and thereby restricting interstate commerce. **(A)** is a frequent incorrect answer on the MBE; the bald statement that something is "not a right" is almost never correct. **(B)** is not the best answer, because here the state is not using the least restrictive means to achieve the objective. **(C)** is a frequent incorrect answer on the MBE; remember there are two P&I clauses – this question involves Article IV Privileges and Immunities. One state is discriminating against another. 14th Amendment Privileges or Immunities involves rights of national citizenship (employment, interstate travel, etc.).

128./C/ This is the best answer because state discrimination on the basis of U.S. citizenship is tested under strict scrutiny (unless it is participation in government). The requirement fails the strict judicial scrutiny standard. **(A)** is incorrect because the state cannot exercise the police power in a manner that violates the Equal Protection clause. **(B)** is incorrect because requiring U.S. citizenship is not a narrowly tailored way of ensuring barbers speak English. **(D)** is incorrect because this is not legislative punishment of a named person.

129./D/ This is the best answer because both (A) and (C) are effective grounds here. **(A)** is a specific protection against discrimination aimed towards out-of-staters, so they violate the constitutional right to travel. **(B)** is incorrect because this clause protects rights of national citizenship, like petitioning Congress. **(C)** protects against invidious discrimination, including interstate travel rights, so it is effective.

130./C/ This is correct because Article IV Privileges and Immunities are in play – discrimination by one state against citizens of other states. **(A)** is incorrect because abstention does not apply here, because the state law is unambiguous. **(B)** is not the best answer because the argument for denial of procedural due process is unsupported. **(D)** is incorrect because it correctly states the original or trial jurisdiction of the U.S. Supreme Court – not the federal district court.

131./B/ The Supreme Court may hear cases appealed from a state's highest court if a constitutional challenge is made, but the state court may not preclude review by applying a procedural rule inconsistently. **(A)** is not the best answer, because the inconsistent application of the rule makes **(B)** a stronger argument. **(C)** is incorrect because the constitutional issue is a First Amendment right, which cannot be foreclosed by inconsistent use of procedural rules. The D cannot avoid the state high court requirement by asserting that the statute is facially invalid. **(D)** is incorrect because the constitutional issue is a First Amendment right, which cannot be foreclosed by inconsistent use of procedural rules. The D cannot avoid the state high court requirement by asserting that the statute is facially invalid.

132./A/ This is the best answer, as in *NY v. U.S.* Congress may not commandeer the legislative process of the states into implementing a federal program. **(B)** is incorrect because the 11th Amendment promotes state sovereign immunity, not federal. **(C)** is incorrect because the case here is ripe, since the state would have to begin building immediately, even though the toxic waste fines are five years away. **(D)** is incorrect because Congress may not commandeer the legislative process of the states into implementing an unfunded federal program.

133./B/ This is the best answer because state laws retroactively impairing an existing government contract need only have a rational basis and here it serves the public need for parks. **(A)** is incorrect because it is overbroad and the state's sovereignty is limited by the federal Constitution. **(C)** is incorrect because laws may usually override equitable principles. **(D)** is incorrect because a state may generally repeal its own laws if there is a rational basis for doing so.

134./D/ The Executive (branch) must execute the laws of the U.S., and the President appointed Attorney General has exclusive prosecutorial discretion. **(A)** is incorrect because the executive branch effectively has prosecutorial discretion. **(B)** is incorrect because the executive branch effectively has prosecutorial discretion. **(C)** is incorrect because only the President is immune for acts done in official capacity, not appointed ambassadors.

135./A/ This general statement is the best answer because Congress has broad ability to investigate for the purpose of finding facts to assist it in passing legislation, but Congress can't ask irrelevant questions unrelated to matters upon which Congress may legislate. **(B)** is incorrect because Congress' power to investigate extends to more than mere expenditures. **(C)** is incorrect because either house may inquire of the Executive Branch. **(D)** is incorrect because either house may inquire of the Executive Branch.

136./C/ This is correct because the legislation here relates to a substantial improvement in commerce. **(A)** is incorrect because the Contract Clause does not apply to the federal Congress. **(B)** is incorrect because it is a restriction on government power, not a clause conferring power. **(D)** is not the best answer because no rights secured by the 14th Amendment are implicated in the facts given.

137./D/ The burden in a discrimination claim is on the challenger to show the lack of a tailored application to a compelling government interest. Even though the law affects religion, it is generally applicable. It will probably be reviewed under rational basis scrutiny, unless intentional discrimination is shown. **(A)** is incorrect because it assumes the government has the burden of proof. **(B)** is incorrect because it assumes the government has the burden of proof. **(C)** is incorrect because the organization will have to show more than just substantial interference.

138./A/ This is the strongest constitutional argument because it has been held that wild animals move in interstate commerce when they cross state lines and are thus subject to the commerce power. **(B)** is generally an incorrect answer on the MBE; "necessary and proper clause" only extends enumerated powers, it does not create new powers. **(C)** is generally an incorrect answer on the MBE; the police power at the federal level is very limited—police power is much more expansive at the state level. **(D)** is a close but still incorrect answer. These animals were killed on private property. Occasionally, the examiners use a similar question involving wild animals on federal land. In that event, the federal property power is the correct answer.

139./D/ This is the best answer because states are not prohibited from subsidizing local industries and "distribute government largesse" to state residents. *Reeves v. Stake.* **(A)** is incorrect because this is not the type of protectionism that the clause seeks to prevent. **(B)** is incorrect because this is not the type of protectionism that the clause seeks to prevent. Other companies are free to lobby their own states to grant them subsidies. **(C)** is not the best answer because this purports to make an exception to standing and does not answer the merits.

140./D/ This is the best answer because a state can burden interstate commerce if their statute is the least restrictive means to achieve a legitimate state interest, such as here. **(A)** is incorrect because the dormant commerce clause does not prevent a state from subsidizing in-state businesses. **(B)** is incorrect because states can discriminate against out-of-state citizens or residents if they are the peculiar source of evil, which here they appear to be. **(C)** is the best incorrect answer because undue statutory burden can be upon one state, it does not have to be a multi-state undue burden.

141./B/ This is correct because the Fifth Amendment Due Process Clause does have equal protection implications, which can support a challenge to the agency's "household" definitions. **(A)** is incorrect because no First Amendment rights are implicated – not even the right of association. **(C)** is incorrect because the Fourteenth Amendment does not apply to the Federal Government. **(D)** is incorrect because the Fourteenth Amendment does not apply to the Federal Government.

142./B/ In *Coleman v. Miller*, the Supreme Court held that the viability of a constitutional amendment is a political question, which prevents a federal court from deciding issues related to viability of the amendments. **(A)** is not the best answer because the suit seeks to enjoin even the consideration of the issue. **(C)** is incorrect because state law does not control federal constitutional amendments. **(D)** is incorrect because in *Coleman v. Miller*, the Court held that the viability of a constitutional amendment is a political question, which prevents a federal court from deciding issues related to viability of amendments.

143./C/ This is the correct answer because the radio station is not a state actor, so the Constitution does not require it to play Jeb's ads. **(A)** is incorrect because it hints at First Amendment doctrine, which does not apply to private parties. **(B)** is incorrect because it hints at First Amendment doctrine, which does not apply to private parties. **(D)** is incorrect because it hints at First Amendment doctrine, which does not apply to private parties.

144./B/ This is the best answer because it argues an undue burden on interstate commerce, just as requiring different size mud flaps on trucks. **(A)** is incorrect because the Equal Protection clause protects people not speedometers. **(C)** is not the best choice because the takings clause is separate from Due Process, and this law survives both analyses. **(D)** is incorrect because Bills of Attainder are legislative punishment of a named individual. The question actually states that the legislature did not name anyone.

145./C/ This is correct because Congress is empowered to spend money for the general welfare of the U.S. This power is extremely broad and extends beyond the regulatory power of Congress. **(A)** is incorrect because Congress' spending power is not limited by commerce or other powers. **(B)** is incorrect because Congress' spending power is not limited by commerce or other powers. **(D)** is incorrect because Congress' spending power is not limited by commerce or other powers.

146./C/ This is the best answer because the present welfare recipients have a property interest likely requiring notice prior to termination. **(A)** is incorrect because such a state action requires procedural due process. **(B)** is incorrect because it disregards Sally's procedural due process rights. **(D)** is incorrect because it denies Sally a pre-deprivation hearing of her due process rights.

147./D/ This is the best answer because Congress has police power over the District of Columbia, and this statute is intended to protect the health and welfare of the citizens of the District. **(A)** is incorrect because the supremacy clause only strikes inconsistent state laws. **(B)** is incorrect because general welfare is a spending provision. **(C)** is not the best answer because it is arguable whether regulation of government property would allow this particular law.

148./A/ This is the best answer because it describes the classic "market participant exception" to the dormant commerce clause. This state purchases the cars and becomes a market participant creating the market with its own funds. **(B)** is incorrect because it ignores the market participant exception to the dormant commerce clause. **(C)** is incorrect because it ignores the market participant exception to the dormant commerce clause. **(D)** is incorrect because it ignores the market participant exception to the dormant commerce clause.

149./B/ This is the correct answer because the taxing power, separate from the power to regulate, is properly used when the dominant intent of a tax is to raise revenue and not merely extract a penalty. **(A)** is not the best answer because the power to tax is independent from the power to regulate. **(C)** is incorrect because the test is whether the tax generates revenue, not significant or substantial revenue. **(D)** is incorrect because taxes are presumed not to be penalties, as long as the tax raises revenue.

150./A/ This is the best answer because the court will apply rational basis scrutiny since the law is not facially discriminatory. **(B)** is incorrect because discriminatory impact requires much higher percentages – nearly 100%. **(C)** is incorrect because discriminatory intent is very difficult to prove and the courts will weigh heavily against this finding. **(D)** is incorrect because the language comes from an exception to discrimination against alienage or citizenship.

151./A/ This is the best answer because education grants to private colleges to improve facilities are generally upheld even if the institution has a specific religious affiliation. **(B)** is incorrect because the state cannot violate the establishment clause by switching the power used, and the property clause is a federal power. **(C)** is incorrect because there is no excessive entanglement in cashing a check, and the grant was part of a larger program. **(D)** is incorrect because there is no excessive entanglement in cashing a check, and the grant was part of a larger program.

152./C/ This is the best answer because the statute is a restriction on marriage and family matters, which must be narrowly tailored to promote a compelling governmental interest with no less restrictive means available. The state can pursue child support non-payment in other ways if a future default occurs. **(A)** is incorrect because a state may not constitutionally enact a law that violates due process. **(B)** is incorrect because a state may not constitutionally enact a law that violates due process. **(D)** is incorrect because there is probably a rational basis for the distinction, and indigents and people with children are not a suspect class.

153./A/ This is the best answer because even if the court would strike down a law banning milk, the Court would not employ strict scrutiny. **(B)** is incorrect because contraceptives are protected by strict scrutiny under substantive due process. **(C)** is not the best answer because tires would probably be protected under the dormant commerce clause due to their necessity for interstate commerce. **(D)** is incorrect because contraceptives are protected by strict scrutiny under substantive due process.

154./A/ This is the best answer because the state may terminate its entire welfare program. **(B)** is incorrect because it contemplates procedural due process issues. **(C)** is incorrect because the Court has not recognized this principle in the context of welfare benefits. **(D)** is incorrect because it contemplates procedural due process issues.

155./A/ Because race is at issue, strict scrutiny applies to this state actor. **(B)** is incorrect because the company is contracting to carry out a public function so it is a state actor. **(C)** is incorrect because one cannot bootstrap a suspect class onto a quasi-suspect class. **(D)** is incorrect because the subject matter of the state function is not related to the company's employment practice.

156./B/ Funding does not make a nursing home a state actor; only if the home were fulfilling a governmental function would it be a state actor. **(A)** is incorrect because the home is not a state actor. **(C)** is incorrect because even if the home were a state actor, it would still need to prove that the hiring practice is to remedy past discrimination. The facts do not state such, only that the employees are members of a racial minority. **(D)** is incorrect because the home is not a state actor.

157./C/ Procedural due process was not provided those employees who were fired. **(A)** is incorrect because arbitrary and capricious suggests that the state lacked any reason for the action. In this case, the state's reason is articulated. **(B)** is incorrect because a state agency is a state actor regardless of the function performed. **(D)** is incorrect because wealth is not a quasi-suspect class, and it ignores the due process neglect.

158./B/ Notice must be reasonably calculated under the circumstances to reach the person deprived of property. Actual notice is usually required. **(A)** is incorrect because posting a hearing date on the website is not reasonably calculated to reach the person being deprived of the property. **(C)** is incorrect because there is no exception to the notice requirement because of necessity. **(D)** is incorrect because this level of proof applies in criminal trials only.

159./C/ Unless the professorship is tenured, the at-will law negates any property interest in a government job. **(A)** is incorrect because employment by itself is not a fundamental right. **(B)** is incorrect because unless the professorship is tenured, the at-will law negates any property interest in a government job. **(D)** is incorrect because the professor was fired for being "lazy", not for his protected right of expression.

160./B/ Desecrating the flag is protected speech, but the method of desecration – shooting a gun in a downtown place – may be prohibited because of the rational basis in protecting public safety. **(A)** is incorrect because there is no "right to be heard." People are free to ignore anyone they like. **(C)** is incorrect because the Second Amendment guarantees the right to ownership but does not protect misuse. Also, a state law prohibiting flag desecration would be struck down because the First Amendment applies to the states. **(D)** is incorrect because prior restraint is only one method of impermissible government interference with fundamental rights.

161./D/ A statute that prefers certain religions must be narrowly tailored to achieve a compelling secular end. This statute fails that test. **(A)** is not the best answer because a certain amount of control over the press, particularly broadcast media, is constitutionally permissible. **(B)** is not the best answer, because AAA does not have standing to assert such a claim, only one of the media that suffered from the Equal Protection violation has that standing. **(C)** is incorrect because the Free Exercise Clause prevents the prohibition of religious beliefs. AAA is not arguing that the statute interfered with its religious beliefs, only with its ability to disseminate information about those beliefs.

162./C/ Whether a party has standing depends on whether there is an injury in fact that is redressable by the court. The stations refused to broadcast the AAA segment based on the Texarkana statute, so the challenger AAA has been harmed by the state. **(A)** is not the best answer because even though the states may have been under no obligation to air the segment in the absence of the statute, the reason they cited for refusing to air it was the statute. **(B)** is incorrect because an organization does have standing if it is directly injured. **(D)** is not the best answer because a standing analysis relates to whether an injury has occurred. Whether the statute actually prohibits stations from broadcasting the segment is a substantive legal defense, not a standing argument.

163./A/ NAAPSTR has not been injured by the broadcast, and thus does not have standing. Simply because an organization lobbies for a statute does not automatically confer standing on that organization in every conflict involving the statute. **(B)** is not the best answer because a private party may file suit based on a civil statute, provided that party has been injured. **(C)** is incorrect because NAAPSTR has not been injured and therefore lacks standing to sue. **(D)** is incorrect because NAAPSTR lacks standing and therefore the suit will never be decided on its merits. Also, atheism is characterized as a religious belief and is thus protected by the First Amendment.

164./B/ The Eleventh Amendment grants states immunity from suits by citizens seeking money damages in federal courts, so a dismissal or remand would result. **(A)** is not the best answer because the suit is barred from federal court by the Eleventh Amendment (although if the case were brought in state court, the Supremacy Clause would apply and so the employees would likely prevail). **(C)** is incorrect because according to the facts, the employees are engaged in interstate commerce – guided tours in parks between two states. Also, the Eleventh Amendment bars a suit in federal court. **(D)** is incorrect because it is too generic. Giving guided tours is not a traditional state function, even if state parks management is. Also, the Eleventh Amendment bars a suit in federal court.

165./A/ Although the Allen Employees may have a claim under the federal act, there is no constitutional requirement that a state pay its employees the same wages as employees of other states, even if those employees perform similar functions. **(B)** is incorrect because Article IV Privileges and Immunities protects citizens of one state from discrimination based on citizenship in another state. It does not protect citizens of Allen from "discrimination" by the State of Allen. **(C)** is not the best answer because Equal Protection prevents one sovereign body from treating two similarly situated persons differently. It does not prevent the State of Allen from paying its own citizens a different wage than the State of Burns pays its own citizens. As long as the State of Allen treats all of its own citizens the same, there is no Equal Protection violation. **(D)** is incorrect because the Eleventh Amendment grants states immunity from suit in federal court, not state court.

166./D/ Any citizen has standing to challenge a prior restraint on protected speech. An overbreadth challenge is appropriate here because the statute appears to prohibit both protected speech and unprotected speech. **(A)** is not the best answer because Rebecca is not unmarried and cannot be personally harmed by the statute. She therefore has no standing to challenge the statute, although the grounds cited would be valid. **(B)** is incorrect because Rebecca has no standing to challenge this statute since she has benefited from the statute, so she has no injury. **(C)** is not the best answer because Rebecca is not currently employed for wages, so she is not eligible for unemployment benefits. She therefore has no standing to challenge the statute because she cannot be injured by it.

167./B/ Since the veto has been overridden, the statute is valid law and trumps the treaty, which was signed earlier. **(A)** is not the best answer. Although **(A)** is true, it is not an argument for why the statute should prevail over the treaty, it is only an argument for why the veto override is successful. **(C)** is incorrect because there is no constitutional provision that negates all treaties relating to trade. Had the treaty been signed after the passage of the statute, then the treaty would prevail. **(D)** is incorrect because it is not an argument for why the importation should cease, but for why it should continue.

168./C/ Article I gives Congress plenary power to regulate the naturalization process. This means that Congress can restrict entitlements for aliens to benefit of U.S. citizens, as this policy would encourage aliens to become citizens. **(A)** is not the best answer, because the reasoning is not specific enough. Congress does have this entitlement right, but there is another option presented that is more tailored to these facts. **(B)** is incorrect because as an alien, Hans is subject to certain restrictions of Congress. **(D)** is incorrect, because neither Hans nor any other alien has to prove citizenship to file a lawsuit in the United States, so long as personal and subject matter jurisdiction requirements are satisfied.

169./D/ The ordinance was an *ex post facto* law. Cheminol was not in violation of any bithium regulations until after the city passed the new lower standard. Cheminol was not given the opportunity to comply with the new standard. **(A)** is not the best answer because the right to regulate does not include the right to pass laws and issue punishments *ex post facto*. **(B)** is incorrect because Cheminol had no notice of the law it was accused of violating, it was an *ex post facto* law. **(C)** is incorrect because a bill of attainder is a law that punishes an individual without a hearing. Cheminol did have a hearing, and the law did not specifically target Cheminol, but was neutral.

170./B/ The city ordinance sets a higher standard of public safety than the federal law, and therefore does not violate the Supremacy Clause. The federal law simply provides a floor below which the state or city law may not go. A higher standard is acceptable. **(A)** is incorrect because if Congress had occupied the field then a city ordinance would be *per se* invalid. This would be a valid constitutional argument. **(C)** is not the best answer because improper legislative procedure would be a legitimate constitutional argument. **(D)** is not the best answer because individuals are protected by the takings clause from government actions that deprive them of use of their property (whether this is a successful takings argument is not the issue, the question calls for the least effective constitutional argument).

171./A/ Unlike the fine for the excessive bithium levels, which was *ex post facto*, Cheminol had a full and fair opportunity to be heard, had notice of the city's cleanup order, and refused to obey. Only then was Cheminol fined the additional $200,000. Therefore, the fine is enforceable. **(B)** is not the best answer because Cheminol did have a property interest – the cost of the cleanup – at stake. **(C)** is incorrect because unlike the fine for the excessive bithium levels, the cleanup order was prospective, and allowed time for Cheminol to comply. **(D)** is incorrect because nothing in the facts indicates that the cleanup order was in conflict with any federal law.

172./C/ The language of the executive agreement only places a burden on the president to create a positive image, not the press. **(A)** is incorrect because executive agreements do have the force of law, although to a lesser extent than treaties or statutes. **(B)** is not the best answer because while true, Congress does not need to override an executive agreement that is not unconstitutional. **(D)** is not the best answer because while the president does have broad discretion, he may not violate the Constitution. Therefore, this is not the best argument for the validity of the agreement.

173./B/ The gender distinction is substantially related to the achievement of an important governmental interest. This would make the distinction constitutionally permissible. **(A)** is not the best answer because it is too general. Collision statistics do not bear any substantial relation to a rule differentiating between men and women over 60 in vision and reflex testing. **(C)** is incorrect because Congress cannot pass a law that the Supreme Court has declared unconstitutional. Gender discrimination in state employment is illegal, and any Congressional edict to the contrary would be overturned. **(D)** is not the best answer because a general history of discrimination against women in those types of jobs does not bear any substantial relationship to a rule regarding eyesight and vision testing.

174./D/ The Takings Clause of the Fifth Amendment, applicable to states and cities via the Due Process Clause of the Fourteenth Amendment, prohibits the taking of private property for public use without just compensation. A regulation can amount to a taking if it deprives the owner of most or all economic use of the property. Chemlab, a chemical manufacturer, has no other use for the property and will have to move. **(A)** is incorrect. The Fifth Amendment applies to state and local bodies via the Due Process Clause of the Fourteenth Amendment. **(B)** is incorrect. Chemlab has been deprived of any economic use of its property and will have to incur great expense to move its factory. **(C)** is not the best answer, because the Takings Clause is applicable even if the law serves a compelling governmental interest (like building a public transportation system through a block of businesses). Just compensation must still be paid.

175./D/ The ordinance is both vague and overbroad. It is vague because ordinary persons must guess at what activities would "create a disturbance" or "hinder the work of city employees." It is overbroad because both protected and non-protected activities appear to be prohibited by the ordinance. **(A)** is incorrect because Equal Protection is not implicated; similarly situated individuals are not being treated differently. **(B)** is not the best answer because while the ordinance does interfere with the right to assembly, it does so only because it is vague and overbroad. Cities and states can regulate assembly and association, as long there is a compelling state interest, there is no attempt to suppress ideas, and there are no less restrictive means available. **(C)** is not the best answer because the government can put reasonable time, place, and manner restrictions on speech. The ordinance does not appear to restrict the content of speech, only the manner in which it is carried out.

176./A/ The U.S. Constitution always trumps state constitutions when they are in direct conflict. The employees have a strong argument under the U.S. Constitution that cannot be countered simply by saying that the Palray State Constitution provides more latitude to the city. **(B)** is incorrect because the federal government has very little police power compared with the states. Also, although a state's police power is bound by federal laws, the question of which entity has more police power is not relevant. The important issue is whether the entity has used its police power in a constitutionally acceptable way. **(C)** is incorrect because a state constitution must always comport with the minimum protections provided by the U.S. Constitution. **(D)** is incorrect because 14th Amendment Privileges or Immunities deals with the rights of national citizenship like the right to travel and vote.

177./C/ Article IV Privilege and Immunities prevents states from discriminating against residents from other states. **(A)** is not the best answer because the Congressional Tax and Spend power relates to federal taxing and spending, not state as here. **(B)** is incorrect because the Commerce Clause applies to the federal government, not the states. **(D)** is incorrect because the Fourteenth Amendment Privileges or Immunities protects rights of national citizenship, like voting and interstate travel. No national right seems implicated here.

178.D/ If a product is purchased outside a state but used in-state, a state use tax is permissible. Also, business conducted within a state may be subject to net income, licensing, and occupational taxes. **(A)** is incorrect because a sales tax can be levied only by the state in which the purchase takes place. Maggie made her purchase in Waldorf, not Statler. **(B)** is incorrect because a sales tax is levied against the buyer, not the seller, even though the seller may be charged with the tax collection responsibility. **(C)** is incorrect because a sales tax can be levied only by the state in which the purchase takes place. Maggie made her purchase in Waldorf, not Statler.

179./A/ The merchant Sid's claim involves the right to pursue a livelihood, which is certainly fundamental, so this seems to be the least effective argument. **(B)** is not the best answer because this argument supports Waldorf's claim that the nonresidents are the particular source of evil. Waldorf would have to make this claim to counter Sid's argument that the tax is discriminatory in violation of the Article IV Privileges and Immunities Clause. **(C)** is not the best answer because if the Act is constitutional, then almost certainly the tax law is. **(D)** is not the best answer because it suggests that Waldorf is using the least restrictive means available to solve the problem. Waldorf would have to make this claim to counter Sid's argument that the tax is discriminatory in violation of the Article IV Privileges and Immunities Clause.

180./B/ The president is only immune from civil suits regarding acts taken while in office, not before. Since the act in question took place two days prior to his inauguration, Executive Immunity does not apply. **(A)** is incorrect because the president is immune from civil suits for acts taken while in office, and in this case the acts in question took place two days prior to his inauguration. **(C)** is incorrect. The issue here is not impeachment, but whether the president has immunity from a civil lawsuit. **(D)** is not the best answer. There is no such rule for waiver of immunity when a crime is involved.

181./A/ Only a majority of House member votes are necessary for Articles of Impeachment, but the Senate must convict by a 2/3 margin for the President to be removed from office. **(B)** is incorrect because the Senate must convict by a 2/3 vote to remove the President from office. Also, he must be impeached before he is removed. **(C)** is not the best answer because although the President has been impeached by a majority of the House, he cannot be removed without a 2/3 vote of the Senate. **(D)** is incorrect because President Brush has been impeached, although he has not been removed.

182./B/ Congress is prohibited from limiting the pardon power of the Executive because it is a political question except in cases of impeachment. **(A)** is not the best answer because the constitution does not delegate this task to a branch of government other than the judiciary, and the issue does not here meet the definition of a political question. **(C)** is incorrect, because the reverse is actually true: the President can only pardon for federal crimes, not state crimes. **(D)** is incorrect. Article IV, Section III is the Federal Property Clause, which has absolutely nothing to do with this impeachment question.

183./D/ If a contract contains racially restrictive covenants, state action is present if a state court enforces the contract, so this is their best argument. **(A)** is not the best answer. A place of public accommodation would include a business or school, but not usually a housing development. **(B)** is not the best answer, because although there are some licensing and zoning contacts between Kelly and the state, these kinds of minor regulations do not constitute significant state involvement. **(C)** is incorrect because housing is not usually a traditional public function.

184./C/ The Act completely eliminates the right of appeal which has been determined to be a Fifth Amendment due process right. **(A)** is not the best answer because federal courts established by Congress may be courts of limited jurisdiction (*i.e.,* Bankruptcy, Admiralty, etc.). **(B)** is not the best answer because Congress does have the power under Article III to limit the jurisdiction of the Supreme Court. **(D)** is incorrect because the Act does not remove federal judges from office, it eliminates the office altogether, which is permissible.

185./B/ The initial fact pattern stated that the Labor and Employment Court had jurisdiction over claims made pursuant to the Labor and Employment Act. This claim is made pursuant to the Minimum Wage Act, over which the court has no jurisdiction. **(A)** is not the best answer because there is immediate harm threatened by the minimum wage increase, and the harm is not speculative. **(C)** is incorrect because the court has no jurisdiction. **(D)** is not the best answer because Dakola's minimum wage will increase as a result of the Supremacy Clause.

186./D/ Courts have been most lenient about public funds for athletic programs made to religious schools at the college level. **(A)** is not the best answer because any aid to religious schools at levels lower than college has been almost totally prohibited. **(B)** is not the best answer because any aid to religious schools at levels lower than college has been almost totally prohibited. **(C)** is not the best answer because any aid to religious schools at levels lower than college has been almost totally prohibited.

187./C/ If Jerry is sincere in his belief, then the law as applied may be a violation of his right to religious free exercise. **(A)** is not the best answer because it is not specific enough. **(B)** is not the best answer because the facts do not suggest that Jerry was trying to express or communicate any information. A freedom of religion argument is more appropriate. **(D)** is not the best answer because a neutral, generally applicable law that does not create any government approval, oversight, involvement, money, etc. does not offend the Establishment Clause.

188./D/ The First Amendment totally prohibits any restriction on religious beliefs. This would include a court examining a belief to determine if it is reasonably religious. Jerry's opinion regarding the sanctity of his beliefs is the only one that matters. **(A)** is not the best answer because it speaks to Jerry's sincerity in his religious belief or whether it is a pretext, which the court may examine. **(B)** is not the best answer because a court may examine the sincerity of a religious belief. **(C)** is incorrect because Jerry is only protected if he actually believes that the ritual is required as part of his faith.

189./C/ Since the state does not impose the tax on Tassen trucks, the tax favors in-state interests over foreign interests and thus is protectionist. **(A)** is incorrect because the privilege tax is not a tax on goods (the goods tax is separate). Therefore, a "goods in the stream of commerce" argument is inapplicable. Privilege taxes are permissible, even if the user does not stop in the state. **(B)** is not the best answer because the state has an interest in preserving its roads. This has a substantial nexus with taxing trucking, which is a direct cause of wear and tear to roads. **(D)** is not the best answer because preserving roads is a legitimate state interest.

190./A/ There is still the issue of whether the tax is fairly apportioned between actors from various states and in-state versus out-of-state actors. Illiho trucks are taxed 20 times higher than trucks from other states, regardless of any actual connection to the proportional amount of use of Tassen roads. **(B)** is incorrect because no federal law is indicated to raise a preemption issue. **(C)** is incorrect, there is still the constitutional issue of apportionment of the tax, even if the imposition of the tax is permissible. **(D)** is not the best answer, because the issue of undue burden on interstate commerce at the imposition of the privilege tax was resolved when the court determined the privilege tax to be valid. If the privilege tax imposed an undue burden on interstate commerce, it would have been struck down in its entirety.

191./B/ The Tassen goods tax is taxing some goods that are in the stream of commerce – here there is no break in transit as the goods pass through the state. This is not permitted under the dormant (or negative) Commerce Clause. **(A)** is not the best answer because it has a wrong conclusion and a tax imposed on goods in the stream of commerce does burden interstate commerce, even though it is not necessarily protectionist. **(C)** is incorrect because it is really just a restatement of (A). Just because a tax is not protectionist does not necessarily end a dormant Commerce Clause inquiry. The tax must also avoid undue burdens on interstate commerce. **(D)** is incorrect because the dormant Commerce Clause regulates the burden placed on interstate commerce, and not taxation of goods in general.

192./D/ Although there is no general federal police power, Congress does have police power over the District of Columbia, as enumerated in Article I. **(A)** is not the best answer because it is not specific enough. Congress has the power to do what is necessary and proper to carry out all of its enumerated powers, but the N&P Clause does not, in and of itself, justify any particular action without reference to an enumerated power. **(B)** is not the best answer because while true, it does nothing to explain why the law is constitutional. **(C)** is not the best answer because it is precisely the argument that was rejected by the Supreme Court when it struck down the federal Prevention of Violence Against Women Act.

193./C/ Poverty is a non-suspect class, which is afforded rational basis judicial scrutiny under Equal Protection jurisprudence. The rational basis test states that the law must be rationally related to a legitimate governmental interest, and the P has the burden of proof. **(A)** is not the best answer, because it combines the rational basis test with intermediate scrutiny. Intermediate judicial scrutiny states that the law must be substantially related to an important governmental purpose, and the state usually has the burden of proof. **(B)** is incorrect, because it confuses the rational basis test with strict scrutiny language, and the proper test is rational basis. **(D)** is incorrect because it states the intermediate judicial scrutiny test, which applies only to quasi-suspect classes of gender and illegitimacy. Poverty is a non-suspect class.

194./A/ A law that deprives a citizen of property prior to providing a meaningful opportunity to be heard must be carefully scrutinized as a potential procedural due process violation. **(B)** is not the best answer because there is no question that states may impose fines for civil traffic violations pursuant to their police powers. **(C)** is not the best answer because there is no indication that the state is discriminating based on classifications of persons, but instead is establishing different procedures based on the severity of the fine involved, which is acceptable. **(D)** is incorrect because no person's liberty is threatened, and no restraint of movement or activity is involved.

195./D/ One element of the *Mathews v. Eldridge* balancing test weighs the administrative burden and cost to the government of providing a pre-deprivation hearing procedure. The facts here support the state's use of a post-deprivation procedure. **(A)** is incorrect. It states the rational basis test, which is not a factor in the *Mathews v. Eldridge* balancing test. **(B)** is incorrect because this fact, if true, would support Joe's argument. One element of the *Mathews* test that weighs in favor of a pre-deprivation hearing is whether there is a high risk of erroneous deprivation. **(C)** is not the best answer because *Mathews* examines the individual interest at stake in each case. To some people, $50 might be a very important property interest, even if others rate it lower.

196./A/ This is the only argument that will carry any weight with a court trying to determine whether certain speech is obscene. If a film has artistic value according to a reasonable person standard, it will not be classified as obscene. **(B)** is not the best answer because even a film depicting "normal" sexual relations can be obscene if it appeals to prurient interest in sex. **(C)** is not the best answer because even a film depicting "normal" sexual relations can be obscene if it appeals to prurient interest in sex and how widely a film is distributed has no bearing on an evaluation of its obscenity. The test is whether the film lacks social value, is patently offensive, and appeals to the prurient interest in sex. **(D)** is not the best answer because the question of whether materials have scientific, artistic, or literary merit is determined by a reasonable person standard, not a local standard. Also, even a film depicting "normal" sexual relations can be obscene if it appeals to prurient interest in sex.

197./C/ The unique test for evaluating a law restricting commercial speech is that the law serves a substantial government interest, directly advances that interest, is narrowly tailored to achieve that interest, and no more extensive than necessary. Only the wording of **(C)** matches the language of the test. **(A)** is incorrect because the determination of what is obscene is a complex standard that states and localities may determine themselves (with certain restrictions). **(B)** is not the best answer because the test refers to a "substantial" government interest, not a "compelling" government interest. **(D)** is not the best answer because the test is whether the law "directly advances" that interest, not whether it is "rationally related."

198./B/ In cases between two states where, as here, one state is suing on behalf of its citizens under the *parens patriae* doctrine, lower federal courts have concurrent jurisdiction with the Supreme Court. **(A)** is not the best answer because it misstates the law. Lower courts have concurrent jurisdiction when one state is a party, or when one state is suing on behalf of its citizens under the *parens patriae* doctrine. If the suit is between two or more states, and neither state is suing on behalf of its citizens, then the Supreme Court has mandatory original jurisdiction. **(C)** is incorrect because Alabraska is suing on behalf of its citizens under the *parens patriae* doctrine, therefore the case does not fall within the Supreme Court's mandatory jurisdiction. **(D)** is incorrect because it misstates the law. The Supreme Court must hear cases between two states, it does not have certiorari discretion.

199./D/ If Virginessee's regulations are less stringent than federal law, they are invalid. Any state law that provides less protection than a federal law on the same direct matter is preempted. **(A)** is incorrect because states are not required to have similar regulations to other states, even if they share a common border. State laws must comport with federal law, not the laws of other states. **(B)** is not correct because legislation is not necessarily invalid when it is recklessly or thoughtlessly enacted. **(C)** is not the best answer because it is too vague – just because the state regulations "do not comport" with the federal regulations does not mean that they are less stringent. If they are more stringent, they are valid.

200./A/ The President may remove administrative appointees, but only if they are not appointed for a fixed term as here. **(B)** is not the best answer because Congressional approval is not required for appointments to administrative agencies like the EPA. **(C)** is incorrect because the President may not dismiss appointees at will if they are appointed for a fixed term. **(D)** is incorrect. Although it is true that the President does not need Congressional approval, he may not remove officials at will it they were appointed for a fixed term.

RIGOS BAR REVIEW SERIES

UNIFORM MULTISTATE BAR EXAM (MBE) REVIEW

CONSTITUTIONAL LAW

Index

CHAPTER 6

CRIMINAL LAW
AND
PROCEDURE

RIGOS UBE REVIEW SERIES

UNIFORM MULTISTATE BAR EXAM (MBE) REVIEW

CHAPTER 6 – CRIMINAL LAW AND PROCEDURE

Table of Contents

I.   MBE EXAM COVERAGE

A. Weight

27 of the 200 MBE objective multiple-choice questions test Criminal Law and Procedure distributed approximately 60% criminal law and 40% criminal procedure. Homicide is the heaviest tested topic. See MEE at 12-487 for prior NCBE exam question issues tested distribution. Working questions helps understand the theory.

B. Emphasis

The MBE focuses on the common law criminal law, some modern statutory modifications, and constitutional criminal procedure. If a statutory law is being tested, the relevant portion of the statute at issue will be provided. Since there is no federal criminal common law, the MBE focuses on the majority state common law principles, and will sometimes refer to the rules embodied in the Model Penal Code (MPC). Exam questions often turn on identifying the elements of each crime.

C. The Call of the Question

1. Criminal Law: The question call will likely be phrased in one of five ways:

a. Outcome: "Should D be found guilty (not guilty) of the crime(s) alleged, it will be because ..., or what rule justifies that outcome?"

b. Best Argument: "What is the best argument for the prosecution/defense?"

c. Most Serious Crime: "Of the alternatives listed, what is the most serious crime of which the D could be convicted?"

d. Best Precedent: "Which criminal precedent best resolves the issue raised by the facts?"

e. Which Crime: "Which of four fact patterns most closely describes a particular crime?"

2. Criminal Procedure: Look for the following calls:

a. Best Instruction to Jury: "What is the best/worst jury instruction that the judge should make regarding the validity of a search?"

b. Admissibility: "Is the evidence offered admissible at trial" or "Which is the strongest argument in favor of excluding the statements from evidence?"

c. Appeal: "Based on the facts of the investigation, arrest, and trial, are there grounds for an appeal by the defendant?"

II. OVERVIEW: GENERAL PRINCIPLES OF CRIMINAL LAW

A. Requirements for Criminal Liability

The elements of a crime are stated in the statute and D may argue a negating defense which attacks an essential element of the state's case. The prosecutor must prove each element beyond a reasonable doubt. These elements are:

1. Action (*Actus Reus*): The prosecutor must prove beyond a reasonable doubt that the D performed each act required by the criminal statute in question.

2. Mental State (*Mens Rea*): The prosecutor must prove the D possessed the mental state required for that specific crime. The specific intent requirement is an application of the common law *mens rea* requirement to criminal law.

> **MBE Tip:** *Mens rea* and *actus reus* should be nearly concurrent. The *mens rea* should be the impetus or activating factor of the *actus reus*. If a D has the intent in his mind to commit larceny, and then three days later (with the intent no longer present) he takes the victim's money by mistake, the earlier *mens rea* will not join with the later *actus reus* to create criminal liability.

3. Result: The prosecutor must prove that the specified crime occurred.

4. Causation: The prosecutor must prove the D's actions caused the result.

> **MBE Tip:** Many UBE questions will set up facts where most necessary elements of a crime are given, but one element is not discussed, not proven beyond a reasonable doubt, or not supported by competent evidence. Look for any missing elements in the fact pattern. Don't skip this step or you'll be missing obvious correct responses.

B. *Actus Reus*

The D must have committed an unlawful act – *actus reus* or "guilty act." A person is not criminally liable for thoughts alone. The definition of the relevant criminal statute will specify what acts are required for a specific crime. There are two questions involving the criminal liability act requirement: (1) When is an act not an act for criminal law purposes? and (2) When will a failure to act serve as a culpable act?

1. Nonvolitional (Involuntary) Act: Although there may be an "act" in the ordinary sense of the word, it may not qualify as an *actus reus* for the purpose of assigning criminal liability to the actor if it is a nonvolitional act.

a. Rule: An involuntary act that was not controlled by the conscious will of the actor does not qualify as an "act" for criminal liability purposes.

b. Example: If a person is sleepwalking, unconscious, having an epileptic seizure, or is acting under physical force by another, his actions are nonvolitional.

c. Exception: If the person knew he had a defect that might make him a danger but failed to take reasonable precautions, he still may be culpable. For example, an epileptic would still be culpable if he failed to take his medication, but continued to drive knowing a seizure was likely and could put other drivers' lives in danger.

> **MBE Tip:** Watch for subtle issues of causation. If the *actus reus* did not cause the crime, the D is not culpable. Scrutinize the fact pattern for something that breaks the chain of causation. For example, if a parent hits a child, but the coroner lists the cause of death as cancer, the parent will not be convicted of homicide.

    2. Omission / Failure to Act: The general rule is that there is no criminal liability for an omission to act, such as failing to intervene to stop a crime. Similarly, there is generally no legal duty to warn or to aid a victim after a crime is committed. However, a failure to assist can be actionable as a crime in certain situations described below. Keep in mind that the D must be physically able to perform the act if he is to be held liable for the failure.

    a. Statute Specifies Failure to Act as *Actus Reus*: When a statute specifically criminalizes the omission (such as requiring a driver to stop at an accident they caused or not paying a speeding ticket) then that failure to act will be the *actus reus* of the crime.

    b. Legal Duty to Act: In some circumstances there is a legal duty to act and D's failure to act may substantially contribute to an illegal result. This legal duty can be based on a contract, a statute, a parental duty to a child, the creation of risk by D, or beginning an undertaking by D.

    (1) Contract: A person hired as a lifeguard has a duty by contract to save swimmers in the area. She must make an attempt to rescue if it is reasonable to do so.

    (2) Statute: Some hospitals must, by statute, treat indigent patients. If employees of such a hospital knowingly turn away someone who then dies because of lack of treatment, they can be liable for homicide.

    (3) Parent for a Child: A family relationship creates a parents' legal duty to care for a child. If a parent neglects to feed her child, seek necessary medical attention, or protect her child from abuse, she can be held criminally liable for that omission.

    (4) Creation of Risk: Danger created by D may impose a duty. At a party, D pushed Betty into the swimming pool as a joke. When he hears her shout, "Help! I can't swim," D now has the duty to rescue her.

    (5) Undertaking: A D may have a duty to assist when she has already begun assisting, particularly if she does so to the victim's detriment, or dissuades other potential rescuers from coming to aid P.

C. *Mens Rea*

    A D who committed the *actus reus* must also possess a specific, unlawful state of mind to be criminally liable. This state of mind is called the "culpable mental state," the "criminal intent," or the "*mens rea*" (guilty mind) and is heavily tested on both the MBE and MEE. The required mental state is included in the elements of certain crimes. For example, criminal liability for burglary requires that the D specifically intended to enter a dwelling at night to commit a crime therein.

> **MBE Tip:** If the question references a statute, look for the wording "knowingly commit," "knowingly cause," or a similar indication of the required intent level.

1. Common Law: Under common law, a variety of terms and definitions may be used for the culpable state of mind, however the most common are general intent, specific intent, malice, recklessness, and absolute or strict liability. Proof of a more deliberate state of mind automatically proves the lesser states of mind.

a. General Intent: This requires only that D intended to commit the act which constituted the *actus reus*. Examples include battery, kidnapping, false imprisonment, or intent to shoot a gun leading to a death.

b. Specific Intent: A "specific intent" *mens rea* requires the actor to actually intend to commit the criminal act or cause the harm constituting the crime. If a crime requires specific intent, the prosecutor must prove that the D actually had the specific intent to commit the crime, such as shoot a particular person. Under the common law, **CAR BAL** – **C**onspiracy, **A**ttempt, **R**obbery, **B**urglary, **A**ssault, and **L**arceny crimes require specific intent.

> **MBE Tip:** CAR BAL intent is another subtle area often tested. Learn the different levels of intent and be able to distinguish crimes based on the presence or absence of intent.

c. Malice: This is ill will or the desire to harm another. Malice is defined as the intentional doing of a wrongful act without just cause or excuse, with an intent to inflict an injury or under circumstances such that the law will imply an evil intent. Under common law, malice is also evidenced by "extreme recklessness" which is an extreme indifference to the consequence of the act, also called a "depraved or wicked heart." For the common law crimes of arson and murder, the prosecutor must prove that the D acted with malice or specific intent.

d. Recklessness: A person is reckless when she consciously disregards a substantial and unjustifiable risk. This disregard must be a substantial deviation from the conduct that a reasonable person would exercise in the same situation. Thus, recklessness is greater than ordinary negligence. The actor must act without regard for the harm that might occur generally but need not specifically intend to cause the particular harm which occurred. The recklessness crimes are manslaughter and battery.

e. Criminal Negligence: This is a level of disregard, indifference, or neglect that is below the standard of recklessness. It involves an act that creates an unreasonable risk of harm (use the tort standard to decide what constitutes "unreasonable") and awareness of the risk by the D. It does not constitute criminal liability at common law, but most states and the Model Penal Code have adopted it.

f. Absolute or Strict Liability: Proof of a particular state of mind is not necessary for a strict liability crime. The conduct alone is conclusively proscribed by the statute. Running a red traffic light or statutory rape are examples of absolute liability crimes.

g. Vicarious Liability: When an employee or agent commits the *actus reus* and some culpability can reasonably be inferred to the employer or principal, vicarious criminal liability may arise. This is a principle similar to *respondeat superior* in civil tort law. However, because the intent does not arise directly from the employer's/principal's conduct, liability under this doctrine is always designated by statute and restricted to relatively minor punishments such as fines.

> **MBE Tip:** A total lack of intent may be at issue in a particular question, such as an unconscious actor. They would not qualify because criminal intent requires a voluntary act. Look for a statement in the facts that the jury believes the D lacked intent.

2. Model Penal Code (MPC) States of Mind: In an effort to simplify and define the common law intent mental states, the MPC defines the potential D's mental states as "purposely," "knowingly," "recklessly," "negligently," and "strict liability." On the MBE and MEE the state of mind is usually included in the definition of each crime. The actual mental state may or may not be clearly specified. Classifications include:

a. Purposely: A person acts purposely when it is his deliberate conscious intent to perform the act and cause the result constituting the crime.

b. Knowingly: A person acts knowingly when he is aware that it is practically certain that his act will cause the result constituting the crime.

c. Recklessly: A person acts recklessly when he consciously disregards a substantial and unjustifiable high risk that his act will cause a result which constitutes a crime. A conscious disregard of the risk must be a gross deviation from what a reasonable person would do under the circumstances.

d. Negligently: A person acts negligently when he should be aware of a substantial and/or unjustifiable risk that his act will cause a result which constitutes a crime. Again, his disregard of the risk must be a gross deviation from what a reasonable person would do under the circumstances. Criminal negligence implies gross negligence as a substantial departure from the ordinary standard of due care.

MBE Tip: Some states have adopted statutes making "criminal negligence" sufficient *mens rea* for crimes such as vehicular homicide or child neglect. On the MBE, look for a statute that refers to this *mens rea*. Absent such a statute, assume that criminal negligence is insufficient to create criminal liability.

---

e. Strict Liability: The MPC adopts essentially the same state of mind approach as the common law requiring no *mens rea* for culpability.

MBE Tip: *Mens rea* can be confusing. For example, it is counterintuitive to think of "recklessness" as a "mental state" when the facts sound like D was not thinking at all at the time. Have a thorough understanding of all levels of *mens rea* and remember that the statute or common law definition of the crime will indicate the required *mens rea*.

---

3. "Mistakes of Fact" May Negate *Mens Rea*: A person's misunderstanding of the factual circumstances may prevent the prosecutor from proving that the person possessed the state of mind required for the particular crime. An example is D takes another's bicycle thinking it was her own. If the crime requires specific intent, an honest mistake will negate that the D possessed specific intent. If the crime requires malice or recklessness, the mistake must be both honest and reasonable.

4. "Mistakes of Law" Do Not Excuse Except in Certain Circumstances: A person's ignorance of the law does not generally vitiate violation of a criminal statute. Examples include hunting or fishing without a license, or possession of a firearm without a required permit. On the MBE, the facts may state that the D did not think his act was a crime. Anyone could say they did not know the law and escape liability, so a mistake of law is not usually a valid defense. There are three exceptions where ignorance of the law could be a defense.

a. Offense Requires Knowledge of the Law:

(1) Rule: The statute may define the crime so that "knowledge of a willful violation" is a required element that the prosecutor must prove. In this circumstance, mistake is not an affirmative defense raised by the D. Instead the burden is on the prosecutor to prove knowledge beyond a reasonable doubt.

(2) Example: An anti-pollution statute might specify that the D "willfully fail to report levels of contaminants." "Willfully" indicates that the D must have knowledge of the requirement and fail to report. To avoid ignorance as a defense, the statute will often require only constructive knowledge, not actual knowledge.

b. Mistake of Law Causes a Mistake of Fact:

(1) Rule: If a person mistakenly thinks that the law provides him with rights, it may negate the *mens rea* in some cases. Again, this is not an affirmative defense, but an element that the prosecutor must prove, for which the defendant can raise a reasonable doubt.

(2) Example: D's car has been lawfully repossessed, but he thinks it is stolen. He finds it, gets in, and drives it away. His mistaken belief that the car is lawfully his property is grounds to negate the *mens rea* for theft.

c. Misinformation from a Public Official:
If a person tries to learn the law by consulting a public official (IRS agent, Department of Land Use inspector, etc.), and that official misinforms the D, this is a defense under the MPC or statutory law but not under the common law. Note that this exception constitutes an affirmative defense rather than negating any element of the crime.

> **MBE Tip:** Usually the exam tests the general rule that a mistake of law is not a "defense." It may negate the required *mens rea*, causing the prosecution to fail in its task of proving all the elements of a crime.

5. Transferred Intent: Mental states are subject to transferred intent. A D cannot avoid criminal liability by claiming that she intended to commit a different crime or intended to commit the same crime against another subject. Therefore, intent will often transfer between similar crimes/victims, unless there is a radical break in the chain of foreseeability.

a. Between Victims:
Intent will transfer between victims. If D intends to shoot Bill, but hit Sam, D's intent will transfer between victims and D will be liable for the intentional shooting of Sam.

b. Between Crimes:
Intent will also transfer between crimes. If the D breaks into a house intending to commit a robbery, but no one is home so he commits larceny instead, intent will transfer.

> **MBE Tip:** Don't try to stretch transferred intent too far. For example, if A throws a rock into a vacant building intending to break a window (intent to do Malicious Mischief) and unbeknownst to him B is inside the building and is hit (Assault), intent does not transfer. A will not be convicted of intentionally assaulting B although he could be found criminally negligent.

D. Causation

The prosecutor must prove beyond a reasonable doubt that the D's actions caused the harmful result required for the particular crime. For example, if the crime charged is murder, someone must have been killed and the D's actions had to have been both the actual and the proximate cause of the resulting death.

1. Actual Cause: To prove actual cause or cause-in-fact, the prosecutor must prove that "but for" the D's actions the harm would not have occurred or that the D's actions were a substantial factor in causing the harm.

a. "But For" Test: "But for" the D's actions, harm to the P would not have occurred. Under the "but for" test, the D is considered the sole cause of the harm.

b. Substantial Factor Test: Even if another event or actor contributed to the harm, the D is still liable if his actions were a substantial factor in causing the harm. If the D's actions were not enough by themselves to cause the harm, but when combined with other forces would produce the harm, the D's actions are considered the cause-in-fact.

> **MBE Tip:** If the harm would have resulted anyway and the D's actions hasten the harm, the D is usually liable. For example, killing a terminally ill person is still murder.

2. Proximate Cause:

a. Rule: The D's actions were the proximate cause of the harm if the harmful result was the natural and probable result of the D's actions. The result cannot be too remote or accidental. Generally, if the D's actions were the actual cause of the harm, the actions will also be the proximate cause of the harm. An example is a third-party victim such as D shooting an unintended bystander or the wrong victim.

b. Exception: Even though the D's actions might have been the actual cause of the harm, there are some results that are so far removed from the D's actions by time, place, or circumstances that it would be unjust to hold the D criminally liable. There may be no proximate cause if:

(1) Intervening Cause: The ultimate harm was set in motion by the D's actions but the harm occurred at the end of an unforeseeable chain of events (*"intervening" cause*); or

(2) Superseding Cause: The ultimate harm was the result of an unforeseeable, independent event beyond the D's control (*"superseding" cause*).

> **MBE Tip:** Be wary of MBE and MEE questions that imply intervening or superseding causes. Rarely will these help the D escape liability, unless the intervening event is wholly independent of the criminal act (example: D poisons V without V's knowledge and V is immediately killed in an unrelated auto accident). Unforeseeable criminal behavior by a third party may produce a superseding cause (example: D scratches V with a fingernail and treating physician recklessly infects V with a deadly disease).

E. Accomplice Liability

One D can be convicted of the crime committed by another D under the theory of accomplice liability if the D aids, abets, facilitates, or encourages the perpetrator in the commission of the crime with culpable intent. If the facts indicate that a D is liable as an accomplice, he is liable for the underlying crime committed. This requires **CIA** – **C**omplicity, **I**ntent specific, and **A**ctive participation.

> **MBE Tip:** Being an accomplice is *not* a separate crime, but merely a means of prosecuting helpers. For example, if D is an accomplice to a burglary, he himself is charged with burglary. Discard an MBE option stating that a D can be "charged with the crime of being an accomplice."

1. Complicity: This is a general agreement to further and cooperate in a future crime. The link between the accomplice and principal may be mere words of encouragement and approval, such as encouraging a group fight resulting in a battery or a homicide, or directing a child to steal.

> **MBE Tip:** Complicity frequently involves the companion crimes of attempt, solicitation, and conspiracy. If complicity is suggested in the fact pattern, remember to look for an accomplice trying to withdraw from complicity before the crime in question occurs. A significant act of warning or prevention of the crime is necessary for the accomplice to avoid liability.

2. Intent Specific: The majority rule under the common law requires that the D specifically intend that the crime be committed.

3. Active Participation: The D must do an overt act to participate and assist the crime (such as getaway driver, lookout, etc.). Usually, mere presence at the scene of the crime is insufficient. Look for evidence of D encouraging the perpetrator to commit the crime.

4. Victim Protected: A person cannot be convicted of a crime if the person is in the class of persons the statute means to protect. For instance, an underage person cannot be convicted of statutory rape even if that person aided, abetted, facilitated, or encouraged the perpetrator to commit statutory rape. She is in the class of persons the law means to protect, thus she is a victim, not an accomplice.

5. Conviction Not Dependent on Fate of Others: Again, the D will be charged, tried, and convicted of the crime committed by the perpetrator, not with the crime of "complicity" or "accomplice." The complicit D can be convicted even if the primary perpetrator is not convicted.

> **MBE Tip:** The exam will often test the "act" requirement for accomplice liability. Remember: a silent onlooker, even one with criminal intent, is not enough for accomplice liability. Verbal encouragement is usually sufficient to fulfill the act requirement.

F. Merger – Lesser Included Crimes

All crimes whose elements are included in a greater crime are implicitly charged by charging the crime with the greater degree. For example, because larceny, assault, and battery all merge into robbery a D cannot be charged with both larceny and robbery. An exception is for burglary that does not merge with any other crime; the underlying crime must be charged separately.

> **STOP!** Go to page 375 and work Learning Questions 1 to 10.

III. AFFIRMATIVE DEFENSES

A. Insanity

The insanity defenses measure whether the D was severely mentally ill at the time of the crime. The D raises the issue of insanity and must either produce a "scintilla" of evidence or raise a "reasonable doubt" as to his sanity (depending on the jurisdiction). The D need not plead "guilty" to raise this defense. Again, depending on the jurisdiction, the D will either have to prove insanity by a preponderance of the evidence, or the prosecutor will have to prove sanity beyond a reasonable doubt. States differ.

1. *M'Naghten* Test: To establish the defense of not guilty by reason of insanity, the *M'Naghten* test requires that the D prove he was unable to comprehend the act or unable to tell right from wrong as a result of severe mental disease or defect at the time of the offense. The defense of insanity must be established by a preponderance of the evidence. This defense puts the mental health of the D at issue, which waives the doctor-patient privilege.

2. Irresistible Impulse: Some states, including half of those that use *M'Naghten*, allow the "irresistible impulse" insanity defense if the D was unable to control his actions. The test provides that even if the D knew that what he was doing was wrong, he was unable to control his actions to conform to what he knew was right.

3. MPC Substantial Capacity Test: This is the default rule and may be an easier standard for D to meet than *M'Naghten*. It applies if the D was then totally incapable of realizing what he was doing, knowing if the action was right or wrong, or being unable to control his actions. The substantial capacity test will find the D not guilty by reason of insanity if he was substantially incapable of knowing right from wrong, or incapable of controlling his actions (essentially combining the *M'Naghten* and irresistible impulse tests).

4. *Durham* Test: This is also called the "Product Rule." When the unlawful act was the product of a mental defect/disease, then the D will not be held criminally liable. This is the most expansive of the insanity tests, and therefore the most criticized and least used.

MBE Tip: It is likely that in law school you learned the test for your particular state's jurisdiction, so make sure you are aware of the MPC substantial capacity test. If the MBE or MEE question does not specifically name the *M'Naghten* or Irresistible Impulse test as the governing law, assume the MPC Substantial Capacity test applies.

---

5. Competence to Stand for Trial: Competence to stand for trial, in contrast, measures the degree of mental illness and cognitive impairment at the time of trial. If a person is unable to understand the proceedings and rationally assist counsel in his own defense, it jeopardizes his/her constitutional right to a fair trial under the 5th Amendment. *Duskey v. U.S.*

B. Diminished Capacity

No act committed by a person while in a state of voluntary intoxication or impairment shall be deemed less criminal by reason of his condition.

1. Specific Intent: If the defined statutory crime requires specific intent (other than *actus reus*), it may be a defense if the D can prove that their capacity was so diminished that they were substantially unable to form the required specific intent.

2. Voluntary Intoxication: Voluntary intoxication such as drinking to strengthen the D nerve to do the crime will never be a valid defense to a crime because the act of becoming intoxicated itself shows disregard for the consequences and thus malice or recklessness. Any resulting diminished capacity is self-inflicted.

MBE Tip: Involuntary intoxication may be a valid defense to all crimes, as it may be considered equivalent to temporary mental illness. An example is ingested drugs dropped into a cup of coffee by someone else. If involuntary intoxication is an option, be wary. Was the D truly not responsible for his/her intoxicated state?

C. Infancy

The level of intent imputed to children, and the venue (juvenile v. adult) court depends primarily upon the age of the child. All children under 18 are tried in juvenile court.

1. Under Seven: Children under the age of seven years are conclusively presumed to be incapable of forming the intent to commit a crime.

2. Seven to Thirteen: Children over seven and under fourteen years old are presumed to be incapable of intending a crime, because of insufficient capacity to understand the act was wrong. The presumption is not automatic and is subject to rebuttal. The prosecutor must submit clear and convincing proof that the child had sufficient capacity to understand the act (or neglect), and to know that it was wrong.

3. Fourteen to Eighteen: There is no presumption of incapacity for children fourteen to eighteen years old. An exception to this is if the crime is a serious violent offense and the D is 16 or 17.

D. Duress

If a D was threatened with imminent death or serious bodily harm to himself or another, and that threat compelled him to commit a crime, the D may raise the defense of duress in certain circumstances. While it depends upon the circumstances, a D may not be held liable for a crime committed where there was extreme coercion to act (or not act).

1. When Available: This defense may apply if the person was threatened with imminent death or great physical harm to himself, a member of his family, or others. In addition, D must reasonably believe that he had no alternative but to commit the crime to avoid the threatened serious harm outlined below.

2. When Not Available:

a. Only Property Threatened: Threats against property are not sufficient to raise the defense of duress.

b. Murder or Manslaughter: Duress is also not an available defense if the crime charged is intentional murder or manslaughter.

c. D Created Situation: The D cannot intentionally or recklessly place himself in a situation where it was probable he would be subject to duress, and then claim the defense.

MBE Tip: The fact pattern on the exam will likely describe a very sympathetic D, who was placed in an intolerable situation of duress. This will tempt you toward acquittal as your response. However, remember that if intentional murder or manslaughter is charged, no amount of duress, however dire, will exonerate the D.

E. Entrapment

Entrapment is a defense when the idea of the crime originated with the police and the D would not have committed the crime in the absence of the enticement of the police. The defense of entrapment is not established by a showing that the law enforcement officials merely afforded the D an opportunity if the D was predisposed to commit the crime.

> **MBE Tip:** An answer which suggests that D is acquitted because of the defense of entrapment is usually wrong unless it is clear that the D was not predisposed to commit the criminal act and the idea to engage in such an unlawful act originated from the law enforcement officer.

F. Defense of Self

1. Reasonable Force: A person who reasonably believes he is being attacked can use reasonable force to protect himself. The D must reasonably believe such force was necessary to protect himself from an imminent, unlawful attack and there was not a feasible escape. There is also a requirement that the amount of force D chose to use was necessary.

a. Must Be Imminent: The threat of future or potential harm is not usually sufficient to justify the present use of defensive force.

b. Proportionality: The D may use only the amount of force that is reasonably necessary to prevent present harm to himself (*i.e.*, force that is proportional to the attack). Preventative deadly force is subject to heightened scrutiny but may be allowed if the attack threatens D with serious bodily harm and there is no alternative. The person claiming the defense cannot have provoked the incident in which they subsequently murdered the victim.

> **MBE Tip:** Use of deadly force in defense resulting in homicide is heavily tested. The defense will be unsuccessful if the deadly force is used merely in defense of property.

2. Honest Mistake: An honest, reasonable mistake as to the facts of a situation may be sufficient for self defense to be available. An example is D's reasonable belief that another party was about to shoot D. If the D makes an honest but *un*reasonable mistake in the amount of force necessary to defend himself, self defense is not available. However, it may reduce the charge from murder to manslaughter as the mistake prevented the formation of the required mental state.

3. Aggressors: Self defense is sometimes available to a first aggressor, but this depends primarily on the subsequent actions of the first aggressor and the victim.

a. Non-Deadly v. Deadly Force: If an aggressor uses non-deadly force, he can claim self-defense if the victim responds with deadly force. However, if the aggressor uses deadly force in the first place, he cannot claim self-defense.

b. Withdrawal by First Aggressor: If the aggressor withdraws or retreats from his aggression and clearly communicates that to the victim, the aggressor regains his right to self defense. In this circumstance, the victim can also no longer claim self defense if he continues the fight.

4. Retreat Rule: Under the MPC, the victim must first try to retreat if it is safely possible to do so, before she is entitled to use deadly force. The common law has no requirement to retreat, especially if the aggression is in D's own home.

G. Defense of Others

1. Others: Under the common law, there needed to be a family or personal relationship between the victim and the third-party defender for the defender to use force to protect the victim. In the modern view, the victim can be a total stranger.

2. Reasonable Force: This standard is essentially the same as for self defense. The force used in defending another must not be unreasonable.

a. Majority View: The majority view determines whether the force amount was appropriate according to a reasonable third-party defender's belief.

b. Minority View: The minority view, in contrast, would allow the third party to use only as much force as the victim himself could use. Thus, if the seeming victim was the original aggressor who had used deadly force, the third party cannot use force because the aggressor had forfeited her right to self defense.

3. Arrest: If the victim is being lawfully arrested, neither the victim nor third party defender are entitled to use force against the police officer.

H. Defense of Property

Deadly force is not privileged to protect property. Reasonable non-deadly force can be used to defend property. If a threat to property also threatens to harm people, the rules for defense of self and others apply. A trespasser without more is not usually deemed an aggressor and thus may use necessary force to repel an attack by the property's owner or tenant.

I. Necessity Defense

Commission of the criminal act was necessary to prevent some greater harm occurring. Emergencies may qualify. Examples are a person driving his car while intoxicated to escape from a kidnapping or starting an arson fire around his house to clear flammable brush in the face of an advancing forest fire. This is often referred to as "the lesser of two evils" defense.

J. Fleeing Felon

1. Private Citizen: If D is fleeing from the scene of a felony, a private citizen may use deadly force if the suspected felon poses an immediate threat to the citizen or others. Note that the citizen must know and be correct in the knowledge that the D is a fleeing felon and poses a serious present threat. The MPC does not allow a private citizen to use deadly force.

2. Police Arrest: In comparison, a police officer may use deadly force if the felony is dangerous and the suspect attacks the officer and/or ignores a command to stop.

STOP! Go to page 376 and work Learning Questions 11 to 20.

IV.   INCHOATE (INCOMPLETE) CRIMINAL OFFENSES

These include offers, plans, and attempts to commit a crime that fails.

A. Solicitation

Common law solicitation consists of encouraging another person to commit a felony or serious misdemeanor with the intent that the other person will commit the crime.

1. Encouragement: The encouragement may consist of only words, either written or spoken. Many different terms have been used besides "encourage:" If you "advise," "command," "convince," "counsel," "entice," "entreat," "incite," "induce," or "urge" another to commit a crime, you are guilty of solicitation.

2. Felony or Serious Misdemeanor: Solicitation can only be charged if the crime solicited is any felony or a serious misdemeanor that breaches the peace or obstructs justice.

3. Intent: The state of mind required for solicitation is specific intent even if the state of mind for the underlying crime is only malice or recklessness.

4. Completion: The crime of solicitation is complete as soon as the other person hears the solicitation, even if that person immediately rejects the criminal encouragement.

5. Protected Class: As with accomplice liability, a person who is in the class of persons to be protected by the law cannot be convicted of solicitation. The prime example is statutory rape solicited upon themselves by a minor.

6. Merger: If the other person agrees to commit the crime, a conspiracy is formed and the solicitation merges into conspiracy and/or into the crime, if the crime is in fact committed. Thus, the solicitor becomes an accomplice to the crime.

7. Renunciation: If the solicitor immediately renounces or disavows the solicitation (for reasons other than fear of criminal prosecution), there is a defense.

> **MBE Tip:** There is some overlap between solicitation, conspiracy, and attempt. Bare solicitation is not automatically attempt, but solicitation plus acts in furtherance create conspiracy. A solicitor may be charged with solicitation even if the solicitee immediately refuses. When the crime is completed, the solicitation charge merges into conspiracy.

B. Conspiracy

Common law conspiracy is an agreement and plan to commit a criminal unlawful act. Most jurisdictions now also require at least one of the conspirators take a substantial overt step in furtherance of the conspiracy. Mere knowledge of or observing the crime is usually insufficient. Examples include providing supplies to use in the crime, staking out the victim or location, making phone calls and arrangements, pre-arranged getaway car driver, etc.

1. Agreement: As long as the parties have a bilateral intent to agree and to commit a specific unlawful act, the conspiracy agreement does not have to be spoken. Feigned agreement, such as when the person agrees to a crime in order to escape the situation and report the conspiracy to law enforcement does not qualify as "conspiracy."

2. Two or More Persons: A conspiracy must consist of at least two people. If the underlying crime such as bribery requires two people, this requirement is met with conspiracy.

a. Common Law: Under the common law "bilateral requirement," if one of the "conspirators" is someone with no intent to commit the crime, there is no conspiracy. For example, if an undercover police officer is one of the "conspirators," the D cannot be charged with conspiracy. However, a person can be convicted of conspiracy even if none of the co-conspirators can be convicted due to incapacity (insanity, infancy, etc.).

b. Modern Rule: The modern rule in most states rejects the "plurality of agreement" rule and one person, with unilateral intent to conspire and intent to commit a crime, can be charged with conspiracy even if the other person had no similar intent to commit a crime.

> **MBE Tip:** Whenever there is a substantial overt step towards a crime that involves planning by more than one person, consider conspiracy as a correct answer.

3. Unlawful Act: Under the common law, the unlawful act did not have to be a crime, but could also be a tort or breach of contract. Under the modern rule, the unlawful act must be a crime.

4. Foreseeable:

a. *Pinkerton* Rule: A conspirator can be held liable for all foreseeable crimes committed in furtherance of the conspiracy, whether or not he specifically agreed to commit that particular crime or there is an escalation.

b. Example: If a bookie sends someone to "collect," he is liable for whatever crimes (burglary, assault, robbery) his messenger commits. Under the MPC/*Pinkerton*, the bookie need only specifically agree to the original crime (extortion, larceny, etc.).

c. Minority Rule: The *Pinkerton* rule has not been adopted in all states. Some states allow a conspirator to only be culpable for those crimes to which he specifically agreed.

> **MBE Tip:** If the MPC is mentioned, *Pinkerton* is in play. All co-conspirators may be charged with all crimes committed. Although it is unlikely that the exam will test the minority view, review the fact pattern for an indication of the jurisdiction. If the jurisdiction has not adopted the MPC or *Pinkerton*, then each co-conspirator can only be charged with the crimes to which he agreed, regardless of how foreseeable the other crimes were.

5. Withdrawal: If a conspirator successfully withdraws, he is not liable for future crimes committed by the other conspirators. The defendant bears the burden of proof.

a. Cease Acts: To successfully withdraw, D must cease to commit any and all acts in furtherance of the conspiracy.

b. Communicate Withdrawal: The D must also communicate his withdrawal to all co-conspirators in time for them to cease to commit acts in furtherance of the conspiracy. Note that merely communicating with an uninvolved third party is insufficient.

c. Take Action: Under the MPC, the withdrawing conspirator must take some affirmative good faith action to stop the conspiracy and prevent the commission of future crimes. Informing the authorities usually qualifies as valid withdrawal.

> **MBE Tip:** Conspiracy is frequently tested. Watch for decoys, like a person who assists without the agreement or knowledge of other conspirators. Such a person cannot be charged with conspiracy, although he may be otherwise chargeable (attempt, aiding & abetting, etc.)

C. Attempt

Common law attempt required that the actor specifically intend to commit the crime and take affirmative steps to bring himself into "close proximity" to completing the crime. Under contemporary law, only a substantial step is required, not "close proximity." Under the MPC, it is an affirmative defense if the person voluntarily abandons the attempt after a substantial step was taken, but before the crime is actually committed.

> **MBE Tip:** Once the actor has expressed intent to commit a specific crime and a substantial step has been taken, the crime of criminal attempt has occurred even if the actor subsequently changes her mind and the underlying crime is abandoned. Decide whether the actor has renounced and abandoned the attempt because of her conscience or because the crime has become too difficult. There is no defense for difficulty, such as factual impossibility.

1. Mens Rea: As with solicitation, specific intent is required for attempt, even if the *mens rea* for the underlying crime is lower (*e.g.* recklessness, negligence).

2. Substantial Step: Any act taken in furtherance of the underlying crime usually qualifies, but not mere preliminary planning prior to the point of no return.

3. Mistake: Factual impossibility does not negate attempt. It is still an attempt when D shoots V thinking V is merely asleep but, in fact, V is already dead. Another exam fact pattern is D tries to shoot V but the gun, unknown to D, was not loaded.

4. Merger: Attempt as a lesser included offense merges with the most serious crime if it is completed. However, attempt does not merge with conspiracy.

> **MBE Tip:** The merger distinction is frequently tested. Conspiracy does not merge with the completed crime, while solicitation and attempt do.

INCHOATE CRIME SAC ANALYSIS CHART

	Initial Act	**Substantial Step Required?**	**Merger?**	**Defenses?**
Solicitation	Encouragement to commit a crime	NO	Merges with conspiracy if solicitee agrees; Merges with completed crime	Renunciation
Attempt	Intent to commit a crime and an act in furtherance thereof	YES	Merges with completed crime	Abandonment
Conspiracy	Agreement to commit a crime (between two or more persons)	YES, in most jurisdictions	Does not merge with completed crime	Withdrawal

V. HOMICIDE CRIMES

> **MBE Tip:** Below we focus on the elements that compose the crimes. The types and degrees (1°, 2°, 3°) of culpability are particularly important. Note however, that the controlling criminal statutes will often be provided in the question. Where they are not, you will likely be examining the more general common law requirements and you can worry less about degrees.

A. Murder

Common law murder is the unlawful killing of another human being with malice aforethought. If a D intends to kill or cause serious bodily harm to someone, but his actions end up killing another person, the D's intent is transferred to the person actually killed.

1. Malice Aforethought: The mental state intent requirement for common law murder can be demonstrated by proving the D had (1) intent to kill, (2) intent to cause serious bodily harm, (3) extreme recklessness, or (4) intent to commit a felony. Any of these four mental states is sufficient. "Malice aforethought" is therefore a somewhat misleading term; it does not require malice, ill will, pre-planning, or intent to kill in all cases.

a. Intent to Kill: This requires proof of the D's conscious intentional desire to kill the victim or his knowledge to a substantial certainty that his actions will result in the victim's death. Thus, actual specific intent to kill is not required. This state of mind can be demonstrated through the D's actions or statements.

b. Intent to Cause Serious Bodily Harm: A D intends to cause serious bodily harm if he intends to inflict an injury which creates a substantial risk of death or causes a protracted impairment to the victim's health.

c. Extreme Recklessness: This is greater than the mental state of recklessness and is shown as total indifference to the clear possibility of someone being killed or seriously injured. This "depraved heart" does not require proving the specific intent to kill or cause serious bodily harm; mere reckless indifference to the value of human life is sufficient. Examples include firing a gun in a public place or driving drunk or at an extremely high speed.

d. Intent to Commit a Dangerous Felony:

(1) Rule: If a human being is killed, intentionally or not, during the commission of a dangerous felony, the intent to commit the felony itself satisfies the malice aforethought requirement. The D will be liable as an accomplice for murders committed by co-participants in the felony. In many states, the D can also be liable for the death of a co-participant killed by police, victims, or other co-participants during the felony.

(2) Example: If the D intends to commit the crime of arson and someone is killed during the arson (from the time of "attempt" to "escape"), the D can also be convicted of felony murder.

> **MBE Tip:** Homicides are frequently tested. Watch carefully for requisite intent to do the act (not to be confused with motive or ill will, which are not required), including intent to cause serious bodily harm, which is sufficient for a murder charge even if death was not actually subjectively intended. For felony murder to apply, the underlying felony must be dangerous and the killing must occur while the felony is in progress.

2. Causation: The prosecution must show that the D's actions were the actual and proximate cause of the victim's death. Actual cause is shown if the victim would not have died but for the D's actions or the D's actions were at least a substantial factor in the victim's death. Proximate cause is shown if the victim's death was the natural and probable result of the D's actions.

3. Human Being: The D must have killed a human being. Under common law, a human being exists between the birth of a live child and legal death.

a. Legal Death – Historically: Legal death was formerly defined as the time when a person stopped breathing and his heart stopped beating.

b. Legal Death – Current View: With current medical technology a person can be kept breathing and his heart beating on life support equipment, so now the test is "irreversible cessation of brain function."

> **MBE Tip:** Causing or hastening the death of a person with a terminal illness is still murder. The inevitable fate of the victim is irrelevant as long as the victim was legally alive at the time of the killing.

4. Statutes: Most states have enacted statutes which divide murder into degrees with varying levels of punishment. Exam questions testing the crime of murder may include the language of a controlling statute.

a. First Degree: First degree murder generally requires specific intent premeditation and deliberation or felony murder.

(1) Premeditation: Some kind of specific intent advance thought or planning to cause death is considered premeditation, even if it is not prolonged. Some states consider that premeditation can occur in an instant.

(2) Felony Murder: If a death occurs during the course of an inherently dangerous felony, the perpetrator may be charged with felony murder regardless of whether the death itself was intentional. Foreseeability of a resulting death is the test, not specific intent. Some states specifically list which particularly dangerous felonies qualify for first degree felony murder. Others hold that a killing during any felony committed in a dangerous manner qualifies as first-degree felony murder.

(3) BARRK Felonies: Most states include **B**urglary, **A**rson, **R**obbery, **R**ape, and **K**idnapping in the category of dangerous felonies. Notice assault or battery alone is not usually sufficient.

> **MBE Tip:** Because of the differing laws in the various states, first degree murder exam questions will most likely include the applicable statute or rule. If it does not, err on the side of the common-sense rule: if the felonies committed seem particularly heinous or there is any suggestion of advance thought prior to the homicide, first degree murder is probably in play.

b. Second Degree: Second degree murder is any common law homicide that does not qualify as first-degree murder, but that rises above manslaughter. Focus on the *mens rea* ("guilty mind") factor to determine where the homicide falls in the spectrum.

B. Manslaughter

Common law manslaughter is killing a human being without malice aforethought but with criminal negligence. The *mens rea* required for murder is absent.

1. Voluntary Manslaughter: This is intentional killing but the mitigating facts substantially reduce the defendant's culpability. The common law majority rule limited excusable provocation to a predetermined list of situations, such as being provoked by deadly force or finding one's spouse in bed with another. The situational commonality is that a prior intent to kill was not then present, such as reckless driving while intoxicated. The majority view today is that excusable provocation is a question of fact for the jury as to whether any provoking event was one that would cause an ordinary reasonable person to lose all self-control.

2. Involuntary Manslaughter: A person kills another human being through a voluntary but reckless act, but not with malice, extreme recklessness, or specific intent such as a speeding accident causing a death. Dropping a brick off a bridge that landed on a passerby's head is an example where the mere reckless behavior is a significant departure from the ordinary care standard or disregard of a situation creating a significant risk of harm. Such action is more than mere negligence or a departure from ordinary care.

3. Heat of Passion: Regardless of whether the provocation was excusable, the jury must also find that the D was actually acting in the heat of passion. The D must have committed the killing shortly after the provoking event while still in a rage. If there was a cooling off period, involuntary manslaughter is not available.

4. Misdemeanor Manslaughter: This is similar to felony murder but the related crime committed was classified as a misdemeanor instead of a felony. Misdemeanor manslaughter has been abolished by statute in most states and is not recognized by the MPC. In those states which still recognize it, the misdemeanor must be conduct that is inherently wrong (such as theft), not merely statutorily wrong (such as driving with an expired license).

C. Negligent Homicide

The MPC requires a gross deviation from a reasonable person standard of care be shown for negligent homicide where premeditation is absent. Most states have statutes proscribing negligent homicide in recognition of the dangerousness of automobiles. The negligence must be a substantial and significant deviation from ordinary care, thus more than ordinary negligence.

> **MBE Tip:** Historically, one quarter or more of the exam questions have tested homicide issues. You need to know this topic cold.

> **STOP!** Go to page 377 and work Learning Questions 21 to 30.

VI. OTHER CRIMES

A. Theft

The English common law recognized larceny, larceny by servant, and larceny by trick. The English Parliament created the crimes of embezzlement and obtaining property by false pretenses. The modern view is to combine all these overlapping offenses into one category known as "theft." Statutory theft generally has degrees of fault based upon the value of the stolen property.

1. Larceny: Common law larceny is the trespassory taking control and carrying away of tangible personal property in the possession of another without permission or consent, and with the intent to permanently deprive that person of his or her property.

    a. Intent to Permanently Deprive: Larceny is a specific intent crime and the D must have intended to permanently deprive the possessor at the time of the taking or at a later time while the D had unauthorized custody of the property. D must intend to keep the property, hold it long enough to deprive the possessor of most of its economic value, or dispose of the property in a manner that would make it unlikely that the possessor would get it back.

        (1) At Time of Taking or a Later Time: D must intend to permanently deprive the possessor at the time of the taking. If he decides to return the property at a later time, it does not negate the intent at the time of the taking.

> **MBE Tip:** Mere intent to borrow another's property negates the element of intent to permanently deprive, and thus is not larceny. However, if the D took the property without the intent to permanently deprive the possessor and later decides to keep the property, he has formed the required intent and it relates back to the time of the taking.

        (2) Mistake of Fact Defense: If in good faith the D mistakenly believes he is entitled to the property or takes the property in satisfaction of a pre-existing claim or debt, the D lacks the intent to permanently take "the property of another." An example is someone taking the wrong coat leaving a restaurant. The person mistakenly believes the coat is hers and there is no intent to deprive. An honest mistake, even if it is not a mistake that a reasonable person would have made, negates intent.

> **MBE Tip:** Larceny is one of those crimes where mistake is a defense because it negates an element of the crime. This is not the case with most other types of crimes. Therefore, it is frequently tested.

    b. Trespassory: This describes the lack of permission from the possessor to enter the property. If express or implied permission is lacking, then entering is automatically trespassory.

c. Taking: The D obtains complete dominion and control over the property. Theft of the property may also be control by another person at the D's direction.

d. Carrying Away: The slightest degree of control and movement of the property satisfies the carrying away requirement. Taking the property out of the store is not required. Even taking the property into one's own hands is sometimes enough, such as a shoplifter putting an item into their pocket.

e. Tangible Personal Property: The common law property excludes real estate, things attached to the real estate such as minerals, trees, etc., and intangibles such as financial rights from larceny. There are other torts and property concepts that cover the improper appropriation or invasion of these kinds of property.

f. In Possession of Another: The property must be owned by another exclusively and must be taken from one who has possession. If the D has joint ownership of the property, he cannot be convicted of larceny under the common law.

> **MBE Tip:** Larceny is a crime of possession; even the true owner can commit larceny against someone who has possession. An example is an owner taking items previously pawned from an inventory display shelf without paying the pawnbroker the agreed-upon redemption amount. This makes it possible to commit larceny by even an owner. It is not a defense that the possessor did not have legal ownership. Be on the lookout for a tricky fact scenario like this.

2. Embezzlement: Embezzlement is when the D wrongfully takes property from a person with whom the D has a fiduciary duty relationship.

a. Intent: There must be the intent to permanently deprive the owner of his or her interest in their property. This may include a fiduciary duty relationship allowing the D access to the converted property. The fiduciary often has control of the property before the embezzlement takes place, such as a bookkeeper who converts an employer's cash receipts.

b. Examples: Examples include an employee taking employer's assets without permission, an agent not remitting cash to the employer received from a third party, an attorney intentionally converting client property for their own use, a guardian misusing custodian funds, or a trustee embezzling trust funds.

c. Unauthorized Use: Use of a client's asset without approval may also be characterized as embezzlement. Examples are a trustee using assets entrusted to the fiduciary such as real property. Living rent free in a client's home and using their automobile without permission may qualify. One UBE question involved substantial long distance phone calls charged to a client by the fiduciary.

> **MBE Tip:** Note this key distinction between larceny and embezzlement. Embezzlement only applies where the taker is a fiduciary who is legally in control of the property when it is taken, such as a lawyer who steals from client's trust accounts. If the taker is a fiduciary but was not in control of the property (*e.g.*, a lawyer who goes into the store of one of his customers and steals from the cash register, rather than from the trust account) the crime is larceny. The chart below itemizes the larceny and embezzlement distinctions.

3. Embezzlement / Larceny Requirement Distinctions Chart:

Embezzlement	Larceny
Property legally in possession of D	Property legally in possession of another
Property "converted" – high standard beyond loan or contrary to trust agreement	Property "carried away" – lower standard, even slight movement or interference will do
Fiduciary relationship – D must be in a position of special responsibility and trust	No fiduciary relationship

4. False Pretenses: The D obtains title and possession to property of another by false pretenses when, with the intent to permanently deprive the owner thereof at the time, he fraudulently induces the victim to voluntarily deliver possession and title of tangible, personal property to the D. Filing a fraudulent insurance claim would qualify. The intent to permanently deprive the owner must be present at the time the D induces the victim to give him the property, not later. The D cannot believe that property belongs to them because that might negate the requisite intent to steal.

5. Larceny by Trick: Larceny by trick is similar to false pretenses, but only requires transfer of possession, not transfer of title. Transfer of title depends on whether the owner expected to regain possession of the property. If he does not expect to get the property back, he has transferred title as well as possession, and the crime is false pretenses.

> **MBE Tip:** Larceny is the most heavily tested of the pure theft crimes (larceny, larceny by trick, embezzlement, false pretenses). Memorize all the above elements of larceny, and when dealing with a larceny question make sure all elements are satisfied.

6. Forgery: This involves the intentional making, altering, or use of a false legal writing in order to commit a fraud, such as a check or promissory note.

7. "Bad Check" Fraud Statutes: Check fraud is specifically prohibited by statute in almost every jurisdiction. Although it is a subset of larceny and forgery, the D need not have actually deprived the victim of any property. If the account has insufficient funds (NSF), the D can still be held liable as long as she had knowledge the charge would create an overdraft which provides the intent to permanently deprive the victim of the funds.

B. Receiving Stolen Property

The crime of receiving stolen property is: (1) the acquisition or control of stolen tangible personal property, (2) knowing the property is stolen, (3) with the intent to permanently deprive the true owner of the property.

1. Acquisition or Control: This can be accomplished by any one of three methods:

a. Actual Possession: The D actually takes physical possession of the stolen property.

b. Deposit on D's Behalf: The thief deposits the stolen property in a place designated by the D.

c. D as Middleman: The D brings together the thief and a designated receiver of the stolen property.

2. Knowledge: The D must actually or constructively believe the property is stolen when he receives the items.

MBE Tip: If the D testifies that they believed the property was not stolen, the prosecutor can still demonstrate that a reasonable person should have known the property was stolen because the D paid an unreasonably low price, or the transaction occurred under suspicious circumstances. Look for this on the exam, as it is a less obvious form of "knowledge."

3. Intent to Permanently Deprive: Receiving stolen goods is a specific intent crime. The D must have the intent to permanently deprive the true owner of his/her property either at the time he received the property or later.

C. Robbery

Common law robbery is the crime of larceny plus (1) the property must be taken from the owner's person or presence and (2) this must be accomplished by force, intimidation, or imminent harm putting the property owner in fear.

1. Person or Presence: Property is on the victim's person when the victim is touching it, such as a wallet, jewelry, or clothing. Property is in the victim's presence when it is in an automobile, room, or residence with the victim.

2. By Force or Intimidation: There must be a causal relationship between the use of force and the taking of the property. Force can be any action, such as bumping into the victim to pick his pocket. Intimidation is any minimal threat of immediate force to harm the victim, his family, anyone in his company, or to destroy his house. The D doesn't have to have the actual ability to carry out the threat as long as he has the apparent ability. For example, a realistic toy gun weapon would suffice as armed robbery.

MBE Tip: Larceny is the foundation of robbery: make sure all larceny elements are met in addition to force or intimidation. If so, larceny merges into robbery. Also note that pick-pocketing without the victim's knowledge or any use of force is larceny, not robbery.

D. Burglary – BEDIN

Common law burglary is the **b**reaking and **e**ntering of the **d**welling house of another with the **i**ntent to commit larceny or a felony inside during the **n**ight.

1. Breaking: This is the physical or constructive opening of anything closed for the purpose of gaining entry. Today "breaking" only requires intent and lack of permission. Force or violence is not required. Nothing need be actually broken or destroyed. The D must only affirmatively open a door or window or enlarge an opening to enter. If the D uses fraud or threat of force to induce someone to let him in, it also constitutes breaking.

2. Entering: Any unlawful physical intrusion beyond that necessary for breaking into the house is entering. If the D has actual or implied consent of the occupants, it is not entry as required by the definition of burglary. The D does not need to fully enter the building; a hand or foot preventing closure of the door is sufficient.

3. Dwelling House of Another: Under the common law, only entry into a building, tent, or houseboat, etc., presently used as a dwelling for habitation or sleeping constitutes burglary. The presence of the inhabitants is not necessary, but the building cannot be abandoned. If the building is both a business and a dwelling, entry into either is burglary.

> **MBE Tip:** Most jurisdictions have eliminated the dwelling requirement for burglary. Breaking and entering any building or structure will usually do. Don't be fooled if one of the MBE options suggests that burglary has not occurred because the structure was not a dwelling, unless the facts specifically state that the common law applies.

4. Intent to Commit a Felony or Larceny: Burglary is a specific intent crime and intent is required at the time of the building entry. If the intent to commit a felony is formed later, the D cannot be charged with burglary. He can, of course, be charged with the felony. If the D enters with the intent to commit a felony but changes his mind and does not commit the felony, burglary can still be charged. Because larceny of low-value property can be a misdemeanor, larceny is specifically included due to the inherent danger present when someone breaks and enters into another's home or business. Persons taking back their own property may lack the intent to steal required for larceny.

5. Night: Under the common law, nighttime is when there is not enough sunlight to spot and recognize the burglar. Most jurisdictions have eliminated the non-daylight nighttime requirement. Burglary in most states may now occur at any time of day or night.

> **MBE Tip:** Burglary is frequently tested, as well as criminal trespass without intent to commit another crime. The time of day may not be stated. Note that burglary does not merge with the crime that the burglar intended to commit once inside.

6. Underlying Crime: The underlying crime does not need to actually be committed. If the D had the intent to commit the crime when he entered and subsequently abandoned the burglary, he can still be charged. Burglary does not merge with any other crimes. The D can be convicted of burglary and the crime the burglar intended to commit when he entered if he actually committed the underlying crime.

7. Statutory Burglary: The statutes in most states recognize degrees of burglary depending on such factors as whether a dwelling or building was entered, the D was armed, or a person was injured during the course of the burglary.

> **MBE Tip:** Intent to commit a felony or larceny at the time of entry is the most frequently tested element of burglary. Intent to commit the crime must exist at the time of entry for burglary to be charged. Conversely, failure to commit the crime does not negate a burglary charge if the intent existed at the time of entry.

E. Battery

Common law battery is the intentional or reckless unlawful application of force to the person of another, directly or indirectly, that results in physical harm or an offensive touching.

1. Intentional or Reckless: Under the minimal "general intent" actual specific intent is not required; only criminal recklessness is required for common law battery. Recklessness is the conscious disregard of a substantial and unjustifiable risk of injury to the victim. There is no "assumption of the risk" defense principle allowed in criminal battery.

2. Unlawful: The touching or force is unlawful unless the victim consents or the contact is privileged as in self defense, defense of others, or law enforcement contacts.

3. To Person of Another: Coming into contact with the property of another is not sufficient. The contact must be with the body of another; an animal does not qualify.

4. Directly or Indirectly: The D can either touch the body of the victim with his own body or strike the victim with an object in his hand or thrown at the victim.

5. Physical Harm or Offensive Touching: Physical harm can be any injury or even temporary pain. Offensive touching can be any contact even if no physical injury or pain results. Some states do not recognize offensive touching in their battery statutes.

F. Assault

Common law criminal assault is either attempted battery or intentionally causing another to become in reasonable apprehension of immediate significant bodily harm. See tort coverage in MBE 1 at 1-34.

1. Attempted Battery: Under the common law, some states recognize the mere attempted battery to be a form of criminal assault. To be charged with criminal attempted battery, the D must specifically intend to batter the victim, must take all steps necessary to batter the victim, even if the actual battery did not subsequently occur.

2. Apprehension: The D must intentionally cause the victim to feel a reasonable apprehension of an immediate battery. The D must specifically intend to cause the victim either bodily harm and/or apprehension of harm. The victim must feel apprehension but the apprehension does not need to be actual fear. The victim must be aware of the threat (an unconscious victim does not qualify) and the threat must be one that would cause a reasonable person to feel apprehension of immediate contact. Vague future threats do not qualify.

3. Merger: Attempted assault merges into battery if the battery is actually completed (on the second swing, so to speak).

> **MBE Tip:** Most states recognize both of the above forms of assault. Some states combine battery and assault in their criminal codes, with degrees depending on the seriousness of the injury or whether a weapon was used. Different weapons may be treated differently. This is another area where the exam question will sometimes include the statute at issue. Always read your facts carefully to make sure you are applying the appropriate rule.

G. Rape

Common law rape is a male's forced sexual intercourse with a female, other than the spouse of the D, without her consent. Modern statutes have expanded the definition of rape to include spouses, males, and other forced sexual acts not amounting to sexual intercourse.

1. Consent: The prosecutor must prove lack of valid consent. There is no valid consent if the victim is extremely intoxicated, unconscious, or mentally impaired, if her consent was obtained by immediate threat of harm to the victim or members of her family, or fraud. Under the common law, the victim had to show she resisted to demonstrate lack of consent. Now physical resistance is not always necessary because the D may coerce the victim by threats, not necessarily with the actual use of force.

2. Statutory Rape: Common law statutory rape is sexual intercourse with a person under a defined statutory age.

a. Consent and Intent Irrelevant: Statutory rape is a strict liability crime regardless of whether the victim actually consented. The crime itself is prohibited no matter what state of mind the D possessed, such as having sex with a victim that D believed was 19 who is really 13. A mistake about the victim's age is not a valid defense.

b. State Law Controls: Modern statutes have expanded statutory rape to include male victims and sexual acts not amounting to sexual intercourse. Many statutes have degrees which depend on the relative ages of the D and victim.

> **MBE Tip:** Rape is not frequently tested. If it is at issue, look for an intoxicated D (voluntary intoxication is not a defense unless D was unaware of having intercourse) or a statutory rape scenario (consent/intent are irrelevant; statutory rape is a strict liability crime).

H. False Imprisonment / Kidnapping

Common law false imprisonment is the intentional detention and unlawful confinement and restraint of a person against their will. Kidnapping is abduction and false imprisonment with movement of the person to another location. A charge of false imprisonment merges into kidnapping once the D moves the victim.

1. Intent: False imprisonment and kidnapping require specific intent on the part of the D to confine the victim or substantial certainty that his actions will result in confinement of the victim.

2. Confinement: The D must block the victim's movement in all directions. Physical force or restraint is not required; threat of immediate physical force or falsely pretending to have lawful authority also qualify. Physical resistance by the victim is not required. Any measurable period of confinement is sufficient. The victim does not have to attempt escape as long as no avenue of escape is known to the victim.

3. Movement: Moving the victim is kidnapping involving abduction.

> **MBE Tip:** The difference between kidnapping and false imprisonment is abduction versus mere restraint. Remember abduction requires either deadly force or a secret place.

4. Consent: Incapacity, deception, or coercion may invalidate the victim's consent.

5. Statutes: Many jurisdictions recognize degrees of kidnapping. Some states do not require abduction or movement while some require substantial movement or the passing of substantial time.

I. Arson

Common law arson is the malicious burning of the dwelling house of another.

1. Malice: The D must either intend to burn the house or manifest extreme indifference to the consequences of his behavior.

2. Burning: Any slight burning or charring is sufficient. The building does not need to be destroyed. Mere blackening by smoke or heat does not suffice under common law, but may under modern statutes.

3. Dwelling House: Common law arson involves the burning of a dwelling house. Most states have eliminated this requirement and arson can be the burning of any structure.

4. Of Another: Common law did not recognize burning one's own house or building, but modern statutes do, especially if the D was trying to reap insurance benefits.

> **MBE Tip:** Arson is similar to burglary in that the common law recognizes the crime only as it pertains to a dwelling, but modern statutes apply it in the context of any building. It is not likely that the common law of arson will be tested, so note the modern improvements.

J. Blackmail and Extortion

This crime occurs when D demands money or other property by threatening future harm.

1. Threat Required: The D may threaten to: cause physical injury, expose derogatory information to a third party, or cause financial harm in the future.

2. Defenses: A mere statement of intent to expose or report derogatory information is only unlawful if related to the D's receipt of property. Also, a reasonable mistake by D or an attempt to recover D's own property is allowed by the MPC.

> **STOP!** Go to page 379 and work Learning Questions 31 to 41.

VII. OVERVIEW: GENERAL PRINCIPLES OF CRIMINAL PROCEDURE

> **MBE Tip:** Criminal procedure questions may include evidence and constitutional law issues.

A. Federal Constitution

The Due Process Clause of the Fourteenth Amendment applies the Fourth, Fifth, and Sixth Amendments of the United States Constitution to the individual states.

1. Fourth Amendment:

a. Secure from Unreasonable Search and Seizure: The Fourth Amendment provides, "The right of the people to be secure in their persons, houses, papers, and effects, against unreasonable searches and seizures, shall not be violated, and no warrants shall issue, but upon probable cause, supported by oath or affirmation, and particularly describing the place to be searched and the persons or things to be seized."

b. State Intrusion on a Legitimate Expectation of Privacy – SIP: There must be (1) a **s**tate action and (2) **i**ntrusion on private citizens who (3) have a **p**rivacy expectation.

(1) State Action: The party making the intrusion must be a state actor. They need not be an official police officer, but can also be such state officials as probation officers, public school teachers, welfare case workers, or fish and game wardens. Private citizens under the direction and/or control of a police officer may be treated as state actors.

> **MBE Tip:** Private citizens are not state actors when they search or record conversations on their own even if they hope to give what they have found or recorded to the police.

(2) Standing Rule: The D may challenge a search and seizure only if (s)he was the person who was searched or seized; an illegal search of the D's sister's apartment discovering evidence incriminating D does not provide him standing to challenge.

> **MBE Tip:** The search of property of another person producing evidence incriminating D is frequently tested.

(3) Legitimate Expectation of Privacy: This is an objective test standard. Would a reasonable person have a legitimate expectation of privacy in this situation? Areas where there is a reasonable expectation of privacy include a person's own home, place of business, automobile (in a limited sense), and personal effects. A search warrant is usually required.

(4) Privacy Expectation Absent:

(a) Public Property: Commercial stores are public places that afford no legitimate expectation of privacy to anyone. Situations such as a drug-smelling dog on public property, a police officer on public property looking over into a private residence and seeing an addict injecting drugs, or a private residence used as a commercial "drug house" do not create a legitimate expectation of privacy that would normally be present in a private residence.

(b) Public Exposure: If the area is exposed to the public, there is no legitimate expectation of privacy. An example would be a private home with the window blinds open. Similarly, a person riding a public bus, a prisoner in a jail cell, a high school student in a public class, etc. may have little or no expectation of privacy.

> **MBE Tip:** Being in a public place does not always vitiate the personal right to privacy. Note that a person can assert a reasonable expectation of privacy and thus a Fourth Amendment claim in a public place such as a phone booth. Similarly, most overnight guests have a reasonable expectation of privacy in a hotel or motel room.

(c) Held Out to the Public: A person does not have a reasonable expectation of privacy for things held out to the public at large. Examples of this are voice or handwriting samples or public utility records.

(d) Open Fields Doctrine: As long as the fields are outside the curtilage of a home (the area of the buildings immediately adjacent to the main dwelling house), there is no reasonable expectation of privacy.

(e) Garbage Left for Collection: A search of curbside garbage or trash does not require a warrant because the creator of the garbage has no reasonable expectation of privacy once the garbage is put out for collection by another party.

(f) Internet Privacy Expectations: Internet hackers and advances in GPS and cell phone technology continue to challenge traditional notions of privacy under the Fourth Amendment. *U.S. v. Jones* 132 S. Ct. 945 (2012) held the attachment of a GPS tracking device to a person's vehicle to monitor the vehicle's movements was a search and seizure.

c. "Plain View" Doctrine: If the evidence in the residence is in plain view of a police officer, there is no Fourth Amendment violation. The police must have been entitled to be in the place where they were, such as a sidewalk viewing of drugs through a window. See further information *infra* under search warrant exceptions.

> **MBE Tip:** The topic of searches is heavily tested and the nuances should be thoroughly understood. First, examine where the search took place and under what circumstances: Was there an expectation of privacy? Do the circumstances suggest that there is a justification for violating that privacy (probable cause, articulable suspicion, etc.)?

2. Fifth Amendment Right: The text of the Fifth Amendment reads as follows: "No person shall be held to answer for a capital, or otherwise infamous crime, unless on a presentment or indictment of a grand jury, except in cases arising in the land or naval forces, or in the militia, when in actual service in time of war or public danger; nor shall any person be subject for the same offense to be twice put in jeopardy of life or limb, nor shall be compelled in any criminal case to be a witness against himself, nor be deprived of life, liberty, or property, without due process of law; nor shall private property be taken for public use, without just compensation." Production of document requests do not violate the Fifth Amendment.

3. Sixth Amendment Right: The text of the Sixth Amendment reads as follows: "In all criminal prosecutions, the accused shall enjoy the right to a speedy and public trial, by an impartial jury of the state and district wherein the crime shall have been committed, which district shall have been previously ascertained by law, and to be informed of the nature and cause of the accusation; to be confronted with the witnesses against him; to have compulsory process for obtaining witnesses in his favor, and to have the assistance of counsel for his defense." The Supreme Court has held some emergency 911 calls may be introduced without violating a D's right to confront and cross–examine a 911 accuser who is not available at trial.

> **MBE Tip:** On the exam, the call of the question often refers to constitutional issues which could be raised in motions or on appeal. Take care to initially distinguish criminal procedure from constitutional law questions and remember to analyze your criminal procedure questions in a constitutional (rights) context. This may also cross-over to evidence.

VIII. SEARCH AND SEIZURE

The Fourth Amendment requires that prior to all searches and seizures, the state actor must have probable cause and a judicial approved warrant or a recognized exception such as the owner-occupant consent. Any trustworthy information may be considered in determining whether probable cause exists, even if the information would not ultimately be admissible at trial. The necessary threshold showing standard of proof is "probable cause." This is less than the preponderance of the evidence in a civil matter, but more than an articulable suspicion.

A. Arrest

Arrest is taking legal custody of a person, depriving him of liberty and requiring him to answer a criminal charge. Police station questioning and line-ups qualify. Arrest must always be reasonable. Arrest without an arrest warrant is considered reasonable if there is probable cause. Excessive force during arrest is not allowed. Deadly force used against a fleeing suspect not posing a risk of death or serious physical injury is unreasonable. Arrest is a heightened form of detention for which the police can move the suspect to jail.

B. Probable Cause to Arrest

In order to have sufficient probable cause to arrest a suspect, it must be likely that:

1. Violation: Sufficient quality and quantity of required evidence that a violation of the law has occurred, and

2. Suspect Committed: The suspect arrested committed some criminal violation. This is also true when there is a seizure of a person to the extent that it is similar to an arrest (detention of the suspect where the suspect does not feel free to leave).

> **MBE Tip:** The fact the officer was wrong does not *per se* mean the search was improper.

C. Warrant

Even if probable cause exists to arrest a person, a warrant or D's express consent is required before a search or seizure can be made unless exceptional circumstances apply.

1. Warrant Required: Prior to the issuance of a warrant, a neutral and detached judge or magistrate must be satisfied that probable cause exists based on the surrounding facts and circumstances. A warrant is required to arrest the suspect if the crime is a misdemeanor unless the crime is committed in the presence of a police officer. In the case of a non-emergency where the suspect is in a home, law enforcement officers must obtain a warrant.

2. Warrant Not Required: An officer must have the occupant's consent or probable cause for a warrantless search or arrest. The burden is on the government to justify a warrantless search or seizure (arrest).

a. Felony Suspect in Public Place: A warrant is usually not required if a felony has been committed and the suspect is in a public place.

b. Misdemeanor in Officer's Presence: A misdemeanor which is committed in a police officer's presence does not require a warrant. For example, if an officer witnesses a minor shoplifting a case of beer from the local mini-mart, the officer does not have to wait for the issuance of a warrant.

c. Exigent Circumstances: This would include circumstances where there is reason to believe the suspect of a serious crime will flee, the police are in hot pursuit, evidence may disappear or someone will be injured if the officer left the scene to get a warrant, or the public safety is jeopardized.

D. Effect of Unlawful Arrest

1. Prosecution Still Valid: The prosecution may move ahead with its case if there is supporting evidence. An unlawful arrest does not necessarily destroy the prosecution's case.

> **MBE Tip:** A frequent wrong MBE criminal procedure answer is "The D cannot be prosecuted due to an illegal arrest." Tainted evidence may be suppressed under the exclusionary rule, but the prosecution may still proceed if there is enough other evidence.

2. Fruits of the Poisonous Tree Excluded: An unlawful arrest may lead to suppression of evidence acquired during the course of the arrest. Evidence most likely suppressed in this instance would be a post-arrest confession or physical evidence of the crime seized during the search incident to arrest.

E. Detentions

Detention is a temporary (brief and reasonable) restraint of a person's liberty (person does not feel free to leave).

1. Investigative *Terry* Stop: In order for there to be an investigative stop by a police officer without the presence of probable cause, there must be "reasonable and articulable suspicion" based on specific and articulable facts known to the officer at the time of the stop, when looking at the totality of the circumstances, including the officer's training.

2. Automobile Stops and Roadblocks: Sobriety roadblocks (where the police stop every car, every other car, or every tenth car, etc.) are allowed under the Fourth Amendment and in the majority of jurisdictions. The police cannot stop a car at random unless they have articulable suspicion. Both the driver and passengers may be ordered to vacate the car during a lawful traffic stop. The U.S. Supreme Court in *Edmond* held that drug roadblocks using drug-sniffing dogs were unconstitutional.

3. Police Station Detention: In order to bring a suspect to the police station for a line-up, fingerprinting, or questioning, an officer must have full probable cause for arrest.

4. Detention During House Search: When police are searching a house for contraband pursuant to a search warrant, they may detain the occupants during the search.

F. Probable Cause to Search

If a search was not valid, the evidence seized is not admissible. In order to have sufficient probable cause to search premises, it must be likely that two circumstances apply:

1. Connected: The items searched for must likely be directly connected to criminal activity. A general search for non-criminal items is not allowed, even if there is a possibility of finding criminally connected items.

2. In the Location: The discovered illegal items must be likely to be found in the place to be searched. The Fourth Amendment does not prohibit searches of property under the control of persons not suspected of a crime at the time of the search.

G. Warrant Search

Most searches must be conducted pursuant to a valid warrant or the voluntary consent of the property owners. Probable cause is the first step toward establishing a valid warrant search.

1. Prerequisites:

a. **Probable Cause:** Warrants must be supported and based upon a showing of particularized probable cause and describe the items sought in the search. This may be shown by an officer's or other's affidavits, and hearsay may be used (*i.e.*, confidential informants who informed an officer).

b. **Neutral Magistrate:** The magistrate determining probable cause at the hearing and issuing the warrant must be neutral, detached, and otherwise unbiased in weighing the quantity and qualitive grounds presented. If the neutrality of the magistrate is challenged, there must be case-specific reasons offered for the alleged bias or independence impairment.

c. **Factors Considered with Informant Tips:** Among the factors to be considered by the judge in issuing a warrant are the following:

(1) **Reliable Information:** The information must be inherently reliable (not obviously false or contrary to logic). This is a vague standard and easy to meet.

(2) **Reliable Informant:** The informant must have been in a position to have a factual basis for the information (*i.e.*, personal knowledge). There must be a factual basis for the credibility of the informant to the extent that he is a reliable witness. However, reliability can also be established if the police have corroborating information independent of the informant's tip suggesting accuracy. The identity of the informant is not always necessary if the information at issue seems quite reliable. The affidavit can be attacked if it contained a false statement that was material to the finding of probable cause.

d. **Knock and Announce Requirement:** The police must "knock and announce that they are the police and state their purpose" when executing the warrant. Force may be used if there is a failure to respond after a reasonable time. An exception to the knock and announce requirement is if an emergency situation requires immediate entry of the premises. Emergencies are generally limited to exigent circumstances involving life, safety, and preservation of property (evidence). A judge may issue a "no-knock warrant" in advance.

e. **Must be Executed Without Delay:** The warrant information or execution must not be stale. If delayed, there may be an absence of current probable cause, which is required on the search date. It also must be reasonably likely the same evidence is still there.

2. Scope of Warrant:
The scope of the authorized search is usually specifically particularized, not overbroad, and contains a description of the items.

> **MBE Tip:** Search warrants are heavily tested. Look for a warrant without a description of the type of items sought. Also asked is a specified home and the police also search other adjacent buildings such as a garage or tool shed. This may be permitted if outbuildings are specified in the warrant; searching another house or a mobile home next door is not.

3. Fruits of Search May Be Seized:
Police may generally seize any contraband that they discover while they are properly executing a warrant. This is true even if the items are not specified in the warrant.

STOP! Go to page 380 and work Learning Questions 42 to 50.

H. Exceptions to a Warrant

1. Search Incident to Arrest: A search may be made prior to the arrest only if the police had probable cause to arrest the person prior to the search. Police are allowed to conduct a warrantless "search incident to" (after) a lawful arrest within reasonable time. If an arrest is unlawful, then any search incident thereto and inventory at the police station is also unlawful.

a. Search Area: Here there is no express warrant limitation and the arrested person and close area may be searched, such as an unlocked glove box or briefcase, but not the entire house. Some cases suggest it is presumed that the entire interior passenger area of a car is considered "within the wingspan" of an arrested driver but engine or trunk areas are normally still excluded as not in plain view.

b. Protective Sweep: A "protective sweep" may be made of the house for dangerous persons. However, the scope of a protective sweep extends only to those places in which a person could reasonably be hiding. The police may effect a pat-down for weapons of anyone present to ensure officer safety. The police may detain other persons present in the house ("investigative detention") for the purpose of ensuring officer safety.

c. Search of Persons While on Premises: If individuals are named in the search warrant, police may search such individuals. The police may also search individuals present on the premises if there is probable cause to arrest them or if the police have a reasonable fear for their own safety sufficient to justify a pat-down search for weapons. Otherwise, the police may not search persons found on the premises who are not named in the warrant.

2. Automobiles:

a. Stop: Possible routine traffic violations justify stopping a vehicle.

b. Search: The police must have probable cause to believe that the vehicle contains contraband or evidence relating to a crime. If an automobile will be unavailable by the time a warrant is obtained, the "exigent circumstances" exception may be applicable. This exception allows an automobile to be searched if the automobile is reasonably believed to have been used in a crime. In 2014 the U.S. Supreme Court in *Riley* held searching a cellphone for suspicious communications at a traffic stop required a prior warrant.

c. Locked Places: There are only a few circumstances under which officers can search an area intended by the owner to be secure from search. Examples are a locked container such as a locked glove box or locked trunk of an automobile. Exceptions include:

(1) Probable Cause: The officers must have clear probable cause to search the trunk or other locked space (mere suspicion is insufficient).

(2) Impound Upon Arrest: This applies when a vehicle has been impounded simultaneous to or subsequent to a valid arrest of the driver and/or owner.

> **MBE Tip:** Automobile and home searches are frequent MBE and MEE questions. All the various exceptions should be noted: articulable suspicion; exigent circumstances; "wingspan" (within suspect's control); plain view; search incident to arrest; search upon impound; and probable cause. In other words, if you see an automobile or home search, have a prepared "laundry list" of exceptions to check before determining that the search is illegal.

3. Stop and Frisk: Police may briefly stop a person without probable cause for arrest if they had an "articulable and reasonable suspicion" of criminal activity. This is also known as a "*Terry* stop and frisk." A brief protective frisk is valid if the police have articulable suspicion that the person may be armed and involved in criminal activity. This protective wand or hand search is limited to a "pat-down" of the suspect's outer clothing for the bulk of concealed weapons, not personal effects. Admissibility of any evidence discovered turns on whether or not the officer "reasonably believed" the item discovered and seized was a possible weapon. *Miranda* warnings are not required.

> **MBE Tip:** A hammer, ax, or similar object may qualify as a weapon for "pat down" purposes.

4. Plain View: Police may make a warrantless seizure only when they are justified in being present on the premises, inadvertently discover illegal contraband or items used in a crime, have knowledge (prior to the search) that the object in plain view is seizable or is contraband, and when the police can show some "exigent circumstance" that requires an immediate seizure. Smelling by drug-sniffing dogs is considered in "plain view."

> **MBE Tip:** Note that this exception only applies if the police initially had probable cause to enter the premises. The exam frequently poses facts where unusual and suspicious circumstances are present, such as a neighbor saw a trespasser in the home or police discovered evidence of forcible entry. The contraband at issue must not be hidden, such as in a box.

5. Inventory:

a. Property at Jail: This search must be incident or related to (after) a lawful arrest and subject to a search policy that is consistently enforced. An inventory list is prepared.

b. Impound of Automobile: An automobile may be inventoried when it is impounded. A locked glove box, trunk or locked containers can then be searched. Generally, the police must allow a third party to move a car. An automobile may be impounded when one of the following is applicable:

(1) Incapacitation: The driver is incapacitated, unconscious, intoxicated, or otherwise unable to move the vehicle. Impound removes the vehicle from the driver's control.

(2) Arrest: The driver is arrested and taken into custody by police, and there is no other unimpaired driver available who could safely operate the vehicle.

(3) Public Danger: The automobile presents a public danger, for example being stalled in the roadway, vehicle accident, or leaking dangerous chemicals.

(4) Criminal Instrumentality: If a vehicle is used in the commission of a crime such as transporting illegal drugs, prostitution location, or used as a "get away" car to facilitate the commission of a crime it may be impounded.

6. Consent: Police can search without a warrant if a search of the person or premises has been consented to by the person or the property owner, or other person with control of or other rights to the premises, such as tenants. The consent must be express and voluntarily and intelligently made. Consent to search may be expressly revoked at any time.

> **MBE Tip:** Consent to search may usually be given by one who actually controls the premises even if not the property owner. This may include family members, housemates (as to common areas), or live-in partners, but usually not short-term guests in hotels.

7. **Exigent Circumstances:** This warrant exception applies if:

    a. In Hot Pursuit Emergencies: Police in an emergency or in hot pursuit of a fleeing felon may conduct an automobile search without a warrant and seize items, and may also pursue the suspect into private dwellings.

    b. Evanescent (Disappearing) Evidence: Police may seize evidence without a warrant if it is likely to disappear before a warrant can be obtained. An example of "disappearing evidence" is a blood sample which may contain traces of drugs or alcohol.

    c. Automobiles: Because automobiles are easily moved, they may sometimes fall under this exigent circumstances exception. Note that there must usually be justification for the impound besides possible vehicle moveability.

    8. Wiretapping / Eavesdropping / Phones: Wiretapping, eavesdropping (including an electronic device on a phone that records the numbers dialed) and other forms of electronic surveillance violate the expectation of privacy and constitute a search under the Fourth Amendment. In 2014 this restriction was extended to searching smartphones and cellphones which the Supreme Court described as containing "the privacies of life." A pre-search warrant supported by probable cause is thus required. The following are exceptions:

    a. Non-Private Public Speech: When the speaker makes no attempt to keep the conversation or his voice private, a warrant is not required. An example is speaking loudly in a restaurant overheard by a police officer.

    b. Consent by One Party: Consent to record by one party to the conversation is adequate to avoid the warrant requirement if there is a fire, medical emergency, crime, disaster, extortion, or hostage situation.

    c. Announcement by One Party: If one party to the conversation announces to the others that the conversation is about to be recorded, the recording becomes admissible. This can be a recorded announcement made at the beginning of the call.

    9. Privacy Interest Required: There must be standing to contest a search involving a violation of the D's reasonable expectation of their own privacy in the invaded place, not the privacy rights of another. Examples of no reasonable expectation of privacy include leaving contraband by a window facing a street or a car owner that lends her automobile to another and is now trying to contest a search of the automobile while in that other person's possession.

    10. Impeachment Purposes: Even though evidence is obtained in violation of the Fourth Amendment, it may be admissible to impeach the D at trial.

STOP! Go to page 381 and work Learning Questions 51 to 57.

IX. CONFESSION AND INTERROGATION

    Coercion by improper police conduct violates the Fifth Amendment's privilege against self-incrimination. Coerced confessions are inherently unreliable and thus inadmissible.

    In order for a confession to be valid, and therefore admissible, there are two requirements. A confession may be introduced against the person who made it only if the confession was (1) voluntary (not coerced by the police) and (2) the suspect was given the *Miranda* warnings prior to interrogation and their subsequent confession.

A. Voluntary

A statement of confession will only be admissible against a D if it was given voluntarily. Even if *Miranda* warnings were administered, an involuntary confession will not be allowed into evidence.

1. Test: The test for determining the "voluntariness" of a confession is the absence of police coercion. An officer cannot threaten a D but may warn or explain the legal consequences of a criminal conviction. If the police improperly coerce a confession, it is involuntary and must be excluded from the prosecution's case in chief; in addition, it cannot be used to impeach the D's testimony.

2. Exception: Note, the key factor here is the possibility of police coercion. Thus, confessions made to a cellmate (suspect brags about the crime), or made by a suspect due to serious mental illness (he heard "voices" telling him to confess) or coercion by the average citizen (a neighborhood acquaintance threatened harm to the suspect if he did not confess), are not considered "police coercion" and may, therefore, be admissible.

> **MBE Tip:** Voluntariness analysis is separate from *Miranda* analysis. Don't be fooled by facts that suggest *Miranda* is satisfied but imply police coercion. If the police fail either the *Miranda* analysis or the voluntariness analysis, the confession/statement will be suppressed.

B. *Miranda* Rights

When a suspect in police custody is questioned, any confession he makes will not be admissible against him unless he has previously received the *Miranda* warnings. The rationale is that questioning of the suspect while in custody is likely to induce confessions made in violation of the Fifth Amendment. The police must give *Miranda* warnings even if the suspect is already aware of his rights or represented by an attorney in another matter.

1. Fifth Amendment Protection: *Miranda* is based in the Fifth Amendment's privilege against self-incrimination (not the Sixth Amendment right to counsel). Excluded is non-assertive conduct such as blood draw, handwriting, fingerprints, DNA samples, etc.

2. Applies to State and Federal Courts: The *Miranda* rules govern the admissibility of confessions in both state and federal courts.

3. In Custody Required: *Miranda* warnings are necessary only when the suspect is taken into police custody for "custodial interrogation" and is not free to leave. If the police stop a drunk driver or question someone at the scene of an ongoing emergency, their statements are not custodial interrogation, so *Miranda* warnings are not then triggered. This is a public safety exception. An objective test is used to determine whether or not the suspect is in custody. A person is "in custody" if a reasonable person in that situation would not have felt free to leave or would have felt compelled to stay until dismissed.

4. Interrogation: Interrogation by the police covers both direct and indirect questions aimed at the suspect. Formal interrogation occurs if the police submit questions to a suspect that are likely to elicit an incriminating response from the suspect.

a. Questioning: It is only where the confession is the result of police questioning that *Miranda* is triggered. If the suspect blurts out a statement of culpability voluntarily without police questioning, it is admissible.

b. Police: *Miranda* rights are triggered only when both the custody and the questioning are conducted by law enforcement authorities. *Miranda* does not apply if Joe Citizen elicits a confession from the suspect after detainment and questioning. The suspect must be aware that the questioners are police.

c. Cellmate Confession: Incriminating statements voluntarily made by a suspect to a non-police cellmate are admissible. If the "cellmate" affirmatively elicits the incriminating statements, however, the environment takes on the character of a custodial interrogation and the admission must be excluded at trial.

5. Four Protected Warnings – RARI: A suspect may exercise his rights at any time. If, during questioning, the suspect at any time exercises his rights to silence or to an attorney, the questioning must cease – even if the suspect originally did not invoke those rights. The four required **RARI** components (*i.e.*, *Miranda* warnings) are:

   a. You have the **Right to remain silent**.

   b. **Anything you say can be used against you** in a court of law.

   c. You have the **Right to the presence of an attorney**.

   d. **If you cannot afford an attorney, one will be appointed** for you prior to questioning if you so choose.

6. Waiver of *Miranda*: The traditional view is that a suspect's waiver of his right to silence and to an attorney during questioning is valid only if it is knowingly, intelligently, and voluntarily affirmatively waived. The suspect's silence is not sufficient. In 2002 the U.S. Supreme Court held the police are not always required to obtain an express waiver from a suspect in custody. The suspect now apparently has a duty to acknowledge the waiving request and affirmatively and unequivocally state he is not waiving his rights. Mere silence by D is insufficient as is "maybe I should talk to a lawyer" and thereafter admits the crime.

7. Grand Jury Testimony Not Protected: A suspect or witness subpoenaed to testify before a grand jury or preliminary hearing is not usually entitled to have an attorney present or receive *Miranda* warnings. They may, however, assert the Fifth Amendment privilege against self-incrimination unless the prosecutor has granted them immunity. A grand jury may indict based upon evidence that would not be admissible at trial, including hearsay.

MBE Tip: *Miranda* rights are heavily tested on the MBE and may cross-over to evidence. The wording used by the suspect to waive invocation of the right to counsel is often fuzzy on the exam. Such a "waiver" is to be carefully scrutinized and if ambiguous is usually ineffective.

C. Effect of Assertion of *Miranda* Rights

This right only applies once the suspect is in physical custodial interrogation. If the suspect clearly and unambiguously invokes his right to silence or right to counsel, the interrogation must cease, even if the suspect previously waived those rights.

1. Right to Silence Invoked: If the suspect invokes his right to silence, the police may resume questioning after waiting several hours and giving new *Miranda* warnings.

2. Right to Counsel Invoked: If the suspect clearly and unequivocally invokes his right to counsel, the police may not resume the interrogation until counsel has been made available to the suspect, or the suspect himself initiates communication with the police.

3. Subsequent Waiver or Assertion of Rights: A suspect who originally asserted his rights is protected for 14 days after release from interrogative custody. *Shatzer.* A suspect who originally waived his rights may later assert their *Miranda* rights. The subsequent assertion must be unambiguous and unequivocal.

4. Confession – *Miranda* Rights – Confession: If the police interrogate a D and secure a confession without *Miranda* warnings, a subsequent *Miranda* warning and second confession do not excuse the prior Fifth Amendment violation. Both confessions are likely tainted and should be suppressed.

> **MBE Tip:** Remember the custodial interrogation requirement applies only to police suspects. A person who happens to be at a crime or an accident scene is usually a mere witness and not entitled to *Miranda* warnings.

D. Impeachment Use

A *Miranda* violating confession may not be introduced in the prosecution's case in chief. In comparison, it may usually be used for rebuttal to impeach D's testimony. Usually this occurs when D voluntarily takes the stand in defense and unequivocally denies doing the same offense they confessed to earlier.

> **MBE Tip:** *Miranda* is heavily tested. Do not confuse the standard for waiver of the right to counsel during questioning (the invocation of rights must be clear and unambiguous, otherwise waiver of the right is presumed) and the standard for waiver of the right to counsel during formal trial proceedings (the waiver must be knowing and intelligent and is never presumed).

E. Confession Admissibility Flow Chart

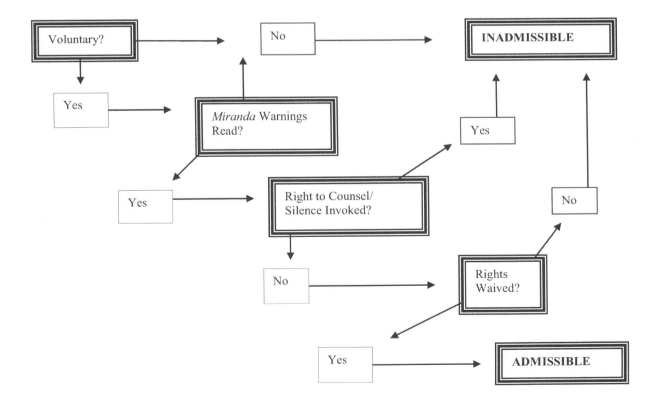

X.   PRE-TRIAL PROCEEDINGS

A.   Sixth Amendment Right to Counsel

Beyond the initial appearance before a court, a criminal suspect has a right to have counsel present at all pre-trial confrontation procedures. Such confrontations include line-ups (witness picks the suspect out of a group of "suspects") and show-ups (witness is shown the suspect and asked whether the suspect is the perpetrator). The right does not apply where a witness views still or moving pictures of the suspect for identification.

B.   Waiver of Right to Counsel

Waiver of one's Sixth Amendment right to counsel during questioning must be affirmatively made, knowingly, and intelligently. In effect, the suspect must be told of this right, understand it, and affirmatively waive it. Silence by a suspect does not usually constitute waiver.

C.   Due Process and Identification Procedures

The danger of some lineup identification procedures is the possibility that a witness will identify the suspect at trial based on what happened at the police station session later and not from remembering the details of the actual crime scene.

1. Totality of the Circumstances: The validity of an identification procedure at the police station is reviewed by a judge based on the multi-factor totality of the circumstances.

2. Lineup Unnecessarily Suggestive: If the lineup identification procedure was so "unnecessarily suggestive" and so "conducive to mistaken identification" as to be deeply unfair to the D, the D may challenge the resulting identification on due process grounds. For example, if the suspect was known to be over 6 feet tall, and the D was placed in a lineup with other men all under 5 feet 8 inches tall, the identification procedure would be suspect.

3. Reliable and Not Conducive to Error: An identification procedure does not violate due process if it is reliable or "not conducive to likely error" even if it is somewhat suggestive. For example, if the witness had a long time to view the incident and suspect under adequate light and close up, then suggestive identification procedures are more likely to be held as fair to the D. Also, an independent source may make an identification at trial even if the identification of the lineup witness is suppressed.

4. Photo Identifications: Where a witness identifies the suspect through the use of photographs, the "totality of the circumstances" test is used to determine whether the D's due process rights have been violated. A due process violation will be found only if the photo identification session is quite likely to have produced a misidentification.

MBE Tip: A motion to suppress may be brought if the identification was unnecessarily suggestive. This is a question of fact. For example, police statements to the witness such as, "We have the man," may qualify if the witness sees the police with only one suspect.

D.   Exculpatory Evidence

The prosecution must disclose to D's counsel all evidence which may be favorable to the D. See *infra* at 354.

E. Indictment or Information

The initial pleading by the state is an "indictment" from a grand jury or an "information" filed by the prosecuting attorney. The indictment or information is a concise and definite statement identifying the D and giving the essential facts constituting the offense charged and signed by the prosecuting attorney. For each offense charged, the prosecution must cite the statute, rule, regulation, or other provision of law that the D is alleged to have violated.

F. Preliminary Hearings

The D has a right to counsel at a preliminary hearing within 30 days of arrest.

1. Probable Cause: If a person is indicted or arrested without being supported by an arrest warrant, a magistrate must evaluate the officer's probable cause at a *Gerstein* hearing. This must occur within 48 hours of detention or the suspect must be released.

2. Bail Hearing: Bail is intended to ensure the D shows up for trial. Bail is generally available in connection with all crimes, except in the case of a capital offense where the death penalty is applicable. Otherwise, bail can be denied to secure a D's presence at trial where flight is feared or to prevent the commission of a serious crime. Examples include a D intimidation or threatening harm to the other party or to a witness. Under these circumstances bail may be denied because it is necessary to prevent an interference with the case proceeding. Bail must not be excessive.

3. Determination of Competence: A hearing may be held by the trial court to determine the D's competence. This is required by the 14th Amendment. The D's ability to understand the nature of the charge and assist counsel during the trial process are the leading factors to be considered. Mental illness or low cognitive ability may qualify.

G. Guilty Pleas

1. Plea Bargain: A plea bargain is viewed as a contract between the prosecutor and the D so a grand jury indictment is not required. The D has the right to counsel in plea negotiations. The plea bargain is presented to the judge, who may or may not accept it.

2. Waiver of Sixth Amendment Right to Trial: A guilty plea waives a D's right to a jury trial as provided under the Sixth Amendment.

3. *Alford* Plea: The D does not admit that they committed the crime, but admits it is more likely than not that they would be convicted.

4. Voluntary and Intelligent: The judge must determine that the plea is voluntary and intelligent by questioning the D. The judge must personally inform the D of the elements of the crime he is charged with, of the D's right not to plead guilty, and of the potential sentence in consequence of pleading guilty or not guilty.

5. Withdrawal of Guilty Plea: The D's guilty plea is subject to collateral attack if the court lacked jurisdiction to take the plea, if there was ineffective assistance of counsel to the extent that the D did not make an intelligent decision, if the plea was not made knowingly or voluntarily, or if the prosecution failed to keep the bargain.

STOP! Go to page 382 and work Learning Questions 58 to 66.

XI. TRIAL

A. Right to a Speedy Trial

The right to a speedy trial is guaranteed by the Sixth Amendment but may be waived by the D. There is no fixed length of time in the federal courts to determine whether or not there has been a speedy trial. It is based on a number of factors discussed below.

1. Factors: There are four **LEAP** factors to be balanced in trial scheduling:

    a. Length of Delay: The length of delay between charging or arrest and trial.

    b. Explanation: The party's explanation of the reason or reasons for the delay are key. If the delay is due to the fault or request of the D, it is unlikely that the speedy trial rule has been violated without other intervening circumstances.

    c. Assertion Time: Whether and when the D asserted the right to a speedy trial is considered. The longer the D waits, the more likely it is that the D was not truly concerned about the speediness of the trial.

    d. Prejudice: Whether the D was prejudiced by the delay is also important.

2. Result of Violation: If the court finds that the D's right to a speedy trial was violated, the charges must be dismissed or the conviction reversed.

B. Right to a Public Trial

The Sixth Amendment provides that the criminally accused have the right to a public trial and a jury finding beyond a reasonable doubt. Thus, any suspect in a criminal prosecution may agree to have a closed trial but may not be forced to have a closed trial. However, a judge does not violate the constitutional rights of an accused if he/she refuses a request for closed trial.

C. Right to a Trial by Jury

All serious criminal cases (*i.e.*, those that involve more than six months in jail) are to be heard by a fair and impartial jury required under the Sixth Amendment. There is no constitutional right to a jury of more than six persons or requirement that the verdict be unanimous. However, there are rules to be followed that have been promulgated by the courts.

1. Jury Size: If the jury is only six persons, the criminal verdict must be unanimous. If a jury is 12 persons, a 9 to 3 vote in favor of conviction is sufficient.

2. Jury Composition / Selection: Jury pools must represent an accurate cross-section of the community, although the actual seated jury doesn't have to. Jurors may be stricken for cause (unlimited) or by peremptorily (limited number). There can be no peremptory challenges based on race or gender. *Batson.*

3. Juror Challenges: Limited preemptory challenges may be made without reason, unless made only for race or gender. The concept is jurors that are potentially biased or prejudiced may deny the D a fair trial based solely on the evidence presented at trial. There is a limited number of other challenges for cause. The D is entitled to be present.

4. Jury Decisions: All essential elements of the offense must be determined by the jury, not the court by directing the verdict. Jury instructions cannot create an irrebuttable conclusive presumption which unconstitutionally shifts the burden of proof to the D.

D. Right to a Separate Trial

A D may be represented by counsel who is also representing another D in the same case. However, if the D's interests may be jeopardized by a joint trial or by joint counsel (particularly in the use of confessions), he/she may move to sever the proceeding into a separate trial and obtain separate counsel.

E. Right to be Present at Trial

The Sixth Amendment provides the basis for the D's right to be present during his trial. The D may forfeit this right by disruptive or threatening behavior.

F. Rights Provided by the Confrontation Clause

The *Crawford* holding provides a criminal D the right to cross-examine witnesses. The testimonial Confrontation Clause allowing full and effective cross-examination is not absolute. For example, a D may voluntarily leave the courtroom. Or, if the D is an alleged child molester, the D may be in another room so that the child would not see him.

G. Right to Counsel

The right to "effective representation" applies at every "critical stage" including police interrogations, probable cause hearing, arraignments, and guilty pleas.

1. Appointment of Counsel: Every D has a right to counsel in any prosecution that could result in imprisonment. If the D is indigent the court will appoint counsel. A D may expressly waive the right to counsel and demand to defend himself (*pro se*) if the waiver was informed and dangers explained by the court. There is no right to be co-counsel with an appointed attorney. Nor does the right to counsel entitle a D to exceptional counsel.

2. Ineffective Counsel: The deprivation of the right to effective counsel applies only if the assistance was not effective and there is a "reasonable probability" that the trial court's outcome would have been different without counsel's misfeasance or nonfeasance.

H. Right to Remain Silent

The Fifth Amendment provides that no person shall be compelled to be a witness against himself in a criminal case; nor may the D's silence be argued by the prosecution as an inference against him. The Fifth Amendment privilege against self-incrimination includes refusing to take the stand at trial. This privilege may be invoked in both criminal and civil settings.

1. D Assertion: The D may assert this privilege and in doing so does not have to take the stand at trial. The prosecutor may not comment on the D's refusal to testify, but this does not block witness testimony about D's words. If the D voluntarily takes the stand to testify, the Fifth Amendment right is waived to all questioning and is subject to cross-examination.

2. Witness: A non-party witness must take the stand (and be sworn in) if called, and after listening to each question individually, may specifically invoke the privilege as it would apply to each question. If the witness is granted immunity by the prosecutor, the witness may be compelled to answer questions.

MBE Tip: Remember, only a witness may selectively invoke the Fifth Amendment after each objectionable question. The D must either refrain entirely from testifying or he has waived the right and must then subject himself to cross-examination and answer all questions.

3. Testimonial Evidence: Only testimonial evidence (the witness' own words) is affected by this trial privilege. This privilege cannot be invoked against physical evidence (fingerprints, blood, or DNA samples) or statements made elsewhere such as at the crime scene or a police station lineup.

I. Sentencing and Penalty Phase

A court may bifurcate the criminal trial with a guilt and penalty phase. The rules against the jury being able to consider prior crimes does not apply to the sentencing phase. [E.R. 1101]

J. Prosecution's Burden of Proof

In order for the D to be convicted of a criminal offense, the prosecution must prove every element of its case beyond a reasonable doubt. In some states, self-defense is not an affirmative defense. The prosecution must disprove self-defense beyond a reasonable doubt. Insanity and duress are affirmative defenses and there the defense has the burden of proof.

STOP! Go to page 384 and work Learning Questions 67 to 73.

XII. DOUBLE JEOPARDY

The Fifth Amendment provides that no person shall "be subject for the same offense to be twice put in jeopardy of life or limb." Via the Fourteenth Amendment, the guarantee applies to state trials as well as federal. The classic application and intent of the Double Jeopardy Clause is to prevent re-prosecution after the D has been acquitted.

A. Jeopardy Attached

Protection against double jeopardy requires prior judicial finality. This does not attach until there is a trial, beyond any grand jury proceeding.

1. Bench Trial: If the case is tried by a judge without a jury, jeopardy attaches when the first witness has been sworn, not pre-trial motions, etc.

2. Jury Trial: If the case is tried by a jury, jeopardy attaches when the jury has been empaneled and sworn (*i.e.*, when the entire jury has been selected and taken the oath).

B. Separate Charges Brought Separately

Prosecuting separate offenses in succession, even if they arise from the same set of factual events, is not usually a double jeopardy violation. Also, if all events necessary for the greater crime have not yet occurred, such as the victim dies two months after an assault acquittal, the defendant may be subsequently prosecuted for murder.

1. Same Facts, Different Crimes: For example, during the course of a bank robbery, the D shoots and kills the teller. The prosecutor is not obligated to try the robbery charge and the murder charge at the same time, because they are separate offenses and neither charge is a lessor included offense. Normally, prosecutors will charge and try separate crimes arising from the same conduct together, but this is not constitutionally required.

2. Same Facts, Different Victims: It also does not violate double jeopardy to try a D for the commission of a crime against two different victims, even if the two victims were harmed under the same factual circumstances, unless they are absolutely indistinguishable. For example, a D could be tried successively for killing a bank teller and also a bystander. However, if a D burglarizes a home shared by three roommates, successive prosecutions cannot be brought by each roommate for burglary because it is one offense.

C. Exceptions

1. Mistrial: If after the trial has begun it is terminated by a necessary mistrial, the prosecution is not barred from retrying the D. This could occur because of "manifest necessity," hung jury, too few jurors left on the panel, or a mistrial at the D's request.

2. After Conviction: Where the D is convicted at trial, and then gets the verdict set aside on appeal, the double jeopardy rule usually does not apply and the state may then re-prosecute. However, if the appellate court reverses the decision because the evidence at trial was insufficient to support a conviction (*i.e.*, the evidence presented at trial was insufficient to convict the D), a retrial is barred.

D. Separate Sovereigns

A conviction or acquittal by one jurisdiction does not bar a re-prosecution by another jurisdiction such as a federal jurisdiction and a state jurisdiction. States and their political subdivisions, such as counties or cities, are regarded as the same for double jeopardy purposes.

E. Lesser Included Offenses

This situation arises where one charge is a required lesser included offense of the other, such as theft and burglary. Lesser included and greater offenses are treated as the same offense and are therefore subject to the double jeopardy rule. For example, if a D is tried for first degree murder and is acquitted, he cannot subsequently be tried for manslaughter of the same victim. If each offense has an element different from the other then they are not the same offense but are separate offenses and are not subject to the double jeopardy rule.

MBE Tip: The subtle distinctions of double jeopardy is a frequent MBE testing topic.

XIII. REMEDY FOR VIOLATIONS OF CONSTITUTIONAL PROTECTIONS: THE EXCLUSIONARY RULE

The exclusionary rule applies following the court grant of a motion to suppress. Evidence obtained by violating the D's constitutional rights may not be introduced by the prosecution at the D's criminal trial for the purpose of providing direct proof of the D's guilt. While there are limited exceptions, it is a powerful tool for the defense.

A. Enforceable Right

The D has a right to a hearing outside the presence of the jury to determine the admissibility of evidence. During that hearing, the D and counsels have a right to argue and testify without fear that anything he says will be admitted against them at trial. The prosecution must prove admissibility is proper by a preponderance of the evidence.

B. Fruits of the Poisonous Tree

In general, all illegally obtained evidence must be excluded; all evidence subsequently flowing from the illegally obtained evidence must also be suppressed. This includes any evidence obtained from an illegal search, arrest, or confession.

C. Limitations on the Exclusionary Rule

A number of exceptions to the exclusionary rule have been carved out. They are generally based on a principle of "harmless error," where the lack or invalidity of a search warrant has not significantly harmed the evidentiary process.

1. Good Faith Reliance on Search Warrant: Evidence is admissible if it is obtained under a good faith reliance on a facially valid warrant that was later proved invalid.

2. Independent Source: Where evidence is obtained from a source independent from the original illegal source, it is admissible.

3. Inevitable Discovery: If the prosecutor can show the police would almost certainly have subsequently discovered the evidence even if they had not violated the constitutional protections, the evidence will be admissible.

4. Live Witness Testimony: A witness identified through illegally obtained evidence may testify if he does so voluntarily. An example is an undercover police agent.

5. Impeachment Purposes: Excluded evidence may be used to impeach the testifying D who opens the door on the subject.

D. Harmless Error

The prosecution must prove on appeal that the evidence at issue that should have been excluded at trial was harmless error. This usually means a showing that there was enough other relevant evidence for the jury to convict the D even without the tainted evidence.

E. Cruel and Unusual Punishment

The 8th Amendment forbids cruel and unusual punishment that is excessively painful or brutal and punishment that was not proportional to the crime.

> **MBE Tip:** Review our Evidence chapter at 4-53 for further cross-over testing details.

XIV. EXCULPATORY EVIDENCE SUPPRESSION – SEIP

A. *Brady*

The U.S. Supreme Court held in *Brady* that the knowing **s**uppression by the prosecution of either **e**xculpatory or **i**mpeachment evidence that is **p**rejudicial to the prosecutor's case against the D violates a D's constitutionally protected due process. Unlike the ethical standard of RPC 3.8, the Supreme Court imposed a materiality requirement on the evidence not disclosed by the prosecutor to defense counsel.

B. Burden on Defendant

This duty to disclose applies to both willful or inadvertent suppression, but there must be a reasonable probability the result of the proceeding would have been different had the evidence at issue been timely produced by the prosecution.

> **STOP!** Go to page 385 and work Learning Questions 74 to 80.

XV. FINAL CHAPTER REVIEW INSTRUCTIONS

1. Completing the Chapter: Now that you have completed your study of the chapter's substantive text and the related Learning Questions, you need to button up federal civil procedure. This includes completing your Magic Memory Outlines® and working all of the subject's practice questions.

2. Preparing Your Own Magic Memory Outline®: This is helpful to your MBE success. The book paper outline works but consider purchasing our software template for your creation process. Do not underestimate the learning and memory effectiveness derived from condensing the text chapter into succinct summaries using your own words. This important exercise is covered in much more detail in the introduction and on the downloaded software.

a. Summarize Knowledge: You need to prepare a summary of the chapter in your own words. An example is on page 6-357. The words in the outline correspond to the bold headings in the text.

b. Capture the Essence: Your job is to summarize the substance of the text by capturing the essence of the rule and entering summarized wording into your own outlines. Use the text coverage to craft your own tight, concise, but comprehensive statements of the law.

c. Boilerplate Rule Statements: Our related MEE volume at 12-491 contains primary issue statements that are helpful in both outline creation and MEE answer boilerplate language rule statements. Take pride in your skills as an author; your Magic Memory Outlines should be the finest written document you have ever created.

d. Focus: Focus your attention and wording on the required technical elements necessary to prove the relevant legal principles. Look for fine-line distinctions. Integrate any helpful "learning question" information into your outline.

3. Memorize Outline: After you have completed your own Magic Memory Outline® for the whole chapter, read it over carefully once or twice. Refer back to your outlines frequently in quick reads during your preparation period.

4. Work Old Questions: The next step is to work all the regular questions in this chapter, beginning on page 6-385. These vary in degree of difficulty, but the ones toward the end tend to concentrate on the most difficult fact patterns and issues. Date and put an X through their numbers as you work each question. Use the Question Map for cross-reference to the textual coverage so you can work on your weak topics. If you use the software, you can click on the questions under the subject and topic you have just studied.

a. Question Details: Again, it is usually worthwhile to review the explanatory answer rationales, as they reinforce the relevant principles of law. If you are still unsure of the controlling rule, refer back to the related portion of the text. This will help you to appreciate the fine-line distinctions on which the MBE criminal law and procedure questions turn.

b. Do a Few Questions at a Time: Work the final chapter practice questions in sequence. Make sure you stop after no more than a few to check the answer rationales. Do this frequently so that the facts of the individual questions are still in your active memory.

c. Mask Down: Lay a mask over the answer rationales. Mask the answers for the questions to be worked. Pull the mask down to expose that question's answer rationale. Do not look down at future answers until after you work the relevant question. Test yourself.

d. Best to Work Them All: We have tried to pick questions from subjects and issues with an average or higher probability of reappearing on the MBE. Work as many as you can, but at least read all of the questions and ponder their answer rationales. Every question and answer has some marginal learning and/or reinforcement value. Many of the actual MBE questions are very similar to the ones in your Rigos UBE Review Series review books.

e. Learn from Mistakes: The objective is to learn from your mistakes by reviewing the explanatory rationales while you still remember the factual and legal details of the question. It is good to miss a few; this will help you become familiar with the MBE fine-line distinctions. The bar examiners' use of distracters, tricks, and red herrings frequently reoccurs.

f. Flag Errors: Put a red star in the margin of the book alongside every question you missed. Missed questions should be worked again the day right before the MBE so that you do not make the same mistakes on the exam.

5. Take the Practice Exam: You can order two optional full simulated MBE exam sets that provide a helpful assessment. They contain 200 questions in random order broken down into two three-hour groups of 100 each. The bold question numbers listed on the right side of the Question Maps refer to these final exam questions. While some practice exam questions in your text are intentionally easier or more difficult and complex than the MBE, both parts of the Final Exam have approximately the same overall difficulty as the actual MBE questions.

6. Make Your Own Exam: The optional UBE Review Series software allows you to pick 5, 10, 20, or 100 questions at random from all seven MBE subjects. This is an important feature because you must become intellectually comfortable with all the different subjects. If you are not an early riser and/or get going slowly when you first get up, try working 10 or 20 questions using the "Make Your Own Exam" software the first thing every morning.

7. Update Your Magic Memory Outline®: The fine-line distinctions in the question and answer rationales will improve your understanding of how the MBE tests the law. Consider updating your Magic Memory Outline® while the question testing environment is still fresh in your mind.

8. Essays: Candidates in jurisdictions that administer the Multistate Essay Exam should refer to the *Rigos UBE Review Series Multistate Essay Exam Review — MEE —* for further depth and practice essay questions. That volume contains sample MEE criminal law and procedure essay questions and answers that relate to this chapter coverage.

9. Performance Questions: Candidates in jurisdictions that administer the Multistate Performance Exam should refer to the *Rigos UBE Review Series Multistate Performance Test Review – MPT* for practice task performance questions.

10. Next Chapter: It is now time to go to the beginning of the next subject in your review. Begin by previewing the chapter. Scan the topical coverage and major issues.

> **MBE Tip:** This Magic Memory Outline® is intended to be the platform upon which you create your own outline. Capture the essence and concentrate on using streamlined wording.

I. MBE EXAM COVERAGE
A. Weight – *33 questions, 2/3 criminal law, 1/3 criminal procedure* ....
B. Emphasis – *Common law, statutory modifications. Elements of crime are heavily tested* ....
C. The Call of the Question ....
   1. Criminal Law – *Five structures to questions* ....
      a. Outcome – *Why or what rule justifies outcome* ....
      b. Best Argument – *For the prosecution or defense* ....
      c. Most Serious Crime – *of which D could be convicted* ....
      d. Best Precedent – *that is helpful/necessary to resolve the issue* ....
      e. Which Crime – *is best described by the facts* ....
   2. Criminal Procedure ....
      a. Best Instruction to Jury – *for the prosecution or defense* ....
      b. Admissibility – *strongest argument for evidence exclusion* ....
      c. Appeal – *grounds present? Offer of proof made below?* ....

II. OVERVIEW: GENERAL PRINCIPLES OF CRIMINAL LAW
A. Requirements for Criminal Liability..
   1. Action (*Actus Reus*) – *Did D perform each act required for the crime?* ....
   2. Mental State (*Mens Rea*) – *Did D have the mental state required* ....
   3. Result – *Can Prosecutor prove that the specific crime occurred* ....
   4. Causation – *Did D's action cause the criminal result* ....
B. *Actus Reus* – *Guilty act required or failure to act* ....
   1. Nonvolitional (Involuntary) Act – *For purpose of assigning criminal liability* ...
      a. Rule – *Involuntary act not controlled by conscious act*..................
      b. Example – *Sleepwalking, unconscious, or epileptic seizure*..............
      c. Exception – *Failure to take medicine or reasonable precautions* ....
   2. Omission/Failure to Act – *General rule is no duty to act, such as intervene* ....
      a. Statute Specifies Failure to Act as *Actus Reus* – *Failing to stop a crime* ....
      b. Legal Duty to Act – *Substantially contribute to an illegal result*.................
         (1) Contract – *Lifeguard, firefighter, or some employee duty* ....
         (2) Statute – *Hospital by statute must treat indigents, or liable*...................
         (3) Parent for a Child – *Neglects to feed children or provide medical aid*.....
         (4) Creation of Risk – *Push a person into a swimming pool* ....
         (5) Undertaking – *Rescuer dissuades another rescuer to come to aid* ....
C. *Mens Rea* – *Specific unlawful state of guilty mind – culpability issue* ....
   1. Common Law – *Malice, reckless, absolute, specific culpable act* ....
      a. General Intent – *Only required is that D intended to commit action*..............
      b. Specific Intent – *Actual intent to commit act or cause harm required* ....

VIII. SEARCH AND SEIZURE

RIGOS BAR REVIEW SERIES

UNIFORM MULTISTATE BAR EXAM REVIEW (MBE)

CHAPTER 6

CRIMINAL LAW AND PROCEDURE

Question Distribution Map

> **MBE Tip:** Numbers immediately following the topic are the chapter question numbers. The **boldface** numbers preceded by "F" are the final exam question numbers. For example, for the topic "II. B. 1. Nonvolitional Act" below, question 148 is in the chapter questions on page 6-404, and question **F102** is in the final exam.

III. AFFIRMATIVE DEFENSES

XIII. REMEDY FOR VIOLATIONS OF CONSTITUTIONAL PROTECTIONS: THE EXCLUSIONARY RULE

XIV. EXCULPATORY EVIDENCE SUPPRESSION – SEIP

MEE Candidates: Please refer to the *Rigos UBE Review Series Multistate Essay Exam (MEE) Review* for practice essay questions and sample answers covering criminal law and procedure.

LEARNING QUESTIONS

1. If a defendant stabs a victim with the intent to kill him, but the victim had already died of a heart attack six hours before, the defendant cannot be found guilty of murder because the prosecution cannot prove
- (A) *Actus reus.*
- (B) *Mens rea.*
- (C) Causation.
- (D) Result.

2. An omission or a failure to act can create criminal culpability if
- (A) A statute or other law creates a duty to act.
- (B) The defendant had a duty under contract.
- (C) The defendant created the risk to the victim.
- (D) All of the above.

3. Under the common law, specific intent is always required to prove the crime of
- (A) Felony murder.
- (B) Manslaughter.
- (C) Robbery.
- (D) Statutory rape.

4. If a crime is one of strict liability, proof of intent to commit the crime
- (A) Must be proven beyond a reasonable doubt.
- (B) Is not required.
- (C) Must be proved by a preponderance of evidence.
- (D) Is impossible to procure.

5. The criminal law doctrine of "transferred intent" means
- (A) Intent to commit one type of crime transfers to any other type of crime.
- (B) Intent to harm one victim transfers to another victim.
- (C) Intent by one conspirator to commit a crime transfers to all other conspirators.
- (D) Intent to seize certain evidence transfers to other unrelated evidence seized.

6. Under the Model Penal Code (MPC), mistake of law can exonerate a defendant if
- (A) The statute does not specify that knowledge of the law is presumed.
- (B) The defendant can prove his mistake by a preponderance of the evidence.
- (C) The defendant was acting upon misinformation from a public official.
- (D) The defendant is a non-U.S. citizen and unfamiliar with the legal system.

7. Suppose A shoots B, intending to kill him, and then 20 minutes later, C shoots B also intending to kill him. Neither wound alone would be fatal, but the two combined cause B to bleed to death. According to the substantial factor test
- (A) A is guilty of murder and C of attempted murder.
- (B) C is guilty of murder and A of attempted murder.
- (C) A and C are both guilty of murder.
- (D) Both A and C are guilty of attempted murder.

8. If Y helps Z commit a burglary by driving Z to the scene and acting as a lookout, and Z completes the crime, Y can be charged with

(A) Burglary.
(B) Accomplice to burglary.
(C) Attempted burglary.
(D) None of the above.

9. If the victim's harm is a natural and probable result of the actions of a defendant, then that defendant's actions are said to be the _____ of the harm.

(A) Presumed cause.
(B) Proven cause.
(C) Actual cause.
(D) Proximate cause.

10. A defendant who breaks into a home intending to steal a stereo and instead steals $500 in cash can be found guilty of both larceny and burglary because

(A) The two crimes are identical.
(B) The elements of burglary have been met.
(C) Larceny is a lesser included offense of burglary.
(D) Burglary does not merge with larceny.

11. In a jurisdiction that has adopted the Model Penal Code, a defendant can be found not guilty by reason of insanity if he

(A) Lacked the capacity to distinguish right from wrong.
(B) Was unable to control his actions as a result of some mental defect.
(C) Lacked the capacity to distinguish right from wrong, was unable to control his actions as a result of some mental defect, or was totally incapable of realizing what he was doing.
(D) Acted out of terror as a result of a threat of substantial physical harm.

12. A criminal defendant must be capable of understanding the criminal proceedings and effectively assisting her lawyer because

(A) If she can't, it violates her constitutional right to a fair trial.

(B) If she can't, she was likely unable to comprehend the nature of her crime at the time she committed it.
(C) She must appear as a witness in her own defense.
(D) She must tell her lawyer when to make objections.

13. Q goes to a bar and orders a large number of virgin (non-alcoholic) daiquiris. Unbeknownst to him, the bartender makes the drinks with alcohol. Q, who never drinks, becomes quite drunk and batters V. On the battery charge, Q will likely be found

(A) Guilty, because intoxication is not a defense.
(B) Guilty, because a reasonable person would have known that the drinks contained alcohol.
(C) Not guilty, because involuntary intoxication is a defense.
(D) Guilty, because battery is a strict liability crime.

14. If a child is 12-years old at the time he is charged with murder

(A) He is conclusively presumed incapable of forming the requisite intent.
(B) He is presumed incapable of forming the requisite intent and the prosecutor must provide clear and convincing proof of capacity.
(C) He is presumed incompetent to stand trial.
(D) He may be tried as an adult.

15. A commits burglary because B threatens to sink A's yacht if A does not comply. Charged with burglary, A will likely be found

(A) Guilty, because duress is not an available defense to burglary.
(B) Not guilty, because under duress A could not have formed the requisite specific intent.
(C) Not guilty, because A was acting under duress.
(D) Guilty, because a threat to property is insufficient for a duress defense.

16. Entrapment is available as a defense when

    (A) Police create the opportunity for the defendant to commit the crime.

    (B) The defendant has a predisposition to committing the crime.

    (C) The police induce the defendant to commit a crime that he otherwise would not have committed.

    (D) The defendant was predisposed to commit the crime, but did not intend to commit that particular crime prior to encountering the police setup.

17. In a loud voice in a busy restaurant, A tells B, "If you don't pay this debt by 5:00 tomorrow, I'm coming to your house to cut your arms off." B, in terror, shoots A. B is charged with murder and argues self-defense. His defense will fail because

    (A) He had a duty to retreat.

    (B) He used deadly force when deadly force was not threatened.

    (C) He was threatened with future, not imminent, harm.

    (D) He recklessly put himself in a dangerous situation.

18. A defendant who makes an honest but unreasonable mistake in using deadly force as self-defense against an aggressor will likely

    (A) Be charged with murder, because mistake is not acceptable when the use of deadly force is involved.

    (B) Be charged with manslaughter, because the mistake negated the required mental state for murder.

    (C) Be acquitted, because he acted in self-defense.

    (D) Be acquitted, because he had no criminal intent.

19. The majority view on defense of others is that a defender may use as much force as he reasonably believes is required to protect the victim. The minority view holds that

    (A) A defender may use as much force as he reasonably believes is required, but only if he has a personal relationship to the victim.

    (B) A defender may not use any force but must summon help from a law enforcement officer.

    (C) A defender must use only non-deadly force unless he has a personal relationship to the victim.

    (D) A defender can only use that amount of force that the victim himself would be legally allowed to use.

20. Quincy personally witnesses Abram robbing Jones, although he sees no weapon. As Abram flees from the scene he runs by Quincy, who hits Abram in the head with a golf club, killing him instantly. If charged with murder, Quincy will likely be

    (A) Convicted, because Abram did not pose an immediate threat.

    (B) Acquitted, because Abram was a fleeing felon.

    (C) Convicted, because private citizens may never use force to apprehend suspects.

    (D) Convicted, because Quincy was not correct in his belief that Abram was a felon.

21. Over a couple of beers, Don tells Mathew that he should go over to his ex-girlfriend's house and beat up her new boyfriend. Mathew says "You're nuts, man, I'm not that stupid" and leaves. Charged with criminal solicitation, Don would likely be

    (A) Convicted, because he intentionally encouraged another to commit a felony.

    (B) Acquitted, because Mathew immediately refused.

    (C) Acquitted, because Don did not offer anything of value to Mathew for committing the crime.

    (D) Acquitted, because the proposed crime was never committed.

22. Sarah, age 14, approaches Ben, age 19, at a party and suggests that they have sex. They have sex. Ben is arrested for statutory rape, and Sarah for solicitation. Ben is acquitted. Sarah will likely be
- (A) Acquitted, because the solicitor cannot be convicted if the solicitee is acquitted.
- (B) Acquitted, because she is within the class of persons that the statute was enacted to protect.
- (C) Acquitted, because she consented and therefore, she was not soliciting a crime.
- (D) Convicted, because the crime of solicitation is completed when the offer is made.

23. "In a criminal conspiracy, every co-conspirator may be charged with each crime committed, whether or not he agreed to each crime." This statement is a description of the
- (A) *Pinkerton* rule
- (B) *M'Naghten* rule
- (C) *Miranda* rule
- (D) *Gerstein* rule

24. If two people commit a crime that by definition requires two persons to commit
- (A) They can also be charged with conspiracy if they had a previous verbal agreement.
- (B) They cannot be charged with conspiracy under any circumstances.
- (C) One person will be charged with solicitation.
- (D) Only one can be charged because the other must be granted immunity and testify.

25. The *mens rea* which must be proven for criminal attempt is
- (A) The same as the *mens rea* for the underlying crime attempted.
- (B) Specific intent.
- (C) Recklessness.
- (D) None, attempt is a strict liability crime.

26. A murder defendant, who did not specifically intend to kill his victim or cause him serious bodily harm, may still be convicted of murder if
- (A) It can be proven that the defendant had a motive for the killing.
- (B) He had recently threatened the victim.
- (C) He was totally indifferent to the possibility of seriously injuring or killing someone.
- (D) He violated a statute.

27. In a murder case, if it is proven that a defendant did not intend to kill his victim, but instead intended only to "shoot him in the leg to scare him" the defendant will likely be convicted of
- (A) Murder.
- (B) Voluntary manslaughter.
- (C) Involuntary manslaughter.
- (D) Negligent homicide.

28. Disconnecting the life support of a victim who is still breathing and whose heart is still beating, but who has irreversible cessation of brain function is not murder because
- (A) The victim is not a legal human being.
- (B) It is voluntary manslaughter.
- (C) There is no causation.
- (D) It is merciful.

29. X is driving 100 mph on a deserted country road late at night. As he comes around a corner, he collides with a vehicle that was pulling out of a driveway, killing a passenger. If the jury finds that X was reckless, he should properly be convicted of
- (A) Second degree murder.
- (B) Involuntary manslaughter.
- (C) Voluntary manslaughter.
- (D) Reckless endangerment.

30. In a jurisdiction governed by the MPC, the *mens rea* for negligent homicide is
- (A) Extreme recklessness.
- (B) Mere negligence.
- (C) A gross deviation from the standard of care.
- (D) Nothing; the MPC does not recognize negligent homicide.

31. Which of the following scenarios would most likely result in a criminal conviction for larceny?

    (A) Tim goes to his neighbor's house, hoping to borrow his weed whacker. His neighbor is not home, but the tool is sitting out. Tim takes it, but it is quite old and it breaks before he can return it.

    (B) Tim goes to his neighbor's house, intending to take back his own weed whacker that the neighbor had borrowed from him months ago. Unbeknownst to Tim, his neighbor had already returned the tool to Tim's wife. Tim mistakes his neighbor's tool for his own and takes it.

    (C) Tim goes to his neighbor's house intending to borrow his weed whacker. His neighbor isn't home, but the tool is sitting out. After a few days, Tim decides that he likes his neighbor's tool better. He returns his own tool to his neighbor, hoping his neighbor won't notice.

    (D) Tim goes to his neighbor's house, intending to steal his weed whacker. He sees the tool in the open garage, and is about to pick it up when he abruptly changes his mind and leaves.

32. An employee who uses his company computer at work to run his own secret for-profit enterprise against company policy would be most appropriately charged with

    (A) Embezzlement.
    (B) Larceny.
    (C) False pretenses.
    (D) Robbery.

33. The difference between larceny by trick and false pretenses is

    (A) One involves fraud; the other does not.
    (B) One involves transfer of title and possession; the other only involves transfer of possession.
    (C) One involves tangible property; the other does not.
    (D) Nothing; they are the same crime.

34. Maurice, a merchant, gets a call from Ron, who in the past has sold him top-quality car stereos at a low price. Ron tells Maurice, "Hey, I got 300 stereos I'll sell you for $10 each that can sell for $50 each." Maurice says "Great! Leave them in my warehouse on Bleecker." Ron does so. But when Maurice sees them, he says, "Half of these are broken – I won't pay." As it turns out, the stereos are stolen. Charged with receiving stolen goods, Maurice will likely be

    (A) Acquitted, because he did not actually take possession.
    (B) Acquitted, because he had no actual knowledge that the property was stolen.
    (C) Acquitted, because he did not complete the transaction.
    (D) Convicted.

35. Stan goes into a liquor store with an unloaded gun in his hand, hoping for a chance to get some cash. He sees the clerk go into the back room, dashes behind the counter, breaks open the cash register, and makes off with $400 before the clerk returns. Charged with robbery, Stan will likely be

    (A) Acquitted, because the clerk was not present.
    (B) Acquitted, because the gun was not loaded.
    (C) Convicted, because he forced the cash register drawer open.
    (D) Convicted, because he was carrying a gun.

36. Biff goes to Jackson's house at 3:30 p.m. intending to break in and take Jackson's computer system. When he arrives, he finds the door wide open and no one at home. He walks in the front room and takes the computer system. The most serious crime that Biff could be convicted of is

    (A) Larceny.
    (B) Robbery.
    (C) Burglary.
    (D) Embezzlement.

37. A defendant can be convicted of common law criminal battery if he possessed a *mens rea* of
  (A) Recklessness.
  (B) Gross negligence.
  (C) Recklessness or specific intent.
  (D) Negligence.

38. To be convicted of criminal assault, a defendant must
  (A) Cause a victim to fear serious bodily harm.
  (B) Cause a victim to fear immediate battery.
  (C) Ultimately succeed in battering a victim.
  (D) Be holding a weapon or object capable of inflicting serious bodily harm.

39. Doug has sexual intercourse with Linda without her consent. She tells him "No" repeatedly, but he is too drunk to realize that she has not consented. Charged with rape, Doug will likely be
  (A) Convicted, because he should not have had intercourse while intoxicated.
  (B) Convicted, because intoxication negates the *mens rea* only when the defendant was too drunk to realize he was having intercourse.
  (C) Acquitted, because Linda did not demonstrate any physical resistance.
  (D) Acquitted, because his intoxication prevented him from realizing there was a lack of consent, which is an element of rape.

40. Kidnapping is defined as the intentional and unlawful confinement of a person with movement of that person to another location. However, a defendant is not guilty of kidnapping if
  (A) The victim is not physically restrained.
  (B) The victim does not attempt escape.
  (C) The victim is only confined for a short time.
  (D) The defendant does not intend to confine the victim.

41. Mel is painting his car in his garage, surrounded by flammable chemicals. He stops for a moment to take a smoke break, sits down, and falls asleep with the lit cigarette in his hand. The cigarette ignites some fumes and burns the garage down. Charged with arson under most modern statutes, Mel will likely be
  (A) Convicted, because his actions were reckless, sufficient *mens rea* for arson.
  (B) Acquitted, because he did not burn down a dwelling.
  (C) Acquitted, because the garage was his own property.
  (D) Acquitted, because he did not intend to start the fire or manifest extreme disregard for the danger.

42. A business owner reviewing an employee's personal emails on a work computer does not violate the Fourth Amendment because
  (A) There is no legitimate expectation of privacy.
  (B) The computer is the property of the owner, and it is therefore the equivalent to a man searching his own wallet.
  (C) The business owner is not a government employee.
  (D) It is not a search.

43. The "Open Fields" doctrine holds that
  (A) If there is no fence or other barrier to private property, an officer may enter the premises and search.
  (B) There is no expectation of privacy in fields not immediately adjacent to a dwelling.
  (C) Items placed in a public garbage can adjoining the main residence is protected from search.
  (D) A car parked in an open field may be searched.

44. In order to have probable cause to arrest, there must be
- (A) A likelihood that a violation of the law occurred.
- (B) A likelihood that a violation of the law occurred and the person arrested committed the violation.
- (C) A warrant.
- (D) A likelihood that the suspect will be convicted.

45. A warrantless arrest is legally permissible if
- (A) The suspect committed a felony and is in a public place.
- (B) The officer has an articulable suspicion that the suspect was involved in a crime.
- (C) The suspect is in a location not under his control.
- (D) The suspect committed a misdemeanor in front of an eyewitness.

46. If a defendant is successful in challenging the validity of the warrant, it will have the following effect
- (A) His case will be dismissed.
- (B) He will be found not guilty, because there will be no evidence against him.
- (C) Any evidence obtained as a result of the arrest will be excluded as tainted evidence.
- (D) No effect.

47. In order to bring a suspect to the police station for a lineup, an officer must have
- (A) An articulable suspicion of wrongdoing.
- (B) Some physical evidence linking the defendant to criminal activity.
- (C) A warrant.
- (D) Full probable cause to arrest.

48. A probable cause affidavit for a search warrant
- (A) Cannot be based on hearsay.
- (B) Must exist before stopping an automobile.
- (C) Must specify the items to be seized and their suspected locations.
- (D) Cannot be based on the testimony of an informant alone.

49. A proper search warrant must specify
- (A) The particular rooms in a structure in which evidence is suspected to be located.
- (B) The particular structure in which evidence is suspected to be located.
- (C) The particular person who owns the structure to be searched.
- (D) The particular crimes which are expected to be charged after the search is completed.

50. Incident to a lawful arrest, a warrantless search may be made
- (A) Of all of the suspect's property.
- (B) Of anything within the suspect's reach.
- (C) Of the suspect's home.
- (D) Of the suspect's car, including the trunk.

51. While executing a search warrant for illegal weapons in Stuart's home, Officer Jones frisked Greg. When he felt a large metal object, he reached in Greg's jacket and found an iron pipe. Later, it was discovered that the pipe had been used as a murder weapon. Greg's motion to exclude the pipe as evidence should be
- (A) Denied, because Officer Jones had the right to pat down Greg to ensure his own safety.
- (B) Granted, because the search of Greg's person was outside the scope of the warrant.
- (C) Denied, because a *Terry* frisk is always valid.
- (D) Granted, because Officer Jones did not have an articulable suspicion to validate the search.

52. To validate an automobile search under the "exigent circumstances" warrant exception, the officer must be able to demonstrate that
   (A) The officer had probable cause to believe the automobile was being used in a crime.
   (B) The automobile was in working order and therefore capable of being moved.
   (C) The driver was acting suspiciously.
   (D) The evidence sought was in plain view.

53. Paul's neighbor notices suspicious persons on Paul's property and calls the police. When they arrive, they find a broken window in the house. They knock, and hearing no answer, enter. Sitting on the living room table, they see a wooden box. Inside, they find a handgun. As a convicted felon, Paul is not allowed to own a handgun. Paul's motion to suppress the handgun as evidence should be
   (A) Granted, because there was no proof that the handgun was Paul's.
   (B) Denied, because the handgun was in plain view.
   (C) Denied, because the police entered illegally.
   (D) Granted, because the handgun was in the wooden box.

54. An automobile may be searched and inventoried when impounded. It may be impounded when
   (A) The driver is unconscious.
   (B) The driver is arrested.
   (C) The driver is unconscious, the driver is arrested, or the automobile is suspected of having been used in a crime.
   (D) The automobile is abandoned in the middle of the freeway.

55. Police may search a house without a warrant if express, voluntary, and knowing consent is given by the owner-occupant. Once consent is given, it may be revoked
   (A) If the officer exceeds the scope of the consent.
   (B) For any reason at any time.

   (C) If it is demonstrated that the person giving the consent did not have authority.
   (D) After a reasonable period of time.

56. An example of evanescent evidence is
   (A) An automobile.
   (B) A handwriting sample.
   (C) A suspect's blood that may contain drugs and/or alcohol.
   (D) A confession.

57. Kyle tells the police that Ted is going to call him in two days to arrange a murder for hire. The police conduct a warrantless wiretap of the phone call, and shortly thereafter arrest Ted for solicitation of murder. Ted's motion to suppress the recording as evidence should be
   (A) Denied, because Kyle consented and the conversation related to a crime.
   (B) Denied, because a wiretap is not a "search" under the Fourth Amendment.
   (C) Granted, because Ted had a legitimate expectation of privacy.
   (D) Granted, because the police had sufficient time to obtain a warrant.

58. A confession will generally be admissible against a defendant if
   (A) It is in the form of a signed affidavit.
   (B) *Miranda* warnings were given.
   (C) The defendant was being interrogated when he confessed.
   (D) *Miranda* warnings were given and the confession was made voluntarily.

59. If it is established that a confession was coerced by the police, then
   (A) It can be used, but a limiting instruction must be read to the jury.
   (B) It is to be excluded from the prosecution's case in chief, but can be used for impeachment purposes.
   (C) The prosecution may still proceed.
   (D) The charges against the defendant are dismissed.

60. Joe is arrested and is read the *Miranda* warnings. He expressly told the arresting officer he would not speak to police until he speaks to a lawyer. While in jail waiting for his lawyer, his "cellmate," an undercover officer, begins asking Joe about his arrest. Two hours later Joe confesses to his cellmate that he is guilty of the crime. The prosecutor wants to put cellmate on the stand as a witness. Joe's motion to exclude the confession should be

(A) Denied, because he received and understood his *Miranda* rights.

(B) Granted, because the questions were a custodial interrogation.

(C) Denied, because Joe did not know that his cellmate was an officer and therefore his confession was voluntary.

(D) Granted, because his confession was coerced.

61. When testifying to a grand jury, a witness has the right to

(A) Receive *Miranda* warnings.

(B) Have an attorney present.

(C) Be confronted with the witnesses against him.

(D) None of these rights.

62. The right to be represented by counsel during formal court criminal proceedings

(A) Must be affirmatively, knowingly, and intelligently waived.

(B) Must be clearly and unambiguously invoked.

(C) Cannot be refused.

(D) Is protected by the Fifth Amendment.

63. Bob, an Asian American, is arrested for armed robbery. An eyewitness who claims the robber was of Asian descent is brought into the police station for a lineup identification. In the lineup are two African Americans, two Caucasian Americans, one Native American, and Bob. Bob's lawyer files a motion to suppress the lineup identification. Under these circumstances

(A) The identification procedure will probably be found unnecessarily suggestive, and the charges will be dismissed.

(B) The identification procedure will probably be found unnecessarily suggestive, and the witness identification will be excluded as evidence.

(C) Another lineup should be prepared for the witness, this time with Bob surrounded by other Asian Americans.

(D) A judge would likely find the lineup identification to be admissible.

64. If a person is indicted or arrested without a warrant

(A) The warrant can be issued *ex post facto*.

(B) An arraignment must be held within 72 hours.

(C) He cannot be detained for more than 24 hours.

(D) A *Gerstein* hearing must be held within 48 hours of detainment.

65. A competency hearing may be held by the trial court in a criminal case to determine

(A) If counsel is competent to provide adequate representation.

(B) If the defendant was of sound mind at the time he committed the crime.

(C) If the defendant is capable of understanding the proceedings and assisting counsel.

(D) If the defendant will be able to receive a fair trial within the jurisdiction.

66. If the prosecution and defendant reach a plea agreement in a criminal action

(A) No further proceedings are necessary.

(B) A judge has discretion to accept or reject the plea.

(C) The defendant still has the right to a jury trial.

(D) The plea agreement may not be withdrawn.

67. If the judge in a criminal case determines that a defendant's right to a speedy trial has been violated,

(A) The conviction is set aside and a new trial is granted.

(B) A trial must be held within 72 hours.

(C) The charges are dismissed or the conviction reversed.

(D) The defendant is entitled to compensation.

68. Brenda, a respected and reputable accountant, is about to be tried for criminal embezzlement. At a pretrial hearing, she requests a closed trial to prevent damage to her reputation in the community. Without comment or explanation, the judge refuses. The judge's decision is

(A) Proper, because there is no constitutional right to a closed trial.

(B) Proper, because sufficient grounds for requesting a closed trial did not exist, therefore the judge had discretion.

(C) Improper, because the judge did not enter written justification in the record.

(D) Improper, because a closed trial must constitutionally always be granted upon request.

69. In a criminal trial with a twelve-person jury, a criminal conviction is only proper if

(A) The verdict is unanimous.

(B) At least 9 jurors vote in favor of conviction.

(C) The jurors are all the same race as the defendant.

(D) The majority of jurors vote in favor of conviction.

70. The Sixth Amendment defendant's right to be present at a criminal trial

(A) Is absolute.

(B) Only applies through the Confrontation Clause, so if there are no witnesses, the trial may be conducted without the defendant.

(C) May be forfeited if the defendant is continually disruptive.

(D) Only applies to felonies.

71. The right to effective counsel in a criminal case after the initial court appearance is violated if

(A) The defendant is convicted despite the existence of questionable evidence.

(B) Counsel neglected to make an appropriate objection.

(C) The defendant can demonstrate that he disagreed with counsel's strategy.

(D) There is a reasonable probability that the case outcome would have been different without counsel's misfeasance or nonfeasance.

72. Marla is on trial for arson. Peter, an eyewitness, takes the stand. To everyone's surprise, on cross-examination it begins to seem as though Peter may have had a hand in the crime. Peter begins to invoke his Fifth Amendment right after each question. Defense counsel requests that the witness be compelled to answer. The judge should

(A) Compel Peter to answer, as failure to do so would violate Marla's rights under the Confrontation Clause.

(B) Compel Peter to answer, as he waived his Fifth Amendment right to remain silent when he took the stand.

(C) Refuse to compel.

(D) Compel Peter to answer, as he is not the defendant on trial and thus the privilege against self-incrimination is not applicable.

73. To secure a conviction in a criminal case, the prosecution must

(A) Prove every element of the charge beyond a reasonable doubt.

(B) Prove key elements of the charge beyond a reasonable doubt.

(C) Prove every element of the charge by clear and convincing evidence.

(D) Prove every element of the charge by a preponderance of the evidence.

74. When a defendant is convicted and the verdict is set aside on appeal
- (A) Double jeopardy bars a retrial.
- (B) A retrial is barred only if the appellate court determines that the trial evidence was insufficient to support a conviction.
- (C) The appellate court may conduct a de novo trial.
- (D) A retrial may be held only if it is conducted by a different sovereign.

75. Kylie is tried for murder and acquitted. Upon an exit poll of the jury, the prosecutor discovers that the jury would have convicted the defendant if they had been presented the opportunity. The prosecutor then files a manslaughter charge against Kylie because she believes it will be easier for the jury to convict. Kylie moves for dismissal. The motion should be
- (A) Denied, because murder and manslaughter are different charges.
- (B) Denied, because the jury made a reversible legal error.
- (C) Granted, because double jeopardy applies.
- (D) Granted, because a lesser charge can only be tried before a greater one, not after.

76. In a criminal case, the prosecution must prove that evidence is admissible
- (A) By a showing of probable cause.
- (B) By a preponderance.
- (C) By clear and convincing proof.
- (D) Beyond a reasonable doubt.

77. Evidence obtained in violation of the Fourth Amendment
- (A) Is always inadmissible.
- (B) Is usually admissible to impeach the defendant.
- (C) Is admissible in the prosecution's case if the trial judge determines that it would be harmless to do so.
- (D) Is admissible if the police believed their actions were proper.

78. "Fruits of the poisonous tree" are
- (A) Criminal charges that are based on excluded evidence.
- (B) Jurors that have personal biases that exclude them from hearing a case.
- (C) Items of evidence that would not have been obtained without the help of prior illegally obtained evidence.
- (D) Arguments that are based on excluded evidence.

79. A live witness who was identified through illegally obtained evidence
- (A) Is considered "fruit of the poisonous tree" and may not testify.
- (B) May testify only to impeach the defendant.
- (C) May testify only in favor of the defendant.
- (D) May testify if she does so voluntarily.

REGULAR QUESTIONS

80. If during trial a criminal defendant's attorney brings a Motion to Suppress evidence hearing
- (A) The defendant's statements at the hearing may not be used against him at trial and the jury may not be present.
- (B) The burden is on the defense to prove evidence inadmissible.
- (C) The defendant does not have a right to counsel.
- (D) None of the above.

81. Tom buys $100 worth of heroin from Mike. When Mike's product turns out to be only non-narcotic powder, Tom goes to Mike's house to break in and get his $100 back. When he arrives on Mike's front porch, he finds the house empty. An envelope containing $500 is wedged halfway under the door. He takes $100 and replaces the envelope under the door leaving $400 therein. Mike's neighbor sees Tom poking around the house and calls the police. As Tom is leaving, the police arrive and arrest him.

On a charge of 1st degree burglary, Tom's best defense is
- **(A)** He lacked intent, since he only went to Mike's house to recover his own property.
- **(B)** He did not enter the house, but only stood out front.
- **(C)** The amount of money taken is so small that it is only a misdemeanor, not a felony.
- **(D)** No one was present in the house at the time.

82. Tom buys $100 worth of heroin from Mike. When Mike's product turns out to be only non-narcotic powder, Tom goes to Mike's house to break in and get his $100 back. When he arrives on Mike's front porch, he finds the house empty. An envelope containing $500 is wedged halfway under the door. He takes $100 and replaces the envelope. Mike's neighbor sees Tom poking around the house and calls the police. As Tom is leaving, the police arrive and arrest him.

Upon Tom's arrest, the police discover the previous transaction between Mike and Tom. According to Tom, he and Mike agreed to meet in a hotel room Mike had reserved and make the exchange. Tom and Mike are both charged with conspiracy to traffic in illegal narcotics. Mike's defense at trial is that although he did originally agree to meet Tom and sell him the drugs, prior to the actual exchange, Mike had a change of heart. He purposely gave Tom fake heroin to prevent him from getting real heroin somewhere else. Mike's defense will likely

- **(A)** Succeed, because he lacked the necessary *mens rea*.
- **(B)** Fail, because he initially agreed to commit the crime, and failure to complete it is not a defense to conspiracy.
- **(C)** Succeed, because no substantial step was taken in furtherance of the crime.
- **(D)** Fail, because he committed fraud.

83. Shawn and Tanya break into Umberto's house at night and are arrested and charged with burglary and conspiracy to commit burglary. At trial, the prosecutor presents evidence that they had planned the break-in but does not successfully demonstrate what they intended to do once inside. Shawn and Tanya will likely be
- **(A)** Convicted, because agreement and substantial step is enough for conspiracy, even if the crime is not committed.
- **(B)** Convicted, because they broke into a dwelling at night and therefore an inherently dangerous situation was created.
- **(C)** Acquitted, because the conspiracy merged with the burglary once it was actually committed.
- **(D)** Acquitted, because the prosecution failed to prove agreement or intent to commit the substantive crime of burglary.

84. Max enters a liquor store, pulls out a gun, and demands that the cashier empty the register. As Max looks around for customers and police, the cashier reaches out and attempts to grab the gun. Max nervously drops it, accidentally discharging it, and a nearby customer is killed. Max is charged with first degree murder. On these facts, he will likely be

(A) Acquitted, because he lacked the necessary intent required for first degree murder.

(B) Acquitted, because the cashier's actions were the proximate cause of the death.

(C) Convicted, because any death that is a natural and probable consequence of a felony is first degree murder.

(D) Convicted, because intent to commit serious bodily harm is assumed when a deadly weapon is used.

85. Lawrence removes Victor's wallet from his jacket pocket while Victor is wearing the jacket. Victor notices Lawrence as he is running away and tackles him after only a few feet. What is the most serious crime of which Lawrence could be convicted?

(A) Larceny.
(B) Burglary.
(C) Robbery.
(D) None of the above

86. William goes to John's home at 10 p.m. to demand repayment of a $50 loan. He knocks repeatedly, but gets no answer. Hearing the cries of a hurt dog coming from inside the house, he breaks a window and crawls in. He finds John's dog underneath a fallen bookshelf, and rescues him. On his way out the front door, he notices $50 cash on a table and takes it. What is the most serious crime of which William could be convicted?

(A) Larceny.
(B) Burglary.
(C) Robbery.
(D) None of the above.

87. Gary walks up to Tim with a hot pink plastic toy gun, points it at Tim, and with a grin on his face states, "Give me your wallet or I'll shoot you." Tim, being rather dim witted, believes the gun to be real and, hands over his wallet. Gary, dumbfounded at his luck, takes the wallet and walks away. What is the most serious crime of which Gary could be convicted?

(A) Larceny.
(B) Burglary.
(C) Robbery.
(D) None of the above.

88. In a jurisdiction which has adopted only the *M'Naghten* test, which of the following scenarios could provide defendant with a colorable insanity defense?

(A) Defendant is charged with first degree murder. He is a clinically diagnosed schizophrenic and claims that demonic voices commanded him to stab the victim.

(B) Defendant is charged with second degree murder. He claims he was enraged over the discovery of his wife's extra-marital affair and lost control, hitting the victim with his fists and breaking his neck.

(C) Defendant is charged with vehicular manslaughter. He is a clinically diagnosed psychotic and claims he thought he was riding a horse in an open pasture, not driving a car.

(D) Defendant is charged with arson. He has been diagnosed as a pyromaniac, unable to control his urges to burn buildings.

89. Gerald tells Nancy that he is planning to confront Dan, a known gang member, and "beat him senseless." Nancy, whose sister was attacked by a member of the same gang, thinks this is a great idea and tells Gerald the name and location of a park which she knows Dan frequents. When Gerald gets there, he assaults Dan in front of Barry. Barry watches the entire attack, smiling, but does nothing to stop it.

On these facts, Nancy can be charged with

(A) Solicitation.
(B) Rendering criminal assistance.
(C) Assault.
(D) None of the above.

90. Gerald tells Nancy that he is planning to confront Dan, a known gang member, and "beat him senseless." Nancy, whose sister was attacked by a member of the same gang, thinks this is a great idea and tells Gerald the name and location of a park which she knows Dan frequents. When Gerald gets to the park he assaults Dan in front of Barry. Barry watches the entire attack, smiling, but does nothing to stop it.

Barry is also charged with assault on a theory of accomplice liability. His best defense to that charge is

(A) He was too frightened to act in Dan's defense.
(B) He did not take any action to assist Gerald.
(C) He owed no legal duty to rescue Dan.
(D) He did not have criminal intent.

91. A bank robbery takes place and two eyewitnesses state the getaway car was a gray Honda Accord. Minutes later, Dave is stopped in his blue Honda Accord 3 blocks from the scene. The officer sees a locked briefcase on the back seat and asks Dave to open it. When Dave refuses, the officer pries the briefcase open and finds cocaine.

Dave's motion to suppress introduction of the cocaine as evidence will most probably be

(A) Granted, because insufficient probable cause existed for the search.
(B) Denied, because the briefcase was in plain view and therefore subject to search.
(C) Granted, because the briefcase was locked and Dave refused consent.
(D) Denied, because the briefcase was within Dave's "wingspan."

92. A bank robbery takes place and two eyewitnesses state the getaway car was a gray Honda Accord. Minutes later, Dave is stopped in his blue Honda Accord 3 blocks from the scene. The officer sees a locked briefcase on the back seat and asks Dave to open it. When Dave refuses, the officer pries the briefcase open and finds cocaine.

Dave is arrested and charged with possession of cocaine with intent to distribute. The prosecutor wants to bolster her case regarding intent and executes a search warrant for Dave's apartment. No drugs or other evidence are found. They do discover, however, that Dave often spends the night at the apartment of his girlfriend, Debbie.

The prosecutor applies for a warrant to search Debbie's apartment for cocaine. The magistrate, a former prosecutor, issues the warrant. In the pantry of Debbie's apartment, a Tupperware container is found containing a small amount of cocaine. The container has Dave's fingerprints on it.

Dave's motion to suppress introduction of the cocaine as evidence will most probably be

(A) Granted, because Debbie was not a suspect and her residence could not be subject to a valid warrant.
(B) Granted, because the warrant was invalid due to lack of probable cause.
(C) Denied, because the warrant was issued subsequent to a valid arrest.
(D) Granted, because the magistrate was biased.

93. A bank robbery takes place and two eyewitnesses state the getaway car was a gray Honda Accord. Minutes later, Dave is stopped in his blue Honda Accord 3 blocks from the scene. The officer sees a locked briefcase on the back seat and asks Dave to open it. When Dave refuses, the officer pries the briefcase open and finds cocaine.

At trial, Dave decides to take the stand. On cross-examination, the prosecutor begins to ask questions about Dave's drug activities, and Dave responds "I refuse to answer on the grounds that I may incriminate myself." The judge orders Dave to answer, and he is convicted, based largely on his own testimony. On appeal, Dave's request that his conviction be reversed will likely be

(A) Granted, because Dave's attorney should have prevented him from taking the stand, and thus was not reasonably effective.

(B) Granted, because a party may invoke the Fifth Amendment selectively as each question is asked.

(C) Denied, because the judge's decision constitutes harmless error.

(D) Denied, because Dave waived his right to avoid self-incrimination once he took the stand.

94. On a tip from a reliable informant that Mark is planning a bank robbery, Officer Lewis, in uniform, pays a visit to Mark's house. Mark is not home, but his wife Sheila answers the door. Officer Lewis informs Sheila of his purpose and requests her consent to search the house. Sheila says "Certainly, we have nothing to hide." and steps aside. Looking in the closet in the master bedroom, Officer Lewis finds floor plans of First National Bank and documents containing strategies for breaking in. When Mark returns home, Officer Lewis arrests him.

On a motion to suppress the evidence found at his home, Mark will most likely

(A) Succeed, because Sheila was not told that she had the right to refuse consent.

(B) Succeed, because Officer Lewis should have first obtained a warrant.

(C) Fail, because consent to search by third persons is effective if they have joint authority over the premises.

(D) Succeed, since the officer had no warrant and the evidence was not in plain view.

95. On a tip from a reliable informant that Mark is planning a bank robbery, Officer Lewis, in uniform, pays a visit to Mark's house. Mark is not home, but his wife Sheila answers the door. Officer Lewis informs Sheila of his purpose and requests her consent to search the house. Sheila says "Certainly, we have nothing to hide." and steps aside. Looking in the closet in the master bedroom, Officer Lewis finds floor plans of First National Bank and documents containing strategies for breaking in. When Mark returns home, Officer Lewis arrests him.

After Mark's arrest without a warrant, he is booked, a criminal complaint is filed charging him with attempted robbery, and he is immediately indicted and arraigned. His trial begins five weeks later. On appeal, Mark could raise the issue that

(A) The delay was a violation of his right to a speedy trial.

(B) A preliminary hearing with live witnesses in front of a magistrate should have been held prior to indictment.

(C) The failure to hold an immediate arraignment was a due process violation.

(D) There was insufficient evidence to file a complaint.

96. Officer Stanley pulls over John's station wagon when he sees it has a broken tail light. Upon approaching the car, Officer Stanley notices Harry sitting on the passenger's side and sees a handgun and several purses sitting in the rear compartment of the station wagon, beyond the back seat. He asks John about the items, and John replies, "Harry did it; all I did was give him a lift." Both are arrested and charged, and four days later make their first court appearance and are indicted.

On appeal, John and Harry can both argue
- **(A)** The failure to hold a *Gerstein* hearing was improper.
- **(B)** The stop was illegal because no articulable suspicion existed.
- **(C)** The illegal items were not within the "wingspan" of any occupant.
- **(D)** The arrest was unlawful because the officer did not have a warrant.

97. Officer Stanley pulls over John's station wagon when he sees it has a broken tail light. Upon approaching the car, Officer Stanley notices Harry sitting on the passenger's side and sees a handgun and several purses sitting in the rear compartment of the station wagon, beyond the back seat. He asks John about the items, and John replies, "Harry did it; all I did was give him a lift." Both are arrested and charged, and four days later make their first court appearance and are indicted.

John is charged with rendering criminal assistance. In a pretrial hearing, John moves to have his statement "Harry did it; all I did was give him a lift" suppressed. John's motion will likely
- **(A)** Fail, because he was not under custodial interrogation at the time he made his statement.
- **(B)** Fail, because it is an exculpatory statement and not a confession.
- **(C)** Succeed, because he had not been read his *Miranda* rights before he made the statement.
- **(D)** Succeed, because it is hearsay.

98. Hank is arrested on suspicion of arson. He is read his *Miranda* warnings and then interrogated. At one point during interrogation, he says to the interrogating officer, "Don't I get a lawyer if you're going to ask me questions?" The officer responds, "Sure, if you really think you need one." John replies, "Well, I guess I don't." He then confesses to the officer and later agreed with the prosecutor to plead guilty to a lesser charge. While awaiting sentencing, a cellmate informs him that he may have legally been hasty in his decision to voluntarily confess to the arson. Hank then requests legal representation and appeals his conviction. An appellate court reviewing the case will likely
- **(A)** Affirm, because he knowingly and voluntarily entered into a beneficial plea bargain agreement.
- **(B)** Reverse, because interrogation continued after he had invoked his right to counsel.
- **(C)** Reverse, because his waiver of the right to counsel during legal proceedings was not knowing and intelligent.
- **(D)** Affirm, because if the right to counsel at trial is not clearly invoked, it is deemed waived.

99. Tom is arrested and charged with vehicular homicide. Despite repeated explanations and warnings by the police and the prosecutor, he chooses to represent himself. During initial proceedings, the court questions Tom and discovers he has only an 8th grade education and no legal knowledge or experience. Over Tom's objections the court appoints counsel based on its reasonable belief that Tom is incapable of adequately representing himself. Tom is convicted. An appellate court will likely
- **(A)** Reverse, because Tom should have been allowed to represent himself.
- **(B)** Reverse, because Tom received ineffective assistance of counsel.
- **(C)** Affirm, because the decision to appoint counsel was harmless error.
- **(D)** Affirm, because the trial judge's decision adequately protected Tom's right to counsel.

100. Tim, while demonstrating the capabilities of his new assault rifle, and believing the rifle to be unloaded pulls the trigger. A single bullet discharges, passes through Mary's body and hits Jack killing them both. Tim is charged with the murder of both victims. Trial for the murder of Mary ends in a hung jury. Prior to the commencement of the trial for Jack's murder, defense counsel in the trial for the murder of Mary, moves for dismissal. The motion will likely be

(A) Granted, because double jeopardy attached after the jury was sworn in Mary's case.
(B) Granted, because Tim lacked the necessary intent for murder.
(C) Denied, because double jeopardy does not apply when the first trial ended in a hung jury.
(D) Denied, because the murder of each victim is a separate crime and double jeopardy does not apply.

101. Officer hears breaking glass and sees Stan run out of a darkened liquor store at 3 a.m. as the alarm blares. Stan runs around the corner, out of Officer's view, and hops into a car. Officer sees the car quickly speed away and pursues, lights flashing. Stan pulls over and Officer arrests him. Seeing nothing in the passenger compartment, Officer pries the trunk of the car open and finds cash and a baseball bat. Stan's motion to suppress the cash and baseball bat as evidence will likely be

(A) Denied, because the officer had probable cause to search the trunk.
(B) Denied, because a search incident to a valid arrest in an automobile always includes the trunk.
(C) Granted, because the trunk area was out of the range of Stan's control.
(D) Granted, because the arrest was illegal and therefore the evidence is fruit of the poisonous tree.

102. Bill commits a burglary and seems to get away with it. Two weeks later, the victim's brother, suspicious of Bill, comes to his house and threatens to kill Bill's daughter if Bill does not confess. Bill goes down to the police station and confesses. Bill's motion to suppress his confession will likely be

(A) Granted, because the confession was coerced.
(B) Granted, because no other evidence linking Bill to the crime existed aside from his confession.
(C) Denied, because the police were not involved in any coercion.
(D) Denied, because Bill's belief that the threat would be carried out was not reasonable.

103. Mike is arrested on suspicion of larceny. After receiving and acknowledging his *Miranda* rights from the police, he is questioned. When he refuses to confess, the officer tells him that he has connections in prison that could make Mike's life in there "very unpleasant" if he does not confess. Mike then confesses. At trial, the confession is not used in the prosecution's case-in-chief but is admitted to impeach his testimony that he has never stolen. On appeal, Mike's conviction will likely be

(A) Affirmed, because he confessed with full understanding of his right to remain silent, and that his statements could be used against him.
(B) Affirmed, because his conviction would probably have been secured regardless of the admittance of his confession, and the decision was harmless error.
(C) Affirmed, because the confession may be admitted to impeach.
(D) Reversed, because a coerced confession is never admissible.

104. In response to an informant's tip, the police go to Dan's house looking for illegal narcotics. Finding only Dan's 12-year-old daughter at home, the police ask her permission to come in and look around. She agrees, and upon entry, the officers find several types of narcotics and drug paraphernalia. At trial, Dan is convicted. In a post-trial motion, Dan argues to suppress the evidence as fruits of an illegal search. After hearing the evidence and arguments of both lawyers, the trial court denied the motion. Dan's appeal on the grounds that the search was illegal should be

    (A) Granted, because his daughter did not have authority to consent to the search and was too young to knowingly consent.

    (B) Granted, because a warrant should have been obtained.

    (C) Denied, because Dan had the opportunity for full and fair litigation of his 4th Amendment claim at the trial level.

    (D) Granted, because the trial court committed reversible error.

105. Michael's wife, Terry, is suffering from terminal end-stage cancer and is in terrible pain. Michael, Terry's sister Brenda, and the doctor discuss Terry's situation in the waiting room. Michael asks the doctor to turn up the intravenous drip of morphine to a lethal level. The doctor initially agrees; Brenda says nothing but nods. However, a few moments later the doctor changes his mind and tells Michael. Michael returns to Terry's room followed by Brenda and the doctor. Michael turns up the drip himself, as Brenda looks on. The doctor tries to restrain Michael and calls security. Terry dies as a result of the morphine overdose.

What is the most serious crime of which Michael can be convicted?

    (A) Involuntary manslaughter.

    (B) Voluntary manslaughter.

    (C) Murder.

    (D) None of the above.

106. Michael's wife, Terry, is suffering from terminal end-stage cancer and is in terrible pain. Michael, Terry's sister Brenda, and the doctor discuss Terry's situation in the waiting room. Michael asks the doctor to turn up the intravenous drip of morphine to a lethal level. The doctor initially agrees; Brenda says nothing but nods. However, a few moments later the doctor changes his mind and tells Michael. Michael returns to Terry's room followed by Brenda and the doctor. Michael turns up the drip himself, as Brenda looks on. The doctor tries to restrain Michael and calls security. Terry dies as a result of the morphine overdose.

In a Model Penal Code jurisdiction, what is the most serious crime of which the doctor can be convicted?

    (A) Attempted murder.

    (B) Conspiracy to commit murder.

    (C) Murder.

    (D) None of the above.

107. Michael's wife, Terry, is suffering from terminal end-stage cancer and is in terrible pain. Michael, Terry's sister Brenda, and the doctor discuss Terry's situation in the waiting room. Michael asks the doctor to turn up the intravenous drip of morphine to a lethal level. The doctor initially agrees; Brenda says nothing but nods. However, a few moments later the doctor changes his mind and tells Michael. Michael returns to Terry's room followed by Brenda and the doctor. Michael turns up the drip himself, as Brenda looks on. The doctor tries to restrain Michael and calls security. Terry dies as a result of the morphine overdose.

What is the most serious crime of which Brenda can be convicted?

    (A) Murder.

    (B) Attempted murder.

    (C) Conspiracy to commit murder.

    (D) None of the above.

108. Eddie (who has previously been twice convicted of bank robbery) convinces Zelda (who has no criminal record) to help him break into Dave's Discount Diamonds and take some jewelry to sell for cash. They enter at night through an open window in an adjacent apartment building and steal $14,000 worth of necklaces, earrings, etc., from the store. Three days later, a police department informant with a 5% history of accuracy tells Officer Briggs that Zelda has stolen jewelry in her apartment. Briggs asks a judge for a search warrant, which is issued. Briggs goes to Zelda's apartment and knocks. Zelda answers and Briggs declares that he has a warrant and is there to search the apartment. He searches the entire apartment, finally finding the jewelry in the freezer. Zelda immediately confesses, but claims that Eddie planned the crime and threatened to kill Zelda's daughter, who was in the next room, if Zelda didn't participate.

On these facts, if Eddie is charged with burglary he will most likely be

(A) Convicted.
(B) Acquitted, because the window was open, so he did not break into the store.
(C) Acquitted, because he did not have intent to commit a felony inside.
(D) Acquitted, because he did not enter a dwelling.

109. Eddie (who has previously been twice convicted of bank robbery) convinces Zelda (who has no criminal record) to help him break into Dave's Discount Diamonds and take some jewelry to sell for cash. They enter at night through an open window in an adjacent apartment building and steal $14,000 worth of necklaces, earrings, etc., from the store. Three days later, a police department informant with a 5% history of accuracy tells Officer Briggs that Zelda has stolen jewelry in her apartment. Briggs asks a judge for a search warrant, which is issued. Briggs goes to Zelda's apartment and knocks. Zelda answers and Briggs declares that he has a warrant and is there to search the apartment. He searches the entire apartment, finally

finding the jewelry in the freezer. Zelda immediately confesses, but claims that Eddie planned the crime and threatened to kill Zelda's daughter, who was in the next room, if Zelda didn't participate.

At trial, Zelda moves for the jewelry to be excluded as evidence because it was obtained due to an improper search. Her best argument in support of her motion is

(A) She did not receive *Miranda* warnings before the search was conducted.
(B) She did not consent to the search.
(C) There was insufficient probable cause for the warrant.
(D) The search was outside the scope of the warrant.

110. Eddie (who has previously been twice convicted of bank robbery) convinces Zelda (who has no criminal record) to help him break into Dave's Discount Diamonds and take some jewelry to sell for cash. They enter at night through an open window in an adjacent apartment building and steal $14,000 worth of necklaces, earrings, etc., from the store. Three days later, a police department informant with a 5% history of accuracy tells Officer Briggs that Zelda has stolen jewelry in her apartment. Briggs asks a judge for a search warrant, which is issued. Briggs goes to Zelda's apartment and knocks. Zelda answers and Briggs declares that he has a warrant and is there to search the apartment. He searches the entire apartment, finally finding the jewelry in the freezer. Zelda immediately confesses, but claims that Eddie planned the crime and threatened to kill Zelda's daughter, who was in the next room, if Zelda didn't participate.

Zelda's defense at trial is that she committed the crime under duress. This defense will likely

(A) Fail, because the threat of harm was not immediate.
(B) Fail, because duress is not available when the crime charged is burglary.
(C) Fail, because the threat of harm was not against Zelda herself.
(D) Succeed.

111. Slick and Stan are in an automobile collision. Slick gets out of his car and runs over to Stan's car, knocking on the window. Stan rolls down his window and Slick screams profanities, shaking his fist. Stan gets out of his car and Slick, seeing Stan's immense stature, backs away toward his own car and tries to get back into it. Stan grabs Slick by the collar and slaps him across the ear. Slick yelps and gets back in his car. If charged with battery, Stan will likely be

(A) Convicted, because he intentionally engaged in a harmful touching.

(B) Acquitted, because Slick was the first aggressor and Stan was acting in self-defense.

(C) Acquitted, because the physical harm to Slick was minor and temporary.

(D) Acquitted, because Slick's aggressive behavior created an assumption of risk of offensive bodily contact.

112. During Tom's trial for robbery, two witnesses testified. Nancy, the victim, stated that Tom pulled a gun on her from behind and said "hand over your purse or I'll kill you" and then grabbed her purse off her shoulder and ran. A passerby testified that Tom ran up from behind, grabbed the purse and ran, but that no weapon or threats were used. Tom can possibly be convicted of

(A) Either robbery or larceny.

(B) Larceny only.

(C) Neither robbery nor larceny.

(D) Both robbery and larceny.

113. Bryce owns a liquor store in the State of Atley, which has a criminal statute making it a strict liability offense to sell alcohol to anyone under the age of 21. Bryce hires Ben to work as cashier. Mel, who is 17, comes in and asks to purchase alcohol. Ben asks to see Mel's identification. Mel shows Ben a phony driver's license. Ben glances at it and sells Mel a six pack of beer. If charged with sale of alcohol to a minor, Ben will likely be

(A) Convicted, because he failed to take the proper steps to ensure that Mel was 21.

(B) Acquitted, because Bryce as the owner of the store is solely responsible.

(C) Acquitted, because Ben believed the identification to be genuine.

(D) Convicted, because Ben made the sale and Mel was underage.

114. Detective Johns received information from Taylor, a police informant who had given reliable information in the past, that Wanda had a large amount of the narcotic PCP in her house. Taylor specified that he knew Wanda socially, and that six weeks prior, he had been at Wanda's home and seen the drugs there, inside a large wooden chest in the living room. Detective Johns, upon inquiry, discovered that Taylor did in fact know Wanda. Johns drew up an affidavit specifying half a kilo of PCP was on the premises, went before a neutral magistrate, and got a search warrant. The next day, in Wanda's house, inside of a shoebox in a basement closet, Johns found a small amount of PCP and a baggie of marijuana.

The warrant procured by Johns is likely

(A) Valid, because it was based on reliable information from a reliable informant.

(B) Valid, because the magistrate was impartial.

(C) Invalid, because there was no corroboration of the informant's claims.

(D) Invalid, because the information was too remote in time to justify a finding of probable cause.

115. Detective Johns received information from Taylor, a police informant who had given reliable information in the past, that Wanda had a large amount of the narcotic PCP in her house. Taylor specified that he knew Wanda socially, and that six weeks prior, he had been at Wanda's home and seen the drugs there, inside a large wooden chest in the living room. Detective Johns, upon inquiry, discovered that Taylor did in fact know Wanda. Johns drew up an affidavit specifying half a kilo of PCP was on the premises, went before a neutral magistrate, and got a search warrant. The next day, in Wanda's house, inside of a shoebox in a basement closet, Johns found a small amount of PCP and a baggie of marijuana.

Assuming the warrant is valid, what is the best argument Wanda could make that the search was improper?

- (A) The warrant was not executed without delay.
- (B) The shoebox was outside the scope of the warrant.
- (C) A warrant alone is not sufficient to search a residence; the officer must also have consent.
- (D) The PCP did not belong to Wanda, but to her brother.

116. In the State of Woollahra, a statute defines bribery as "the offer and acceptance of money in exchange for the consideration of a public official in the course of his or her duties." Belinda, a lobbyist for the Save the Spotted Owl Society, offers Sophie, a Senator, a $500 "campaign contribution" to vote yes on an important legislative bill. Sophie takes the money without comment, but then votes no on the bill. Both Belinda and Sophie are charged with bribery and conspiracy to commit bribery. Sophie will likely be

- (A) Acquitted, because she did not vote yes and so there is no proof of conspiracy.
- (B) Convicted, because an agreement was made and money was exchanged, which is a substantial step in furtherance.
- (C) Acquitted, because bribery as defined by the statute requires the agreement of two persons.
- (D) Convicted, because she considered Belinda's request and took the money.

117. Q and R are hanging out at Q's house looking at Q's rifles. Q, intending only to demonstrate the action on his newest rifle acquisition, fires a shot toward his neighbor's yard, even though he knows his neighbor is at home and likely to be out in his yard. The bullet hits S, a water meter reader in the neighbor's yard. What is the most serious crime of which Q can be convicted?

- (A) Murder.
- (B) Voluntary manslaughter.
- (C) Involuntary manslaughter.
- (D) Q cannot be convicted.

118. Q and R are hanging out at Q's house looking at Q's rifles. Q, intending only to demonstrate the action on his newest rifle acquisition, fires a shot toward his neighbor's yard, even though he knows his neighbor is at home and likely to be out in his yard. The bullet hits S, a water meter reader in the neighbor's yard. If Q had intended to shoot his neighbor, and shot the water meter reader by mistake, the appropriate charge would be

- (A) Murder.
- (B) Voluntary manslaughter.
- (C) Involuntary manslaughter.
- (D) Negligent homicide.

119. Tim shoplifts a candy bar from a convenience store, in full view of a video camera. Officer Bevis is watching and follows Tim out of the store and down the street. Just as Tim gets home and closes his front door, Bevis knocks on it. Tim opens the door and Bevis arrests him. Upon searching Tim's home, Bevis finds an empty candy bar wrapper but no receipt.

Tim's argument that the warrantless arrest was unlawful will likely
- (A) Fail because he committed a misdemeanor in an officer's presence.
- (B) Succeed, because Bevis did not knock and announce his intentions.
- (C) Succeed, because once a suspect is home a warrant is always required.
- (D) Fail, because Bevis had an articulable suspicion.

120. Tim shoplifts a candy bar from a convenience store, in full view of a video camera. Officer Bevis is watching and follows Tim out of the store and down the street. Tim gets home and closes his front door, Bevis knocks on it. Tim opens the door and Bevis arrests him. Upon searching Tim's person, Bevis finds an empty candy bar wrapper but no receipt.

If Tim loses his argument that his arrest was unlawful, his motion to exclude the candy bar wrapper as incriminating evidence will likely be
- (A) Granted, because an officer may only pat-down for weapons incident to an arrest
- (B) Granted, because Officer Bevis could not have specified the location of the candy bar wrapper prior to the search.
- (C) Denied, because a full bodily search is usually permissible incident to a lawful arrest.
- (D) Granted, because Officer Bevis did not have a reasonable apprehension of danger.

121. Officer Stevens properly obtained a warrant to search the home of Trey Parkins looking for cocaine. After a thorough home search turned up nothing, Stevens noticed a mobile home, parked 500 feet from Parkins' house. Stevens called in the license number and learned the mobile home was owned by Parkins. He searched the mobile home and found heroin.

A motion to suppress the heroin as evidence should be
- (A) Denied, because the mobile home was an adjacent outbuilding.
- (B) Granted, because the mobile home was outside the scope of the warrant.
- (C) Granted, because heroin was not specified in the warrant as an item to be seized.
- (D) Denied, because Parkins owned the mobile home.

122. Officer Stevens properly obtained a warrant to search the home of Trey Parkins looking for cocaine. After a thorough home search turned up nothing, Stevens noticed a mobile home, parked 500 feet from Parkins' house. Stevens called in the license number and learned the mobile home was owned by Parkins. He searched the mobile home and found heroin.

During the motion to suppress hearing, it is revealed that the search occurred 35 days after the warrant was obtained. This presents a problem for the prosecution primarily because
- (A) The case will be dismissed because the Sixth Amendment right to a speedy trial has been violated.
- (B) It conclusively establishes a presumption of police misconduct that the jury must consider.
- (C) It means that the defense may argue police misconduct to the jury in closing arguments.
- (D) All of the evidence obtained as a result of the warrant is now probably fruit of the poisonous tree.

123. In a jurisdiction governed by the Model Penal Code, Ted and Sandra go on vacation, leaving their 10-year-old daughter Lea in charge of the house and their 9-month-old infant. While they are away, the infant becomes ill. The illness is treatable, but Lea ignores the baby's cries and watches TV. The infant dies of fever.

Ted and Sandra are charged with negligent homicide. It is likely that
- (A) The case will be dismissed because the MPC does not impose criminal liability for negligence, only tort liability.
- (B) They will be acquitted, because the prosecution will not be able to prove that Ted and Sandra were practically certain that their act would result in the death of their infant.
- (C) They will be convicted, because their actions were a substantial and significant departure from the ordinary standard of due care.
- (D) They will be convicted, because child neglect is a strict liability crime.

124. In a jurisdiction governed by the Model Penal Code, Ted and Sandra go on vacation, leaving their 10-year-old daughter Lea in charge of the house and their 9-month-old infant. While they are away, the infant becomes ill. The illness is treatable, but Lea ignores the baby's cries and watches TV. The infant dies of fever.

If Lea is charged with criminally negligent homicide, she will likely be
- (A) Convicted, unless the defense can prove by clear and convincing evidence that she did not know her actions were wrong.
- (B) Acquitted, unless the prosecution can prove by clear and convincing evidence that she knew her actions were wrong.
- (C) Acquitted, because she is conclusively presumed incapable of forming the intent to commit a crime.

- (D) Acquitted, unless the prosecution can prove beyond a reasonable doubt that she knew her actions were wrong.

125. In a jurisdiction governed by the Model Penal Code, Ted and Sandra go on vacation, leaving their 10-year-old daughter Lea in charge of the house and their 9 month old infant. While they are away, the infant becomes ill. The illness is treatable, but Lea ignores the baby's cries and watches TV. The infant dies of fever.

Ted confesses to the police. Sandra requests her own lawyer and moves for a separate trial. The motion should be
- (A) Denied, because she cannot establish any facts that distinguish her case from Ted's.
- (B) Denied, in the interests of judicial economy.
- (C) Granted, because two defendants can never be tried together if their interests conflict in any way.
- (D) Granted, because Ted's confession jeopardizes Sandra's interests.

126. A criminal statute in the State of Nalya makes it a gross misdemeanor to sell firearms to anyone under 18. Violators are strictly liable for the crime. Pete's Gun Emporiorama has a strict policy to check for identification before making any sale. Bubba works at Pete's, but routinely fails to check for identification of young-looking people. The owner Pete has knowledge of Bubba's transgressions, but does not take any action to remedy the situation. One afternoon, Bubba comes in to work after a lunch consisting of a six-pack of beer. At work, he sneaks another two beers and promptly passes out behind the counter. Dale, who is 14, comes in to the store and sees Bubba's condition. He takes a $500 handgun out of the unlocked case and, misreading the sign, leaves $50 cash on the counter, thinking it is payment in full.

Bubba is arrested for violating the statute. He will likely be

(A) Acquitted, because he lacked the requisite intent.
(B) Convicted, because voluntary intoxication is never a defense.
(C) Acquitted, because he did not perform the *actus reus*.
(D) Convicted, because the statute makes this a strict liability crime.

127. A criminal statute in the State of Nalya makes it a gross misdemeanor to sell firearms to anyone under 18. Violators are strictly liable for the crime. Pete's Gun Emporiorama has a strict policy to check for identification before making any sale. Bubba works at Pete's, but routinely fails to check for identification of young-looking people. The owner Pete has knowledge of Bubba's transgressions, but does not take any action to remedy the situation. One afternoon, Bubba comes in to work after a lunch consisting of a six-pack of beer. At work, he sneaks another two beers and promptly passes out behind the counter. Dale, who is 14, comes in to the store and sees Bubba's condition. He takes a $500 handgun out of the unlocked case and, misreading the sign, leaves $50 cash on the counter, thinking it is payment in full. Dale is charged with larceny. His best defense is

(A) He was mistaken as to the price, which negated the "trespassory" element of larceny.
(B) As a minor, he was legally incapable of forming the necessary intent.
(C) He was under duress because his friend Xavier told him if he didn't get a gun, Xavier would wreck his car.
(D) The gun did not work and therefore was not worth $5, let alone $500.

128. A criminal statute in the State of Nalya makes it a gross misdemeanor to sell firearms to anyone under 18. Violators are strictly liable for the crime. Pete's Gun Emporiorama has a strict policy to check for identification before making any sale. Bubba works at Pete's, but routinely fails to check for identification of young-looking people. The owner Pete has knowledge of Bubba's transgressions, but does not take any action to remedy the situation. One afternoon, Bubba comes in to work after a lunch consisting of a six-pack of beer. At work, he sneaks another two beers and promptly passes out behind the counter. Dale, who is 14, comes in to the store and sees Bubba's condition. He takes a $500 handgun out of the unlocked case and, misreading the sign, leaves $50 cash on the counter, thinking it is payment in full.

Pete is arrested and charged with violating the gun sale statute. He will likely be

(A) Acquitted, because he was unaware of the existence of the statute.
(B) Convicted, because he knew of Bubba's transgressions and failed to supervise Bubba, which led to the violation.
(C) Convicted, because as the owner of the shop he is responsible for the "sale."
(D) Acquitted, because the statute only imposes liability for the act of a sale.

129. A criminal statute in the State of Nalya makes it a gross misdemeanor to sell firearms to anyone under 18. Violators are strictly liable for the crime. Pete's Gun Emporiorama has a strict policy to check for identification before making any sale. Bubba works at Pete's, but routinely fails to check for identification of young-looking people. The owner Pete has knowledge of Bubba's transgressions, but does not take any action to remedy the situation. One afternoon, Bubba comes in to work after a lunch consisting of a six-pack of beer. At work, he sneaks another two beers and promptly passes out behind the counter. Dale, who is 14, comes in to the store and sees Bubba's condition. He takes a $500 handgun out of the unlocked case and, misreading the sign, leaves $50 cash on the counter, thinking it is payment in full.

If Dale is acquitted on the larceny charge, then re-arrested and charged with violation of the gun sale statute, he will likely be

(A) Acquitted, because the statute only criminalizes the sale and says nothing about the purchase.
(B) Convicted, because he is strictly liable for violating the statute.
(C) Acquitted, because double jeopardy prevents prosecution of the misdemeanor.
(D) Acquitted, because he was acquitted on the larceny charge.

130. Cisco and Hopalong are sitting in a coffee shop. Cisco says, "Hey, wanna know how we can make some fast money?" Hopalong says, "Sure, lay it on me." Cisco says, "I know where this rich dude's kid goes to school, out at Westside. We can grab him outside and hang on to him until the old man pays up big." Hopalong frowns and says, "No way. I'm on parole. Find another toady." Hopalong then leaves, but Cisco decides to do the job anyway.

That afternoon, as Cisco is waiting outside the school, Hopalong shows up. They nod at each other quickly. Cisco shifts his eyes toward a young boy, and Hopalong pulls him into the van. They drive into a far corner of the school parking lot and wait.

Cisco makes a call on his cellular phone to the boy's father and demands a ransom. Much to their dismay, however, when they put the boy on the phone to prove they have him, they realize they have grabbed the wrong child. They quickly hang up the phone and release the boy. However, the father has caller ID and Cisco and Hopalong are quickly apprehended.

Hopalong and Cisco are both charged with kidnapping the boy. They will likely be

(A) Acquitted, because they did not move the boy to a different location.
(B) Convicted.
(C) Acquitted, because their mistake as to the boy's identity negated their intent to kidnap him.
(D) Acquitted, because they only held the boy for a brief period.

131. Cisco and Hopalong are sitting in a coffee shop. Cisco says, "Hey, wanna know how we can make some fast money?" Hopalong says, "Sure, lay it on me." Cisco says, "I know where this rich dude's kid goes to school, out at Westside. We can grab him outside and hang on to him until the old man pays up big." Hopalong frowns and says, "No way. I'm on parole. Find another toady." Hopalong then leaves, but Cisco decides to do the job anyway.

That afternoon, as Cisco is waiting outside the school, Hopalong shows up. They nod at each other quickly. Cisco shifts his eyes toward a young boy, and Hopalong pulls him into the van. They drive into a far corner of the school parking lot and wait. Cisco makes a call on his cellular phone to the boy's father and demands a ransom. Much to their dismay, however, when they put the boy on the phone to prove they have him, they realize they have grabbed the wrong child. They quickly hang up the phone and release the boy. However, the father has caller ID and Cisco and Hopalong are quickly apprehended.

Hopalong and Cisco are also both charged with conspiracy to commit kidnapping. They will likely be

(A) Convicted, since they had a tacit agreement to commit the crime.

(B) Acquitted, since they made no agreement prior to the act.

(C) Acquitted, because conspiracy merges with the completed crime.

(D) Convicted, since two of them were involved.

132. Cisco and Hopalong are sitting in a coffee shop. Cisco says, "Hey, wanna know how we can make some fast money?" Hopalong says, "Sure, lay it on me." Cisco says, "I know where this rich dude's kid goes to school, out at Westside. We can grab him outside and hang on to him until the old man pays up big." Hopalong frowns and says, "No way. I'm on parole. Find another toady." Hopalong then leaves, but Cisco decides to do the job anyway.

That afternoon, as Cisco is waiting outside the school, Hopalong shows up. They nod at each other quickly. Cisco shifts his eyes toward a young boy, and Hopalong pulls him into the van. They drive into a far corner of the school parking lot and wait. Cisco makes a call on his cellular phone to the boy's father and demands a ransom. Much to their dismay, however, when they put the boy on the phone to prove they have him, they realize they have grabbed the wrong child. They quickly hang up the phone and release the boy. However, the father has caller ID and Cisco and Hopalong are quickly apprehended.

Hopalong is also charged with battery. By state statute, offensive touching is not recognized as a form of battery. Hopalong's best defense would be

(A) The boy did not feel any apprehension.

(B) He did not have the specific intent to harm the boy.

(C) He did not inflict any physical harm.

(D) Battery is a lesser included offense of kidnapping.

133. Aaron fires a shotgun into a dwelling at night, killing someone sleeping inside. He is charged with murder. He may succeed in having the charge reduced from second degree murder to involuntary manslaughter by arguing

(A) The victim was a trespasser who assumed the risk.

(B) He believed the house to be abandoned.

(C) He was intoxicated and failed to form the requisite intent.

(D) He did not have specific intent to kill.

134. Beaker is a veteran police officer of 20 years. One night while off duty, he is pulled over. He consents to the standard battery of intoxication tests including a blood alcohol test, which comes back above the legal limit. Beaker is arrested for drunk driving. As the officer puts the handcuffs on, he says, "You know the routine. Do I have to go through it?" Beaker says, "No, I'm quite familiar, thanks." The officer then questions him and says, "You know Honeydew (the prosecutor). If you admit it, he'll probably cut you a break." Beaker then confesses.

Beaker's motion to suppress the confession should be

(A) Denied, because he acknowledged and voluntarily waived his *Miranda* rights, and his statement was voluntary.

(B) Denied, because it could be demonstrated by a preponderance of the evidence that he was familiar with the *Miranda* warnings.

(C) Granted, because his confession was coerced.

(D) Granted, because the *Miranda* warnings were not read.

135. Beaker is a veteran police officer of 20 years. One night while off duty, he is pulled over. He consents to the standard battery of intoxication tests including a blood alcohol test, which comes back above the legal limit. Beaker is arrested for drunk driving. As the officer puts the handcuffs on, he says, "You know the routine. Do I have to go through it?" Beaker says, "No, I'm quite familiar, thanks." The officer then questions him and says, "You know Honeydew (the prosecutor). If you admit it, he'll probably cut you a break." Beaker then confesses.

Beaker also moves to suppress the blood alcohol content (BAC) test administered at the scene as fruits of the poisonous tree. That motion should be

(A) Denied, because Beaker consented to the test and it was administered prior to the arrest.
(B) Denied, because only the confession itself is inadmissible; physical evidence obtained as a result of an illegal confession is admissible.
(C) Granted, because blood alcohol tests are inherently unreliable.
(D) Granted, if Beaker had strong evidence indicating that he had not been drinking.

136. Ted and Daniel are at a restaurant. Mitch approaches from behind and, thinking Ted is someone else, he playfully reaches out to smack Ted lightly on the shoulder. Ted has Mitch arrested for battery. On these facts, Mitch will likely be

(A) Convicted, because he intentionally slapped Ted, an offensive touching.
(B) Convicted, because there is an eyewitness and battery is a strict liability offense.
(C) Acquitted, because Mitch's mistake as to Ted's identity negates the *mens rea*.
(D) Acquitted, because the slap was not serious enough to cause pain.

137. Tanya has a plan to get rid of both her troublesome husband and her demanding boyfriend and make some easy money in the process. First, she takes out a hefty life insurance policy on her husband, with herself as the beneficiary. The policy states that the proceeds will not be paid in the event that the beneficiary causes the death. She then calls her boyfriend who comes over while her husband is out. Tanya tells her

boyfriend, "Hey, if you really want us to be together, I know a way. Take these shears and cut the brake line in his car. By the time he gets to the bottom of the hill, our troubles will be over." The boyfriend hesitates, and Tanya says if he doesn't agree, she will kill herself. He then agrees.

The boyfriend waits in the bushes until the husband returns, cuts the brake line, and leaves. The next day, the husband is killed when his brakes fail as he drives down the steep hill from his house. The police rule the death an accident, and Tanya applies for and receives the insurance proceeds. She then tells the police that she suspects someone murdered her husband. She gives them the shears and name of her boyfriend. Betrayed, the boyfriend confesses and tells the entire story. Tanya is arrested.

As to the death of her husband, Tanya could potentially be convicted of

(A) Murder.
(B) Conspiracy and murder.
(C) Solicitation, conspiracy, and murder.
(D) Solicitation and conspiracy only.

138. Tanya has a plan to get rid of both her troublesome husband and her demanding boyfriend and make some easy money in the process. First, she takes out a hefty life insurance policy on her husband, with herself as the beneficiary. The policy states that the proceeds will not be paid in the event that the beneficiary causes the death. She then calls her boyfriend who comes over while her husband is out. Tanya tells her boyfriend, "Hey, if you really want us to be together, I know a way. Take these shears and cut the brake line in his car. By the time he gets to the bottom of the hill, our troubles will be over." The boyfriend hesitates, and Tanya says if he doesn't agree, she will kill herself. He then agrees.

The boyfriend cuts all the lines below the car he could find. The next day, the husband is killed when his brakes fail as he drives down the steep hill from his house. The police rule the death an accident, and Tanya applies for and receives the insurance proceeds. She then tells the police that she suspects someone murdered her husband. She gives them the shears and name of her boyfriend. Betrayed, the boyfriend confesses and tells the entire story. Tanya is arrested.

The boyfriend's best defense to a murder charge would be

(A) He did not think that the husband would actually be killed in the collision.

(B) He was under duress as a result of Tanya's threat to harm herself.

(C) He is only 17.

(D) He actually cut the line to the air conditioning, not the brakes.

139. Tanya has a plan to get rid of both her troublesome husband and her demanding boyfriend and make some easy money in the process. First, she takes out a hefty life insurance policy on her husband, with herself as the beneficiary. The policy states that the proceeds will not be paid in the event that the beneficiary causes the death. She then calls her boyfriend who comes over while her husband is out. Tanya tells her boyfriend, "Hey, if you really want us to be together, I know a way. Take these shears and cut the brake line in his car. By the time he gets to the bottom of the hill, our troubles will be over." The boyfriend hesitates, and Tanya says if he doesn't agree, she will kill herself. He then agrees.

The boyfriend waits in the bushes until the husband returns, cuts the brake line, and leaves. The next day, the husband is killed when his brakes fail as he drives down the steep hill from his house. The police rule the death an accident, and Tanya applies for and receives the insurance proceeds. She then tells the police that she suspects someone murdered her husband. She gives them the shears and name of her boyfriend. Betrayed, the boyfriend confesses and tells the entire story. Tanya is arrested.

The insurance company could press charges against Tanya for

(A) False pretenses.

(B) Embezzlement.

(C) Larceny.

(D) Larceny by trick.

140. Tanya has a plan to get rid of both her troublesome husband and her demanding boyfriend and make some easy money in the process. First, she takes out a hefty life insurance policy on her husband, with herself as the beneficiary. The policy states that the proceeds will not be paid in the event that the beneficiary causes the death. She then calls her boyfriend who comes over while her husband is out. Tanya tells her boyfriend, "Hey, if you really want us to be together, I know a way. Take these shears and cut the brake line in his car. By the time he gets to the bottom of the hill, our troubles will be over." The boyfriend hesitates, and Tanya says if he doesn't agree, she will kill herself. He then agrees.

The boyfriend waits in the bushes until the husband returns, cuts the brake line, and leaves. The next day, the husband is killed when his brakes fail as he drives down the steep hill from his house. The police rule the death an accident, and Tanya applies for and receives the insurance proceeds. She then tells the police that she suspects someone murdered her husband. She gives them the shears and name of her boyfriend. Betrayed, the boyfriend confesses and tells the entire story. Tanya is arrested.

Unbeknownst to Tanya, her husband had been secretly tape-recording the goings-on in the house because he suspected her of having an extra-marital affair and plotting his death. The police find the tape recorder and seize it. Tanya's motion to suppress the recording of her conversation with her boyfriend about the killing should be

(A) Granted, because neither party to the conversation consented to having it recorded.

(B) Granted, because tape recordings are never admissible evidence.

(C) Denied, because Tanya had no legitimate expectation of privacy.

(D) Denied, because her husband made the recording.

141. Jamie and Franz are enjoying a quiet evening at home upstairs in their spacious 10-bedroom mansion. Suddenly, Jamie hears a noise downstairs. Franz goes to check it out and comes back saying he saw a man creeping around downstairs in the dark. Jamie says, "Let's take the back stairs and go to the neighbors' house." Franz grabs his gun and says, "No way, I'll see what's going on." Franz heads downstairs and finds the man in the kitchen. He calls out, "Hey, what are you doing?" The man turns around with something in his hand that looks like a gun. Franz shoots the man in the chest and he dies almost instantly. When Franz turns on the light, he realizes to his horror that the man was holding a zucchini – he was unarmed and looking for food.

Franz could be charged with
(A) First degree murder.
(B) Second degree murder.
(C) Involuntary manslaughter.
(D) None of the above.

142. Jamie and Franz are enjoying a quiet evening at home upstairs in their spacious 10-bedroom mansion. Suddenly, Jamie hears a noise downstairs. Franz goes to check it out and comes back saying he saw a man creeping around downstairs in the dark. Jamie says, "Let's take the back stairs and go to the neighbors' house." Franz grabs his gun and says, "No way, I'll see what's going on." Franz heads downstairs and finds the man in the kitchen. He calls out, "Hey, what are you doing?" The man turns around with something in his hand that looks to Franz like a gun. Franz shoots the man in the chest and he dies almost instantly. When Franz turns on the light, he realizes that the man was holding a zucchini – he was unarmed and just looking for food.

Franz argues self-defense. In a jurisdiction governed by the MPC, his defense will likely

(A) Succeed, because he was defending in his own home and his mistake about the weapon was honest and reasonable.
(B) Succeed, because self-defense is conclusively presumed when one is threatened in one's own home.
(C) Fail, because he did not retreat when Jamie suggested it.
(D) Succeed, because the amount of force used was reasonable.

143. Heidi is schizophrenic. She often sees people and hears voices that are not there telling her to do things that she knows are wrong. One day she hears a voice tell her, "If you don't burn down that bank across the street, you're going to die." Heidi cannot resist the voice but waits until the bank closes so that at least no one will be killed. She throws a firebomb in the window and the building goes up in flames. Unbeknown to Heidi a night watchman is trapped inside and dies.

Heidi will have an insanity defense in a jurisdiction governed by
(A) *M'Naghten*
(B) Irresistible impulse
(C) Irresistible impulse and MPC Substantial Capacity
(D) MPC Substantial Capacity only.

144. Heidi is schizophrenic. She often sees people and hears voices that are not there telling her to do things that she knows are wrong. One day she hears a voice tell her, "If you don't burn down that bank across the street, you're going to die." Heidi cannot resist the voice but waits until the bank closes so that at least no one will be killed. She throws a firebomb in the window and the building goes up in flames. Unbeknown to Heidi a night watchman is trapped inside and dies.

If her insanity defense is unsuccessful, Heidi will likely be convicted of
(A) Arson.
(B) Arson and murder.
(C) Arson and manslaughter.
(D) Manslaughter.

145. Heidi is schizophrenic. She often sees people and hears voices that are not there telling her to do things that she knows are wrong. One day she hears a voice tell her, "If you don't burn down that bank across the street, you're going to die." Heidi cannot resist the voice but waits until the bank closes so that at least no one will be killed. She throws a firebomb in the window and the building goes up in flames. Unbeknown to Heidi a night watchman is trapped inside and dies.

Heidi requests a 12-person jury, but her request is refused by the judge. The judge's decision is
  (A) Proper, because there is no constitutional right to a 12-person jury and the defendant has a right to be in the proceeding.
  (B) Improper, because a defendant in a capital case has the right to a 12-person jury.
  (C) Improper, because a jury request may not be refused for any reason.
  (D) Proper, because there is no absolute constitutional right to a jury trial.

146. Kylie is 15 but looks older and has a fake driver's license that states she is 21. She approaches Ben in a bar and strikes up a conversation. They hit it off and begin dating. After six dates, Ben suggests they have sexual intercourse, which they do. Kylie's mother discovers the relationship and confronts her. Kylie denies that she consented, and her mother calls Ben. He is shocked and dismayed to learn her true age, and truthfully insists that he had no idea she was underage. Ben is charged with statutory rape. He will likely be
  (A) Convicted, because he was reckless in having intercourse without verifying her age.
  (B) Convicted, because Kylie did not consent.
  (C) Acquitted, because he made an honest, reasonable mistake of fact about Kylie's age.
  (D) Convicted, because he is strictly liable.

147. Tamara is an epileptic. She must take her medicine regularly to avoid seizures. One afternoon, she is in a hurry to beat the traffic out of town and leaves the house without taking her medication on time, figuring she can take it at the first rest stop. She gets on the freeway and suddenly blacks out. When Tamara awakens, she is in the hospital. Her father tells her she had a seizure while driving and collided with another vehicle, killing the driver.

Tamara is charged with vehicular manslaughter. She will likely be
  (A) Convicted, because she was reckless in driving without taking her medication.
  (B) Convicted, because she failed to act when she had a legal duty.
  (C) Acquitted, because she lacked the proper *mens rea* for manslaughter.
  (D) Acquitted, because she acted involuntarily and thus is not culpable.

148. Tamara is an epileptic. She must take her medicine regularly to avoid seizures. One afternoon, she is in a hurry to beat the traffic out of town and leaves the house without taking her medication on time, figuring she can take it at the first rest stop. She gets on the freeway and suddenly blacks out. When Tamara awakens, she is in the hospital. Her father tells her she had a seizure while driving and collided with another vehicle, killing the driver.

While in the hospital and being administered medication, Tamara has another attack. The nurse comes in to restrain her, and Tamara's arm jerks and hits the nurse across the face, breaking his nose. Tamara is charged with battery of the nurse. She will likely be
  (A) Convicted, because battery is a strict liability crime.
  (B) Acquitted, because there is no causation.
  (C) Acquitted, because she acted involuntarily.
  (D) Acquitted, because Tamara acted in self-defense.

149. Sanford, Byron, and Reese all own stores down near the waterfront receiving docks. Sanford hears about a shipment of brand-new clock radios that has just been received and decides to help himself to a few cases to boost his sagging appliance business. He tells Reese his plan; Reese says nothing. Sanford drives over to the docks late one night, and much to his surprise, boxes and boxes are just sitting on the docks. He loads his pickup truck with boxes. When he gets back to his store, however, he realizes that he has locked himself out. He parks the truck inside Byron's warehouse.

When Byron and Reese show up the next morning to open their stores, Sanford asks Byron if he would be willing to hang on to the radios until Sanford can find a locksmith. Byron asks him where the radios came from. Sanford says, "I took them from a shipment that came in last night." Byron thinks that Sanford means he ordered them and they were finally delivered. Reese, who knew beforehand what Sanford had planned, says nothing and goes into his own store. The police eventually track the missing radios to Byron's store.

Charged with receiving stolen goods, Byron will likely be
- (A) Convicted, because he had control of the goods.
- (B) Acquitted, because he did not know or have reason to know that the goods were stolen.
- (C) Acquitted, because he only planned to hold the goods temporarily.
- (D) Convicted, because he is strictly liable.

150. Sanford, Byron, and Reese all own stores down near the waterfront receiving docks. Sanford hears about a shipment of brand-new clock radios that has just been received and decides to help himself to a few cases to boost his sagging appliance business. He tells Reese his plan; Reese says nothing. Sanford drives over to the docks late one night, and much to his surprise, boxes and boxes are just sitting on the docks. He loads his pickup truck with boxes. When he gets back to his store, however, he realizes that he has locked himself out. He parks the truck inside Byron's warehouse.

When Byron and Reese show up the next morning to open their stores, Sanford asks Byron if he would be willing to hang on to the radios until Sanford can find a locksmith. Byron asks him where the radios came from. Sanford says, "I appropriated them from a shipment that came in last night." Byron thinks that Sanford means he ordered them and they were finally delivered. Reese, who knew beforehand what Sanford had planned, says nothing and goes into his own store. The police eventually track the missing radios to Byron's store.

Under an accomplice theory, Reese can be charged with
- (A) Larceny only.
- (B) Receiving stolen goods only.
- (C) Larceny and receiving stolen goods.
- (D) Nothing; Reese cannot be charged.

151. Sanford, Byron, and Reese all own stores down near the waterfront receiving docks. Sanford hears about a shipment of brand-new clock radios that has just been received and decides to help himself to a few cases to boost his sagging appliance business. He tells Reese his plan; Reese says nothing. Sanford drives over to the docks late one night, and much to his surprise, boxes and boxes are just sitting on the docks. He loads his pickup truck with boxes. When he gets back to his store, however, he realizes that he has locked himself out. He parks the truck inside Byron's warehouse.

When Byron and Reese show up the next morning to open their stores, Sanford asks Byron if he would be willing to hang on to the radios until Sanford can find a locksmith. Byron asks him where the radios came from. Sanford says, "I appropriated them from a shipment that came in last night." Byron thinks that Sanford means he ordered them and they were finally delivered. Reese, who knew beforehand what Sanford had planned, says nothing and goes into his own store.

The police eventually track the missing radios to Byron's store.

In addition to larceny, Sanford is also charged with solicitation (asking Byron to hold the goods). On the solicitation charge, Sanford will likely be
- (A) Convicted.
- (B) Acquitted, because the solicitation merged with the completed crime.
- (C) Acquitted, because what he asked Byron to do was not a crime.
- (D) Acquitted, because the solicitation was unsuccessful.

152. Sanford, Byron, and Reese all own stores down near the waterfront receiving docks. Sanford hears about a shipment of brand-new clock radios that has just been received and decides to help himself to a few cases to boost his sagging appliance business. He tells Reese his plan; Reese says nothing. Sanford drives over to the docks late one night, and much to his surprise, boxes and boxes are just sitting on the docks. He loads his pickup truck with boxes. When he gets back to his store, however, he realizes that he has locked himself out. He parks the truck inside Byron's warehouse.

When Byron and Reese show up the next morning to open their stores, Sanford asks Byron if he would be willing to hang on to the radios until Sanford can find a locksmith. Byron asks him where the radios came from. Sanford says, "I appropriated them from a shipment that came in last night." Byron thinks that Sanford means he ordered them and they were finally delivered. Reese, who knew beforehand what Sanford had planned, says nothing and goes into his own store. The police eventually track the missing radios to Byron's store.

As it turns out, the "shipment" of radios was actually part of a massive sting operation by the police and were just useless casings that had been discarded by the manufacturer. Sanford's best defense to the larceny charge would be

- (A) Entrapment.
- (B) Because the radios were discarded before the police got them, they were not in the possession of another.
- (C) He honestly and reasonably believed the radios were being given away, because they were just sitting on the docks.
- (D) He was under duress because his business was failing.

153. Sanford, Byron, and Reese all own stores down near the waterfront receiving docks. Sanford hears about a shipment of brand-new clock radios that has just been received and decides to help himself to a few cases to boost his sagging appliance business. He tells Reese his plan; Reese says nothing. Sanford drives over to the docks late one night, and much to his surprise, boxes and boxes are just sitting on the docks. He loads his pickup truck with boxes. When he gets back to his store, however, he realizes that he has locked himself out. He parks the truck inside Byron's warehouse.

When Byron and Reese show up the next morning to open their stores, Sanford asks Byron if he would be willing to hang on to the radios until Sanford can find a locksmith. Byron asks him where the radios came from. Sanford says, "I appropriated them from a shipment that came in last night." Byron thinks that Sanford means he ordered them and they were finally delivered. Reese, who knew beforehand what Sanford had planned, says nothing and goes into his own store. The police eventually track the missing radios to Byron's store.

Charged with larceny and receiving stolen goods under an accomplice theory, Reese will likely be
- (A) Convicted, because he knew and approved of both crimes.
- (B) Acquitted, because he took no action.
- (C) Convicted, because he assisted.
- (D) Acquitted, because an accomplice cannot be charged unless he specifically agrees to a crime.

154. Sarah and Kelly live and work in Waratah State, the penal code of which makes it a crime to "Knowingly buy, sell, transport, or distribute marijuana." The state courts have interpreted "distribute" as "disperse, share, or give." Sarah and Kelly have lockers next to each other at work. One day, Sarah notices that Kelly has a baggie in her locker of some dried green leafy substance. She asks Kelly about it; Kelly tells her the substance is marijuana. Kelly then asks Sarah if she would like to try some. Sarah refuses and starts to leave. Kelly says, "You better not say anything, or I'll flush it all down the toilet and you'll look like an idiot." Sarah tells her boss, who calls the police. They come and search Kelly's locker and arrest her after finding the baggie of marijuana.

Charged with violation of the penal code section mentioned above, Kelly will likely be

(A) Convicted, because she transported marijuana.
(B) Acquitted.
(C) Convicted, because she solicited Sarah.
(D) Convicted, because she possessed marijuana.

155. Sarah and Kelly live and work in Waratah State, the penal code of which makes it a crime to "Knowingly buy, sell, transport, or distribute marijuana." The state courts have interpreted "distribute" as "disperse, share, or give." Sarah and Kelly have lockers next to each other at work. One day, Sarah notices that Kelly has a baggie in her locker of some dried green leafy substance. She asks Kelly about it; Kelly tells her the substance is marijuana. Kelly then asks Sarah if she would like to try some. Sarah refuses and starts to leave. Kelly says, "You better not say anything, or I'll flush it all down the toilet and you'll look like an idiot." Sarah tells her boss, who calls the police. They come and search Kelly's locker and arrest her after finding the baggie of marijuana.

If the prosecutor wants to secure the severest possible sentence for Kelly, she may also charge

(A) Attempt to distribute and conspiracy to distribute.
(B) Attempt to distribute and solicitation.
(C) Solicitation only.
(D) Attempt to distribute, conspiracy to distribute, and solicitation.

156. Sarah and Kelly live and work in Waratah State, the penal code of which makes it a crime to "Knowingly buy, sell, transport, or distribute marijuana." The state courts have interpreted "distribute" as "disperse, share, or give." Sarah and Kelly have lockers next to each other at work. One day, Sarah notices that Kelly has a baggie in her locker of some dried green leafy substance. She asks Kelly about it; Kelly tells her the substance is marijuana. Kelly then asks Sarah if she would like to try some. Sarah refuses and starts to leave. Kelly says, "You better not say anything, or I'll flush it all down the toilet and you'll look like an idiot." Sarah tells her boss, who calls the police. They come and search Kelly's locker and arrest her after finding the baggie of marijuana.

Kelly moves to suppress the marijuana as evidence because it was obtained in violation of the Fourth Amendment. Her motion should be

(A) Denied, because there was probable cause and exigent circumstances.
(B) Denied, because her employer was the owner of the locker and could give valid consent to the search.
(C) Granted, because she had a legitimate expectation of privacy.
(D) Granted, because the police should have obtained a warrant.

157. Stedman plans to kidnap Susie. He follows her for weeks, learning her routine. He buys chain and padlocks. He prepares a room in his home to use as a holding pen; he soundproofs it and boards up all the windows. He waits in an alley with his van late one evening as Susie is leaving work. He waits for her to walk by, and when she does, he runs up behind her and grabs her. But hearing his footsteps, Susie had time to grab her pepper spray. She blasts him in the face and runs for it. Stedman does not run after her. He decides it is too much trouble and goes home.

Charged with kidnapping, Stedman will likely be
- (A) Convicted, because he had intent, and confined the victim.
- (B) Convicted, because a victim's escape does not negate the act of kidnapping.
- (C) Acquitted, because he abandoned his crime and turned himself in.
- (D) Acquitted, because the prosecution cannot prove result.

158. Stedman plans to kidnap Susie. He follows her for weeks, learning her routine. He buys chain and padlocks. He prepares a room in his home to use as a holding pen; he soundproofs it and boards up all the windows. He waits in an alley with his van late one evening as Susie is leaving work. He waits for her to walk by, and when she does, he runs up behind her and grabs her. But hearing his footsteps, Susie had time to grab her pepper spray. She blasts him in the face and runs for it. Stedman does not run after her. He decides it is too much trouble and goes home.

However, if charged, Stedman will likely be convicted of
- (A) Attempted battery assault, attempted kidnapping, and battery.
- (B) Attempted kidnapping only.
- (C) Attempted kidnapping and battery.
- (D) Battery only.

159. Roger and Pete are long time friends and belong to the same bowling league.

One evening, Pete tells Roger he is feeling ill and is not going bowling. Not having much fun alone, Roger leaves the bowling alley early and goes by Pete's house to see if he is feeling better. As he approaches the front door, Roger hears his own wife, Sarah, laughing. He peeks in the window and sees Pete and Sarah. Sarah is half undressed with a glass of wine in her hand. In a rage, Roger kicks in the door, picks up a chair, and hurls it at Pete. Pete is knocked unconscious. He then pushes Sarah to the hardwood floor and hits her repeatedly in the face. Pete suffers minor injuries; Sarah dies several days later of massive head trauma.

Choose the precedent that best resolves this case.
- (A) A finds out from an anonymous letter that B has been molesting A's daughter. A grabs a gun, drives to B's house, and kills him. A is guilty of voluntary manslaughter.
- (B) After following her for several weeks, A finally confirms his long-held suspicion that his wife has been having an affair. He goes home and sits with his gun, which he bought when he first began to suspect the affair. When his wife comes home, he asks her about the affair, and she denies it. They argue for over an hour, and then he shoots her. A is guilty of first-degree murder.
- (C) A has a prized record collection that took years to accumulate. B, the babysitter, listens to them one night and accidentally scratches a particularly valuable one. A comes home, discovers what B has done, and hits her across the face. She is thrown against a concrete wall and dies of massive head trauma. A is guilty of second-degree murder.
- (D) Distraught over his wife's death, A has several drinks at a bar and gets in his car to go home. On his way home, a child runs into the street unexpectedly. Because of his diminished capacity, A is not able to stop in time and hits the child, who dies several days

later of head trauma. A is guilty of involuntary manslaughter.

160. Roger and Pete are long time friends and belong to the same bowling league. One evening, Pete tells Roger he is feeling ill and is not going bowling. Not having much fun alone, Roger leaves the bowling alley early and goes by Pete's house to see if he is feeling better. As he approaches the front door, Roger hears his own wife, Sarah, laughing. He peeks in the window and sees Pete and Sarah. Sarah is half undressed with a glass of wine in her hand. In a rage, Roger kicks in the door, picks up a chair, and hurls it at Pete. Pete is knocked unconscious. He then pushes Sarah to the hardwood floor and hits her repeatedly in the face. Pete suffers minor injuries; Sarah dies several days later of massive head trauma.

Which fact, if proved by the prosecution, should most persuade a jury to convict Roger of murder?
- (A) He is a former professional boxer.
- (B) He had actually known about the affair for months.
- (C) He had displayed a severe temper in the past.
- (D) His wife had a life insurance policy designating him as beneficiary.

161. Roger and Pete are long time friends and belong to the same bowling league. One evening, Pete tells Roger he is feeling ill and is not going bowling. Not having much fun alone, Roger leaves the bowling alley early and goes by Pete's house to see if he is feeling better. As he approaches the front door, Roger hears his own wife, Sarah, laughing. He peeks in the window and sees Pete and Sarah. Sarah is half undressed with a glass of wine in her hand. In a rage, Roger kicks in the door, picks up a chair, and hurls it at Pete. Pete is knocked unconscious. He then pushes Sarah to the hardwood floor and hits her repeatedly in the face. Pete suffers minor injuries; Sarah dies several days later of massive head trauma.

Which fact, if proved by the defense, should most persuade a jury to acquit Roger?
- (A) He had gotten drunk at the bowling alley before he stopped by Pete's house.
- (B) He neither believed that his wife would die from the injuries nor intended to kill her.
- (C) He had never been violent in the past.
- (D) His wife had come at him with a knife.

162. Xander was sick and tired of his store getting burglarized every other week. He set up a shotgun, pointed at knee level and rigged it to fire if the door was forced open. Glen, a career burglar, comes by for his usual "hit" on Xander's store. He kicks open the door and is shot in the thigh. Unwilling to summon help because of fear of getting caught, he hobbles home and eventually bleeds to death. Xander will likely be convicted of
- (A) Murder.
- (B) Involuntary manslaughter.
- (C) Negligent homicide.
- (D) None, because he acted in defense of his property.

163. Carey is a heavy narcotics user and also an alcoholic. He constantly has a red nose and haggard, half-open eyes. His clothing frequently smells of liquor and he has permanent slurred speech. He often stumbles and lurches when he walks because of decreased coordination and motor function. One morning, Carey is on his way to the liquor store, sober but not planning to remain that way. Meanwhile, Officer Tompkins is sitting in an unmarked police car across from the liquor store, taking her breakfast break. She watches Carey stumble and weave down the street, trip over the curb, and head into the liquor store. Officer Tompkins cannot see the sales counter; she can see only a few feet past the front door.

Carey approaches the clerk, who looks skeptical. The clerk asks Carey if he has been drinking. Carey tells him no. The clerk puts Carey through a couple of tests that the police use to determine intoxication, and Carey passes them. The clerk smells no trace of alcohol on Carey's breath, although his clothes have a faint stench. The clerk sells Carey a bottle of vodka but forgets to give Carey his receipt. Carey leaves. Officer Tompkins sees Carey emerge with the paper bag containing the vodka in his hand, from which he removed the cap and takes a sip. She immediately makes her move and arrests Carey, then takes him in handcuffs into the store and arrests the surprised clerk.

Charged pursuant to a state statute that prohibits the "knowing sale of alcohol products to any intoxicated person or any person having the appearance of being intoxicated" the clerk will likely be

(A) Convicted.
(B) Acquitted, because Carey was in fact not intoxicated.
(C) Acquitted, because he took reasonable steps to verify that Carey was not intoxicated.
(D) Acquitted, because no one actually witnessed the sale, and so there is no evidence of the crime.

164. Carey is a heavy narcotics user and also an alcoholic. He constantly has a red nose and haggard, half-open eyes. His clothing frequently smells of liquor and he has permanent slurred speech. He often stumbles and lurches when he walks because of decreased coordination and motor function. One morning, Carey is on his way to the liquor store, sober but not planning to remain that way. Meanwhile, Officer Tompkins is sitting in an unmarked police car across from the liquor store, taking her breakfast break. She watches Carey stumble and weave down the street, trip over the curb, and head into the liquor store. Officer Tompkins cannot see the sales counter; she can see only a few feet past the front door.

Carey approaches the clerk, who looks skeptical. The clerk asks Carey if he has been drinking. Carey tells him no. The clerk puts Carey through a couple of tests that the police use to determine intoxication, and Carey passes them. The clerk smells no trace of alcohol on Carey's breath, although his clothes have a faint stench. The clerk sells Carey a bottle of vodka but forgets to give Carey his receipt. Carey leaves. Officer Tompkins sees Carey emerge with the paper bag containing the vodka in his hand, from which he removed the cap and takes a sip. She immediately makes her move and arrests Carey, then takes him in handcuffs into the store and arrests the surprised clerk.

Charged pursuant to a state statute that prohibits public intoxication, Carey will likely be

(A) Convicted, because he appeared intoxicated.
(B) Acquitted, because he was not intoxicated.
(C) Convicted, because he had planned to drink the rest of the vodka in a nearby park.
(D) Convicted, because he drank alcohol in public.

165. Carey is a heavy narcotics user and also an alcoholic. He constantly has a red nose and haggard, half-open eyes. His clothing frequently smells of liquor and he has permanent slurred speech. He often stumbles and lurches when he walks because of decreased coordination and motor function. One morning, Carey is on his way to the liquor store, sober but not planning to remain that way. Meanwhile, Officer Tompkins is sitting in an unmarked police car across from the liquor store, taking her breakfast break. She watches Carey stumble and weave down the street, trip over the curb, and head into the liquor store. Officer Tompkins cannot see the sales counter; she can see only a few feet past the front door.

Carey approaches the clerk, who looks skeptical. The clerk asks Carey if he has been drinking. Carey tells him no. The clerk puts Carey through a couple of tests that the police use to determine intoxication, and Carey passes them. The clerk smells no trace of alcohol on Carey's breath, although his clothes have a faint stench. The clerk sells Carey a bottle of vodka but forgets to give Carey his receipt. Carey leaves. Officer Tompkins sees Carey emerge with the paper bag containing the vodka in his hand, from which he removed the cap and takes a sip. She immediately makes her move and arrests Carey, then takes him in handcuffs into the store and arrests the surprised clerk.

At trial, the clerk testifies that he was told that he was only prohibited from making sales to persons actually intoxicated. When asked who told him that, he states that he was confused by the statute's wording and therefore called a member of the liquor control board to request an interpretation. If true, in a jurisdiction that has adopted the MPC this would

(A) Exonerate the clerk, because he made a mistake of fact.
(B) Exonerate the clerk, because he was acting on misinformation from a public official.
(C) Not exonerate the clerk, because ignorance or mistake of law is not an excuse.
(D) Not exonerate the clerk, because the statute was clear.

166. Talia is walking home from her bus stop late at night on a brightly lit street when she stops and sets her purse down to dig out her door keys from her pocket. Corey, a thrice-convicted pickpocket comes up from behind her and snatches her purse off the ground. When she pursues him, he tosses a stick at her to slow her down, but she ducks and it just misses hitting her. She continues to pursue him, but after a few blocks gets too tired and stops.

She goes immediately to the police station and reports the theft. She describes Corey's hair, face, and clothes in detail. Two officers are radioed his description

and told to pursue him. Talia waits at the police station to give a full report and looks at some mug shots. As Talia is going through the mug shots, the officers bring Corey in in handcuffs saying, "We've got the purse snatcher." A few pages later, Talia identifies Corey's mug shot from the book.

On these facts, Corey could be convicted of

(A) Larceny and robbery.
(B) Robbery and battery.
(C) Robbery only.
(D) Larceny and attempted battery.

167. Talia is walking home from her bus stop late at night on a brightly lit street when she stops and sets her purse down to dig out her door keys from her pocket. Corey, a thrice-convicted pickpocket comes up from behind her and snatches her purse off the ground. When she pursues him, he tosses a stick at her to slow her down, but she ducks and it just misses hitting her. She continues to pursue him, but after a few blocks gets too tired and stops.

She goes immediately to the police station and reports the theft. She describes Corey's hair, face, and clothes in detail. Two officers are radioed his description and told to pursue him. Talia waits at the police station to give a full report and looks at some mug shots. As Talia is going through the mug shots, the officers bring Corey in in handcuffs saying, "We've got the purse snatcher." A few pages later, Talia identifies Corey's mug shot from the book.

On a charge of assault, Corey would likely be

(A) Convicted, because he threw the stick at her intending to slow her down.
(B) Acquitted, because he never touched her.
(C) Acquitted, because he did not verbally threaten her, so she was never in apprehension of a battery.
(D) Convicted, because he took her property.

168. Talia is walking home from her bus stop late at night on a brightly lit street when she stops and sets her purse down to dig out her door keys from her pocket. Corey, a thrice-convicted pickpocket comes up from behind her and snatches her purse off the ground. When she pursues him, he tosses a stick at her to slow her down, but she ducks and it just misses hitting her. She continues to pursue him, but after a few blocks gets too tired and stops.

She goes immediately to the police station and reports the theft. She describes Corey's hair, face, and clothes in detail. Two officers are radioed his description and told to pursue him. Talia waits at the police station to give a full report and looks at some mug shots. As Talia is going through the mug shots, the officers bring Corey in in handcuffs saying, "We've got the purse snatcher." A few pages later, Talia identifies Corey's mug shot from the book.

Corey's motion to suppress Talia's mug shot identification as evidence should be
- (A) Denied, because she got such a good look at him that she would have identified the photo anyway.
- (B) Denied, because there was no intentional police misconduct.
- (C) Granted, because the totality of the circumstances suggest that the photo session was likely to produce a misidentification.
- (D) Denied, because there was other independent evidence to suggest Corey's guilt.

169. State X has adopted the MPC. Tad is driving in X with a .03 blood alcohol level. By state statute anyone driving with a .02 alcohol level or above has "conclusively committed a misdemeanor," although Tad is unaware of this because the statute was enacted only four months ago. He swerves to avoid a cat and hits a child that has suddenly run into the road. The child is killed.

Charged with misdemeanor manslaughter, Tad will likely be

- (A) Acquitted, because he did not know of the new law and did not intend to kill the child.
- (B) Convicted, because the killing occurred while Tad was committing a misdemeanor that was inherently wrong.
- (C) Convicted, because this is the type of crime the misdemeanor manslaughter rule is intended to prevent.
- (D) Acquitted, because the MPC does not recognize the misdemeanor manslaughter rule.

170. State X has adopted the MPC. Tad is driving in X with a .03 blood alcohol level. By statute anyone driving with a .02 alcohol level or above has "conclusively committed a misdemeanor," although Tad is unaware of this because the statute was enacted only four months ago. He swerves to avoid a cat and hits a child that has suddenly run into the road. The child is killed.

Charged with violating the .02 blood alcohol rule, Tad will likely be
- (A) Acquitted, because his friend had told him the statutory limit was .06.
- (B) Convicted, because he is strictly liable.
- (C) Acquitted, because he was unaware of the recent statute's enactment.
- (D) Acquitted, because he did not know his level was above .02.

171. Shana gets mugged in broad daylight and Oliver witnesses it. As the mugger struggles to take Shana's purse, he reaches in his coat pocket and pulls out a lead pipe. Oliver intervenes, knocking the pipe out of the mugger's hand and striking him several times in the face and stomach with his fist. The mugger falls to the ground, bleeding. He dies later that day from internal injuries. Charged with second degree murder, Oliver will likely be

- (A) Acquitted, because he used reasonable force to defend Shana.
- (B) Convicted, because Shana was a stranger, and not part of Oliver's family.

(C) Convicted, because only the police may use force in the prevention of a crime.

(D) Convicted, because the amount of force was disproportional.

172. Avery, Hewlett, and Packard are bankers who have developed a plan for early retirement. Avery has designed a computer program that moves small amounts of money, undetectable as individual transactions, into a secret account that will aggregate over time into a hefty nest egg. Hewlett installed the program in a low-profile corner of the mainframe. Packard set up the secret account. They meet to check the account periodically, although they have not yet built up enough of a balance to bother making a withdrawal. Mac, a co-worker, gets wind of the plan and threatens to expose the group. Hewlett pulls Mac into a secluded storeroom and says, "You'd better be careful, or you're gonna get it."

When Packard gets wind of Hewlett's threat, he decides he is getting in over his head. He closes the account and goes to the police. At the station, he sits down with an inspector who questions him as he tells the whole story. Meanwhile, Avery secretly removes an office computer from a storage room and takes it home so that he can better monitor the progress of his program, intending to return it when the job is done. When he uses it and realizes how fast it is, he decides to keep it. As Hewlett is leaving work, he punches Mac in the face without warning and says "Just a reminder." Avery, Hewlett, and Packard are arrested later that evening.

Charged with assault of Mac, Hewlett will likely be

(A) Convicted, because Mac had apprehension of harm.
(B) Convicted, because Hewlett threatened deadly force.
(C) Acquitted, because the threat of harm was not immediate.
(D) Acquitted, because Mac did not believe the threat to be serious.

173. Avery, Hewlett, and Packard are bankers who have developed a plan for early retirement. Avery has designed a computer program that moves small amounts of money, undetectable as individual transactions, into a secret account that will aggregate over time into a hefty nest egg. Hewlett installed the program in a low-profile corner of the mainframe. Packard set up the secret account. They meet to check the account periodically, although they have not yet built up enough of a balance to bother making a withdrawal. Mac, a co-worker, gets wind of the plan and threatens to expose the group. Hewlett pulls Mac into a secluded storeroom and says, "You'd better be careful, or you're gonna get it."

When Packard gets wind of Hewlett's threat, he decides he is getting in over his head. He closes the account and goes to the police. At the station, he sits down with an inspector who questions him as he tells the whole story. Meanwhile, Avery secretly removes an office computer from a storage room and takes it home so that he can better monitor the progress of his program, intending to return it when the job is done. When he uses it and realizes how fast it is, he decides to keep it. As Hewlett is leaving work, he punches Mac in the face without warning and says "Just a reminder." Avery, Hewlett, and Packard are arrested later that evening.

With respect to taking the computer, Avery can be charged with

(A) False pretenses.
(B) Larceny.
(C) Embezzlement.
(D) Burglary.

174. Avery, Hewlett, and Packard are bankers who have developed a plan for early retirement. Avery has designed a computer program that moves small amounts of money, undetectable as individual transactions, into a secret account that will aggregate over time into a hefty nest egg. Hewlett installed the program in a low-profile corner of the mainframe. Packard set up the secret account. They meet to check the account periodically, although they have not yet built up enough of a balance to bother

making a withdrawal. Mac, a co-worker, gets wind of the plan and threatens to expose the group. Hewlett pulls Mac into a secluded storeroom and says, "You'd better be careful, or you're gonna get it."

When Packard gets wind of Hewlett's threat, he decides he is getting in over his head. He closes the account and goes to the police. At the station, he sits down with an inspector who questions him as he tells the whole story. Meanwhile, Avery secretly removes an office computer from a storage room and takes it home so that he can better monitor the progress of his program, intending to return it when the job is done. When he uses it and realizes how fast it is, he decides to keep it. As Hewlett is leaving work, he punches Mac in the face without warning and says "Just a reminder." Avery, Hewlett, and Packard are arrested that evening.

In a jurisdiction that has adopted the *Pinkerton* rule, Packard can be charged with

(A) Conspiracy, embezzlement, larceny, and battery.
(B) Conspiracy only.
(C) Conspiracy and embezzlement.
(D) Conspiracy and attempted embezzlement.

175. Avery, Hewlett, and Packard are bankers who have developed a plan for early retirement. Avery has designed a computer program that moves small amounts of money, undetectable as individual transactions, into a secret account that will aggregate over time into a hefty nest egg. Hewlett installed the program in a low-profile corner of the mainframe. Packard set up the secret account. They meet to check the account periodically, although they have not yet built up enough of a balance to bother making a withdrawal. Mac, a co-worker, gets wind of the plan and threatens to expose the group. Hewlett pulls Mac into a secluded storeroom and says, "You'd better be careful, or you're gonna get it."

When Packard gets wind of Hewlett's threat, he decides he is getting in over his head. He closes the account and goes to the police. At the station, he sits down with an inspector who questions him as he tells the whole story. Meanwhile, Avery secretly removes an office computer from a storage room and takes it home so that he can better monitor the progress of his program, intending to return it when the job is done. When he uses it and realizes how fast it is, he decides to keep it. As Hewlett is leaving work, he punches Mac in the face without warning and says "Just a reminder." Avery, Hewlett, and Packard are arrested later that evening.

Packard pleads guilty, Avery and Hewlett plead not guilty. Avery and Hewlett move to suppress Packard's confession to the police. The motion should be

(A) Denied, because it did not occur during a custodial interrogation.
(B) Denied, because Packard is the only defendant with the right to move to suppress his own confession.
(C) Granted, because Packard was never read his *Miranda* rights.
(D) Granted, because Packard was coerced.

176. Ray and Belinda are walking along the pier late at night. Thinking it will be a funny joke Belinda blindfolds Ray, telling him she has a surprise for him, and neglects to warn him that he is about to step off of the pier. Ray falls a couple of feet and lands in relatively deep water. Ray begins to shout that he can't swim. Belinda thinks he is playing a joke on her for revenge, so she does nothing. When she doesn't hear him after a couple of minutes, she becomes concerned, but it is too late. Ray has drowned. Charged with murder, Belinda moves for dismissal, arguing that the prosecution cannot prove *actus reus*. The motion will likely be

(A) Granted.
(B) Denied, because the prosecution need not always prove *actus reus*.
(C) Denied, because she intended to cause serious bodily injury.
(D) Denied, because her failure to act was the *actus reus*.

177. Lonnie and Burt are getting divorced, and Lonnie has moved out. Burt has told Lonnie that she may not reenter the house without his permission, and Lonnie tells him she will not. Lonnie mistakenly believes that half of everything in the house is hers. One day she comes by when Burt is not home and, using her old key, she takes some of Burt's prized and expensive artworks, such as his rare "Dogs Playing Poker" and a velvet Elvis painting that he acquired before the marriage.

What is the most serious crime with which Lonnie can be charged?
  (A) Larceny.
  (B) Larceny by trick.
  (C) Burglary.
  (D) Lonnie cannot be charged.

178. Lonnie and Burt are getting divorced, and Lonnie has moved out. Burt has told Lonnie that she may not reenter the house without his permission, and Lonnie tells him she will not. Lonnie mistakenly believes that half of everything in the house is hers. One day she comes by when Burt is not home and, using her old key, she takes some of Burt's prized and expensive artworks, such as his rare "Dogs Playing Poker" and velvet Elvis paintings that he acquired before the marriage.

What is Lonnie's best defense at trial?
  (A) She was mistaken as to her legal status regarding the property, and regarding her legal right to enter the house.
  (B) She was under duress as a result of the divorce proceedings.
  (C) She believed that Burt had possession of some of her property, and she thought this would make them even.
  (D) She was drunk, and her judgment was impaired.

179. Lonnie and Burt are getting divorced, and Lonnie has moved out. Burt has told Lonnie that she may not reenter the house without his permission, and Lonnie tells him she will not. Lonnie mistakenly believes that half of everything in the house is hers. One day she comes by when Burt is not home and, using her old key, she takes some of Burt's prized and expensive artworks, such as his rare "Dogs Playing Poker" and velvet Elvis paintings that he acquired before the marriage.

Lonnie's defense counsel fails to call any witnesses, make any objections, or perform more than a cursory cross-examination. Lonnie is convicted. On appeal, Lonnie argues ineffective assistance of counsel. The argument will likely
  (A) Prevail, because his misconduct is *per se* evidence of ineffective assistance of counsel.
  (B) Prevail, only if she can show that there is a reasonable probability that the outcome would have changed if her attorney had performed differently.
  (C) Fail, unless she can conclusively prove that she would have been acquitted if her attorney had performed differently.
  (D) Fail, because she admitted that she took the items in question.

180. In which of the following circumstances is the defendant most likely to be convicted of the charged crime?
  (A) Alma intends to shoot Bertha but misses and hits the tire of a passing car. The car veers out of control and crashes, killing the driver. Alma is charged with murder.
  (B) Celine intends to drive to Dave's house and kill Dave with a knife. She pulls a knife out of her kitchen drawer and heads for her car but changes her mind and goes back in the house. Celine is charged with attempted murder.

(C) Ernie intends to surprise Fabian, putting a bucket full of confetti over the door that will spill when Fabian comes through. The bucket accidentally comes loose and falls on Fabian's head, cutting him. Ernie is charged with battery.

(D) Gunther intends to shoot Helga, but the gun misfires. Helga knocks the gun out of Gunther's hand and stabs him in the leg with a knife, intending to wound him so that he can be subdued. Gunther dies from the stab wound. Helga is charged with murder.

181. Intending to play a joke on Kim, Zed took Kim's dog's collar and set it on the back porch, intending to make her think her dog had gotten out into the huge fenced back field and would have to be chased down and retrieved. Kim saw the collar and thought her dog had been stolen. She had a heart attack and died. Zed, charged with involuntary manslaughter, should argue

(A) He did not intend for Kim to die.
(B) There is no causation.
(C) He did not know she had a weak heart.
(D) His actions were not reckless.

182. David mistakenly believed that Sean had stolen his lawnmower. He crept into Sean's garage late at night to look around. His flashlight batteries burned out and he lit a match. When he didn't find the mower, he blew out the match, dropped it, and left. The match, still smoldering, fell into a small pool of flammable solvent, igniting some old newspapers and burning down Sean's house. David is charged with arson. He will likely be

(A) Convicted, because he was trespassing when fire was started.
(B) Convicted, because his actions were the actual cause of the fire.
(C) Acquitted, because he did not act with intent or with extreme indifference to the consequences of his behavior.
(D) Convicted, because he was negligent.

183. Intending to teach the mischievous neighborhood kids a lesson, Mr. Hooper sets a bear trap in his yard, hoping to injure one of the kids to keep them all from trespassing on his property. A child with a rare physiological disorder where his blood fails to clot gets a leg caught in the trap and bleeds to death at the hospital. Hooper is charged with murder. He will likely be

(A) Acquitted, because he never intended to kill the child.
(B) Acquitted, because the fact that the child had a rare disorder was the superseding cause of the death.
(C) Acquitted, because the death was unforeseeable.
(D) Convicted.

184. Intending to set fire to Glen's cabin, so that he and Glen can split the insurance money, William pours gasoline all over the cabin and tries to light a match. However, it suddenly and violently begins to rain. William cannot get the match lit and the gasoline is washed from the cabin. He comes to his senses and walks away, leaving the empty gas can a mile away behind a tree. Three days later, a bolt of lightning strikes a tree near the gas can, which heats up and, explodes the trace gasoline left in it, starting a massive forest fire and incinerating the cabin.

William is likely not guilty of arson because

(A) Glen had agreed to the crime.
(B) The lightning strike was a superseding cause.
(C) The actual destruction of the cabin was too remote in time from William's attempt.
(D) He was not acting out of malice.

185. Intending to set fire to Glen's cabin, so that he and Glen can split the insurance money, William pours gasoline all over the cabin and tries to light a match. However, it suddenly and violently begins to rain. William cannot get the match lit and the gasoline is washed from the cabin. He comes to his senses and walks away, leaving the empty gas can a mile away behind a tree. Three days later, a bolt of lightning strikes a tree near the gas can, which heats up and, explodes the trace gasoline left in it, starting a massive forest fire and incinerating the cabin.

Charged with attempted arson, Glen will likely be
- (A) Convicted.
- (B) Acquitted, because he took no substantial step toward accomplishing the crime.
- (C) Acquitted, because William and Glen agreed to the crime and the attempt merges with the conspiracy.
- (D) Acquitted, because William abandoned the attempt before it was completed.

186. In Telstra State, it is a felony to impersonate a police officer. Not aware of this law, Tony, Tina, and Tommy all plan to impersonate police officers, crash their friend's party (where illegal drugs will be in use) and scare everyone for a good laugh. They rent realistic looking police uniforms and wear sunglasses so they won't be recognized.

On September 8, they go to the party in the uniforms. They knock on the door, and when it is opened, several partygoers scream, "Raid!" Total chaos ensues, and several attendees try to descend the fire escape in the back. They all fall to their deaths. Thinking no one recognized them, the three impersonators flee in horror, and hide the police uniforms at Tony's house.

On October 4, officers show up at Tony's door on a completely unrelated case – they have suspicion that Tony's house contains illegal weapons, but no probable cause or warrant. Tony initially consents to the search, confident that he has no such weapons. However, as the police begin searching, Tony remembers the uniforms and tells them, "Okay, you've had your chance, I want you to leave now." But the officers refuse and continue searching. When they find the uniforms, they remember the police report regarding the deaths at the house party the month before. They take Tony in for questioning. They read him his *Miranda* rights and tell him if he doesn't confess, he could be in for some

"cruel and unusual punishment." He confesses in a signed affidavit.

The same day, the police station receives a letter, postmarked October 1. It is the confession of Tina, who was overcome by guilt but too terrified to turn herself over to the police in person. She recounts the events, including the flight and stashing the uniforms at Tony's house. She includes Tony's address. Tina and Tommy are arrested later that day.

Charged with felony murder, Tony, Tina, and Tommy will likely be
- (A) Convicted.
- (B) Acquitted, because the deaths were unintentional.
- (C) Acquitted, because the felony committed was not inherently dangerous.
- (D) Acquitted, because the deaths occurred after, not during, the felony.

187. In Telstra State, it is a felony to impersonate a police officer. Not aware of this law, Tony, Tina, and Tommy all plan to impersonate police officers, crash their friend's party (where illegal drugs will be in use) and scare everyone for a good laugh. They rent realistic looking police uniforms and wear sunglasses so they won't be recognized.

On September 8, they go to the party in the uniforms. They knock on the door, and when it is opened, several partygoers scream, "Raid!" Total chaos ensues, and several attendees try to descend the fire escape in the back. They all fall to their deaths. Thinking no one recognized them, the three impersonators flee in horror, and hide the police uniforms at Tony's house.

On October 4, officers show up at Tony's door on a completely unrelated case – they have suspicion that Tony's house contains illegal weapons, but no probable cause or warrant. Tony initially consents to the search, confident that he has no such weapons. However, as the police begin searching, Tony remembers the uniforms and tells them, "Okay, you've had your chance, I want you to leave now." But the officers refuse and continue searching.

When they find the uniforms, they remember the police report regarding the deaths at the house party the month before. They take Tony in for questioning. They read him his *Miranda* rights and tell him if he doesn't confess, he could be in for some "cruel and unusual punishment." He confesses in a signed affidavit.

The same day, the police station receives a letter, postmarked October 1. It is the confession of Tina, who was overcome by guilt but too terrified to turn herself over to the police in person. She recounts the events, including the flight and stashing the uniforms at Tony's house. She includes Tony's address. Tina and Tommy are arrested later that day.

Charged with conspiracy, Tony, Tina, and Tommy will likely be
- (A) Acquitted, because by definition, three persons were not required to commit the crime.
- (B) Acquitted, because each acted separately from the other.
- (C) Acquitted, because they did not know the act they conspired to commit was unlawful.
- (D) Convicted.

188. In Telstra State, it is a felony to impersonate a police officer. Not aware of this law, Tony, Tina, and Tommy all plan to impersonate police officers, crash their friend's party (where illegal drugs will be in use) and scare everyone for a good laugh. They rent realistic looking police uniforms and wear sunglasses so they won't be recognized.

On September 8, they go to the party in the uniforms. They knock on the door, and when it is opened, several partygoers scream, "Raid!" Total chaos ensues, and several attendees try to descend the fire escape in the back. They all fall to their deaths. Thinking no one recognized them, the three impersonators flee in horror, and hide the police uniforms at Tony's house.

On October 4, officers show up at Tony's door on a completely unrelated case – they have suspicion that Tony's house contains illegal weapons, but no probable cause or warrant. Tony initially consents to the search, confident that he has no such weapons. However, as the police begin searching, Tony remembers the uniforms and tells them, "Okay, you've had your chance, I want you to leave now." But the officers refuse and continue searching. When they find the uniforms, they remember the police report regarding the deaths at the house party the month before. They take Tony in for questioning. They read him his *Miranda* rights and tell him if he doesn't confess, he could be in for some "cruel and unusual punishment." He confesses in a signed affidavit.

The same day, the police station receives a letter, postmarked October 1. It is the confession of Tina, who was overcome by guilt but too terrified to turn herself over to the police in person. She recounts the events, including the flight and stashing the uniforms at Tony's house. She includes Tony's address. Tina and Tommy are arrested later that day.

Tony's motion to suppress the uniforms as evidence should be
- (A) Granted, because he withdrew his consent for the search.
- (B) Granted, because the uniforms were outside the scope of the search.
- (C) Denied, because their discovery was inevitable and Tina's letter was an independent source.
- (D) Denied, because Tony could not withdraw his consent once it was given.

189. In Telstra State, it is a felony to impersonate a police officer. Not aware of this law, Tony, Tina, and Tommy all plan to impersonate police officers, crash their friend's party (where illegal drugs will be in use) and scare everyone for a good laugh. They rent realistic looking police uniforms and wear sunglasses so they won't be recognized.

On September 8, they go to the party in the uniforms. They knock on the door, and when it is opened, several partygoers scream, "Raid!" Total chaos ensues, and several attendees try to descend the fire escape in the back. They all fall to their deaths. Thinking no one recognized them, the three impersonators flee in horror, and hide the police uniforms at Tony's house.

On October 4, officers show up at Tony's door on a completely unrelated case – they have suspicion that Tony's house contains illegal weapons, but no probable cause or warrant. Tony initially consents to the search, confident that he has no such weapons. However, as the police begin searching, Tony remembers the uniforms and tells them, "Okay, you've had your chance, I want you to leave now." But the officers refuse and continue searching. When they find the uniforms, they remember the police report regarding the deaths at the house party the month before. They take Tony in for questioning. They read him his *Miranda* rights and tell him if he doesn't confess, he could be in for some "cruel and unusual punishment." He confesses in a signed affidavit.

The same day, the police station receives a letter, postmarked October 1. It is the confession of Tina, who was overcome by guilt but too terrified to turn herself over to the police in person. She recounts the events, including the flight and stashing the uniforms at Tony's house. She includes Tony's address. Tina and Tommy are arrested later that day.

Tina's motion to suppress her confession as evidence should be
- (A) Granted, because she was not aware of her *Miranda* rights.
- (B) Granted, because her boyfriend coerced her into confessing.
- (C) Denied, because she was not in custody and confessed voluntarily.
- (D) Denied, because without it, Tommy could not be prosecuted.

190. In Telstra State, it is a felony to impersonate a police officer. Not aware of this law, Tony, Tina, and Tommy all plan to impersonate police officers, crash their friend's party (where illegal drugs will be in use) and scare everyone for a good laugh. They rent realistic looking police uniforms and wear sunglasses so they won't be recognized.

On September 8, they go to the party in the uniforms. They knock on the door, and when it is opened, several partygoers scream, "Raid!" Total chaos ensues, and several attendees try to descend the fire escape in the back. They all fall to their deaths. Thinking no one recognized them, the three impersonators flee in horror, and hide the police uniforms at Tony's house.

On October 4, officers show up at Tony's door on a completely unrelated case – they have suspicion that Tony's house contains illegal weapons, but no probable cause or warrant. Tony initially consents to the search, confident that he has no such weapons. However, as the police begin searching, Tony remembers the uniforms and tells them, "Okay, you've had your chance, I want you to leave now." But the officers refuse and continue searching. When they find the uniforms, they remember the police report regarding the deaths at the house party the month before. They take Tony in for questioning. They read him his *Miranda* rights and tell him if he doesn't confess, he could be in for some "cruel and unusual punishment." He confesses in a signed affidavit.

The same day, the police station receives a letter, postmarked October 1. It is the confession of Tina, who was overcome by guilt but too terrified to turn herself over to the police in person. She recounts the events, including the flight and stashing the uniforms at Tony's house. She includes Tony's address. Tina and Tommy are arrested later that day.

Tony's motion to suppress his own confession should be

    (A) Denied, because he was administered his *Miranda* rights and waived them by confessing.

    (B) Granted, because he did not have a lawyer present when he confessed.

    (C) Denied, because the amount of police coercion involved was not enough to cause a reasonable person to confess.

    (D) Granted, because the police coerced him into confessing.

191. Theodore and Franklin get into a heated argument about who can eat the most boiled eggs in a sitting. Theodore, in a rage, picks up a baseball bat and hits Franklin, splitting his skull open. Franklin dies on the way to the hospital. In order to successfully reduce Theodore's crime from murder to voluntary manslaughter, his attorney must demonstrate

    (A) That a reasonable person would have reacted similarly.

    (B) That Theodore was acting in the heat of passion.

    (C) That Theodore was acting in the heat of passion and that a reasonable person would have reacted similarly.

    (D) That Theodore's actions were reckless, not intentional.

192. Danny, a 25-year-old-male shoe salesman, is obsessed with women's feet to the point of compulsion. He is particularly enamored of the feet of Trisha, a frequent customer whom he believes is 17 (she is actually 15). One night, he follows Trisha home, in the hope of gaining access to her bedroom and fondling her feet. He is concerned that his actions are wrong but cannot stop himself. Once all the lights go out, he slides open a window and enters the house.

Danny accomplishes his objective of fondling Trisha's feet, but a neighbor spotted him sneaking in the window and he is quickly arrested. Although he was unaware of this, there is a state statute that makes it a strict liability gross misdemeanor to touch a child under 16 unknown to the perpetrator on any part of the body. It is a felony to touch a child under 16 on the breasts, genitals, or buttocks.

Danny should be charged with

    (A) Burglary and the misdemeanor of the touching of a child.

    (B) Burglary only.

    (C) Misdemeanor touching of a child only.

    (D) Neither burglary nor misdemeanor touching of a child.

193. Danny, a 25-year-old-male shoe salesman, is obsessed with women's feet to the point of compulsion. He is particularly enamored by the feet of Trisha, a frequent customer whom he believes is 17 (she is actually 15). One night, he follows Trisha home, in the hope of gaining access to her bedroom and fondling her feet. He is concerned that his actions are wrong but cannot stop himself. Once all the lights go out, he slides open a window and enters the house.

Danny accomplishes his objective of feet fondling, but a neighbor spotted him sneaking in and he is quickly arrested. Although he was unaware of this, there is a state statute that makes it a strict liability gross misdemeanor to touch a child under 16 unknown to the perpetrator on any part of the body. It is a felony to touch a child under 16 on the breasts, genitals, or buttocks.

In a jurisdiction that has adopted only the *M'Naghten* test, Danny's insanity defense will

    (A) Succeed, if he can demonstrate that it was impossible for him to resist the urge to touch Trisha's feet.

    (B) Succeed, if he can prove he has a mental disease or defect.

    (C) Fail, because he knew right from wrong.

    (D) Fail, because he is strictly liable.

194. Danny, a 25-year-old-male shoe salesman, is obsessed with women's feet to the point of compulsion. He is particularly enamored of the feet of Trisha, a frequent customer whom he believes is 17 (she is actually 15). One night, he follows Trisha home, in the hope of gaining access to her bedroom and fondling her feet. He is concerned that his actions are wrong but cannot stop himself. Once all the lights go out, he slides open a window and enters the house.

Danny accomplishes his objective of feet fondling, but a neighbor spotted him sneaking in and he is quickly arrested. Although he was unaware of this, there is a state statute that makes it a strict liability gross misdemeanor to touch a child under 16 unknown to the perpetrator on any part of the body. It is a felony to touch a child under 16 on the breasts, genitals, or buttocks.

If the prosecution can prove that Danny intended to fondle Trisha's genitals when he entered the house, but then he got scared and decided not to, he can be charged with

(A) Burglary and felony touching of a child.
(B) Burglary and attempted felony touching of a child.
(C) Burglary only.
(D) Attempted felony touching of a child only.

195. Keenan goes to Damon's house, hoping to convince Damon to loan Keenan his portable stereo. Unbeknownst to Damon, Keenan has no intention of returning the stereo, as he is about to leave town for good. Unbeknownst to Keenan, Damon knows Keenan is about to leave town. Also, the stereo is broken and useless. The two of them chat for a while and Keenan asks if he can borrow the stereo. Damon says, "Heck, you're such a good friend, you can have it for $10 bucks." Keenan figures this is a good deal. He gives Damon the money and takes off. In this jurisdiction, larceny is punishable by 2 years in prison, false pretenses by 1 year in prison, larceny by trick by 6 months in prison and a $2,500 fine.

Charged with burglary, Keenan will likely be

(A) Convicted.
(B) Acquitted, because he did not intend to commit a felony at the time of entry.
(C) Acquitted, because he did not break and enter.
(D) Acquitted, because he obtained the stereo by legal means.

196. Keenan goes to Damon's house, hoping to convince Damon to loan Keenan his portable stereo. Unbeknownst to Damon, Keenan has no intention of returning the stereo, as he is about to leave town for good. Unbeknownst to Keenan, Damon knows Keenan is about to leave town. Also, the stereo is broken and useless. The two of them chat for a while and Keenan asks if he can borrow the stereo. Damon says, "Heck, you're such a good friend, you can have it for $10 bucks." Keenan figures this is a good deal. He gives Damon the money and takes off. In this jurisdiction, larceny is punishable by 2 years in prison, false pretenses by 1 year in prison, larceny by trick by 6 months in prison and a $2,500 fine.

As a prosecutor, you would most likely charge Damon with

(A) Larceny.
(B) Larceny by trick.
(C) False pretenses.
(D) Nothing – he has not committed a crime.

197. Keenan goes to Damon's house, hoping to convince Damon to loan Keenan his portable stereo. Unbeknownst to Damon, Keenan has no intention of returning the stereo, as he is about to leave town for good. Unbeknownst to Keenan, Damon knows Keenan is about to leave town. Also, the stereo is broken and useless. The two of them chat for a while and Keenan asks if he can borrow the stereo. Damon says, "Heck, you're such a good friend, you can have it for $10 bucks." Keenan figures this is a good deal. He gives Damon the money and takes off. In this jurisdiction, larceny is punishable by 2 years in prison, false pretenses by 1 year in prison, larceny by trick by 6 months in prison and a $2,500 fine.

Damon is indigent and requests an attorney at the initial appearance, but he is told he does not qualify to receive one because it is believed he has a hidden fortune. In a subsequent plea agreement, Damon pleads guilty to larceny by trick. What punishment can he most likely expect?

(A) Six months in prison.
(B) $2,500 fine.
(C) Six months in prison and a $2,500 fine.
(D) No punishment, his conviction will likely be overturned.

198. Keenan goes to Damon's house, hoping to convince Damon to loan Keenan his portable stereo. Unbeknownst to Damon, Keenan has no intention of returning the stereo, as he is about to leave town for good. Unbeknownst to Keenan, Damon knows Keenan is about to leave town. Also, the stereo is broken and useless. The two of them chat for a while and Keenan asks if he can borrow the stereo. Damon says, "Heck, you're such a good friend, you can have it for $10 bucks." Keenan figures this is a good deal. He gives Damon the money and takes off. In this jurisdiction, larceny is punishable by 2 years in prison, false pretenses by 1 year in prison, larceny by trick by 6 months in prison and a $2,500 fine.

Keenan is acquitted on the burglary charge. The prosecutor charges him with attempted larceny. He will most likely be

(A) Convicted, because he attempted to gain possession of the stereo by fraud without intent to return it.
(B) Acquitted, because the prosecution violates double jeopardy.
(C) Acquitted, because he is actually guilty of attempted false pretenses, a more serious crime.
(D) Convicted, because he took substantial steps toward committing the crime.

199. Barry and Sandra are out on a date. They have several drinks and go back to her apartment. Barry pushes Sandra onto the bed and tries to undress her over her sincere protestations. Finally, she kicks him in the stomach and he leaves in agony. Sandra files a police complaint against Barry.

Barry is subsequently charged with attempted rape of Sandra. His best defense would be

(A) He honestly and reasonably believed she had consented.
(B) He is impotent and therefore rape of Sandra was impossible.
(C) He was intoxicated.
(D) His actions did not constitute attempted rape.

200. Barry and Sandra are out on a date. They have several drinks and go back to her apartment. Barry pushes Sandra on to the bed and tries to undress her over her sincere protestations. Finally, she kicks him in the stomach and he leaves in agony. Sandra files a police complaint against Barry.

During Barry's trial, he repeatedly protests his innocence during the prosecution's case, and addresses the jury directly, yelling, "You can't do this to me!" Finally, the judge has him removed from the courtroom. His conviction will likely be

(A) Affirmed, because the judge had discretion to have him removed.
(B) Overturned, because a defendant has a constitutional right to be present at trial.
(C) Overturned, because his behavior was grounds for a mistrial.
(D) Overturned, because of ineffective assistance of counsel.

RIGOS BAR REVIEW SERIES

UNIFORM MULTISTATE BAR EXAM REVIEW (MBE)

CHAPTER 6 – CRIMINAL LAW AND PROCEDURE

Answers

Question Answer Rationales

> **MBE Tip:** Put a piece of paper over the answers and "mask down" while working through the questions so you don't accidentally peek at the next answer.

1. **/C/** Since the defendant did not cause the death, he cannot be found guilty of murder. However, he may be found guilty of attempted murder. **(A)** is incorrect because the defendant performed the act of stabbing the victim. **(B)** is incorrect because the defendant had the intent to kill. **(D)** is not the best answer because although the defendant did not cause it, the result of death has been achieved.

2. **/D/** All of these three situations create a duty to act, so this is the best answer. **(A)** is incorrect because this situation creates a duty to act. **(B)** is incorrect because this situation creates a duty to act. **(C)** is incorrect because this situation creates a duty to act.

3. **/C/** Robbery requires the *mens rea* specific intent under the common law. **(A)** is incorrect because felony murder does not require any specific intent. **(B)** is incorrect because manslaughter could be the result of recklessness. **(D)** is incorrect because statutory rape is a strict liability crime not requiring intent.

4. **/B/** Strict liability means the defendant is guilty regardless of his state of mind, so in effect intent is not required. **(A)** is incorrect because proof of intent to commit the crime is not required under strict liability. **(C)** is incorrect because proof of intent to commit the crime is not required under strict liability. **(D)** is incorrect because proof of intent to commit the crime is not required under strict liability.

5. **/B/** This is a correct statement about the doctrine of transferred intent between victims. **(A)** is a misstatement of the law; intent transfers only to similar crimes. **(C)** describes a different principle of transfer between conspirators. **(D)** is nonsensical – "intent" by police to seize evidence is not usually analyzed, only procedure.

6. **/C/** Misinformation from a public official may exonerate a defendant by negating the *mens rea* of the crime. **(A)** is incorrect because the *mens rea* specified in a law has no bearing on whether a mistake of law is permitted. **(B)** is incorrect because a mistake of law is generally not a defense. **(D)** is incorrect because ignorance of the legal system is not usually a defense.

7. **/C/** The substantial factor test for causation states that if the defendant's actions were not enough by themselves to cause the harm, but combined with other forces do produce the harm, the defendant's actions are considered the cause in fact. **(A)** is not the best answer because under the substantial factor test, both are guilty of murder. **(B)** is not the best answer because under the substantial factor test, both are guilty of murder. **(D)** is not the best answer because under the substantial factor test, both are guilty of murder.

8. **/A/** An accomplice is charged with the underlying burglary crime committed. Because there is no such thing as an actual criminal charge of "accomplice" alone. **(B)** is incorrect because attempt is an inchoate crime, and cannot be charged if the crime is completed, as here, so **(C)** is incorrect. Y can be charged with one of the named offenses, so **(D)** is incorrect.

9. **/D/** The statement is the definition of proximate cause. **(A)** is incorrect because "presumed cause" is not genuine criminal law terminology. **(B)** is incorrect because "proven cause" is not genuine criminal law terminology. **(C)** is incorrect because "actual cause" is the direct cause of the harm, not simply the "natural and probable result."

10. **/D/** Burglary, unlike other crimes, does not merge with larceny even though larceny is an element of burglary. **(A)** is incorrect because burglary has additional elements to larceny. **(B)** is not the best answer because the facts indicate a burglary has occurred. **(C)** is incorrect because a defendant cannot be convicted of both a lesser included and greater offense, and because larceny is not a "lesser included" offense to burglary.

11. **/C/** The Model Penal Code (MPC) recognizes all three of these conditions as potentially acceptable for an insanity defense. **(A)** is not the best answer because it is incomplete. **(B)** is not the best answer because it is incomplete. **(D)** is incorrect because Option D describes the defense of duress, not insanity.

12. **/A/** This is the standard for defendant's competency to stand trial, which is constitutionally required. **(B)** is incorrect because "competency to stand trial" and "insanity at the time the crime was committed" are examined as separate issues. **(C)** misstates the law – a defendant need not usually appear as a witness. **(D)** is incorrect – usually the lawyer will use her own judgment to determine when to object.

13. **/C/** Voluntary intoxication is not a valid defense, but involuntary intoxication caused by another, as here, can be a defense to any crime, equivalent to temporary insanity. **(A)** is incorrect because involuntary intoxication may be a defense. **(B)** is not the best answer because no such reasonableness standard is required for involuntary intoxication. **(D)** is incorrect because battery is not a specific intent crime.

14. **/B/** Children ages 7-14 are presumed incapable of intending a crime, but the presumption is rebuttable. **(A)** is incorrect because it describes the rule for children under 7. **(C)** is incorrect because children may be tried if they are capable of understanding the proceeding. **(D)** is incorrect because children under 18 are tried in juvenile court unless they are accused of serious violent crimes and are 16 or 17.

15. **/D/** Duress as a valid defense requires an imminent threat of serious bodily harm or death to oneself or a third party which the defendant reasonably believed would be carried out. Property damage threats are insufficient. **(A)** is incorrect because duress as a defense is available for all crimes except murder and manslaughter. **(B)** is incorrect because duress does not negate required intent, it is a defense to the crime. **(C)** is incorrect because duress requires imminent threat of serious bodily harm or death to oneself or a third party that the defendant reasonably believed would be carried out.

16. **/C/** This is the best answer presented because it is the only correct scenario for a viable entrapment defense. **(A)** is incorrect because mere creation of the opportunity to commit a crime is not usually enough for entrapment. **(B)** is incorrect because a predisposition helps to establish that there was no entrapment. **(D)** is incorrect because predisposition to commit the crime negates a police entrapment defense.

17. /C/ This is the best answer because a threat of harm must be imminent for self-defense to be applicable. **(A)** is not the best answer because even if B had retreated, and then shot A, he would not be entitled to effectively argue self-defense. **(B)** is not the best answer because an imminent threat of serious bodily harm is sufficient to justify the use of deadly force. **(D)** is not the best answer because one may always act reasonably in self-defense, even if one has not chosen the wisest course of action beforehand.

18. /B/ This is the best answer because mistake about the amount of necessary force does not exonerate a defendant, but can be sufficient for reducing the charge from murder to manslaughter. **(A)** is not the best answer because an honest mistake about the amount of necessary force will likely be sufficient to reduce the charge from murder to manslaughter. **(C)** is incorrect because deadly force may only be used in self-defense if deadly force is threatened. **(D)** is incorrect, because the intent here was to inflict serious bodily harm or death.

19. /D/ This is the best answer because it accurately states the minority view of imputing the victim's status on the D. **(A)** is incorrect because today the defender need not have a personal relationship to the victim in any jurisdiction. **(B)** is not the best answer because the defender may always act if reasonable, rather than waiting for police. **(C)** is incorrect because the amount of force allowed does not turn on the defender's relationship to the victim.

20. /A/ This is the best answer because although Abram is a fleeing felon (he committed a robbery), Quincy has no basis for the belief that Abram is an immediate threat. **(B)** is not the best answer because Quincy has no basis for the belief that Abram is an immediate threat. **(C)** misstates the law; a citizen may use force to apprehend a fleeing felon if that felon poses an immediate threat. **(D)** is incorrect because Quincy witnessed Abram committing robbery, which is a felony.

21. /A/ Don has committed textbook solicitation by intentionally encouraging another to commit a felony or serious misdemeanor. **(B)** is incorrect because solicitation is complete once the offer has been made, regardless of acceptance or refusal. **(C)** is incorrect because no value need be offered for solicitation, mere words of encouragement are enough. **(D)** is incorrect because while solicitation does merge with conspiracy if the encouraged crime is committed, solicitation is itself a crime regardless of the ultimate result.

22. /B/ One who is in the class of persons that a statute was enacted to protect cannot be charged with solicitation because statutory rape laws were enacted to protect minors. **(A)** misstates the law: the solicitor can be convicted regardless of the outcome of charges against other parties. **(C)** is incorrect because statutory rape is a strict liability crime, so intent is irrelevant. **(D)** correctly states the law, but is not the best answer because of the protected persons exception.

23. /A/ This is the correct response; the statement describes the *Pinkerton* conspiracy rule. **(B)** is incorrect because *M'Naghten* is a rule regarding the defense of insanity. **(C)** is incorrect because *Miranda* concerns reading of constitutional rights to a suspect. **(D)** is incorrect because *Gerstein* has to do with the requirement of holding a probable cause hearing within 48 hours of a warrantless arrest.

24. /B/ If a crime by its definition requires two persons to commit, those two persons cannot be convicted of both the underlying crime and conspiracy. **(A)** is incorrect because if a crime by its definition requires two persons to commit, those two persons cannot be convicted of both the underlying crime and conspiracy. **(C)** is not the best answer because it is not always true that there is solicitation just because there is a two-person crime. **(D)** is incorrect because other evidence may be sufficient to convict both.

25. /B/ This is the best answer because the *mens rea* for attempt is always specific intent, regardless of the *mens rea* for the underlying crime. **(A)** is incorrect because the *mens rea* for attempt is always specific intent, regardless of the *mens rea* for the underlying crime. **(C)** is incorrect because the *mens rea* for attempt is always specific intent. **(D)** is incorrect because the *mens rea* for attempt is always specific intent.

26. /C/ This describes the *mens rea* of extreme recklessness, which is sufficient malice aforethought to support a charge of murder. **(A)** is incorrect because the motive in this alternative suggests specific intent to kill, which the facts of the problem already preclude. **(B)** is incorrect because threats without specific intent to kill (which the facts already preclude) are not enough. **(D)** is incorrect because only if the defendant violated a statute while committing a dangerous felony at the time (felony murder) would this apply, which the facts do not specify.

27. /A/ Intent to cause serious bodily harm (substantial risk of death or prolonged injury to victim) is sufficient *mens rea* for murder; here the facts make it clear that D intended to shoot the victim. **(B)** is incorrect because here intent to cause serious bodily harm is sufficient *mens rea* for murder. **(C)** is incorrect because here intent to cause serious bodily harm is sufficient *mens rea* for murder. **(D)** is incorrect because here intent to cause serious bodily harm is sufficient *mens rea* for murder and there is no negligent homicide under the common law.

28. /A/ The two negatives cancel themselves out and a "human being" legally exists between live birth and legal death, which is usually described as irreversible cessation of brain function which here applies. **(B)** is incorrect because legal culpability for any death depends first upon the status of the victim as a human being. **(C)** is not the best answer because there is causation to the extent that the heart and lungs ceased to function as a result of the action of the defendant. **(D)** is not the best answer because it is a moral, not a legal, consideration.

29. /B/ The *mens rea* for involuntary manslaughter is mere recklessness. **(A)** is not the best answer because second degree murder requires at least extreme recklessness. **(C)** is not the best answer because voluntary manslaughter is intentional but was committed in the heat of passion. **(D)** is not the best answer because reckless endangerment does not involve a death.

30. /C/ This is correct; The MPC requires that a gross deviation from the "reasonable person" standard of care must be shown. **(A)** is incorrect because it overstates the *mens rea* requirement. **(B)** is incorrect because it understates the *mens rea* requirement. **(D)** is incorrect because the MPC recognizes negligent homicide, as opposed to the common law, typically as it relates to the operation of vehicles.

31. **/C/** Larceny is the taking and carrying away of property in the possession of another with the intent to permanently deprive the owner. Although Tim initially intended to borrow the tool, his subsequent intent to permanently deprive the owner of their property relates back to the time of the taking. **(A)** is incorrect because there was never an intent to permanently deprive the owner of their property. **(B)** is incorrect because Tim's reasonable mistaken belief of ownership negates the element of property "in possession of another." **(D)** is not the best answer because Tim does not "carry away" the tool.

32. **/A/** Unauthorized use of an employer's property is a form of embezzlement. An employee is usually in a fiduciary relationship with the employer. **(B)** is incorrect because no tangible property has been carried away. **(C)** is not the best answer because the employee has not induced the employer to surrender title to any tangible property which is false pretenses. **(D)** is incorrect because no property was not taken by force from a person's body or presence.

33. **/B/** False pretenses is when a defendant fraudulently induces an owner to transfer title and possession to personal property. Larceny by trick is similar, but involves only transfer of possession, not title. **(A)** is incorrect because both crimes involve fraudulent conduct. **(C)** is incorrect because either crime can involve personal property. **(D)** is incorrect because larceny by trick is similar, but involves only possession, not title.

34. **/D/** Maurice has committed the crime of receiving stolen goods. Constructive knowledge such as unreasonably low price is sufficient for "knowing" that the goods were stolen. A $10 price for goods worth $50 seems to qualify. **(A)** is incorrect because the delivery of goods by the thief to a location designated by the defendant is enough for receipt. **(B)** is not the best answer because even if the defendant did not have actual knowledge, he had constructive knowledge due to the unreasonably low price, which is sufficient. **(C)** is incorrect because the crime is complete when property is received, regardless of whether the defendant paid for it or sold it himself.

35. **/A/** Robbery is larceny by force or intimidation from a personal victim or in the presence of a person. There must be a causal relationship between the use of force and the taking of property. **(B)** is irrelevant because the clerk was not present, so the quality or amount of force used is not at issue. **(C)** is incorrect because the force must be used against the person for robbery to be in play. **(D)** is irrelevant because the clerk was not present, so the quality or amount of force used is not at issue.

36. **/C/** Entering the dwelling house of another with the intent to commit a felony or larceny inside is burglary. No forced entry is required, and in most jurisdictions, a nighttime entry is no longer necessary. **(A)** is not the best answer because although larceny has occurred, it is not the most serious crime he has committed. **(B)** is incorrect because no person was present as is required for robbery. **(D)** is incorrect because no fiduciary relationship is indicated in these facts.

37. **/C/** Recklessness or specific intent must be present to warrant a criminal battery charge. **(A)** is not the best answer because there is more than one correct *mens rea* listed in the available responses. **(B)** is incorrect because gross negligence is usually insufficient for criminal battery. **(D)** is incorrect because negligence is insufficient for criminal battery.

38. **/B/** Assault is defined as the intentional creation of apprehension of an immediate battery. **(A)** is incorrect because a threat of serious bodily harm is not required, just as it is not required for a battery conviction. **(C)** is incorrect because if the defendant succeeds in battering the victim after an attempted battery assault, the assault merges with the battery. **(D)** is incorrect because threat of serious bodily harm is not required, just as it is not required for a battery conviction.

39. **/B/** Intoxication is not a defense to rape unless the defendant is so intoxicated that he does not realize that he is having intercourse. **(A)** is incorrect because having consensual intercourse while intoxicated is not illegal and the prosecution has the burden to show the victim did not consent. **(C)** is incorrect because physical resistance is no longer generally required to be proven by the victim. **(D)** is incorrect because intoxication is not a defense to rape unless the defendant is so intoxicated that he does not realize that he is having intercourse.

40. **/D/** For a charge of kidnapping, specific intent or substantial certainty that confinement of the victim will result is required. **(A)** is incorrect because physical restraint is not necessarily required; a threat may be enough. **(B)** is incorrect because the victim need not attempt to escape. **(C)** is not the best answer because any measurable confinement time can qualify.

41. **/D/** This is the required *mens rea* for arson. **(A)** is incorrect because recklessness is not a sufficient *mens rea* for arson. **(B)** is incorrect because most modern statutes have eliminated the "dwelling" requirement for arson. **(C)** is incorrect because most modern statutes have eliminated the exception for arson if burning down one's own property.

42. **/C/** This is the best answer, because no matter how egregious a violation of privacy, if there is no state action (a government officer, police, etc.), the Fourth Amendment does not apply. **(A)** is not the best answer because there may be a limited expectation of privacy at a place of business. **(B)** is incorrect because the search is not of the computer, but of the messages, which amount to the "personal effects" of the employee. **(D)** is incorrect because reviewing personal communications is a search, like wiretapping.

43. **/B/** This is a correct statement of the "Open Fields" doctrine which limits a legitimate search to those areas within the curtilage of the main house. **(A)** is not the best answer because it misstates the doctrine – entry of premises is not permitted. **(C)** is incorrect because the garbage placed in a public garbage can loses its residential protection. **(D)** is incorrect because it is not a correct statement of the Open Fields doctrine. Also, a car is still somewhat private even if parked in an open field – an articulable suspicion would still be required.

44. **/B/** For probable cause to arrest, there must be both a likelihood of violation of the law and a likelihood that the person arrested committed the violation. A warrant is not always required, such as if the arrest is of a felony suspect in a public place, or a misdemeanor suspect when the misdemeanor was committed in the officer's presence. **(A)** is incorrect because another element is required for probable cause to arrest. **(C)** is not the best answer because a warrant is redundant; procurement of a warrant must be based on probable cause. **(D)** is incorrect because probable cause does not require a likelihood of conviction.

45. **/A/** A person committing a felony in a public place may be arrested without a warrant, although a *Gerstein* hearing must be held within 48 hours to establish probable cause. **(B)** is incorrect because articulable suspicion, required for a *Terry* frisk, is not probable cause, which is required for an arrest. **(C)** is incorrect because the suspect could be in a dwelling other than his own in which case a warrant would be required. **(D)** is incorrect because the misdemeanor exception applies only when the misdemeanor is committed in front of a police officer, not a private citizen.

46. **/C/** This is the only correct alternative. Illegally obtained evidence will be excluded, but the case will go forward. **(A)** is incorrect because an unlawful arrest does not result in dismissal of the case. **(B)** is incorrect because there may be other evidence independent of the unlawful arrest. **(D)** is incorrect because any evidence seized during a search subsequent to arrest would be excluded as fruit of the poisonous tree.

47. **/D/** Full probable cause to arrest must exist before any detention where the suspect does not feel free to leave such as a police organized line up. **(A)** is incorrect because it understates the standard – full probable cause to arrest must exist. **(B)** is incorrect because it understates the standard – full probable cause to arrest must exist. **(C)** is incorrect because it overstates the requirement – if an officer has full probable cause to arrest, he may detain the suspect, even without a warrant.

48. **/C/** This is the best answer because it is the only true alternative. The warrant must contain a description of the items sought. **(A)** is incorrect because hearsay may be acceptable evidence for establishing search warrant probable cause. **(B)** is incorrect because an articulable suspicion is usually sufficient justification to stop an automobile. **(D)** is incorrect because if an informant is historically reliable and the information he provides appears reliable, his affidavit may be sufficient for probable cause.

49. **/B/** The only correct statement in that a proper search warrant must specify the particular location to be searched. **(A)** is incorrect because the warrant need not identify the particular rooms. **(C)** is incorrect because who owns the property may not be relevant and need not usually be specified. **(D)** is incorrect because charges must be included in an indictment or information, but not a search warrant.

50. **/B/** Incident to lawful arrest, an officer may search within the suspect's reach, or "wingspan." **(A)** is incorrect because a search of all the suspect's property would require probable cause or a warrant. **(C)** is incorrect because a search of the suspect's home would require probable cause or a warrant. **(D)** is incorrect because a search of the suspect's trunk or anything out of his "wingspan" would require probable cause or a warrant.

51. **/A/** While executing a valid search warrant, an officer may conduct a protective sweep of the premises or home for dangerous persons and a pat-down of other persons present. Since the warrant was for illegal weapons, Officer Jones was likely reasonable in conducting the pat-down. **(B)** is incorrect because the warrant was for illegal weapons and Officer Jones was likely reasonable in conducting the pat-down. **(C)** is incorrect because it misstates the law; a *Terry* frisk requires an articulable suspicion to be valid and "always" is an absolute word. **(D)** is incorrect because the warrant was for illegal weapons and Officer Jones was likely reasonable in conducting the pat-down.

52. **/A/** "Exigent circumstances" usually exist when an automobile is believed to have been used in a crime. Generally, this means that the automobile itself constitutes culpable evidence, and it might be unavailable by the time a warrant is obtained. **(B)** is incorrect because simply that the car appears to be in working order is not enough. If it were enough, the exigent circumstances exception would automatically apply to all vehicles, and that is too broad. **(C)** is incorrect because it describes a probable cause situation and is not the best answer. **(D)** is incorrect because it describes the "in plain view" exception to requiring a search warrant, so it is not the best answer.

53. **/D/** Contraband hidden in a container is not in plain view, even if the container is, so therefore the handgun suppression motion should be granted. **(A)** is incorrect because it goes to proving the criminal charge, not to the validity of the search. **(B)** is incorrect because contraband hidden in a container is not in plain view, even if the container itself is. **(C)** is not the best answer because given the circumstances; the police had probable cause to enter.

54. **/C/** The most correct alternative because a vehicle may normally be impounded under any or all three of these circumstances. **(A)** is incorrect because, while impound is proper, there is no grounds stated here to justify a search. **(B)** is not the best answer because it is not as complete an answer rationale as C and someone else could drive the car. **(D)** is incorrect because here the vehicle may not always be impounded if it can be towed to a safer location.

55. **/B/** This is the broadest and best answer because a non-warrant search is permissive. When a consent search is conducted, there are usually no limitations on when and why consent may be revoked. **(A)** is not the best answer because there are no limitations on when and why consent may be revoked. **(C)** is not the best answer because there are no limitations on when and why consent may be revoked. **(D)** is not the best answer because there are no limitations on when and why consent may be revoked.

56. **/C/** Evanescent evidence is physical evidence that might "disappear" or "dissipate" before a warrant can be obtained, thus justifying the police to conduct a warrantless seizure. **(A)** is incorrect because an automobile is evidence that will not "disappear," (although it could be moved or destroyed) which is the definition of evanescent evidence. **(B)** is incorrect because a handwriting sample can always be reproduced. **(D)** is incorrect because a confession is not physical evidence.

57. **/A/** Consent to record by one party when the conversation relates to a fire, medical emergency, crime, disaster, extortion, or hostage situation is sufficient to avoid the warrant requirement. **(B)** is incorrect because a wiretap is a search. **(C)** is not the best answer because consent by one party when the conversation relates to a fire, medical emergency, crime, disaster, extortion, or hostage situation is enough to avoid the warrant requirement. **(D)** is not the best answer because consent by one party when the conversation relates to a fire, medical emergency, crime, disaster, extortion, or hostage situation is sufficient to avoid the warrant requirement.

58. **/D/** The best answer because both the *Miranda* warning and voluntary confession circumstances weigh in favor of a confession's admissibility. **(A)** is not the best answer because signed affidavits do not make confessions any more or less admissible. (B) is not the best answer. *Miranda* warnings are a requirement for admissibility, but the facts here do not specifically say anything about whether the confession was voluntary. **(C)** is not the best answer because it does not include the required *Miranda* warnings.

59. /C/ The coerced confession may not be used by the prosecution for any purpose, but the prosecutor's case may be able to proceed on other evidence. **(A)** is incorrect because the prosecution may not use a coerced confession for any purpose. **(B)** is not the best answer because the prosecution may not use a coerced confession for any purpose. **(D)** is incorrect because the case may proceed on other evidence.

60. /B/ Despite the situational trickery, this is a custodial interrogation because the "cellmate" has drawn the confession out of Joe through interrogation while he was under custody. **(A)** is not the best answer because the D had demanded his *Miranda* rights and could not be interrogated without his lawyer. **(C)** is incorrect because of the special exception of a police officer cellmate interrogation. **(D)** is not the best answer because a confession must be both voluntary and obtained in compliance with *Miranda*.

61. /D/ A grand jury witness has none of these rights and cannot be compelled to provide potentially incriminating evidence unless the witness is granted immunity. **(A)** is incorrect because a grand jury witness does not have the right to receive *Miranda* warnings. **(B)** is incorrect because a grand jury witness does not ordinarily have the right to have an attorney present. **(C)** is incorrect because a grand jury witness does not have the right to be confronted with the witnesses against him.

62. /A/ The waiver of the right to counsel during formal court proceedings must be affirmative, knowing, and intelligent. **(B)** is incorrect because clear and unambiguous invocation only applies to the right to counsel during questioning. **(C)** is not the best answer because on rare occasions a judge will permit a *pro se* criminal defendant. **(D)** is incorrect because the right to counsel during formal proceedings is protected by the Sixth Amendment.

63. /B/ This kind of unbalanced lineup would be conducive to mistaken identification, and thus excluded since the witness at trial might identify Bob based on the police station session rather than memory of the crime. **(A)** is incorrect because the charges would not necessarily be dismissed; another, independent identification would still be admissible. **(C)** is not the best answer because the witness has already identified Bob based on the tainted session, and this would influence her. **(D)** is not the best answer because under the circumstances, it is unlikely a judge would find this lineup acceptable.

64. /D/ A *Gerstein* probable cause hearing must be held within 48 hours of detainment upon any warrantless arrest or indictment. **(A)** is incorrect because warrants must be issued prior to arrest. **(B)** is incorrect because it misstates the deadline for an arraignment, which is 14 days. **(C)** is not the best answer because a suspect arrested on probable cause without a warrant may be detained for 48 hours until a *Gerstein* hearing is held.

65. /C/ A competency hearing is held to determine whether the defendant is competent to stand trial. **(A)** is incorrect because a competency hearing relates to the competency of the defendant, not counsel. **(B)** is not the best answer because competency relates to the defendant's ability to stand trial, not the defendant's state of mind when he allegedly committed the crime. **(D)** is incorrect because a competency hearing relates to the defendant's competency, not the question of a fair trial in the jurisdiction.

66. /B/ A judge always has the final say in whether to accept or reject a plea bargain, even if both sides agree. **(A)** is incorrect because the plea agreement must be presented to a judge. **(C)** is incorrect because a voluntary and intelligent plea agreement waives the Sixth Amendment jury trial right. **(D)** misstates the law: a plea may be withdrawn if the court lacked jurisdiction, the defendant received ineffective assistance, etc.

67. /C/ This is the best answer because it is the only proper remedy for violation of the right to a speedy trial. **(A)** is incorrect because a new trial is not held. **(B)** is incorrect because once the defendant's rights violation has occurred, any trial held subsequently will still be in violation. **(D)** is not the best answer because compensation is not ordinarily granted for constitutional rights violations in the context of a criminal proceeding.

68. /A/ There is no D constitutional right to a closed criminal trial, only to an open trial. **(B)** is incorrect because the judge has discretion. **(C)** is incorrect because the judge has discretion and written justification for this type of bench decision is not required. **(D)** is incorrect because there is no constitutional right to a closed trial, only an open trial.

69. /B/ On a 12-member jury, a 9 to 3 guilty vote is sufficient to convict the criminal D. **(A)** is incorrect because only the minimum 6-member jury need be unanimous. **(C)** is incorrect because selecting jurors based on race violates *Batson*. **(D)** is incorrect because a conviction by a majority is not enough in a criminal case.

70. /C/ The criminal's right to confront adverse witnesses may be forfeited if the defendant is continually disruptive. **(A)** is incorrect because the right to be present at trial may be forfeited if the defendant is continually disruptive. **(B)** is incorrect because it misstates the law; the right to be present at trial is independent of the Confrontation (of witnesses) Clause. **(D)** is incorrect because provided the defendant does not forfeit his right to be present at trial, it is otherwise available for every criminal proceeding regardless of the charge level.

71. /D/ The test for the required ineffective assistance of counsel is that there is a reasonable probability of a different outcome had counsel been competent. **(A)** is not the best answer because questionable evidence might have been ignored or discounted by the fact finder. **(B)** is incorrect because failing to make an appropriate objection may have had no effect on the outcome of the case. **(C)** is incorrect because counsel's strategy may have been correct; it might have been misfeasance to obey the client.

72. /C/ A witness may invoke the Fifth Amendment privilege selectively, it is only the defendant who waives the Fifth by voluntarily taking the stand. **(A)** is incorrect because the Confrontation Clause does not entitle a defendant to the answer to every question posed to a witness (for example, the information may be privileged). **(B)** is incorrect because a witness may invoke the Fifth Amendment privilege selectively; it is only the defendant who waives the Fifth by taking the stand. **(D)** misstates the law because the Fifth Amendment privilege applies to any person testifying in a criminal or civil proceeding.

73. /A/ Every element in a criminal case must be proven beyond a reasonable doubt. **(B)** is incorrect because every element must be proven beyond a reasonable doubt, even if not "key." **(C)** misstates the standard of proof, which is "beyond a reasonable doubt." **(D)** misstates the standard of proof, which is "beyond a reasonable doubt."

74. /B/ A retrial is barred only if the appellate court reverses specifically because the evidence was insufficient to support a conviction. **(A)** is incorrect because double jeopardy is not offended if the verdict is merely set aside. **(C)** is incorrect because an appellate court reviews the record, it does not restart the trial process. **(D)** is not the best answer because "separate sovereigns" is not the only exception that would allow a retrial.

75. **/C/** Double jeopardy prevents subsequent prosecution of two separate charges based on the same core factual events unless each charge has an element separate from the other. Here manslaughter is a lesser included crime in murder. **(A)** is incorrect because whether or not the charges are different, double jeopardy is usually offended if the charges arise from the exact same factual events. **(B)** is incorrect because an acquittal may never be reversed. **(D)** is incorrect because regardless of whether the lesser or greater offense is tried first, double jeopardy prevents subsequent prosecution of the other if arising from the same factual events.

76. **/B/** In a criminal case the prosecution must demonstrate evidence admissibility by a preponderance of the evidence. **(A)** misstates the admissibility standard of proof. **(C)** misstates the admissibility standard of proof. **(D)** misstates the standard of proof for evidence admissibility.

77. **/B/** Generally, such tainted evidence will be admissible for impeachment purposes, if it directly contradicts the defendant's testimony. **(A)** is incorrect because evidence obtained in violation of the Fourth Amendment is admissible in some circumstances. **(C)** is incorrect because the harmless error analysis is at the appellate, not the trial, level. **(D)** is incorrect because there is only a limited exception based on the good faith reliance of the police on a facially valid search warrant – such good faith does not generally exonerate illegal behavior.

78. **/C/** Evidence that is obtained through illegal sources or resulting therefrom are "fruits of the poisonous tree" and are generally excluded under the "fruits of the poisonous tree" doctrine. **(A)** is not the best answer because the doctrine relates to excluded evidence, not charges. **(B)** is incorrect because the doctrine relates to excluded evidence, not jurors. **(D)** is not the best answer because the doctrine relates to excluded evidence, not arguments.

79. **/D/** A live witness may always testify voluntarily, regardless of how she was discovered, such as an undercover police agent. **(A)** is incorrect because a live witness may always testify voluntarily, regardless of how she was discovered. **(B)** is incorrect because a live witness may testify voluntarily on any subject, regardless of how she was discovered. **(C)** is incorrect because a live witness may testify voluntarily on any subject, regardless of how she was discovered.

80. **/A/** A motion to suppress hearing to determine if evidence is admissible must be conducted outside the presence of the jury, and the defendant's statements therein may not be used as evidence at the trial. **(B)** is incorrect because the burden is on the prosecution to justify admissibility if the defense raises the issue. **(C)** is incorrect because the defendant does have the right to counsel in an evidence suppression hearing. **(D)** is incorrect because the statements may not be used against the defendant at trial and the jury may not be present.

81. **/B/** This is the best answer, because some states recognize degrees of burglary based on whether the defendant enters another's property, so this might not be considered 1st degree burglary. **(A)** is not the best answer because even if he could prove that Mike unlawfully deprived him of his property, it is possible to commit burglary against someone who is not the true owner of the property taken. **(C)** is incorrect because misdemeanor larceny is a sufficient underlying offense to burglary, because of the danger created by breaking and entering a dwelling. **(D)** is incorrect because persons need not actually be present in a dwelling for a burglary to be committed.

82. **/B/** This is the best response because conspiracy involves an agreement between two or more persons to commit an unlawful act, and a substantial step in furtherance of the conspiracy. Actual commitment of the crime is a separate offense, unless it merges. **(A)** is insufficient because Mike did have the necessary *mens rea* at the time the conspiracy was formed. **(C)** is not the best answer because reserving the hotel room is a substantial step. **(D)** is incorrect because whether or not he committed fraud is not relevant to the issue of conspiracy to commit the drug offense.

83. **/D/** This is the best answer because the prosecution must prove all required elements, and an element of burglary is intent to commit a felony or larceny which the facts state was not demonstrated by the prosecution. **(A)** is incorrect because the agreement must include the *mens rea* of a crime as well as the *actus reus*. **(B)** is incorrect because it describes a factor in determining the degree of burglary, not an element of the crime. **(C)** is incorrect because conspiracy does not merge with burglary and could be a separate charge.

84. **/C/** This is the best answer because it is an accurate restatement of the felony-murder rule. **(A)** is not the best answer because while intent is normally required for murder, the felony-murder rule is an exception. **(B)** is incorrect, because the cashier's actions were reasonable and predictable under the circumstances. **(D)** is incorrect, because the felony-murder rule does not "assume" intent, it eliminates the element of intent. Intent is rarely assumed; it is either an element of the offense or it is not.

85. **/A/** Larceny is the best answer, because Lawrence committed the taking and carrying away of the property of another with intent to steal. That he only made it a few feet does not negate the charge. **(B)** is incorrect because burglary involves entering a structure. **(C)** is not the best answer because although the property was taken from Victor's person, there was no force or threat of force used, a required element of robbery. **(D)** is incorrect because one of the listed crimes has been committed.

86. **/A/** Larceny is the best answer, because William has committed the trespassory taking and carrying away of the property of another with intent to steal. His belief that the property was rightfully his does not invoke the recapture of chattels rule because he was not in pursuit of the chattel directly after the taking. **(B)** Burglary is not the best answer because at the time he entered the dwelling, he did not have intent to commit a crime therein, only to rescue an animal. **(C)** Robbery is not the best answer because the owner of the property was not present and no force was used or threatened against him. **(D)** is incorrect because William is guilty of one of the listed crimes.

87. **/C/** This is the best answer because he has committed robbery, defined as larceny with the two additional elements of 1) taking the property from person or presence of the owner, and 2) accomplishing the property taking by force or intimidation and/or putting the owner in fear. The reasonable person standard is not applied in this situation – it does not matter that a reasonable person would not have had any apprehension of harm. It is enough that the apprehension was created in the particular victim. **(A)** is not the best answer because of the additional elements elevating this action from larceny to robbery. **(B)** is not the best answer because burglary requires entry in to a dwelling or structure with intent to commit a crime. **(D)** is incorrect because Gary is guilty of one of the listed crimes.

88. **/C/** This is the best answer because it describes the requisite state of mind to pass the *M'Naghten* test: the presence of a mental disease or defect coupled with an inability to comprehend the nature and quality of the act. **(A)** is not the best answer because it suggests an acknowledgement of awareness that an act is incorrect, which is overridden by an uncontrollable urge created by mental illness. In a jurisdiction governed by the "irresistible impulse" test, this argument might be successful. **(B)** is not the best answer because there is no mental disease or defect at work. At best the defendant's sudden violent outburst might save him from a first-degree premeditated murder charge. **(D)** is not the best answer because it suggests an acknowledgement of awareness that an act is incorrect, which is overridden by an uncontrollable urge created by mental illness. In a jurisdiction governed by the "irresistible impulse" test, this might be successful.

89. **/A/** This is the best answer because Nancy's conduct may meet the elements for solicitation liability; she has encouraged Gerald to commit the substantive crime. **(B)** is not the best answer because rendering criminal assistance usually occurs after a crime has been committed, in concealing or assisting flight from a crime. **(C)** is incorrect because Nancy's statement to Gerald did not initiate the attack. **(D)** is incorrect because Nancy is guilty of one of the listed crimes.

90. **/B/** Conspiracy requires complicity, intent, and active participation; here, this is the best answer because some specific action, even if it is just words of encouragement, is required to create accomplice liability. **(A)** is not the best answer because Barry's smile during the attack suggests that he was not frightened. **(C)** is not the best answer because a "no legal duty to rescue" defense is applicable to a tort action, while the criminal law has numerous exceptions. **(D)** is not the best answer because onlookers who hope for the criminal result are considered to have the same criminal intent as the actor.

91. **/C/** This is the best answer because the right of officers to search automobiles under exigent circumstances (with probable cause) but without a warrant does not apply to locked briefcases. **(A)** is not the best answer because the eyewitnesses' description of the car and the proximity of the car to the scene, arguably established sufficient probable cause. **(B)** is incorrect because the plain view rule applies to contraband that is in plain view (*e.g.*, a clear baggie containing suspected drugs) not to locked solid containers that happen to be visible. **(D)** is incorrect because Dave was not yet under arrest, so the "wingspan" exception allowing a warrantless search incident to an arrest is not applicable.

92. **/B/** This is the best answer, because there was no evidence that there was cocaine at Debbie's apartment and the prosecutor was merely speculating that drugs might be there. **(A)** is not the best answer because a suspect's residence is not the only location that can be subject to a valid warrant. **(C)** is not the best answer because a valid arrest alone is not sufficient for a valid warrant. **(D)** is not the best answer, because the standard for evaluating bias is whether the magistrate had a "stake in the outcome of the case" not simply that the magistrate may be sympathetic to prosecutors in general.

93. **/D/** This is the best answer, because defendants have a right not to take the stand at trial and remain silent, but once they voluntarily take the stand, Fifth Amendment protection against self-incrimination is waived. **(A)** is not the best answer because there are no facts suggesting that Dave's attorney did not advise him properly, and a client always has the controlling right to decide whether to testify in a criminal trial. **(B)** is incorrect because only witnesses, not defendants, may take the stand and invoke the Fifth Amendment as each question is asked. **(C)** is not the best answer because it is too random and there are no facts to suggest that Dave's testimony was not critical to his conviction. The outcome might have been different if he had decided not to testify.

94. **/C/** This is the best answer because voluntary consent is effective if the person consenting has authority over the premises/property to be searched. **(A)** is incorrect because knowledge of the right to refuse a search is only one element in evaluating the voluntary nature of consent; it is not an absolute requirement for a valid consent search. All other facts suggest that the consent was given voluntarily. **(B)** is not the best answer because although a warrant could be obtained on reliable information from a dependable informant, it is not required if voluntary consent is obtained. **(D)** is not the best answer, because a search by consent usually applies to all places which could reasonably contain the items seized, and all property over which the consenting party has authority, so the bedroom closet seems to qualify.

95. **/B/** This is the best answer because in a felony case, a *Gerstein* preliminary hearing must be held (usually with witnesses) for a magistrate to determine whether there is probable cause to believe that the defendant committed the crime charged when a D is arrested without a warrant. **(A)** is incorrect because five weeks does not seem to be an unreasonable trial delay. **(C)** is incorrect because arraignment always follows the indictment/filing of information. **(D)** is not the best answer because the extensive documentary evidence combined with the statement of a reliable informant is probably enough for the filing of a complaint.

96. **/A/** This is the best answer because whenever a warrantless arrest is made, a *Gerstein* hearing is required to be held within 48 hours in front of a magistrate to establish probable cause. **(B)** is incorrect because the broken taillight is an infraction that makes the stop legal. **(C)** is incorrect because the "wingspan" rule applies to search incident to arrest, and in any event is trumped by the "plain view" rule. **(D)** is incorrect because arrest warrants are not required in exigent circumstances with probable cause. In this case, the exigent circumstance of the suspects being in a car justifies immediate arrest.

97. **/A/** This is the best answer because confessions in the absence of *Miranda* warnings are only excluded if they are given during interrogation when the suspect is not free to leave. Voluntary utterances prior to arrest are neither custodial nor the result of interrogation and are admissible. **(B)** is incorrect because the statement is incriminating as to the charge – rendering criminal assistance. **(C)** is not the best answer because an officer is only required to administer *Miranda* warnings upon arrest. **(D)** is not the best answer because an admission by a party opponent is not hearsay.

98. /C/ This is the best answer because waiver of the right to counsel must always be knowing and intelligent, and is particularly scrutinized when a guilty plea consent agreement is entered; here, all four of the RARI *Miranda* requirements were not met. **(A)** is incorrect because an advantageous plea agreement does not negate any constitutional improprieties that may have occurred in reaching the plea. **(B)** is not the best answer because John's question was not a "clear invocation" of the right to counsel. **(D)** is not the best answer, because the facts in this alternative deal with the right to counsel during formal court proceedings, not interrogation. Also, the rule for the right to counsel during formal proceedings is quite the contrary – waiver must be voluntary, knowing, and intelligent.

99. /A/ This is the best answer because even if a judge reasonably believes a criminal defendant will do an incompetent *pro se* job, the right to demand self-representation is absolute. **(B)** is incorrect because there are no facts given here that indicate that the appointed attorney was ineffective. **(C)** is not the best answer because no facts indicate whether the error affected the outcome. **(D)** is incorrect because while the right to counsel may have been protected, the right to demand self-representation was violated.

100./C/ This is the best answer because re-prosecution after a hung jury is not considered double jeopardy. **(A)** is not the best answer because while it is true that double jeopardy attaches after the jury is sworn, a hung jury negates it. **(B)** is not the best answer because the hung jury in Mary's trial suggests that Tim's intent is at least a debatable issue, and thus is an unlikely candidate for judgment as a matter of law. **(D)** is not the best answer because two crimes are different for double jeopardy purposes only if each requires proof of one additional fact that the other does not.

101./A/ This is the best answer, because although normally an automobile search incident to arrest is restricted to areas within the suspect's control and excludes locked containers, the existence of probable cause – seeing the burglary – overrides this restriction. **(B)** is not the best answer, because in an automobile search incident to arrest, the trunk may not be searched unless probable cause exists and "always" is an absolute word. **(C)** is not the best answer because the "wingspan" or "control" rule only applies when the officer does not have probable cause to believe the locked trunk may contain evidence of a crime. **(D)** is incorrect because the officer's observance of Stan's actions and behavior likely gave him significant cause to arrest.

102./C/ This is the best answer because police coercion is required for a confession to be considered involuntary and here the coercion was induced by a private party. **(A)** is not the best answer because the police did not participate in the coercion. **(B)** is not the best answer because the facts given here are insufficient to make this determination, and a confession need not be corroborated by other evidence to be admissible. **(D)** is incorrect because there is not factual support for the alternative's rationale and belief in the likelihood of a threat is probably not relevant to the issue of voluntariness of a confession.

103./D/ This is the best answer because the facts suggest that the confession was coerced by improper police conduct. **(A)** is incorrect because the *Miranda* requirements are separate from voluntariness requirements. Even a confession procured in compliance with *Miranda* is not admissible if coerced. **(B)** is not correct because the facts do not suggest this, and a constitutional violation is not usually "harmless error." **(C)** is incorrect – a coerced confession may not be admitted in direct, although a confession in violation of *Miranda* may be admitted to impeach.

104./C/ This is the best answer because a defendant may not usually successfully argue a search and seizure claim in an appeal if she had opportunity for full and fair consideration of the issue at the trial court level and did not there raise the issue timely, thereby preserving it for appeal consideration. This is usually true even if the appellate court believes that the trial court reached the incorrect result. **(A)** is not the best answer because while these may be good arguments at the trial court level, they may not usually be considered in an appeal proceeding if they were fully litigated below. **(B)** is not the best answer because a consent search is at least theoretically permissible, and therefore a warrant is not an absolute prerequisite for searching a house. **(D)** is incorrect because the issues in controversy were fully litigated below.

105./C/ This is the best answer because Michael had intent to kill his wife, which is defined as "malice aforethought," despite his good and merciful intentions. The fact that Terry would have died shortly anyway does not negate causation because her death was hastened. **(A)** is incorrect because the *mens rea* for involuntary manslaughter is recklessness. **(B)** is incorrect because voluntary manslaughter is committed in the heat of passion, and the facts here indicate premeditation. **(D)** is incorrect because Michael is guilty of one of the listed crimes.

106./D/ "None of the above" is the best answer because the doctor fulfilled the MPC requirements for withdrawal from a conspiracy; he ceased participation and attempted to prevent illegal acts of other conspirators. He did this before a substantial step was taken in furtherance of the crime. **(A)** is incorrect because the doctor withdrew from the crime before a substantial step was taken, and thus has an affirmative defense. **(B)** is incorrect because conspiracy also requires an overt step in furtherance of the conspiracy, and the doctor withdrew immediately. **(C)** is incorrect because the doctor did not perform the *actus reus* for murder.

107./C/ This is the best answer because Brenda "agreed" through her nodding during the discussion and her subsequent actions. Verbal or written agreement is not always required for conspiracy to commit murder. Conspirators are directly liable for all foreseeable crimes to which they agree, even if they do not personally commit the act. **(A)** is incorrect because murder requires malice aforethought. **(B)** is not the best answer because mere acquiescence to save her sister more unnecessary pain is not malice aforethought. **(D)** is incorrect because Brenda may be guilty of one of the listed crimes.

108./A/ This is the best answer, because Eddie has fulfilled all the requisite elements for a burglary. He broke in (physical force is not required) without permission, entered a building at night (although most jurisdictions no longer require it to be at night), and had the intent to commit larceny at the time of entry. **(B)** is incorrect because today "breaking" only requires lack of permission to enter; no actual force is needed. **(C)** is not the best answer, because intent to commit any larceny is sufficient for a burglary charge. **(D)** is incorrect because the store was connected to an apartment building (and furthermore, most jurisdictions have eliminated the "dwelling" wrongful entry requirement; any physical structure will do).

109./C/ This is the best answer because a proper warrant based on the word of an informant requires that (1) the informant be reliable and (2) the information received appear reliable under the circumstances. Neither requirement appears to be fulfilled here. **(A)** is incorrect because *Miranda* warnings are required before a custodial interrogation, and have nothing to do with a search. **(B)** is not the best answer because a warrant search does not require consent although the warrant was not proper and therefore a lack of consent could be a viable argument, but it is not the best argument, as the call of the question demands. **(D)** is incorrect because "outside the scope" means any location not named in the warrant, or any hiding place that could not reasonably contain the items to be seized. The freezer qualifies as a reasonable hiding place.

110./D/ The defense will likely succeed based on the available facts. The threat of serious bodily harm or death against one's family member is sufficient to qualify as duress if the belief that the threat will be carried out is reasonable. Here, no facts indicate otherwise. **(A)** is incorrect because the threat of harm is probably imminent if, as here, the threatened person is in the next room. **(B)** is incorrect because only murder and manslaughter exclude duress as a defense. **(C)** is not the best answer because threatened harm against a family member is usually sufficient for duress.

111./A/ Stan will likely be convicted on these facts. He intentionally and harmfully touched Slick's body directly, which constitutes all the elements of battery. **(B)** is incorrect because Slick had retreated back to his car and was no longer a threat to Stan, so Stan cannot claim self-defense. **(C)** is incorrect because even minor and temporary pain is sufficient for battery. **(D)** is incorrect because there is no "assumption of risk" principle in criminal battery; assumption of risk is a tort principle that does not apply here.

112./A/ This is the best answer because Tom can be convicted of robbery or larceny depending on whom the jury believes. Robbery is larceny by force in a person's presence, so if Nancy's testimony is believed, Tom will be convicted of robbery. If the purse was simply taken with no force involved, Tom will be convicted of larceny. **(B)** is incorrect because if Nancy is believed, robbery is proved. **(C)** is incorrect because on these facts, either robbery or larceny has been committed. **(D)** is incorrect because larceny is a lesser included offense to robbery, so Tom could not be convicted of both crimes.

113./D/ A strict liability crime requires no *mens rea* for culpability. The mere *actus reus* is enough. It does not matter whether Ben knew or should have known that Mel was underage, the fact that he made the sale to a person under 21 is all that is required for statutory liability. **(A)** is not the best answer because although Ben could have avoided culpability by ensuring that Mel was 21, his failure to do so is not the reason for his culpability – the statute is strict liability. **(B)** is incorrect because the *actus reus* of the statute is the sale of alcohol, regardless of who is the owner of the store. **(C)** is incorrect, because this is a strict liability statute, culpability is not at issue.

114./D/ Probable cause sufficient for a warrant exists when information is presented that would lead a reasonable person to conclude that seizable evidence will be found. The six-week delay raises serious doubts as to whether the evidence would still be in Wanda's home and a small amount of drugs found is not even close to half a kilo as stated in the warrant application. **(A)** is incorrect because a warrant must be based on probable cause to be valid regardless of whether other formalities are observed. **(B)** is incorrect because a warrant must be based on probable cause to be valid regardless of whether other formalities are observed. **(C)** is not the best answer because reliable information from a reliable informant is sufficient and usually needs no corroboration.

115./B/ This is the best answer because the warrant specified ½ kilo of PCP, which could not possibly fit in a shoe box. Even a search pursuant to a proper warrant is limited to those places where the evidence to be seized could reasonably be. **(A)** is incorrect because one day later is not sufficient delay to invalidate a warrant. **(C)** is a misstatement of the law. Consent is not required if a warrant is valid. **(D)** is irrelevant to the inquiry. To whom the drugs belong has no bearing on the validity of the search, only to Wanda's ultimate culpability.

116./C/ If a crime by its definition requires two persons agreement to commit, both must agree and the facts do not indicate Sophie agreed. **(A)** is incorrect because a conspiracy can be formed by agreement and a substantial step, even if the crime is not completed. **(B)** is not the best answer because if a crime by its definition requires two persons to commit, those persons cannot be convicted of both the underlying crime and conspiracy. **(D)** is not the best answer because if a crime by its definition requires two persons to commit, those persons cannot be convicted of both the underlying crime and conspiracy.

117./A/ Q is likely guilty of murder. Extreme recklessness is sufficient *mens rea* for murder, and Q's actions seem to fit the definition. **(B)** is not the best answer because extreme recklessness is sufficient *mens rea* for murder. **(C)** is not the best answer because extreme recklessness is sufficient *mens rea* for murder. **(D)** is incorrect because Q can be convicted of murder by causing the death through his extreme recklessness.

118./A/ Intent to kill transfers from one victim to another. If Q intended to kill or inflict serious bodily harm on his neighbor, that intent would transfer to the meter-reader, and Q could be charged with her murder. **(B)** is incorrect because the doctrine of transferred intent applies here. **(C)** is incorrect because the doctrine of transferred intent applies here. **(D)** is incorrect because the doctrine of transferred intent applies.

119./A/ When a suspect commits a misdemeanor in an officer's presence, the officer need not wait for a warrant to arrest. **(B)** is incorrect because the "knock and announce" requirement relates to search warrants, not arrests when the crime was conducted in an officer's presence. **(C)** is not the best answer, because while generally a suspect at home can only be arrested pursuant to a warrant, in this case Tim's arrival at home was a technicality, the officer was in continuous pursuit. **(D)** is incorrect because articulable suspicion is a lesser form of probable cause and is not enough to arrest.

120./C/ Incident to a lawful arrest, an officer may conduct a full search of the suspect. **(A)** is incorrect because incident to a lawful arrest, an officer may conduct a full search of the suspect. **(B)** is incorrect because being able to specify the location of evidence to be seized is a rule relating to the formalities of obtaining a search warrant. **(D)** is incorrect because incident to a lawful arrest, an officer may conduct a full search of the suspect even if there is not an apprehension of danger.

121./B/ This is the best answer because the mobile home was sufficiently independent and remote from the house and was not specified in the warrant. **(A)** is incorrect because the mobile home was sufficiently independent and remote from the house and was not specified in the warrant. **(C)** is not the best answer because fruits of a search may be seized. **(D)** is incorrect because a warrant to search a particular dwelling does not cover every dwelling or building owned by that person (*e.g.*, property on another block, in another state.)

122./D/ A warrant must be executed without unreasonable delay to avoid becoming stale. If not, the warrant could be declared invalid and all the evidence obtained therefrom would be inadmissible. **(A)** is incorrect because the right to a speedy trial only attaches after arrest/detention. **(B)** misstates the law, no such conclusive presumption exists. **(C)** is not the best answer because excluded vital evidence is a more serious problem than counsel's potential arguments.

123./C/ This is the best answer because the parents' actions appear to meet the test for criminal negligence under the MPC of creating an unreasonable risk of harm and awareness of the risk. **(A)** is incorrect because the MPC does recognize criminal negligence, although the common law does not. **(B)** is incorrect because it describes the *mens rea* "knowingly" under the MPC. **(D)** is not the best answer because it misstates the law.

124./B/ A child between 7 and 14 is presumed incapable of intending a crime, but the presumption may be rebutted by the prosecution if they can present clear and convincing evidence. **(A)** is incorrect because the burden of proof is on the prosecution. **(C)** is incorrect because it describes the rule for a child under 7 years and here the D was 10. **(D)** is incorrect because the standard is "clear and convincing evidence," not "beyond a reasonable doubt."

125./D/ If a defendant's interests are threatened by a joint trial, a motion for separate trial and counsel should be granted. **(A)** is not the best answer because Sandra's interests are threatened, and she should receive a separate trial. **(B)** is not the best answer because Sandra's interests are threatened, and she should receive a separate trial. **(C)** misstates the law; joint trials are permissible, if the conflicting interests are negligible or collateral.

126./C/ The criminal statute proscribes the sale of firearms to minors. Bubba was apparently unconsious and could not knowingly perform the *actus reus* of the sale of a firearm to a person under 18, so he cannot be criminally liable. **(A)** is incorrect because strict liability requires no proof of intent. **(B)** is incorrect because Bubba did not perform the *actus reus* of the sale, so he cannot be criminally liable. **(D)** is incorrect because Bubba did not perform the *actus reus* of the sale, so he cannot be criminally liable.

127./A/ If Dale actually believed that anyone who paid $50 had permission to take the gun, then he would have believed that he had permission, and thus the taking was not trespassory. **(B)** is incorrect because only infants under 7 are conclusively presumed incapable of intending a crime. **(C)** is incorrect because duress is only a defense if there is an imminent threat of harm to persons, not property. **(D)** is not the best answer because the intent at the time of the crime was not trespassory, so the actual value is not relevant.

128./D/ Like Bubba, Pete did not commit the act of a sale, and the statute does not impose liability for failing to supervise, or any kind of liability to an owner as *respondeat superior*. **(A)** is incorrect because ignorance of the fact that certain behavior is proscribed is almost never a defense. **(B)** is incorrect because Pete did not commit the *actus reus* of a sale, and the statute does not impose liability for failing to supervise, or any kind of liability to an owner as *respondeat superior*. **(C)** is incorrect because Pete did not commit the *actus reus* of a sale, and the statute does not impose liability for failing to supervise, or any kind of liability to an owner under the doctrine of *respondeat superior*.

129./A/ The purchase of firearms by minors is not proscribed, only the sale. **(B)** is incorrect because the purchase of firearms by minors is not proscribed. **(C)** is incorrect because each offense – larceny and the gun sale statute – contains an element that the other does not, and therefore double jeopardy is not offended by prosecution of both. **(D)** is incorrect because acquittal on one charge does not exonerate a defendant charged with a wholly separate crime, even if it arises from the same circumstances.

130./B/ The thugs appear to have committed all the elements of kidnapping. They moved him to another part of the parking lot (any movement is kidnapping). **(A)** is incorrect because the Ds had specific intent, which transfers from victim to victim. **(C)** is incorrect because their identification error does not negate intent. **(D)** is incorrect because the defendants confined him against his will and a lengthy period is not required.

131./A/ Although Hopalong initially refused, his actions in meeting up with Cisco by the school and their shared nod are enough to prove an agreement existed and a substantial step was taken. **(B)** is incorrect because Hopalong's actions in meeting up with Cisco by the school and their shared nod are enough to prove an agreement existed and a substantial step was taken. **(C)** misstates the law, conspiracy does not merge. **(D)** is not the best answer, since two participants do not automatically create a conspiracy. The defining characteristics of a conspiracy are an agreement and a substantial step taken in furtherance.

132./C/ If offensive touching is excluded by statute, then inflicting physical harm is the only way to achieve a battery. **(A)** is incorrect because apprehension is an element of assault, not battery. **(B)** is not the best answer because recklessness is also sufficient *mens rea* for battery, so specific intent is not required. **(D)** is incorrect because battery is not a lesser included offense of kidnapping.

133./B/ If he believed the house was empty, it would reduce his *mens rea* in the crime from extreme recklessness to mere recklessness, which could reduce the charge to involuntary manslaughter. **(A)** is incorrect because there is no assumption of risk principle in criminal liability. **(C)** is incorrect because voluntary intoxication is not a defense unless it prevents the defendant from realizing what he is doing. In this case, voluntary intoxication, followed by firearm use, would seem to constitute extremely reckless behavior. **(D)** is incorrect because it is too simplistic and specific intent is not required for murder; extreme recklessness will suffice.

134./D/ *Miranda* warnings must be read to the suspect even if the police know or have reason to know that a suspect is familiar with his rights, otherwise a confession is not valid. **(A)** is incorrect because *Miranda* warnings must be read to the suspect even if the police know or have reason to know that a suspect is familiar with his rights. **(B)** is incorrect because *Miranda* warnings must be read to the suspect even if the police know or have reason to know that a suspect is familiar with his rights. **(C)** is not the best answer because a suggestion of a possible beneficial plea agreement does not usually amount to coercion.

135./A/ Fruits of the poisonous tree are items of evidence obtained as the result of an illegal search or confession – the blood alcohol content (BAC) was obtained independently and is admissible. **(B)** misstates the law – physical evidence obtained as a result of an illegally procured confession is fruit of the poisonous tree. **(C)** is irrelevant and a factual misstatement. **(D)** is not the best answer because it goes to the weight of the tainted evidence, not admissibility.

136./C/ This is the best answer, because Mitch did not intentionally or recklessly injure Ted. He made a mistake of fact that negated the *mens rea* for battery. If Ted and Mitch were friends, the touching would not have been offensive. **(A)** is not the best answer because although Mitch intentionally slapped Ted, he would not have done it if he realized Ted was a stranger. **(B)** is incorrect because it misstates the law, battery requires intent or recklessness. **(D)** is incorrect because slapping a stranger, even a light slap, could be categorized as an offensive touching.

137./B/ Tanya and her boyfriend had a conspiracy agreement to commit an unlawful act, murder, and completed that act. **(A)** is not the best answer because conspiracy also applies. **(C)** is incorrect because conspiracy does not merge with the completed crime, but solicitation does. **(D)** is incorrect because co-conspirators are liable for the crimes to which they agreed (and in some jurisdictions, all foreseeable crimes).

138./D/ This is the best defense because, if the jury believes it could negate causation and the boyfriend then likely can be convicted of only attempted murder at best. **(A)** is not the best answer because his actions constituted extreme recklessness. **(B)** is incorrect because duress suffered by another is not usually a defense to murder or manslaughter. **(C)** is not the best answer because if the prosecution could prove by clear and convincing evidence that D knew his actions were likely deadly, he would be culpable, minor or not.

139./A/ Tanya intended to permanently deprive the insurance company of title to and possession of its property by way of fraud, so false pretenses is the best answer. **(B)** is incorrect because the company gave up the money voluntarily. **(C)** is incorrect because the company gave up the money voluntarily. **(D)** is incorrect because larceny by trick results when the true owner only gives up possession of his property, not title because he expects to get it back. The company did not expect the money would be returned by Tanya at the time they gave it to her.

140./D/ A private party made the recording – not the police – so there is no state action, and thus no Fourth Amendment violation. **(A)** is incorrect because a private party made the recording so there is no state action, and thus there is no Fourth Amendment violation. **(B)** misstates the law – tape recordings are certainly admissible if authenticated and relevant. **(C)** is incorrect because a private party made the recording so there is no state action, and thus there is no Fourth Amendment violation.

141./B/ On these facts, Franz is probably culpable for second-degree murder because he did intend to shoot the gun at a person. **(A)** is incorrect because Franz did not premeditate or plan the killing. **(C)** is incorrect because Franz's act was deliberate and not reckless. **(D)** is incorrect because Franz is chargeable with one of the listed offenses.

142./C/ The MPC requires a victim to retreat if it is possible to do so safely before the use of deadly force is permitted and Jamie's advice to leave suggests there was an option available to the subsequent confrontation so the mistaken death was avoidable. **(A)** is not here the best answer, although it would be, had Franz been unable to retreat. **(B)** misstates the law because there is no "conclusive presumption." **(D)** is not the best answer because – setting aside Franz's mistake – a gun versus a zucchini is not reasonable force.

143./C/ The most complete alternative because irresistible impulse and substantial capacity both recognize a defense where the defendant was unable to control her actions as the result of a considerable mental disease or defect. **(A)** is incorrect because the *M'Naghten* test only allows the defense where the defendant cannot determine right from wrong. **(B)** is incorrect because the "irresistible impulse" and "substantial capacity" tests both recognize a defense where the defendant was unable to control her actions as the result of a considerable mental disease or defect. **(D)** is incorrect because the "irresistible impulse" and "substantial capacity" tests both recognize a defense where the defendant was unable to control her actions as the result of a mental disease or defect.

144./B/ Heidi intentionally burned a structure, which is arson. Because arson is an inherently dangerous felony, she is also guilty of felony murder. **(A)** is not the best answer because Heidi is also guilty of felony murder. **(C)** is not the best answer because Heidi is guilty of felony murder, not manslaughter. **(D)** is not the best answer because Heidi is guilty of arson and felony murder, not manslaughter.

145./A/ There is a constitutional right to a minimum 6-person jury, the verdict of which must be unanimous. **(B)** is incorrect because there is only a constitutional right to a 6-person jury. **(C)** is incorrect; although a request to have a jury trial should not be refused, but a request as to jury size may be. **(D)** is incorrect because there is a constitutional right to a 6-person jury, the verdict of which must be unanimous.

146./D/ Statutory rape is a strict liability crime. **(A)** is incorrect because *mens rea* is of no consequence in a strict liability crime. **(B)** is not the best answer because on a charge of statutory rape, consent is irrelevant. **(C)** is incorrect because *mens rea* is of no consequence in a strict liability crime.

147./A/ Putting herself in a position where she was likely to be a danger makes Tamara reckless, which is sufficient *mens rea* for involuntary manslaughter. **(B)** is not the best answer because it is the definition of a criminal act of omission. Although Tamara's failure to take her medication did lead to the criminal act, the failure to take it was not itself the criminal act. **(C)** is incorrect because Tamara's recklessness put her in a position where she was likely to be in danger to herself and others. **(D)** is not the best answer – although she did act involuntarily at the time of the accident, her act of driving without her medication was voluntary.

148./C/ This time, Tamara is off the hook. She is not culpable for failing to take her medicine, and so she is not culpable for any involuntary acts she may commit while having an attack. **(A)** is incorrect because it misstates the law – battery requires intent or recklessness. **(B)** is incorrect because there is causation – her arm hit his nose and broke it. **(D)** is incorrect because first aggressor is a self-defense principle. Tamara did not act in self-defense, she acted involuntarily.

149./B/ To be convicted of receiving stolen goods, the defendant must have known, or the prosecution must be able to show that a reasonable person should have known, that the goods were in fact stolen. It does not appear from the circumstances here that Byron had any reason to suspect that the goods were stolen. **(A)** is incorrect because it does not appear from the circumstances that Byron had any reason to suspect that the goods were stolen. **(C)** is incorrect because receiving stolen goods is completed once the goods are received, regardless of how long the defendant plans to keep them. **(D)** misstates the law.

150./D/ Reese committed no act of assistance or encouragement, so he cannot be charged as an accomplice, even if he had criminal intent. **(A)** is incorrect because Reese committed no act of assistance or encouragement, so he cannot be charged as an accomplice, even if he had unexpressed criminal intent. **(B)** is incorrect because Reese committed no act of assistance or encouragement, so he cannot be charged as an accomplice, even if he had unexpressed criminal intent. **(C)** is incorrect because Reese committed no act of assistance or encouragement, so he cannot be charged as an accomplice, even if he had unexpressed criminal intent.

151./B/ Solicitation merges with the crime solicited, if the crime was actually completed. **(A)** is incorrect because solicitation merges with the crime solicited, if the crime is completed. **(C)** is not the best answer because it misstates the facts. **(D)** is not the best answer because it misstates the facts.

152./C/ If Sanford honestly and reasonably believed that the radios were being given away, it would negate the *mens rea* intent to deprive the true owner at the time of the taking, a required element of larceny. **(A)** is incorrect because Sanford was predisposed to commit the crime. **(B)** is not the best answer because at the time of the taking, Sanford believed the radios were in possession of another. Also, the police were in possession of them. **(D)** is incorrect because only threat of serious bodily harm to oneself or another qualifies for a duress defense.

153./B/ An accomplice must take some kind of affirmative action to be culpable, even if it is just verbal encouragement; here, Reese merely had knowledge. **(A)** is incorrect because mere criminal intent and knowledge are not enough without some action. **(C)** misstates the facts – Reese did not assist. **(D)** is incorrect because agreement is an element of conspiracy – an accomplice can assist without agreement.

154./B/ Interpreting the statute strictly, Kelly should be acquitted, because on the facts given, there is no evidence that she did any of the acts specified. **(A)** is incorrect because she did not transport it (at least there is no evidence of that stated). **(C)** is incorrect because solicitation does not create liability for the underlying crime if the crime is incomplete. **(D)** is incorrect because the statute does not proscribe possession.

155./B/ Kelly had intent to distribute and made a substantial step of solicitation which was offering Sarah the drugs. **(A)** is incorrect because there was no agreement. Even if there were, the crime of distribution by definition requires two people to accomplish so conspiracy could not be charged. **(C)** is incorrect because Kelly's act is enough for attempt. She also intentionally verbally enticed Sarah to take part, which completes solicitation, even though Sarah refused immediately. **(D)** is incorrect because there was no agreement. Even if there were, the crime of distribution by definition requires two people to accomplish so conspiracy could not be charged.

156./A/ Under the circumstances, there was probable cause to search the locker and Kelly's statement of possible destruction gave the police reason to believe that the evidence would be destroyed if there were any delay and the police did not create the exigent circumstances. **(B)** is incorrect because even at work, there is a limited expectation of privacy in a locked locker. **(C)** is incorrect because under the circumstances, there was probable cause to search the locker and Kelly's statement gave the police reason to believe that the evidence would be destroyed if there were any delay. **(D)** is incorrect because under the circumstances, there was probable cause to search the locker and Kelly's statement gave the police reason to believe that the evidence would be destroyed if there were any delay.

157./D/ To be convicted of kidnapping, the defendant must actually achieve the result that the crime prohibits. **(A)** is incorrect because kidnapping includes confinement *and* movement of the victim. **(B)** is not the best answer because the defendant must first complete the act of kidnapping before this rule comes into play. **(C)** is incorrect because it misstates the facts – he did not turn himself in.

158./C/ He has fulfilled the elements for attempted kidnapping: intent and a substantial step toward completion; and battery: an intentional unlawful offensive direct touching to the person of another. **(A)** is incorrect because attempted battery assault followed immediately by a battery merges with the completed battery. **(B)** is incorrect because Stedman has fulfilled the elements for attempted kidnapping: intent and a substantial step toward completion; and battery: an intentional unlawful offensive direct touching to the person of another. **(D)** is incorrect because Stedman has fulfilled the elements for attempted kidnapping: intent and a substantial step toward completion; and battery: an intentional unlawful offensive direct touching to the person of another.

159./A/ Voluntary manslaughter is an intentional killing in the heat of passion due to excusable provocation. Generally, the provocation must be at least extreme enough to cause a reasonable person to lose self-control. **(B)** is not the best answer because there is no surprise – A has known for some time and even bought the gun, a sign of some premeditation. **(C)** is not the best answer because the provocation is not severe enough. **(D)** is not the best answer because the killing was not intentional.

160./B/ Had Roger known about the affair instead of being surprised, this would tend to negate the "heat of passion" element of voluntary manslaughter – he would have had time to cool down from his anger. **(A)** is not the best answer because Roger's ability to inflict more severe injury than another man could is irrelevant – in the heat of passion all self-control and judgment is lost. **(C)** is not the best answer because Roger's propensity for violence is irrelevant – in the heat of passion all self-control and judgment is lost. **(D)** is not the best answer because this kind of insurance arrangement is common between spouses. The insurance alone does not prove that the killing was premeditated rather than in the heat of passion.

161./D/ If Roger hit his wife after she came at him with a knife, she would be the aggressor, and Roger's use of force would be reasonable and proportional to hers. Therefore, Roger would have been acting in self-defense, and under those facts should be acquitted. **(A)** is incorrect because voluntary intoxication is not a defense. **(B)** is incorrect because even if he did not believe she would die, he did intentionally inflict serious bodily harm, which is sufficient *mens rea* for murder or manslaughter. **(C)** is incorrect because past tendency for peacefulness does not excuse current acts of violence.

162./A/ Xander set his trap with intent to cause serious bodily harm and knew almost to a certainty that such harm would be inflicted. Glen's failure to seek medical attention is irrelevant because he would not have died but for the injuries inflicted by Xander. **(B)** is incorrect because it presumes that Xander acted without intent. **(C)** is incorrect because it presumes that Xander acted without intent. **(D)** is incorrect because deadly force may never be used in defense of property.

163./A/ The statute as written prohibits the knowing sale of alcohol to a person who appears intoxicated as well as those actually intoxicated, so the clerk has committed the offense. **(B)** is incorrect because the statute as written prohibits the knowing sale of alcohol to a person who appears intoxicated as well as those actually intoxicated. **(C)** is incorrect because the statute as written prohibits the knowing sale of alcohol to a person who appears intoxicated as well as those actually intoxicated. **(D)** is not the best answer because Carey went into the store empty handed and calmly emerged with a paper bag containing a brand-new bottle of vodka. This is probably enough circumstantial evidence to convict.

164./B/ The statute as written prohibits the *actus reus* of public intoxication, which suggests intoxication in fact and the facts indicate Corey was not intoxicated. **(A)** is incorrect because the appearance of intoxication is not prohibited. **(C)** is not the best answer because Carey cannot be convicted for what he planned to do, only what he actually did (the *actus reus*). **(D)** is not the best answer because the statute prohibits public intoxication, not public drinking, and Carey could not have been intoxicated immediately after taking one sip of alcohol.

165./B/ Under the MPC, a person who in good faith consults a public official and receives misinformation has a defense. **(A)** is incorrect because the clerk acted on a mistake of law, not fact. **(C)** is incorrect because under the MPC, a person who consults a public official and receives misinformation has a defense. **(D)** is not the best answer, because regardless of the clarity of the statute, apparently the clerk honestly did not understand, reasonably sought clarification, and the official misinformed the clerk.

166./D/ The best answer because the theft itself was larceny and the subsequent tossing of a stick an attempted battery. **(A)** is incorrect because larceny is a lesser included offense to robbery and so he could not be convicted of both. **(B)** is incorrect because he did not actually touch Talia, so he cannot be charged with battery. **(C)** is incorrect because although he initially committed only larceny by snatching the purse with no preceding or concurrent use of force, he later used force in throwing the stick, and therefore could be charged with attempted battery.

167./A/ When Corey threw the stick, he intentionally caused Talia reasonable apprehension of immediate bodily harm. **(B)** is incorrect because in assault there is no touching requirement – only the apprehension of a touching by the victim. **(C)** is incorrect because verbal threats are not required – a simple swing of the fist will do. **(D)** is incorrect because taking property relates to larceny or robbery, not assault.

168./C/ No matter how certain a victim might be that an identification is accurate, when circumstances make it quite likely that the lineup or show-up will produce a misidentification the motion to suppress will ordinarily be granted. Here, the appearance of the officers with the suspect prior to the mug shot ID was highly suggestive to the victim. **(A)** is incorrect because whether the victim would have properly identified the defendant in spite of an improper lineup identification session is impossible to know. **(B)** is incorrect because the intent of the police is irrelevant if the identification session was truly tainted. **(D)** is not the best answer because the availability of other evidence to suggest guilt weighs in favor of, not against, suppressing a possibly illegal piece of evidence (because the value of that other evidence is necessarily decreased).

169./D/ The MPC does not recognize the misdemeanor-manslaughter rule and the child's death would have occurred even if D was cold sober. [Note: A combination of **(B)** and **(C)** would probably be enough for a misdemeanor manslaughter conviction in a state that recognized the rule.] **(A)** is incorrect because even if the MPC recognized the misdemeanor-manslaughter rule (it doesn't), the rule would likely be enforced like the felony murder rule and intent would not be an element of the crime. **(B)** is incorrect because the MPC does not recognize the misdemeanor-manslaughter rule. **(C)** is incorrect because the MPC does not recognize the misdemeanor-manslaughter rule.

170./B/ The word "conclusively" in the statute makes the offense a strict liability misdemeanor. **(A)** is incorrect because mistakes of law based on misinformation are only excused if the misinformation came from a public official. **(C)** is incorrect because ignorance of a law is generally not a defense. **(D)** is incorrect because intent is irrelevant to a strict liability crime.

171./A/ Reasonable force was used here in defense of others and this is an available defense to charges of murder or manslaughter. **(B)** is incorrect because modern statutes no longer require the person defended to be a friend or family member. **(C)** is incorrect because it misstates the law – force may be used by private persons in self-defense or defense of others. **(D)** is incorrect under the circumstances, the defensive use of fists was reasonable and proportional to the mugger, armed with a deadly weapon.

172./C/ To be convicted of assault, the D must have created an apprehension of immediate harm or an offensive touching. Vague future threats do not constitute assault, no matter how serious. **(A)** is incorrect because to be convicted of assault, the D must have created an apprehension of immediate harm or an offensive touching. **(B)** is incorrect because to be convicted of assault, the D must have created an apprehension of immediate harm or an offensive touching. **(D)** is not the best answer because regardless of Mac's belief, a vague future threat cannot constitute assault.

173./B/ Avery committed a trespassory taking and carrying away of tangible personal property in the possession of another with the intent to permanently deprive the owner. Although he intended to return it at the time of the taking, he later changed his mind and decided to keep it, which intent relates back to the time of taking and creates a larceny. **(A)** is incorrect because the employer did not voluntarily transfer possession and title to Avery. **(C)** is not the best answer because embezzlement does not involve property in the control of the owner, but rather in control of the fiduciary. **(D)** is incorrect because Avery did not break and enter the building without the owner's permission.

174./C/ Although the *Pinkerton* rule allows a co-conspirator to be prosecuted for all foreseeable crimes committed by any other co-conspirator, Packard successfully withdrew (stopped his unlawful activity and took steps to prevent other crimes) prior to the larceny and battery. **(A)** is incorrect because Packard withdrew before the larceny and battery, however, he did conspire to embezzle and did embezzle. **(B)** is incorrect because regardless of the fact that the money was never in Packard's hands, he did deprive his employer of it, so he has also committed embezzlement. **(D)** is incorrect because regardless of the fact that the money was never in his hands, he did deprive his employer of it, so attempted embezzlement merges into the completed crime of embezzlement.

175./A/ Packard voluntarily appeared at the police station and gave the confession of his own free will. Although police questioned him, he was not "in custody" or arrested until later nor was he told he was not free to leave so the custodial interrogation requirement is missing. **(B)** is incorrect because it misstates the law: any evidence offered against a defendant may be subject to suppression, regardless of the source. **(C)** is incorrect because Packard was not in custody, which is a prerequisite for *Miranda* to be at issue. **(D)** is incorrect because it misstates the facts: there is no evidence here of coercion.

176./D/ Belinda created the danger and thus had a duty to rescue, thus her failure to act becomes the *actus reus* of the crime. **(A)** is incorrect because Belinda created the danger and had a duty to rescue, thus her failure to act becomes the *actus reus* of the crime. **(B)** misstates the law – the prosecution must always prove *mens rea, actus reus,* causation, and result. **(C)** is not the best answer because intent is not enough without action, and also because it misstates the facts.

177./C/ Lonnie committed burglary when she entered Burt's residence without permission with the intent to commit larceny therein. The fact that she has a key or that she used to live there is irrelevant; she currently does not have permission so any entry, forced or not, after she had agreed to the contrary is considered breaking and entering. **(A)** is not the best answer because Lonnie has also committed burglary, of which larceny is a lesser included offense. **(B)** is incorrect because larceny by trick involves obtaining property by fraud perpetrated on the owner. **(D)** is incorrect because Lonnie can be charged with one of the listed crimes.

178./A/ Although ignorance of the law is not a defense to violation of that law, mistake of the law or one's legal status may create a mistake of fact which negates the *mens rea* of the crime. If Lonnie believed she had a legal right to enter the house and take the property, this would negate the *mens rea* for burglary and larceny. **(B)** is incorrect because duress is only available if there is a threat of serious bodily harm to oneself or another. **(C)** is incorrect because a belief that one is "owed" is not a defense to theft, unless one believes that the specific property taken is one's own. **(D)** is incorrect because voluntary intoxication is not a defense unless one is unaware of one's actions entirely.

179./B/ To win an ineffective assistance of counsel argument, the defendant must be able to show that counsel was not reasonably effective and that there is a reasonable probability that the trial court outcome would have changed. **(A)** is incorrect because the defendant must be able to show that counsel was not reasonably effective and that there is a reasonable probability that the outcome would have changed. **(C)** is incorrect because the defendant must be able to show that counsel was not reasonably effective and that there is a reasonable probability that the outcome would have changed. **(D)** is not the best answer because admitting the *actus reus,* causation, and result is only part of proving culpability – *mens rea* and defenses can still be argued.

180./A/ Alma's intent to murder transfers from Bertha to the driver of the car, and so Alma is guilty of the driver's murder just as she would be guilty of Bertha's murder. **(B)** is not the best answer because Celine withdrew long before she actually committed the crime, and that is an affirmative defense. **(C)** is not the best answer because Ernie had no intent to injure Fabian and was not reckless in his actions. **(D)** is not the best answer because Helga used reasonable proportional force in self-defense to Gunther's attack with a gun.

181./D/ To prove involuntary manslaughter, the prosecution must prove that the defendant acted recklessly, disregarding a significant risk of harm or departing from the ordinary standard of care. Zed's best defense is that the joke was harmless, and that an ordinary reasonable person would agree his actions were not reckless. **(A)** is incorrect because intent is not an element of involuntary manslaughter. **(B)** is incorrect because Zed's actions were the proximate and actual cause of the death. **(C)** is incorrect because there is a stronger response that relates directly to an element of the crime – intent.

182./C/ This answer correctly describes the *mens rea* for arson, and David's actions do not meet the test. **(A)** is incorrect because it is irrelevant whether or not David was trespassing. **(B)** is not the best answer because causation is not enough to convict without the required *mens rea* which is not present. **(D)** is not the best answer because mere garden variety negligence is not enough to prove criminal arson.

183./D/ Hooper intended to cause serious bodily harm, which is *mens rea* enough for murder. **(A)** is incorrect because intent is not required. **(B)** is incorrect because to exonerate a defendant, a superseding cause must be so far removed from the defendant's actions as to make it unjust to hold the defendant criminally liable. **(C)** is incorrect because serious bodily injury at least was foreseeable, and therefore so was a death.

184./B/ Even though William's actions were the actual cause of the fire, the lightning striking near the empty gas can and exploding into the forest fire was too remote from William's actions to be attributed to him. **(A)** is not the best answer because a defendant need not be acting contrary to the victim's interests to be convicted of arson. **(C)** is not the best answer because remoteness in time need not necessarily mean lack of causation; William could have started a slow burning fire that took days to smolder. **(D)** is incorrect because "malice" means only intent, not actual ill will or hatred.

185./A/ As a co-conspirator, Glen is culpable for all crimes agreed to (or all foreseeable crimes, if the *Pinkerton* rule governs). William is guilty of attempted arson (intent and substantial step) so Glen is guilty also. **(B)** is incorrect because a co-conspirator need not take any steps to be culpable as long as another co-conspirator does so. **(C)** misstates the law: conspiracy and attempt do not merge. **(D)** is incorrect because William abandoned, but did not withdraw – he did not take steps to make sure the crime would not take place (*i.e.*, contacting the police).

186./C/ Felony murder requires that the deaths occur during the course of an inherently dangerous felony which does not appear to be the situation here. **(A)** is incorrect because impersonating a police officer is not an inherently dangerous act. **(B)** is incorrect because felony murder requires no showing of intent. **(D)** is not the best answer because the felony was still going on at the time the deaths occurred.

187./D/ The three defendants clearly agreed to commit this illegal action together. **(A)** misstates the law: if three persons were all required to commit the crime, then they could not be guilty of conspiracy. If three are not required, then conspiracy is available. **(B)** is incorrect because three co-conspirators can act separately in furtherance of the same crime and still be guilty of conspiracy. **(C)** is incorrect because ignorance of the law is generally not a defense.

188./C/ If the prosecution can prove that illegally obtained evidence would have inevitably been discovered because of Tina's letter, the evidence is likely admissible. **(A)** is incorrect because Tina's letter would likely have led the police to Tony's house looking for the uniforms anyway. **(B)** is incorrect because fruits of a search are usually admissible, as long as the evidence is discovered in a location that could reasonably contain the evidence that is the original object of the search. **(D)** is incorrect because the evidence was obtained illegally after Tony validly withdrew his consent which requires the police to stop searching immediately.

189./C/ A voluntary, spontaneous confession when the defendant is not in custody is admissible in the absence of *Miranda* warnings, which are required only prior to a custodial interrogation. **(A)** is incorrect because a voluntary, spontaneous confession when the defendant is not in custody is admissible in the absence of *Miranda* warnings. **(B)** is incorrect because coercion must be by the police or other state actor to render a confession inadmissible. **(D)** is incorrect because the fact of a confession's necessity to the prosecution's case does not affect the issue of whether it was illegally obtained.

190./D/ The definition of a voluntary confession is the absence of police coercion. **(A)** is incorrect because if police coercion is present, the confession is inadmissible, regardless of *Miranda* analysis. **(B)** is not the best answer because the absence of a lawyer does not by itself prove inadmissibility of the confession. **(C)** is incorrect because there is no "threshold" by which coercion producing a confession goes from legal to illegal – any coercion is improper.

191./C/ To reduce the crime from murder to voluntary manslaughter, Theodore must have been acting in the heat of a passion that would have caused a reasonable person to react in a similar manner. **(A)** is incorrect because it only addresses one element of the required test. **(B)** is incorrect because it only addresses one element of the test acting in the heat of passion. **(D)** is incorrect because the *mens rea* for voluntary manslaughter is intent, not recklessness.

192./C/ Danny has violated the statute and committed a misdemeanor, and is strictly liable. **(A)** is not the best answer because he did not intend to commit a felony at the time of entry and should not be charged with burglary. **(B)** is incorrect because Danny is strictly liable for the misdemeanor touching of a minor. **(D)** is incorrect because Danny is strictly liable for the misdemeanor touching of a minor.

193./C/ The *M'Naghten* test only allows an insanity defense where a mental disease or defect prevented the defendant from being able to tell the difference between right and wrong. **(A)** is incorrect because "irresistible impulse" is not recognized under the *M'Naghten* test. **(B)** is not enough – the mental disease/defect is only part of the defense. **(D)** is not the best answer because strict liability means only that the prosecution need not prove *mens rea*: defenses are still available to the defendant.

194./B/ The intent to commit a felony turns this entry into a burglary. Also, he has likely taken enough steps toward commission of the felony touching to be charged with that. **(A)** is incorrect because Danny did not commit the *actus reus* of the touching and cannot be charged with that. **(C)** is not the best answer because Danny can also be charged with the attempted felony touching. **(D)** is incorrect because Danny entered the house without permission with the intent to commit a felony, so he can be charged with burglary.

195./C/ Keenan was present with the permission of Damon, so he did not break and enter. **(A)** is incorrect because Keenan had Damon's permission to be on the premises. **(B)** is incorrect because Keenan intended to commit larceny (larceny by trick). **(D)** is incorrect because intent at the time of entry is the proper inquiry for burglary.

196./C/ Damon has deprived Keenan of possession and title to his money (he does not intend to give the money back) by way of fraud or false pretenses. **(A)** is incorrect because Damon had Keenan's permission to take the money. **(B)** is not the best answer because Keenan did not expect to get his money back at some future date. **(D)** is incorrect because Damon has committed one of the listed crimes.

197./D/ The right to counsel is protected by the Sixth Amendment and may only be waived affirmatively, knowingly, and intelligently. **(A)** is incorrect because his conviction will likely be overturned due to a flagrant Sixth Amendment violation. **(B)** is incorrect because his conviction will likely be overturned due to a flagrant Sixth Amendment violation. **(C)** is incorrect because his conviction will likely be overturned due to a flagrant Sixth Amendment violation.

198./B/ Larceny is a lesser included offense to burglary and would have been available during the burglary prosecution as a lesser charge. Since Keenan was acquitted on the burglary charge, he cannot be charged with larceny based on the same set of facts without offending double jeopardy. **(A)** is incorrect because Keenan was acquitted on the burglary charge and cannot be charged with larceny based on the same set of facts without offending double jeopardy. **(C)** is incorrect because possible guilt of a more serious crime does not preclude prosecution of a lesser crime—it is at the discretion of the prosecutor. **(D)** is not the best answer because Keenan was acquitted on the burglary charge and cannot be charged with larceny based on the same set of facts without offending double jeopardy.

199./A/ Honest belief of consent may be a valid defense to a rape charge.; here however it seems unlikely to prevail since the facts imply force was used. Still, given the other three alternatives, it appears choice A is the best answer. **(B)** is incorrect because impossibility does not preclude a charge for attempt. **(C)** is incorrect because voluntary intoxication is not a defense unless the defendant was totally unaware of his actions. **(D)** is incorrect because these facts could support a charge of attempted rape.

200./A/ When a defendant is being severely disruptive, he waives his right to be present at trial and the judge has discretion to have him removed. **(B)** is incorrect because severe disruption by a defendant can constitute waiver of his right to be present at trial. **(C)** is not the best answer because the defendant's own behavior caused the disruption and the judge had discretion to remove him. **(D)** is incorrect because no facts indicate that counsel was ineffective in defending Barry.

Index

CHAPTER 7

FEDERAL CIVIL

PROCEDURE

RIGOS UNIFORM BAR EXAM (UBE) REVIEW SERIES

MULTISTATE BAR EXAM (MBE) REVIEW

CHAPTER 7

FEDERAL CIVIL PROCEDURE

Table of Contents

This chapter is updated for the 2020 NCBE testable civil procedure issues. Federal jurisdiction, pre-trial procedures, and motions are heavily tested. Particular FRCP numbers are not necessary in your essay answers. It may help to diagram the interaction between the parties. The *Erie* doctrine holds a federal court should apply federal procedural law and the substantive law of the state in which it sits. There is no general federal common law.

> **MBE Tip:** There are usually 27 multiple-choice civil procedure questions on every MBE exam. See MEE at 13-513 for prior NCBE exam question issues tested distribution. Questions may also include topics from evidence, conflict of laws, and occasionally torts issues.

I. COMMENCEMENT OF ACTION

A. Filing

A federal civil action is commenced by filing a complaint in a U.S. district (trial) court.

B. Pre-Filing Notice Requirements

In unusual situations, P may be required to give notice to D before formally commencing a lawsuit by filing.

1. Federal Tort Claims: Tort claims against the federal government must be submitted administratively before any lawsuit is commenced. If the federal government rejects the tort claim notice or fails to make a final decision within six months, P may file suit.

2. Waiver: P's failure to comply with a pre-filing notice requirement is an affirmative defense, but D may waive the defense by not moving to dismiss within a reasonable time. If D pleads a defense, but then engages in discovery, pretrial motions, or other conduct inconsistent with an intent to seek a dismissal, the court may deny a later motion to dismiss.

C. Relationship to Service

After filing the complaint, the P must present a completed summons to the federal district court clerk for their signature. A copy of the complaint papers are then to be served upon D. P generally has 90 days after filing to effect service, but the court has discretion to extend this deadline. However, if P fails to serve D before the deadline, the complaint will be treated as if it were never filed for statute of limitations purposes.

II. JURISDICTION, SERVICE, AND VENUE

> **MBE Tip:** Every Civil Procedure question raises jurisdiction issues. Be sure to separately address personal jurisdiction issues and subject matter jurisdiction issues.

A federal court may not assert personal jurisdiction unless the D named: (1) is given adequate notice and opportunity to be heard; and (2) has sufficient minimum contacts with the state where the district court sits when the claim is commenced. An action commenced without jurisdiction will be dismissed, and any judgment entered without jurisdiction is void.

A. Service of Process – FRCP 4 and 5

Notice to D is essential to create constitutional personal jurisdiction. To satisfy due process requirements, notice must be reasonably calculated, under the circumstances, to reach the intended person and provide notice of the lawsuit. There are three acceptable methods of satisfying the service requirement: (1) D's waiver of service; (2) personal, hand-to-hand delivery, either to D voluntarily present in the forum or to someone authorized by law to accept service for D; and (3) any method allowed under the state law where the district court is located or where D is served.

> **MBE Tip:** A P must comply with state rules regarding service. Some states allow service of process by certified mail; others do not. Also, state law varies on whether service is effective if P substantially complies with procedural requirements but commits some minor error.

1. Waiver of Service: P may mail D a written notice of suit, copy of the complaint, and request that D waive service. If D agrees they are rewarded with 60 days to file their answer, rather than the usual 21 days. The court may impose the costs of service and related attorney fees upon a D who receives such a notice but refuses to waive personal service. A waiver of service does not waive any defenses, including lack of personal jurisdiction.

2. Personal Service on Individuals: Personal service upon individuals must be made within the state where the District Court sits and is accomplished in the following ways:

a. Delivery to the Person: Delivering hand-to-hand service of both the summons and complaint upon the D personally, regardless of where it is accomplished (*e.g.*, at home, at work, on the street), is generally effective, including "transient jurisdiction."

b. Abode Service: Leaving a copy of the summons and complaint with a resident of suitable age and discretion at the D's place of abode (home) is also valid personal service. It is insufficient to leave the papers at a home in which D does not actually reside, or to leave the papers with a person who does not also reside in the home. A hotel is not considered an abode unless the D has resided there for a long continuous period of time.

> **MBE Tip:** There is no bright-line rule on whether a person is of "suitable age and discretion." Service upon D's teenage child is probably effective, but consider the rule before dismissing it.

c. Authorized Agent Service: An individual D may be served through an agent so authorized by contract or other express appointment.

d. Who May Serve Papers: Summons and complaints may be served by any non-party over 18 who has no interest in the action. P may not personally serve the papers. The person serving the pleadings must complete and file an affidavit of service with the court.

e. Territorial Limits: D must be served within the state. An exception applies if a third-party D or indispensable party is joined under Rule 14. See *infra* at 471. Their service may be made within 100 miles of the district court issuing the summons, even outside the state.

> **MBE Tip:** The "100 mile bulge" third party rule is a heavily tested issue in civil procedure.

f. Community Property Considerations: Service of process on either spouse is usually presumed sufficient to support an action on a community asset or obligation. This presumption may be overcome by proof that the judgment is based solely on the separate obligation of one spouse. To be safe, most Ps serve both spouses personally or leave papers at their place of residence with a person of suitable age and discretion then residing therein.

3. Service by Publication: Service by publication is allowed under some circumstances, such as a showing that D has fled. In general, though, publication is not sufficient if D's name and address are ascertainable. Publication may be proper where the D has concealed himself or left the state to avoid creditors, or has fled from service.

4. Service on the Federal Government: P may serve the federal government by: (1) personal delivery or certified mail service upon the United States Attorney's Office for the district in which the action is brought; and (2) sending a copy of the summons and complaint by registered or certified mail to the U.S. Attorney General. If the complaint challenges an order by a non-party federal agency itself or a particular employee, the summons and complaint must also be sent to that particular agency and officer.

5. Service on Corporations and Other Business Associations: The summons and complaint are to be delivered to an officer or managing general agent of the business. Under the local option, most states require business entities to designate a registered agent and address for receipt of service of process and/or that service on the state government corporate division is adequate. Corporations served must identify any 10% or above ownership interests of any parent corporation.

6. Specific Situations: Required methods of service may vary for special situations, such as property interests where simply publishing notice may suffice. Trustee or Personal Representatives are served, not the beneficiaries. Service on an *in rem* (property) D or a foreigner under the Hague Convention rules may be difficult and not likely to be tested.

7. Insufficiency of Service of Process: Service deficiencies must usually be asserted by D in the first pleading or such is deemed waived unless a later filing would not delay proceedings. Once the action has been properly commenced, papers may be served pursuant to less rigorous requirements including simple personal or electronic deliveries and mailings to opposing counsel of record.

8. Time Limit for Service: If the D is not served within 90 days of the complaint being filed, the court must dismiss the action on motion or *sua sponte* without prejudice.

> **STOP!**   Go to page 513 and work Learning Questions 1 to 7.

B. Minimum Contacts (General Jurisdiction)

1. Generally: A federal court may not assert personal jurisdiction over a non-resident D unless the D has minimum contacts with the forum state where the district court is located. Minimum contacts creating general jurisdiction does not offend traditional notions of fair play and substantial justice. *International Shoe.* State long-arm statutes normally govern.

2. Domicile: A person domiciled in a state, even if she has temporarily left, is subject to jurisdiction in that state. This is determined at the time of filing.

3. No Contacts, But In-State Service: Service upon a nonresident who is voluntarily present in the state is sufficient to confer personal "tag" jurisdiction. [*Burnham*]

4. Consent or Waiver: Jurisdiction exists if D consents to jurisdiction, or fails to challenge personal jurisdiction by a pre-answer motion or in the answer itself. FRCP 12.

5. Consent by Contract: Consent by contract is normally effective, *e.g.*, "The parties agree that litigation arising out of this contract will be conducted in Florida in accordance with Florida law, and the parties consent to personal jurisdiction in Florida."

C. Long-Arm Jurisdiction (Specific Jurisdiction)

1. Generally: State long-arm statutes may provide that a person or entity submits to jurisdiction in that state by engaging in any of a long list of enumerated acts of conduct. Common provisions allow the assertion of jurisdiction over a person who:

    a. Business: Transacts business within the state.

    b. Tort: Commits a tort within the state.

    c. Property: Owns or uses any real property situated within the state.

    d. Insurance: Contracts to insure any person or risk within the state.

2. Jurisdiction is Specific to In-State Activity: Jurisdiction under a long-arm statute is specific jurisdiction: jurisdiction to adjudicate a specific dispute arising out of D's activity in that state. Thus, if P seeks to base jurisdiction upon a business transaction, the dispute must arise from a transaction within the state. For jurisdiction based upon property in the state, P must only show that the dispute arises out of the ownership or use of that property.

3. Transacting Business: See also the corporate chapter in MEE at 1-87 for business entity internal governing issues.

    a. Factors Considered: Factors considered under the "transacts business" clause determination vary. Courts commonly require the following three **PAF** elements:

        (1) Purposefully: The nonresident D or foreign corporation must purposefully act or consummate a transaction in the forum state. Mere general advertising is not sufficient, but targeted internet order marketing or on-the-ground live sales staff usually qualifies.

        (2) Arise From: The cause of action must arise from, or be connected with, an act or transaction involving the privilege of doing business in that state.

        (3) Fundamental Fairness: The assumption of jurisdiction in the forum state must not offend traditional notions of fair play and substantial justice. In a plurality opinion, the Supreme Court held that merely placing products in the stream of commerce without more is an insufficient nexus. [*Asahi Metal*] Consideration is now given to a variety of factors including the quality, nature, and extent of the in-state activity, the relative convenience of the parties, the benefits and protection of state laws, and basic fairness. Substantial, systematic, and continuous targeted in-state presence is usually sufficient. [*Nicastro*]

    b. Physical Presence not Required: The P's claim must arise from the D's actions occurring in the forum state, but D's physical presence in the state is not required. Extensive telephone or advertising via mail solicitations to in-state buyers may support jurisdiction.

    c. Internet Transactions: In general, the test to determine whether D's website is sufficient to support personal jurisdiction is how "active" and "targeted" to a particular market the website is. A "passive" website, which merely provides occasional information to web surfers, but does not ordinarily allow for ordering or selling online will not usually reach the minimum contacts requirement. In comparison, an active website that both solicits business and takes orders may be sufficient to support jurisdiction. Ongoing internet communications and newsletters that are systematic and continuous are in the gray area.

   d. Registered Agent Distinguished: An out-of-state corporation's appointment of a registered in-state agent for service of process does not provide minimum contacts.

> **MBE Tip:** If D's officer was served in the state, the long-arm considerations are not necessary.

   4. Commission of a Tortious Act:

   a. Generally: If D commits a tort in the state, jurisdiction usually attaches. A classic example is a nonresident motorist who causes an automobile accident.

   b. Product Liability Cases: Product liability questions may involve products manufactured out-of-state that injure in-state residents. If D transacted business "in-state," the court may assert personal jurisdiction under the relevant long-arm statute. P must show that D placed the product in the "stream of commerce" in that particular state, making it reasonably foreseeable that the product would be used in-state if it is not clear that D was transacting business in-state.

   5. Ownership or Use of Property: Specific jurisdiction under a long-arm statute may be based upon D's ownership or use of property (real or personal) in the state. However, D's ownership of property in State X does not give a federal court sitting in State X jurisdiction over D for any lawsuit against D in State X. The court has jurisdiction only to resolve disputes arising out D's ownership or use of the in-state property. For example, if D's property is emitting noxious fumes, the court would have jurisdiction over D to resolve a dispute about the fumes, but not a dispute unrelated to the property.

   6. Insuring Risk: Jurisdiction exists when an out-of-state D insures an in-state property or other risk. The classic example is a suit by an insured State X resident to recover on a policy written by an out-of-state insurer.

   7. Full Jurisdiction Obtained: Assuming the requirements of the long-arm statute have been satisfied, and assuming minimum contacts exist, the court obtains full jurisdiction and can proceed to determine all issues properly presented.

> **MBE Tip:** Civil procedure questions will involve federal courts, but your minimum contacts analysis must focus on the state where the court sits. Note that long-arm statutes grant specific jurisdiction over only the individual transactions creating it; long-arm statutes do not grant general jurisdiction.

D. Challenges to Personal Jurisdiction, Consolidation, and Waiver

   Unlike challenges to subject matter jurisdiction, challenges to personal jurisdiction (*e.g.*, improper service of process, no minimum contacts) may be deemed waived under certain circumstances. Challenges to personal jurisdiction are subject to the consolidation and waiver provisions in FRCP 12.

   1. Appearance: The filing of a formal Special Notice of Appearance is not a waiver of the right to raise a timely objection to personal jurisdiction. However, if an objection is not timely asserted by motion or responsive pleading, the objection is waived under FRCP 12.

   2. Method: Personal jurisdiction may be objected to by motion or in the answer to the complaint. If the challenger uses a motion, it must be in a pre-answer motion. Once an answer has been filed, it is too late to raise the issue in a subsequent motion.

3. Exception: An exception is made for judgments entered by default, which may be vacated for lack of personal jurisdiction within the longer time allowed by FRCP 60.

4. Timeliness, Consolidation: A challenge to personal jurisdiction (whether based upon lack of notice, improper service, or lack of minimum contacts) must be asserted in a timely manner – by motion before filing an answer, or in the answer itself. An untimely challenge is deemed waived. Consolidation and waiver provisions in FRCP 12 apply.

5. Waiver: A challenge to personal jurisdiction may also be waived:

a. By Waiting Too Long to Move for Dismissal: D must make a timely objection to personal jurisdiction in the answer or by motion and must also move to dismiss within a reasonable time. If D pleads the defense but then engages in discovery, pretrial motions, etc., a later motion to dismiss may come too late. Note that if a case is dismissed prior to trial, it is treated for purposes of the statute of limitations as if it had never been commenced. Thus, courts are hesitant to grant a dismissal if D went through lengthy pretrial proceedings until the statute of limitations expired, thereby preventing P from re-filing the case.

b. By Seeking Affirmative Relief: D may waive the defense by seeking affirmative relief from the court, on the theory that D has consented to jurisdiction.

> **MBE Tip:** Personal jurisdiction is a popular bar topic. A challenge to personal jurisdiction must be made in the answer (or by motion before the answer) or else it is waived.

E. *In Rem* Jurisdiction

A court lacking personal jurisdiction may take action in regard to D's real property in the state, pursuant to its *in rem* powers. The court may take such action (*e.g.*, a partition or a quiet title remedy) without additional contacts because the property alone supplies sufficient contacts. Due process, however, still requires that D be given notice and opportunity to be heard. Modern long-arm statutes generally grant personal jurisdiction over D in the place of *in rem* jurisdiction.

F. Subject Matter Jurisdiction – FARS

Subject matter jurisdiction is the court's authority to hear and decide a particular case. Parties cannot create subject matter jurisdiction by consent. Subject matter jurisdiction (unlike personal jurisdiction) can be challenged at any time, even by post-trial motion or appeal. Federal district courts have subject matter jurisdiction over only certain defined categories of cases. The common **FARS** grounds for federal subject matter jurisdiction are:

1. Federal Question: District courts may hear any case arising under the constitution, a federal statute or international treaty regardless of amount. Examples include federal trademark, patent, or copyright disputes. The mere existence of an affirmative defense under federal law is not sufficient to create federal question jurisdiction.

2. Amount and Diversity Jurisdiction: District courts may hear cases between citizens of different states if the amount in controversy exceeds an aggregated $75,000. Court costs, punitive damages, and post-judgment interest do not count toward this amount in controversy threshold. Separate claims of $75,000 or below may not be aggregated unless all Ds are jointly and severally liable. The state substantive law governs. State citizenship is determined at the time suit is filed, not when the claim occurred. Diversity must be "complete"; no P may be a citizen of the same state as any of the Ds. An estate executor is a party to an action only as a representative and thus treated as a citizen of the same state as the decedent.

3. <u>R</u>emoval Jurisdiction: D in a state court case has 30 days from receiving the complaint to "remove" the case to federal district court. A notice of removal must be filed and served on the P who may object within 30 days of receiving the initial state court complaint. Subject matter jurisdiction in areas of context-specific federal concerns must exist. However, if party diversity is the only basis for federal jurisdiction, the case may not be removed if it was filed in a state where at least one D is a citizen.

4. <u>S</u>upplemental Jurisdiction: A federal court may have jurisdiction over claims directly related to the main claim where federal subject matter jurisdiction exists. The test is whether the additional stand-alone claim is so related as to form part of the same case or controversy. The court may decline to exercise supplemental jurisdiction if the state-based claim substantially predominates over the federal question claim.

5. Actions Against Corporations: Dual citizenship is possible. For diversity jurisdiction, a corporate D's "residence" is in the state of incorporation and/or where its headquarters' principal place of business where the officers direct, control, and coordinate the corporate "nerve center" activities [*Hertz*]. This complicated the previous "muscle test" approach that designated the state where most corporate activities took place.

6. Exceptions: Domestic relations and probate matters are ineligible for federal jurisdiction and must be tried in state courts. P may pre-emptively defeat diversity by naming a non-diverse party as a co-D as long as doing so does not constitute fraudulent joinder; conversely, Ds may not defeat diversity by interpleading a non-diverse party as a third-party D.

MBE Tip: The P designates the state forum and may never remove the case to federal court.

G. Venue and Change of Venue

Venue refers to where proceedings will take place. Which federal district court should hear the case, assuming the parties have not designated a particular forum by contract?

1. Basis: There are three general grounds for establishing proper venue.

a. Residence of D: Venue is proper in a federal district court if any D resides in that district, provided that all Ds reside in the state where that district is located. A corporate D may be deemed to reside in any district where it is subject to personal jurisdiction

b. Location of Events or Property: Venue is also proper in a federal district where "a substantial part of the tortious act, events, or omissions giving rise to the claim occurred, or a substantial part of the property that is the subject of the action is situated."

c. Personal Jurisdiction: If there is otherwise no district where venue is proper, venue is proper in any district where any D is subject to personal jurisdiction.

2. Improper Venue: If the case was filed by the P in an improper venue, the court may either transfer the case to a district where venue is proper or dismiss the case.

3. Forum *Non Conveniens*: Even if venue is proper, the court may nonetheless transfer the case to another district where venue is also proper if there is a compelling reason why the case should be heard there instead. D's burden is heavy when moving for transfer on forum *non conveniens* grounds. Calendar congestion may be considered by the court.

MBE Tip: Many federal civil procedure questions have multiple jurisdiction and venue issues. Look for facts indicating the parties are from different states.

STOP! Go to page 514 and work Learning Questions 8 to 15.

III. PLEADINGS AND MOTIONS

When the FRCP or a court order sets a deadline by stating a number of days, that period begins on the day after the order and includes weekends or holidays. The parties may file electronically by midnight on the last day of the period. Parties may request extensions by motion before the deadline. After the deadline, a court may grant a retroactive extension only through a motion demonstrating excusable neglect. Courts may extend all sorts of deadlines except those for judgment as a matter of law, a motion for a new trial, or a motion for relief from judgment.

A. Complaint and Answer – FRCP 3, 4, and 5

1. Complaint Contents – JARR: The first step in an action is the filing of the formal complaint and securing from the court a properly issued summons that is served on D within 90 days of filing. Despite the liberal rules about "notice pleading," a complaint must give the D fair notice of all material elements of each claim and the factual and legal basis for each count pled in the complaint. Undisclosed claims may not be asserted at trial. If the P is a corporation, all related entities owning 10% or more of its stock must be disclosed. [FRCP 7.1] The complaint must include statements of:

a. Jurisdiction: Subject matter and personal over Ds is required.

b. Allegation of Facts Underlying the Claim: Plausibility is required.

c. Right to Relief: The legal theory must be specified (tort law, breach of contract, etc.). If the claim is based on a statute, the particular statute should be specified.

d. Relief Requested: P must specify the remedy or relief that they desire.

2. Joinder of Claims: P may assert multiple claims or theories of recovery in a single complaint, even if the claims do not all arise out of one transaction or occurrence. Alternative or inconsistent allegations are now allowed if not unreasonable. The court may later order separate trials in the interest of convenience, judicial economy, or to avoid prejudice.

3. Single Complaint: P must assert in a single complaint all claims arising out of one transaction or occurrence. "Claim splitting" is not allowed. For example, P may not file two separate lawsuits based upon one car crash, one for property damage and one for personal injury. The first judgment in the first lawsuit would preclude the second lawsuit.

4. Pre-Answer Motion to Dismiss: D may move to dismiss under FRCP 12 for lack of jurisdiction, insufficiency of service, failure to join a party, or failure to state a claim upon which relief can be granted (there is no interpretation of the facts under which the P could prevail). No "special appearance" by D is required. D does not waive the deficiency (typically lack of personal jurisdiction) by filing a motion to dismiss.

> **MBE Tip:** A D who files a pre-answer motion to dismiss should allege all available defenses under FRCP 12, as certain omitted defenses cannot be made in a subsequent motion.

5. Answer: The D must serve an answer to the complaint within 21 days (60 days if D resides outside the U.S.). If D waived formal service, he is rewarded with a full 60 days to respond (90 days if residing outside of the U.S.). General denials of allegations are allowed based on lack of knowledge. Affirmative defenses (*e.g.*, the statute of limitations), must be expressly pleaded or may be deemed waived. If an answer contains counterclaims, it may be amended once as a matter of right if the P's answer to the counterclaims has not been served.

6. Post-Answer Motion to Dismiss: A summary judgment motion supported by affidavits (see *infra* at 480) or a 12(c) motion for judgment on the pleadings may be filed after the pleadings are closed. This motion may thus be made after or with the answer.

B. Notice Pleading – FRCP 8

The federal courts use the system of "notice pleading," which requires merely general plausible allegations. Inconsistent claims or defenses may be pled in the alternative. General damages including pain and suffering, any disability, and loss on a contract, do not ordinarily need to be specified in detail. The court usually should allow leave to amend when justice so requires. Certain claims and defenses, however, must be specially pleaded.

C. Pleading Special Matters – FRCP 8 and 9

Fraud, breach of trust, mistake, and any denial of contract capacity need to be pleaded with particularity and the relevant facts explained in detail. Similarly, time, place, conditions precedent, and application of foreign laws should be explained. Any special damages such as lost wages, medical expenses, and lost profits should also be specified in the complaint. [FRCP 9] Affirmative defenses (*e.g.*, assumption of risk, contributory negligence, fault of nonparty, fraud, and statute of limitations) must likewise be specifically pleaded. [FRCP 8(c)]

D. Signing of Pleadings, Sanctions – FRCP 11

All pleadings filed must be signed by the attorney of record. There must be a reasonable inquiry into the factual basis or legal merits of a claim prior to filing. Pleadings must be well grounded in fact and warranted by existing law or a good faith argument for an extension or modification of existing law. General denials usually violate the rule. If the document is frivolous, Rule 11 sanctions may be imposed on the attorney signing the document. The Rule 11 motion pleadings may be served on opposing counsel but should not be filed with the court for 21 days to allow the opposing party 21 days to withdraw or correct the pleading.

E. Challenges to the Pleadings – FRCP 12

1. In General: Pleadings may be challenged by a Rule 12 motion to dismiss. Rule 12 motions do not go to the facts, but rather address whether the law allows the specific claim or defense (*e.g.*, improper jurisdiction, venue, service, or expired statute of limitations). A 12(b)(6) motion is for failure to state a claim upon which relief can be granted.

2. Motion to Dismiss for Failure to State Claim: 12(b)(6) is the most common motion under FRCP 12 tested on the UBE. The ground rules are as follows.

a. Purpose: The rule offers a quick and convenient way for the D to avoid a claim when it is clear that the plaintiff will never prevail regardless of the facts proven at trial or there is no remedy. Typical examples are claims barred by the statute of limitations, or causes of action that are not recognized under the applicable substantive law of the jurisdiction.

b. Drastic Remedy: Judges consider dismissals for failure to state a claim a drastic remedy and grant them sparingly, only after careful scrutiny. The effect of granting the motion is to deny the P his or her day in court to present their detailed case.

c. Truth Inference: For purposes of deciding a 12(b)(6) motion, all the factual allegations in the complaint will be assumed as true. But the P still must plead a claim that is factually plausible above the speculative level. Furthermore, the court may disregard legal conclusions that are unsupported by any relevant factual allegations (*Twombly*).

d. Amendment Allowed: Courts will generally allow a P to amend the complaint, in lieu of granting a dismissal. This relief may apply if by amendment the P may be able to state a new or additional cause of action.

e. Too Vague: Despite notice pleading rules and P's ability to amend pleadings, courts will occasionally dismiss because the complaint was too vague to satisfy the D's due process right to notice (of both the fact of the claim and the nature of the claim).

f. Conversion to Motion for Summary Judgment: When reviewing a 12(b)(6) motion, a court may consider only matters presented in the pleadings. If the parties introduce matters outside the pleadings, a court may then consider the 12(b)(6) motion to have been effectively converted into a motion for summary judgment and consider the extrinsic evidence. A court may then postpone the motion for summary judgment to allow discovery to proceed. A court may consider all documents attached to the original pleadings without triggering the conversion to a motion for summary judgment.

g. Document Referenced: If the pleadings only reference a document without actually attaching a copy of that document, a court may consider that document only if it is integral to the case in order for the motion to remain a 12(b)(6) motion.

3. Other Rule 12 Motions: A 12(c) motion is for judgment on the pleadings. The standard is the same as a 12(b)(6) motion; however, the timing differs. Ds typically raise 12(b)(6) motions in response to a P's initial complaint; Ps typically raise 12(c) motions in response to the D's answer that triggered the close of the pleadings stage. In the interests of justice (FRCP 1), courts will usually re-characterize one as the other if a party labels their motion incorrectly. A 12(f) motion is used to strike invalid defenses or redundant, impertinent, or scandalous matters.

F. Consolidation and Waiver of Certain Defenses – FRCP 12

1. In General: Under FRCP 12, certain defenses must be raised timely and consolidated with certain other defenses, or they are deemed waived. These rules promote judicial economy by avoiding piecemeal challenges to the court's authority to proceed with the case. The ground rules for FRCP 12 are as follows:

2. FRCP 12 Defenses: Defenses that may be subject to the waiver provisions if not asserted timely in the defendant's answer include (1) lack of personal jurisdiction, (2) insufficient service of process, (3) lack of minimum contacts, and (4) improper venue.

3. Lack of Subject Matter Jurisdiction: Lack of subject matter jurisdiction can be raised at any time, even after judgment. Consolidation and waiver provisions do not apply.

4. Lack of Personal Jurisdiction or Improper Venue: Lack of personal jurisdiction or improper venue may be challenged in two ways:

a. Challenge by Motion: D may challenge personal jurisdiction or venue by motion, prior to filing an answer. D must include all challenges to service of process, minimum contacts, and venue. Any challenges not included in the motion are waived.

b. Challenge in Answer: D must include in the answer all challenges to service of process, minimum contacts, and venue. Any challenges not included in the answer are waived except lack of jurisdiction. If the challenges are asserted in the answer, P may wait and file the actual motion to dismiss and/or for a change of venue later, to allow extra time to research and draft the motion.

G. Counterclaims – FRCP 13

Counterclaims are causes of action made by the D against the P. There are two types of counterclaims: permissive and compulsory.

1. Compulsory: The D must bring compulsory counterclaims against P if they arose out of the same transaction or occurrence as P's claim. They cannot be brought separately later by the D. Logically, P's complaint tolls the statute of limitations on any compulsory counterclaim by the D, or the P could prevent D's counterclaim by filing at the last minute.

2. Permissive: Permissive counterclaims arise from a separate set of facts.

H. Crossclaims – FRCP 13

Crossclaims are made by a D against other co-defendants. Crossclaims must arise from the same transaction or occurrence as the P's claim. Crossclaims are never compulsory.

I. Amended Pleadings – FRCP 15

1. Generally: A pleading may be amended as a matter of right (without leave of court) only: (1) once, before a responsive pleading is served, or (2) if no responsive pleading is permitted and the action is not yet on the trial calendar, within 21 days after it is served.

2. Leave of Court: Otherwise, pleadings may be amended only by leave of court, or with the written consent of opposing counsel. FRCP 15 specifies that "leave shall be freely granted when justice so requires." Generally, judges will deny leave to amend only if made in **BUUF** – **b**ad faith, **u**ndue delay, **u**nfair prejudice, or **f**utility.

3. Claims, Defenses, or Parties: Courts are usually more willing to allow amendments adding claims or defenses than to allow amendments adding new parties.

4. Relating Back: When the statute of limitations is close, a significant issue may be whether an amendment relates back to the date of the original pleading?

a. New Claim or Defense: An amendment adding a new claim or defense relates back if it arises out of the same transaction or occurrence, even if the amendment was necessitated by inexcusable neglect, or was the result of a conscious litigation strategy.

b. New Party: An amendment adding a new party relates back only if (a) it arises out of the same conduct, transaction, or occurrence of the original pleadings, (b) the added party receives due notice, and (c) it is not unfair because the added party knew or should have known that, but for mistaken identity, the action would have been brought against him.

c. New Party – Restriction: An amendment adding a new party does not relate back if the amendment was necessitated by inexcusable neglect, or was the result of a conscious decision, strategy, or tactic.

d. New Party – Practical Effect: Courts almost never allow a claim against a new D to relate back if it would have otherwise been barred by the statute of limitations.

MBE Tip: Look for the statute of limitation running on the original claim shortly after the filing of the complaint or adding a new party.

J. Appearance and Default – FRCP 55

A default judgment prevents the losing party from asserting defenses that might have otherwise been raised and compulsory counterclaims arising from the original action. A default judgment is preclusive if the court had rightful jurisdiction over the D, and the D had proper notice and opportunity to appear. By failing to contest P's claims, D in theory is deemed to have admitted their truth.

1. General Overview: A summons instructs D to serve an answer within 21 days (60 days if residing outside the U.S.). A D who waives service has 60 days to respond (90 days if residing outside the U.S.). If D fails to respond timely, P is entitled to a default judgment. P need not give D notice of the motion for default judgment.

2. Appearance: Even if D fails to file a timely answer, P must give D written notice at least 7 days prior to the hearing for default if D has "appeared" in the action. D may then prevent default judgment by serving and filing an answer before the hearing on P's motion. D's counsel formally "appears" in an action by serving and filing a notice of appearance, but informal settlement negotiations between counsels may constitute substantial compliance, if D was aware of P's claim indicated a clear intention to defend against it.

3. Entry and Judgment Amount: If the amount of a default judgment is uncertain, the court may order hearings or other procedures to determine the proper amount of damages. Normally the court will award the amount requested in the complaint.

4. Minors, Incompetents, and Members of Military: Minors, incompetents, and members of the military are protected against the entry of a default judgment.

5. Motions to Vacate – In General: The clerk grants a party's default upon motion. If the judge has not yet entered the formal judgment against the defaulting party, FRCP 55(c) allows the default to be set aside for "good cause." More commonly, a D learns of a default after the judgment against them has been entered. D's remedy then, if any, is a motion to vacate the default judgment pursuant to FRCP 55(c) or 60(b), which may also be termed a motion for relief from judgment or a motion to vacate judgment.

6. Motions to Vacate – For Lack of Personal Jurisdiction: A motion to vacate a default judgment is often based upon an alleged lack of personal jurisdiction, for example if P resorted to substitute service (*e.g.*, by publication) without using due diligence to locate D for personal service. A default judgment without personal jurisdiction may be vacated on motion of D, if filed within a "reasonable" time. Lack of personal jurisdiction is sufficient to vacate the judgment; D need not defend on the merits of the case.

7. Motions to Vacate – Other: Non-jurisdictional grounds to vacate default judgments are typically based upon D's admission of error, for example not receiving service, losing a summons, or inadvertently failing to promptly retain counsel. When ruling on a motion to vacate, the court will examine the specific facts and take into account the following:

a. Meritorious Defense: Whether D has a plausible defense going to the merits of the case. If D has no defense, there is no point in vacating the default judgment.

b. Reason for D's Failure to Appear: Stubbornness or failure to appreciate the seriousness of a summons will not support D's motion to vacate. However, the courts may forgive misunderstanding or miscommunications among attorneys, clients, and insurers.

c. D's Diligence: If D did not move to vacate the judgment promptly upon learning of the default judgment, the court will be less inclined to vacate the judgment.

d. Effect Upon P: Similarly, if P will be prejudiced by vacating the default judgment, the motion to vacate may be denied. This might apply if so much time has passed that crucial evidence is no longer available.

> **STOP!** Go to page 515 and work Learning Questions 16 to 26.

IV. PARTIES

MBE Tip: The subject of parties has appeared only rarely on past exams, and questions have focused on joinder of parties and class actions. Only the most basic rules are covered below.

A. **Generally** – FRCP 17

1. Real Party in Interest: Every action must be prosecuted in the name of the real party in interest. This is roughly the equivalent of requiring that P must have "standing." Executors and administrators or estates, guardians, trustees of trusts residence determines if diversity jurisdiction applies. It is not necessary to join individual beneficiaries.

2. Capacity: Both P and D must have the "capacity" to sue or be sued. Minors and incompetent persons lack capacity and must sue or be sued via a guardian *ad litem*.

B. **Compulsory Joinder of Indispensable Parties** – FRCP 19

1. Generally: Although Ps generally decide whom to name as a party, FRCP 19 requires that persons needed for just adjudication must be joined as parties if feasible. This is generally used to require joinder of other Ds, but it may require the joinder of Ps as well. If the parties do not voluntarily comply, the court will order joinder of a necessary party.

2. Complete Relief: Joinder is necessary if, in the person's absence, complete relief cannot be accorded among those who are already existing parties.

3. Rights Are Being Adjudicated: Joinder is necessary if the person claims an interest relating to the action and must be a party to adequately protect her interests. Joinder is also required when necessary to protect a party from multiple or inconsistent obligations.

   a. Indispensable Parties: In a contract dispute, all parties to the contract must usually be joined. In a property or fund dispute, all affected owners are usually necessary parties and must be joined. In an insurance dispute, all named insureds must be joined.

   b. Parties Who Are Not Indispensable: In a tort case, all the tortfeasors need not be joined. State law usually allows a P to sue multiple tortfeasors separately.

4. Dismissal in Absence of Indispensable Party: A court may order joinder. If a person cannot be joined, thereby preventing the action from proceeding "in equity and good conscience," the court will dismiss the entire action. A person cannot be joined if the person is not subject to service of process or if venue would be improper.

C. **Permissive Joinder of Parties** – FRCP 20

1. Common Question of Law or Fact: FRCP 20 allows persons to join in an action if they have claims (or have claims asserted against them) arising from the same transaction or occurrence, involving some common question of law or fact. This rule encourages all interested persons to be joined in a single action to promote judicial economy.

2. Separate Trials: The court may, on motion, order a separate trial if the presence of a party would cause embarrassment, delay, undue expense, or prejudice.

D. **Impleader (Third Party Claim)** – FRCP 14

1. Generally: Impleader occurs when D1 brings D2 into a civil lawsuit, on the theory that D2 is derivatively liable for all or part of P's original claim for indemnification or contribution. D1 is the "third party P," and D2 the "third party D."

2. Procedure: D1 may bring in D2 by serving D2 a summons and third-party complaint within 14 days after serving its original answer. The 100-mile-bulge service rule of FRCP 4(k)(1)(B) applies to service made within 100 miles of the issuing district court. *Supra* at 460. The court may deny third-party joinder if bringing in D2 would be unduly prejudicial, but joinder does not destroy original diversity jurisdiction.

3. Insurer as Party: In tort cases, D1's insurer may not be brought in as a party. Under FRE 411, the jury may not be made aware of the presence or absence of insurance, due to the possibility of prejudice. An exception exists if the insurer would be directly liable to P.

E. Interpleader – FRCP 22

If a party is subject to multiple potential liability, parties may be joined if they may be potentially liable to or benefit from a claim. An example is insurance policy proceeds maximum coverage allocation to multiple beneficiaries. The proceeds would be deposited into the registry of the court pending a resolution of the case.

F. Substitution of Parties – FRCP 25

1. Grounds: A pleading may add a new substituted P or D if a party dies, becomes incompetent, the interest is transferred, or a public officer ceases to hold office.

2. Procedure: A D who is substituted in after the action is commenced must be served with a summons and complaint in the same manner as the original D.

3. Time: FRCP 25 allows the motion to substitute up to 90 days from the service of death notice or the underlying suit will be dismissed.

G. Class Actions – FRCP 23

1. Generally: One or more persons may sue or be sued as the representative of a class of Ps or Ds who have a common interest in the suit. Class actions allow for the efficient pursuit of claims that have a significant aggregate effect, but would be too small individually to justify legal redress. Courts have considerable discretion to decide whether a case may proceed as a class action, appoint class counsel, and award reasonable attorney fees.

2. Requirements: A court will only certify a class action if **CULP** is satisfied:

a. Common Questions: There must be important questions of law and/or fact common to all members of the class who have personal and particularized damages.

b. Usual Claim: The claims or defenses of the representative parties are usual and typical of the claims or defenses of all the other definable class members.

c. Large Membership: The class is so numerous that joinder of all members is impractical. State courts decide if there are sufficient class members, but for federal district court jurisdiction, the 2005 Class Action Fairness Act sets a minimum of 100 class members and a $5 million claim floor, exclusive of interest and costs.

d. Protection: The representative parties must appear to fairly and adequately protect the interests of all the class members.

3. Examples: CULP requirements were satisfied for a suit by customers of a paint that caused mold and mildew. CULP requirements were not satisfied in a discrimination suit brought by university professors, as the court held that the facts and legal issues were likely to differ. The Ps were allowed to proceed individually, but class action status was denied.

4. Additional Required Factors: Beyond the CULP requirements, a case may proceed as a class action only if the case fits within at least one of three categories:

> **a. Risks of Separate Actions:** Separate actions would create the risk of: (1) inconsistent judgments, which would establish confusing standards of conduct for the party opposing the class; or (2) inadvertently affecting the rights or remedies of those who do not sue. For example, if all claims would be paid from a common fund on a first-come, first-served basis, the fund might be exhausted before all claimants have had an opportunity to litigate.

> **b. Conduct of Opposing Party:** The class action's opponent has made final injunctive or declaratory relief appropriate. An example is company-wide discrimination against a large number of employees, who now seek a common class-action remedy.

> **c. Common Questions:** The questions of law or fact common to class members must trump questions affecting individual members. A court determines whether a class action is the best way to adjudicate the controversy fairly and efficiently by considering the possibility of individual claims, whether any litigation is already commenced, and possible difficulties in the management of a class action. Sexual discrimination has so much individual variability that class action status was denied by the Supreme Court in *Walmart v. Duke* (2011).

5. Member Notice Requirements:

> **a. In "Common Questions":** For "common questions" class actions, the best notice practicable must be given to all class members who can be identified through reasonable effort. Each member must be notified that he or she may opt out of the class, and that the class judgment recovery will include all members who do not affirmatively request exclusion.

> **b. Not In "Common Questions":** For other types of class actions, notice requirements are decided by the court. Typically, the class members are given notice of the proceedings, but they do not have the right to opt out and pursue individual claims.

6. Implicit Requirements: In addition, most courts require class actions to meet certain requirements that are not explicitly detailed in the FRCP but are known as "implicit" requirements. One of these implicit requirements is common to all lawsuits, namely, that the representative class member's claim not be moot. In addition, the representative of the class must have standing, as required of all plaintiffs in any sort of lawsuit. Finally, there must be a defined class, the standards for defining that class must be feasible, and the representative must be a member of that defined class.

H. Intervention – FRCP 24

A third party may be adversely affected by the outcome of a proceeding, including any effect applicable to *res judicata* or collateral estoppel. They may file a motion seeking the official status of an intervening third party in the litigation by showing they are practically and importantly affected negatively by the disposition of the litigation and there are common questions of law and fact. A motion to intervene may be denied if it would unduly delay or prejudice the rights of the original parties in the action.

> **STOP!** Go to page 518 and work Learning Questions 27 to 31.

V. DISCOVERY – FRCP 26-37

A. Methods and Scope of Discovery – PRIDE

A party may obtain discovery of any non-privileged matter relevant to any party's claim or defense in the action.

1. Methods: In federal district court, five methods of **PRIDE** discovery are authorized following the initial disclosures (see *infra* at 476): **P**roduction of documents, **R**equests for admission, **I**nterrogatories, **D**epositions, and **E**xaminations (parties only). Production of documents, requests for admission, and interrogatories must be submitted or formally objected to within 30 days. Responding parties usually bear their own production costs. Trial court discovery decisions are subject to a high "abuse of discretion" standard.

2. Discovery Conference Required: Discovery may proceed at any speed and in any order, except that a party generally may not conduct any discovery before the initial FRCP 26(f) mandatory discovery conference is held between counsel and any possibilities for settlement explored. The parties are encouraged to agree by stipulation to a detailed discovery plan and schedule. Stipulations are usually binding.

> **MBE Tip:** By local rule, many district courts establish discovery schedules and deadlines. Mention the possibility of local rules when responding to a question about discovery, particularly with respect to the timing, sequence, and deadlines.

3. Discovery vs. *Ex Parte* Contacts: In certain situations, counsel must use formal discovery rather than seeking information on an informal, *ex parte* basis. *Ex parte* contacts are improper when dealing directly with the opposing party and with the opposing party's experts, consultants, management-level employees, and treating physicians (except in workers' compensation cases). *Ex parte* contacts are proper with ordinary lay witnesses, and with lower-level former employees of a corporation.

4. Scope of Discovery Generally: The scope of discoverable information is broad, even beyond what would be admissible at trial. FRCP 26 requires only that information sought via discovery be relevant, and likely to "lead to" the discovery of admissible evidence.

5. Privileges Apply: Trial privileges (attorney-client, physician-patient, married husband-wife during marriage, etc.) apply during discovery. Confidential communications protected by a privilege at the event date are not discoverable unless the privilege has been waived.

6. Protective Orders – DUOP: The court may enter a protective order to bar or limit proposed discovery that is **D**uplicative, **U**nduly burdensome, **O**ppressive, or to **P**rotect secret processes, software code, formulas, customer lists, or other trade secrets, and software.

7. Work-Product: An attorney's work-product is not discoverable unless it is the only source of the information. This includes all notes, investigative reports, legal research, impressions, and expert opinions prepared in anticipation of litigation or specifically for trial.

 a. What is Protected: Documents and tangible items, including investigative reports, witness statements, notes, research, photographs, videotapes, charts, diagrams, etc. are protected. If these were not prepared by a lawyer, but at the direct request of the attorney, they are usually protected as well. A report prepared by an expert not expected to testify is not usually discoverable. Note that the physical things themselves are protected, but not the facts therein, nor the sources of those facts. For example, an attorney's notes from interviewing a witness are work product, but opposing counsel may interview the same witness.

 b. In Anticipation of Litigation: The immediate prospect of likely litigation ahead usually suffices to trigger the "anticipation" rule, even if the litigation was not then actually commenced. This requires the suspension of any existing document destruction policy.

> **MBE Tip:** When a lawyer retains a consultant or investigator, the court will usually grant protection under the Work-Product Rule without sharing it with your opponent.

c. Distinguish from Attorney-Client Privilege: The Work-Product Rule should not be confused with attorney-client privilege. The Work-Product Rule prevents the opposing party from discovering materials prepared in anticipation of litigation. The attorney-client privilege only protects confidential communications between attorney and client, but it applies at all stages of both civil and criminal proceedings. Usually a privilege log must be prepared and available to the court for review.

d. Court-Ordered Disclosure: Upon a showing of "substantial need," usually that the work-product is the only source of certain information, the court may order disclosure. The petitioning party must show the importance of the information to their case, and their difficulty obtaining equivalent information from other sources. In general, there is no justification for disclosure of a statement by a person who is available to be deposed.

e. Legal Malpractice: Where an attorney's work-product is directly at issue (*e.g.*, in a malpractice action), the normal protections may evaporate.

f. Waiver by Disclosure to Witnesses: An attorney may waive the work-product privilege by allowing a witness to see work-product materials in preparation for testifying or giving a deposition. This "opens the door." Also, opposing counsel has the right to examine and even introduce into evidence any materials used to refresh a witness' memory while testifying.

g. Attorney's Thought Processes: The courts tend to protect attorneys' impressions, legal theories, and strategies, even on the basis of "substantial need."

8. Insurance Availability: Production of any insurance policy that may satisfy all or part of a judgment is a mandatory initial disclosure.

> **MBE Tip:** Remember that evidence regarding insurance is not admissible at trial on the issue of liability or negligence, but discovery may exceed the scope of what may be admitted at trial.

9. Using FOIA in Lieu of Discovery: When a P has a suit pending against a governmental entity, or a suit can be reasonably anticipated, the P may also use the Freedom of Information Act (FOIA) to obtain information. However, the scope of discovery allowed under the FOIA is no broader than it would be under the civil discovery rules; privileges and the Work-Product Rule still apply.

B. Discovery With Regard to Experts

1. Testifying: Expert witnesses who will testify must be disclosed 90 days before trial and are required to disclose their subject matter, substance of opinion, and grounds thereto. They may be formally deposed, but *ex parte* contact is improper. Failure to disclose an expert witness prior to trial may prevent her testimony, or may result in other sanctions.

2. Consulting: Discovery upon the opponent's experts not expected to be called at trial requires a showing of exceptional circumstances. The opinions of consulting experts are protected on the theory that they are part of the party's legal "team" and thus their opinions constitute a lawyer's work-product. A showing of undue hardship and inability to obtain information elsewhere may constitute "exceptional circumstances."

3. Fact or "Occurrence": A witness who would otherwise qualify as an expert witness, but who instead testifies on the basis of personal involvement in the case (*e.g.*, a treating physician or project engineer), is termed a "fact expert" or an "occurrence expert." The test is whether opinions were obtained for the specific purpose of preparing for litigation. Fact experts are treated as ordinary lay witnesses without other "expert" protections. Labeling a fact expert a consultant cannot shield him from discovery. A fact expert may still be called as a witness by the opposing party and questioned regarding their professional expertise.

C. Mandatory Initial Disclosures – FRCP 26(a)

In most federal civil actions, a party has a duty to disclose automatically certain basic information within 14 days after the initial discovery conference.

1. Included: This includes identity of witnesses with discoverable information, physical and electronic documents in the parties' possession, custody, or control, other tangible things the party may rely upon, and numerical computations of each category of damages. A summary of the subject the fact witness will testify about must be disclosed.

2. Expert Testimony Requirements: Required disclosure details of any anticipated expert testimony includes the expert's qualifications, compensation, factual bases for all expert opinions to be made, and the data used in forming the expert's opinion.

> **MBE Tip:** This basic information must be disclosed even if opposing counsel does not formally request same.

D. Depositions – FRCP 30 and 45

A deposition is a recorded oral and/or video examination, and may be taken of anyone, even if the deponent is not a party. Venue is proper where the action is pending or the deponent resides, is employed, or regularly does business. A subpoena must issue from the court where the action is pending. A subpoena *duces tecum* is a court summons requesting the scheduled deponent produce specified documents and tangible things for inspection at the deposition.

1. Subpoena Required: Service of the deposition subpoena is required to compel the attendance of a non-party and the designated non-party deposition location must be within the state or less than 100 miles of where the witness lives, works, or regularly does business. A non-party deponent must be tendered a check for payment of the attendance fee and mileage costs at the time of service. A motion to quash or limit the subpoena may be filed by the deponent.

2. Recording Testimony: The questions and answers are recorded by a court stenographer, and videotaping is allowed. The deposition is limited to one day of 7 hours.

3. Transcript: The witness' testimony is under oath and the deposition transcript is submitted to the witness for review and correction prior to official publication.

4. Conduct During Depositions: Objections by counsel and instructions to a witness not to answer are only allowed to assert a privilege, object to the form of the question, or to request a protective order from the court. Witnesses must answer without evasion; private consultation between counsel and the deponent is not allowed.

5. Use of Deposition as Evidence at Trial: A deposition transcript is an out-of-court statement and thus objectionable as hearsay. However, exceptions to the hearsay rule apply, usually allowing impeachment of the witness. A deposition by a party may be introduced in place of live testimony or introduced as an admission by a party-opponent. If the deposition is by a nonparty, it will usually be admissible under FRE 801 to show prior inconsistent or consistent statements if the witness testifies at trial. If the deponent is unavailable for trial, the deposition will be admissible as former testimony.

E. Interrogatories – FRCP 33

1. Generally: Interrogatories are written questions propounded to an opposing party. They can be addressed only to the parties to the lawsuit, and must be answered within 30 days of service. Interrogatories may be included with other written discovery requests. Written supplementation is required if the answering party becomes aware of discoverable matter or additional experts expected to testify after the first answer was submitted. Answers to interrogatories are not objectionable hearsay; they constitute admissions by party opponents.

2. Scope of Inquiry: Scope of discovery rules apply to interrogatories that are limited to 25 questions including all discrete subparts. Questions may inquire about facts, or about the application of law to fact ("Do you contend that the facts alleged in the complaint give the plaintiff a cause of action under the Consumer Protection Act?"). Inquiries about pure contentions of law, however, are not allowed ("Do you claim that Statute X prevails over Statute Y?").

F. Production of Documents – FRCP 34

Requests to produce, copy, and inspect documents must be answered within 30 days. The location of the requested information must be identified, and the other party must be allowed to examine and copy the records. Insurance contracts are discoverable.

G. Physical and Mental Examinations – FRCP 35

A party who places their physical or mental condition in controversy may be required to submit to a physical or mental examination (an independent medical exam, or "IME"). The examination cannot be conducted solely upon the demand of the party seeking discovery but may be agreed to by stipulation. If the parties do not agree, a motion for the examination may be filed, and the court may grant same for good cause.

H. Requests For Admission – FRCP 36

Admissions of factual evidence are deemed admitted if not affirmatively denied or objected to within 30 days, unless the court permits a withdrawal or amendment. Failure to respond timely is deemed an admission. As with interrogatories, the party seeking discovery cannot ask for an admission on a pure issue of law such as "do you admit that 42 U.S.C. § 1983 applies?" One party may not request the other to admit to ultimate conclusions of law, *e.g.*, negligence or proximate cause.

I. Supplementation of Responses – FRCP 26(e)

A party has no general duty to supplement discovery responses (including initial disclosures) unless:

1. Materially Incomplete or Incorrect: The party later learns that a prior discovery response was in some material way incorrect or incomplete; and

2. Not Already Rectified: The information needed to correct or complete the response has not already been provided via other discovery or in writing.

J. Discovery Abuse – POSE – FRCP 37

In moving for a protective or to compel order of the court, counsel must certify that they have conferred with opposing counsel, or at least attempted to, in an effort to resolve or narrow the discovery dispute. If this is not successful and a discovery motion is filed, the court may award sanctions for abuse of the discovery process ("discovery sanctions").

1. Protective Orders: If A believes B seeks excessive discovery or protected information, A may file a motion for a protective order to limit the scope of discovery, based upon applicable law (*e.g.*, work product rule, privilege, software code, trade secret).

2. Orders Compelling Discovery: If B resists A's request for discovery, A may seek a court order compelling B to cooperate or produce the specified evidence.

3. Sanctions for Violation of Order or Rule: If a party refuses to comply with a protective order or an order compelling discovery, the court may impose sanctions on a party and/or their attorney. On appeal such sanctions are reviewed for abuse of discretion.

    a. Discretion: The court has broad discretion to determine the severity of the sanctions. The court may exclude non-produced evidence at trial, find a party in contempt, or require the payment of costs and attorney fees incurred in attempting to secure discovery.

    b. Scale of Severity: Costs and attorney fees incurred in bringing the sanctions motion are considered routine in successful motions. Harsher sanctions usually require explicit findings by the trial court.

    c. Ultimate Sanctions: If a P engages in particularly egregious discovery abuse, the ultimate sanction is a dismissal with prejudice. For a D who engages in particularly egregious discovery abuse, the ultimate sanction is a default judgment in favor of the P.

4. Exclusion of Witness: If a party fails to identify a witness prior to trial, the court may refuse to allow the party to call the witness to testify at trial.

K. Spoliation

The duty to preserve relevant evidence arises when it becomes apparent that the opposing party has a legal claim or defense expectancy that likely involves the particular evidence at issue. A "litigation hold" should preserve all relevant evidence and documents.

1. In General: Intentional destruction of relevant evidence ("spoliation") is dealt with more harshly than other abuses of the discovery process. In considering appropriate sanctions, courts consider both the level of the spoliator's culpability and the degree of prejudice the destruction has caused the other party. In addition to routine sanctions, the court may refuse to allow the offending party to introduce related evidence (*e.g.*, if D destroyed the car, D's photo of the car will not be admitted).

2. Negative Inference: Evidence of the destruction is admissible to suggest that the destructive party had something to hide such as a "smoking gun" or dangerous product memorandums. Opposing counsel may be allowed a jury instruction inviting the jury to infer that the evidence must have been unfavorable to the party who destroyed it.

3. Electronically Stored Documents: The foregoing rules apply with equal force to electronically stored documentary files such as digital copies of paper records and emails. Thus, a party to litigation has a duty to preserve even emails that may be relevant to the case.

4. Implications for Practice: Never destroy relevant evidence, delete computer files or advise a client to do so. Clients must be advised to retain all documents, physical and electronic, that might be arguably relevant to the case. The duty to retain comes into existence when awareness of the opposing parties' documentation expectation is clear.

5. Civil vs. Criminal Cases: Spoliation is usually used in the context of civil cases, but the same general rules apply to criminal cases. The State's duty to preserve exculpatory evidence in criminal cases stems from the defendant's constitutional right to due process. A violation of that duty may have consequences not associated with civil cases.

STOP! Go to page 519 and work Learning Questions 32 to 39.

VI. PRE-TRIAL PROCEDURES

A. Preliminary Equitable Relief – FRCP 65 and 66

A party may seek a preliminary injunction and/or temporary restraining order to restrain the other party from acting while the case is pending. If the requesting party eventually prevails on the merits, the court will usually make the preliminary injunction permanent.

1. Requirements – RAMP: In considering a preliminary injunction motion (and perhaps prejudgment attachment of assets), the court considers the following **RAMP** factors.

a. Risk of Irreparable Harm: The movant must show irreparable injury, money damages are inadequate as a remedy, or that a particular asset will disappear.

b. Appropriate Weight of Harm Distribution: The potential harm P will suffer without an injunction issuing outweighs the harm D will suffer if restrained.

c. Merits Success Likelihood: P must at least show that she is reasonably likely to succeed on the merits at trial.

d. Public Interest: Whether the injunction will serve or harm the public interest. The court may require the movant provide a security amount.

2. Temporary Restraining Order: If immediate and irreparable harm may occur before notice and opportunity to be heard can be afforded to the opposing party, the court may issue a temporary restraining order (TRO) *ex parte* (without the opposing party being heard).

a. Showing Required: The moving party must submit an affidavit setting forth the specific facts and reasons why a TRO should be issued, the efforts made (if any) to notify the opposing party of the motion for a TRO, and the justification for issuing the TRO *ex parte*. An example is a wife being battered by her ex-husband could apply for a TRO without the husband's attorney being given written or oral notice of the motion.

b. Limited Duration: A TRO must usually expire no later than 14 days after it is issued. A motion to dissolve requires 2 days prior notice. The court will hold a hearing to determine if the TRO should be dissolved or converted to a preliminary injunction.

B. Dismissals

1. Voluntary Dismissal – FRCP 41(a): Actions may be dismissed voluntarily by the P, but the D may object if a counterclaim has been asserted. P may voluntarily dismiss as a matter of right, unless D has served a responsive pleading such as an answer or motion for summary judgment. Otherwise, P must either have all parties stipulate to the dismissal or obtain leave of court. P's first voluntary dismissal is generally without prejudice, and P may refile the action. If P takes a second voluntary dismissal, however, the dismissal usually operates as adjudication on the merits, and P cannot thereafter file the action a third time.

2. Involuntary Dismissal – FRCP 41(b): The D may move the court for an involuntary dismissal of P's case. Grounds include failure to prosecute (undue delay), failure to comply with a civil or court rule, and P's violation of the "two dismissal rule." Dismissal operates as an adjudication on the merits and by default is with prejudice unless the order specifically states the dismissal is without prejudice to P re-filing. D may move for a dismissal at the close of P's case, on the basis that P has failed to demonstrate any right to relief. Such a dismissal is also with prejudice (P may not refile), unless the court orders otherwise.

3. Coordination with Statute of Limitations: If a case is dismissed under FRCP 41, it is treated as if it had never been commenced for purposes of the statute of limitations. The statute is not tolled between the time of filing and the dismissal. Thus, even if a dismissal is without prejudice, the statute of limitations may bar P from refiling if significant time passed.

MBE Tip: The voluntary and involuntary dismissal rules and P re-filing are heavily tested.

C. Summary Judgment – FRCP 56

Summary judgment is a procedural device designed to avoid the time and expense of an unnecessary trial. Either party may file a motion for summary judgment at any time until at least 30 days after close of formal discovery. This subject is heavily tested.

1. Motion: A motion for summary judgment argues that the case presents the absence of any genuine dispute of material fact so the trier of fact has nothing to decide. Therefore, the moving party is entitled to a judgment as a matter of law. The factual question is resolved on the basis of the evidence available as presented in argumentative briefs viewed in the light most favorable to the non-movant party.

2. Issue of Material Fact: In most debatable cases, the question is whether the claims involve any genuine disagreement about material facts to be determined at trial. The non-moving party must have had adequate opportunity to develop opposing facts.

a. Affirmative Showing: The party opposing the motion may not simply rest on unsupported allegations in the pleadings but must affirmatively show that the case involves designated genuine dispute of material fact that could affect the trial's outcome.

b. Materiality: Only material issues of fact remaining will preclude summary judgment. Minor, inconsequential issues do not preclude summary judgment being granted.

c. Admissible Evidence Only: In determining whether there are issues of fact, the court will consider only evidence that would be admissible at trial under the Rules of Evidence. Sworn affidavits from witnesses and deposition testimony in defending a summary judgment motion are usually considered if based upon personal knowledge and likely admissible at trial. Expert's sworn affidavits of opinion require a compelling showing of authority.

d. Self-Contradiction: A party cannot create an issue of fact and prevent summary judgment simply by offering different versions of the same story, *e.g.*, by submitting an affidavit that contradicts his prior deposition statements or prior admissions.

e. Credibility: The court does not ordinarily consider credibility. Even if one affidavit of a witness or party lacks apparent credibility, if the issue is material, a factual issue will be deemed to exist.

f. Typical Factual Issues: Certain issues, if disputed, are routinely considered material factual issues precluding summary judgment of dismissal. Examples include an oral contract, negligence, proximate cause, reasonableness, and state of mind such as intent, consent, knowledge, notice, mistake.

g. Any Doubt: Any doubt should be resolved in favor of the non-movant party thereby allowing a trial or at least further discovery.

3. Summary Judgment When Law Compels Result: Summary judgment may also be appropriate when discovery reveals that one party will prevail regardless of some disputed issues of fact. An example is where D has an ironclad affirmative defense (*e.g.*, the statute of limitations has run, or P signed a valid release) that P cannot overcome no matter how favorable the facts are for P. Summary judgment will likely be granted, because a trial would serve no useful purpose and waste judicial resources.

4. Reconsideration: The court has discretion to reconsider an earlier summary judgment decision by evaluating new evidence creating material questions of facts. The movant should renew their motion within 28 days after judgment entry.

D. Pre-Trial Conference

The assigned judge will normally hold a pre-trial conference to discuss the scheduling, proposed witness list, document review, etc. required in the proceedings. Motions *in limine* to admit or exclude trial evidence may be heard. Normally, a final pre-trial order is issued after the conference. An order issued after a "final" pre-trial conference, shortly before the trial itself, will not be modified except as to prevent "manifest injustice." [FRCP 16]

> **STOP!** Go to page 521 and work Learning Questions 40 to 44.

VII. TRIALS

A. Burden of Proof

1. More Likely Than Not: The preponderance of evidence – more likely than not – is the required proof standard. This applies to both P's claims and D's counterclaims.

2. Special Situations: Libel, slander, and fraud must be pled with particularity and require a higher clear, cogent, and convincing evidential showing.

B. Procedure

1. Pre-Trial Order Controls: As discussed above, the court has normally already determined what may and may not be admitted and scheduling issues.

2. Opening Statement: The party with the burden of proof presents the opening statement portion of the trial. The statement should be limited to the facts that a party reasonably intends to introduce in their own case. Opening statements should not contain personal opinions which usurp the jury's function or evidence not likely to be admitted.

3. Timeliness of Trial Objections: In order to preserve the right to challenge a judgment by post-trial motion or by an appeal, counsel must voice objections to trial rulings at the earliest practicable opportunity, not by first-time post-trial motion or on appeal.

a. Rulings on Evidence: The preferred practice is to object before the witness answers the question "what did he tell you?" If the basis for the objection, here hearsay testimony, does not become apparent until later, counsel must move to strike the inadmissible hearsay at the earliest opportunity. An example is "John told me . . . ."

b. Other Rulings: Counsel may seek other rulings during the course of trial including whether witnesses will be excluded from the courtroom, testimony will be taken out of the usual order, etc. Objecting "on the record" at the earliest opportunity is required.

c. Constitutional Exception: An exception is made for constitutional issues, which may be raised for the first time on appeal.

4. Mistrials: The court *sua sponte* or either counsel may move for a mistrial on the basis of major misconduct by the court, counsel, parties, or witnesses. Examples include unwarranted statements by counsel, and jurors text messaging or conducting internet research.

a. Motion: A motion for a mistrial initiated by counsel is similar to a motion for a new trial; the difference is largely one of timing. A motion for a mistrial is made during the trial itself and, if granted, renders the trial proceeding void. A motion for a new trial is made at the conclusion of the trial and, if granted, results in a new trial.

b. Timeliness: In order to be timely, a motion for a mistrial should be made as soon as practicable after the relevant misconduct occurs. Counsel should not wait until the conclusion of the trial to voice an objection.

C. Jury Trials – FRCP 38 and 39

1. Of Right: Unlike some state's rules, in federal court any party may demand in a formal pleading that the judicial factual determinations be made by a jury of one's peers. This demand must be affirmatively made within 14 days of the complaint or answer being filed. Failure to timely comply with this demand requirement is deemed a waiver of a jury, and the case is tried before a judge as a "bench trial." [FRCP 38] Unless the parties stipulate otherwise the jury shall have at least six but no more than twelve members, and each juror must participate unless excused. The verdict must be unanimous. [FRCP 48]

2. Legal or Equitable Decisions: Juries are to decide questions of fact such as whether a breach of contract or tort occurred and the extent of the resulting damages. Judges decide questions of law, admissibility of evidence, federal tort negligence claims, and equitable actions such as specific performance or injunctive relief. The trial court has wide discretion to decide if the predominant nature of the case is legal or equitable. If both are present in the case the judge will usually let the jury decide the factual issues first so that the court's conclusion does not encroach in the jury's determination of their charge. If mixed factual and legal issues are presented, the jury may usually hear the whole action.

3. Docket Designation: FRCP 39 provides that upon receiving a jury demand, the action must be so designated on the docket. Even if the jury option is not properly demanded by a party, the court may decide to try any issue with an advisory jury.

4. Jury Selection: *Voir dire* is a process in which both parties' counsel interview and select jurors. The jury pool is to be drawn from a fair cross-section of the community. Questions are directed to the potential juror by the attorneys and judge.

a. Peremptory Challenge: A "peremptory challenge" is a trial lawywer disqualification of a prospective juror for which no particular reason or cause needs to be stated. In a civil case, each party (not each side) is usually entitled to three peremptory challenges.

b. Restriction: The courts have created constitutional restrictions on the exercise of a party's peremptory challenges. Most notably, a peremptory strike cannot be based solely upon race or gender, but such factors as a juror's education or religion may be proper.

c. Challenge for Cause – LIB: A prospective juror may be peremptorily challenged "for cause." There is usually no limit on the number of challenges for cause, but since peremptory challenges are still available to either side the court may deny the peremptory request. If the challenge to strike is granted, the particular juror is removed from the case. Valid **LIB** bases for challenge include:

(1) Lack of Qualifications: Under 18, not a U.S. citizen, unable to communicate in English, or a convicted felon.

(2) Incapacity: Being of unsound mind or body, and thus rendered incapable of serving as an objective juror.

(3) Bias, Actual or Implied: A potential juror or their spouse employed by, or related to, a party in the case could be considered to have created an "implied" or "perceived" bias that merits striking a potential juror for cause. Another frequent "for cause" reason is that a juror's answers make it clear their impartiality in deciding the case is at risk, including in a murder case a juror's opposition to the death penalty.

5. Jury Instructions: FRCP 51

a. Generally: Jury instructions are the formal instructions given to the jury by the judge before the jury begins their deliberations. The instructions are read orally by the judge and provided to the jurors in writing. Typically, instructions cover the role of the jury, the burden of proof, the required elements of P's cause of action, the required elements of defenses asserted by D, and any special instructions tailored to the individual case.

b. Content of Instructions: Jury instructions must accurately reflect applicable law and must be sufficient to permit each party to argue its theory of the case. The instruction narrative should be phrased in neutral language and not be argumentative.

c. Timing and Procedure: Proposed jury instructions and any answers to written questions are to be submitted after all trial evidence has been presented, but before counsels' final jury arguments are made. As a practical matter, the timing and procedure for proposing instructions is usually governed in more detail by local rule, and may even vary by the preferences of individual judges. At the time set by the judge, counsel generally meet with the judge to work out the language of the jury instructions that the court will give.

d. Objections to Proposed Instructions: Counsel must be given an opportunity to object on the record or challenge proposed instructions, or to the court's refusal to give a proposed instruction. In this context, the objection is often termed an "exception."

(1) Timeliness: The principle of timeliness applies. To preserve a point for appeal, an exception must be taken at the earliest opportunity. An exception made after the verdict is returned is usually too late.

(2) Preserve for Appeal: To preserve a point for appeal, exceptions and objections must also be made and entered into the record. If the court has determined the content of the instructions in chambers with counsel, as is often the case, counsel must request an opportunity to go "on the record" with a court reporter to voice any exceptions.

6. Counsel's Closing Argument: Each party addresses the jury at the end of the trial. The party with the burden opens and closes the comments on the evidence and the law as contained in the court's instructions. Counsel may only refer to evidence actually presented during the trial and generally may not comment on insurance.

7. Jury Deliberations: Jury deliberations are held in private. No other persons may be in the room. Court personnel may not discuss the case with jurors and may not pressure the jury to reach a verdict more quickly. The jurors are instructed that they are to consider only the evidence presented in the courtroom. The jurors may not conduct their own factual investigations or legal research, such as using the internet. They are not to discuss the case with anybody outside the jury room until a verdict is reached.

8. Verdict: At least 6 of the 12 maximum jurors must participate in the verdict which must be unanimous unless the parties stipulate otherwise. When deliberations have concluded and the necessary votes have been cast, the presiding juror (the "jury foreman") reads the verdict. A special verdict is composed of answers to specific questions of fact. Unless the parties stipulate otherwise, the verdict must be unanimous. In the absence of a verdict, a mistrial is declared. Usually, either party may poll the jury after the reading of the verdict.

9. Juror Misconduct, Setting Aside the Jury Verdict:

a. Improper Actions: A party may move to set aside a verdict on the basis of juror misconduct or other improper actions by jurors. Whether the motion is granted will depend on the severity of the misconduct and the degree of prejudice to the losing party. Bases for this include discussing the case with friends or family before the verdict, independent investigation of the facts (*e.g.*, by looking up trial relevant information on the internet or visiting the scene of the accident), legal research conducted by jurors, nonjurors present during deliberations and reaching a verdict "by chance or lot" (*e.g.*, rolling dice or flipping a coin).

b. Improper Reasoning or Thought Process: Courts are reluctant to set aside a verdict on the basis of improper or illogical reasoning. Examples include failing to exactly follow jury instructions, failing to understand or consider specific evidence, attributing too much or too little importance to specific evidence or testimony, and calculation of damages. Similarly, the court will not entertain challenges to a juror's motives, intentions, or beliefs.

c. Life Experiences: As part of the deliberation process, the jurors may share their own life experiences with other jurors. For example, "I once had an injury similar to the plaintiff's injury, and I was not in any pain." The court will not ordinarily set aside a verdict solely on this basis.

d. Bias or Prejudice: Traditionally, a juror's bias or prejudice against a party has not been considered a sufficient basis to set aside a verdict. It was believed that the *voir dire* process was sufficient to eliminate jurors with bias or prejudice. However, some courts have set aside verdicts on the basis of bias or prejudice that was deliberately concealed during *voir dire*, but which was expressed either during deliberations or outside the courtroom.

e. Error in Recording or Reporting Verdict: A clerical error in recording or reporting the verdict (*e.g.*, clerk types $5,000 instead of $50,000, so the incorrect number is read aloud by the bailiff in court) may serve as grounds to set aside the verdict.

f. Procedure: Normally, a motion to set aside the verdict is brought as a motion for a new trial under FRCP 59, subject to time limits and other procedural requirements.

STOP! Go to page 522 and work Learning Questions 45 to 50.

VIII. JUDGMENT AS A MATTER OF LAW (JMOL) – FRCP 50

A. Terminology

The procedures formerly known as motions (1) for a directed verdict (after P or D rests his case), and (2) for judgment notwithstanding the jury verdict, are now obsolete. Both have now been consolidated into a single procedure known as a motion for "judgment as a matter of law (JMOL)." In writing an answer to an essay question avoid using the obsolete terms.

B. Purpose and Timing

1. Purpose: The motion for JMOL is a procedural device to keep a case from being decided by the jury when there is no rational factual basis by which a reasonable jury could base a finding against the non-moving party. One party has failed to produce material evidence to demonstrate that there are legally sufficient material facts in dispute.

2. Timing: Either party may submit a motion for JMOL after either P or D rests their cases, and also at the close of evidence, but it should strategically be made before the case is submitted to the jury. In order to submit a motion for JMOL after the jury verdict, the party must have requested JMOL at the close of evidence before the jury began deliberations. The motion deadline after entry of the verdict is 28 days. A court may also *sua sponte* enter JMOL.

3. Comparison to Summary Judgment: JMOL is merely summary judgment that is based upon all the evidence as presented at trial rather than merely the admissible evidence obtained through discovery. Moving for JMOL both before submission to the jury and after the verdict is desirable to preserve the ability to appeal an earlier adverse summary judgment.

> **MBE Tip:** The new term – judgment as a matter of law – JMOL – should be used on the MEE exam. The former terminology, if used in the facts of the question, are likely distractors.

C. Test For Sufficiency of the Evidence

1. Generally: The court's decision to grant a JMOL is based upon whether the evidence is sufficient to submit the case to the jury. The test for sufficiency is that it may be said, as a matter of law, that there is no evidentiary basis or reasonable inference therefrom to sustain a verdict against the non-moving party.

2. Burden on Motion: The burden is on the moving party. A motion for JMOL admits the truth of the evidence offered by the opposing party and all reasonable inferences derived therefrom. All evidence is interpreted against the moving party and favorably towards the opposing party. The non-moving party must be fully heard on all significant issues. In close cases, doubts are usually resolved in favor of submitting the case to the jury.

3. Credibility Disregarded: Credibility is not usually taken into account when ruling on a motion for JMOL. The court will not grant the motion simply because it believes one party's witnesses and does not believe the other party's witnesses.

4. No Weighing of Evidence: When ruling on a motion for JMOL, the court also does not "weigh" the parties' evidence. The question is simply whether the party opposing the motion for JMOL has produced enough evidence to submit the case to the jury.

IX. VERDICTS AND JUDGMENTS (OTHER THAN JMOL)

A. Jury Trials

The jurors may be asked to return a general verdict (in favor of one party) or a special verdict composed of answers to specific questions of fact. A special verdict question may be the determination of the proper judgment amount to be entered. It is also possible to have the jury answer interrogatories. The verdict is memorialized in a formal, final judgment.

B. Bench (Judge) Trials – FRCP 52

In a trial without a jury, the trial court judge must prepare written "findings of fact" and "conclusions of law" after the close of the trial to support their verdict. This findings and conclusions document is filed with the written judgment.

C. Entry of Judgment – FRCP 58

The date a judgment is formally "entered" is of great significance because it starts the time running for most post-trial events, *e.g.*, motions for new trial, motions to vacate, and appeals. A judgment is not entered when the jury returns a verdict, or when the judge announces his/her decision orally. "Entry" occurs when the judgment is reduced to writing, signed by the judge, and delivered to the clerk of court for filing in the judgment registry. Money judgments are "stayed" automatically for 14 days after entry. [FRCP 62]

D. Costs and Attorney Fees

1. Litigation Costs: The prevailing party is usually entitled to recover costs, called "taxable costs," that are assessed by the clerk, from the losing party. Costs are specified by statute, and are relatively modest. Examples are fees for filing, factual witnesses, statutory compensation, and service of process expenses. It is not necessarily abuse of discretion for the district court to award expert witness fees. To challenge costs claimed by a prevailing party, a losing party would file a "motion to determine taxable costs."

2. Attorney Fees: Under the so-called American rule, each side bears its own attorney fees, unless otherwise provided by statute or by contract between the parties. Specialized statutes (*e.g.*, consumer protection, anti-discrimination, breach of fiduciary duty, family law, and probate) may allow an award of reasonable attorney fees.

X. POST-TRIAL MOTIONS

A. Motion for New Trial – FRCP 59

1. Grounds – JET: The grounds for a new trial include irregularity in the proceedings, misconduct by persons involved in the trial (including prevailing parties, attorneys, witnesses, and jurors), significantly excessive or inadequate damages (remittitur, additur), and newly discovered evidence that is very significant and probably could not be discovered earlier with reasonable diligence. New trial motions are usually more likely to be granted than JMOLs.

a. Juror Misconduct: See Juror Misconduct, Setting Aside the Verdict *supra.*

b. Errors of Law: Errors of law (the same sorts of errors that could be raised on appeal) may also serve as the basis for a motion for new trial. Thus, a motion for a new trial can often be a quick and inexpensive substitute for an appeal.

c. **Timeliness:** The principle of timely objection applies. Thus, in order to preserve the right to move for a new trial on the basis of an event or error occurring during trial, an objection should be made during trial, and as soon as practicable after the event occurs.

2. Timing and Procedure: A motion for new trial is filed after conclusion of the trial, but no later than 28 days after entry of judgment. The motion may be supported by the trial record, additional affidavits, or both. The court itself may also propose a new trial on all or some of the issues *sua sponte* within 28 days after entry of judgment, and the parties are entitled to notice and a hearing. The time requirements are rigorously enforced.

B. Relief or Correction of Judgment – FRCP 60

1. Grounds: Relief from a final judgment may be granted for a just cause or valid reason such as clerical errors, improper service, excusable neglect or irregularity in obtaining the judgment, fraud or misrepresentation by an opposing party, lack of jurisdiction, clerical or other mistake, and new evidence that could not be discovered earlier with reasonable diligence. Unlike a motion for new trial, a motion to vacate for relief is not a substitute for an appeal and cannot be based upon errors of law.

2. Timing and Procedure: A motion for final judgment relief, a.k.a. a motion to vacate a judgment, must be brought promptly within a reasonable period of time. Motions based upon newly discovered evidence, mistake, excusable neglect, irregularity, fraud, or misconduct by an opposing party, must be brought within one year after entry of judgment. The principle of timely objection applies. A motion to vacate should be brought as soon as practicable after the basis for the motion becomes apparent.

C. Harmless Error – FRCP 61

The harmless error doctrine provides that minor, or harmless, errors during a trial do not require reversal of the judgment by an appellate court.

1. Clear Showing of Error Necessary: The court considers the entire record, but the standard is clear error, where the trial court's findings are clearly erroneous or there was not substantial evidence to support the jury's verdict. Alleged errors or defects that do not affect any party's substantial rights such as admitting or excluding evidence or witness credibility are usually to be disregarded in determining if a judgment or order from a court below should be disturbed.

2. Example: In comparison, an improper denial of a request for a jury trial under FRCP 39 is usually grounds for at least a remand with instructions.

> **STOP!** Go to page 523 and work Learning Questions 51 to 58.

XI. APPEALS

A. When an Appeal is Allowed – Final Judgment Rule

1. Appeal as of Right: An appeal is allowed as a matter of right from the final judgment, or from any other decision that terminates the action (*e.g.*, a complete dismissal).

2. Collateral Order Doctrine: Generally, only final judgments are appealable. This is a final determination of all issues involved in the case. However, the appellate court has discretion to allow immediate review of interlocutory (*i.e.*, non-final) decisions of substantial importance to the outcome of the case, to prevent the possibility of irreparable harm, or to review a matter collateral to the merits. The procedure is also called "discretionary review." Even if denied, such a request preserves the issue at play for review later.

3. Extraordinary Writs: In rare situations, a party may seek review of the district court's action before entry of judgment by seeking the "extraordinary writs" of mandamus and prohibition from the court of appeals. These writs are available only when no other form of review, such as an appeal, is available to remedy the error effectively, and justice requires that the writ be issued.

a. Writ of Mandamus: A writ of mandamus directs the district court to take some action that is required under the law.

b. Writ of Prohibition: By contrast, a writ of prohibition involves a court of appeals ordering the district court to refrain from taking an action that is contrary to law, *e.g.*, a court action beyond the scope of its subject matter jurisdiction.

B. Appeal Procedure

The Federal Rules of Appellate Procedure (FRAP), supplemented by any local circuit rules, control. Entry of judgment starts the clock running for the time parties may appeal.

1. Time for Notice of Appeal: An appeal is commenced by serving and filing a Notice of Appeal. The notice is filed in the district trial court, not the appellate court. Unless ordered to the contrary by the district judge, an appeal notice must be filed within 30 days after entry of final written judgment or order of summary judgment. This is 30 days after the written judgment is filed, unless the government is a party, in which case either side has 60 days.

a. Post-Trial Motions: If a motion for a new trial has been filed, the 30-day appeal period begins to run when the order disposing of the post-trial motion is entered.

b. Cross Appeals: Cross-appeals must be filed 30 days after entry of judgment or 14 days after initial notice of appeal, whichever is later.

2. Extension of Time: The district court may extend the appeal time period limit in extraordinary circumstances. Usually this requires a showing of good cause or excusable neglect. Generally, the principle of finality will prevail over a party's right to file an untimely appeal.

3. Standard of Review: The emphasis is on questions of law, not questions of fact.

a. Discretionary Rulings: Many rulings are within the discretion of the trial court and are thus reviewed only for a clear "abuse of discretion" below. Here, the appellate court will often defer to the trial court's understanding of the entire case. Examples are rulings with regard to discovery, granting or denial of a continuance, admissibility, relevance or prejudice of evidence, sanctions under FRCP 11, and rulings on motions to amend pleadings.

b. Factual Determinations: Factual determinations generally enjoy less deference on appeal than judgments covered by "abuse of discretion" review. Factual findings from a jury on appeal are reviewed for "substantial evidence," and typically enjoy more deference than factual findings from a judge's bench trial, which are reviewed for being "clearly erroneous." Substantial evidence review assesses whether there was sufficient evidence to persuade a fair-minded, rational person of the truth of the premise. Reversals on factual issues are very rare because the trier of fact is deemed to be in a better position than the appellate court to resolve factual issues such as witness credibility and veracity.

    c. Pure Questions of Law: Pure questions of law are reviewed *de novo* (*i.e.*, without deference to the trial court's ruling below). Examples are plain error in the interpretation of statute or court rule, constitutional considerations, application of case law, substantive content of jury instruction, and interpretation of contract ambiguity.

    d. Raised Below: Except for jurisdictional or constitutional questions, the alleged error for review must have been raised below in the trial court proceeding.

    e. Sustain on Any Theory: To avoid a remand, the trial court decision may be affirmed by an appellate court on a theory different from the trial court's.

    4. Circuit Court of Appeals: District Court decisions are reviewed by the United States Circuit Courts of Appeals. This first level of appeal is of right.

    5. United States Supreme Court: Review of Court of Appeals decisions is usually discretionary.

    a. Conflict: A petition for review may be granted if the Circuit Court of Appeals decision conflicts with another Circuit's decision (or a Supreme Court decision).

    b. Question of Law: Review may be granted if a state's highest court has held a federal statute or treaty invalid.

    c. Substantial Public Interest: Review may also be granted if there is an issue of substantial interest that should be determined by the Supreme Court.

XII. PRECLUSION

    To achieve judicial economy, prevent repetitive litigation, and promote finality, litigants should get only one opportunity to try their case. The claim for relief is merged into the final judgment if the P wins and barred by the judgment if P loses their case. A grant of a motion for summary judgment or declaratory judgment usually qualifies as a final judgment. These doctrines do not usually apply if the claim asserted or parties are different.

A. *Res Judicata*

    Upon conclusion of the litigation at trial and the entry of a valid and final judgment, the final judgment is binding and conclusive between the parties in this action and any persons in privity with the parties. No second "bite of the apple" is allowed.

    1. Same Facts: The same operative occurrence or transaction involving the same issue may not serve as the basis for a second lawsuit. *Res judicata*, which is pled as an affirmative defense, can bar attempts to do so. Thus claim-splitting of compulsory counterclaims [FRCP 13] is not allowed. However, *res judicata* does not bar the assertion of claims in different facts including permissive counterclaims in later lawsuits.

    2. Claim Preclusion: *Res judicata* is often referred to as a rule of "claim preclusion." Claims that were or could have been litigated in the case are merged into the judgment and may not be litigated again. Courts use a "transaction or occurrence" test. For example, if P obtains a judgment against D, she may not sue D again in an attempt to get more damages for the same injury. All damages from a claim must be sought in a single lawsuit. Similarly, if the earlier claim was unsuccessful, a second claim on the same facts is barred.

3. Non-Party: A new P not involved in the original case as a party is not usually bound by the prior judgment.

> **MBE Tip:** *Res judicata* requires both that the same claim previously was litigated on the merits and the current claim involves the same parties or one in privity with those original parties. The **s**ame claim and **s**ame parties are necessary. **SS** is the acronym.

B. Collateral Estoppel

Collateral estoppel is essentially a restriction on the relitigation of specific issues of fact or law that were actually decided and necessary to the outcome in the first lawsuit between the parties. The prior litigation cannot have been concluded by a mere default judgment or settlement between the parties.

1. Same Issue: An issue that was actually or necessarily fully litigated and decided in reaching a final prior judgment is not subject to relitigation between the same parties. Note that this may not preclude a subsequent claim by a non-party not involved in the first claim unless there is a substantial legal relationship between the parties such as successive property owners, or the non-party had control over the prior litigation.

2. Issue Preclusion: Collateral estoppel is often referred to as a rule of "issue preclusion."

a. Example: If P sues D for flood damages, and D unsuccessfully claims immunity, D may not claim immunity in a subsequent suit by P for damages from a second flood. D is barred from later claiming immunity again, as the same identical issue was resolved in the earlier suit.

b. Non-Mutual Offensive Use: Third parties in a different later lawsuit against D may attempt to prevent D from asserting the same immunity defense. The controlling issue must have been actually litigated and necessary to decide that issue in the first action (non-mutuality preclusion).

> **MBE Tip:** Remember the collateral estoppel acronym **SAFEN**. The **s**ame facts and questions as in the prior case, that was **a**ctually at issue in litigation resulting in a **f**inal binding judgment in which the issue was **e**ssential and **n**ecessary to the decision.

3. Non-Mutual – Defensive Use: Courts seem more inclined to allow defensive use of non-mutual collateral estoppel where D was previously exculpated against other claimants than offensive where the D was previously held liable. The court has discretion and much depends upon whether D in the first action vigorously litigated the core liability issue.

> **MBE Tip:** *Res judicata* and collateral estoppel are tested on every exam, often combined with jurisdiction issues.

> **STOP!** Go to page 7-524 and work Learning Questions 59 to 80.

XIII. FINAL CHAPTER REVIEW INSTRUCTIONS

1. Completing the Chapter: Now that you have completed your study of the chapter's substantive text and the related Learning Questions, you need to button up federal civil procedure. This includes completing your Magic Memory Outlines® and working all of the subject's practice questions.

2. Preparing Your Own Magic Memory Outline®: This is helpful to your MBE success. The book paper outline works but consider purchasing our software template for your creation process. Do not underestimate the learning and memory effectiveness derived from condensing the text chapter into succinct summaries using your own words. This important exercise is covered in much more detail in the introduction and on the downloaded software.

a. Summarize Knowledge: You need to prepare a summary of the subject in your own words. An example is found at page 7-493. The words in the outline correspond to the bold headings in the text.

b. Capture the Essence: Your job is to summarize the substance of the text by capturing the essence of the rule and entering summarized wording into your own outlines. Use the text coverage to craft your own tight, concise, but comprehensive statements of the law.

c. Boilerplate Rule Statements: Our related MEE volume at 13-517 contains primary issue statements that are helpful in both outline creation and MEE answer boilerplate language rule statements. Take pride in your skills as an author; your Magic Memory Outlines should be the finest written document you have ever created.

d. Focus: Focus your attention and wording on the required technical elements necessary to prove the relevant legal principles. Look for fine-line distinctions. Integrate any helpful "learning question" information into your outline.

3. Memorize Outline: After you have completed your own Magic Memory Outline® for the whole chapter, read it over carefully once or twice. Refer back to your outlines frequently in quick reads during your preparation period.

4. Work Old Questions: The next step is to work all the regular questions in this chapter, beginning on page 7-528. These vary in degree of difficulty, but the ones toward the end tend to concentrate on the most difficult fact patterns and issues. Date and put an X through their numbers as you work each question. Use the Question Map for cross-reference to the textual coverage so you can work on your weak topics. If you use the software, you can click on the questions under the subject and topic you have just studied.

a. Question Details: It is usually worthwhile to review the explanatory answer rationales, as they reinforce the relevant principles of law. If you are still unsure of the controlling rule, refer back to the related portion of the text using the Question Map for cross-reference. This will help you to appreciate the fine-line distinctions on which the MBE civil procedure questions turn.

b. Do a Few Questions at a Time: Work the final practice questions in sequence. Make sure you stop after no more than a few to check the answer rationales. Do this frequently so that the facts of the individual questions are still in your active memory.

c. Mask Down: Lay a mask over the answer rationales. Mask the answers for the questions to be worked. Pull the mask down to expose that question's answer rationale. Do not look down at future answers until after you work the relevant question. Test yourself.

d. Best to Work Them All: We have tried to pick questions from subjects and issues with an average or higher probability of reappearing on the MBE. Work as many as you can, but at least read all of the questions and ponder their answer rationales. Every question and answer has some marginal learning and/or reinforcement value. Many of the actual MBE questions are very similar to the ones in your Rigos UBE Review Series review books.

e. Learn from Mistakes: The objective is to learn from your mistakes by reviewing the explanatory rationales while you still remember the factual and legal details of the question. It is good to miss a few; this will help you become familiar with the MBE fine-line distinctions. The bar examiners' use of distracters, tricks, and red herrings frequently reoccurs.

f. Flag Errors: Put a red star in the margin of the book alongside every question you missed. Missed questions should be worked again the day right before the MBE so that you do not make the same mistakes on the exam.

5. Take the Practice Exam: You can order two optional full simulated MBE exam sets that provide a helpful assessment. They contain 200 questions in random order broken down into two three-hour groups of 100 each. The bold question numbers listed on the right side of the Question Maps refer to these final exam questions. While some practice exam questions in your text are intentionally easier or more difficult and complex than the MBE, both parts of the Final Exam have approximately the same overall difficulty as the actual MBE questions.

6. Make Your Own Exam: The optional software allows you to pick 5, 10, 20, or 100 questions at random from all seven MBE subjects. This is an important feature because you must become intellectually comfortable with all the different subjects. If you are not an early riser and/or get going slowly when you first get up, try working 10 or 20 questions using the "Make Your Own Exam" software the first thing every morning.

7. Update Your Magic Memory Outline®: The fine-line distinctions in the question and answer rationales will improve your understanding of how the MBE tests the law. Consider updating your Magic Memory Outline® while the question testing environment is still fresh in your mind.

8. Essays: Candidates in jurisdictions that administer the Multistate Essay Exam should refer to the *Rigos UBE Review Series Multistate Essay Exam Review — MEE —* for further depth and practice essay questions. That volume contains sample MEE criminal law and procedure essay questions and answers that relate to this chapter's coverage.

9. Performance Questions: Candidates in jurisdictions that administer the Multistate Performance Exam should refer to the *Rigos UBE Review Series Multistate Performance Test (MPT) Review* for practice performance task questions.

Magic Memory Outlines®

I. COMMENCEMENT OF ACTION

    A. Filing – *complaint commences a federal civil action* ....

    B. Pre-Filing Notice Requirements – *unusual, if only individual parties* ....

        1. Federal Tort Claims – *government defendant claim notice usually required*.......

        2. Waiver – *if D fails to move for dismissal timely*...

    C. Relationship to Service – *filed complaint must be served on D within 90 days* ....

II. JURISDICTION, SERVICE, AND VENUE

    A. Service of Process – *reasonably calculated to reach D* ....

        1. Waiver of Service – *request from P to D requesting service waiver* ....

        2. Personal Service on Individuals – *in the state of the District Court*.....................

            a. Delivery to the Person – *summons and complaint served upon D* ....

            b. Abode Service – *leave with resident of suitable age and discretion* ....

            c. Authorized Agent Service – *appointed by D* ....

            d. Who May Serve Papers – *any non-party with no interest in action*...............

            e. Territorial Limits – *within state or 100 miles (bulge rule) from court* ....

            f. Community Property Considerations – *service on either spouse adequate for community assets*..

        3. Service by Publication – *if D has concealed or fled state to avoid service* ....

        4. Service on the Federal Government – *summons and complaint to U.S. Attorney*...

        5. Service on Corporations and Businesses – *corporate officer or managing agent*..

        6. Service in Specific Situations – *in rem or foreign government* ....

        7. Insufficiency of Service of Process – *ongoing pleadings, motion, etc.* ....

        8. Time Limit for Service – 90 *days and court may then dismiss complaint* ....

    B. Minimum Contacts – *required for court to impose personal jurisdiction*..................

        1. Generally – *minimum contacts with forum state required*...................................

        2. Domicile – *subject to jurisdiction - permanent residents*.....................................

        3. No Contacts, But In-State Service Obtained – *service in state on nonresident* ...

        4. Consent or Waiver – *failure to challenge in pre-answer motion* ....

        5. Consent by Contract – *parties' agreement to personal jurisdiction issues* ....

    C. Long-Arm Jurisdiction – *engaging in a list of enumerated acts of conduct in state*..

        1. Generally – *in-state transact business, commit tort, own property, or similar* ....

VII. TRIALS

RIGOS UNIFORM BAR EXAM (UBE) REVIEW SERIES

MULTISTATE BAR EXAM (MBE) REVIEW

CHAPTER 7

FEDERAL CIVIL PROCEDURE

Question Distribution Map

> **MBE Tip:** Numbers immediately following the topic are the chapter question numbers. The **boldface** numbers preceded by "F" are the final exam question numbers. For example, for the topic "I. A. "Filing" below, question 1 is in the chapter questions on page 7-513, and for the topic II. F. 5. "Actions Against Corporations" question **F4** is in the final exam on page 574 in MBE Volume 1.

III.   PLEADINGS AND MOTIONS

VII. TRIALS

Multiple-Choice Questions

LEARNING QUESTIONS

1. A federal civil action at law is formally commenced by filing a complaint
- (A) In a state court.
- (B) In a U.S. district court.
- (C) With the United States Supreme Court.
- (D) In a court where the plaintiff resides.

2. Mike was riding his bicycle when he was hit by a car being driven by an FBI agent who was chasing after a suspect. Under the Federal Tort Claims Act, in order to file a lawsuit against the government, Mike must
- (A) First file an administrative claim with the FBI in order to recover his damages.
- (B) File a lawsuit in a state court in which the damages took place.
- (C) File a lawsuit in federal district court where the damages occurred.
- (D) File a lawsuit with the United States Supreme Court.

3. Which provision of the U.S. Constitution is met by the requirement that service of process be performed when filing a lawsuit:
- (A) Sixth Amendment right to counsel.
- (B) Fifth Amendment protection against self incrimination.
- (C) Substantive due process.
- (D) Procedural due process.

4. Peter Plaintiff is suing his Homeowner's Association for negligence. Peter has hired an attorney, but in order to save money, Peter has his niece Alice serve the summons and complaint on the president of the HOA. Alice is an attorney, but is not representing Peter. Service of process is

- (A) Improper because Alice is an attorney.
- (B) Improper because the summons and complaint must be mailed, not personally served.
- (C) Proper because it may be performed by anyone who is not a party to the cause of action.
- (D) Proper because Alice is over 18.

5. Jack arrives at the home of Mr. and Mrs. Big to deliver a summons and complaint. He knocks on the door, only to discover that the couple has gone out for the evening and hired a 16-year-old babysitter to watch over their 8-year old daughter. Jack leaves the summons and complaint with the babysitter. Service of process is
- (A) Improper because the babysitter is not over 18.
- (B) Proper because anyone who is old enough to be trusted with a minor child is presumed old enough to accept service of process.
- (C) Improper because the babysitter does not reside at the home.
- (D) Improper because a party accepting service must be related to Mr. and Mrs. Big.

6. Dodge and Penny were married in the State of Columbia where they both then resided. Four years ago Dodge ran off with his secretary and then moved out of state. Even though Penny received a substantial award for child support during their divorce, Dodge has not paid any of the money he owes her. Although Dodge has been very careful about not returning to Columbia, Penny heard from a mutual friend that Dodge would be having a layover at the local airport while travelling on a business trip. Penny arranged to have a summons and complaint served on Dodge while he was at the local airport. Service of process is

(A) Proper, because a defendant may be served within the state, even if they are not a resident of that state.
(B) Improper, because Dodge is not a resident of the State of Columbia.
(C) Improper, because Dodge must be served at his home.
(D) Improper because airports are considered to be federal lands not subject to the jurisdiction of a state's courts.

7. When filing a lawsuit against a corporation, delivery of a summons and complaint on a corporation is best performed by

(A) Delivery to the corporation's attorneys.
(B) Delivery to the warehouse where the corporation stores and ships its goods.
(C) Delivery to the corporation's state designated registered agent.
(D) Delivery to the corporation's office or general managing agent.

8. Ted originally lived in the State of Washington before moving last year to California, where he bought a house and got a California driver's license. For the last four months, Ted has been working a temporary job in Arizona, where he has been staying with friends, but he has recently decided to take an extended vacation in Nevada. The Franchise Tax Board in California wants to file a lawsuit against Ted for failing to pay state taxes. Which state has sufficient minimum contacts in order for California to assert personal jurisdiction over Ted?

(A) Washington.
(B) California.
(C) Arizona.
(D) Nevada.

9. A state's Long Arm Statute generally provides that a person submits to jurisdiction in that particular state by engaging in which of the following activities?

(A) Transacting business within the state.
(B) Committing a tort within the state.
(C) Owning or using real property located within the state.
(D) All of the above.

10. Frass Canyon is a winery which is located in the Santa Inez Valley of California, north of Los Angeles. Although Frass Canyon has a website, its website contains only the location and operating hours of the tasting room and a short description of the types of varietals that Frass Canyon makes available each year. Frass Canyon does not sell wine through its website, although it does welcome inquiries by providing a contact email and phone number.

Keith is a resident of New Jersey who recently obtained a bottle of Frass Canyon's Pinot Noir. Unfortunately, after drinking the wine he came down with a serious case of botulism and nearly died. Keith filed a case against Frass Canyon in the United States District Court of New Jersey, claiming that the winemaker's website grants the United States district court jurisdiction under New Jersey's Long Arm Statute. Keith's case will

(A) Be tried in federal court in New Jersey because Keith and Frass Canyon are from different states and Keith will likely be able to prove more than $75,000 in damages.
(B) Be tried in federal court in New Jersey because posting a web page which is available to the general public is sufficient to transact business in a foreign state.
(C) Be dismissed for lack of personal jurisdiction because Frass Canyon has insufficient minimum contacts with New Jersey.
(D) Be dismissed because merely placing goods in the stream of commerce is insufficient to grant a court in New Jersey personal jurisdiction over Frass Canyon.

11. A challenge to personal jurisdiction
   (A) Is deemed waived if an attorney files a notice of appearance with the court.
   (B) Must be made in the first motion to dismiss filed before the answer or in the defendant's answer to the complaint.
   (C) May be made at any time during the proceeding.
   (D) May be raised on appeal.

12. A challenge to subject matter jurisdiction
   (A) May be brought at any time, even by post-trial motion or appeal.
   (B) Is deemed waived if an attorney files a notice of appearance with the court.
   (C) Must be made in the first motion to dismiss filed before the answer to the complaint or in the defendant's answer to the complaint.
   (D) Must be raised on appeal.

13. Buyer, a resident of New York, purchased a $120,000 automobile in New Jersey from an auto dealer. The car carried a two-year repair policy issued by an insurance company in New York. The car engine blew up and Buyer filed suit in federal court against the seller alledging $75,010 damages. The seller impleaded the insurance company operating in both states as a third party. A motion to dismiss for lack of diversity was filed. The court will likely
   (A) Grant the motion because Buyer and the Insurance Company lack diversity.
   (B) Grant the motion because the amount the insurance company could be liable for is less than $75,000.
   (C) Deny the motion to dismiss.
   (D) Deny the motion to dismiss as the $75,010 meets the minimum required jurisdiction amount.

14. Miles has a house in Vancouver, WA but works in Portland, OR. Rather than deal with the daily commute across the Columbia River bridge, Miles rents a room in a house from a co-worker who lives in Portland but returns to his house in Vancouver every weekend and stays there on holidays and on his vacation time. One evening while returning to his home in Vancouver, Miles loses control of his car and causes a significant amount of damage to an Oregon house belonging to Maya. Maya sues Miles for the damage caused to her home. Maya should file her lawsuit in the federal district court of
   (A) District of Washington.
   (B) District of Oregon.
   (C) District of Washington and Oregon.
   (D) Any of the above.

15. Acme Springs, Inc., is a manufacturing corporation whose articles of incorporation were filed in Delaware and whose corporate offices are located in New York City. Acme does all of their manufacturing in New Jersey, where they also have a small warehouse and ship products to their customers. Jack lives in Massachusetts and wants to file a product liability claim against Acme. Venue is proper in
   (A) Delaware.
   (B) New York.
   (C) New Jersey.
   (D) Any of the above.

16. A complaint filed by a plaintiff against a defendant must include statements of
   (A) An allegation of facts underlying the claim and the remedy the lawsuit desires.
   (B) Subject matter and personal jurisdiction; an allegation of facts underlying the claim; the legal theory granting the plaintiff a right to relief; and the remedy the lawsuit desires.
   (C) The legal theory granting the plaintiff a right to relief and the remedy that the lawsuit desires.
   (D) Subject matter and personal jurisdiction; the legal theory granting the plaintiff a right to relief; and the remedy that the lawsuit desires.

17. Shirl is in her car waiting at a stop light when she is rear-ended by Thorne, who was texting while driving and failed to notice the stopped car in front of him. Although Shirl's car was totaled, she felt fine after the accident and never went to see a doctor. Shirl hires an attorney and successfully sues Thorne to recover the damages to her car. However, six months after receiving a judgment, Shirl begins having trouble with her back and neck, and decides to file a lawsuit against Thorne for personal injury.

Shirl's lawsuit for personal injury will

(A) Succeed because she won her claim for damages to her car.

(B) Succeed because even though she did not plead injury damages in her first case, it is plausible that she would have been injured if her car was totaled.

(C) Be precluded by the first judgment.

(D) Fail because if she did not feel the need to go to a hospital, then her injuries could not have arisen six-months later.

18. You have been retained by a local client that has just received a summons and complaint for a lawsuit in federal district court. The client has not waived service. How long do you have to file an answer?

(A) 120 days.

(B) 90 days.

(C) 60 days.

(D) 21 days.

19. Matt bought a car from Acme Motors at his local dealership. Matt was employed during the recession and needed a reliable car in order to assist with his job hunting. After explaining his circumstances to a saleswoman at the Acme Motors dealership, he was assured that they could find him a vehicle that he could afford. Matt found a car that he liked and was assured by the finance staff at Acme Motors that everything would be taken care of. However, Matt quickly discovered that the payments on his new car were much more than he would ever be able to afford, and two months later the car was repossessed. Acme Motors is now threatening Matt with the costs of collection and attorney's fees.

Matt files a lawsuit against the dealership, alleging fraud in the transaction. However, in his complaint, Matt only specified the elements of fraud and a general description of what happened between him and the Acme Motors dealership.

Acme Motors files a motion to dismiss Matt's complaint. Their motion will most like be

(A) Granted, because fraud must be pleaded with particularity and the relevant facts explained in detail.

(B) Granted, because Matt has failed to state a claim on which relief may be granted.

(C) Dismissed, because notice pleading only requires statements consisting of general plausible allegations.

(D) Dismissed, because Matt has given Acme Motors fair notice of all material elements of each claim, the factual basis for each, and the legal basis for each.

20. Attorney Toby was hired by his new client Jake to file a product liability claim against Toy Company, a large manufacturer. Toby took Jake at his word as to all the details of what happened and failed to investigate the legal merits of Jake's claim before signing the complaint.

What is the best course of action for the Toy Company's attorney?

(A) File a motion for default judgment.

(B) File Rule 11 motion for sanctions.

(C) File a Rule 12 motion to dismiss.

(D) File a Rule 12(b)(6) motion for failure to state a claim on which relief may be granted.

21. Mark is a junior in-house-counsel for a cell phone carrier, Galaxy Communications (GC). He receives a summons and complaint from Pete, a customer who complains that GC misrepresented its pricing structure by failing to disclose additional fees that would be charged to the customer.

While reviewing the summons and complaint, as well as Pete's cell phone contract, Mark discovers that Pete agreed to resolve any dispute through mandatory binding arbitration. Mark also finds that the arbitration occurred six-months ago, resulting in a decision against Pete.

Mark's best course of action would be

(A) To file a motion for default judgment.

(B) To file a Rule 11 motion.

(C) To file a Rule 12 motion.

(D) To file a Rule 12(b)(6) motion.

22. According to Rule 12, which defenses must be raised in either the answer to the complaint or by motion before the answer is filed or else these defenses are deemed waived?

(A) Lack of proper venue.
(B) Lack of personal jurisdiction due to insufficient service.
(C) Insufficient process.
(D) All of the above.

23. Janie and Deb own neighboring houses which border a lake with steep banks. Although Deb's house is on the lake, the easiest way to get down to a beach is by a small footpath which crosses through Janie's property. Deb occasionally used the path for the six years she has owned the house and was shown the path down to the beach by the previous owner of her house, who owned the property for fifteen years. Janie recently discovered that Deb has been using the footpath, and files an action for trespass. In response, Deb files an action against Janie in order to move the court for a declaratory judgment establishing an easement by prescription. Deb's claim against Janie is a
(A) Crossclaim.
(B) Compulsory Counterclaim.
(C) Permissive Counterclaim.
(D) Impleader.

24. The City of Berkeley filed a foreclosure action against Property Owner for failure to pay property taxes for a period of more than three years. Property Owner believed that her property taxes were being paid as part of her mortgage payment, so she filed a lawsuit against her mortgage company, Freedom Funding, for failure to pay the property taxes. Property Owner's claim against Freedom Funding is a
(A) Crossclaim.
(B) Compulsory Counterclaim.
(C) Permissive Counterclaim.
(D) Joinder of an indispensable party.

25. Sundale Daily News is a news organization which publishes a daily paper. They ran a story about Celine, who came home one day from work only to discover a man floating face down in her swimming pool. In this story the newspaper strongly implied that Celine had killed the man because of jealousy over the man refusing to leave his wife. However, Celine had never met the man before, and the county prosecutor's office declined to press charges.

A year after the story in the Sundale Daily News ran, Celine hired an attorney, Jessie, to file a lawsuit against the newspaper for the tort of libel and assert a claim for intentional infliction of emotional distress. However, Jessie became distracted with other matters and neglected to file Celine's lawsuit until shortly before the two-year statute of limitations was due to expire. Three months after filing the lawsuit Jessie realizes that he forgot to include the claim for intentional infliction of emotional distress. Jessie amends his pleadings to include the claim for intentional infliction of emotional distress.

Jessie's attempt to amend the complaint pleadings to include a new claim will likely be
(A) Denied because the statute of limitations has run.
(B) Denied because a judge could find bad faith, undue delay, or unfair prejudice.
(C) Allowed because the new claim relates back to the same transaction or occurrence.
(D) Allowed because a pleading may be amended as a matter of right before a responsive pleading is served.

26. Stacy and Carey were long time business associates and friends who one day had a significant disagreement. Stacy filed a lawsuit against Carey by having a summons and complaint served upon him. Carey accepted the summons and complaint but failed to file an answer. Carey did not contact Stacy in any way to discuss the lawsuit in order to come to some kind of agreement. Stacy filed a motion with the court for a default judgment but did not give Carey notice of the motion.

When Carey received a notice that the default judgment against him has been entered with the court, Carey filed a motion with the court seeking to vacate the entry of the default judgment because he never received notice of Stacy's motion. Carey's motion to have the default judgment overturned will

(A) Fail, because the court did not have jurisdiction over Carey.

(B) Fail, because a plaintiff need not give the defendant notice of the motion for default judgment.

(C) Succeed because Stacy's failure to deliver her motion to Carey for default judgment violated Carey's procedural due process rights.

(D) Succeed because Carey has a meritorious defense, and thus it would be against the interest of justice not to allow it to be asserted.

27. Which of the following lawsuits would a court be most likely to allow to proceed?

(A) A majority shareholder files a lawsuit on behalf of a corporation due to a breach of contract claim against a supplier without first making a written demand on the board of directors.

(B) A limited partner in a limited partnership files a lawsuit on behalf of the partnership against a former employee who breached a confidentiality agreement.

(C) A man who was adjudged mentally incompetent files a tort lawsuit against the city for failing to repair the sidewalk in front of his house.

(D) A trustee of a family trust files a lawsuit against an accounting firm for embezzlement of the trust's funds.

28. Susumu, Yuki, and Naoto each own land sharing a common boundary on which there is a small lake. Susumu was surprised when several animals on his land were found dead near the edge of the lake. There is no river leading into or out of the lake. Susumu discovers that the lake has been polluted, and strongly suspects that Yuki has been illegally dumping into the lake, so he files a lawsuit against her. What is the status of Naoto?

(A) Naoto is an indispensable party.

(B) Naoto is a third-party plaintiff.

(C) Naoto is a third-party defendant.

(D) Naoto is a non-indispensable party.

29. Jake works for Boing Aircraft Company as a welder. While working on the assembly floor, Jake was seriously injured when a pressure valve on the welding equipment malfunctioned. The welding equipment was manufactured by Acme Welding, Inc. from Texas and supplied to Boing Aircraft by Precision Welding Supplies. In addition to a workman's compensation claim against Boing Aircraft, may Jake join Acme Welding and Precision Welding Supply in his federal lawsuit in a product liability action?

(A) No, because in the interests of promoting judicial efficiency, disparate claims may not be joined, even if they arise from the same transaction or occurrence.

(B) No, because Acme Welding and Precision Welding Supply are not indispensable parties, and therefore Jake must sue each party separately.

(C) Yes, because Acme Welding and Precision Welding Supply are indispensible parties to the lawsuit.

(D) Yes, because Jake's injury and the issue of product liability claim arose from the same occurrence.

30. Plaintiff sues D1 for the tort of negligence. D1 then delivers a summons and third-party complaint to D2 on the theory that if D1 is held liable, then D2 will be liable to D1 in whole or in part for indemnification or contribution. D2 in turn then sues D1's insurance company and attempts to implead them in as D3. D2's motion to the court to implead D3 will be

(A) Granted, because the insurance company is a non-indispensible party.

(B) Granted, because the insurance company is an indispensible party.

(C) Denied because of the risk of prejudice.

(D) Denied because the insurance company was not involved with the tort.

31. A court will only certify a class in a lawsuit if which of the following factors are satisfied?

(A) There are common questions of law and/or fact to the class; the class members are so numerous that joinder of all parties is impractical; and the representative parties will fairly and adequately protect the interests of all the class members.

(B) The claims or defenses of the representative parties are typical of the other class members; the class is so large that joinder of all parties is impractical; and the representative parties will fairly and adequately protect the interests of all the class members.

(C) There are common questions of law and/or fact to the class; the claims or defenses of the representative parties are typical of the other class members; the class is so large that joinder of all parties is impractical; and the representative parties will fairly and adequately protect the interests of all the class members.

(D) There are common questions of law and/or fact to the class; the class is so large that joinder of all parties is impractical; and the representative parties will fairly and adequately protect the interests of all the class members.

32. Which of the following methods of discovery is not permitted in federal district court?

(A) Production of Documents.
(B) Interrogatories.
(C) Examinations (physical and mental)
(D) Letters of Request

33. Which of the following is not protected by federal privilege and would be discoverable?

(A) Statements made by a doctor to his patient while he was seeking medical treatment for an injury.
(B) A contentious conversation between an attorney and his client which occurred in a public coffee shop.
(C) The contents of a conversation which occurred between a husband and a wife while the couple was married, but the couple is currently divorced.
(D) Notes prepared by a non-testifying expert which are to be used as part of attorney's defense in a negligence case.

34. Doctor Lewis and Doctor Carter were at a local emergency room who treated Jeannie. Jeannie was injured in a car accident when her vehicle was broadsided by a driver who failed to stop for a red light. Doctor Greene also treated Jeannie but was primarily responsible for supervising doctors Lewis and Carter.

Jeannie developed complications during surgery resulting in injuries which has left her permanently disabled. Jeannie filed a lawsuit against the driver of the other vehicle. The driver in turn alleged that doctors Lewis and Carter were contributorily negligent in some way for Jeannie's injuries. During discovery, Jeannie's attorney has listed that he plans on calling doctors Lewis and Carter to testify. Jeannie's attorney has also hired Dr. Greene as an expert regarding the standard of care of emergency physicians. Jeannie's attorney does not plan on calling Dr. Green to the stand during trial.

Defense counsel wants to call Dr. Green to the stand to testify as a lay witness. Jeannie's attorney objects on the grounds that Dr. Green is an expert, and his opinions constitute work product.

What result?

(A) Doctor Green may be called to testify as a lay witness due to his personal involvement in treating Jeannie.
(B) Doctor Green may only be called to testify as an expert witness regarding the standard of care performed by doctors Lewis and Carter.
(C) Doctor Green's opinions constitute work product and he may not be called to the stand to testify.
(D) Doctor Green may not be called to testify unless opposing counsel can make a showing of undue hardship and the inability to obtain information elsewhere.

35. Maggie was friends with Ashley, who was dating Razor. Razor breaks up with Ashley and begins dating Maggie. Maggie is awakened late one night to discover that her car is on fire. Maggie's dog, Fluffy, has also gone missing. The police conduct an investigation but fail to turn up any suspects.

Bliss, a friend of both Maggie and Ashley, tells Maggie that she was driving Ashley home from a bar late one night when Ashley asked if they could make a stop. Bliss parked in front of Maggie's house and Ashley got out of the car. A few minutes later, Ashley ran back towards the car.

Maggie files a lawsuit against Ashley for the destruction of her car. Bliss is deposed as a non-party witness and testifies under oath as to the events which occurred outside of Maggie's house. The deposition is videotaped, and a transcript is produced by a court stenographer. Bliss reviews the transcript before it is published.

During cross examination Bliss testifies that although she was with Ashley that night, they really went to a rock concert several towns away and were nowhere near Maggie's house on the night in question. Maggie's lawyer attempts to introduce the transcript of Bliss' deposition. Defense counsel objects on the basis that the deposition transcript is an out of court statement and thus hearsay.

What result?
- **(A)** The transcript is inadmissible because a deposition may not be taken of a person who is not a party to the action.
- **(B)** The transcript is inadmissible because it constitutes hearsay.
- **(C)** The transcript is admissible as a prior inconsistent statement made by a nonparty.
- **(D)** The transcript is admissible because Bliss was under oath and the transcript was produced by a court stenographer.

36. Amy Attorney is defending her best friend Sheldon, against a lawsuit filed by Leonard. Leonard claims that Sheldon breached a contract wherein Sheldon agreed to sell to Leonard a mint-in-box Kenner Star Wars Millennium Falcon which was released in 1979. Sheldon asking price was $100, but he changed his mind after discovering that the toy was really worth $5000, and now denies having made the offer to Leonard.

Howard was in the room when Sheldon offered to sell the toy to Leonard.

During discovery, both parties submit interrogatories. Which individual(s) should an interrogatory not be propounded to?
- **(A)** Howard.
- **(B)** Sheldon.
- **(C)** Leonard.
- **(D)** Both Sheldon and Leonard.

37. In a civil case alleging invasion of privacy and intentional infliction of emotional distress, what court procedure would be used by the plaintiff's attorney to request copies of the defendant's phone records from a third-party telephone company?
- **(A)** Subpoena.
- **(B)** Request for production of documents.
- **(C)** Interrogatories.
- **(D)** Subpoena *duces tecum*.

38. Jeff is a somewhat eccentric guy who lives by the beach and spends most of his free time bowling with his best friend Walter. Maude was driving her BMW late one night when she broadsided Jeff's Pontiac LeBaron as he was coming out of bowling alley parking lot.

Jeff was treated and released from a local emergency room, but several weeks later began experiencing pain in his left knee. He filed a lawsuit against Maude to recover the damages to his car and for the pain and injury to his knee, which prevented him from going bowling.

During a deposition, Maude's lawyer, Brent, became so fed up with Jeff's ranting and raving that he files a petition with the court requesting a mental examination of Jeff.

Brent's motion to the court will be
- **(A)** Granted, because a party seeking discovery may obtain one physical and mental examination as a matter of right.
- **(B)** Denied, because Jeff has not placed his mental condition at controversy in the case he filed.

(C) Granted, provided that Brent can prove to the court that Jeff is not competent.

(D) Granted, because a physical or mental exam may be conducted solely upon the demand of a party seeking discovery.

39. Joe is a new attorney working for Frontier Auto, a company which manufactures off-road sports utility vehicles. Joe's office receives a letter demanding the payment of medical bills by Sarah, who was injured when her 2006 Frontier SUV's power suddenly turned off while she was driving on a freeway at 70 mph.

In researching the matter, Joe discovers that Frontier Auto's engineers knew of a defect with the fuse panel on their year 2004 - 2008 SUVs. However, the head of the electrical engineering department elected not to inform anyone outside of his department of the situation, and in fact instructed the engineers of his department to quietly fix the problem. Joe also discovered that Sarah's letter was not the first such letter received by Frontier Auto, and that every time the company had denied that the accidents were a result of their vehicles.

In order to ensure that no one discovers the actions of the electrical engineering department, Joe orders the head of that department to delete any emails of his knowledge of the fuse panel problem, and to shred any documents generated by his department which might be potentially related to the fix.

Joe's actions were
(A) Proper, because a company has no legal duty to retain records for longer than five years.
(B) Proper, because no lawsuit had been filed.
(C) Improper, because only paper copies can be destroyed, but electronic records must be preserved.
(D) Improper, because it was apparent that the opposing party has a legal claim.

40. What are the elements that a court will consider when deciding whether to issue a preliminary injunction?
(A) Whether money damages alone would be an adequate remedy should the plaintiff be injured.
(B) Whether the harm suffered by the defendant if restrained outweighs the harm the plaintiff will suffer without an injunction issuing; the likelihood the plaintiff will be able to succeed on the merits; and whether the injunction is in the best interests of the public.
(C) The risk of irreparable harm to the moving party; whether the harm the plaintiff will suffer without an injunction outweighs the harm the defendant will suffer if restrained; the likelihood that the Plaintiff will succeed on the merits; and whether the injunction will harm the public interest.
(D) Whether the plaintiff is able to show that they will be able to succeed on the merits; and whether issuance of the injunction will harm the public interest.

41. A Temporary Restraining Order (TRO) must expire no more than _____ days after it is issued.
(A) 5 days.
(B) 10 days.
(C) 14 days.
(D) 21 days.

42. Under what circumstances may a plaintiff not voluntarily dismiss a lawsuit which has been filed without being prejudiced in bringing the claim again?
(A) Where the defendant has served an answer or a motion for summary judgment.
(B) Where the defendant has asserted an affirmative defense.
(C) Where the plaintiff has already taken one voluntary dismissal, but now seeks to dismiss their cause of action a second time.
(D) Where the plaintiff has failed to prosecute their case.

43. Which of the following reason(s) is/are grounds for defendant to move for an involuntary dismissal of the plaintiff's case?

    (A) Plaintiff has voluntarily dismissed the same claims twice before.

    (B) Plaintiff has failed to comply with a court order.

    (C) At the close of Plaintiff's case, on the basis that the Plaintiff has failed to demonstrate any right to relief.

    (D) All of the above.

44. Which of the following would not be considered by a federal court when deciding whether to grant a party's motion for summary judgment?

    (A) A Memorandum of Points and Authorities prepared by defense counsel, arguing that there are no triable issues of fact and that the settled facts require a summary judgment for the moving party.

    (B) A declaration submitted by a witness which was allegedly made under oath.

    (C) Financial records which were deemed admissible at trial after being unsuccessfully opposed by a Motion *in limine*.

    (D) An excerpt from a deposition which was conducted under oath.

45. In a civil tort suit for conversion of property, the burden of proof which must be satisfied by the plaintiff is

    (A) Reasonable suspicion.

    (B) Clear, cogent, and convincing.

    (C) More likely than not.

    (D) Beyond a reasonable doubt.

46. During a trial for the tort of libel, a secretary for the defendant was being questioned on the witness stand by the plaintiff's counsel when she made the following statement.

> "I heard Mr. Reese tell Mr. Finch to go ahead and publish the article, even though Mr. Reese knew the article was likely not true, and there could be problems later on."

Defense counsel didn't object at the time this statement was made, but while preparing for trial the next day, he realizes that the secretary's statement was hearsay and that he made a mistake by not objecting.

What steps can defense counsel take to preserve the issue for appeal?

    (A) None.

    (B) File a motion for a mistrial.

    (C) File a motion for a new trial.

    (D) Appeal the case on the basis that the judge committed a reversible error by allowing the statement to be entered into evidence.

47. When is the proper time to bring a motion for a mistrial?

    (A) At the conclusion of the trial.

    (B) After the opposing side has presented their case.

    (C) On appeal.

    (D) During the trial itself.

48. On which basis may a prospective juror, be challenged "for cause?"

    (A) Lack of qualifications.

    (B) Incapacity.

    (C) Bias – Either actual or implied

    (D) All of the above.

49. At the conclusion of a criminal trial for first degree murder, the prosecutor made the following statements during his closing argument:

"I don't believe the defendant when he said that he came home and there was an intruder in the house. Do you? There were no fingerprints other than the defendant's and his murdered wife. If there was an intruder in the house, then why wasn't there a single shred of evidence? The defense counsel is simply trying to throw sand in the face of the jury in order to distract you from the fact that the defendant is without a doubt, guilty. In fact, the defendant is about as guilty as anyone I ever prosecuted."

What is the defense counsel's best course of action?

(A) File a motion for a new trial.
(B) Immediately object and file a motion for a mistrial.
(C) Nothing, because the prosecutor's statements were proper.
(D) File for a motion for summary judgment.

50. Which of the following actions is the least viable basis for a party to move to set aside a verdict on the basis of juror misconduct?

(A) The jury fails to follow the jury instructions.
(B) A juror discusses the case with friends and family before the verdict.
(C) It is discovered during deliberations that a juror intentionally concealed his bias toward the plaintiff.
(D) The jury foreman misreads the verdict, stating that the plaintiff is to be awarded $10,000, when the jury agreed that the plaintiff should be awarded $100,000.

51. A motion for a "judgment as a matter of law" includes a

(A) Motion for a Directed Verdict.
(B) Motion for a Judgment Notwithstanding the Jury Verdict.
(C) Neither A or B.
(D) Both A and B.

52. A motion made to the court to keep a case from being decided by a jury when there is no factual basis by which the jury could reasonably reach a finding against the non-moving party is known as a

(A) Summary judgment.
(B) Judgment notwithstanding the jury verdict.
(C) Judgment as a matter of law.
(D) Directed verdict.

53. What is the primary purpose served by a motion for a judgment as a matter of law?

(A) To avoid the time and expense of an unnecessary trial.
(B) To keep a case from being decided by a jury when there is no rational basis by which the jury could

reasonably base a finding for the non-moving party.
(C) To serve as a remedy for misconduct by the court, counsel, parties, witnesses, or any other major irregularity in the trial.
(D) To obtain relief from a judgment that resulted from mistake, excusable neglect or irregularity, fraud, newly discovered evidence, or misconduct by an opposing party.

54. When is the latest time that a party may bring a motion for a judgment as a matter of law before the court?

(A) After the plaintiff has rested their case.
(B) After the defendant has rested their case.
(C) Before the case has been submitted to the jury.
(D) After the case has been submitted to the jury.

55. What is the primary difference between a motion for a judgment as a matter of law (JMOL) and a motion for summary judgment?

(A) A JMOL motion is made during or after the trial.
(B) A JMOL motion is brought before the trial starts.
(C) A JMOL motion is brought after the jury verdict has been read.
(D) A JMOL motion is raised on appeal.

56. A retail painting dealer advertised extensively on their website. Buyer saw a $195 painting he believed was a classic. He went into their retail shop and indicated to the sales person that he wanted to buy the painting and put $195 cash on the counter. The salesman said "that painting costs $195,000, not $195, even though he admitted that the student they had used to post the paintings on their website may have made a mistake. Buyer sued for specific performance and the jury ultimately decided that they were going to enforce the $195 purchase price. The seller then moved for judgment as a matter of law and the trial judge granted the motion because she believed that the buyer was aware a serious

mistake had been made. On the appeal, the most likely outcome is
- (A) Sustain the trial judgment verdict.
- (B) Reverse the trial judge's verdict.
- (C) Remand the case for a new jury trial.
- (D) Decline to act at all since it is clear the judge and jury did not agree on the insight to be afforded the evidence presented by both plaintiff and defendant.

57. Donna is suing Ralph for breach of contract. Ralph pleads a defense of mistake. The jury was instructed to render a verdict on both the breach of contract and the mistake defense, but not on the restitution claim. The jury returns, finding in favor of Donna for breach of contract, but also in favor of Ralph for mistake.

The jury was asked to return a
- (A) General verdict.
- (B) Judgment as a matter of law.
- (C) Special verdict.
- (D) Formal verdict.

58. A reviewing court may set aside or vacate a trial court's findings of fact:
- (A) If a mistake was made below.
- (B) If the reviewing court disagrees on principle with the trial court's findings.
- (C) If the trial court's findings are clearly erroneous.
- (D) If the trial court's findings are reasonably erroneous.

59. Tony sued Mary for negligence and won the case after a full trial on the merits. The judgment was promptly filed. Mary is unhappy with the verdict and comes to you as her lawyer to determine what she can do next. The date her judgment was formally entered is important because
- (A) This starts the time running for her to file a motion for new trial.
- (B) This starts the time running for her to file an appeal.
- (C) Both (A) and (B).
- (D) None of the above.

60. Entry of a judgment occurs:
- (A) When it is in writing, signed by the attorneys, and recorded in the judgment registry.
- (B) When the judge announces his/her decision.
- (C) When it is in writing, signed by the judge, and recorded in the judgment registry.
- (D) Both (A) and (C).

61. Patricia, the Plaintiff's attorney, won her personal injury case against Dennis, the Defendant's attorney. During the case Patricia filed pleadings and used ABC Service of Process, Inc. to serve the Defendant in a timely manner. She hired expert witnesses and secured lay witnesses who were at the car crash to testify on the Plaintiff's behalf. Patricia may recover the following litigation cost(s) from Dennis:
- (A) Service of process.
- (B) Witnesses.
- (C) Filing.
- (D) All of the above.

62. Siblings Arnie and Betty were in heated litigation against each other. They both hired attorneys to represent them. Betty claimed that Arnie breached his fiduciary duty when their mother, Pamela, died and Arnie was named Executor of her estate. Betty alleged that, among other things, Arnie started spending their mother's money before all the debts and taxes had been paid. Betty prevailed and is seeking attorney's fees from Arnie.

May Betty seek an award of reasonable attorney's fees from Arnie?
- (A) Yes, under the "American Rule," the losing party pays reasonable attorney's fees of the prevailing party.
- (B) Yes, if there is a specialized statute for Betty's claim that allows an award of reasonable attorney fees.
- (C) No, each party is responsible for its own attorney fees.
- (D) No, there is no specialized statute allowing such an award for Betty's claim.

63. Plaintiff Paul underwent surgery for a tumor. Rick, M.D. performed the surgery. Paul had complications after the surgery that resulted in almost constant pain and that required him to take a leave of absence from work. Paul is suing Rick, alleging that the surgery Rick performed has put him in a far worse position now than he was before the procedure was performed. During the *voir dire* in this medical malpractice case, Donald, a retired surgeon turned horticulture enthusiast, was a prospective juror. When asked his occupation on *voir dire*, he answered "horticulturist" and did not mention his past occupation as a surgical doctor. When asked if any close family members or friends were a part of the medical profession, he simply replied, "I have known a lot of people in the medical field."

After the trial had been in progress about two weeks, respondent's attorney discovered Donald's past occupation. He immediately called the matter to the attention of the trial judge and the plaintiff's attorney.

What is respondent's best recourse?
  (A) File a motion for a mistrial and include evidence that shows juror misconduct.
  (B) Wait until the case is over and judgment has been rendered, and then file a motion to vacate judgment if the judgment is not in respondent's favor.
  (C) File a motion to appeal.
  (D) Submit a writ of prohibition, asking the court to take action on this matter.

64. A motion for a new trial must be filed
  (A) At least 28 days after the entry of judgment.
  (B) No later than 28 days from when the jury returns the verdict.
  (C) No later than 28 days after the entry of judgment.
  (D) None of the above.

65. Tom Trustee brought an action against Doug Debtor/Defendant seeking to deny his discharge in bankruptcy, stating that he willfully delayed in and failed to provide records pursuant to a court order. Doug failed to answer and a default judgment was entered against him. Ten months later Doug filed a motion, stating that he was confused over conflicting advice from his attorney. Tom argues that Doug's motion is untimely and that he did not provide pertinent records, which compromised Tom's efforts.

What motion did Doug most likely file and how will the Court likely rule?
  (A) Motion for a new trial; in favor of the Tom because Doug did not raise error of law.
  (B) Motion to vacate judgment; in favor of Doug because his relief is based on excusable neglect.
  (C) Motion for appeal; in favor of Doug because he has a matter of right to appeal.
  (D) Harmless error; in favor of Tom because Doug's delay did in fact substantially affect Tom's rights.

66. Which of the following may serve as a basis for a motion for new trial?
  (A) Harmless error.
  (B) Lack of jurisdiction.
  (C) Material issues of fact.
  (D) Errors of law.

67. A defendant put several witnesses on the stand to disprove the prosecutor's case. After one of the witnesses testified, it was brought to the judge's attention that the testimony of this witness was mistakenly allowed to be heard by the jurors and should be stricken. The judge ordered the testimony stricken from the record and told the jury to ignore the testimony. At the end of the trial, the jury found the defendant guilty. The defendant is seeking a reversal on the judge's decision to strike this testimony.

Was this a proper action by the judge?
  (A) Yes, if this error was harmless and did not affect the defendant's substantial rights.
  (B) Yes, collateral estoppel gives the judge the discretion to order the testimony stricken.
  (C) No, because the judge could find the testimony of this witness is needed for fairness sake since the witness has already been heard.
  (D) No, because this testimony should be included as a matter of right.

68. Kevin represents Dahlia, who is suing George. On day three of the trial, George's attorney seeks to admit a copy of a document as new evidence that helps his client. Kevin does not object and the evidence was admitted. The trial lasted for eight days. After the judgment returned in George's favor, Kevin realized this evidence should not have been admitted because it was not an original document and the original was available. Kevin filed a motion for a new trial based on this error 20 days later. In the motion he objects to the admissibility of this document.

Kevin's motion for a new trial will be
- **(A)** Granted to preserve his motion as a matter of right.
- **(B)** Granted because he filed it within 28 days after the entry of judgment.
- **(C)** Denied because his objection was not timely.
- **(D)** Both (A) and (B).

69. When appealing an issue that is separate from the merits of the case, which of the following allows for such an appeal?
- **(A)** Discretionary ruling.
- **(B)** Collateral order doctrine.
- **(C)** Supplemental Jurisdiction.
- **(D)** Motion to dismiss for failure to state a claim.

70. You represent a client in a highly contentious case that has gone on for three weeks. Everyone is tired, including the judge. In an attempt to bring the case to a close quickly and prevail, the opposing party files and serves you with an order compelling disclosure of attorney-client privileged materials. The judge enforces the order. What is your best response?
- **(A)** File a post-trial motion.
- **(B)** File a cross-appeal to get this decision before an appellate court.
- **(C)** Use collateral estoppel to stop the proceedings.
- **(D)** Get an appellate court to use its discretion to review this decision before the trial is over.

71. A Notice of Appeal is filed in
- **(A)** The appellate court.
- **(B)** The State Supreme Court.
- **(C)** The trial court.
- **(D)** Any of the above.

72. In rare circumstances, a party may seek review of a district court's action by seeking "extraordinary writs" from the court of appeals. When must you seek such a review?
- **(A)** Before entry of judgment.
- **(B)** Only after entry of judgment.
- **(C)** At any time.
- **(D)** Writs have been phased out in the federal rules so they are no longer available.

73. The U.S. State Office of Well Springs comes to you to represent them in defending a litigation matter. The matter involves citizens opposing work with which the U.S. State Office wants to move forward. At the end of the trial, the judge ruled in the citizens' favor. You seek to appeal the adverse judgment. Generally, how long do you have to file the appeal?
- **(A)** 60 days.
- **(B)** 30 days.
- **(C)** 28 days.
- **(D)** 14 days.

74. The United States Supreme Court may review a Court of Appeals decision when
- **(A)** There is an issue of substantial interest that should be determined.
- **(B)** A state court has decided the constitutionality of a federal law.
- **(C)** The Circuit Court of Appeals decision conflicts with another Circuit Court's decision.
- **(D)** All of the above.

75. Max and Linda are neighbors and have been in dispute as to their property boundary line. Two cherry trees, a raspberry bush, and a tulip bed all sit along the property line in question. One of the cherry trees blocks Linda's view of her favorite mountain. When Max was out of town, she had one cherry tree and the raspberry bush removed. Upon his return, Max sued Linda for damages for destroying his cherry tree. During the litigation, Max determined the true boundary line by hiring a professional to do a land survey. Both the trees and bush were on Max's property. He was successful and now decides to also sue Linda for removing his raspberry bush.

Max's cause of action for the raspberry bush is likely to

(A) Succeed because he won the previous litigation, which will serve as the basis for the second lawsuit.
(B) Succeed because even without the previous litigation, Max has all the evidence he needs to win again on the same liability issue.
(C) Fail because the statute of limitation will have run by then.
(D) Fail because Max cannot get more damages for the same injury.

76. One year went by after Linda lost her claim in court against her neighbor, Max, for destroying his cherry tree. On the other side of Linda's property, her neighbor, Sven, had grown prize-winning roses that ran along the side of Linda's property. Sven had already surveyed his property and knows that the roses are completely on his property. However, Linda's dog has repeatedly pricked itself with the thorns on the roses when it buries bones amidst the roses. When Sven is at work one day, Linda mows over the roses. Sven brings suit on the same grounds that Max did: suing for damages for destroying the roses on his property.

Sven's cause of action for the roses is likely to

(A) Succeed because Max's previous victory will serve as a basis for Sven's lawsuit.
(B) Succeed because Sven was not a party involved in the previous litigation and thus can bring this claim on the same type of issue.
(C) Fail because his issue will be precluded; he cannot get a second "bite at the apple."
(D) Fail because Linda will make defensive use of collateral estoppel.

77. When challenging a claim preclusion, the doctrine you are addressing is
(A) Collateral estoppel.
(B) Res judicata.
(C) Either (A) or (B).
(D) Both (A) and (B).

78. Donna sues Albert for breach of contract. Albert pleads a defense of mistake and an affirmative defense that Donna aided in the mistake. The issues of breach and mistake defenses are litigated. The jury found that no mistake was made by either party, and Donna prevailed on a general verdict. The judgment was necessarily against Albert on the breach of contract and the mistake defenses.

Subsequently, Donna sues Albert for breach in another, similar contract.

May Albert assert a mistake defense in this second suit?
(A) Yes. The second suit is different enough to not be preclusive.
(B) Yes. Albert may argue that mistake was not a necessary issue to the first action.
(C) No. *Res judicata* precludes Albert from attempting to assert the same defense.
(D) No. Albert is collaterally estopped from claiming mistake again.

79. Which of the following are elements of issue preclusion?
(A) An issue actually litigated AND necessary to the prior judgment.
(B) An issue actually litigated BUT NOT necessary to the prior judgment.
(C) An issue actually litigated and no final judgment has been entered yet in the first case.
(D) None of the above.

80. Landlord was sued by Tenant for premise non-habitability. Tenant stated that rodents were found in her apartment. Landlord countered that Tenant was to blame for the rodent infestation in her own apartment. This assertion was litigated. In discovery, it was found that Tenant did not dispose of her trash properly and caused the inhabitability herself. Landlord prevailed at trial.

A few months later, a second tenant sued Landlord due to rodents and other pests in his apartment. In this second lawsuit, Landlord asserts that same defense without a separate investigation.

In this second lawsuit
- **(A)** Landlord may make a defensive use of non-mutual collateral estoppel.
- **(B)** Landlord can preclude Tenant on the basis that a second bite of the apple is not allowed.
- **(C)** Tenant may attempt to prevent Landlord from asserting this same defense.
- **(D)** Both (A) and (C) are correct.

REGULAR QUESTIONS

81. Defendant is Caucasian and is on trial for a robbery which occurred in an Asian neighborhood. During potential jury member *voir dire*, the prosecuting attorney and the defendant's attorney questioned an Asian store owner, whose store is not in the neighborhood where the defendant allegedly committed the robbery. The prosecuting attorney would like this prospective juror on the jury. However, the defendant's attorney uses his first peremptory challenge against this prospective juror, basing his decision on race. He states that the Asian store owner may overly identify with the victims of this crime.

Since this is the attorney's first peremptory challenge, the judge will
- **(A)** Allow this challenge since he is entitled to three peremptory challenges.
- **(B)** Allow this challenge because the attorney has cause and there is no limit to the challenges for cause.
- **(C)** Deny the challenge because the jury must contain a diverse group to adequately represent a jury of the defendant's peers.
- **(D)** Deny the challenge because there is a restriction on basing peremptory challenges on a criteria such as race.

82. Seller retails antique automobiles in Miami, Florida. One day Brian and Betty from New York together walk into Seller's retail store and place two orders. Brian purchased a 1940 Ford coupe for $50,000 and Betty purchased a 1957 Chevrolet hardtop for $40,000. Both paid by check and left together. Five days later Brian's check bounced and three days later Betty's bank returned her check NSF. Seller initiates a lawsuit in federal district court against both Brian and Betty. Is federal jurisdiction proper?
- **(A)** No, because Brian and Betty are both residents of New York so diversity is lacking.
- **(B)** Yes, because the amount of damages Seller suffered exceeded $75,000, diversity is present, and allowing one suit promotes judicial economy.
- **(C)** No, because the $75,000 threshold is not met in this case.
- **(D)** Yes, because the facts in both incidents were identical, their fraud occurred at the same time, and there is diversity jurisdiction between the seller and all buyers.

83. A careless neighbor failed to maintain his house adequately for years, and as a result it became an eyesore in the community. When a fastidious next-door neighbor tried to sell her house, she received only offers well under her remaining mortgage balance and heard constant comments from potential buyers about the undesirability of living next to the careless neighbor's eyesore of a house. After the summer buying season ended, the fastidious neighbor spent the autumn and winter in despair, and ended up receiving counseling for depression. In the next spring, the fastidious neighbor decided to sue the careless neighbor for nuisance and for negligent infliction of emotional distress (NIED).

Which of the following represents the argument least likely to succeed at having the case disposed of under a FRCP 12(b)(6) motion to dismiss for failure to state a claim for which relief can be granted?

(A) State law requires a zone of danger or some kind of impact for NIED claims.

(B) The careless neighbor did not have a duty to the fastidious neighbor to maintain his own house to any particular standard.

(C) The allegation that potential buyers bid low only because of proximity to the careless neighbor's eyesore of a house does not seem very probable.

(D) These two neighbors, like all neighbors in their home owners' association, had signed a covenant committing to arbitrate disputes between them that involve property issues.

84. A man was driving through Kansas on his way from Nebraska, where he lived, to visit a relative living in Oklahoma. The man bought a sandwich at a local deli owned by a family that operated the business through a closely-held corporation. After he finished his sandwich, the man thought he noticed some of the family members leaving the restroom without washing their hands. The sandwich made him very, very sick during his visit to Oklahoma, where he incurred over $100,000 in medical expenses. Upon returning home to Nebraska, the man consulted with a local attorney to inquire about suing the Kansas deli in federal court to recover for the medical expenses and for pain and suffering. The local attorney called and sent a demand letter to the deli.

Around the same time, the man learned that the CEO of the closely-held corporation that owned the deli was going to attend a 5-N Club event in Nebraska. The man's attorney decided to conduct service of process on the CEO at that event. Just to be safe, though, the attorney also had service of process hand-delivered to one of the family's teenage boys who was a member of the local high school's 5-N Club. The complaint itself alleged that the family members running the deli were participants in a new social movement that discourages hand-washing because this practice allegedly washes away healthy bacteria needed for healthy skin, and that this unhygienic practice led to the food poisoning in the sandwich. Deli's attorney called the plaintiff's lawyer to discuss the case.

The deadline for the deli's formal answer passed, the court clerk entered default against the deli, and then immediately the man's attorney applied and moved for default judgment that was subsequently granted. At what point did the deli have the best chance to change the outcome of this case?

(A) The deli should have moved to dismiss the case for defective service of process because the complaint was served upon a minor, the high school-aged teenager, and because the district court in Nebraska did not have personal jurisdiction over the corporation running the deli.

(B) The deli should have moved to dismiss the case for defective service of process on the CEO who was merely visiting Nebraska and because the district court in Nebraska did not have personal jurisdiction over the corporation running the deli.

(C) The deli should have moved to dismiss for failure to state a claim for which relief can be granted because the allegation of the family's participation in the unsanitary social movement was allegedly spurious, salacious, and obviously a sensational lie.

(D) The deli could have the default judgment set aside because the man's attorney did not notify the deli of the application and motion for default judgment.

85. A landlord sued a former tenant for missed rent payments and because they damaged the property as they left the premises. At one point the landlord moved for default judgment. In what situation will the landlord have to provide the former tenant with notice of the application or motion for default judgment?

(A) The former tenant offered to pay the landlord only for the missed rent payments if the landlord would withdraw the lawsuit.

(B) The landlord knows the former tenant's new address in the same city where the landlord's own rented property is located.

(C) The former tenant is currently serving in the military, but stationed in the U.S., and the landlord knows the former tenant's contact information at that particular military base.

(D) The landlord is aware that the former tenant arguably has some convincing defenses to the landlord's claims, so therefore the landlord has a duty to provide the former tenant with notice so that the ultimate legal decision is reached to the greatest degree possible on the merits and substantive claims involved in the lawsuit.

86. A wealthy Iowa couple passed ownership of an apartment building to their children in a trust. The apartment building was located in Council Bluffs, Iowa, near the state's western border with Nebraska. The children continued living in Iowa after their parents passed away, but years later the trustee moved across the river to Omaha, Nebraska, where there were better restaurants. Long after that, the Council Bluffs City Council decided to build a new city hall right next to the apartment building, but while the old building on the city property was undergoing demolition to make way for the new city hall, the apartment building sustained major damage to its exterior. After unsuccessfully exhausting administrative channels for compensation, the trustee sued the city government in federal court to recover for the damage to the apartment building, relying upon her Nebraska residency and the hundreds of thousands of dollars in damages to justify diversity jurisdiction. What will happen if the city alleges that the children, whose state of residency is Iowa where the city is located, are the real parties in interest as the beneficiaries of the trust?

(A) Complete diversity requires that none of the plaintiffs share any citizenship with any of the defendants; because the children as nominal plaintiffs share citizenship with the city, the federal district court will dismiss the case for refiling in state court despite the Nebraska citizenship of the trustee.

(B) Although the children are residents of the same state as the city that is being sued, because the trustee is considered the real party in interest, the trustee's Nebraska residency will still justify diversity jurisdiction and the case will proceed in the federal district court.

(C) Although both the children are the real parties in interest and the trustee is only a nominal plaintiff, because the trustee initiated the lawsuit, when evaluating whether diversity is satisfied, only the trustee's citizenship as the nominal plaintiff will be considered.

(D) Because the children, who are the real parties in interest, still live in the same state as the city that is being sued, diversity jurisdiction has been defeated and so the federal district court will dismiss the case for refiling in an Iowa state court.

87. An angel investor sued a venture capitalist for tortious interference with a business expectancy. The case involved a contract between the angel investor and an agritourism business, the valuation of which would be critical to the case. The venture capitalist's attorney hired a testifying expert and a separate consulting expert to deal with the valuation issue. Also involved in the case were two CPA accountants. The angel investor brought her own CPA to her attorney to advise her attorney on the valuation issue. The other CPA was with an outside firm who had done work for the agritourism business before the lawsuit arose. Which type of communication will not be discoverable?

(A) An email between the testifying expert and the consulting expert who had been retained by the venture capitalist's attorney.

(B) A final report produced by the consulting expert that the testifying expert viewed and used to form her opinions about the valuation issue.

(C) An email between the angel investor's attorney and the accountant at the accounting firm.

(D) An email between the angel investor's attorney and the accountant whom the angel investor had brought to the attorney to advise the attorney.

88. An autonomous unmanned aerial delivery vehicle crashed into the rear section of a lady's luxury sports car as she was driving, causing an accident that injured her and totaled her expensive automobile. As a result, the lady sued the owner of the aircraft, an online retail corporation, to obtain compensation for the injuries she suffered and for the damages to her expensive vehicle. The corporation's legal team sent over a set of interrogatory questions including this one: "Do you the owner of the sports car make regular use of any electronic devices or software that compile data about your driving or about your travel locations?" The lady in good faith had her attorney answer no to this question, but six weeks into discovery she found out that a stargazing app on her cellphone had been regularly compiling her locations for years, and that she could readily download it in comma-separated-value (.csv) format. For the purposes of the stargazing app, though, the compiled locational data was accurate only to a kilometer radius and updated only every hour. Which of the following is true?

(A) The lady has a legal obligation to correct the interrogatory response by indicating that she has made use of an app that compiles such data.

(B) The lady has a legal obligation to turn over the location data only if a reasonable person would conclude that the information would materially help the corporation's defense, and the low granularity stargazing locational data probably would not be so helpful in this regard.

(C) If the corporation's legal team does not submit a final Request for Supplementation at the end of the discovery phase, then the lady need

not ever disclose the locational data.

(D) The lady has a legal obligation to provide the location data, but may charge the corporation for her and her attorney's efforts in doing so.

89. An employee has been working for a wholesale corporation for five years managing orders from retail stores and purchases from factory suppliers. Three years ago at the advice of the corporation's in-house counsel, the owner and CEO of the corporation had the employee sign a non-competition and non-disclosure agreement in exchange for that year's rather large holiday season bonus. In subsequent years, though, and after substantially smaller bonuses, the employee's relationship with the owner/CEO soured. One Monday in April, the employee failed to show up for work, and after re-establishing communication with a few factory suppliers and retail store owners, the in-house counsel discovered that they were under the mistaken impression that the corporation had begun doing business under a new trade name. Upon further investigation into public documents, the in-house counsel found out that the allegedly new trade name had recently been registered as an LLC by the employee. In which situation will the in-house counsel most likely be able to convince a judge to issue a temporary restraining order (TRO) preventing the employee from operating the new LLC?

(A) On the same Monday that the employee fails to show up for work, the in-house counsel files a motion requesting a TRO. The motion also includes evidence that the employee had absconded with $17,000 from one of the corporation's business accounts.

(B) Three months after the first Monday in April when the employee failed to show up for work, the in-house counsel filed a motion requesting a TRO. The motion also includes evidence that 75% of the corporation's retail store owners had ceased doing business with the corporation and were now dealing with the new LLC, and that the employee was doing this work within the geographical radius proscribed by her non-competition agreement.

(C) On the same Monday that the employee fails to show up for work, the in-house counsel files a motion for a TRO alleging that the operation of the new LLC will cause "irreparable harm" to the corporation.

(D) Three days after the employee's initial failure to show up for work, the in-house counsel files a motion requesting a TRO. The motion includes evidence that retail store owners had already begun failing to make payments on accounts payable due on that date and were instead making payments to an account at a bank located in a small island nation well-known as a tax haven.

90. A concerned citizen was out sailing on the bay one fine late-summer evening. All of the sudden his sailboat jerked sharply upward, split, and sank, throwing him into the water where he gashed his leg on a piece of debris. While all of this was happening, his attention was fixed not so much on his sailboat or himself, but on the strange miniature submarine-looking craft that seemed to have appeared underneath and then come up under his sailboat.

After the local coast guard rescued him using an amphibious vehicle, he discovered that that strange looking craft that sank his sailboat was an autonomous unmanned submarine owned and operated by the National Sea and Sky Bureau (NSSB), a federal agency. The citizen immediately had his attorney file a lawsuit against the NSSB requesting monetary damages as compensation for the loss of the sailboat and for his personal injuries, and an injunction against operating such autonomous unmanned submarines in areas like the bay that people frequent with their recreational boats.

Around the same time, the citizen told his attorney, his wife, and his son, that while a piece of debris in the water did gash his leg, that was actually the second time that

evening that he had suffered a gash to that area. Earlier while working the sails, a metal piece on the boom had caught on his leg and caused a smaller gash in the same area. During the first week after the accident, the citizen's son made a public comment to an online newspaper story about the incident that briefly mentioned his father's earlier injury from the boom. After his attorney learned of this comment two weeks later and questioned his client's son about it, though, the son took the initiative to delete it without the attorney suggesting he do so.

As the initial discovery process began, the citizen began to feel more and more eager to advance the cause of defending the safety of recreational boaters and told his attorney that he looked forward to the jury trial portion of the case when they could expose the dangers of autonomous unmanned watercraft. The attorney informed his client that juries do not judge federal tort claims. How could a jury still become involved in the case?

(A) The judge could impanel an advisory jury to offer a non-binding opinion about the appropriate level of damages as well as whether the judge should issue the requested injunction.

(B) The judge would need an advisory jury to decide whether the NSSB could compel the citizen's son to testify to the gash from his sailboat that the citizen had suffered earlier that same day.

(C) The judge could have an advisory jury offer a non-binding opinion about the appropriate level of monetary damages that the federal government ought to give the citizen.

(D) The judge would need an expert advisory jury to determine whether the attorney violated the Rules of Professional Conduct by questioning the son about the comment he made to the online newspaper article about his father's boat collision.

91. The Rowther family had been operating their family farm on Mannar Island for generations. A few months ago they reached an agreement with a new shipping company, Kappal Inc., to have the farm's products transported to the mainland for sale. Which issue in a subsequent dispute between the Rowther family and Kappal Inc. would likely constitute a genuine issue of material fact enabling the Rowther family's case to overcome a motion for summary judgment submitted by the company?

(A) Whether the law of the destination mainland district or the law of Mannar Island should apply to resolve the case.

(B) Whether the Rowther family had orally expressed to Kappal Inc. their total reliance on Kappal Inc.'s services in delivering their produce to the distribution company or whether the contract merely required transport to the port facility on the mainland.

(C) In which interpretation direction arguably ambiguous language should be resolved concerning when Kappal Inc. had a duty to pick up the items to be transported.

(D) Determining whether the decline in agritourism business due to rotting and smelly produce sitting around is a natural and necessary result of Kappal Inc.'s failure to transport or was a natural result that did not necessarily result from Kappal Inc.'s conduct.

92. The jury deliberated for five days in a high stakes and heavily publicized criminal trial. The jury foreman was frustrated because he was unable to break a deadlock between two groups of jurors. To resolve the disagreement, both sides agreed to appoint one person to represent their position and the two were to do internet research on the main issue in dispute. On Saturday and Sunday, the two designated jurors jointly researched the main issue in the trial. They both read and agreed upon how most jurors had decided the same issue in other cases. On Monday morning they jointly reported a summary of their research to the other jurors. On re-vote a few prior "guilty" jurors converted to "not guilty." The foreman immediately reported to the judge "we have researched the legal issue over the internet and now finally have agreed on an innocent verdict."

The court would likely

(A) Enter the jury verdict in the judgment registry.

(B) Overturn the innocent verdict on a JNOV motion.

(C) Order a new trial and enter an order prohibiting the current jury members from doing independent investigation during the proceeding.

(D) Order a new trial with new jurors.

93. A whitewater rafting guide arrived at the river put-in point with his guests and realized that his assistant had forgotten to bring lifejackets. Needing the money to pay for his son's tutoring before a major exam, and not wanting to disappoint customers, he decided to conduct the raft trip without lifejackets. After a customer fell into the water and nearly drowned, the customer sued the rafting guide for negligence. The jury returned a verdict in favor of the customer, awarding $20,000 in compensatory damages and $1.2 million in punitive damages. What motion should the rafting guide's attorney now make to have the best chance of striking or substantially reducing the punitive damages?

(A) A motion for judgment as a matter of law (JMOL) because the award of punitive damages was not supported by clear and convincing evidence.

(B) A motion for a new trial because the award of punitive damages was not supported by clear and convincing evidence.

(C) A motion for JMOL because the award of punitive damages was not supported by a preponderance of the evidence.

(D) A motion for a new trial because the award of punitive damages was grossly excessive, shocking the conscience.

94. What principle generally defines those expenses which are "taxable," i.e., those costs that a prevailing party may typically have a non-prevailing party pay as part of the judgment of a lawsuit?

(A) Costs that are reasonable.

(B) Costs assessed by the clerk.

(C) Costs assessed by the judge.

(D) Costs that the prevailing party requested the non-prevailing party to cover at the time the cost was incurred.

95. A car driver hit a biker on the street, causing some injuries. The biker sued the car driver, but the car driver felt guilty about his negligence, did not want to increase costs for himself or for the biker, and so decided to allow the biker to win by default rather than paying any attorneys to engage in emotionally-wrenching settlement negotiations. Later the biker realized that some of his injuries were far more serious than he had originally thought. When the biker sued the car driver again to recover for the additional cost of the unexpected injuries, the car driver initially was sympathetic, but began to suspect that the biker was trying to blame other health problems on the injuries from the collision. A day after the cross-summary judgment hearing at which both parties' motions failed, the car driver moved to dismiss the case based upon res judicata, a.k.a. claim preclusion. What will be the result of the car driver's motion?

(A) The court will dismiss the lawsuit.

(B) The court will re-open the summary judgment hearing.

(C) The court will deny the motion for dismissal and allow the lawsuit to move into trial on all claims.

(D) The court will consider the car driver's motion to be actually an assertion of collateral estoppel, a.k.a. issue preclusion. The judge will partially grant the motion to dismiss as to the extent of any injuries that could have been reasonably anticipated at the time of the first lawsuit, but will allow to proceed to trial claims for injuries the extent of which could not have been reasonably anticipated at the time of the first lawsuit.

96. Manny Mazina was turning a new page in his life book, and decided to pursue certification in network management in order to establish a sound career for the sake of his family. He was running out of money though and borrowed money with a promise

to repay, from his cousin Ted Tibako in order to pay for the Net Squared certification test and study materials. After passing the test, Mazina immediately found a good job at one of the many Maple Valley tech startups in a neighboring state.

Engrossed in his new work and growing family, Mazina did not notice when his cousin Tibako back in their home state of Ogima began trying to contact him to ask for the money back. Eventually Tibako sued Mazina for the money lent. Mazina likewise did not notice the summons, and eventually Tibako obtained a default judgment against him. What is not a good argument Mazina should make to vacate that default judgment?

(A) Mazina argues that according to the laws of the State of Ogima, the statute of limitations on such debts had passed before Tibako filed the lawsuit.

(B) Mazina argues that the summons was probably left with Tibako's part-time butler who was fired soon after when the summons allegedly was served on someone in his household, and that the amount of money Tibako claimed he owed him was incorrect.

(C) Mazina argues that he wants to settle the case rather than having to face the default judgment.

(D) Mazina argues that the summons was left with the part-time butler whom he subsequently fired, and that he had already paid off the debt before leaving the State of Ogima for Maple Valley by hiring the moving company operated by Tibako's son to transport his household goods to Maple Valley, an arrangement that Mazina claims Tibako suggested to him as an alternate means to pay off the debt.

97. The Chief Information Officer (CIO) at one of the world's top aerospace engineering companies received a warning from an unknown "security firm" that her company's systems were vulnerable due to a zero-day exploit the existence of which had not yet been released to the public. The CIO received similar warnings daily, and dismissed it as just another attempt to pass off a known vulnerability as a new one in order to get the standard monetary reward for reporting such vulnerabilities. In truth, though, it was a new exploit, and two weeks later unknown malicious actors exfiltrated terabytes of files containing very sensitive trade secrets of the company using that very same exploit. The company fired the CIO, who had an employment contract allowing termination only for a cause such as gross negligence in performing one's duties. The CIO sued the company for violating her employment contract and for engaging in gender discrimination. Both parties agreed to a bench trial rather than a jury trial.

Organizations advocating better protections for customers' private information became worried when a judge ruled that the CIO had not been grossly negligent in ignoring the security firm's warning. If such organizations were to file amicus curiae briefs to the company's appeal, what is the most likely grounds upon which they might be able to convince an appellate court to overturn the trial court's judgment?

(A) After a bench trial, the judge concluded that in fact there was no evidence that the malicious actors had done any harm to the company. Negligence requires a harmful result, and so because there was no result, there could have been no negligence.

(B) The CIO won the case through a default judgment resulting from the company having engaged in widespread and egregious discovery abuse.

(C) After the CIO received the company's answer, the trial judge permitted the CIO to amend her pleadings to allege gender discrimination in addition to violation of her employment contract.

(D) After the bench trial, a key part of the judge's final decision was the finding that in the past, the company had not similarly punished previous CIOs when similar situations had arisen.

98. Dana Driver and Patty Passenger were in Dana's car on the way to a shopping center for the day after Thanksgiving sale. While driving they were intensely discussing the items the newspaper had indicated were to be on sale. A large truck failed to stop at an intersection and collided with their car. Dana sued the trucking company and at trial, the court held Dana was not contributorily negligent. Subsequently Patty sued Dana for her physical injuries. Upon Dana's motion to dismiss, the court will likely

(A) Dismiss Patty's suit because of *res judicata.*

(B) Dismiss Patty's suit because she is collaterally estopped.

(C) Allow Patty's suit only if Patty was not aware of the first lawsuit.

(D) Allow Patty's suit against Dana.

99. Great Expectations was a corporation listed on the New York Stock Exchange that published record earnings for the year which caused its stock price to double. The Securities and Exchange Commission received rumors that the management had fabricated transactions to artificially inflate earnings and brought suit alleging a federal security act violation. Great Expectations vigorously litigated the issue in a jury trial but lost. The stock collapsed.

David Derivative was a class action lawyer who observed the trial. Upon the verdict being published, he began to contact the institutions who owned blocks of Great Expectations shares. He was able to convince over 500 of them to join a class action he filed against Great Expectations. After Great Expectations put in a general denial, David filed a motion seeking a declaratory judgment that Great Expectations not be allowed to relitigate the issue of whether they had fabricated earnings. The court would likely

(A) Grant the motion because the derivative action is on behalf of the 500 corporate owners.

(B) Deny the motion because a class action may not use collateral estoppel offensively.

(C) Deny the motion because the shareholders are in effect the corporation, so it violates the separation of interest requirement of collateral estoppel.

(D) Grant the motion seeking offensive collateral estoppel.

100. Which type of expense is taxable, i.e., the prevailing party may usually recover this cost after winning the lawsuit?
- (A) Legal research and consulting costs.
- (B) Fee for non-party witness who did not testify.
- (C) Fee for a testifying expert.
- (D) Postage fees.

101. Saveright, Inc. is a manufacturing company that manufactures a brand of space heaters which are marketed as very efficient. They claim their space heaters provide a measureable cost savings to customers. Saveright does not directly advertise in any state, but has an exclusive distribution deal with BigBox Stores, LLC, a nationally recognized chain of discount stores with more than a thousand stores spread across all fifty states in the country.

Tracy, a resident of State A, wants to file a product liability lawsuit against Saveright, Inc. after the space heater she bought caught fire and caused extensive damage to her house. Saveright is incorporated in State B, but its primary distribution warehouse is in State C. BigBox Stores, LLC is a limited liability company formed under the laws of State D.

In which federal district court should Tracy file her case?
- (A) State A.
- (B) State B.
- (C) State C.
- (D) State D.

102. A neighbor with a private residence lived next to a gravel pit that a company had owned and operated for many years. Neighbor and gravel pit employees together co-own a common driveway to reach to the rear of both of their individual properties. The company has depleted most of the gravel in the front of the pit and recently begun to mine the gravel towards the rear of the property. This has resulted in more trucks using the rear portion of the driveway with more frequency. Neighbor sued the company alleging excessive use of the common driveway and nuisance. The court denied all requested relief. Neighbor then sold his property to a new resident. The gravel truck traffic continued and increased somewhat. Two years later the new owner filed suit against the company, which filed a motion to dismiss. A court would likely hold the second lawsuit is
- (A) Barred by the doctrine of collateral estoppel.
- (B) Not barred because the plaintiff is a different party.
- (C) Allowed only if the truck traffic has increased.
- (D) Not barred if the truck traffic is a nuisance.

103. Deckard is a Nevada resident who owns a large ranch located in the State of California that borders a piece of property he owns in the State of Nevada. Rachel is a neighboring landowner who owns property only in California.

Deckard frequently travels to Reno for business and has found that it is more convenient for him to fly his private plane to Reno than to drive there. He thus had a small airstrip and hangar constructed on his property in Nevada. Rachel hates the noise created by Deckard's airplane, files a lawsuit in the federal district court of California to enjoin Deckard from using his property as an airport.

What is the most likely result?
- (A) Rachel's case will proceed because noise is equivalent to toxic fumes, and thus Deckard can be enjoined from using his property as an airport.
- (B) Rachel's case will be dismissed because the California court may assert *in rem* jurisdiction over the property in California.
- (C) Rachel's case will be dismissed because the behavior complained of does not arise out of Deckard's ownership or use of the California property.
- (D) Rachel's case will proceed because California's long-arm statute gives a court in California jurisdiction over any defendant who owns real property in California.

104. A New York City cab stopped to pick up a passenger on 53rd and Lexington. As soon as the passenger entered the back door of the cab the driver accelerated trying to get through a yellow light at the intersection. A UPS van was at the cross street and, late in his deliveries, entered the intersection a little too soon. An accident resulted injuring both the cab driver and passenger. The cab driver sued UPS and at trial prevailed with the court holding there was no contributory fault.

Two months after the verdict the passenger sued the cab company and driver. The attorney for the cab company filed a declaratory judgment motion seeking a holding that the decision in the prior action collaterally estopped the passenger claim for damages against the defendants. The court will likely hold collateral estoppel

- **(A)** Bars the passenger's suit in total.
- **(B)** Bars the suit against cab company, but not the driver.
- **(C)** Bars the suit against the driver, but not the cab company.
- **(D)** Does not bar the suit against either defendant.

105. A screenwriter was a resident of New York who was vacationing in Florida. While at a theme park, a display collapsed, seriously injuring the screenwriter. The theme park was owned by a corporation incorporated in Delaware with their corporate headquarters in New Jersey but had locations all across the country from Hollywood to Coney Island. The screenwriter was treated by a Florida physician who transferred her to the Moya Clinic in Minnesota. The screenwriter recovered and moved to California, where there were more job opportunities. The screenwriter's lawyer filed a lawsuit against the corporation in a federal district court in California. The complaint alleged the damages exceeded $75,000 and was based upon diversity jurisdiction. The corporation moved to dismiss the claim for lack of proper jurisdiction. The motion should be

- **(A)** Denied because proper diversity exists.
- **(B)** Granted because both parties are located in Florida and the accident occurred there.
- **(C)** Granted because the accident occurred in Florida.
- **(D)** Denied because the injured party lived in New York.

106. A single parent was a resident of New York and employed by a corporation as a low wage salesperson. The parent contracted fibrosis from working at one of the corporation's stores located in New Jersey. The parent filed an action for damages against the corporation in U.S. District Court in New York alleging violation of a federal workplace environmental standard. The corporation filed a motion seeking a transfer to the district court in Florida, the site of its corporate headquarters, on the basis of *forum non conveniens*, or in the alternative to the district court in New Jersey, the state in which the alleged environmental violation occurred. The court may

- **(A)** Dismiss the New York action since D has no connections with New York and the claimed damages did not arise from events there.
- **(B)** Retain jurisdiction in New Jersey or transfer the lawsuit to either New York or Florida.
- **(C)** Retain jurisdiction in New York.
- **(D)** Transfer the lawsuit to New Jersey or Florida.

107. While in the process of moving from Mississippi to Ohio to take possession of newly-inherited land, an impoverished apartment renter realized he could not afford to pay for the transportation of his one-of-a-kind Scheinweg piano, designed in an Art Nouveau style with keys made from mammoth tusk ivory, that long of a distance. While the renter was still in Mississippi, a New England piano store chain contracted with the renter to buy the piano and subsequently transferred $80,000 to the renter's bank account. The renter later received an offer from a relative in Nevada to restore the piano and move it for free to Ohio in order to keep it in the family. When the piano store chain's movers showed up to the Mississippi apartment to pick it up, the renter had already moved to Ohio and the piano was already in Nevada. The piano store chain initiated a lawsuit in an Ohio federal district court requesting specific performance of the sale. The federal judge of this court

- **(A)** May deny the renter's objection that the court in Ohio has no jurisdiction, but must submit the request for specific performance to a jury.

(B) May deny the renter's objection that the court in Ohio has no jurisdiction, may deny the renter's asserted right to a jury trial, and may grant specific performance of the sale.

(C) Must grant the renter's request that the venue be moved to a federal court in Mississippi, New England, or Nevada.

(D) May deny the piano store chain's requested specific performance but must submit the issue of restitution to a jury if either party asserts their right to a jury trial.

108. Betty Buyer ordered 250 widgets from Sally Supplier located in an adjoining state to be delivered three months hence. The contract price was $20 per widget or $5,000 in total. Supplier demanded and Betty agreed to pay 20% or $1,000 cash down to "finalize" the order. Betty paid the $1,000.

Three months passed and Sally did not deliver the widgets even though Betty was able to verify Sally had at least 10 of the units in inventory. Two more months went by and Betty brought suit in federal district court satisfying diversity jurisdiction. Betty sought damages for the seller's non-performance, a return of the $1,000 she paid, and an order of specific performance. She also noted a demand for a jury trial. Sally filed a motion to strike the jury demand, thereby requiring a bench trial over all issues. The court should

(A) Deny the motion only as it relates to the specific performance claim.

(B) Grant the motion over all aspects of Betty's claims.

(C) Deny the motion for all aspects of the case.

(D) Deny the motion only as it relates to Betty's monetary damages.

109. A seller from Vermont sells computer equipment to a buyer in California. The seller's invoice specifies payment is due in 30 days, any delinquencies are to bear interest of 1% per month, and buyer pays all collection costs and up to $5,000 punitive damages. In January, the buyer purchased from the seller $31,000 of notebook tablets and in February $39,000 of colored printers. Receiving no payment, the seller refused to ship any more merchandise to the buyer. In July, the seller filed a collection suit in federal district court. At the filing date there was $3,700 interest accrued, $900 in costs incurred attempting to collect the funds, and $500 in court filing and service charges was incurred by the seller. For federal diversity jurisdiction purposes, the amount in controversy is deemed to be

(A) $35,600.

(B) $73,700.

(C) $74,600.

(D) $80,100.

110. Acme Corporation entered into a joint one–year loan agreement with creditors First and Second Bank to borrow $80,000 and executed a promissory note which specifically named both creditors in total. As between themselves, the two creditors agreed to each bear any loss 60% and 40% respectfully. Acme's main corporate place of business was in California, and First and Second Bank headquarters are in New York. One year goes by and Acme does not make payment. First and Second Bank file suit in federal court. For federal jurisdiction purposes what is the amount in controversy?

(A) $40,000 each for First and Second Bank.

(B) $80,000 for First and Second jointly.

(C) $32,000 for First Bank.

(D) $48,000 for Second Bank.

111. David, Kim, and Joey all inherited a piece of real property which is located in the state of Massachusetts from their father, who passed away five years ago after battling a long illness. David lives in Texas, Kim lives in Tennessee, and Joey lives in Washington. None of the children has travelled to Massachusetts since their father's funeral, nor have any of them had any business dealings with that state.

A neighbor seeks to bring an action with regards to a boundary dispute with the property. The action is best filed in which state?

(A) Washington

(B) Massachusetts

(C) Texas

(D) Tennessee

112. Adam and Alice are married and residents of New Jersey. Their attorney is located in New York, and both their wills appoint him their personal representative. On New Year's Eve the couple drove into New York to party on Broadway. At 12:00 a.m. they walked across Broadway at 50th to get to their car when they were run down by a drunk New Yorker. They both died as a result of the collision and their personal representative and executor filed a wrongful death action in New York Federal District Court. The complaint specifies that the actual damages were to be determined at trial. The defendant New York driver filed a motion to dismiss based upon lack of diversity. The court should

(A) Grant the motion to dismiss as the personal representative and driver are both residents of New York.
(B) Deny the motion to dismiss.
(C) Grant the motion to dismiss since a judgment under $75,000 damages is possible.
(D) Deny the motion to dismiss because the controversy at issue does not involve a federal question.

113. Larry and Loretta fell in love while attending law school in Boston. They were both hired by prestigious New York law firms and moved to Manhattan. They both worked in excess of 60 billable hour weeks with an objective to be promoted from associate to partner. Unfortunately, they drifted apart personally and two years later Larry had an affair with a brand-new associate at his law firm named Lois. Loretta had become tired of the law firm mindset and her husband Larry. She moved back to Boston and filed for divorce in federal district court alleging their marital estate exceeded $75,000. If Larry files a motion to dismiss, the federal court should

(A) Deny the motion because the total amount at issue exceeds the minimum jurisdiction amount.
(B) Grant the motion because half of the amount at controversy does not exceed $75,000.
(C) Grant the motion because federal jurisdiction is lacking.
(D) Deny the motion because the parties were residents of different states at the time suit was commenced.

114. Paradise City is a delightful place to live whose water supply comes exclusively from Paradise Lake. Three separate gold mining companies conducted operations at the far end of the Lake which lead to significant degradation to the water quality. Paradise hired an engineer who concluded all three mining companies had contributed to the degradation in about equal amounts. Based upon the engineer's opinion Paradise purchased a $150,000 water filtration unit that corrected the problem and filed a federal claim against all three mining companies. If the gold mining companies move to dismiss the court will likely

(A) Grant the motion because each company's damages inflicted were only $50,000.
(B) Deny the motion if Paradise alleges all three defendants are jointly and severally liable.
(C) Deny the motion pending the jury trial decision of whether joint and several liability existed.
(D) Grant the motion because Paradise has the burden to allocate relative fault.

115. A family business operating in Vancouver, Washington, suffered a major embezzlement perpetrated by a CPA. The CPA was employed by a large auditing firm located in Portland, Oregon, ten miles to the south across the Columbia river from Vancouver. The complaint naming the auditing firm as the D was filed in the federal district court for Washington and properly served upon the auditing firm in Portland alleging common law inadequate supervision of their agent, the CPA. The CPA lived in Vancouver and was not named personally as a defendant. However, the auditing firm brought her in as a third-party defendant under the theory that she should personally be held liable to the auditing firm if they were found liable to the family business. The CPA's lawyer moved to remand the whole case to a Washington State court because both the family business and the CPA were citizens of Washington State, so diversity is lacking and the matter did not involve a federal question or state long arm statute. The motion will likely be

(A) Granted because both the family business and the CPA are residents of Washington State.

(B) Granted because the family business should have named the CPA as a co-defendant as an indispensable party in its original complaint.

(C) Denied because the CPA was served within 100 miles of the court.

(D) Denied because a third-party impleaded defendant does not affect diversity.

116. Victoria was an old Volvo sports car buff who lived in Seattle, which is located in the federal Western District of Washington. She had long desired to buy a 1972 Volvo P1800 sports coupe which was the last year Volvo made this classic model. Victoria found a well-cared-for P1800 across the state in Spokane, Washington which is located in the federal Eastern District of Washington. The seller of the automobile was a Chicago, Illinois, corporation that was incorporated in Delaware and distributed their cars nationally through independent antique car distributors. One mile from the seller's garage in Spokane the car exploded and Victoria was seriously injured. If Victoria wants to sue the corporation that sold her the Volvo sports coupe, the correct venue to bring suit is

(A) The District Court in Chicago, Illinois.

(B) The Eastern District Court of Washington.

(C) The Western District Court of Washington.

(D) The District Court of Delaware.

117. A group of dissident shareholders of Mega Buck, Inc. are filing a federal lawsuit under the 1934 Securities and Exchange Act which provides for a one-year statute of limitations. On January 1, 2015 their lawyer filed their complaint alleging fraud on the part of defendant "Mega Bank" in February, 2014.

Two months went by before the dissident shareholders' lawyer realized the suit named the wrong defendant. On March 1, 2015 they amended their complaint changing only the defendant's name from "Mega Bank" to "Mega Buck." Defendant files a motion to dismiss the amended complaint as in violation of the law's one-year statute of limitations. The court should

(A) Grant the motion because more than one year has expired.

(B) Deny the motion because the action will be treated as having been commenced on January 1, 2015.

(C) Deny the motion because making the typographical error was gross negligence by the shareholders' lawyer.

(D) Grant the motion because this is a different party.

118. Last month Dean got really drunk while out partying with friends. Although he tried to carefully drive home in an attempt to avoid attracting attention of the police, Dean swerved his car in an attempt to avoid hitting something "large and fuzzy" which darted across the road. As a result, Dean collided with John's house. The car landed in the middle of John's daughter's bedroom. Fortunately, she had been sleeping with her parents that night, and was not injured, but John was very angry and went out onto the front lawn to confront Dean.

John began screaming at Dean in the middle of the night. After exiting his car, Dean punched John, knocking John to the ground, and then sat on top of John until the cops arrived. Dean was arrested and charged with DUI. John filed a civil lawsuit against Dean, alleging in his complaint only the torts of battery, assault, and trespass to land. However, during the trial John's attorney began arguing that Dean was liable for causing John intentional infliction of emotional distress.

What result?

(A) The claim for intentional infliction of emotional distress will be allowed because the tort can be reasonably inferred from the damages complained of.

(B) The claim for intentional infliction of emotional distress will be allowed because the notice pleading rules are very liberal.

(C) The claim for intentional infliction of emotional distress will not be allowed because all claims arising out of one transaction or occurrence must be included in a single complaint.

(D) The claim for intentional infliction of emotional distress will not be allowed because it was not included in the complaint.

119. A businesswoman operated a corporation that purchased and sold used helicopters in Texas. Most of the purchases were made in Nevada where airlines stored their used aircraft. The businesswoman traveled to Georgia to investigate two used helicopters she saw advertised in an internet advertisement. She bought one of the two helicopters for $90,000, but never had any other connections to Georgia. That summer she vacationed in South Carolina where she was injured in an automobile accident caused by a Georgia resident who was also vacationing in South Carolina. The Georgia resident refused to pay for the injuries he had caused. The businesswoman therefore brought suit in Georgia state court where juries historically have rendered very liberal judgments for Ps. The Georgia resident filed a motion to dismiss for lack of personal jurisdiction over the businesswoman, a resident of Texas.

Does Georgia have jurisdiction over this action?

(A) Yes, because the tortfeasor is a Georgia resident.

(B) Yes, because the businesswoman took advantage of Georgia by doing business there.

(C) No, unless the businesswoman's Georgia activities were systematic and continuous.

(D) No, because the businesswoman should have filed the case in South Carolina state court, the jurisdiction where the accident occurred.

120. Acme Corporation has filed a federal diversity lawsuit against their former employee Iola whom they allege has used their federal copyrights and patents after she left to work for a competitor. Acme headquarters are in New York and Iola now lives in Maine. Maine law specifies service by certified mail is adequate if a person follows the federal post office rule of requiring a signature for the certified delivery. Acme used this system for service on Iola. Iola puts in a special notice of appearance and filed a motion to dismiss on the basis that the federal rule of personal service was not met. Regarding the motion to dismiss, the federal district should

(A) Deny the motion since the service complied with local Maine law.

(B) Grant the motion because it does not appear service met the federal court rule of valid service.

(C) Deny the motion for the moment but allow plaintiff to make the argument later after more facts are known in the case.

(D) Grant the motion unless Acme can show prejudice if they are required to comply with the federal rule of personal service.

121. Albert was operating his vehicle in a non-negligent manner in New York state when he was hit from behind by Driver who was under the influence of alcohol. Albert suffered serious injury. Driver learned that a lawsuit was imminent and moved to a new home in New Jersey to avoid service of the complaint. Albert hired a lawyer who filed a diversity action in federal court. A process server went to Driver's new home in New Jersey and knocked on the door. No one came to the door, but the next-door neighbor heard the commotion and came out on her front porch. She told the process server "Driver lives there but he is at work, so slide the papers under his door." The process server did as instructed. Driver's lawyer filed a motion to dismiss. The court should

(A) Grant the motion unless reliance upon the neighbor's direction was justified.

(B) Deny the motion because the Driver's lawyer filing a motion would strongly imply Driver had knowledge of the claim.

(C) Grant the motion because service was inadequate.

(D) Deny the motion because service was adequate.

122. Plaintiff filed a complaint in Federal District Court naming Defendant. Plaintiff then hired a process server to deliver and serve the summons and complaint on Defendant personally. Defendant heard rumors that Plaintiff had filed a complaint against him and fled the state. A five-month period passed and despite numerous attempts, service on Defendant was not accomplished. Dismissal of the complaint is

(A) Mandatory.
(B) Not mandatory if the Plaintiff shows good cause for the service failure.
(C) Mandatory unless Defendant's attorney agrees to accept service on behalf of their client.
(D) Mandatory unless P objects.

123. Floor Mart is a large national retail corporation with headquarters in Alabama. P purchased a lawnmower at his local Floor Mart store in Texas. When he started to use the mower on his home's lawn the machine blew-up, throwing off the cutting blades into P's leg. P suffered substantial damages and filed a federal lawsuit for damages in Texas. P mailed the complaint to Floor Mart in Alabama by first-class mail. He also paid a process company to personally serve the sales clerk that had sold him the lawnmower. Service is most likely

(A) Adequate.
(B) Adequate only if the sales clerk admits they received the complaint.
(C) Inadequate.
(D) Adequate only if the U.S. Postal Service authority will testify that the mailman delivered the documents in his regular mail delivery.

124. A corporation, registered in Delaware with its principal place of business in Indiana, sells its collectible card game products and offers its gaming services only over the internet. Which of the below situations is most likely to subject that corporation to personal jurisdiction in a Kansas state court? Assume that the corporation has never physically sold any of its products in Kansas.

(A) The corporation pays a marketing company to place advertisements for its products alongside search results that are related to the type of product the corporation sells.

(B) The corporation poaches an employee with valuable skills from a Kansas-based competitor, and immediately after coming to Indiana that employee posts trade secret-protected software code from the Kansas-based competitor in an online open-source forum without specifying the competitor's name.
(C) Kansas residents use the corporation's online platform to play with their collectible cards in tournaments featuring cash prizes over the internet and have won some of the tournaments.
(D) The corporation's official blog posted an assertion that it has "better customer service than all its competitors," one of whom everyone knows to be a well-respected Kansas-based business offering similar products and services.

125. Patricia Plaintiff has sued Donna Defendant. Which of the following arguments, assuming each is factually true, would least likely allow Donna Defendant to have the case dismissed involuntarily against the wishes of Patricia Plaintiff?

(A) Patricia Plaintiff and her counsel have engaged in egregious discovery abuse, refusing to turn over documents to Donna Defendant even after specifically ordered to do so by the judge.
(B) Six years after the initial filing of the lawsuit, and after Patricia Plaintiff and her counsel had requested trial to be postponed twice before in years past, the court schedules a pre-trial conference, and two hours before the conference Patricia Plaintiff's counsel requests that the clerk postpone the conference and does not show up to the conference when the judge conducts it anyway.
(C) Patricia Plaintiff admits in a deposition that she waited to file suit against Donna Defendant until after the statute of limitations had elapsed on an unrelated possible claim Donna Defendant may have had against Patricia Plaintiff.
(D) Patricia Plaintiff's counsel provides a friendly witness with a script prior to a deposition, the judge orders Patricia Plaintiff to pay a monetary

sanction for such misconduct, and Patricia Plaintiff does not pay the sanction by the deadline specified.

126. Which of the below is an impermissible question to include in an interrogatory to the opposing party?

    (A) "Do you contend that this jurisdiction's binding precedents have merged and made indistinguishable the standards for evidence admissibility with regard to partially-integrated and completely integrated contracts?"

    (B) "Do you contend that Parties to this contract all intended it to be a completely integrated contract?"

    (C) "Please state the name and address of each person who had knowledge of the pre-contract negotiations."

    (D) "Please state the name and address of each person who attended the July 14, 20xx, contract negotiation meeting."

127. On a Friday afternoon an attorney is rushing to catch a plane for a scheduled vacation with his wife. It is the last day on which a tort lawsuit can be filed against an insurance company, and the attorney finished drafting the summons and complaint before handing the documents off to his assistant for proofreading. He then tells his assistant to contact him on his cell phone after proofreading while he drives to the airport.

The attorney's assistant proofs the documents and then calls the attorney saying "I did not find any errors." He then tells her to sign his name to the summons and complaint, and then file them with the court. The legal assistant does so, and the attorney spends the next week on vacation.

However, a sharp-eyed court clerk who processing the documents and who is familiar with the attorney notices that the signature on the summons and complaint do not match with the attorney's past filings.

What will the court likely do in this case?

    (A) The court will file Rule 11 sanctions against the attorney for failing to make a reasonable inquiry into the factual basis of his claims.

    (B) The court will strike the proceedings because of the lack of a proper signature.

    (C) The court will allow the pleadings because the attorney directed that the papers be signed.

    (D) Assist the client in filing a malpractice claim against the attorney for failure to properly file their case before the statute of limitations expires.

128. Seven years ago, a billionaire tech-mogul bought a mansion in a prestigious neighborhood. When he bought the property, an old row of lilac bushes planted just inside his land roughly marked the boundary between his property and the plot of his neighbor, a wealthy clothing magnate. A month after purchasing the mansion, the tech-mogul tore out the lilac bushes and planted a line of blackberry bushes in its place. In the intervening seven years, the bushes had grown into the clothing magnate's property. One day the clothing magnate learned that the tech-mogul believed he owned all the land covered by the blackberry bushes.

Upon hearing the tech-mogul claim ownership of his land by asserting ownership over the entire blackberry patch that was now extending into his property, the clothing magnate decided to take action. He had his attorney file a quiet title action with the property boundary marked by where the old line of lilac bushes had been. After notifying the tech-mogul of the action and receiving objections from his attorney, the clothing magnate's attorney promptly served an interrogatory asking "Do you the tech-mogul claim ownership of all land upon which the current blackberry patch sits?" and a request for admission asking "Do you the tech-mogul admit that soon after you bought your property ten years ago, you tore out a row of lilac bushes that marked the boundary with the clothing magnate's property?" Five weeks later after a motion to compel, the tech-mogul responded "yes" to the interrogatory question, and "no" to the request for admission. What is the most likely result assuming local court rules mirror the FRCP?

(A) The tech-mogul may continue to pursue a claim of ownership over the entire blackberry patch, and the clothing magnate must produce evidence that the tech-mogul tore out the old lilac bush.

(B) The tech-mogul may not pursue a claim of ownership over the entire blackberry patch as a result of spoliation: destroying evidence of the lilac bushes as the original property boundary.

(C) The tech-mogul may have to pay the clothing magnate's attorney's fees for the motion to compel, and in his dispute with the clothing magnate he will be deemed to have admitted that he tore out the boundary-marking lilac bushes.

(D) The tech-mogul may not continue to pursue a claim of ownership over the entire blackberry patch due to his late response, or dispute that the lilac bushes formed the boundary, but he may still dispute that he tore them out with intent to obfuscate the boundary.

129. Frugal with her personal expenses while initially getting her tech startup going, a software programmer decided to reward herself with a luxurious sports coupe after her company went public. One day as she was racing down Interstate 12 going twenty miles over the speed limit, she approached a car in her lane traveling below the speed limit. Although she braked, she still hit the car, causing an accident. In a subsequent lawsuit, the driver of that car had his attorney send the programmer a request for admission that the programmer was exceeding the speed limit just prior to the collision. After the programmer denied speeding, the other driver hired an investigator to find out whether any security cameras or other video footage had caught the programmer speeding just before the accident, and sure enough, the investigator did find such footage. The other driver's attorney then requested monetary and evidentiary sanctions for discovery abuse for having deliberately misstated the truth in a request for admission. Which monetary sanction would a judge not award?

(A) The billing for the attorney's fees that the other driver's attorney incurred preparing for requests for admission sent by the programmer's attorney.

(B) The billing for the time the other driver's attorney spent preparing the part of the motion for sanctions requesting attorney's fees.

(C) The investigator's billing for time spent to discover the footage.

(D) The investigator's expenses incurred to discover the footage.

130. A soldier in the Army recently deployed with his unit to Afghanistan. The day before he left, the soldier was served with a Summons and Complaint by the homeowner's association (HOA) with authority over his condominium residence property. The complaint alleged past due HOA dues, and demanded a lien be placed on the soldier's home. Before he left, the soldier attempted to contact the HOA to discuss the details of the lawsuit and arrange a payment plan with the HOA.

After 30 days, the HOA had not received any response from Harry concerning their lawsuit, so the HOA's attorney filed a motion for a default judgment. The motion for default will likely be:

(A) Granted, because the soldier was properly served with the summons and complaint.

(B) Granted, because the soldier has failed to timely file an answer within the required 21 days.

(C) Denied, because the soldier is in the military.

(D) Denied, because the soldier has "appeared" in action.

131. A motion to quash or limit a subpoena issued to a non-party deponent may be filed by

(A) The Deponent.
(B) The Defendant.
(C) The Plaintiff.
(D) Any of the above.

132. A daredevil established himself as a hang glider test pilot for a more regular income. One day he became seriously injured in a crash. The daredevil wanted his attorney to sue the manufacturer of the hang glider's nose wires, believing the crash to have resulted from a product defect rather than any problems caused by the previously-untested and brand-new hang glider design he had been flying. The daredevil's attorney retained two experts, one to address the testing of new hang glider designs, and the other to address issues around nose wire manufacture. The attorney had them draw up the detailed reports. In response to the manufacturer's motion for summary judgment, the attorney submitted the experts' reports as critical elements to substantiate the claimed product defect claim. Why would a judge refuse to consider the experts' reports at the summary judgment motion stage?

(A) The attorney needed also to submit a report from a licensed physician that would address the daredevil's injuries.

(B) The two experts whom the attorney had retained were impermissibly coordinating their efforts for the case.

(C) The attorney should have had the experts submit affidavits of their opinions, not just notarized reports.

(D) The attorney should have submitted the full reports earlier to the other side as part of the initial disclosures.

133. What is the penalty for a person who fails to comply with a properly issued subpoena to appear at a deposition?

(A) The party who wishes to call that person as a witness will be prevented from doing so at trial.

(B) The party wishing to interview that person will be allowed to infer that person's failure to appear at the deposition constitutes an admission on their part.

(C) The court will issue an order for the person to appear at the deposition.

(D) The court will hold the person failing to obey the subpoena in contempt.

134. A young couple moved into a neighborhood and set up a day care business in their house. When they bought their house, they knew that it was only three blocks away from a pre-existing day care business operated by an older couple. Shortly after starting their own day care business, another family in the neighborhood approached the young couple to take care of their daughter. This other family in the neighborhood who were of the Pelasgian ethnicity had first tried to place their daughter in the older couple's day care. When the older couple claimed to have no more openings, the Pelasgian family did not believe them, and so the Pelasgian family decided to go with the young couple's day care instead.

Subsequently, the young couple placed billboards along the major roads through the neighborhood advertising that they do not refuse children based upon race or ethnicity, unlike "another unnamed" day care operation in the neighborhood. But every driver in that tight-knit neighborhood knew exactly which other day care operation the young couple's advertisement was referring to. Over the next couple weeks, the older couple saw their business drop off sharply, and whereas once they did not have enough openings for new children, now for the first time in years they were struggling to maintain profitability.

The older couple decided to sue the young couple for libel. The case became the sensation of local media. Some neighbors sided with the young couple, claiming that they too had noticed subtle instances of prejudice from the older couple; other neighbors sided with the older couple, observing to everyone's disbelief that, contrary to the present sad state of the older couple's business, their business had been booming just two months earlier precisely because the older couple has been so friendly toward everyone regardless of race or ethnicity.

At the close of evidence in a lengthy jury trial involving testimony from a variety of neighbors, the young couple family moved for judgment as a matter of law (JMOL) in order to rid themselves of the claims against them. Which fact is most likely to prevent the young couple's motion for JMOL from succeeding?

(A) The only evidence that the older couple could find of the younger at least negligently claiming that the older couple was biased against ethnic Pelasgians is that the young couple should have known that at the time of the billboards, the older couple's day care could very likely have been full, and so there was a perfectly legitimate reason to decline to accept the other family's daughter.

(B) The daughter's father who testified at the trial was known in the neighborhood as a hothead who frequently would get angry at shop clerks for allegedly cheating him out of mere cents when giving him his change from a purchase.

(C) The older couple asserted that the monetary damages their business suffered could be attributed solely to the allegedly libelous billboards precisely because they identified this amount of loss as greater than that which their business would have suffered due solely to the arrival of a new competitor in the neighborhood.

(D) Overall and on net balance in light of testimony from a wide cross-section of the neighborhood's residents, the judge believes that the older couple was not biased against any race or ethnicity.

135. A company is one of the world's top developers of education tools for primary school students. Its CEO and in-house counsel concluded that it would be best for its business plan to develop and sell its software on the traditional closed source model, not the open source model. Six months ago, the company released a newly updated version of its main classroom learning suite that enables students to 3D print the designs and other items that they create with the visual arts and technologies portion of the software suite. Two months ago, the company's main competitor quite surprisingly released a new version of its software suite that was radically different from previous versions, but uncannily similar to the company's latest version.

In response, the company's CEO and in-house counsel decided to pursue various legal claims against the competitor including trade secret misappropriation. The in-house counsel warned the CEO that during the discovery process, the competitor could move to compel the company to provide its source code to the competitor with the justification that the competitor could then compare the source code for its software against the source code of the company's software in order to prove that they were different and therefore that the competitor did not infringe upon any of the company's intellectual property rights. The in-house counsel assured the CEO, though, that there are measures they can take to prevent the competitor's own software developers from learning any more of their company's source code than they already did (assuming that somehow they had illegitimately obtained some of it already). Which of the following suggestions will best protect the documents from being viewed by the competitor's software programming team?

(A) Mark the documents containing the source code "CONFIDENTIAL," subject them to a protective order as trade secrets, and then hand them over to the head of the competitor's in-house counsel team.

(B) Before a software developer has the source code compiled, the developer sends the finished source code to the company's in-house counsel, thereby attaching attorney-client privilege to it, and then the in-house counsel sends the source code off to be compiled.

(C) Require all software developers to store documents containing source code only on hard disks that are fully encrypted, with only the company's in-house counsel possessing the unlocking password. As a matter of standard business practice, the in-house counsel unlocks the drives at the beginning of each work day.

(D) Have the company's in-house counsel review each document containing source code and offer an opinion about how useful it might be to pursue a patent on it.

136. An engineer runs a 3D printing business in Franklin State that takes orders over the internet and in person. Her shop specializes in intricate, delicate printing with metal materials. She advertises her business on the internet using keyword targeting services running within popular search engines; none of the keywords that she pays for are geographic or locational. Because metal products are so heavy and the designs are so delicate, most of her customers come by in person to pick up what they have ordered.

One day she received an order over the internet for a specialized joint costing $1,200 to be used in a robotic arm. The billing address was in Franklin State and, as usual, the customer indicated that she wanted to come by in person to pick up the joint. Subsequently over the phone the customer revealed that she was in the process of moving to the nearby State of Texatoba where she planned to open up a manufacturing business that needed robotic arms. If the engineer's product worked well, the customer planned to order many more.

Unfortunately, when the customer tested the first robotic arm using the specially-manufactured joint, it did not work correctly, and actually caused some damage to the customer's new shop in Texatoba State instead. The customer immediately initiated a tort and breach of contractual warranties lawsuit against the engineer at the local state court in Texatoba. The engineer was sure that the problem did not arise from the joint she had produced. As a consequence, her attorney was easily able to draft a substantive answer. In addition, though, the engineer's attorney did not believe that the Texatoba state court had personal jurisdiction over the engineer or her business, but the attorney needed more time to find out where the customer was when the customer submitted the initial order for the robotic arm joint, and to

research controlling case law and how it might apply to the unique facts of this situation. What should the engineer's attorney do to have the claims against the engineer dismissed?

(A) First file the substantive answer challenging the customer's claims, and then after enough discovery and research submit a motion to dismiss based upon a lack of personal jurisdiction.

(B) Move for a new trial in the State of Franklin, where the case should properly have been brought.

(C) Move for voluntary dismissal.

(D) File an answer that generally asserts a lack of personal jurisdiction but leave the particular details and arguments in light of case law to a later motion to dismiss.

137. A Kentucky-based psychiatrist offers specialized marriage counseling to members of a particular religion online, maintains an online discussion forum over related issues, and sells books she wrote through her website, some of which the psychiatrist claims were signed by a now-deceased leader of that religion. A customer lives in Wyoming. Never before has the psychiatrist offered counseling services to anyone in Wyoming, and there is no evidence of anyone else in Wyoming interacting online through the psychiatrist's website. If a dispute arises between the two, which situation will most likely subject the Kentucky-based psychiatrist to personal jurisdiction in a Wyoming state court?

(A) The psychiatrist advertises endorsements from various regional religious bodies, including one for the Rocky Mountain area, and the customer now wants to sue the psychiatrist over the bill for a set of counseling sessions.

(B) The customer bought a used copy of one the psychiatrist's books from a famous third-party online book-selling powerhouse that was advertised to have been signed by the now-deceased religious leader; however, the customer alleges that the copy she received was unsigned. The customer was unable to obtain a signed copy from the bookselling powerhouse, and now has sued the psychiatrist for specific performance to obtain a signed copy.

(C) The customer wants to sue the psychiatrist for negligent infliction of emotional distress allegedly arising from the psychiatrist's arguably heretical advice offered in a book that the customer bought through the psychiatrist's website.

(D) The psychiatrist belongs to a network of counselors providing specialized services to adherents of their religion; another Wyoming-based psychiatrist in this network recommended the Kentucky-based psychiatrist to the customer in Wyoming. Subsequently, the customer experienced a setback in her family situation due to the Kentucky-based psychiatrist allegedly misinterpreting their religion's arbitration rules.

138. An entrepreneur in Hawai'i over the internet sells cutting-edge, trendy dongles that add a variety of different functionalities to electronic devices. Because he operates from an island, though, when customers buy from his website, the dongles they receive come directly from mainland distributors with whom the entrepreneur has made shipping arrangements. The entrepreneur advertises this service on his website so that customers know from the start that their orders will not arrive more slowly because the business is located offshore. All online orders require buyers to click through a sales contract with choice of jurisdiction and choice of law clauses specifying Hawai'i as the venue for all disputes arising from the contract, and the laws of Hawai'i as governing this dispute resolution.

A customer lives on the mainland in Oregon and ordered a specialized image projection dongle from the entrepreneur's website. Although the customer has wanted to vacation all her life in Hawai'i, she has never been there, and was pleased to learn that her shipment would not take longer than usual because of the location of the entrepreneur's business. After receiving her dongle, though, the customer claimed to the entrepreneur that it was defective, a charge that the entrepreneur denied. The customer began posting negative criticism about the entrepreneur's product on prominent websites, upon which the entrepreneur decided to sue her in a Hawai'i state court for defamation.

The customer made a special appearance to challenge the Hawai'i state court's exercise of personal jurisdiction over her. What is the likely result assuming that the state court's rules follow the FRCP?

(A) The customer will see the case dismissed: Hawai'i state courts have no personal jurisdiction over her because she would need to have bought from the physical store in order to have sufficiently minimal contacts to warrant the local state court asserting personal jurisdiction over her.

(B) The customer will not be able to have the case dismissed because of lack of personal jurisdiction: The choice of jurisdiction clause in the online order form process creates sufficiently minimal contacts between her and Hawai'i to justify such personal jurisdiction.

(C) The customer will see the case dismissed: Hawai'i state courts have no personal jurisdiction over her because selling over the internet alone is not enough to convey personal jurisdiction over buyers in the seller's jurisdiction.

(D) The customer will see the case dismissed because choice of jurisdiction clauses in click-through online agreements are insufficient to create the minimum contacts necessary for personal jurisdiction; the choice of jurisdiction clause would have had to have been contained in a less pro forma contract for which there must be some evidence of actual bargaining that involved the choice of jurisdiction clause.

139. Two friends, one an engineer, the other a sailor, founded a light manufacturing 3D printing LLC together with each owning 50%. Business took off and was so successful that the two hired employees to do their work for them. At that point, the founders withdrew to management roles, with the engineer doing most of that work. The sailor decided to live off his share of the profit, spending most of the year boating around the world and withdrawing money directly from corporate accounts when he came ashore again after periods of time that would range unpredictably from a week to six months.

At one point, the sailor suddenly withdrew such a large amount of money from the corporate account, with no notice to the engineer, that the engineer was only able to make payroll that month by using money from her personal savings account. The sailor immediately went back out to sea before the engineer could reach him to discuss the matter. At that point, the engineer felt she needed to deal with this problem by dissolving the corporation and taking over most of its assets to continue the business by herself. What should the engineer's personal attorney recommend she do in addition to filing a formal legal complaint?

(A) File a motion to dissolve the corporation along with a motion for a permanent injunction preventing the sailor from withdrawing money from corporate accounts.

(B) File a motion to dissolve the corporation along with a motion for collateral estoppel to prevent the sailor from withdrawing money from corporate accounts.

(C) File a motion to dissolve the corporation along with a motion for a temporary restraining order (TRO) preventing the sailor from withdrawing money from corporate accounts.

(D) File a motion requesting summary judgment on an accompanying motion to dissolve the corporation and file a motion for a preliminary injunction preventing the sailor from withdrawing money from corporate accounts.

140. There are four factors for determining whether a class action is the best way to adjudicate the controversy fairly and efficiently under the Common Question certification. Which one of the following choices is not one of those four factors?

(A) The degree to which a class action would prevent prejudice to non-class parties opposing the class action who could face incompatible standards of conduct if the various claims were brought separately and not as class actions.

(B) The desirability or undesirability of concentrating the litigation of the claims in the particular forum.

(C) The likely difficulties for the court in managing a class action lawsuit.

(D) The class members' interests in individually controlling the prosecution or defense of separate actions.

141. A new widely marketed communications device leveraged a previously-unused stretch of electromagnetic spectrum. Years later complaints began to arise that the use of this stretch of spectrum was causing medical problems in users of the device. Some users had developed cancer, others had various internal organs shut down, while still others developed unsightly but benign tumors. An attorney brought a class action suit against the service providers with whom these customers had contracts primarily to compel the service providers to switch to a safer part of the spectrum. A secondary objective was to recover monetary damages from both the service providers and the manufacturer to compensate the victims for their health problems. For which of the following reasons would a court most likely deny class-action status to this complaint?

(A) The complaint did not detail with particularity the reasons why the common questions of law and/or fact outweigh questions affecting individual members.

(B) The class members did not all suffer the same sorts of injuries.

(C) The complaint did not obtain advance approval from a large representative sample of the plaintiff class.

(D) The plaintiffs' attorney did not provide notice to the class members advising them of their right to opt out of class inclusion.

142. All class action lawsuits must be certified in at least one of three required categories. Which of the following is not one of those three categories?

(A) There would be prejudice to potential class members if their actions were brought as individual actions because doing so would be dispositive of their interests or substantially impair or impede the ability of potential class members to protect their interests.

(B) There would be prejudice to non-class members due to incompatible standards of conduct resulting from the class members' actions being brought as individual actions.

(C) It is both possible and feasible to define a clear class using objective criteria and the members of that class have the same exact set of common questions of fact and/or law.

(D) The class members request primarily injunctive or declarative relief, not primarily monetary damages, because the defendant's actions have made such relief appropriate.

143. On a steep hillside, the downslope property owner began digging into the hillside in order to lay a foundation for a new house. The upslope property owner became very worried that the digging would cause instability in the hill, ruining the foundation of the upslope property owner's own house, and so the upslope property owner sought a preliminary injunction preventing the downslope owner from continuing with excavation until the plan could be verified to not undermine lateral support. Why might an appeals court overturn the preliminary injunction if the downslope owner were to file an interlocutory appeal challenging it?

(A) The trial judge issuing the preliminary injunction generally concluded that the upslope property owner was likely to win on the merits and would suffer irreparable harm if the injunction were not granted, and that the public interest was not adversely affected.

(B) The same trial judge who issued the preliminary injunction in this case did not issue a preliminary injunction in a case the previous year that was arguably identical.

(C) The upslope owner did not first obtain a temporary restraining order (TRO) before requesting the preliminary injunction.

(D) The trial judge issued the preliminary injunction in an ex parte proceeding taking place after the upslope property owner had made reasonable efforts to serve process on and provide the downslope property owner with notification of the case and the request for a preliminary injunction.

144. Around election time, a part-time journalist for the website of a city neighborhood wrote a story about the neighborhood's representative to the city council. The journalist alleged the representation pushed city hall to green-light a local businessperson's application to spot-zone a plot of land to build denser residential housing. The journalist alleged that the representative had received a kick-back in the form of the businessperson purchasing all the paintings that the representative's son had produced last year to adorn the businessperson's establishments. The representative was outraged and decided to sue the original journalist as well as other journalists who re-published the article all together as a class under state law for defamation and under federal law for interfering with an election by publishing false information. The representative made sure to specially-plead the defamation claim and filed suit in federal court.

The representative conducted service of process on the journalist the same way the journalist published the defamation: over the internet, on a government website that linked to the original article, to the re-published articles, and to the journalists' social media profiles. Which of these statements about the representative's case is false?

(A) The class in a class action suit can only be plaintiffs; defendants cannot be a class, and so the representative has to sue the journalists separately.

(B) The representative did not have to specially-plead the defamation claim.

(C) The representative could not conduct service of process by publication over the internet on a government website.

(D) The federal court can dismiss the defamation claim allowing refiling in state court even though the representative's election-law claim is a federal question and the representative demonstrated how the state law defamation claim satisfies the requirements for supplemental jurisdiction.

145. A plaintiff and a defendant are involved in a tort case in which the plaintiff alleges that the defendant shined a laser into the plaintiff's home, severely damaging the plaintiff's eye. The defendant is suspicious that the plaintiff actually had pre-existing eye problems that the plaintiff is blaming on the laser incident. In order to search for evidence of such a pre-existing condition, the defendant has demanded through the discovery process that the plaintiff turn over all documents relating to any "complementary or alternative medicine" (CAM) products or services enjoyed by the plaintiff that the plaintiff has possession of or access to. What is the best reason to justify the defendant's discovery request?

(A) The CAM records are likely to be admissible evidence.

(B) The CAM records could possibly contain evidence of the plaintiff having sought treatment products or services for eye conditions prior to the lasing incident.

(C) CAM records are not protected by the physician/patient privilege at all; therefore, they should be as discoverable as receipts and other records from regular retail stores and non-medicinal service providers like haircutters.

(D) The request for the plaintiff's CAM records must be reasonably calculated to lead to the discovery of information relevant to any one of the party's claims or defenses.

146. A defense attorney directly contacted the represented plaintiff in a personal injury lawsuit. In the conversation the plaintiff made some admissions that could undermine the veracity of their case. Defense attorney now wants this information admitted into evidence as admissions of a party opponent. What motion should plaintiff's counsel file to suppress this evidence?

(A) A writ of mandamus to compel the court to suppress the evidence.

(B) A motion *in limine* to request that the court suppress the evidence.

(C) A subpoena *duces tecum* to compel the defense attorney to submit an affidavit about his actions that the court needs to consider when deciding on the motion to suppress.

(D) A motion for application of the collateral estoppel doctrine to stop the defense attorney from having the evidence admitted.

147. Starting in the spring and as the summer progressed, a sailboater grew increasingly angry at a specific motorboater who would constantly go too fast thereby producing large waves which interfered with sailing. Not only that, the motorboater would play "chicken" with the sailboater, sitting in his path and then zooming out of the way at the last second. One day in August, the motorboater was taking a nap on his craft as the sailboater approached. Thinking this was just another game of chicken, the sailboat actually hit the motorboat. After the collision, the motorboater sues the sailboater claiming property and personal injury damages, accusing him of "boat rage," and the sailboater raises counter-claims for similar damages, accusing the motorboater of negligence and harassment. Both boaters had insurance. What is true about how their insurance will be relevant to the lawsuit?

(A) If the lawsuit goes to trial before a jury, neither party's insurance may be admitted into evidence, and similarly neither party has to inform the other of even the existence of an insurance policy during the discovery process.

(B) Neither party's insurance may be admitted into evidence during a jury trial, but if either claims damages in excess of the other's coverage limits, then the party facing the claim of excess damages must disclose the existence of an insurance policy and its coverage limits.

(C) Although neither party's insurance may be admitted into evidence during a jury trial, because the sailboater is facing a monetary damages claim, the sailboater must disclose the existence of his insurance policy and its coverage limits, but the motorboater need not disclose the existence of his insurance policy and its coverage limits because he initiated the lawsuit.

(D) Although neither party's insurance may be admitted into evidence during a jury trial, each will have to provide the other with a copy of any insurance policies that may cover any part of the final judgment immediately at the beginning of the discovery process.

148. As the jury in a defamation case entered the jury room to reach a final judgment in the case, the defense attorney noticed something peculiar about one of the juror's eyeglasses. After doing some research herself while the jury was deliberating, the defense attorney concluded that the eyeglasses were high-tech eyeglasses of the sort that can record surroundings and access the internet. The jury reached a verdict holding the defendant, a high-profile public figure in the entertainment business, liable for defaming a local political activist. The defense

attorney brought this information about the juror's high-tech eyeglasses to the attention of the court, and after some light questioning the juror admitted to having recorded the proceedings and to having accessed information about the defendant over the internet using the eyeglasses. Apart from appealing this final judgment, what other post-trial motion could the defense attorney submit in order to overturn the unfavorable verdict against her client?

(A) A Motion to Vacate the Judgment because of the newly discovered evidence of the juror's misconduct.

(B) A Motion for Involuntary Dismissal because of the juror's failure to comply with a civil rule.

(C) A Motion for Judgment as a Matter of Law (JMOL) because the entire case arose from exaggerated media reporting and none of the actual evidence could reasonably be interpreted to implicate the defendant.

(D) A Motion to Set Aside the Verdict because of the juror's misconduct.

149. A wealthy family owned a chain of petroleum refineries, and sold most, but not all, of them to a large corporation. Ten years later, a local environmental group discovered that massive chemical pollution from one of the refineries had polluted a whole municipality's groundwater supply. The family and the corporation subsequently engaged in long bouts of litigation leading to trial over whether that specific polluting refinery had even been a part of the sale in the first place; neither party wanted ownership. One day after a jury concluded that the polluting refinery had not been a part of the sale and that the wealthy family still owned it, the wealthy family discovered that one of the jurors had concealed that he had been an employee of the corporation ten years ago working behind the scenes doing due diligence on the disputed refinery transaction, and soon thereafter had left the corporation with the only copies of many documents relating to it. Which of the following motions would the wealthy family not have the ability to file in order for the purpose of overcoming that specific jury's verdict?

(A) A motion for mistrial because of the juror's misconduct.

(B) A motion for a new trial because of the juror's misconduct.

(C) A motion for setting aside the verdict because of the juror's misconduct.

(D) A motion to vacate the judgment due to the new evidence.

150. As a piano mover was hammering back on the legs of a piano he was placing in a temporary performance venue, somehow the piano fell, smashing his toes. The performance company had an on-site safety consultant who immediately came to the scene of the accident to evaluate the condition of the piano and any other relevant aspects of the scene. After the piano mover sued the performance company for negligently having him set up a piano that allegedly had structural issues with its legs and frame in the past, the company's defense attorney retained the same consultant as a mere consulting expert, not as a testifying expert or fact/occurrence expert. What is the best reason a court might order the consultant to produce her observations for discovery?

(A) The piano mover's attorney alleges that the safety consultant fabricated her observations to make them more favorable to her employer.

(B) The only first-hand observations of the condition of the piano as it lay in the area where it fell, besides the piano mover's own testimony, come from the consultant's notes.

(C) Because of the accident, the piano mover has been unemployed for over a year, creating a situation in which the piano mover will lose his house if the case drags on because of the piano mover having a difficult time producing evidence comparable to the consultant's observations.

(D) Through publicly-available court documents of previous cases, the piano mover's attorney can demonstrate that in the past the performance company has typically had the safety consultant serve as a testifying expert, not as a mere consulting expert.

151. A former employee sued his employer claiming that the corporation breached his employment contract by firing him without cause when allegedly according to the contract he could be fired only for cause. After losing his job, the employee left work at the corporate headquarters in Illinois and immediately moved back to Oregon where he had grown up but where the corporation had absolutely no operations, sales, or marketing. The corporate attorney viewed this former employee's contract claim, which the employee had filed in an Oregon state court, as absurd – Like all mid-level managers, his employment was at-will, as specified in the written employment contract and in the employee handbook. At the same time, the former employee began posting scandalous claims about the corporation all over the internet. In response to the lawsuit, the corporation immediately filed an answer that, *inter alia*, requested a permanent injunction forbidding any more disparaging internet posts. Among these possible developments in the case, which is the most probable?

(A) The corporation can have the case dismissed under a 12(b)(6) for failure to state a claim upon which relief can be granted.

(B) The corporation can have the case dismissed because the Oregon state court lacks personal jurisdiction over the action.

(C) Seeing the writing on the wall, the former employee can succeed on a motion for voluntary dismissal under 41(a) in order to file the case in a jurisdiction more likely to yield a satisfactory outcome.

(D) The former employee can amend his pleadings to add a claim of employment discrimination based upon national origin.

152. An auto mechanic, living and working in Franklin State, was driving one of his personal refurbished antique cars in neighboring Jefferson State one day when a student rear-ended him there. The student lived in Madison State and had world-wide insurance for himself and his car provided by a company that had its headquarters and all its insured motorists also in Madison State, but that was registered in Dayton State. In which location would a state court most likely conclude that it does not have personal jurisdiction over the insurance company if the auto mechanic were to sue the student's insurance company for not paying his medical bills for treating resulting from the collision?

(A) Franklin State
(B) Jefferson State
(C) Madison State
(D) Dayton State

153. Which of the following is an acceptable method for the recording of testimony during a deposition?

(A) Court stenographer.
(B) Audio recording.
(C) Videotaping.
(D) Any of the above.

154. The friends of a plaintiff pulled a prank on him by convincing a skydiving company located in Franklin State to rig the plaintiff's parachute so that it would not deploy upon yanking the chord, but rather deploy automatically at a lower altitude. The plaintiff experienced extreme emotional distress during the five seconds between yanking the chord unsuccessfully and it later automatically deploying, and allegedly the plaintiff suffered injury as a result of a landing velocity that was abnormally fast due to the low-altitude parachute deployment. The plaintiff did not sue his friends, but did sue the skydiving company in Franklin State court, noting the court's jurisdiction, alleging these facts, and asking for $14,000 in monetary damages due to physical and emotional injuries as well as any further relief the court might deem appropriate. What would be the best reason for the skydiving company to file a 12(b)(6) motion to dismiss for failure to state a complaint on which relief can be granted?

(A) The plaintiff can sue only his friends; the skydiving company cannot be held liable as a mere agent for their prank.
(B) The plaintiff did not also sue his friends whose joinder is compulsory.
(C) The damages alleged included a phrase that was too vague about

damages or any other relief that a court might judge to be appropriate.
(D) The plaintiff's complaint did not make any legal claims.

155. If a plaintiff sues a defendant in Franklin State, what would not be a proper justification for venue in the courts of Franklin State?

(A) The property that is the subject of the lawsuit is located in Franklin State.
(B) Although the defendant corporation is registered in Delaware, its main place of business is Franklin State.
(C) The defendant has at least minimal contacts with Franklin State so as to justify venue.
(D) The defendant lives in Franklin State.

156. A former employee sued her former employer for dismissing her without cause. Both sides agree that her employment contract allowed dismissal only for cause. While the employer's defense attorney was deposing the former employee, the defense attorney began asking the former employee incessant questions about the former employee's personal relationships with individuals both at and outside of the workplace, about what she told her spouse about her job, and even asked her questions such as "You generally did not feel that your supervisors supported your career, right?" and "How many sick days did you use?" Which of the following does not provide a valid justification for the former employee's attorney to instruct her not to answer?

(A) Do not respond to questions about your personal relationships with individuals at and outside of work.
(B) Do not respond to questions about what you told your spouse about your job.
(C) Do not respond to the question about supervisors not supporting your career.
(D) Do not respond to the question about how many sick days you used.

157. One evening after eating at a specific restaurant, a large number of that restaurant's patrons became sick with food poisoning. One of the patients who had suffered the most sued the restaurant to recover damages for permanent physical injuries. (The patient had parts of some internal organs removed.) If the restaurant's defense attorney submits a motion to compel the plaintiff to submit to a medical examination, which is the best reason for which the court would order the plaintiff to submit to the examination?

(A) The examination will likely lead to the discovery of admissible evidence.

(B) The examination will provide better evidence for trial than answers to other forms of discovery such as interrogatories.

(C) The defendant's proposed examining physician has testified to her competence to conduct the examination at a hearing on the matter.

(D) The court has verified that the pleadings put the injury in controversy and that the pleadings demonstrate good cause to order the examination.

158. If suing the U.S. government in general or a specific government agency, which statement below accurately describes the minimum level of service of process required with regard to the specific governmental entity identified in the option?

(A) While service of process may be mailed via registered or certified mail to the district U.S. Attorney's office and to the Attorney General's office in Washington D.C., any government official must be personally served.

(B) When mailing service of process to the Attorney General's office in Washington D.C., it must be registered or certified, but mailing service of process to the district U.S. Attorney's office need not be registered or certified.

(C) When suing a specific agency, service of process may be performed via announcement in a local newspaper of record in the

jurisdiction of the agency's headquarters after three unsuccessful attempts at service of process directly to the agency itself.

(D) When mailing service of process to an agency, it must only be sent via registered or certified mail.

159. Two neighbors, Scutarius and Ezquerra, disliked each other. One day as Scutarius was driving down the road in front of their houses, Ezquerra tossed a heavy pinecone at Scutarius, hitting his vehicle and damaging it. Scutarius sued Ezquerra for battery and to recover for the damage to his vehicle. In his answer, Ezquerra denied throwing anything and concurrently filed a 12(c) motion for judgment on the pleadings. Scutarius then introduced into evidence footage from his dashboard camera showing Ezquerra off to the side of the road facing his vehicle and throwing the pinecone at it. Which outcome at this point is most likely?

(A) The judge will grant the motion for judgment on the pleadings because Scutarius should have referred to the footage evidence from the dashboard camera in his original claim, and so he cannot introduce it now.

(B) The judge will grant the motion for judgment on the pleadings, but in favor of Scutarius even though Ezquerra filed it because the footage conclusively proves that Ezquerra committed the tort for which Scutarius sued him.

(C) The judge will render summary judgment in favor of Scutarius, and then move into discovery and trial on the issue of damages.

(D) The judge will sanction Ezquerra's attorney for filing an answer that turned out to be a lie.

160. After a plaintiff filed a complaint, the defendant immediately filed an FRCP 12(c) motion for judgment on the pleadings. What will be the likely result?

(A) The judge will stay the 12(c) motion for judgment on the pleadings until after the defendant files an answer, at which point the pleadings close and a 12(c) motion becomes appropriate.

(B) The judge will treat the 12(c) motion for judgment on the pleadings as a 12(b)(6) motion to dismiss for failure to state a claim.

(C) The court will deny the 12(c) motion because it should have been filed after the pleadings were closed, and prevent the defendant from filing a subsequent 12(b)(6) motion.

(D) The court will treat the 12(c) motion for judgment on the pleadings as a motion for summary judgment.

161. Which type of judgment is most similar to a FRCP 12(c) motion for judgment on the pleadings?

(A) Judgment as a matter of law.

(B) Summary judgment.

(C) Dismissal.

(D) Rule 12(b)(6) motion for failure to state a claim for which relief can be granted.

162. A large yacht hit and ran over a small fishing boat, after which the fisherman sued the yacht owner. In which situation has the fisherman put his injuries at issue enough for the yacht owner to have the right to compel the fisherman to undergo a medical examination?

(A) The fisherman claims emotional damages arising from his experience struggling, injured, in the freezing, hypothermia-inducing, water calling for help.

(B) There are questions about whether the fisherman's surgeon chose the best means to address his internal injuries.

(C) The yacht owner wants the fisherman to undergo medical evaluation by a neurologist to investigate whether the yacht owner suffered a mini-stroke that caused him to fail to get his fishing boat out of the way of the yacht.

(D) There are questions about the degree to which the fisherman's injuries have disabled him by impairing his ability to work as a fisherman.

163. Which type of expense is non-taxable; i.e., the losing party to a lawsuit typically does not have to pay this cost to the prevailing party?

(A) Consulting expert fees.

(B) Hybrid fact/occurrence expert fees.

(C) Court-appointed expert fees.

(D) Transcript fee to depose a testifying expert.

164. Plaintiff is a woman who was injured in an automobile accident. Defendant is an insurance company that issued a liability coverage policy to the other driver involved in the accident. During discovery, a dispute has come up involving whether or not the insurance company has fully complied with all of Plaintiff's requests to produce records and documents. Plaintiff filed a subpoena and wishes to depose Defendant's custodian of records. Defendant insurance company has so far failed to comply.

What is the Plaintiff's best course of action?

(A) File a motion seeking summary judgment as to liability.

(B) File a motion seeking a default judgment against the Defendant for failing to produce its custodian of records.

(C) File a motion seeking a court order compelling Defendant to produce the witness so that the witness may be deposed.

(D) File a motion seeking sanctions against the insurance company for failing to produce their custodian of records for a deposition.

165. For the last five years, BigUSA Bank has been providing financing to Mark's Auto Dealerships, LLC, which is owned and operated by Mark. When Mark's Auto Dealerships defaulted on its obligations, BigUSA Bank brought suit. Throughout the discovery process, Mark asserted that law enforcement officials had seized records from his office that were essential to complying with discovery and that such records were no longer in his possession. Mark also provided only boilerplate objections to discovery responses, claimed that the discovery requests were impossible to understand, and sought a protective order. The court denied this request, and the parties agreed to exchange documents by a date certain.

When Mark failed to produce on that date, BigUSA Bank brought a motion to compel discovery. Mark again asserted that relevant documents had been confiscated by government authorities and that he had produced all documents which were in his possession. The court granted BigUSA Bank's motion to compel and ordered Mark to provide full, complete, and unequivocal answers to written discovery, and not to assert boilerplate objections. The court also ordered Mark to produce a privilege log for any documents withheld from production, and specifically provided that failure to comply would result in sanctions being imposed.

On the deadline set for complying with the court's order, Mark provided supplemental, yet deficient, responses. Mark also provided a "search warrant inventory" that listed items seized by the government during raids on his business. The search warrant inventory revealed that contrary to Mark's previous assertions, Mark's computers had not been seized, and Mark has had possession and control during the entire course of the lawsuit. As a result, BigUSA Bank moved for sanctions. Mark then produced an external hard drive containing more than a million files and folders, but in a form so scrambled that neither the author, recipient, nor date of any of the emails can be determined.

What is the most severe sanction the court may impose under these circumstances?
- (A) The court may exclude any evidence produce by Mark.
- (B) The court may enter a default judgment in favor of BigUSA Bank.
- (C) The court may award BigUSA Bank costs and attorney's fees for bringing the sanction motion against Mark.
- (D) The court may find Mark in contempt.

166. Which sort of legal action does not require the plaintiff to provide clear, cogent, and convincing evidence in order to prevail, but rather requires the plaintiff to prove only a preponderance of the evidence?
- (A) Overturning a fraudulent election result.
- (B) Altering child custody.
- (C) Defamation.
- (D) Interference with a business expectancy.

167. Which standard of evidence or proof is the default standard in civil lawsuits?
- (A) Substantially more likely than not that it is true.
- (B) More likely than not.
- (C) Sufficiently strong to command the unhesitating assent of every reasonable mind.
- (D) No substantial doubt.

168. A set of locks separated a lake from a nearby bay leading into the ocean. One day a group of tourists was walking along the locks when a sailor on a boat in a lock swung a rope, hitting some of the tourists and knocking them into the water. The tourists suffered injuries from hitting the walls of the lock and the propeller of the boat in the water. One of the tourists now wants to sue the private corporation managing the locks for not installing proper fences to protect pedestrians from falling in. The tourist's attorney researched details of the boat and discovered that the boat was owned by a small LLC with no assets or income, and the boat itself had now become an immobile derelict liability for the harbor it barely reached after leaving the locks. The corporation owning the locks did not want to implead the LLC because the corporation did not want to face any negative publicity from arguably suing one of its customers. If the tourist sues the lock management corporation for negligence and requests compensation for lost wages due to missing work because of the injuries, what could be the next step?
- (A) Despite neither party having requested the joinder of the LLC owning the boat, the court must compel the LLC to join as a defendant because the LLC is indispensable – without the LLC,

full relief could not be afforded to the parties.

(B) Despite neither party having requested the joinder of the LLC owning the boat, the court may compel the LLC to join as a defendant only if the LLC claims an interest in the matter.

(C) Despite neither party having requested joinder of any of the other injured tourists, the court must compel the other injured tourists to join the lawsuit as plaintiffs because if the other tourists were not joined, the corporation would run the risk of multiple lawsuits from the same set of facts yielding inconsistent judgments.

(D) Only upon the request of the corporation may the court compel the other tourists to join the lawsuit as plaintiffs in order to avoid the risk of inconsistent judgments.

169.   After the dissolution of a partnership between two professionals, the senior partner sued the junior partner to obtain what she believed to be her fair share of the partnership assets, which she had not received.   The litigation dragged on for years. Eventually the senior partner passed away due to natural causes before the lawsuit could conclude. The senior partner was survived by her spouse and children as heirs and beneficiaries to her estate. What happens to the lawsuit now?

(A) The lawsuit is automatically dismissed, leaving the junior partner with no liability.

(B) The lawsuit continues, but the junior partner may face a lower degree of eventual liability because at this point the junior can be liable to the senior partner's heirs and beneficiaries only to the extent he would have been liable if the heirs and beneficiaries had initiated the lawsuit themselves after the passing away of the senior partner.

(C) Because there is more than one heir and beneficiary to the senior partner's estate, the lawsuit continues but as a class action lawsuit.

(D) The survivors are successors to the lawsuit, and if the junior partner eventually loses and faces liability, then the junior partner will be liable to the same degree as if the senior partner had lived to see the conclusion of the lawsuit.

170.   What act would likely constitute D's sufficient appearance such that P must then provide D with notice of an application or motion for default judgment?

(A) D's protective parents directly called P and threatened to defend their child to the utmost no matter the cost.

(B) D's attorney informed P's attorney in a phone call of D's intent to defend the default motion, and then later both attorneys realized that D's attorney would have to withdraw from representation due to a non-waiveable conflict of interest.

(C) D called P directly and generally expressed deep anger at P but did not discuss the lawsuit in particular.

(D) Prior to being served with the summons and complaint, D had not retained any attorney for any purpose; after receiving the summons and complaint, D consulted with but ultimately did not retain an attorney.

171.   What is P's default burden of proof for the claims in a hearing on a motion for default judgment?

(A) A preponderance of the evidence.

(B) The burden of proof is the same as the one required for the plaintiff to overcome a Rule 12(b)(6) motion.

(C) There is no burden of proof.

(D) By clear, cogent, and convincing evidence.

172.   A case has been filed between the Estate of Ed and Allegiance Pharmaceutical Corporation.   Ed was a patient who had been prescribed Allegiance's newest wonder-drug, Prolixenol, which is designed to inhibit the body's absorption of fat. Unfortunately, after a year of taking the drug, Ed unexpectedly died from damage to his spleen.

Ed's spleen was preserved after the autopsy because the medical examiner who performed the autopsy noticed some irregularities with the organ. He became more suspicious once he discovered that Ed had been on Prolixenol for the last year. It was on this basis that Ed's family filed the lawsuit against Allegiance.

During discovery, the spleen was delivered to Allegiance's laboratory for testing to confirm the link between Prolixenol and the damage to Ed's spleen. Members of Ed's family decided that they wanted an independent laboratory to examine Ed's spleen as well. Unfortunately, the spleen has gone missing from the laboratory.

In such circumstances Ed's Estate would be entitled to

(A) Sanctions against Allegiance for failing to comply with an order compelling discovery by losing a key piece of evidence.

(B) A default judgment against Allegiance.

(C) A jury instruction inviting the jury to infer that the evidence must have been unfavorable to the plaintiff.

(D) Preventing Allegiance from introducing a lab report that contains the results of Allegiance's own testing of Ed's spleen.

173. A waiter had worked at a specialty cuisine restaurant for years, but then adopted a new dieting lifestyle that was at odds with the restaurant's cuisine. Nevertheless, the waiter needed the job and continued working there. The restaurant's managers, however, could not tolerate one of their employees dissenting from the cuisine, and so the waiter was let go.

The former waiter sued the restaurant for religious discrimination, and at first the restaurant's managers ignored the lawsuit, thinking it ridiculous to consider a dieting lifestyle a religion. When protestors started showing up on the public sidewalk outside the restaurant, its managers began negotiating with the former waiter, but by then the deadline for submitting an answer to the complaint had passed, the clerk

entered default, and the former waiter's attorney provided the restaurant with notice of the default judgment. Which is the best argument to make in the restaurant's motion to set aside the entry of default?

(A) The court has the authority to excuse the restaurant's neglect in filing an answer because the restaurant's first attorney unwisely advised the restaurant to ignore the former waiter's frivolous claim, and the law favors the resolution of cases on the merits.

(B) The court has good cause to set aside the entry of default because the former waiter had promised not to continue pursuing the case so long as the restaurant was negotiating in good faith, but the former waiter had not told his attorney of this promise.

(C) The court has just cause to set aside the entry of default because the former waiter had not stated a claim for which relief can be granted – a dieting lifestyle is not a religion, and no previous cases had even come close to providing a basis for such a theoretical cause of action.

(D) The restaurant has a meritorious defense because the plaintiff should have known when adopting the new dieting lifestyle that doing so would create intolerable workplace tension.

174. Under which circumstances would a client's duty to preserve relevant evidence arise?

(A) When a client receives a pre-litigation letter that asserts the rights of an opposing party.

(B) A client suspects they might be sued and goes to their attorney for advice.

(C) Once the client has been formally served with a summons and complaint.

(D) Any of the above.

175. The State's duty to preserve exculpatory evidence in criminal cases stems from which Constitutional right of the Defendant?

- (A) Due Process.
- (B) Equal Protection.
- (C) Right Against Self Incrimination.
- (D) Right to Counsel.

176. A motion *in limine* to exclude otherwise relevant evidence in a jury trial may be brought

- (A) Before trial begins.
- (B) During the trial, but before the evidence in question is presented.
- (C) At any time.
- (D) Either (A) or (B).

177. Larry the Larcenor was picked up by the police after neighbors in a high-end residential area reported a suspicious person skulking around. In Larry's possession were several tablet computers and jewelry, to which Larry could give no reasonable explanation as to where or how he had obtained the items. In addition to criminal charges for burglary and grand larceny, Larry faced a civil action for conversion filed by one of the victims.

Larry wanted a jury to resolve the civil case, but never affirmatively mentioned it to the court. When he discovered that his trial would only be before a judge, Larry loudly and angrily protested.

What can Larry do?

- (A) File an interlocutory appeal with the appellate court.
- (B) Accept the bench trial.
- (C) File a motion for a mistrial.
- (D) File a motion for summary judgment.

178. Cathy Cautious was driving down Ventura Highway well under the posted speed limit. Hot Rod Henry was following her in his souped-up 1932 Ford Deuce Coupe and became increasingly frustrated because Cathy was going too slow. Hot Rod pulled into the oncoming lane to pass but misjudged and hit a truck coming in the other direction. His car bounced back into Cathy's lane, pushing her car into the ditch. Cathy was injured and retained a New York lawyer named Alice by signing a standard representation agreement.

The document specified Alice was to receive a $5,000 retainer and $10,000 advance against a fee of $250 per hour, or 40% of any recovery if higher. Alice spent 20 hours making two telephone calls and writing a three-page demand letter after conducting some research on the law. This resulted in a $100,000 settlement offer, which Cathy orally approved. The D sent the $100,000 check to Alice's law firm. Alice deposited the $100,000 into her law firm trust account. Alice then sent Cathy a statement indicating she was to receive $40,000 of the settlement for her fee. Cathy was outraged that 20 hours of a lawyer's time should cost as much as Alice was charging and contested the fee. She also filed a bar grievance against Alice.

To minimize the risk of professional discipline, Alice should be advised to

- (A) Remit $115,000 to Cathy.
- (B) Remit $65,000 to Cathy and transfer $40,000 to the law firm operating account.
- (C) Remit $65,000 to Cathy and transfer $5,000 to the law firm operating account.
- (D) Remit $100,000 to Cathy and transfer $10,000 to the law firm operating account.

179. A journalist for an online publication hired a private investigator (PI) to procure salacious photographs of a politician widely rumored to frequent the seedy side of town discreetly. The PI successfully snapped numerous such pictures, and the journalist published the sensational photographs. In order to avoid the bad press resulting from suing a publication, the politician decided to sue just the PI for committing the tort of invasion of privacy. The PI, however, feels she was just doing her job, so what sort of measure should the PI take to obtain at least partial compensation from the journalist and/or the publication?

- (A) Compulsory joinder of the journalist and/or the publication.
- (B) Permissive joinder of the journalist and/or the publication.

(C) Impleader of the journalist and/or the publication.

(D) Interpleader of the journalist and/or the publication.

180. A trespasser entered the property of a family and, while stumbling around, knocked over an outdoor table that had an expensive antique vase on it that had been filled with summer flowers. In their initial complaint, the family sued the trespasser for the damage he had caused. The trespasser counter-sued, accusing the family of maintaining a property with inherently and unreasonably dangerous conditions. After several months had passed, each party filed motions for summary judgment as part of which the family specified that they wanted to recover the value of the expensive antique vase, to recover the value of the lost flowers, and to obtain compensation for the damage caused to the side of their house by the table and vase hitting it. What major flaw with their case does the family now have?

(A) The family did not disclose the types and specifically claimed amounts of monetary damages, nor the types of evidence to prove those damages, during the initial disclosure period.

(B) The family did not retain a testifying expert to certify the high value of the antique vase.

(C) The family did not bring in their home insurance company to intervene in the case as a result of the trespasser's counterclaim.

(D) The family did not challenge the trespasser's counterclaim by filing a motion for judgment on the pleadings because under the common law, only if the family had willfully acted to bring about injury to a trespasser, or if the family had known that the trespasser would come around and certain other conditions were met, would the family be liable.

181. At the close of evidence in a trial involving whether the defendant had formed a general partnership with the plaintiff, the judge held the initial hearing with counsels on jury instructions. In this court, all such hearings are held on the record. Prior to this hearing, the judge had 1) issued a set of standard, generic jury instructions, 2) required the parties to submit all additional jury instructions that they would like to have submitted to the jury, and 3) required the parties to submit exceptions to both the standard instructions and to the other party's requested additional instructions.

At the initial hearing, defense counsel took exception to all of opposing counsel's requested additional jury instructions and argued that they either did not accurately reflect governing law or they were unclear/confusing. The judge ruled to accept all those additional instructions offered by plaintiff's counsel. Defense counsel then offered slight modifications to some of the plaintiff's accepted additional instructions, and the judge did accept those modifications at the second hearing on jury instructions. After that, the jury began deliberations and reached a verdict in favor of the plaintiff. Which additional measure would not have helped strengthen the defendant's case?

(A) The defense attorney should have specified that by offering amendments to the plaintiff's instructions, the defense was not waiving the original exceptions to those instructions.

(B) The defense attorney should have offered additional requested jury instructions favorable to the defendant that would reflect the theories of the case advanced by the defendant and offered alternatives to all the ones offered by plaintiff's counsel that defense counsel took exception to.

(C) The defense attorney should have taken exception again to the jury instructions when they were read aloud to the jury.

(D) The defense attorney should have taken exception again to the jury instructions upon the reading of the verdict in favor of the plaintiff.

182. A wealthy young couple decided to buy a second vacation home in a neighboring state for $180,000. During the closing process, the escrow company received a contract digitally signed by both of the couples authorizing the release of the purchase price to the seller. When the young couple discovered that the money had been released from escrow, they were angry, asserting that they had not actually created those digital signatures to authorize the completion of the sale. After suing both the escrow company and the seller, the escrow company submitted a Rule 12(b)(6) motion to dismiss for failure to state a claim for which relief can be granted. During the hearing on the 12(b)(6) motion, consideration of which matter would have the motion automatically converted the proceeding into a motion for summary judgment?

(A) The court takes judicial notice of the fact that multiple informational websites produced by local city, county, and state governments in the area warn real estate buyers that by dealing with an escrow company, they are disclaiming any right to sue the escrow company over whether an agreement with the other party to an escrow agreement is a valid contract or not.

(B) The court considers digital files supplied by the escrow company demonstrating that at the beginning of their dealings, the couple digitally agreed to the use of digital signatures through a particular third-party service provider for future dealings with the escrow company.

(C) The court considers not only the pleading itself, but also examines digital and hard-copy versions of the contract even though such copies of the contract were not attached to the original pleadings.

(D) The court considers copies of the initial buy-sell agreement between the couple and the seller that the couple authorized with wet signatures and that the couple referred to in their original pleadings but did not attach to the initial pleadings.

183. A wealthy person set up a testamentary trust for the students at a private school for poor children whose parents were narcotics addicts. After the trust had operated for a decade, the trustee decided to invest all the trust's assets in a local tech startup the trustee was sure would take off. On the day of the startup's IPO, the trustee was in an office with the school administrator and exclaimed as the startup's shares declined in value unexpectedly, "Wow, I made a really poor decision, didn't I!" Then the administrator said, "Well, I should never have given permission for you to make that investment anyway."

A few days later the administrator decided to sue the trustee for breach of fiduciary duty. Before the trustee filed an answer, the trustee filed a motion *in limine* to exclude from evidence the trustee's alleged statement about the poor decision that the trust's attorney had quoted in the original complaint. What will be the most likely effect of the trustee's motion *in limine*?

(A) The court will exclude the alleged statement from evidence as hearsay.

(B) The court will require the trust's attorney to re-draft the complaint to exclude the hearsay statement.

(C) The court will deny any subsequent motion by the trustee to dismiss for lack of personal jurisdiction.

(D) The court will allow the trustee's alleged statement to enter evidence only if the administrator's subsequent statement is also admitted.

184. A blogger filed a class action lawsuit on behalf of other local bloggers against all the police departments in a state to enjoin them from unconstitutionally confiscating bloggers' recording devices and detaining bloggers in jail overnight for recording police actions. As part of the class action certification process, the court agreed that all the cases involving confiscation involved some common questions of law and fact. The court also certified that the blogger's case was usual for cases in the class, that the blogger had the wherewithal to represent the bloggers, and that there were more than fifty bloggers represented. Which is a reason the court could still dismiss the class action lawsuit?

(A) Although a minimum of fifty bloggers could be represented, the actual number was difficult to define because of much uncertainty over who exactly counts as a "blogger."

(B) A litigant cannot bring a class action lawsuit against a class of defendants such as all the police departments in a state.

(C) The representative blogger did not inform other bloggers of their right to opt out by the required deadline.

(D) A litigant cannot file class action criminal lawsuits.

185. What distinguishes the class action certification type(s) that require opt out notice, enabling those potentially in the class to leave the class and pursue separate legal action on their own, from those type(s) that require only notice to the class members, but do not provide a mechanism for the class members to leave the class?

(A) The class(es) that require opt out notice are pursuing primarily monetary damages.

(B) The class(es) that require opt out notice are pursuing primarily equitable, i.e. injunctive, relief.

(C) The class(es) that require opt out notice require only that there are some common questions of law or fact, not that those questions predominate over other issues that are unique to each member of the class.

(D) The class(es) that require opt out notice are cases involving classes of defendants who have a due process right to be able to opt-out since they are unwilling defendants rather than willing plaintiffs to the case.

186. A state law prohibits employment discrimination against people based upon genetic makeup. Federal law does not explicitly prohibit discrimination based on genotype, but does prohibit employment discrimination based upon ethnicity, which arguably overlaps as an issue with genotype. A prospective hire sued a company in federal court for not hiring him due to his genotype. Specifically, the prospective hire alleged that the company did not want to pay higher health insurance rates because of a genetic condition the prospective hire had

that was more prevalent among those of his ethnicity than in people of other ethnicities. The prospective hire did not mention this fact in the complaint, but some of the company's senior executives had recently posted publicly on social media sites links to internet articles about the increased costs companies face in paying higher health care premiums when employees have genetic conditions that are more prevalent among some ethnicities than among others.

The company moved to dismiss for lack of subject matter jurisdiction in federal court – there was no diversity of the parties, and the prospective hire's genetic discrimination claim was not recognized by federal law. How should the court evaluate the company's motion to dismiss?

(A) The court should treat as true all allegations in the non-moving parties' pleadings, including the allegation that the company engaged in ethnic discrimination because of the issue overlap with genotype.

(B) As in a Rule 12(b)(6) motion to dismiss for failure to state a claim for which relief can be granted, the court should not consider documents not attached to the pleadings, such as the social media posts.

(C) After the prospective hire submits the social media posts in response to the company's motion to dismiss, the court should convert the company's motion into a motion for summary judgment and then view all evidence in as favorable a light to the non-moving party; i.e., the prospective hire.

(D) The court should engage in a balanced review of the allegations in the complaint and the company's motion to dismiss, and consider documents submitted by the prospective hire in response to the motion to dismiss, such as evidence of the social media posts.

187. A shipping company provided the captain of a container vessel with a satellite telephone for use while out on the open ocean. After a year of work, the captain sued the shipping company for unpaid overtime, and during the discovery phase, he requested the production of the satellite phone call logs in order to demonstrate the long hours the captain was working. The shipping company first responded that it would be unduly burdensome to produce such documents. The captain filed a motion to compel production of the call logs, and after the court indicated its intent to grant the motion, the parties entered into a consent order for the shipping company to produce the documents within twenty days of the order. The shipping company did not produce the documents by the specified deadline. The captain then filed a motion for sanctions, at which point the attorney for the shipping company notified the captain for the first time that she (the attorney) had just learned that such call logs were regularly deleted a week after the calls occurred. At this point, what will most likely happen?

(A) The court will sanction the shipping company for providing incorrect responses to discovery requests.

(B) The court will sanction the shipping company for evidence spoliation because the call logs were deleted.

(C) The court will sanction the captain for submitting unduly burdensome and oppressive discovery requests for production of the documents.

(D) The court will sanction the shipping company for failing to override standard deletion policies and specially retain all documents, including the call logs, connected with the captain's activities because the shipping company should have expected possible litigation over its failure to pay the captain for his overtime work.

188. The logo for this year's city music festival incorporates an image of a cello player from the previous year with an overlay of the title of the festival. At the festival this year, unfortunately, a clarinet player created a very public scene arguing with a family member in between sets next to the stage. The next day, the local newspapers and blogs carried news of the disturbance, with the outdated logo of the festival accompanying all the articles.

The cello player in the logo sued one of the city newspapers for publication in a false light, claiming damages arising from the costs of the personal and marriage counseling needed after the publication. The cello player and the newspaper settled. Six months later, a music festival in a nearby town turned down the cello player's participation out of concern over possible public disturbances and spectacles. Now the cello player wants to sue all the nearby newspapers and many of the prominent blogs for defamation, with what result?

(A) Because the damages are new, occurring after the settlement, the claims against all Ds can proceed.

(B) Because the cello player settled with one of the city newspapers, the claim against that particular newspaper cannot proceed, but the claims against the other newspapers and blogs can proceed.

(C) Being in the same industry, the area newspapers are all in effective privity with each other, so the claims against them cannot proceed due to the earlier settlement with one of the prominent city newspapers, but the claims against the blogs can proceed.

(D) Because a settlement acts as a final adjudication on the merits, and because the facts are all the same, the cello player will be able to move quickly into the summary judgment phase and automatically obtain favorable judgments against all the defendants.

189. One stretch of a set of train tracks in Franklin State runs across an easement over land owned by a timber company registered in Madison State and headquartered in Jackson State. A train one day collided with a tree that had fallen on the tracks. The train company, which was also registered in Madison State but headquartered in Franklin State, sued the timber company in a Madison State court; they settled. Six months later, the timber company sued the train company in Franklin State court for clearing land beyond its easement to straighten out rail lines at locations that included the place where the train collided with the fallen tree. As part of this case, the timber company revealed its intent to back out of the previous settlement deal because the tree had fallen on a stretch of track that had exceeded the easement; if the train company had not exceeded the easement, there never would have been an accident. What will happen to the timber company's claim?

(A) The Franklin State court will remand the case to federal court because the train tracks cross state lines.

(B) The Franklin State court will likely *sua sponte* transfer the venue for the case to Madison State, which is where the parties are both registered, and the state whose jurisdiction both parties had accepted for claims between them in the past.

(C) The Franklin State court will require the compulsory joinder of an ATV tour business that runs vehicles through the forest and regularly across the train tracks.

(D) The Franklin State court will dismiss the timber company's claim as it relates to the place where the collision occurred but will allow claims as they relate to all other locations to proceed.

190. Two friends, one a law student, the other a storeowner, had a habit of trespassing over a private landowner's undeveloped property to get to a particularly spectacular cove on the beach. One day as they were going down a steep slope there at dusk, they both ran into a new barbed wire fence, which was hidden in the underbush by the landowner, thereby injuring them both. The storeowner sued the property owner for maintaining a dangerous premises and won at summary judgment when the court noted the camouflage with which the property owner set up the barbed wire fence. The law student then sued the property owner. What is the court's most likely next step?

(A) The court will dismiss the law student's claim.

(B) The court will require the law student to prove privity with his friend, the storeowner.

(C) The court will rule in favor of the law student at summary judgment.

(D) The court will entertain discovery into when, and for what reason, the property owner installed the barbed wire.

191. During *voir dire* for a murder trial, a potential juror is questioned about his beliefs and opinions regarding the death penalty. Defendant's attorney informs the potential juror that the sentencing options include the death penalty and life without parole. When asked his general thoughts about these options, the potential juror replied that if the defendant were found guilty, he would sentence the defendant to death without exception. When asked how the potential juror came to such a strong opinion, he briefly mentioned a personal experience on the topic that ultimately convinced him of the need for the death penalty to stop criminals from murdering again.

Upon hearing this potential juror's opinion, the defendant's attorney challenges this potential juror for cause. Which cause will the attorney likely proffer?

(A) Lack of qualification, since the potential juror is only making his statement based on personal experience and not researched facts.

(B) Bias, since his answer makes it clear that he cannot be impartial in this murder trial.

(C) Incapacity, since he will be incapable of serving as an objective juror.

(D) If the attorney has already used three challenges, he may not proffer a cause.

192. During the trial of a well-known auto insurance carrier being sued for failure to reimburse its insured for injuries incurred in an auto accident, the attorneys engaged in the *voir dire* process. The attorney for the insurance company questioned a potential juror about her feelings toward insurance companies. She was vague but stated that insurance companies have a heavy burden on their shoulders and do the best they can given the high volume of cases they must handle. The attorney for the insured asked what her relationship has been with auto insurance carriers. She simply stated that her experiences have been positive and valuable. This potential juror was allowed onto the jury.

The *voir dire* process took a few days to complete. Just before the attorneys completed this process, the attorney for the insurance company realized that the potential juror has been married to one of its long-time executives for twenty years. The insurance company's attorney brought this information to the attention of the other attorney and the judge. The insured's attorney sought to strike this potential juror for cause. The judge granted the attorney's request.

The judge's decision is best described as
- (A) Correct because she is likely to be biased, being a relative of an employee of the defendant.
- (B) Correct because she was not forthcoming in her experience with insurance companies.
- (C) Incorrect because constitutionally, there is a restriction placed on challenges based solely on relationship with one of the parties.
- (D) Incorrect because she is not an actual employee of the insurance company.

193. A defendant's attorney in a negligence case questions a potential juror during *voir dire*. The case focuses on a property owner who neglected to place a fence around his empty backyard swimming pool. A youth had wandered onto the property from the neighbor's yard and fell in. Thankfully, the youth survived with only a sprained ankle and broken arm.

The attorney asked questions to a potential male juror. While conversing with the potential juror, the juror never smiled and maintained a flat calm affect. The attorney could not get a feel for the personality of this potential juror. Attorney used his second peremptory challenge.

Is this a proper use of a peremptory challenge?

- (A) No, because the attorney must have a more substantive reason for challenging this potential juror.
- (B) No, because there is no actual indication that the potential juror is incapable of serving as an objective juror.
- (C) Yes, because the peremptory challenge is protected constitutionally.
- (D) Yes, because the attorney does not need to give a specific reason.

194. There are two defendants in an auto accident and three plaintiffs. There was a three-car pileup on southbound Interstate 5, just north of the University District. Traffic was stop and go, and driver #3 was the most rear vehicle. He hit the car in front of him containing driver #2, who then hit the car in front of her, containing driver #1 and two passengers. Everyone in driver's car #1 is suing driver #2 and driver #3 for compensatory damages.

The defendants have separate attorneys who begin the *voir dire* process by asking several potential jurors many questions around auto accidents and their opinions of what constitutes a safe driver.

At the end of this process, the attorney for driver #2 makes two peremptory challenges before the judge. These challenges are granted. Next, the attorney for driver #3 also makes two peremptory challenges.

How will the judge likely rule upon these latter two peremptory challenges?
- (A) The judge will likely grant these as well, since each party gets three peremptory challenges.
- (B) The judge will likely grant one and deny the other, since each side only gets three peremptory challenges.
- (C) The judge will likely deny both challenges because the attorney did not state a reason for the challenges.
- (D) The judge will likely deny both challenges but allow the attorney to argue first at trial, to be fair and equitable.

195. During *voir dire* in a six-juror civil case, the defendant's attorney interviewed a prospective juror. The case centers on a slip-and-fall in a pet store. There was an "accident" by a dog in an aisle that the customer slipped on and fell to the ground, hitting his head and knocking out his two front teeth. The defendant's attorney asked the prospective juror questions about her own experience with falling because of a slippery floor and sympathy for those who have been hurt. She described her own traumatic experience that left a permanent scar on her forehead.

The same attorney questioned the next prospective juror, asking him about his falling experience. The juror replied that he used to get very embarrassed when he would fall and did not like anyone acknowledging that he fell because it indicated a lack of control on his part.

The defendant's attorney questioned several more jurors and used three peremptory challenges, all on prospective male jurors. However, the plaintiff's attorney wants at least two of these men on the jury. What is the plaintiff's attorney best response?

- (A) State that the defendant's attorney is biased, and this bias is restricted when striking prospective jurors.
- (B) Move for a mistrial.
- (C) Argue that the defense attorney's challenges are constitutionally restricted.
- (D) Ask that the jury be increased to twelve jurors instead of six.

196. A well-known painter brought an action against two married debtors to seek collection. The debtors bought a number of paintings from the painter. They paid the first installment when due but failed to complete the final payment, which was a hefty sum. The husband claimed one of the paintings was torn upon arrival and thus refused to pay any more money for the paintings. The wife believed they should pay the money, but the husband was adamant that he would not pay for a sub-par product. They argued bitterly and decided to do nothing. They did not respond to the painter's action in any way, and the judge entered a default judgment in favor of the painter.

Which of the following responses is likely the best response the debtors can make?

- (A) File a motion for appeal on day 24 after the default judgment was entered.
- (B) File a motion for a new trial on day 30 after the default judgment was entered.
- (C) File a cross appeal on day 45 after the default judgment was entered.
- (D) File a motion to vacate judgment on day 60 after the default judgment was entered.

197. A local fraternal Tigers club wants to put on its second annual summer festival in the Green Hill neighborhood. The festival committee has been gathering volunteers to handle all aspects of the festival. The committee itself is checking with the city to be sure that the festival conforms to all the zoning laws. When the local residents learned of the preparation for the festival, they protested because last year, the parking in front of their homes became impossible during the days the festival lasted. Some residents had to park more than a mile away from their homes. The residents filed suit and requested an injunction to stop the festival this year. After a heated debate and hearing between the angry residents and the committee, the residents lost and sought to appeal the judgment against them. How many days do they have to file an appeal?

- (A) 60.
- (B) 61.
- (C) 30.
- (D) 31.

198. Five friends got together for a spirited 4th of July gathering: Ted, Bill, Jack, Thelma, and Betty. The men purchased fireworks in advance for the gathering. They were all in Ted's backyard the evening of the 4th, when they all started lighting fireworks, except Betty. She stayed a comfortable distance away from the fireworks.

After some time, Thelma walked over to Betty and cajoled her into participating. Reluctantly, Betty got up. As they walked toward Ted, Jack, and Bill, the men began lighting another firework. The firework malfunctioned and exploded, injuring everyone.

Thelma and Betty bring suit against Ted, Jack, and Bill for compensatory damages. The trial court rules in favor of Betty and calculates contributory negligence to Thelma. Thelma, Ted, and Bill all file motions. Thelma filed hers 15 days after the entry of judgment; Ted filed his 29 days after the entry of judgment; Bill filed his 60 days after the entry of judgment; and Jack filed his 90 days after the entry of judgment.

Which of the below is likely the correct motion document filed by the four parties and how might the court rule on their motions?

    (A) Thelma – notice of appeal, arguing against contributory negligence; allowed.

    (B) Ted – motion for new trial, arguing error of law; granted.

    (C) Bill – notice of cross appeal, arguing Betty was also negligent; allowed.

    (D) Jack – motion to vacate judgment, arguing error of law; granted.

199. A married couple commenced a bitter divorce. The husband's attorney filed numerous motions, some of which were valid but many that were not. These motions required the wife to appear in court with her attorney and/or require the attorney to draft numerous responses. Either way, the wife's attorney bills mounted rapidly. Towards the end of the dissolution schedule, the wife's attorney sought an award of reasonable attorney fees because of the frivolous and excessive motions from the husband.

The wife's attorney will likely:

    (A) Fail; each party is responsible for their own attorney fees.

    (B) Fail; there is no provision to collect attorney fees.

    (C) Succeed; a specialized statute may accommodate the attorney's request.

    (D) Succeed; if the husband ends up being the losing party.

200. A homeowner living in New Jersey installed a do-it-yourself security system using off-the-shelf equipment and downloadable software, all originally manufactured and produced by a company in Pennsylvania. The homeowner went on a short vacation after properly activating the security system. Upon her return she discovered that thieves had broken into her home and stolen many personal possessions while she was away. That same day, headlines blared that other buyers of the security system were having the same problems; apparently burglars with hacking skills had discovered a way to deactivate the security system. The homeowner sued the company in federal district court for selling a defective security system.

In her brief to the court, the plaintiff homeowner's attorney cited an unpublished opinion previously issued by a different district court in the same circuit. This case allegedly allowed a similar claim – in which D's security system had a flaw that criminals took advantage of – to go to trial. The D company in this lawsuit discovered, however, that in that earlier case the other supplier defendant had advance notice from a white hat hacker of the security system flaw but had failed to fix it. The homeowner's attorney had failed to disclose this critical distinguishing fact to the court. The D company raised these distinguishing facts for the first time in a motion for judgment as a matter of law at the close of evidence, lost that motion, and then lost the subsequent jury verdict. Two months later, what is the defendant company's best chance for a more favorable outcome?

    (A) Motion for a new trial.

    (B) Renewed motion for JMOL.

    (C) Motion for relief from judgment.

    (D) File an appeal.

Multiple-Choice Answers

1. **/B/** A federal civil action is commenced by filing a complaint in a United States district court, which is the trial court of the federal court system. **(A)** is incorrect because while state courts have concurrent jurisdiction over some federal causes of action, a complaint filed in state court does not create a "federal civil action." **(C)** is incorrect because the Supreme Court is an appellate court and can only generally review matters that have obtained a final resolution in a lower court. **(D)** is incorrect because a civil action must be filed in any U.S. district court in which the D resides, or with a district court located near a substantial part of the events, omissions, or property giving rise to the underlying dispute occurred.

2. **/A/** Under the Federal Tort Claims Act, Mike must first file an administrative claim with the FBI. If the FBI rejects his claim, Mike then has six months to file a lawsuit in federal district court. The same procedure applies if the FBI fails to render a decision on Mike's claim within six months of the day he submitted it to the FBI. **(B)** is incorrect because state courts do not have jurisdiction over federal tort claims. **(C)** is incorrect because under the Federal Tort Claims Act, a claim must be submitted administratively before any lawsuit is commenced. **(D)** is incorrect because the Supreme Court is an appellate court and does not have original jurisdiction over trial court matters involving torts of federal agencies.

3. **/D/** Notice and an opportunity to be heard are key elements of requiring service according to the forum rules. **(A)** is incorrect because the Sixth Amendment right to counsel applies to a D in a criminal case, not a civil case. **(B)** is incorrect because the Fifth Amendment protection against self incrimination applies only to a witness' testimony or similar statements. **(C)** is incorrect because substantive due process looks at the right which is being infringed and asks if the government may infringe on that right.

4. **/C/** Service of process within 90 days may be performed by any person over 18 who does not have an interest in the lawsuit or is not a party to the lawsuit. **(A)** is incorrect because merely being an attorney does not disqualify a person from serving papers in most jurisdictions. Although an attorney representing a party in a lawsuit may not serve the summons and complaint in many states, that does not preclude the attorney from having his/her paralegal, legal intern, or family member from performing this service of process function. **(B)** is incorrect because service of process by mail is not usually allowed unless specifically permitted by the law of the state in which the federal court sits. **(D)** is not the best answer because being over 18 in and of itself is not sufficient to serve process. The person performing the legal service of process must also not be a party to the lawsuit.

5. **/C/** Leaving a copy of the summons and complaint at the residence of the D is permitted, so long as the documents are given to a person of suitable age and discretion who resides at the same residence of the Ds, but here the babysitter does not reside there, so proper service was not accomplished. **(A)** is incorrect because there is no bright-line rule stating that the individual accepting the papers must be over 18 years of age. **(B)** is incorrect because the person accepting the summons and complaint must of a responsible age and reside at the same address as the D. Note that serving a D's parents is not sufficient if the D no longer lives there. **(D)** is incorrect because a party accepting service can share a residence with a D but does not have to be related to them.

6. **/A/** Personal service on individuals must be performed within the state the lawsuit is being filed in. A D does not have to be a resident of that a particular state in order to be subject to jurisdiction of that state's courts. **(B)** is incorrect because as long as a non-resident is physically present in a state, even if only for a brief time, personal service is proper. **(C)** is incorrect because a person may be served a copy of the summons and complaint at any place so long as it is within the boundaries of the state the lawsuit is being filed in. Work, home, a courthouse, or even on the street are all places where a D may be personally served. **(D)** is incorrect because although airports are not federal lands, even federal lands are considered to be within the boundaries of the states in which they are located for service of process purposes.

7. **/D/** Every corporate business entity must be served by delivering the summons and complaint to an officer or a managing or general agent and, if required, to a registered agent. **(A)** is incorrect because the service should be delivered to the corporate officer or general managing agent. **(B)** is incorrect because the summons and complaint should be delivered to the corporate officer or general managing agent. **(C)** is not the best answer because the summons and complaint should preferably be delivered to the corporate officer or general managing agent, even though many states allow service on a registered agent.

8. **/B/** A person remains domiciled in a state if he/she has left the state only temporarily. **(A)** is incorrect because by purchasing property in California and getting a California driver's license, Ted has demonstrated an intent not to return to Washington. **(C)** is incorrect because Ted has taken no steps to establish a permanent residence in Arizona, but Arizona could likely claim long-arm jurisdiction over the income earned there. **(D)** is incorrect because a vacation, even an extended one, is not normally sufficient to establish residence.

9. **/D/** D is correct because transacting business within a state, committing a tort within a state, and owning and using real property within a state are all common provisions that allow the assertion of jurisdiction over a foreign party (i.e. someone who is not a resident of the state). **(A)** is incorrect because transacting business is not the sole basis over which a state typically asserts long arm jurisdiction. **(B)** is incorrect because committing a tort within a state is not the sole basis over which a state typically asserts long arm jurisdiction. **(C)** is not here the best answer because owning or using real property located within the state is not the sole basis over which a state typically asserts long arm jurisdiction.

10. **/C/** In general, the test to determine whether Frass Canyon's website is sufficient to support personal jurisdiction is how "active" and "targeted" the website is. More than "a purchase" is required. Considering that Frass Canyon's website has almost no functionality and exists merely to provide information, the conclusion cannot reasonably be reached that Frass Canyon has taken any affirmative steps to transact business in the state of New Jersey, and so therefore likely has insufficient minimum contacts. **(A)** is incorrect because although a federal district court may have subject matter jurisdiction to hear Keith's case against Frass Canyon, New Jersey's Long Arm Statute would not apply, and so a court in New Jersey would not be able to assert jurisdiction over the case. **(B)** is not correct because the lack of functionality of Frass Canyon's website would make it difficult for a federal district court located in New Jersey to assert that Frass Canyon is purposely availing themselves of the forum state of New Jersey in such a way that would not offend traditional notions of fair play and substantial justice. **(D)** is not the best answer because it is too general and according to the plurality opinion in *Asahi Metal*, merely placing goods in "the stream of commerce" is insufficient minimum contacts for a court to assert personal jurisdiction over a foreign D.

11. **/B/** is the correct statement of the personal jurisdiction challenge rule as presented by FRCP 12. **(A)** is incorrect because the mere appearance of a D does not waive their right to assert a challenge to personal jurisdiction. **(C)** is incorrect because a challenge to personal jurisdiction must be made by the first motion to dismiss brought before the court or in the D's answer to the complaint. **(D)** is incorrect because a challenge to personal jurisdiction must be made by the first motion to dismiss brought before the court or in the D's answer to the complaint.

12. **/A/** Unlike personal jurisdiction, subject matter jurisdiction can be challenged at any time, even by post-trial motion or on appeal. **(B)** is incorrect because subject matter jurisdiction can be challenged at any time. **(C)** is incorrect because subject matter jurisdiction can be challenged at any time. **(D)** is not the best answer because a challenge to subject matter jurisdiction "may" be raised on appeal but is not required (as in "must"), and alternative A is a more accurate statement of when a challenge to subject matter jurisdiction may be raised.

13. **/C/** Although there is not citizenship diversity between the buyer and the insurance company (both are New York residents) supplemental jurisdiction would likely be invoked as the potential insurance recovery is part of the same controversy between the buyer and seller that do have diversity. **(A)** is not the best answer because supplemental jurisdiction will likely apply here. **(B)** is incorrect because supplemental jurisdiction applies even if the third-party claim is less than $75,001 because the claim in chief exceeds $75,000. **(D)** is not the best answer because the thrust of the question is on supplemental jurisdiction, not the original claim amount.

14. **/B/** Since venue in federal district court requires either a federal question or complete diversity of the parties and damages exceeding $75,000, the only way for Maya to get into federal district court would be for her and Miles to be considered citizens of different states and for her to show that Miles caused more than $75,000 in damages to her house. Although Miles is domiciled in Vancouver, Washington because he owns property there and has displayed intent to make Vancouver his fixed and permanent home, Miles lives in Portland for the purposes of his job and can be said to reside there. **(A)** is not the best option for Maya because venue is proper in a district in which any D resides even though a substantial part of the property that is subject to the cause of action is situated in that same district. **(C)** is not the best answer because under the facts provided a federal district court in the District of Washington would have no basis for establishing venue. **(D)** is incorrect because Maya's best chance for getting her claim heard by a federal district court would be to show that she and Miles are residents of different states and so her lawsuit should be filed in federal district court in the District of Oregon so diversity is satisfied.

15. **/D/** Under the *Hertz* decision it is possible for a corporation to be a resident of more than one state for the purpose of establishing venue. A corporate D's residence can be the state of incorporation, the state in which the corporation has its principal place of business ("nerve center"), or the state in which most of the actual work of the company is performed ("muscle center"). **(A)** is incorrect because the residence of a corporate D is not limited to the state in which its articles of incorporation were filed. **(B)** is incorrect because the residence of a corporate D is not limited to the state in which its corporate offices are located. **(C)** is incorrect because the residence of a corporate D is not limited to the state in which its manufacturing or shipping is performed.

16. **/B/** The best answer because a complaint must state the material elements of each claim, the factual and legal basis for each, and the court's ability to assert jurisdiction (both subject matter and personal). **(A)** is incorrect because the subject matter and personal jurisdiction of the court over the D must be stated, as well as the legal basis that gives the P a right to relief. **(C)** is incorrect because the subject matter and personal jurisdiction of the court over the D must be stated, as well as an allegation of the facts underlying the claim. **(D)** is incorrect because an allegation of the facts underlying the claim must be stated.

17. **/C/** P must assert in a single complaint all claims arising out of one transaction or occurrence. "Claim Splitting" is not allowed. **(A)** is not correct because the P cannot wait to bring suit on a separate claim if that claim arises from the same transaction or occurrence. **(B)** is not the best answer because plausibility is only required when alleging the facts which underlie a legal claim. If Shirl fails to include allegations of personal injury at the same time she makes her complaint for property damage, then she is precluded from later raising the personal injury claim if the personal injury claim arose from the same transaction or occurrence. **(D)** is incorrect because a P cannot wait to bring suit on a separate claim if that claim arises from the same transaction or occurrence.

18. **/D/** A D must file an answer within 21 days of service of the complaint. [FRCP 12(a)] **(A)** is incorrect because an answer must be filed within 21 days. **(B)** would only be correct if the D has waived service and/or resides outside of the U.S. **(C)** is not the best answer because the 60-day period only applies either if the D resides outside of the U.S. or if the D has waived service.

19. **/A/** When alleging fraud or mistake, a party must state with particularity the factual circumstances constituting fraud or mistake. However, malice, intent, knowledge, and other conditions of a person's mind may be alleged generally. [FRCP 9] **(B)** is not the best answer, because although Matt's complaint may fail to state a claim on which relief may be granted, the reason is because Matt has failed to plead fraud with particularity, and Matt has failed to explain the relevant facts in detail. **(C)** is incorrect because fraud, breach of trust, mistake, and any denial of mental capacity are exceptions to the "notice pleading" rule. **(D)** is incorrect because of the rule that fraud must be pleaded with particularity.

20. **/B/** Attorneys have an affirmative duty to make a reasonable inquiry into the factual basis or legal merits of a claim prior to filing a pleading. Rule 11 sanctions are therefore appropriate. If discovered by the opposing party, that party must bring a motion before the court in order for the court to impose sanctions. **(A)** is incorrect because a motion for default judgment is only brought if an opposing party had notice of an impending lawsuit and yet fails to timely file any pleading in response. **(C)** is not the best answer because a Rule 12 motion to dismiss does not ordinarily address the facts alleged, but rather focuses on whether the law allows the assertion of the specific claim or defense. **(D)** is not the best answer because in a 12(b)(6) motion, all of the factual allegations in the complaint will usually be accepted as true. In this question, attorney Toby has failed to do any investigation whether or not the facts he is alleging have any basis on real events. Keep in mind that professional responsibility rules prohibit an attorney from knowingly making a false statement to the court or to opposing counsel.

21. **/D/** By agreeing to mandatory binding arbitration, Pete has "signed away" his right to go to trial. Therefore, his complaint fails to state a claim on which relief may be granted. Here a Rule 12(b)(6) motion seems to be the best course of action. **(A)** is not the best answer because a motion for default judgment is appropriate when the D has failed to file an answer or has otherwise failed to appear after delivery of a summons and complaint. **(B)** is not the best answer because a Rule 11 motion is appropriate where the complaint was not grounded in fact and warranted by existing law or a good faith argument for an extension or modification of existing law. There is nothing in the given facts that indicates that the pleading was frivolous. **(C)** is not the best answer because Rule 12 motions concern defenses that must be raised timely and consolidated with other defenses or they are deemed waived. Given the facts at hand, Mark is not asserting any defenses here.

22. **/D/** According to the waiver provisions of Rule 12(h), the following defenses should be raised in the first responsive pleading before the court (either by answer or by motion before filing the answer) or else they are deemed waived: (1) lack of personal jurisdiction, (2) insufficient service of process, (3) lack of minimum contacts, and (4) improper venue. **(A)** is incorrect because it is not complete. **(B)** is incorrect because it is not complete. **(C)** is incorrect because it is not complete.

23. **/B/** Counterclaims are causes of action brought by the D against the P. Compulsory counterclaims are any claims arising out of the same transaction or occurrence which are deemed waived if not asserted in the D's answer. Since Deb's action in order to obtain an easement by prescription arises out of the same transaction or occurrence as Janie's action for trespass, Deb's claim against Janie is likely deemed a compulsory counterclaim. **(A)** is incorrect because a crossclaim involves a claim made by a D against other co-Ds, none of which are present here. **(C)** is not the best answer because permissive counterclaims arise from a separate set of facts, none of which are present in the given question. **(D)** is not the best answer because impleader is a term used to describe how crossclaims are brought against third-parties.

24. /A/ Crossclaims are made by a D against other co-Ds and arise from the same transaction or occurrence as the P's claim. Here, Property Owner would become a third-party P against Freedom Funding, who becomes the third-party D. This situation could also be referred to as "impleading" Freedom Funding. **(B)** is not the best answer because counterclaims are causes of action made by the D against the P. Compulsory counterclaims are any claims arising out of the same transaction or occurrence as the P's claim. In the given fact pattern, we have a D who has filed a claim against a third-party that was not originally a party to the lawsuit. **(C)** is not the best answer because a permissive counterclaim is brought by the D against the P and involved claims that arise from a separate set of facts from that involved in the lawsuit originally brought by the P against the D. **(D)** is incorrect because it is not clear Freedom Funding is an indispensable party to the dispute between the City's claim against the property owner for delinquent taxes.

25. /C/ Even if the complaint amendment was necessitated by inexcusable neglect or was the result of a conscious litigation strategy, an amendment adding a new claim or defense usually relates back to the time it was filed if it arises out of the same transaction or occurrence. **(A)** is not the best answer because even though the statute of limitations period on Celine's claim has run, the new claim is allowed to relate back to the filing date of the original claim if it arises out of the same transaction or occurrence as the original complaint. **(B)** is not the best answer because there is no evidence in the given facts that Jessie's failure to include the claim of intentional infliction of emotional distress was the result of bad faith or undue delay, or that unfair prejudice will result to the newspaper. **(D)** is incorrect since a D must file an answer within 21-days after receiving the summons and complaint, and the window on amending a complaint in this fashion has long since closed.

26. /B/ According to FRCP 55, if a D fails to respond timely to a summons and complaint, the P is entitled to a default judgment. The P need not give notice to the D of the motion for default judgment unless they have formally appeared in the matter. **(A)** is incorrect because there is no indication from the given facts that jurisdiction is at issue in this case. **(C)** is not the best answer because Carey's due process rights were satisfied when he accepted the summons and complaint. **(D)** may have some grain of truth to it, but a party who wishes to mount a defense upon receiving a summons and complaint has a duty to respond timely, otherwise they may forfeit their rights.

27. /D/ FRCP 17 requires that every action be prosecuted in the name of the real party in interest. (D) is correct because it is the responsibility of the Trustee to manage the trust for the benefit of the beneficiaries and this duty gives the trustee agency authority to conduct lawsuits and take actions to prevent the waste of trust assets. **(A)** is incorrect because although a majority shareholder has a significant ownership interest in a corporation, only an officer of the corporation or the board of directors may institute a lawsuit on behalf of the corporation. Through a Shareholder Derivative Action, a shareholder may institute a lawsuit on behalf of a corporation if the board's failure to enforce a corporate right damages the corporation itself. However, the shareholder(s) must first put a written demand on the corporate directors and/or officers to pursue the claim. **(B)** is incorrect because limited partners lack agency authority to act on behalf of the limited partnership, and thus lack standing to sue on behalf of organization. **(C)** is incorrect because a person who has been adjudged mentally incompetent lacks capacity and must sue through a *guardian ad litem*.

28. /A/ FRCP 19 requires that all persons needed for just adjudication must be joined as parties if feasible. In a dispute involving real property, all affected property owners must usually be joined. Naoto is therefore likely an indispensable party. **(B)** is incorrect because a third-party P is typically a D in a lawsuit who files a claim against a third-party (not presently a party to the lawsuit) that the D believes bears some degree of legal responsibility. The D then becomes the "third-party P" while the third-party becomes the "third-party D." **(C)** is incorrect because a third-party P is typically a D in a lawsuit who files a claim against a third-party (not presently a party to the lawsuit) that the D believes bears some degree of legal responsibility. The D then becomes the "third-party P" while the third-party becomes the "third-party D." **(D)** is incorrect because an affected property owner is an indispensible party and must be joined to the lawsuit in order for the rights of all parties to be justly adjudicated.

29. /D/ FRCP 20 allows parties to be joined in a lawsuit if there are claim arising from the same transaction or occurrence, or involving some common question of law or fact. Here Jake's injury arises from using defective equipment manufactured by Acme Welding, Co, and supplied by Precision Welding to the Boing Aircraft Co. FRCP 20 encourages all interested parties to be joined in a single action in the interest of promoting judicial economy. **(A)** is incorrect because parties may be joined in an action if they have claims arising from the same transaction or occurrence, involving some common question of law or fact. Here, Jake's workman's compensation claim arises out of the same common questions of fact as does the product liability claim. **(B)** is incorrect because although Acme Welding and Precision Welding Supply are not indispensable parties, it is in the interest of judicial economy that common questions of law or fact be litigated in one action. **(C)** is incorrect because Acme Welding and Precision Welding Supply are not indispensible parties. However, they may be joined in Jake's lawsuit against Boing Aircraft because a product liability action against them would involve common questions of law or fact that will necessarily be raised against Boing Aircraft Co.

30. /C/ In tort cases, D1's insurer may not be brought in as a party under FRE 411 because the jury may not be informed of the presence or absence of insurance due to the possibility of prejudice. **(A)** is not the best answer because theoretically, even though an insurance company becomes an indispensable party through contract with their insured, public policy prohibits the jury from being made aware of the presence or absence of insurance due to the possibility of prejudice **(B)** is not the best answer because technically the insurance company would be an indispensible party to any action involving an insured client, but mention to the jury of the presence or absence of insurance of D1 is prohibited by FRE 411. **(D)** is irrelevant because whether or not an insurance company was directly involved with a tort committed by D1 has no effect on their liability to D1. FRE 411 prohibits a jury from being made aware of the presence or absence of insurance coverage by D1 due to the possibility of resulting prejudice.

31. /C/ All four of these **CULP** requirements must be satisfied in order for a court to certify a class in a class action lawsuit. **(A)** is not correct because it is missing the usual claim requirement necessary for a court to certify a class in a class action lawsuit. **(B)** is not correct because it is missing the usual claim requirement necessary for a court to certify a class in a class action lawsuit. **(D)** is not correct because it is missing the usual claim or defense requirement necessary for a court to certify a class in a class action lawsuit.

32. **/D/** In federal district court the five **PRIDE** methods of discovery which are authorized following the initial disclosures and mandatory discovery conference are **p**roduction of documents, **r**equests for admission, **i**nterrogatories, **d**epositions, and **e**xaminations (physical and mental). Letters of request are a procedural device of the Hague Convention used to gather evidence and are not part of the rules of U.S. federal civil procedure. **(A)** is incorrect because this is an acceptable method of discovery in federal district court. **(B)** is incorrect because this is an acceptable method of discovery in federal district court. **(C)** is incorrect because this is an acceptable method of discovery in federal district court.

33. **/B/** Asserting the attorney-client privilege applies where there is an attorney-client relationship, and then only to communications intended as confidential. The presence of third persons may destroy the privilege. In a public place there is no expectation of privacy, therefore the communication is not privileged. **(A)** is not the best answer because the physician-patient privilege applies to statements made by the patient to the doctor for the purposes of seeking treatment and may be less applicable to statements made by the doctor. If asked, the physician may assert the privilege on behalf of the patient but may not waive the privilege on behalf of the patient. **(C)** is not the best answer because the contents of a conversation between a husband and a wife, which occurs while the couple is married, is normally covered by the marital communication privilege. The privilege applies to spousal marital communications during marriage even though the couple may later separate or divorce. **(D)** is not the best answer because the opinions of consulting experts – even if not testifying – are protected on the theory that the expert is part of the attorney's "legal team" and thus their opinions constitute attorney work product.

34. **/A/** Dr. Green's personal involvement in Jeannie's treatment makes him a fact witness, or a fact expert. Labeling a fact expert a consultant cannot be used to shield the witness from discovery. **(B)** is not correct because Dr. Green's personal involvement with Jeannie's treatment qualifies him as a fact witness. **(C)** is incorrect because although he has been hired as an expert witness by Jeannie's attorney, Dr. Green's personal involvement in Jeannie's treatment qualifies him as a fact expert. Fact experts are treated as ordinary lay witnesses without the other expert protections and cannot be shielded from discovery. **(D)** is incorrect because it refers to the burden which must be met in order for opposing counsel to gain access to materials prepared by an expert witness that will not be testifying at trial.

35. **/C/** Although a deposition transcript is an out-of-court statement and thus objectionable as hearsay, exceptions to the hearsay rule apply. Bliss' prior inconsistent statement can be used for the purposes of impeachment under FRE 801(d)(1). Bliss is not a party to the action, so her deposition testimony cannot be used as an admission by a party-opponent. **(A)** is incorrect because a deposition may be taken of anyone, even if the deponent is not a party to the action. **(B)** is correct in that the deposition transcript is an out of court statement and thus constitutes hearsay if the person offering the statement is trying to use it to prove the truth of the matter being asserted. However, exceptions to the hearsay rule apply – especially those allowing the impeachment of a witness. **(D)** is incorrect because the fact that the deponent gives their testimony under oath and the testimony is recorded by a court stenographer does not make that testimony equivalent to testimony which is given in court.

36. **/A/** Interrogatories are written questions which can only be propounded to parties in the lawsuit. Howard is not a party to the contract dispute between Sheldon and Leonard, only a potential witness, and thus cannot receive an interrogatory. **(B)** is incorrect because as parties to the lawsuit, Sheldon and Leonard may have interrogatories propounded to them. **(C)** is incorrect because as parties to the lawsuit, Sheldon and Leonard may have interrogatories propounded to them. **(D)** is incorrect because as parties to the lawsuit, Sheldon and Leonard may have interrogatories propounded to them.

37. **/D/** A subpoena *duces tecum* is a court summons ordering the recipient to appear before the court and produce documents or other tangible evidence for use at a hearing or trial. It is not just used to compel a party to bring documents and objects when appearing at a deposition but may be used to request copies of documents from someone who is not a party to the action. **(A)** is not the best answer because a subpoena is a court summons ordering the recipient to appear before the court, usually to compel testimony by a witness under a penalty for failing to appear. **(B)** is not the best answer because a request for production of documents may only be addressed to an opposing party, not to an individual or organization who is not a party to the lawsuit. **(C)** is not the best answer because interrogatories are written questions which can only be addressed to parties to the lawsuit.

38. **/B/** A physical or mental examination may be agreed to by stipulation or ordered by the court for good cause, but a party must place their mental or physical condition at issue in order this to apply. In this case, only Jeff's physical injuries are at issue in his lawsuit against Maude, not his mental state. Although eccentric, there is no indication that Jeff lacks capacity to participate in his case against Maude. [FRCP 25] **(A)** is incorrect because a physical or mental examination must be agreed to by stipulation or ordered by the court for good cause. **(C)** is not correct because Jeff's competency is not at issue in this case. **(D)** is incorrect because a physical or mental examination cannot be conducted solely upon the demand of the party seeking discovery but must be agreed to by stipulation or ordered by the court for good cause.

39. **/D/** Joe's actions constitute spoliation. Although no lawsuit had been filed, the duty to retain relevant evidence arises when it becomes apparent that the opposing party has a legal claim [or defense expectancy] that likely involves the particular evidence at issue. **(A)** is incorrect because so long as the company is in possession of the records, even if there is a company policy to destroy records after a certain amount of time, the company may not destroy records to comply with the company's policy once it has become apparent that the opposing party has a legal claim. **(B)** is incorrect because the duty to preserve evidence arises as soon as it becomes apparent that the opposing party has a legal claim, whether or not a lawsuit has actually been filed. **(C)** is incorrect because the duty to preserve evidence applies equally to both paper copies of documents and electronically stored documents.

40. **/C/** In considering whether to issue a preliminary injunction permanent, all four of these factors are considered. **(A)** is incorrect because this answer choice does not include three of the factors that a court takes into account when considering a preliminary injunction motion - whether the harm the P will suffer without an injunction issuing outweighs the harm the D will suffer if restrained; whether the P is able to show that they will be able to succeed on the merits; and whether issuance of the injunction will harm the public interest. **(B)** is incorrect because this answer choice fails to take into account that a court will also consider whether the harm the P will suffer without an injunction issuing outweighs the harm the D will suffer if restrained. **(D)** is incorrect because this answer choice fails to take into account that a court will also consider the risk of irreparable harm to the moving party; and whether the harm the P will suffer without an injunction issuing outweighs the harm the D will suffer if restrained.

41. **/C/** The primary purpose served by a Temporary Restraining Order (TRO) is to preserve the situation and prevent significant harm to the moving party while allowing the opposing party time to receive notice of a legal proceeding and an opportunity to be heard within 14 days. A TRO may be issued by a court ex parte (i.e., without the presence of an opposing party) upon motion or affidavit by a party seeking the TRO. **(A)** is incorrect because 14-days is the maximum length a TRO can last. During the 14-day period, the court must hold a hearing on the issue of whether the TRO should be dissolved or converted to a preliminary injunction. **(B)** is incorrect because 14-days is the maximum length a TRO can last. During the 14-day period, the court must hold a hearing on the issue of whether the TRO should be dissolved or converted to a preliminary injunction. **(D)** is incorrect because 14-days is the maximum TRO length. During the 14-day period, the court must hold a hearing on the issue of whether the TRO should be dissolved or converted to a preliminary injunction.

42. **/A/** The P may voluntarily dismiss an action one time as a matter of right, unless the D has served an answer containing a counterclaim or motion for summary judgment. [FRCP 41(a)] **(B)** is incorrect because the D's affirmative defense is not sufficient to bar the other party from taking a voluntary dismissal. **(C)** is not the best answer because a P who seeks to take a second voluntary dismissal is free to do so, but the dismissal will operate as an adjudication on the merits and the P will not be allowed to file the action a third time. **(D)** is not the best answer, under FRCP 41(B), a P's failure to prosecute their case (or undue delay) may be grounds for an involuntary dismissal.

43. **/D/** The D may move for an involuntary dismissal of the P's case on any of the following grounds: 1) Where the P has previously voluntarily dismissed two actions asserting essentially the same claims; 2) Where the P has failed to comply with a civil rule; 3) Where the P has failed to comply with a court order; and 4) At the close of the P's case, on the basis that the P has failed to demonstrate any right to relief. [FRCP 41(b)] **(A)** is not the best answer because it is an incomplete alternative. **(B)** is not the best answer because it is an incomplete alternative. **(C)** is not the best answer because it is an incomplete alternative.

44. **/B/** In determining whether there are remaining issues of fact, the court will consider only evidence that would be admissible at trial under the Federal Rules of Evidence. [FRCP 56] A witness declaration would arguably be hearsay and thus not admissible. **(A)** is not the best answer because such a memorandum would likely be admissible at trial. **(C)** is not the best answer because financial records would likely be admissible at trial. **(D)** is not the best answer because a deposition conducted under oath would normally be admissible at trial.

45. **/C/** The preponderance of the evidence, or more likely than not, is the required proof standard in most civil suits. **(A)** is incorrect because "reasonable suspicion" is a relatively low standard of proof used by law enforcement to determine whether a brief investigative stop or search is warranted. **(B)** is incorrect because "clear, cogent, and convincing" is the burden of proof used in special situations, such as cases involving libel, slander, and fraud. **(D)** is incorrect because "beyond a reasonable doubt" is the standard which must be met by the prosecution in proving each and every element against a D in a criminal charge.

46. **/A/** In order to preserve the right to challenge a judgment by post-trial motion or by an appeal, counsel must voice objections to trial rulings as soon as is practicable. Ideally this is done as soon as the objectionable question is asked, but before the witness answers. An attorney must make an objection in order to preserve an issue on appeal. In this case, since defense counsel failed to object in a timely manner, the secretary's statement entered into evidence can be considered by the jury. **(B)** is not the best answer because a motion for a mistrial is brought on the basis of misconduct by the court, counsel, parties, or witnesses, or as the result of any other major irregularity in the trial. In this case, it was the defense counsel who failed to take a necessary action, but a failure to object to an offered piece of evidence does not result in misconduct, even if the evidence would otherwise be inadmissible. **(C)** Is not the best answer because objections to trial rulings cannot be voiced for the first time by post-trial motion or on appeal. A motion for a mistrial is made at the conclusion of the trial and if granted results in a new trial. **(D)** is not the best answer because although the judge decides issues of law, it is not the judge's responsibility to police the actions of the attorneys in order to ensure that parties receive a trial that precisely follows all applicable rules. Attorneys must exercise due diligence in prosecuting or defending their cases in order to ensure the best possible representation for their clients.

47. **/D/** In order to be timely, a motion for a mistrial should be made as soon as practicable after the misconduct occurs. Counsel should not wait until the conclusion of the trial to voice an objection. **(A)** is not the best answer because this describes the timing for when a motion for a new trial should be made, not a mistrial. **(B)** is not the best answer because a motion for a mistrial should be made as soon as practicable after the misconduct occurs. Counsel should not wait either until opposing counsel has finished presenting their case, or until the conclusion of the trial. **(C)** is not the best answer because counsel should not wait until the conclusion of the trial to voice an objection.

48. **/D/** A prospective juror may be challenged "for cause" on the basis that they lack qualifications (e.g., under 18, not a US citizen, unable to communicate in English, or a convicted felon); lack capacity (e.g., being of unsound mind or body); or actual or implied bias (such as being either employed by or related to a party in the case). **(A)** is not the best answer because it fails to take into account either lack of capacity or bias. **(B)** is not the best answer because it is incomplete – It fails to take into account either lack of a juror's qualifications or actual or implied bias. **(C)** is not the best answer because it fails to take into account either the juror's lack of qualifications or the lack of capacity of the juror.

49. **/B/** During a counsel's closing argument, counsel may only refer to evidence actually presented during the trial and may not interject his personal opinions as to the guilt or innocence of the parties or the credibility of the evidence. In order to be timely, a motion for a mistrial should be made as soon as practicable after the misconduct occurs. Counsel should not wait until the conclusion of the trial to voice an objection. **(A)** is not the best answer because a motion for a new trial is made at the conclusion of the trial, and if granted, results in a new trial. Counsel should not wait until the conclusion of the trial to voice an objection to conduct that would result in a mistrial. **(C)** is incorrect because although counsel is generally given wide latitude by a judge when making opening and closing arguments, in this case the prosecutor's statements clearly crossed a line. **(D)** is not the best answer because a motion for summary judgment argues that the case presents no genuine issues of material fact, and that the moving party is entitled to judgment as a matter of law. But in this case, a trial has been conducted, so there were clearly issues of material fact that need to be decided.

50. **/A/** The court will not usually set aside a verdict on the basis of improper or illogical reasoning. A jury who fails to follow the jury instructions is an example of this. Others examples include failing to understand or consider specific evidence, attributing too much or too little importance or weight to specific evidence, and improperly calculating damages. **(B)** is not correct because a juror who discusses a case with friends or family before the reading of the verdict has committed juror misconduct. **(C)** is not correct because a court may set aside a jury verdict on the basis of bias or prejudice that was deliberately concealed during *voir dire*, but which was expressed either during deliberations or outside the courtroom. **(D)** is not correct because a clerical error in recording or reporting the verdict may serve as grounds to set aside the verdict.

51. **/D/** The new Federal Rule 50 now consolidates these two previously separate motions for judgments as a matter of law during and following jury trials. [FRCP 50] The Directed Verdict motion must be made before the jury retires while the Judgment Notwithstanding motion is made after the jury returns their verdict. **(A)** is incorrect because it is not a complete answer. **(B)** is incorrect because it is not a complete answer. **(C)** is incorrect because both of these motions are now consolidated into a Judgment as a matter of law.

52. **/C/** Judgment as a matter of law (JMOL) is the correct terminology. **(A)** is incorrect because a summary judgment motion is made before the start of trial and is used to avoid the time and expense of an unnecessary trial when the case presents no genuine issues of material fact, and where the moving party is entitled to judgment as a matter of law. **(B)** is incorrect because a motion for a judgment notwithstanding the jury verdict (JNV) has been consolidated with motion for a directed verdict and is now an obsolete term. **(D)** is incorrect because a motion for a directed verdict has been consolidated with a motion for a judgment notwithstanding the jury verdict and is now an obsolete term.

53. **/B/** This is the best answer. In a motion for a judgment as a matter of law the moving party argues that the non-moving party has failed to produce material evidence to demonstrate that there are facts in dispute, and therefore there is no reason that the case should be decided by a jury. **(A)** is not the best answer because it describes the purpose of a motion for summary judgment, which is usually filed after discovery, but before a trial has commenced. **(C)** is not the best answer. This best describes the function served by a motion for a mistrial, which is brought during a trial and before a jury has read its verdict. **(D)** is not the best answer. This choice describes the function served by a motion to vacate judgment, which is filed after the judgment has been entered.

54. **/D/** Whenever a party wishes to preserve review of such an adverse ruling on appeal (which is rather often), that party should motion for judgment as a matter of law both before the jury verdict under FRCP 50(a) and after the jury verdict under FRCP (50(b). JMOLs are frequently advisable even after the jury verdict. **(A)** is not the best answer because it ignores the fact that a JMOL may be brought after the plaintiff has rested their case. **(B)** is not the best answer because it ignores the fact that a JMOL may be brought after the defendant has rested their case. **(C)** is incorrect because it ignores the fact that it is frequently not only possible, but advisable, to motion for JMOL after the jury verdict.

55. /A/ A motion for a JMOL is essentially a delayed motion for summary judgment. A motion for a JMOL is made during the trial, instead of beforehand, and is based upon the failure of one party to produce enough evidence to create reasonable issues of substance for submission to the jury. **(B)** is not the best answer because a motion for summary judgment is brought before the start of trial, not a motion for a JMOL. **(C)** is not the best answer because a JMOL motion is brought during trial. Although a motion for a JMOL may be made after the case has been submitted to the jury, the party bringing the motion should not wait until after the verdict has been read. **(D)** is not the best answer because a motion for a JMOL cannot be raised on appeal.

56. /B/ The most likely ruling by the court of appeals here is to reverse the trial judge's ruling granting the motion for a judgment notwithstanding the jury's verdict. The test is whether any reasonable jury could have found as they did. The jury apparently considered all aspects of the bargain and even though the trial judge apparently disagreed, found for the buyer. **(A)** is incorrect because the factual issues and determinations thereof are for the jury, not the judge. **(C)** is incorrect because for a new trial to be ordered usually requires some defect in the jury proceedings beyond the judge's second opinion, and here the facts do not indicate any such basis. **(D)** is almost nonsensical because mere disagreement between the judge and jury is not a proper reason for an appellant court to refuse to rule on a *bona fide* appeal.

57. /C/ One of the two types of verdicts that a jury may return is a special verdict composed of answers to specific questions of fact. Note the judge will decide the equitable issue of the restitution claim later so the court's conclusion does not encroach into the jury's determination of their charge. **(A)** is incorrect because a general verdict is in favor of one party. **(B)** is incorrect because JMOL is a procedural device to keep a case from being decided by the jury when there is no rational factual basis by which the jury could reasonably base a finding against the non-moving party. **(D)** is incorrect because a verdict is memorialized in a formal judgment.

58. /C/ Findings of fact, whether based on oral or other evidence, must not be set aside unless clearly erroneous, and the reviewing court must give due regard to the trial court's opportunity to observe the credibility of the witnesses at trial. **(A)** is incorrect because the court may correct a clerical mistake or a mistake arising from oversight or omission below whenever one is found in the judgment, order, or other part of the record (see FRCP 60; and please don't get this confused with "Error in Recording or Reporting Verdict," covered in the text under Section VII). **(B)** is incorrect because a reviewing court may not set aside the trial court's decision based on principle or morality. **(D)** is incorrect because "reasonably erroneous" is too low a standard; "clearly erroneous" is the required threshold to overturn the trial court.

59. /C/ Once the judgment has been formally entered, the time limitation starts running for most post-trial events, including a motion for a new trial or filing an appeal. **(A)** is an incomplete answer because it fails to include the appeal time limit. **(B)** is an incomplete answer because it fails to include the motion for a new trial. **(D)** is incorrect because "a" and "b" are both important reasons the appeal date is important.

60. /C/ Entry of judgment occurs when it is in writing, signed by the judge, and delivered to the clerk of the court for entry in the judgment registry. **(A)** is incorrect because attorneys are not required to sign the judgment for entry, just the judge hearing the case. **(B)** is incorrect because the decision/judgment must be reduced to writing for it to be entered. **(D)** is incorrect because it includes the incorrect (A) answer.

61. **/D/** These are all examples of costs that the prevailing party may recover from the losing party: filing, factual witnesses, and service of process. Note that fees paid expert witnesses may also be recovered if the trial court feels it is not unreasonable. **(A)** is incorrect because while each answer listed is one type of litigation cost normally recoverable by the prevailing party, on its own, the alternative is incomplete. **(B)** is incorrect because, while each alternative listed is one type of litigation cost normally recoverable by the prevailing party, on its own, the alternative is incomplete. **(C)** is incorrect because while each answer listed is one type of litigation cost normally recoverable by the prevailing party, on its own, the alternative is incomplete.

62. **/B/** The best answer because there may be certain specialized statutes (including breach of fiduciary duty, as alleged here) that allow for an award of reasonable attorney fees. **(A)** is incorrect because under the American rule, each side bears its own attorney fees. In contrast, the English rule may require that the losing party pay the attorney's fees of the prevailing party. **(C)** is not the best answer because it is incomplete. While the American rule usually directs each side to bear its own attorney fees, there are some exceptions through specialized statutes. **(D)** is incorrect because there may be a specialized statute under which Betty can seek reasonable attorney's fees.

63. **/A/** Misconduct by jurors is grounds for requesting the court to declare a mistrial and order a new trial. [FRCP 59] **(B)** is not the best answer because a motion to vacate a judgment focuses more on misconduct by an opposing party and respondent would not want to wait until after the trial is over. **(C)** is incorrect because there must be a judgment entered to be able to appeal. **(D)** is incorrect because a writ of prohibition seeks a district court to refrain from taking an action that is contrary to law. Here, it is not the court that took some action to be refrained from, the juror committed misconduct.

64. **/C/** A motion for a new trial must be filed no later than 28 days after entry of judgment. **(A)** is incorrect because this alternative states that the motion cannot be made before 28 days after entry of judgment. **(B)** is incorrect because the 28-day clock starts running on the day the judgment is entered, not when the jury returns the verdict. **(D)** is incorrect because it excludes the 28-day limitation.

65. **/B/** Doug has one year to file a motion to vacate the judgment. He filed ten months from entry, which is timely. In addition, excusable neglect is a valid reason for the court to grant relief. [FRCP 60] **(A)** is not the best answer because a motion for a new trial must be filed no later than 28 days from judgment entry and so if he had filed a motion for a new trial, the court would deny his claim based on timeliness, not for failure to raise error of law. **(C)** is incorrect because a motion for appeal must generally be filed within 30 days after entry of judgment. **(D)** is incorrect because harmless error is grounds for filing a motion for a new trial. It is not the motion itself.

66. **/D/** This is the best answer because errors of law will generally be legitimate grounds to grant a new trial. **(A)** is incorrect because harmless errors during a trial do not require a judgment reversal or serve as a basis for a new trial. **(B)** is incorrect because lack of jurisdiction is a valid for reason for a motion to vacate judgment, not a motion for a new trial. **(C)** is not the best answer because material issues of fact are considered by the fact finder in their decision.

67. **/A/** Harmless errors during a trial do not require reversal of judgment and are usually to be disregarded when they do not affect any party's substantial rights. Since the D put on several other witnesses and this one witness was mistakenly put on, there would be a harmless error corrected. **(B)** is incorrect because collateral estoppel does not apply here as it regards the relitigation of specific issues of fact or law that were necessary to the outcome in the first lawsuit. **(C)** is not the best answer because the court considers the entire record when making a decision like this and taking all the testimony in totality, one witness who was found to be mistakenly put on the stand does not likely rise to the level of affecting the D's substantial rights. **(D)** is incorrect because while an appeal may be a matter of right, errors during a trial do not require reversal of the judgment by an appellate court.

68. **/C/** With reasonable diligence, Kevin should have realized that the evidence should not have been admitted. Thus, he should have objected during the trial to preserve the issue. One year from judgment entry is the outer time limit to file the motion. **(A)** is incorrect because in order to preserve the right to a new trial, Kevin should have objected during the trial or as soon as practicable; here five days lapsed between the evidence being admitted and the end of the trial. **(B)** is incorrect because while Kevin followed proper procedure, he did not preserve his right to request a new trial based on this error. **(D)** is incorrect as it includes the other two incorrect answers.

69. **/B/** B is the correct answer because the collateral order doctrine is an exception so that a party does not have to wait for a final judgment before appealing. **(A)** is incorrect because discretionary rulings merge into the trial court's final judgment and are grounds for an appeal after the entry of judgment. **(C)** is incorrect because it concerns jurisdiction that a federal court has over claims related to other claims where federal subject matter jurisdiction exists. **(D)** is incorrect because a 12(b)(6) motion to dismiss is a way for the D to avoid a claim when it is clear that the P will not prevail.

70. **/D/** Discretionary review allows an appellate court to immediately review an interlocutory decision of substantial importance to the outcome of the case in the trial court. **(A)** is incorrect because irreparable harm could occur if this decision is not appealed before the case is over. **(B)** is incorrect because a cross-appeal is only filed after the entry of judgment. **(C)** is incorrect because collateral estoppel is a restriction on the relitigation of specific issues of fact or law that was necessary to the outcome in the first lawsuit between the parties. Here, we are still in the same litigation case.

71. **/C/** The notice is filed in the trial court within 30 days and the clerk normally forwards it onward to the higher court. **(A)** is incorrect because the appeal notice is not filed in an appellate court. **(B)** is incorrect because one must appeal to be heard before the State Supreme Court and the notice is not filed in an appellate court. **(D)** is incorrect because this answer includes "a" and "b" as possible correct answers.

72. **/A/** A party may seek review of the district court's action before entry of judgment. **(B)** is incorrect because after entry of judgment is too late to seek review. **(C)** is incorrect because the review must be sought before entry of judgment. **(D)** is incorrect because although it is rare, extraordinary writs are still used when there is no other form of review available, such as an appeal.

73. **/A/** Since the government is a party, the time to file a notice of appeal is expanded from 30 to 60 days. **(B)** is not the best answer because the government is a party. **(C)** is incorrect because 28 days is the time period for filing a motion for a new trial. **(D)** is incorrect because cross-appeals are to be filed 14 days after the initial notice of appeal, or 30 days after the entry of judgment.

74. **/D/** All the answers stated in A, B, and C are valid reasons for the U.S. Supreme Court to grant discretionary review of Court of Appeals decisions. **(A)** is not the best answer because this is only one of the reasons presented that would allow the U.S. Supreme Court to grant discretionary review. **(B)** is not the best answer because this is only one of the reasons presented that would allow the U.S. Supreme Court to grant discretionary review. **(C)** is not the best answer because this is only one of the reasons presented that would allow the U.S. Supreme Court to grant discretionary review.

75. **/D/** According to the rule of "claim preclusion," if a P obtains a judgment against a D, he may not sue the D again in an attempt to get more damages for the same injury. The raspberry bush claim for damages should have been brought in the first lawsuit because it arises from the same factual occurance. **(A)** is incorrect because the same occurrence/transaction may not serve as the basis for a second lawsuit. **(B)** is incorrect because upon conclusion of the litigation, the judgment is conclusive and a litigant can't get a second "bite of the apple." **(C)** is incorrect because there is no indication from the facts given that timing is at issue in this case.

76. **/B/** A subsequent claim on the same issue by a non-party not involved in the first claim is not precluded under the doctrine of collateral estoppel. **(A)** is not the best answer because as a non-party, Sven is not bound by the prior judgment. **(C)** is incorrect because there is nothing in the facts that say Sven has litigated this issue with Linda before. **(D)** is incorrect because defensive use of non-mutual collateral estoppel characterizes a situation when the D was previously acquitted against other claimants. Here the facts state that Linda lost in the previous litigation.

77. **/B/** *Res judicata* is often referred to as a rule of claim preclusion that prevents a claimant from splitting their cause of action. **(A)** is incorrect because collateral estoppel is often referred to as issue preclusion. **(C)** is incorrect because it includes as a possibility an incorrect answer. **(D)** is incorrect because it includes as a possibility an incorrect answer.

78. **/D/** Since both the breach and the mistake defenses were actually litigated and necessary to the judgment, Albert is likely barred from claiming mistake as a defense in the subsequent lawsuit, as the identical issue was resolved in the earlier suit. **(A)** is incorrect because there is no indication from the facts given that there is a different issue at hand. **(B)** is incorrect because the facts given state that the mistake defense was an essential issue in determining the outcome of the first case. **(C)** is incorrect because *res judicata* is about precluding an entire claim, not the direct issue of a mistaken defense.

79. **/A/** Two of the elements of issue preclusion are that the issue was actually litigated and that the issue was necessary to the prior judgment. **(B)** is incorrect because the issue must have been necessary to the prior judgment. **(C)** is incorrect because issue preclusion requires that you have two lawsuits. **(D)** is incorrect because one of the other alternatives is the correct answer.

80. **/D/** Since this issue was actually litigated and necessary to decide the issue in the first action, Tenant may attempt to prevent Landlord from asserting this same defense. The court may consider Landlord's attempt of non-mutual collateral estoppel, but since the issue litigated was the culpability of the P, there will need to be another investigation. **(A)** is not the best answer because it is not as complete an answer as D which includes preclusion of asserting the same defense. **(B)** is incorrect because this second lawsuit is actually Tenant's first "bite of the apple." **(C)** is not the best answer because it is not as complete an answer as D which includes preclusion of asserting the same defense.

81. **/D/** There is a constitutional restriction that peremptory challenges cannot be used solely based on race or gender. [FRCP 47 refers to 28 U.S. Code § 1870] **(A)** is incorrect because while the attorney is entitled to three peremptory challenges, they may not be based on race, as is stated here. **(B)** is incorrect because for the challenge to be allowed based on cause, the prospective juror would need to lack the qualifications, be of unsound mind or body, or be actually or impliedly bias. There is no indication from the facts stated here that any of these factors are present. **(C)** is incorrect because there is no predefined level of diversity in the federal rules to which a jury must rise.

82. **/C/** The best answer because these are separate purchases and potential liabilities, and under these facts the claim amounts are not to be aggregated. **(A)** is not the best answer because the claims are not properly aggregated under these facts. **(B)** is incorrect because here there is only separate claims, so the actionable claim does not exceed the $75,000 threshold level. **(D)** is incorrect because the facts indicate two separate transactions, so the claim amounts in controversy are not to be aggregated.

83. **/C/** The fastidious neighbor D does not have to make factual allegations that are likely or probable; Ps need only have made factual allegations that are plausible, but they must be more than merely conceivable in order to meet the notice-pleading requirements of the FRCP and survive a FRCP 12(b)(6) motion to dismiss. [FRCP 12(b)(6)] **(A)** is not the correct answer because the D careless neighbor could have the case dismissed for failure to make a factual allegation necessary to satisfy one of the essential elements of the claim under FRCP 12(b)(6). **(B)** is not the best answer because when a judge considers a 12(b)(6) dismissal motion, she must assume all factual allegations in the complaint, like those in option C, to be true in favor of the non-moving party. There is no such presumption, however, for questions of law such as whether a duty exists, and so a judge has more leeway when responding to this argument to rule in favor of the D who submitted the 12(b)(6) motion. **(D)** is not the correct answer because a 12(b)(6) motion to dismiss is the appropriate motion if the parties had contractually agreed to submit such disputes to arbitration.

84. **/D/** Because the deli made an informal appearance by communicating with the man and the man's attorney, the man's attorney should have notified the deli of the application and motion for default judgment at least 7 days before the hearing. [FRCP 55(b)(2)] **(A)** is incorrect because the process server must be 18 or older; the individual who receives residential service of process need only be of suitable age, and could be a teenager. **(B)** is incorrect because conducting service of process on an officer of a corporation, such as a CEO, while that officer is in-state allows that local state's courts (and therefore the federal district court in the same area) to assert personal jurisdiction over the corporation of which the officer is an employee without having to satisfy any long-arm statute requirements. **(C)** is incorrect because in a 12(b)(6) motion to dismiss for failure to state a claim for which relief can be granted, all factual allegations are assumed to be true, and so no matter how spurious the allegation that the family participated in the unsanitary social movement was, the allegation that the family did not wash their hands had to be assumed to be true for the purpose of deciding on the 12(b)(6) motion to dismiss.

85. **/A/** A party moving (or, to use the terminology of the FRCP, "applying") for default judgment must provide notice to the other party at least 7 days prior to the default judgment hearing if, and only if, the other party has "appeared" in the case. The appearance can be a formal Notice of Appearance or filing an answer, or an informal appearance such as the non-moving party having engaged in communication and serious settlement negotiations with the moving party as in this instance. [FRCP 55] **(B)** is incorrect because merely having location knowledge does not obligate the party applying or moving for default judgment to inform the other party of the motion. **(C)** is not the best answer because here the landlord could not proceed with default judgment motion at all; Ps may not usually obtain default judgment against military service members. **(D)** is incorrect because even if the moving party knows that the non-moving party might have good defenses, the moving party does not have to notify the non-moving party of the motion if the non-moving party has not appeared.

86. **/B/** The trustee of the trust is considered the real party in interest, and so diversity citizenship jurisdiction is proper and the case will proceed in federal court. [FRCP 17] **(A)** is incorrect because FRCP 17(a)(1) explicitly states that a trustee need not join the persons, here the children, who are beneficiaries of the trust for whose benefit the action is brought. **(C)** is incorrect because the trustee is considered the real party in interest, and the outcome will not turn on the fact that the trustee initiated the lawsuit. **(D)** is incorrect because the trustee's Nebraska citizenship will be enough to maintain diversity jurisdiction.

87. **/D/** Although the angel investor's CPA had not communicated with the angel investor's attorney at the attorney's request, because the attorney communicated with the CPA for the purpose of providing legal advice to the angel investor, this communication would be protected by attorney-client privilege. [FRCP 26] **(A)** is incorrect because this communication does not involve an attorney; therefore, it could not enjoy protection from discovery through either attorney-client privilege or the work product doctrine. **(B)** is incorrect because although typically the actual text of a consulting expert's full opinion is not discoverable, the testifying expert will have to disclose all elements of the basis for her opinions, as well as facts and data used in forming her opinions; because the consulting expert's report was used as a basis for the testifying expert's opinions, it will be discoverable. **(C)** is incorrect because generally communications between an attorney and third parties who are not that attorney's clients are discoverable.

88. **/A/** Although typically a party needs to supplement a discovery response only if the party learns that that previous response was materially incomplete, the threshold for the duty to supplement interrogatories is lower. A party must supplement an interrogatory response if the new information might lead to other discoverable matters. Even the low granularity locational data might lead to more discoverable information. [FRCP 26] **(B)** is incorrect because the duty to supplement interrogatory responses arises at a lower threshold than the materiality threshold of the duty to supplement other types of discovery responses. **(C)** is incorrect because the duty to supplement discovery responses does not arise only after the requesting party proactively requests supplementation; it arises as soon as the responding party learns of information that could supplement earlier responses. **(D)** is incorrect because the default rule in discovery is that the responding party pays for their own costs to provide the response.

89. **/D/** Although the in-house counsel waited three days to request the temporary restraining order, she has provided evidence that the corporation had already suffered irreparable harm due to the payments made to offshore bank accounts and that this harm would continue without immediate intervention. [FRCP 65] **(A)** is not the best answer because although the employee had caused serious harm, that serious harm had already occurred and was not likely to reoccur. **(B)** is incorrect because the corporation waited so long to request a motion for a TRO. It would be difficult for the in-house counsel to convince a judge that a TRO preventing "immediate" harm, rather than a preliminary injunction, is necessary after the corporation had waited so long to request the TRO. **(C)** is incorrect because a judge would likely want an allegation detailing the specific harm the TRO would prevent rather than a general claim of "irreparable harm."

90. **/A/** A judge could impanel an advisory jury for either or both specified reasons, though the judge would not have to abide by an advisory jury's opinions. Juries do not rule on whether injunctions should be granted, but a judge may impanel an advisory jury to offer an opinion about whether equitable relief such as an injunction should be granted. [FRCP 39] **(B)** is incorrect because advisory juries do not offer binding opinions that decide issues, nor do juries of any sort decide issues concerning what sort of testimony is admissible at trial. **(C)** is not the best answer because, while generally accurate, option (A) lists both possible situations in which a judge may impanel an advisory jury and is thus a more complete answer. **(D)** is incorrect because there is no such thing as an "expert advisory jury."

91. **/B/** Whether the parties to the contract added an oral component to the agreement is a typical sort of issue of material fact that would likely enable the claim that it supports to overcome a motion for summary judgment allowing further discovery. [FRCP 56] **(A)** is not the correct answer because the choice of governing law is a question of law that a judge may determine as part of summary judgment motion, not a genuine dispute of material fact that would enable a claim to survive summary judgment. **(C)** is not the correct answer because the resolution of ambiguous written contract language is a question of law, not a question of fact. **(D)** is not correct because whether damages are direct (a natural and necessary result) or consequential (a natural but not necessary result) is usually a question of law, not a question of fact.

92. **/D/** The best answer because it is unlikely the same jurors can disregard their researched opinion in deciding the matter. **(A)** is incorrect because here the judge knows the verdict is tainted. **(B)** is not the best answer because the incident of juror misconduct taints the whole verdict. **(C)** is not as good an answer as (D) because it does not seem likely the existing jurors could independently re-consider the conclusion they reached after being influenced by the actual research of their designated peers.

93. **/D/** One of the grounds upon which a party may move for a new trial is if the damages awarded were grossly inadequate or grossly excessive "shocking the conscience" of the court. [FRCP 59] **(A)** does represent a possible evidentiary standard for granting a motion for JMOL under FRCP 50, but is not the best answer because of the much higher burden of persuasion on the movant when seeking a successful motion for JMOL as compared to the lower burden of persuasion when seeking a successful motion for a new trial. JMOL requires the movant to demonstrate that no "substantial" evidence supports the non-movant's position, and that a reasonable person "must" judge in favor of the movant. On the other hand, trial judges have "broad discretion" to rule on a motion for new trial based upon whether not doing so would be a "miscarriage of justice." When considering motions for JMOL, trial judges do not have the discretion to weigh the evidence; they must come to purely legal conclusions while viewing the evidence in favor of the non-movant. Furthermore, because JMOL is a legal conclusion, appellate courts review such decisions *de novo*, whereas they review a trial court judge's ruling on a motion for a new trial only for abuse of discretion. In general, motions for JMOL are less likely to succeed than motions for a new trial. **(B)** is incorrect because the "clear and convincing" evidentiary standard does not govern the award of a motion for a new trial. Trial judges may award motions for new trials based upon their "inherent power" to reconsider cases in order to prevent a miscarriage of justice. **(C)** does represent possible evidentiary standards for granting a motion for JMOL under FRCP 50 but is not the best answer because of the much higher burden of persuasion on the movant when seeking a successful motion for JMOL as compared to the lower burden of persuasion when seeking a successful motion for a new trial. JMOL requires the movant to demonstrate that no "substantial" evidence supports the non-movant's position, and that a reasonable judge "must" rule in favor of the movant. On the other hand, trial judges have "broad discretion" to rule on a motion for new trial based upon whether not doing so would be a "miscarriage of justice." When considering motions for JMOL, trial judges do not have the discretion to weigh the evidence; they must come to purely legal conclusions while viewing the evidence in favor of the non-movant party. Furthermore, because JMOL is a legal conclusion, appellate courts review such decisions *de novo*, whereas they review a trial court judge's ruling on a motion for a new trial only for abuse of discretion. In general, motions for JMOL are less likely to succeed than motions for a new trial.

94. **/B/** Another way to restate this principle is that these costs are necessary and approved by the court clerk. [FRCP 54] **(A)** is incorrect because costs that are recoverable by default are not subject to a reasonableness standard; they are automatic, necessary costs. **(C)** is incorrect because these sorts of expenses are considered "non-taxable" costs that typically require more justification be shown the judge to recover from the losing party. **(D)** is incorrect because there is no such requirement in order for the prevailing party to recover "taxable" costs.

95. **/C/** As an affirmative defense, *res judicata* must be plead in or before the answer. By the time that the second lawsuit had passed the summary judgment stage, the car driver had waited too long to plead *res judicata*, so a court would likely continue into trial on all the claims raised in the second lawsuit. [FRCP 12] **(A)** is incorrect because here the car driver waited too long to assert *res judicata*. **(B)** is incorrect because courts do not normally re-open concluded summary judgment hearings. **(D)** is incorrect because the fact that the injuries from the original collision worsened does not give the biker the right to make claims on newer injuries (or extent of injuries) that arose from the same occurrence, even if the future extent of those injuries could not have been reasonably anticipated at the time of the first lawsuit.

96. **/C/** A desire to settle a case after default judgment has already been issued does not constitute a sufficient meritorious defense to warrant vacating the default judgment and thus is not here a good argument. [FRCP 55 and 60(b)] **(A)** is incorrect because the passing of a statute of limitations alone is likely a sufficient reason to have a default judgment vacated. **(B)** is incorrect because first a judge would likely find Mazina's reason for not learning of the summons to be excusable, and second because disputing the amount of a loan is considered a meritorious defense sufficient to have a default judgment on a debt vacated. **(D)** is incorrect because it also reflects both of the requirements for overturning a default judgment: first, an excusable reason for not filing an Answer (the issues with the butler), and second a meritorious defense in Mazina's counter-claim that he in fact had already paid off the debt.

97. **/B/** Appellate courts grant more deference to trial courts' factual determinations than to trial judges' discretionary rulings such as sanctions for discovery abuse. Within the range of types of discretionary rulings, appellate courts grant less deference to discretionary rulings such as FRCP 41(B) Involuntary Dismissal and FRCP 37 Discovery Sanctions that act as or in place of an adjudication on the substantive merits of the case than they grant to discretionary rulings such as allowing pleadings to be amended that do not affect the overall outcome of the case. [FRCP 37] **(A)** is incorrect because such factual determinations below receive more deference than the judges's discretionary rulings, and so appellate courts are much less likely to overturn a trial court's ruling because of such factual rulings. **(C)** is incorrect because such discretionary rulings that do not approach the status of a final adjudication receive more deference than discretionary rulings that do act as final adjudications. **(D)** is incorrect because it is a factual determination below to which appellate courts grant the highest possible degree of deference.

98. **/D/** Patty was not involved in the lawsuit against the trucking company so she is not precluded from asserting a claim against Dana even though the first claim held Dana was not contributorily negligent. **(A)** is incorrect because Patty was not a party to the first action. **(B)** is incorrect because Patty was not a necessary party to the first action. **(C)** is not the best answer because Patty was not a necessary party to the first action.

99. **/D/** The D's vigorous litigation defense here in the first lawsuit and the liability commonality is probably sufficient to allow the P to invoke the doctrine of offensive collateral estoppel, and it would serve to maximize judicial economy. **(A)** is not the best answer because the government agency is not in privity with the shareholders. **(B)** is incorrect because there is no rule a class action may not attempt to use offensive collateral estoppel. **(C)** is incorrect because collateral estoppel does not include a "separation of interest" requirement.

100. **/B/** Even if a witness did not testify, the losing party may still have to pay for that witness' court-regulated witness fee. [FRCP 54] **(A)** is incorrect because legal research and consulting fee costs are non-taxable expenses that a losing party by default typically does not have to pay. **(C)** is incorrect because testifying expert fees are non-taxable expenses that the losing party by default typically does not have to pay. **(D)** is incorrect because postage fees are non-taxable expenses that the losing party typically does not have to pay.

101. /A/ Although Saveright does not directly advertise in any state, it is placing its goods in the stream of commerce of State A through its exclusive distribution deal with BigBox Stores, making it reasonably foreseeable that the space heaters would be used in State A. **(B)** is not the best answer since it is likely to be far easier for Tracy to file her lawsuit in State A because she is a resident of that state and diversity is not at issue here. **(C)** is not the best answer because although Saveright may be considered to be a resident of State C under the "muscle center" test for the purposes of establishing diversity, diversity is not at issue here. It is likely far easier for Tracy to file her lawsuit in State A because she is a resident of that state. **(D)** is not the best answer because from the given facts, BigBox Stores is not being implicated in Tracy's lawsuit.

102. /A/ While the new resident was not a party to the first lawsuit, he is in privity with the first owner as a successive owner of the same property and therefore collaterally estopped. **(B)** is incorrect because the new resident is in privity with the P in the first action. **(C)** is not the best answer because the company is a co-owner of the road, not a mere easement holder where excessive use might be actionable. **(D)** is not the best answer because whether a nuisance or not, the new resident moved to the nuisance

103. /C/ A state's long-arm statue does not give a federal court sitting in a state jurisdiction over a D for any lawsuit arising in that state. The court has jurisdiction only to resolve disputes arising out of the D's use of the in-state property. Deckard is not using his property in California as an airstrip, therefore his ownership or use of the property in that state is not implicated. **(A)** is not the best answer because even if it is true that noise is equivalent to toxic fumes, the noise Rachel is complaining of is not coming from Deckard's property located in California, but instead is arising out of his use of his Nevada property. **(B)** is not the best answer because although a California court may assert *in rem* jurisdiction over real property located in the state of California where the court lacks personal jurisdiction, the property at issue here is located in Nevada, not California, which is outside of the jurisdiction of a federal district court located in California. **(D)** is not the best answer because the activity complained of must be related to the property creating the jurisdiction.

104. /D/ The passenger was not a party to the first lawsuit and therefore is not collaterally estopped. **(A)** is incorrect because the passenger's suit is not barred at all. **(B)** is incorrect because the passenger was not a party to the first lawsuit. **(C)** is not the best answer because there is no bar even if the cab company was not a party in the first suit.

105. /A/ Diversity jurisdiction requires both parties be citizens of different states when the claim is commenced. The P's residence is determined by the state of residence at the time the lawsuit is filed, not when the incident occurred, here California. The D corporation's residence is their state of incorporation or where their corporate headquarters are located performing ("nerve center") activities. Here that is Delaware or New Jersey, not the place the accident occurred. **(B)** is incorrect because the state where the injury occurred is not necessarily controlling for diversity purposes. **(C)** is incorrect because Florida does not control. **(D)** is incorrect – even though accurate – because it is the state of residence at the time of filing that is determinant.

106. /D/ Venue is proper where the events occurred, where D's corporate headquarters are located, or where a corporation is registered; so here, New Jersey and Florida are possible venues. **(A)** is incorrect because the action requested is to transfer the claim, not dismiss it. **(B)** is incorrect because venue is not proper in P's residence of New York. **(C)** is incorrect because there is no venue based solely on P's residence.

107. /B/ Although none of the events occurred in Ohio, and although the renter moved to Ohio only after the cause of action arose, jurisdiction is decided at the time the lawsuit begins, by which point the renter had already moved to Ohio. Furthermore, jurisdiction over D is sufficient; jurisdiction over P is unnecessary. Also, because the piano store chain requested only equitable relief (specific performance) the judge has the authority to deny the renter's asserted right to a jury trial. **(A)** is incorrect because the judge may rule on specific performance without a jury trial, even if the renter requests one because it is not a factual question for the jury. **(C)** is incorrect because the judge may retain jurisdiction in Ohio. **(D)** is incorrect because restitution remedies (e.g., rescission, cancellation, and reformation), such as the court ordering the renter to return the $80,000 to the piano store chain, are equitable remedies that a judge need not submit to a jury even if a party asserts their right to a jury trial.

108. /C/ Where both equitable – here specific performance – and legal issues – here damages for breach – are presented in the same claim, the jury may hear the whole facts because whether the inventory at question is owned by Betty will be determined by the jury and thus the motion to strike should be denied. [FRCP 38] **(A)** is not the best answer because the court is likely to deny the motion to strike the jury demand over all aspects of the case. **(B)** is incorrect because the court will likely deny the motion to strike. **(D)** is incorrect because it is likely the court will allow the jury to decide both the legal and equitable claims.

109. /C/ Satisfying federal diversity jurisdiction requires that the amount in controversy must exceed $75,000. Individual claims may be aggregated together to meet the minimum threshold as between the same P and D. Punitive damages, post-judgment interest, and court and service costs cannot be included in the amount in controversy; however, interest and costs specified in a contract are included in the amount in controversy. **(A)** is incorrect because multiple claims between the same P and D may usually be aggregated. **(B)** is incorrect because it does not include the collection costs specified in the contract, which unlike court costs are included in the amount of controversy. **(D)** is incorrect because court costs such as for filing and conducting service of process are not included in the amount in controversy.

110. /B/ Contract claims held jointly require all indispensible parties be joined. Here there is only one claim being asserted, so the amount in controversy requirement of $75,000 minimum is met. **(A)** is incorrect since the aggregate claim is being brought by the joint claimants collectively. **(C)** is incorrect because the proration among collective contract claimants is not determinant of the jurisdiction amount. **(D)** is incorrect because the proration among collective contract claimants is not determinant of the jurisdiction amount.

111. /B/ A state's *in rem* powers allow a state to take action over a piece of real property located within a state, even if the court lacks personal jurisdiction over the parties owning the property. However due process still requires that the Ds be given notice and an opportunity to be heard. **(A)** is not the best answer because a court in Massachusetts lacks personal jurisdiction over a D in Washington without an applicable long-arm statute. **(C)** is not the best answer because a court in Massachusetts lacks personal jurisdiction over a D in Texas without an applicable long-arm statute. **(D)** is not the best answer because a court in Massachusetts lacks personal jurisdiction over a D in Tennessee without an applicable long-arm statute.

112./B/ For diversity jurisdiction a personal representative is treated as a citizen of the same state as the decedent they represent – here New Jersey – so the diversity requirement is met. **(A)** is incorrect because the personal representative is treated as a state citizen of the decedent they represent. **(C)** is incorrect because the federal court will accept the damage amount as pleaded unless they appear terribly unrealistic. **(D)** is incorrect because there does not have to be a federal question if the jurisdiction is allowed under the diversity rules.

113./C/ The best answer because domestic relations and probate matters by policy are ineligible for federal jurisdiction and must be filed in state court. **(A)** is not the best answer because an exception to federal jurisdiction exists for domestic relations matters even if the $75,000 plus minimum amount is met. **(B)** is not the best answer because irrespective of the amount in controversy, a federal court will not ordinarily hear a domestic relations matter. **(D)** is incorrect because diversity of residence is not sufficient if the matter involves domestic relations.

114./B/ If Paradise's position alleging that all Ds are jointly and severally liable is not patently unreasonable the court will likely deny the motion to dismiss based upon the jurisdiction amount requirements. **(A)** is incorrect because Paradise has not unreasonably alleged all Ds are jointly and severally liable for the whole $150,000 because water is fungible. **(C)** is not the best answer because initial jurisdiction is determined before trial. **(D)** is not the best answer because Paradise is alleging joint and several liability and if this theory is correct there will be no judgment proration.

115./D/ Ps do have the ability to forum shop and to choose whether to pursue claims against multiple Ds separately or as part of one action. Even if a D successfully impleads a third-party D whose original inclusion in the P's claim would have defeated diversity, that successful impleader will not defeat diversity. [FRCP 14] **(A)** is incorrect because the family business did not name the CPA as a D in its original suit. **(B)** is incorrect because Ps do not have a duty to include all potential Ds in the same action. Usually P may pursue related claims in different actions against different Ds. **(C)** is incorrect because the bulge rule operates only for purposes of service of process and evaluating personal jurisdiction; it does not have any role in evaluating diversity jurisdiction in such a situation.

116./B/ For venue purposes, a corporation is deemed to be a resident of any district in which there is minimum contacts and that was the place of the dispute's events; here the car sale and injury was in the Eastern District of Washington. Note that the corporation defendant could move to transfer the case to another district on the basis of *forum non conveniens*, such as the Western District of Washington where Seattle is located, since P would have this same right. **(A)** is incorrect because it is the wrong venue. **(C)** is incorrect because it is the wrong venue. **(D)** is incorrect because it is the wrong venue.

117./B/ The best answer because the claim or defense arose out of the same claim and the added party knew or should have known that, but for mistaken identity, the original pleading would have named them. **(A)** is incorrect because the amendment will likely be allowed. **(C)** is not the best answer because while the new party is different, the motion to dismiss will likely be denied. **(D)** is incorrect because the amendment will likely be allowed

118. /D/ Undisclosed claims may not be usually asserted at trial, therefore the claim for intentional infliction of emotional distress will likely not be allowed. **(A)** is not the best answer because a complaint must always give the D fair notice of all material elements of each claim, the factual basis for each, and the legal basis for each. **(B)** is not the best answer because despite the liberal rules about "notice pleading," a complaint must always give the D fair notice of all material elements of each claim, the factual basis for each, and the legal basis for each. **(C)** is not the best answer because although this statement is generally true, it misses the issue here of whether undisclosed claims may be asserted at trial.

119. /A/ Although a Georgia state court likely could not assert personal jurisdiction over the businesswoman if she had been the D and the Georgia resident had proactively as the P sued her, here the businesswoman voluntarily submitted to the jurisdiction of the Georgia state court by filing a case there as the P, and of course the Georgia court has personal jurisdiction over the D tortfeasor as a Georgia resident. **(B)** is incorrect because this business act does not grant the Georgia court jurisdiction over the P; the P filing in the Georgia court does so, and this act has nothing to do with the issue of whether the Georgia court has personal jurisdiction over the D. **(C)** is incorrect because the businesswoman voluntarily filing her action in the Georgia state court alone provides the court with personal jurisdiction over her. **(D)** is incorrect because the P is the "master of her complaint" and so may bring her action in any court that may have personal jurisdiction over the D.

120. /A/ Acme Corporation's motion to dismiss should be denied in that the service on a Maine's resident was adequate as required by Maine law even though not as exacting as the federal rule. **(B)** is not the best answer because it appears the actual service was adequate under state law which is recognized by FRCP 4. **(C)** is incorrect because the method of service seems proper under state law, so more facts would not change the holding that service was adequate. **(D)** is incorrect because FRCP 4 specifically authorizes any service method allowable under Maine law, where Iola was served.

121. /C/ The best answer because FRCP 4 specifies service may be adequate if the summons and complaint is left with a resident of D's abode who is of suitable age and discretion. A neighbor does not meet this requirement as they do not reside in the D's residence. **(A)** is incorrect because the neighbor's suggestion is not determinant if the P service met the service requirements of FRCP 4. **(B)** is not the best answer because the implication of service knowledge is not the FRCP 4 requirement. **(D)** is incorrect because delivery to non-D is only proper if the individual served resides in D's abode.

122. /B/ Dismissal because of not effecting service within 90 days may not result if P can show good cause for the failure. **(A)** is incorrect in that while dismissal is the general rule, this alternative omits the exception. **(C)** is not the best answer because FRCP 4(m) does not list this as an exception. **(D)** is not the best answer because the rule dictates dismissal is mandatory and a general objection is likely insufficient.

123. C/ Corporations, unlike individuals in some circumstances, must be served by leaving the process with a corporate officer, or general or managing agent. Service on a mere sales clerk or by non-certified mail does not seem to meet the requirement of FRCP 4(h) that prefers service on an officer, a managing agent, or some other authorized corporate agent. **(A)** is incorrect because here service seems inadequate. **(B)** is incorrect because the issue here is whether the store sales agent communicated the papers to top management and a mere acknowledgement of receipt by the sales clerk seems inadequate. **(D)** is incorrect because, even if the post office said there was delivery to the corporation, there is no showing a corporate officer or agent received the process.

124./C/ Providing such services to Kansas residents and sending winnings back to them is the situation most likely to subject the corporation to personal jurisdiction in a Kansas state court. **(A)** is incorrect because merely advertising generally on the internet, when that advertising is not geographically-targeted, will not subject the corporation to personal jurisdiction in a Kansas state court. **(B)** is not the best answer because the employee arguably did not directly target the Kansas-based competitor with his actions. **(D)** is not the best answer because the corporation did not directly target the Kansas-based competitor specifically.

125./C/ Such conscious litigation timing strategies are permissible. **(A)** is incorrect answer because a judge could dismiss a case after such egregious discovery abuse and refusal to comply with the judge's order. **(B)** is incorrect because in *Link v. Wabash R. Co.*, the Supreme Court allowed a judge's dismissal of P's case after P's lawyer failed to show up at such a pre-trial conference. **(D)** is incorrect because in *Innospan v. Intuit* the 9th Circuit dismissed the P's case after P's counsel had engaged in such misconduct and P failed to timely pay the resulting monetary sanctions.

126./A/ This question is purely one of law, not fact, and thus is an impermissible question in an interrogatory seeking facts. **(B)** is not the best answer because it focuses more on a factual issue, the Parties' intent, rather than on a legal issue, whether the contract was actually completely integrated. **(C)** is incorrect because, although arguably over-broad, the question seems relevant and the party issuing the interrogatory may compel a response. **(D)** is incorrect because it more specifically requests a clearly-definable list of individuals.

127./B/ Pleadings and sanctions must actually be signed by the attorney of record, or the pleadings may be stricken. [CR 11] **(A)** is not the best answer because there is no indication from the given facts that the attorney failed to make a reasonable inquiry into the factual or legal merits of a claim prior to fling his pleading. **(C)** is not the best answer because the attorney must actually sign the pleadings and cannot simply direct them to be signed by a non-lawyer assistant. **(D)** is not the best answer because although this seems here possible to happen, the malpractice claim against the attorney will be brought by the client, and not by an action of the court which is ultimately at issue in this question.

128./C/ Both interrogatories and requests for admission require responses within 30 days according to the FRCP; the tech-mogul's response after five weeks, therefore, was late. His late response does not extinguish any claims he may have, such as ownership over the whole blackberry patch due to perhaps adverse possession, but a judge may require him to pay the clothing magnate's attorney fees to sanction him for the late response. In addition, after 30 days all requests for admission not responded to are deemed to have been admitted. Therefore, the tech-mogul will be deemed to have admitted that he tore out the lilac bushes and that those bushes marked the boundary. **(A)** is incorrect because the clothing magnate does not have to produce evidence that the tech-mogul tore out the old lilac bush since the tech-mogul is deemed to have admitted it after failing to respond to the request for admission within 30 days. **(B)** is incorrect because a judge would likely not deem the tech-mogul's yard work seven years ago to amount to spoliation. **(D)** is incorrect because the tech-mogul's late response likely will not prevent him from continuing to assert ownership over the blackberry patch perhaps through a claim of adverse possession.

129. /A/ When the D has misstated the truth in a request for admission, P's attorney still may not recover attorney's fees incurred responding to requests for admission sent in the opposite direction from D. **(B)** is not the correct answer because the other driver's attorney likely would be able to recover attorney's fees for the time spent preparing his own request for attorney's fees in this situation. **(C)** is incorrect because these are direct costs incurred proving the matter wrongly denied in response to a request for admission. Such costs are typically awarded in such discovery abuse situations. **(D)** is incorrect because the investigator's expenses would typically be awarded in such a discovery abuse situation.

130. /C/ Federal law protects members of the military against the entry of a default judgment. **(A)** is not the best answer because although the soldier was properly served with a copy of the summons and complaint, federal law protects members of the military against the entry of a default judgment. **(B)** is not the best answer because the federal law which protects members of the military from the entry of default judgment overrides the rule requiring the D to file an answer to a summons and complaint within 21 days. **(D)** is not the best answer although informal negotiations may in some circumstances constitute an effective appearance.

131. /A/ A motion to quash or limit a subpoena may be filed by the deponent. **(B)** is not the best answer, because although a motion to quash or limit the subpoena may be brought by any party affected by the subpoena, the fact pattern does not tell us which party issued the subpoena. **(C)** is not the best answer because the fact pattern does not tell us which party issued the subpoena, even though a motion to quash or limit the subpoena may be brought by any party affected by the subpoena. **(D)** is not the best answer because the fact pattern does not tell us which party issued the subpoena, even though a motion to quash or limit the subpoena may be brought by any party affected by the subpoena.

132. /C/ Only admissible evidence may be considered in a motion for summary judgment. For expert testimony to be admissible, a sworn affidavit with the expert's particularized qualifications and opinions must have been submitted to the court; a mere report, even if notarized, is not sufficient. [FRCP 56] **(A)** is incorrect because even if substantively a judge concluded that such physician testimony was required to meet the necessary burden of proof at the summary judgment phase, such a necessity would not dictate that the judge refuse to consider the other two experts' testimony if they were sworn. **(B)** is incorrect because experts are permitted to coordinate their opinions and testimony for a case. **(D)** is incorrect because the full expert's reports do not have to be disclosed at the initial disclosures stage.

133. /D/ A court which has issued a subpoena may hold a person in contempt who, having been served, fails without adequate excuse to obey the subpoena or an order related to it. **(A)** is incorrect, because a court will instead hold the party in contempt for failure to comply with a court order. **(B)** is incorrect because the failure of a person to comply with a properly issued subpoena does not usually allow the opposing party to infer any sort of admission. **(C)** not the best answer because it is through a court's contempt powers that the court may issue an order for the person to appear, pay fines, or perhaps even impose a jail sentence.

134. /C/ In a defamation claim like libel, one of the essential elements is proving damages. JMOL requires assessing whether the non-moving party, in this case the older couple, has produced enough evidence to submit the case to the jury. In carefully arguing a critical damage issue, the older couple has satisfied at least one critical element of a defamation claim, thereby significantly helping prevent the young couple's motion for JMOL from succeeding. [FRCP 50] **(A)** is incorrect because when assessing whether to grant JMOL, a judge will interpret the evidence reasonably in favor of the non-moving party, in this case the older couple. A judge would possibly conclude that such failure to consider the possibility that the older couple might refuse to take on an additional child merely because their business was full as a reasonable ground upon which to conclude that the young couple was sufficiently negligent for a defamation claim when they made the claim that the older couple was prejudiced against Pelasgians. **(B)** is incorrect because a judge does not consider witness credibility when assessing whether to grant JMOL. **(D)** is incorrect because a judge may not weigh the evidence when assessing whether to grant JMOL; the judge must conclude that no reasonable jury could conclude otherwise. It is insufficient merely that the judge has come to her or his own subjective conclusion.

135. /A/ Implementing this procedure during discovery will enable only an opposing party's in-house counsel and perhaps a select few other officers to view the documents containing the source code. Because of the protective order details and the CONFIDENTIAL marking, they will not have the right to share the source code with their own developers and could face liability for doing so. [FRCP 26] **(B)** is incorrect because in-house counsel acting merely as a conduit for documents does not usually provide protection under the attorney-client privilege. **(C)** is not the best answer because in a discovery dispute, a judge could compel in-house counsel to decrypt the disks and documents containing the source code so that they can be available for the opposing party's discovery efforts. **(D)** is not the best answer because in such a situation, the attorney-client privilege would protect only the attorney's opinion; it would still not protect the document containing the source code itself.

136. /D/ Although the affirmative defense of lack of personal jurisdiction must be plead in or before the answer, it is not necessary to file the motion to dismiss based upon this lack of personal jurisdiction at or before the answer. As long as the answer contains a general challenge based upon personal jurisdiction, the actual motion to dismiss with the detailed factual and case law analysis arguing in support of the challenge may be filed later. [FRCP 12] **(A)** is incorrect because a D must assert a lack of personal jurisdiction at or before the answer in order to avoid involuntarily waiving this affirmative defense. This option does not explicitly indicate that that challenge to personal jurisdiction was in the answer, and so this option seems a better choice. **(B)** is incorrect because a motion for a new trial is filed near, at, or just after the end of a trial due to issues completely unrelated to personal jurisdiction such as errors of law and juror misconduct. If the case were to move to a state court in Franklin, it would result from a motion for change in venue, or from dismissal without prejudice from the courts of Texatoba and re-filing anew in Franklin; it would not result from a motion for new trial. **(C)** is not the correct answer because only the customer as P could request to have the case voluntarily dismissed.

137./A/ Here, the psychiatrist deliberately targeted Rocky Mountain states like Wyoming for her online services, and the dispute arose from those services. **(B)** is not the best answer because the degree to which sellers may face personal jurisdiction merely through the product entering the stream of commerce has not yet been fully clarified by the Supreme Court. **(C)** is not the best answer because recent Supreme Court cases suggest that selling just one item into a jurisdiction does not subject the seller to even specific personal jurisdiction in that area. **(D)** is not the best answer because it is unlikely that a court would consider the Kentucky-based psychiatrist to have "purposefully availed" herself of the benefits and protection of Wyoming law.

138./B/ The choice of jurisdiction clause in the online click-through agreement creates minimum contact between the buyer and the jurisdiction named in that clause to justify that specified court system asserting personal jurisdiction over the buyer. [FRCP 4] **(A)** is not the correct answer because personal jurisdiction can arise from minimum contacts that took place only online; physical interaction such as buying directly from a store, is not necessary. **(C)** is not the correct answer because though this answer alone may be correct, in the specific facts of this case the outcome will differ because of the choice of jurisdiction clause. **(D)** is not correct because the law does not set such a high bar for the minimum contacts sufficiently necessary to create personal jurisdiction.

139./C/ Since the sailor will likely not be in attendance at the hearings because he is at sea and out of communication, the engineer should file the motion for dissolution and at the same time file procedural motions that are *ex parte* such as a motion for default judgment and a request for a TRO. [FRCP 55 for default judgment, and FRCP 65 for equitable relief] **(A)** is not the best answer because it does not have the engineer beginning with ex parte motions like those for default judgment and a TRO. **(B)** is incorrect because collateral estoppel works in an entirely different situation and with regard to an entirely different set of issues. It is not type of equitable relief, but rather merely the term to refer to the prohibition on re-litigating specific factual issues in a second lawsuit that a trier of fact already ruled upon in a prior lawsuit. **(D)** is not the best answer because it would have the engineer filing a motion for summary judgment and requesting a preliminary injunction before filing a motion for default judgment and requesting a TRO, when actually the order should be the reverse, and in fact, if the default judgment and TRO motions are successful, then there will be no need for a summary judgment motion and the TRO could turn into a permanent, not just preliminary, injunction.

140./A/ This factor actually does not ordinarily get considered when assessing whether a class action can be brought under the Common Questions category; instead, it is one of the two types of Risks of Separate Actions class action categories. The missing fourth factor that this extraneous standard replaced is: The extent and nature of any litigation concerning the controversy already begun by or against class members. [FRCP 23(b)] **(B)** is incorrect because this is actually one of the factors considered when assessing whether a class action fits under the 23(b)(3) Common Questions category. **(C)** is incorrect because this is actually one of the factors considered when assessing whether a class action fits under the 23(b)(3) Common Questions category. **(D)** is incorrect because this is actually one of the factors considered when assessing whether a class action fits under the 23(b)(3) Common Questions category.

141./B/ The fact that the putative class members suffered very different sorts of injuries would likely cause class-certification to fail for not meeting the "P" element of the CULP acronym which requires that the representative parties adequately represent the interests of all the class members; having such different injuries would likely be considered a serious difficulty to any one party being able to represent the interests of the other putative class members. [FRCP 23] **(A)** is incorrect because this complaint primarily seeks injunctive relief against using the new stretch of spectrum, making it the most common sort of class-action category of the three. The "C" in CULP requires only that some important questions of law and/or fact be common, a standard that this claim satisfies. **(C)** is incorrect because FRCP 23 does not require advance approval by class members. **(D)** is not the best answer because opt out notice is only required after the court has determined that class action status is to be certified.

142./C/ This requirement is not explicitly listed in any FRCP section, and so it is not one of the three types of class certifications under FRCP 23(b). The first part of this option, the requirement of a definable class, is actually an implicit requirement for class action lawsuits that many courts impose, but it is not one of the three types of certifications. The four options in this question actually leave out one of the three types of certifications under FRCP 23(b), that of an action for monetary damages in which the common questions "predominate" over areas of difference and bringing the lawsuit as a class action is a superior means to fairly and efficiently adjudicate the controversy. [FRCP 23(b)] **(A)** is incorrect because it is one of the three types of class action certifications. **(B)** is incorrect because one of the three types of class actions, and is grouped with the certification laid out in the previous option. **(D)** is incorrect because it is one of the three types of class action certifications.

143./A/ When reviewing preliminary injunctions, appellate courts require specific findings on all four of the preliminary injunction requirements. They require this degree of specificity in order to have a record upon which to assess whether trial judges abused their discretion, which is the standard of review for matters relating to such issues as injunctions, discovery, and evidence admissibility. This preliminary injunction will fail under such scrutiny because the trial judge only "generally" made conclusions, and furthermore did so only in regard to three of the four preliminary injunction requirements. There was no mention of the balance of the hardships tipping in favor of the upslope property owner. [FRCP 65] **(B)** is incorrect because, assuming that the trial judge provides comprehensive reasons covering each of the four elements of a preliminary injunction, an appellate court will not question a trial judge's discretion in this regard. Although outside observers may view the cases as nearly if not exactly identical, an appellate court would likely defer to the trial judge's exercise of discretion as the trier of fact. **(C)** is incorrect because a party need not first obtain a TRO before having the right to request a preliminary injunction. **(D)** is incorrect because although TROs are typically thought of as the sort of injunction relief available through an ex parte proceeding, trial judges may also issue preliminary injunctions through ex parte proceedings if the moving party for the preliminary injunction makes reasonable efforts, as stated in this option, to notify the other party of the proceeding to determine whether a preliminary injunction should be issued.

144./A/ Class action lawsuits can involve both classes of Ps and/or classes of Ds. [FRCP 23] **(B)** is incorrect because it is true; while defamation and fraud both require a clear, cogent, and convincing standard of proof/evidence, only fraud requires special pleading, while defamation does not. **(C)** is incorrect because service of process by publication in which the journalist's home address should be easily ascertainable and the journalist easily approachable, is not permitted. **(D)** is incorrect because it is true; federal courts have discretion over whether to exercise supplemental jurisdiction over state law claims and may refuse to do so even if the state law claim arises out of the same set of facts and arguably satisfies the requirements for supplemental jurisdiction.

145./B/ FRCP 26 states that "Parties may obtain discovery regarding any non-privileged matter that is relevant to any party's claim or defense...Relevant information need not be admissible at the trial if the discovery appears reasonably calculated to lead to the discovery of admissible evidence." Seeking treatment for eye conditions prior to the lasing incident is relevant to the P's claim that the laser caused severe eye damage, and therefore requesting this information from the CAM providers seems reasonably calculated to lead to the discovery of admissible evidence. Although Physician-Patient Privilege by default prohibits such information from even discovery, let alone admissibility, when the medical condition is at issue in the case then such related evidence is both discoverable and admissible. [FRCP 26(b)(1)] **(A)** is incorrect because it is too strict: The matter requested through discovery need not likely be admissible evidence itself. Its discovery need only be "reasonably calculated" to "lead to the discovery of admissible evidence" whether or not the actual admissible evidence came from the initially discovered material or material that was discovered later only because the initial material led to knowledge of the existence of the later-discovered material. **(C)** is not the best answer because CAM records probably are protected by Physician-Patient Confidentiality. **(D)** is incorrect because the formulation is incorrect. The standard is not whether the discovery "must be" reasonably calculated to yield information that is "relevant to any one of the party's claims or defenses" as this option incorrectly states; rather, the standard is that the request must "appears" reasonably calculated to lead to the discovery of admissible evidence.

146./B/ Suppressing evidence is the proper function of a motion *in limine*. **(A)** is incorrect because a writ of mandamus is used to direct the district court to take some required action that does not apply in this context. **(C)** is incorrect because such an affidavit would not be needed for the court to determine whether to suppress the evidence; a motion *in limine* more directly pursues the goal of having the evidence suppressed. **(D)** is incorrect because collateral estoppel prevents issues from being re-litigated; it does not prevent evidence from being admitted.

147./D/ Each party to a lawsuit has a proactive duty to disclose to the other parties any insurance policies that may cover any part of any final judgment, and to provide copies of those insurance policies. This duty arises at the beginning of the discovery process. [FRCP 26] **(A)** is incorrect because whereas insurance coverage cannot usually be admitted into evidence, it must be disclosed during discovery. **(B)** is incorrect because the duty to disclose one's insurance policy does not arise only if the other party claims monetary damages in excess of coverage limits. There are no conditions on the duty to disclose insurance during discovery; this duty is absolute. **(C)** is incorrect because again, there are no conditions upon whether the duty to disclose insurance during discovery may arise; this duty is absolute.

148./D/ A Motion to Set Aside the Verdict, which is equivalent to a Motion for a New Trial, would be the only proper motion in this situation. One of the standard grounds to grant such a motion is severe juror misconduct prejudicing the losing party. [FRCP 59 for Motion for a New Trial and Motion to Set Aside the Verdict] **(A)** is not the best answer because the sort of newly discovered evidence that would substantiate a motion to vacate is evidence concerning the substantive merits of the case itself, not collateral evidence of juror misconduct. [FRCP 60] **(B)** is incorrect because it is misconduct by one of the parties to the case, not by jurors, that provides the grounds for involuntary dismissal. [FRCP 41(b)] **(C)** is incorrect because requesting JMOL is not a post-trial motion, which is what the question asked for. An attorney may file a motion for JMOL after the case has been submitted to the jury, but after the jury has announced its judgment a JMOL is no longer possible. [FRCP 50]

149./A/ There is no specific FRCP the text of which explicitly sets out a motion for "mistrial," which arises from very much the same sort of reasons as a motion for a new trial. Instead, the official comments to FRCPs 47 and 48, which govern jury formation, in passing mention such a motion. The rule that a motion for mistrial is only made before the final verdict comes from the general practice of common law, not from any specific language in the FRCP. Because the jury had already issued a verdict in this refinery case, a motion for mistrial could not be filed; instead, motions to set aside the verdict and for a new trial would be appropriate. **(B)** is not the correct answer because at this point the wealthy family would have justification to file a motion for a new trial. [FRCP 59] **(C)** is incorrect because the likely remedy is a motion for mistrial. **(D)** is incorrect because the wealthy family could also file this motion due to the discovery of the new evidence that had been in the possession of the juror. [FRCP 60]

150./B/ This option, combined with any indications that the company's legal team might be deliberately engaging the safety consultant as a consulting expert rather than as a testifying expert so as to prevent discovery of the consultant's observations, represents the paradigmatic example of the sort of "exceptional circumstances" that justify discovery of a mere consulting expert's observations. [FRCP 26] **(A)** is not a correct answer. Because the expert has been designated as a mere consulting expert, even if parts of the observations were fabricated, they would by default not come to light through discovery at all, let alone come into evidence, and so they would not affect judgment of the merits of the case. **(C)** is incorrect because this incident may seem to represent an "exceptional circumstance," but it does not best represent the sort of exceptional circumstance for which the exception allowing discovery into the materials of consulting experts was created. **(D)** is not correct because it is not an "exceptional" circumstance in and of itself. True, it may provide some foundation for believing that the company may be trying to shield the consultant's materials from discovery by retaining her as a mere consulting expert rather than as a testifying expert, but here it is not the best answer.

151./D/ Although the discrimination claim seems very separate from the breach of contract claim, and although the corporation has already answered, a judge would likely allow the new claim in the interests of judicial economy in order to consolidate claims between the same two parties into the same case. [FRCP 15] **(A)** is not the correct answer because no matter how absurd the claim may seem to the D, to evaluate such a motion all the P's allegations are assumed to be true; therefore, this 12(b)(6) motion would likely not succeed. **(B)** is not the correct answer because the corporation waived its ability to object for lack of personal jurisdiction due to requesting affirmative relief, specifically a permanent injunction. **(C)** is not the correct answer because the corporation has filed an answer, and so the D has the right to object to a P's motion for voluntary dismissal.

152. /A/ Although the student's coverage is world-wide, there are no other connections between the insurance company and Franklin State; therefore, a state court there would be the most likely of the four states' courts to conclude that it does not have personal jurisdiction over the insurance company. **(B)** is incorrect because the accident occurred in Jefferson State and so a state court there would more likely conclude appropriately that it has personal jurisdiction over the parties to the case resulting from the collision and also over any conflicts arising from that case. **(C)** is incorrect because the insurance company is headquartered in this state and does all its business there; therefore, state courts in Madison State would have not just specific jurisdiction over specific issues arising from the insurance company's connections to the state, but actually general jurisdiction as well. **(D)** is incorrect because the insurance company is registered in Dayton State; therefore, it would be considered an appropriate state in which to sue the insurance company for any matter because courts there would also have general jurisdiction over the D.

153. /D/ Unless the court orders otherwise, deposition testimony may be recorded by audio, audiovisual, or stenographic means. [FRCP 30] **(A)** is not the best answer because audio recording and videotaping are also acceptable methods for the recording of deposition testimony. **(B)** is not the best answer because a court stenographer and videotaping are also acceptable methods for the recording of deposition testimony. **(C)** is not the best answer because court stenographer and audio recording are also acceptable methods for the recording of deposition testimony.

154. /D/ The P's complaint did not include any allegations specifying the exact legal claims that the P believes the alleged facts support; however, a judge would likely allow the P to amend his complaint to specify what he believes to be the legal basis for his claims. [FRCP 12(b)(6)] **(A)** is incorrect because the skydiving company, in addition to his friends, could plausibly be held liable for the P's injuries. **(B)** is incorrect because the friends' joinder is not compulsory; the P could sue them separately at a different time. **(C)** is incorrect because specific money amounts for specific damage types would likely be clarified later prior to trial.

155. /C/ The minimal contacts standard is the correct answer because it contains the least justification under these facts. Minimal contacts is not a standard for venue directly; instead, minimal contacts are one way to justify personal jurisdiction, and personal jurisdiction is one way to justify venue. **(A)** is incorrect because it is proper venue to hold the lawsuit in the courts of the state in which property is located. **(B)** is incorrect because venue over corporate Ds may be conferred either by jurisdiction of registration or the jurisdiction in which the corporation's main place of business is located. **(D)** is incorrect because such residency provides one reason to justify jurisdiction in the courts of the state of residence.

156. /A/ In response to such abusive questioning, the former employee's attorney still may not instruct the former employee not to answer since the inquiry does involve the work place at issue in the case. The former employee's attorney in this situation has a difficult decision to make: Does the attorney allow the abusive questioning to continue, or does the attorney stop the interrogation and request a protective order from the court that would risk sanctions if the court does not agree that the attorney had "substantial justification" stopping the deposition and/or requesting a protective order. [FRCP 30] **(B)** is not correct because such a question impinges upon the marital communication privilege, and a deponent's attorney may instruct the deponent not to answer a question that would reveal privileged matters. **(C)** is not correct because it is a leading question, and so the former employee's attorney may object to its form. **(D)** is not correct because it is a vague question (during what period of time were the sick days used), and so the former employee's attorney may object to the form of the question.

157. /C/ Although having a proposed examining physician testify at such a hearing would be rare, the P could challenge the D's proposed physician to verify at a hearing her competence to conduct the examination and to verify that a medical condition is in controversy; such testimony at a hearing could provide the good cause showing necessary to compel an examination. [FRCP 35] **(A)** is not the best answer because the party moving to compel the examination must show "good cause" for the examination; "good cause" is a higher standard than the much lower standard applicable to what sorts of materials a party has a right to obtain through discovery. **(B)** is not the best answer because courts will usually require parties moving to compel an examination to exhaust other discovery means such as interrogatories first before permitting them to compel an examination. **(D)** is not the best answer because the party moving to compel a physical or mental examination must make an affirmative showing that good cause for the examination exists; the court merely relying on the pleadings does not usually provide such an affirmative showing.

158. /D/ Service of process sent to any branch of any government must be registered or certified. [FRCP 4] **(A)** is incorrect because in no situation is personal hand-to-hand service of process to a government agency or official absolutely necessary. **(B)** is incorrect because all mailed service of process to any government agency or official must be registered or certified whether it be in Washington D.C. or local. **(C)** is incorrect because there is no option to conduct publication service of process on government agencies or officials via a newspaper announcement.

159. /C/ A summary judgment need not determine all the factual issues; a judge may grant summary judgment on a certain subset of facts, such as those that determine overall liability, but continue into discovery and usually conduct a bench trial on the issue of damages. [FRCP 56] **(A)** is incorrect because Ps need not disclose all their evidence in their initial complaint. **(B)** is incorrect because the addition of evidence beyond the factual allegations contained in the pleadings according to FRCP 12(d) converts a motion for judgment on the pleadings into a motion for summary judgment. **(D)** is not the best answer because Ezquerra could have lied to his attorney, in which case the attorney would not be responsible for the falsity of Ezquerra's answer.

160. /B/ The FRCP in general encourage judges not to determine outcomes based solely upon errors in how attorneys label their motions; in accordance with FRCP 1, in the "interests of justice" a judge may re-characterize an incorrectly labeled motion as one appropriate for that particular stage in a lawsuit. [FRCP 1 and FRCP 12] **(A)** is not the best answer because FRCP 1 also encourages judges to move lawsuits along as quickly as possible, so a delay would be less likely than re-characterizing the motion as a 12(b)(6) motion. **(C)** is not the best answer because judges will not prevent parties from filing motions in such a harsh manner. **(D)** is incorrect because this sort of re-characterization occurs if the party making the motion wishes to introduce evidence beyond the factual allegations contained in the pleadings.

161. /A/ Judgment as a matter of law is most similar to judgment on the pleadings because success on both requires a judge to conclude that even if everything the P claims were true, the law would still compel a judgment in favor of the D; also, both are judgments that prevent the P from refiling or amending the claims. [FRCP 12(c) and FRCP 50] **(B)** is incorrect because summary judgment requires the judge to rule on legal issues upon which disagreement over the outcome may be more reasonable. **(C)** is incorrect both because dismissal is not even a form of judgment, which is what the question asks for, and furthermore a case's first order of dismissal will typically allow the P to refile, whereas Ps will not be able to refile at least part and probably none of the claims that fail due to a judgment on the pleadings. **(D)** is incorrect because a D's successful 12(b)(6) motion means that the P failed even to articulate a cognizable claim; for judgment on the pleadings, however, the P has articulated a cognizable claim, yet nevertheless the law compels judgment against those claims. Furthermore, a successful 12(c) motion prevents the P from amending or refiling, whereas Ps are typically allowed to amend their pleadings after a D's successful 12(b)(6) motion.

162. /D/ In this factual situation, the fisherman's injuries are in controversy because the extent of those injuries will control a critical element of the damage calculation: the compensation for lost wages. [FRCP 35] **(A)** is incorrect because the fisherman claims emotional damages arising from his experience struggling in the freezing, hypothermia-inducing water while injured and calling for help. **(B)** is incorrect because in this situation the surgeon's chosen treatment method is in controversy, not the nature and extent of the injuries themselves. **(C)** is not the best answer; it stands out as a situation in which the D is attempting to fabricate new issues rather than claiming a medical examination is needed to investigate a claim actually advanced and put into controversy by the P.

163. /A/ Losing parties in a lawsuit do not usually have to pay fees for the prevailing side's consulting experts. [FRCP 54] **(B)** is incorrect because hybrid fact/occurrence experts are considered regular witnesses in this situation, and so the losing party may have to pay the normal witness fee for hybrid fact/occurrence experts. **(C)** is incorrect because court-appointed expert fees are usually taxable, and so the losing party typically may have to pay such fees. **(D)** is incorrect because although testifying expert fees are non-taxable, the cost of transcribing their deposition is a taxable cost that losing parties typically have to pay.

164. /C/ A court order compelling discovery is the proper remedy where a party resists a discovery request. **(A)** is not the best answer because filing a summary judgment motion is likely not yet ripe. **(B)** is not the best answer because a default judgment is reserved for those cases where a party has engaged in particularly egregious discovery abuse. **(D)** is not the best answer because a motion for sanctions is brought only *after* the other party has failed to comply with an order compelling discovery.

165. /B/ The ultimate sanction against D who engages in particularly egregious discovery abuse is the entry of a default judgment in favor of the P. [FRCP 37] **(A)** is not the best answer because although it is within the court's power to exclude evidence, it is not the most severe sanction the court may impose. **(C)** is not the best answer because costs and attorney's fees of bringing the sanctions motion are considered routine sanctions. **(D)** is not the best answer because although it is within the court's power to hold a party that fails to comply with a discovery order in contempt, it is not as severe a sanction as an outright order of dismissal.

166. /D/ Only a few types of civil claims, including defamation (libel or slander) and fraud, require the P to satisfy the clear, cogent, and convincing standard of evidence; the rest, like interference with a business expectancy, a.k.a. contractual interference, require P to prove only by a preponderance of the evidence. [Neither the FRCP nor the FRE explicitly mandate any general or default standard of evidence or proof.] **(A)** This sort of civil action imposes a clear, cogent, and convincing standard of evidence. **(B)** This sort of civil action imposes a clear, cogent, and convincing standard of evidence. **(C)** Defamation is one of the more well-known sorts of civil claims that impose on the proponent a clear, cogent, and convincing standard of evidence.

167. /B/ "More likely than not" represents another way of phrasing the "preponderance of the evidence" standard that generally governs most civil claims. [Neither the FRCP nor the FRE explicitly mandate any general or default standard of evidence or proof.] **(A)** is incorrect because this phrase is another way to express the clear, cogent, and convincing standard of evidence that governs a small subset of civil claims, such as defamation, fraud, and changes in child custody, but that does not generally govern most other types of civil claims. **(C)** is incorrect because this phrase is another way to express the clear, cogent, and convincing standard of evidence that governs a small subset civil claims, such as defamation, fraud, and changes in child custody, but that does not generally govern most other types of civil claims. **(D)** is incorrect because this represents another way of referring to the clear, cogent, and convincing standard of evidence or proof.

168. /C/ Even if neither party requests that the other tourists be joined as Ps, a court must join the other tourists in order to prevent the corporation from running the risk of facing inconsistent judgments. Although state laws usually allow Ps to sue multiple Ds separately in tort cases, any potential P whose situation meets the compulsory joinder requirements must be joined. [FRCP 19] **(A)** is incorrect because this case involves a tort claim, negligence, and state laws usually allow Ps to sue multiple Ds separately for tort claims and do not subject such tort claims to compulsory joinder of multiple Ds. **(B)** is incorrect because this tort joinder may be ordered regardless of whether the LLC claims an interest in the matter. **(D)** is incorrect because courts must (not may) *sua sponte* compel parties to join lawsuits if their participation is indispensable; it is not required that any original party to the lawsuit request such compulsory joinder.

169. /D/ If a party to a lawsuit passes away, then the heirs and beneficiaries to that party's estate may usually be substituted into the lawsuit as successors to the original party's claims. [FRCP 25] **(A)** is incorrect; the claims persist to benefit the heirs and beneficiaries of the original party's estate. **(B)** is incorrect; there is no degree to which the D's potential liability may decrease merely because the original P has passed away. **(C)** is incorrect because this sort of situation does not become a class action.

170./B/ Although D's attorney will have to withdraw, attorneys act as agents for their clients, and this attorney's call to opposing counsel effectively constitutes the D himself expressing an intent to defend himself in the action even if the attorney will have to withdraw; therefore, this act arguably provides P with sufficiently clear intent of D to defend himself such that P will have to provide D with notice of any subsequent application or motion for default judgment. [FRCP 55] **(A)** is not the best answer because D himself must make his intent to defend himself clear; his parents cannot do that for him, and the facts do not say the child was a minor or lacked capacity. **(C)** is incorrect because merely expressing general anger does not express clear intent to defend oneself in a lawsuit. **(D)** is incorrect because D merely consulting with but never retaining an attorney does not come anywhere close to providing P with sufficient notice of D's intent to defend himself such as to compel P to provide D with a notice of motion for default.

171./C/ By default, P need not prove the allegations in the complaint in order to prevail on a motion for default judgment; D's failure to contest the claims acts as an admission of their truth. According to FRCP 55(b)(2)(C)-(D), a court may require P to prove some matters, in which case the burden would typically be by a preponderance of the evidence, and P needs to supply proof of damage claims through at least an affidavit, but there is by default no required burden of proof for the claims themselves. [FRCP 55] **(A)** is incorrect because by default P does not need to prove the original claims in the complaint in order to prevail on a motion for default judgment. **(B)** is incorrect because in a hearing on a motion for default judgment, P need not even meet this low pleading standard in order to prevail. **(D)** is incorrect because P actually does not have any burden of proof in this situation.

172./C/ Evidence of the destruction is admissible to suggest that the party who spoliated the evidence had something to hide; hence the jury should be given an instruction that allows them to infer that the Ed's missing spleen information must have been unfavorable to Allegiance. **(A)** is not the best answer because although sanctions for violation of an order compelling discovery may be appropriate, the better option would be to allow the jury to infer that Allegiance intentionally destroyed Ed's spleen in order to hide something important. **(B)** is not the best answer because a default judgment in favor of the P is the ultimate sanction a court may award for discovery abuse. Whether or not missing evidence rises to that level would be a question for the court to decide. **(D)** is not the best answer because although a court will most likely refuse to allow the offending party to introduce related evidence, such as Allegiance's own lab report about the spleen, a negative inference is probably more effective under the circumstances.

173./B/ This option correctly states the standard, "good cause," and correctly states a situation meeting that standard; i.e., one in which miscommunication between the non-moving party and their attorney resulted in the restaurant's managers reasonably expecting that the former waiter would not act outside of the negotiations by pursuing a default judgment during the negotiations. [FRCP 55(c) and FRCP 60(b)] **(A)** is not the best answer because it states only one element of the overall standard, and a court would be much less likely to consider an attorney's unwise advice in this situation to constitute sufficiently good cause to set aside the entry of default than ongoing negotiations good cause to set aside the entry of default. **(C)** is incorrect because it misstates the standard to set aside an entry of default, which under FRCP 55(c) is simply "good cause." On the other hand, "just cause" is the standard to set aside default judgment under FRCP 60(b). **(D)** is not the best answer because it only states one element of the overall standard, and courts are more likely to consider affirmative defenses raising factual issues not addressed in the original complaint as constituting sufficiently plausible meritorious defenses to set aside default judgment.

174./D/ Under FRCP 37, the duty to retain relevant evidence arises when it becomes apparent that an opposing party has a legal claim or defense that likely involves the particular evidence at issue. **(A)** by itself is not the best answer because the duty to retain is created when awareness of the opposing party's documentation expectation is clear to the potential spoliator. **(B)** by itself is not the best answer because the duty to retain is created when awareness of the opposing party's documentation expectation is clear to the potential spoliator. **(C)** by itself is not the best answer because the duty to retain is created when awareness of the opposing party's documentation expectation is clear to the potential spoliator.

175./A/ In order to preserve the D's Constitutional right to due process, the State has a duty to preserve exculpatory evidence in criminal cases. **(B)** is not the best answer because equal protection is not implicated by the State's duty to preserve exculpatory evidence. **(C)** is not the best answer because the D's Fifth Amendment right against self incrimination is a right afforded the D, and not a duty of the State which is triggered by its possession of exculpatory evidence. **(D)** is not the best answer because the D's right to counsel is a right afforded the D, and not a duty of the state which is triggered by its possession of exculpatory evidence.

176./D/ Although a motion *in limine* is typically brought before trial begins, such a motion may be filed at any time before the pertinent evidence has been brought before the court. While it's true that a judge may instruct a jury to ignore evidence that has been objected to, in practice it is very difficult to "un-ring the bell." **(A)** is not the best answer because a motion *in limine* may be brought during trial, but before the pertinent evidence has been presented. **(B)** is not the best answer because a motion *in limine* is typically brought before trial begins. **(C)** is not the best answer because a motion *in limine* must be brought before the pertinent evidence has been presented to the jury.

177./B/ Unlike some states, a federal court demand for a jury trial by either party is allowed. Failure to comply with this demand requirement is deemed a waiver of a jury and the case is tried before a judge as a bench trial. The demand must be served no later than 14 days after service of the last pleading directed to the issue upon which a jury decision is requested; this is usually the D's Answer. **(A)** is not the best answer because although an appellate court has discretion to allow immediate review of non-final decisions of substantial importance to the outcome of the case in order to prevent the possibility of irreparable harm, the rule governing the demand for a jury trial is well-settled law. **(C)** is not the best answer because a motion for a mistrial (i.e., a motion for a new trial) is generally brought only where there has been an irregularity in the proceedings, where there has been misconduct by persons involved in the trial, or where there is newly discovered evidence that could not have been discovered earlier with reasonable diligence. **(D)** is not the best answer because a motion for summary judgment is a procedural device designed to avoid the time and expense of an unnecessary trial. A criminal D has a constitutional right to a jury trial, and so a motion for summary judgment would be inappropriate in a criminal case.

178./C/ The best answer because when a client objects to the proposed fee, the lawyer should transfer any uncontested fee amount from the law firm trust account to the operating account, remit the mutually agreed upon amount to the client, and interplead the remaining sum in controversy into the registry of a court pending a resolution of the fee dispute. The $5,000 retainer amount is presumably earned upon receipt in New York and many other states in return for the lawyer agreeing to take on the matter, associate their name with the cause, and make themselves available to the P. The earned amount should have been deposited into the law firm operating account upon receipt. Sixty percent of the $100,000 and the unused $10,000 advance are clearly due to the client. Similarly, the lawyer is clearly due at least $250 per hour for the 20 hours spent or $5,000. **(A)** is incorrect because only the undisputed portion of the fee should be remitted to the client. **(B)** is incorrect because the contested fee in trust should not be transferred to either party but may be impleaded into a court registry if agreement on the amount distribution cannot be reached. **(D)** is incorrect because it is not required that all the contested fee be immediately remitted to the unhappy client. [MRPC 1.15]

179./C/ One of the keys to identifying when impleader is most relevant arises from recognizing when indemnification or contribution might be an issue. In this case, the PI feels as if the journalist and/or publication should share at least some of the liability, and so she should engage in third party practice as the third-party P to join the journalist and/or the publication as third party Ds. [FRCP 14] **(A)** is incorrect because tortfeasors are not subject to compulsory joinder. **(B)** is incorrect because the P, not the D, has the discretion to decide whether to join multiple tortfeasors in the same lawsuit. **(D)** is incorrect because interpleader results from a situation in which a party could potentially face double liability to two different parties and interpleads the other two parties to compel them to solve the dispute between them; in this situation, there is no risk of any party facing double liability.

180./A/ Because the family did not disclose the types and amounts of damages, nor the evidence such as expert testimony, or receipts and repair bills, to substantiate these claims, the family will not be able to claim these damages at a later point in the lawsuit as it moves into the summary judgment and then, possibly, trial phases. [FRCP 26(a) for initial disclosure requirements, and FRCP 37 for the denial of these claims] **(B)** is not the best answer; although bringing in such an expert could even be required, the introduction of this expert represents just one sort of initial disclosure that would be needed in order to make the case for the claimed damages. **(C)** is incorrect – third parties may intervene upon their own initiative, and an original party does not have a responsibility to solicit a third party's intervention. **(D)** is not the best answer because this sort of motion does not represent a critical flaw in the family's case, but rather merely a potentially-missed opportunity.

181. /D/ After the jury verdict was entered, taking exception to the previous jury instructions in and of itself would not of itself preserve those exceptions for appeal. [FRCP 51] **(A)** is not the best answer because it is a best practice to state explicitly that one is not waiving one's original exceptions to an opposing party's jury instructions by offering amendments to those instructions after the judge has accepted them. **(B)** is not the best answer because it is a best practice to avoid being deemed to have abandoned a theory of the case by failing to request jury instructions that reflect those theories advanced by one's side in a case. Similarly, at the close of the earlier hearings on jury instructions, counsel should reiterate on the record both exceptions to any accepted instructions and exceptions to the judge's refusal to accept the instructions requested by one's own side. **(C)** is not the best answer because counsel should either take this measure, or alternatively counsel could at an earlier hearing on jury instructions request that the judge make a ruling that counsel does not need to take exceptions to jury instructions as those instructions are read to the jury in order to preserve those exceptions for appeal.

182. /D/ The best answer here is the copy of the wet-signature initial buy-sell agreement that was incorporated by reference in the pleadings but was not attached to the pleadings. This document arguably is not essential to the motion, and although it was referenced in the pleadings, it was not attached. If the court begins considering it, the 12(b)(6) motion will automatically convert to a motion for summary judgment. [FRCP 12(d) and 56] **(A)** is incorrect because courts may take judicial notice of publicly available documents, especially those available from government sources, without triggering the automatic conversion to summary judgment. **(B)** is incorrect because such permission arguably is essential to the case, so it need not have been explicitly referenced in the complaint or attached to the pleadings to be considered in a 12(b)(6) motion, and the couple has not indicated any intent to challenge the validity of those digital files. If, however, the couple were to dispute the validity of those digital files, then the motion would convert to a motion for summary judgment. **(C)** is incorrect because although the digitally-signed agreement in dispute that authorized the release of funds from escrow was not attached to the pleadings, the pleadings did reference this contract, and the contract is essential to the case, so a court may consider it without triggering automatic conversion to a motion for summary judgment.

183. /C/ Filing pre-trial motions such as motion *in limine* to exclude evidence could constitute constructive waiver of the right to protest the court's assertion of personal jurisdiction. Filing such evidence motions reasonably creates the expectation in the opposing party that the moving party intends to carry through with the case rather than challenging it on jurisdictional grounds. [FRCP 12(h)] **(A)** is incorrect because a court would likely admit the evidence here at issue, even though it is hearsay, as a present sense impression. **(B)** is incorrect because courts would not require Ps to redraft complaints in such a situation; courts typically allow Ps to redraft complaints after a D's successful 12(b)(6) motion for failure to state a claim for which relief can be granted. **(D)** is incorrect because the admissibility of one specific piece of evidence does not depend upon whether roughly equivalent evidence offered by the opposing side is equally admitted; there is no such rule mandating or permitting such conditional admittance.

184. /A/ The class of bloggers does not seem to constitute a sufficiently definable class, arguably violating one of the implicit requirements of class action lawsuits. [FRCP 23] **(B)** is incorrect because a class action lawsuit may be brought against a class of Ds. **(C)** is incorrect because such opt out notice is required only for the third type of certification of class action lawsuits, the common question certification when the common questions trump issues unique to each individual situation. Such common question class actions are brought for damages, whereas this class action against the police departments falls under the conduct of the opposing party certification because it primarily aims to obtain equitable – i.e., injunctive – relief. **(D)** is incorrect because although this lawsuit arises from issues pertaining to criminal procedure – i.e., for what reasons police may constitutionally detain suspects, the lawsuit itself is a civil lawsuit.

185. /A/ The CULP factors are requirements for all class action lawsuits. The "C" in CULP stands for the requirement that the class member's claims have "some" common questions of law or fact. In addition to CULP, there are three types of class action certifications, one of which (1) requires not only that there are some common questions, but that those questions predominate over issues that are unique to each member's case. This certification differs from the other two certifications: (2) the risk of separate actions creating inconsistent equitable results for either Ps or Ds; and (3) when the opposing party's conduct warrants injunctive relief, in that these other two award injunctive relief. [FRCP 23(b)] **(B)** is incorrect because the two types of certification that award primarily equitable – i.e., injunctive – relief do not require mandatory opt out notice. **(C)** is incorrect because the type of certification that requires opt out notice is the type that also requires not just that there are common questions, but that they predominate. **(D)** is not the best answer because although class actions in which Ds are the class could require opt out notice, the key distinguishing factors in whether a case requires opt out notice are whether: (1) the certification requires that common questions predominate; and (2) that the class action is pursuing primarily monetary damages.

186. /D/ Among 12(b) motions such as motion to dismiss for lack of subject matter jurisdiction, only 12(b)(6) motions to dismiss require the truth inference under which the court may not doubt the veracity of claims made in the complaint. Other 12(b) motions, such as this motion to dismiss for lack of subject matter jurisdiction, do not require such a truth inference. [FRCP 12(b)] **(A)** is incorrect because the truth inference does not apply in the case of a motion to dismiss for lack of subject matter jurisdiction. **(B)** is incorrect because only a 12(b)(6) motion becomes a motion for summary judgment when matters outside the pleadings are considered; courts may look outside the pleadings to evaluate other 12(b) motions, such as the motion to dismiss for lack of personal jurisdiction. **(C)** is incorrect because only 12(b)(6) motions can convert to motions for summary judgment; other 12(b) motions such as motion to dismiss for lack of subject matter jurisdiction do not convert in this way.

187./A/ The court will most likely sanction the shipping company for providing incorrect responses to discovery requests by ordering them to pay at least for the legal fees incurred by the captain's attorney in preparing, filing, and arguing the motion to compel and the motion for sanctions. The initial discovery response was incorrect in that it implicitly acknowledged the contemporaneous existence of documents that later were claimed not to have ever existed at the time litigation had started, but by the time of the first response the shipping company should have ascertained whether such documents even existed. There is a duty to supplement a prior discovery response when a party learns it was in some material way incorrect or incomplete. [FRCP 26 and FRCP 37] **(B)** is incorrect because the logs were deleted as part of the standard records retention and deletion policy and were not destroyed deliberately with intent to frustrate litigation, which would be required to constitute evidence spoliation. **(C)** is incorrect because there is no indication the captain knew that the call logs were kept for only a week after initial creation, so the captain's initial document production request and subsequent motions prior to learning of retention policy were all reasonable. **(D)** is not the best answer because it is not clear in this situation that a court would impose such a burden on a party to retain call logs well before litigation had begun merely because the shipping company should have known that the captain had a legal claim to overtime compensation that the company was not providing.

188./B/ Even though the damages are new, the cello player will not be able to bring a new claim for defamation against that particular city newspaper from which the cello player obtained the earlier settlement for the publication in a false light claim because both claims result from the same occurrence and so is barred by the principle of *res judicata*. **(A)** is incorrect because "the same occurrence" does include the after effects – i.e., the damages – and so the cello player's claim against the city newspaper is barred by *res judicata*, but the claims against all the other Ds can proceed. **(C)** is incorrect because although privity can affect whether claims against a party are barred by *res judicata*, the newspapers are not in privity with each other simply by involvement in the same industry in the same geographic area. **(D)** is incorrect because the settlement acts as a final adjudication on the merits only between the two parties to the settlement; the cello player will have to litigate fully or separately settle the cases against the blogs and the other newspapers.

189./D/ The collision would not have occurred but for the train company moving the tracks outside of the easement, so the timber company should have raised the easement violation for this location as a compulsory counterclaim. *Res judicata* will bar the timber company from any claims relating to that specific site – i.e., a court will enforce the original settlement agreement – but claims relating to other sites can continue as normal. **(A)** is incorrect both because remand is when a case moves from federal court to state court, while removal is in the opposite direction, and because the mere fact of the train tracks crossing state lines is not the sort of cross-state activity that creates jurisdiction for federal courts for claims such as these. **(B)** is incorrect because the timber company's easement claims directly concern property located in Franklin State; therefore, Franklin State will exercise *in rem* jurisdiction over disputes involving the property. **(C)** is incorrect; there is no basis to assert that a tour business with little or no connection to the facts in dispute should be joined, even if the business uses the same land.

190. /C/ Collateral estoppel – i.e., issue preclusion, which in this case is offensive – will prevent the property owner from denying that putting up the barbed wire was willful misconduct for which a property owner may be liable for unsafe conditions, even to trespassers. The prior lawsuit with the storeowner resolved that specific issue against the owner, so the law student need not prove it for his case. Considering that it is one of the main elements of his claim, a court may award summary judgment in such a situation. **(A)** is incorrect because typical reasons to dismiss, such as 12(b)(6) failure to state a claim for which relief can be granted, or *res judicata*, a.k.a. claim preclusion, do not apply. **(B)** is incorrect; privity is required for *res judicata*, a.k.a. claim preclusion; however, it is not required for collateral estoppel, a.k.a. issue preclusion, to have effect. **(D)** is incorrect; this is the very issue that is precluded because the previous lawsuit with the storeowner conclusively ruled on it.

191. /B/ The potential juror made it clear that impartiality is at risk if he is seated when he stated that he would sentence the D to death without exception. **(A)** is incorrect because lack of qualification usually concerns a potential juror being under 18 years of age, not a U.S. citizen, unable to communicate in English, or a convicted felon. The facts of this scenario do not support any of these situations. **(C)** is incorrect because incapacity has to do with being of unsound mind or body. Just because someone feels strongly about employing the death penalty does not necessarily mean they are of unsound mind or body. **(D)** is incorrect because the three challenge maximum applies only for peremptory challenges.

192. /A/ Bias can be actual or implied. Here, the bias is implied since she has been married to an executive of the insurance company for a long time. **(B)** is not the best answer because under the rules for challenges, the onus is not on the potential juror to know what background information ought to be shared and how much ought to be shared. **(C)** is incorrect because the Constitutional restriction is on peremptory challenges based solely on race or gender. The facts here do not support those categories. **(D)** is incorrect because while she is not employed by the company, she has received benefits from her husband being a long-time executive of the insurance company, which is likely sufficient to show potential bias.

193. /D/ A peremptory challenge is a challenge to a potential juror for which no particular reason needs to be stated. **(A)** is incorrect because a peremptory challenge does not require a substantive reason, as opposed to a challenge for cause. **(B)** is incorrect because a question of incapacity falls under a challenge for cause, not a peremptory challenge. **(C)** is not the best answer because there is a constitutional restriction on the exercise of peremptory challenges, not a protection of them.

194. /A/ In a civil case, each party, not just each side, gets three peremptory challenges. **(B)** is incorrect because the attorney has not reached the three challenge maximum. **(C)** is incorrect because an attorney does not need to give a specific reason for a peremptory challenge. **(D)** is incorrect because there is no offsetting a denial to peremptory challenges by allowing the denied attorney to argue first.

195. /C/ This is the best answer because the P's attorney could make the argument that these peremptory challenges are based solely on gender, which the Constitution restricts. **(A)** is incorrect because bias refers to a prospective juror's bias or the judge's bias, not the attorney. **(B)** is incorrect because mistrials are requested on the basis of misconduct during the actual trial, not during *voir dire*. **(D)** is not the best answer because increasing the jury size does not help remedy what the P wants: two of the male jurors who have been challenged.

196. /A/ A motion for appeal must be filed within 30 days after entry of the final judgment, and this is the couple's best response. **(B)** is incorrect because one must file a motion for a new trial no later than 28 days from the entry of judgment. **(C)** is incorrect because one must file a cross appeal within 30 days after the judgment has been entered, and here they would need another party to file an appeal first. **(D)** is incorrect because while they have one year to file a motion to vacate judgment, they also need a specific reason to justify filing this motion. The facts do not support such a motion, and thus this is not the best response.

197. /C/ Generally, a notice for appeal must be filed no later than 30 days after entry of judgment. **(A)** is incorrect because the government is not a party in this scenario even though the government enjoys 60 days to file a notice of appeal. **(B)** The document that would be permissible to file in 61 days is a motion to vacate judgment, not a notice of appeal. **(D)** is incorrect because the stated time period is one day late of the 30-day cut-off to file a notice for appeal.

198. /A/ Thelma's appeal notice was timely filed within 30 days. **(B)** is incorrect because a motion for a new trial must be filed no later than 28 days after entry of judgment. [FRCP 59] **(C)** is incorrect because a notice of cross–appeal must be filed 30 days after entry of judgment or 14 days after the initial notice of appeal, whichever is later. **(D)** is incorrect because a motion to vacate cannot be based on an error of law. [FRCP 60]

199. /C/ A specialized statute for the attorney's request in family law that may allow an award of reasonable attorney fees is the best answer. **(A)** This alternative may be a general rule, but there are some statutes that allow for an exception, so here this is not the best answer. **(B)** is incorrect because the facts of the case seem to support the likelihood of collecting reasonable attorney fees. **(D)** is incorrect because the alternative infers possible facts that are not in the scenario.

200. /C/ The homeowner's attorney in effect misrepresented the unpublished opinion by omitting key details of that case which would have distinguished it from the situation in the case at bar. Misrepresentation by an opposing party is one reason to file a motion for relief from judgment, and the deadline for such a motion is a year after entry of judgment, so here it is timely. [FRCP 60] **(A)** is incorrect because a motion for a new trial must be filed within 28 days of entry of judgment; in this situation, the company has waited two months, which is too long. **(B)** is incorrect because a renewed motion for JMOL has the same deadline as a motion for new trial; these two motions are often filed together. **(D)** is incorrect because the deadline to file for an appeal is 30 days after entry of judgment; waiting two months is again too long a period of time.

CHAPTER 7

FEDERAL CIVIL PROCEDURE

Index

RIGOS UBE REVIEW SERIES

UNIFORM MULTISTATE BAR EXAM REVIEW (MBE)

Volume 2 Index

General MBE Information

Evidence

Constitutional Law

Criminal Law and Procedure

Federal Civil Procedure

RIGOS UNIFORM BAR EXAM (UBE) REVIEW SERIES

2020 MBE REVIEW

COURSE EVALUATION FORM

Thank you for choosing the MBE section of the Rigos UBE Review Series updated for the new 2020 NCBE content specification outline changes! We hope you feel that these structured materials have given you the knowledge, tools, and confidence to tackle the multiple-choice questions on the MBE!

We constantly strive to provide the best possible bar exam study materials available. We want to hear from you! If you would kindly take a few minutes to fill out the form below and mail it back to us at 310 Sander Building, 4105 East Madison, Seattle, WA 98112, or fax it to us at (206) 624-9320. Let your voice be heard in the effort to continually improve the Rigos UBE Review Series MBE book. THANK YOU!

****

For each of the categories listed below, please rate your opinion of the Rigos Bar Review Series MBE Review on a scale of 1 to 5.

5 = Excellent	4 = Very Good	3 = Good	2 = Fair	1 = Poor

How do you rate the overall Rigos UBE Series?

Arrangement of Materials	5	4	3	2	1
Writing Style / Typography	5	4	3	2	1
Textual Format	5	4	3	2	1
Ease of Use	5	4	3	2	1
Professionalism	5	4	3	2	1

How do you rate the Rigos UBE Series materials in terms of accuracy (typographical, legal rule, etc.)?

Chapter Texts	5	4	3	2	1
MBE Tips and Suggestions	5	4	3	2	1
Questions / Answers	5	4	3	2	1
Magic Memory Outlines®	5	4	3	2	1
Question Distribution Maps	5	4	3	2	1

How do you rate the helpfulness of each component of Rigos UBE Series?

Chapter Texts	5	4	3	2	1
Acronyms – Mnemonics	5	4	3	2	1
Magic Memory Outlines®	5	4	3	2	1
Question Distribution Maps	5	4	3	2	1
Questions/Answers	5	4	3	2	1
MBE Secret Weapon	5	4	3	2	1

How well has Rigos UBE Series prepared you for each of the following aspects of the MBE?

Substantive Knowledge	5	4	3	2	1
Helpful Exam Tips	5	4	3	2	1
Time Management	5	4	3	2	1
Avoiding Common Mistakes	5	4	3	2	1
Confidence Level	5	4	3	2	1

Continued on back of page

What is the likelihood that you would do each of the following?

Recommend Rigos Bar Review Series to others	5	4	3	2	1
Keep Rigos Bar Review Series for future reference	5	4	3	2	1
Use other products from **Rigos** in the future	5	4	3	2	1

Did you study all of the text coverage?
Yes _____ No _____

Did you work all of the learning and practice questions?
Yes _____ No _____

Did you prepare a Magic Memory Outline® for all seven subjects in the MBE?
Yes _____ No _____

Did you take the Practice and Final Exams?
Yes _____ No _____

Can you rate the individual chapters of the Review Series:

VOLUME 1

Contracts & UCC Sales Article 2	5	4	3	2	1
Torts	5	4	3	2	1
Real Property & Future Interests	5	4	3	2	1

VOLUME 2

Evidence	5	4	3	2	1
Constitutional Law	5	4	3	2	1
Criminal Law and Procedure	5	4	3	2	1
Federal Civil Procedure	5	4	3	2	1

Did you use the "Make Your Own Exam" drill software feature?
Yes _____ No _____

Did you use our Secret Weapon procedure during the MBE exam?
Yes _____ No _____

Did you pass the MBE?
Yes _____ No _____ Don't know yet _____ MBE Score _____

If you have any additional comments, critiques or suggestions for improvement about Rigos Uniform Bar Exam Review Series MBE Review, please tell us about them below and earn our check for $25.00. Please feel free to attach pages.

_____

Please provide us the information below. It will allow us to send you $25.00, follow up on your suggestions, and express our thanks for your interest.

NAME: _____

PHONE: _____ EMAIL: _____

LAW SCHOOL: _____ GRAD DATE: _____ ADDRESS: _____

MBE SCORE: _____ NOT RECEIVED YET _____